RISE OF THE NEW YORK SKYSCRAPER, 1865–1913

RISE OF THE NEW YORK
SKY

YALE
UNIVERSITY
PRESS
NEW HAVEN
&
LONDON

SCRAPER

1865–1913

SARAH
BRADFORD
LANDAU
&
CARL W.
CONDIT

Designed by Richard Hendel.
Set in Bodoni Antiqua by
Keystone Typesetting, Inc.
Printed by Thomson Shore.
The paper in this book meets the
guidelines for permanence and
durability of the Committee on
Production Guidelines for
Book Longevity of the Council
on Library Resources.

Library of Congress Cataloging-in-Publication Data
Landau, Sarah Bradford
  Rise of the New York skyscraper, 1865–1913 /
Sarah Bradford Landau and Carl W. Condit.
     p. cm.
  Includes bibliographical references and index.
  ISBN 0-300-06444-6 (cloth : alk. paper)
  1. Skyscrapers—New York (N.Y.)—History. 2. New
York (N.Y.)—Buildings, structures, etc.   I. Condit,
Carl W.   II. Title.
NA6232.L36 1996
720′.483′097471—dc20   95-34061
                                                  CIP

A catalogue record for this book is available from the
British Library.

10 9 8 7 6 5 4 3 2 1

TO SIDNEY

CONTENTS

*"The Tall Building Problem." An artist's composite
view comparing building heights (left to right):
World (1889–90), American Surety (1894–96),
Trinity Church (1844–46), Park Row (1896–99),
American Tract Society (1894–95), St. Paul (1895–
98), Sun (in front; as enlarged c. 1867), and U. S.
Capitol. The Park Row and St. Paul buildings were
under construction when this view was published.
After "The Lofty Buildings of New York City,"*
Scientific American *75 (10 October 1896), 277.*

PREFACE

A hundred years ago people were already worried about the healthfulness and architectural quality of New York's skyscrapers. The following speculation was published in 1894: "Isn't it rather presumptuous then to take it for granted that our successors will be so satisfied with what we have done that they will permit it to endure for centuries. New York may become a really civilized city within a hundred years, and then how much of our work will be tolerated? Daylight and fresh air and leisure to grow wise may become valuable and our crude expression of an ostentatious art may be intolerable to a generation whose ear is attuned to a purer accent of divine speech."[1] Although those of the city's early office towers that do survive have lasted but a single century, we are ready to answer the question. Not only do we tolerate the "crude" efforts of the first skyscraper era, we admire them. Indeed, we regret the destruction of such masterworks as the Produce Exchange and the Singer Tower. Moreover, many might consider the city less "civilized" than in 1894; its citizens show no signs of being "attuned to a purer accent of divine speech," and though daylight and fresh air are indeed precious commodities, their accommodation through the enactment of zoning laws and largely ineffectual planning efforts in the twentieth century has not necessarily brought better buildings. At the moment of this writing, city agencies and civic organizations are marshaling efforts to protect the historic skyscrapers of lower Manhattan as part of a campaign to revitalize the area.

Putting aside for the moment that gloomy assessment, we wish to say something at the outset about the derivation and usage of the word *skyscraper*. No one questions that unusual height is a skyscraper's outstanding characteristic, although just how high a building should be before it warrants that distinction has been endlessly debated. *Skyscraper* was not in fact commonly used to describe tall buildings with any frequency until the later 1880s, when Chicago's concentration of high buildings attracted attention. The second edition of the *Oxford English Dictionary* records the earliest known occurrence of the word (1788) as the name given to a horse that in 1789 won the Epsom Derby; in 1826 high-standing horses were referred to as sky-scrapers. In 1794 the word was used to describe a "triangular sky-sail"; by 1800, a hat or bonnet; in 1857, a "very tall man"; in 1866, fly balls in baseball and cricket. The earliest citation provided by the *OED* for buildings is from an article published in the *American Architect and Building News* on 30 June 1883. John Moser, in an essay titled "American Architectural Form of the Future," discusses the need for a towering structure to distinguish monumental public buildings, and he cites the Hartford, Connecticut, Capitol as coming closest to the desired heroic effect: "This form of sky-scraper gives that peculiar refined, independent, self-contained, daring, bold, heaven-reaching, erratic, piratic, Quixotic, American thought. . . . The capitol building should always have a dome. I should raise thereon a gigantic 'sky-scraper,' contrary to all precedent in practice, and I should trust to American constructive and engineering skill to build it strong enough for any gale." We might add, parenthetically, that the phrases "building skyward" and "sky building" were used that same year in reference to New York City buildings.[2] By 1891 *skyscraper*, more often than not hyphenated as *sky-scraper*, was being applied to buildings, especially in Chicago, with some frequency.[3]

Serious development of the skyscraper building type started with the elevator-office buildings that began to rise in New York around 1870 (see Chapter 4). Of course, long before that there was the occasional unconventionally high building—a fourteen-story sugarhouse was built on Duane Street near Broadway around 1840, for example, well before the day of the elevator, and then rebuilt immediately after a fire.[4] By 1875 New York City had sprouted ten-story, elevator-served office buildings. Chicago's first such building, Burnham & Root's Montauk Block, was completed only seven years later. (For that matter, an aberrantly tall flats complex known as the Queen Anne Mansions, with ten- and twelve-story sections and a passenger elevator, existed in London by 1877).[5] Chicago zoomed ahead heightwise in the 1880s, although New York's World, or Pulitzer, Building (1889–90), at 309 feet from sidewalk to lantern base and with a story count variously reported as eighteen to twenty-six, seems to have overtopped all others at the time. An ordinance passed in 1893 that limited building height in Chicago allowed New York City to take the lead. In the space of less than forty-five years, from 1870 to 1913, New York grew from a city of five- and six-story buildings to a mega-metropolis with fifty-story skyscrapers.

As of mid-1909, the Peoples Gas Building (1910–11) was expected to be the largest, though not the tallest, skyscraper yet built in Chicago.[6] It was to rise twenty-one stories to the legal height limit and contain nearly 708,000 square feet of floor space. By that date New York could boast a massive thirty-three-story office block incorporating 500,000 square feet of floor area (the City Investing Building) and also a forty-seven-story tower (the Singer); by the end of the year construction would begin on a skyscraper that would reach forty stories at its highest point and contain 1,250,000 square feet of usable floor space (the Municipal Building). Chicago had a height limit; New York City did not. We have recorded in some detail the attempts of architects, engineers, and concerned citizens to impose some legislative limits in New York City, efforts that began in the early 1880s, long preceding the passage of the zoning law in 1916.

The question of primacy in skyscraper design—Chicago versus New York—was set aside long ago as unresolvable, and in our view it is probably not important. Readers looking to answer that question definitively will be disappointed, although to be sure, we would be less than candid if we did not admit to having undertaken this study partly to right the balance. As witnessed by the article quoted above and by the last six chapters of this book, the New York skyscraper's bad press began in the 1890s. By 1897 Chicago was being held up as the model against which New York's skyscrapers were found wanting, a judgment that has endured to this day. It was born in the articles of such critics as Montgomery Schuyler and Peter B. Wight and supported by the writings and fine design of Louis Sullivan, and it was afterward nurtured by scholars. By contrast, New York's early skyscrapers were from the beginning disparaged as inferior in design and sometimes even held up to ridicule, as when Schuyler, criticizing the American Surety Building's lack of a steep roof, dubbed that building an "uncompromising parallelopiped" and described the Park Row Building as a "horned monster."[7] As a result, while recent books celebrate the city's Art Deco towers of the 1920s and 1930s and the careers of a few of New York's early skyscraper architects, serious examination of the formative, early phase of the city's skyscrapers has only now reached the dimensions of a full book on the subject.[8] That the subject deserves a book-length study will, we trust, be demonstrated here. For despite its perceived problems, the invention of the New York skyscraper—a saga of ingenuity and greed if ever there was one—is one of the most fascinating and professionally challenging developments in the annals of architecture, combining as it does the histories of engineering, architectural style, land use, and law.

Our primary aim has been to examine as thoroughly as possible both the physical and formal development of this new building type in New York and the ways in which it affected the city. In spite of the outpouring of books on skyscrapers—especially Chicago's—since the late 1920s, there has been no adequate coverage of the history of construction technology or of the mechanical utilities with respect to their contributions to the skyscraper, advances without which the high office or residential building would have been dangerous and uninhabitable. To that end, we have investigated fireproofing techniques as they evolved in the period, as well as the various mechanical utilities—including elevator transportation, central heating, ventilation, lighting, and plumbing—that made construction of the high office building feasible. We also examine how skyscrapers transformed the appearance and shape of the city, especially lower Manhattan; how they were squeezed and shoehorned into every available inch of space, however oddly shaped; and the means by which a building's light and air were safeguarded before there was protection by legislation.

Our study can be described as "formalist," but not in the conventional sense of that term, for along with their architectural aspect— which is by no means neglected—we also consider what one scholar facetiously described as the "hardware" of these buildings, their structural composition. We tell you how big these new high-rise buildings were, how they were anchored to the ground, how they were framed, how their framing was constructed to resist wind pressure, and even how many pounds of pressure per square foot they were built to sustain. In the past, so-called skyscraper construction has been too narrowly defined. As our early chapters disclose, iron floor framing was in wide use for commercial structures by the end of the 1850s; all that remained was to eliminate bearing walls. The general public mistakenly reveres steel as the consummate ingredient; however, although rolled and built-up steel beams did indeed completely replace wrought iron for all framing members after the turn of the twentieth century, the essential forms of the various structural elements were developed in iron long before that, beginning in the 1850s.

Wherever possible we attempt to elucidate correlations between structure and architectural design, although not because we feel compelled to by the outmoded notion that functional, or "rational," expression is essential to skyscraper design or to the progress of modernism. Schuyler and others criticized New York's early skyscrapers for being unnecessarily layered in their exterior design, but in fact the city's building code dictated specific wall thicknesses at specific heights, diminishing as the building rose higher, and it is our observation that these shifts in thickness as well as the actual layered framing of the skyscraper encouraged the horizontal expression of their design. Throughout this study we have linked form to legal provisions, something that has heretofore been neglected except with respect to skyscrapers built after the zoning law was enacted. We therefore discuss in some detail the building laws that were enacted over the years, with particular attention to the 1892 code that legitimized skeleton construction (see Chapter 6).

The skyscraper building type owes its existence and much of its character more to the desire for money and prestige, to advances in technology, and to adventurous real estate speculation than to abstract ideals or theories of style or aesthetics. Architectural design, however, was and still is the essential means of conveying status, inviting the public's attention, and advertising the city as the nation's leading commercial center. One need only look at a photograph of Joseph Pulitzer's gold-domed World Building (see Fig. 7.4) or walk through the spectacular lobby-arcade of the Woolworth Building (see Fig. 11.25) to receive those messages. For those reasons the evolution and specifics of architectural style and planning have not been neglected in this study. We are in full agreement on these matters and have combined our resources to this end.

A word is in order about some issues not specifically addressed in this book, such as the idea of the skyscraper as a focus of capitalistic and elitist values. We have taken capitalism for granted; elitism, although a provocative notion, appears only by inference. Nor do we deal with the history of unions or of the construction industry, certainly worthwhile subjects, although occasionally a labor dispute or a safety record may figure in our account of the construction of a particular building. Nor do we endeavor to support the provocative thesis put forward by Thomas Bender and William R. Taylor that New York was a city that resisted verticality, that it instead remained committed to the horizontal expression of its "urban order" well beyond the time that it could have constructed very tall buildings and buildings of marked vertical design.[9] Indubitably, the city's legacy from colonial times was low buildings and private dwellings, reinforced by the grid plan with narrow lots imposed in 1811. The perception may be accurate that buildings remained low longer than necessary, given the advanced state of technology by the end of the 1850s, but it is equally true that a severe financial depression in 1857 and the onset of civil war in the 1860s acted to slow construction. There were also concerns to be overcome about the safety of tall buildings. As for New York's resistance to Sullivan's "uncompromising" vertical design, we point out that New York already had its own vertical design (see Chapters 1, 3, 5) and that resistance to Sullivan was as much an indication of independence as it was commitment to Beaux-Arts teachings and urban scale. (We might also note that Chicago had no lack of horizontally designed skyscrapers.) Design horizontality was also affected by mandated structural requirements (see Chapter 7).

Our collaboration began twelve years ago with the idea that Condit would handle the technological side of the story and that Landau would contribute the architectural history perspective. In the course of events, however, each collaborator independently produced a voluminous set of notes that addressed all of the aspects described in this introduction, although Condit's were far more concerned with technology. Landau integrated the two sets of notes and wrote the book. In the process, she grew increasingly more interested in technology and became an avid reader of the engineering journals—valuable sources that have been overlooked by most historians of nineteenth-century architecture. She has also contributed to that side of the story. For example, the section on Manhattan's geology, and a substantial part of the discussion of fireproofing in Chapter 2, otherwise based on Condit's researches; the section on the Phoenix column in Chapter 3; and the impact of the building code on the construction of Sullivan's Bayard Building, discussed in Chapter 8, are the result of her investigations.

The structural engineers as well as the architects who contributed to the design of these buildings are duly credited in our story. The engineers deserve more study than we have been able to give them; indeed, the phenomenal rise of the city's skyscrapers on sites that were constricted, or where bedrock lies far below the ground surface, or which were otherwise problematic, reveals just how vital were the contributions of these professionals. Before the 1880s, the architect often served as his own engineer, as did, for example, Robert G. Hatfield, George B. Post, and even Richard Morris Hunt (see Chapters 3 and 4). The polytechnically trained central Europeans, who started coming to the United States in the 1840s, were important contributors, notably the architect Leopold Eidlitz and also his brother Marc Eidlitz, whose firm was for many years a leading New York City building contractor. The changeover to reliance on engineering expertise was highlighted in 1894, when Kimball & Thompson engaged foundation engineer Charles Sooysmith to advise on the underpinning of the Manhattan Life Building; the result was the first use of pneumatic-caisson foundations for an office building (see Chapter 7).

By the end of the nineteenth century, the engineer's contribution was generally understood to be essential, the architect's superficial: "The modern office building is a purely American type. It is not so much the development of an architectural style as it is an engineering accomplishment, and owes its existence, primarily, to engineering inventions. It is the product of many brains, and the architects' contribution has been mainly in connection with the exterior design."[10] The professional journals frequently pointed out how little artistic leeway the architect had due to exigencies of site, rental values, need for light, building code requirements, and so forth. His responsibilities entailed following a prescribed program, providing for the client's needs, and getting the most out of the available space.

We have also paid attention to those who built these skyscrapers, the corporate and investment interests that financed them. Cass Gilbert put it very well when he described the skyscraper as the "machine that made the land pay." Man may once have been inspired to ascend toward heaven, God, whatever, by building high; but in the end it was not divine thoughts but money, ambition, and the desire for power that created the skyscraper. The story of Frank W. Woolworth's insistence that his building overtop every other skyscraper, as recounted in Chapter 11, may represent the most extreme expression of those motives, but it reveals nothing new about New York City.

Our book opens with a chapter describing conditions in the city between 1850 and 1870 and examining the evolution of building types and architectural styles that formed the background for the high-rise office skyscraper. At intervals throughout our study, related building types, specifically the warehouse, the varieties of hotel, and the apartment house, are discussed when necessary to establish their relationship as precedents and parallels to the office skyscraper; our focus, however, is the office skyscraper. Chapter 2 is devoted to the technological preparations for the skyscraper and also addresses the below-ground conditions that affect building foundations and the development of those mechanical utilities that would make the skyscraper possible. (It and Chapter 6 are the most technically oriented in the book.)

The next three chapters consider the evolution of the tall office building, from the early history of iron construction in New York City and its application to commercial buildings before 1870 (Chapter 3) to the "first skyscrapers" of the 1870s (Chapter 4), the three most significant of which are analyzed in depth, and the mammoth, form-setting structures of the 1880s (Chapter 5). Chapter 5 concludes with an analysis of the controversial Tower Building, the first completely skeleton-framed building constructed without masonry adjuncts. Chapter 6 addresses technological progress as it affected skyscrapers from about 1889 to 1895, the planning and construction of the high building, the building code and the issues of health and safety that had begun to plague the New York skyscraper, and architectural design.

The next two chapters investigate the city's monumental high-rise buildings of the 1890s, emphasizing, among other aspects, their representation of corporate power and authority during the first half of the decade (Chapter 7) and their construction on speculation by anonymous real estate interests in the second half (Chapter 8). Chapter 9 assesses the situation at the turn of the century, focusing on the diminishing role of the architect, the economy of the skyscraper, and the mounting pressure for height limitation. Chapter 10 examines the major works of the first decade of the twentieth century, among them the Times and West Street buildings; includes an assessment of the hotel skyscraper as it had developed since the 1880s; and considers efforts to effect urban planning and height control legislation in that decade. The Singer and Metropolitan Life towers are reserved for Chapter 11, where they are closely considered along with other culminating works, including the Woolworth Building, that bring to a close the first skyscraper age. Our study concludes at the end of 1913—the point when recommendations later to be incorporated in the zoning law are put forward by the city's heights of buildings commission. Throughout we have relied on contemporary sources and criticism, quoting our sources liberally in order to convey the flavor of the times.

The audience we address includes professionals, students, and anyone interested in the history of architecture and urbanism, technology, urban planning, and corporate and financial affairs, as well as skyscraper and New York City buffs. Our book is meant to serve both as a readable text and as a reference work, and we hope that it will stimulate interest in undertaking further study of the individuals, real estate entities, corporations, designers, and constructors involved with skyscraper building in the period we treat, as well as of the architectural and technological innovations that made skyscrapers possible.

For the reader's information, we should mention that building story counts vary from source to source and map to map. In the case of the Bankers Trust Building, for example, the count is variously reported as anywhere between thirty-two and forty-one. In that particular case, the building is extant and for the most part unchanged except superficially, so it was possible to consult the building manager, who confirmed that there were thirty-one usable floors above the sidewalk level, with six storage levels in the pyramid roof. (If the four usable below-ground floors are counted, the number swells to forty-one.) As a rule we have not included underground stories in our counts; we consider as the first story the lowest to project fully, or nearly so, above the sidewalk. The highest that we include is the topmost usable floor, unless otherwise indicated.

Our presentation has as a rule been chronological, using wherever possible the date of filing of the new-building permit or a more reliable source, if that exists, as the guide to sequence. In the interests of greater cohesiveness, however, we have occasionally deviated from strict chronology, as for example in Chapter 4, where later enlargements of the key buildings are taken out of order, and Chapter 7, where it was convenient to group together some smaller structures. When information is derived from general sources, from sources too numerous to cite, or from the particular expertise and previous publications of a coauthor (as in the early chapters), endnote citations are minimal, and general and chapter bibliographies supply the sources. (Inevitably, in a work of this magnitude and undertaken over a long period, sources get lost, and that has happened once or twice.) Chapter bibliographies include sources consulted for more than one building or topic and also useful items not cited in endnotes. If the source is limited to a single aspect and is thus cited in an endnote, it does not appear in the bibliography. If a building no longer extant is illustrated, then the word *demolished* appears in the figure caption; otherwise demolition is indicated in the text or endnotes.

A book in the making for as many years as this one has benefited from the assistance of many institutions and individuals. We are grateful to the American Council of Learned Societies for a fellowship awarded to Landau in 1985–86. The book is made possible in part from public funds that the New York State Council of the Arts provided in 1987–88 to assist Landau's work. And we are pleased to acknowledge the College of Fellows Fund of the American Institute of Architects for grants given to Landau in 1984 and 1985. A Mellon Junior Faculty Fellowship at New York University awarded for the spring semester of 1984 facilitated Landau's researches. The project also received support in the form of a grant from the National Endowment for the Humanities. It is a pleasure to acknowledge the help of Eugene Ferguson (history of central heating); Robert Vogel and Neal FitzSimons (history of the elevator); Harold Mayer (bibliographical data); the staff of Northwestern University Library, particularly Janet Ayers, Rolf Erickson, and Richard Olsen; and Richard Parmelee (behavior of early iron frames).

We are especially grateful to Raymonde Gautier for research assistance, and also to the staff members of all the libraries and archives where our research was carried out. We thank particularly Dale Neighbors, Mary Beth Betts, Wendy Shadwell, Mariam Touba, and Laird Ogden (The New-York Historical Society); William O'Malley (Avery Architectural and Fine Arts Library, Columbia University); Kenneth Cobb (Municipal Archives); and Marjorie Pearson, Merry Neisner, Gale Harris, Margaret McMahon, Caroline Kane, and David Breiner (New York City Landmarks Preservation Commission). Others kindly provided information on specific buildings and topics: Giorgio Cavaglieri (Astor Library);

Kathleen Curran (Astor Library and Academy of Music); Arline Schneider of the Equitable Life Assurance Society Archives; Pamela Dunn Lehrer of the New York Life Insurance Company Archives; Marian Stewart and Gretchen Gross of the Mutual Life Insurance Company Archives; Charles L. Sachs (Schermerhorn Row and Seamen's Savings Bank); Fred Schekter (Bennett Building); Frank P. Farinella and Walter E. Sam of Hurley & Farinella, Architects (Potter Building); Jane Cohn of Haines Lundberg Waehler (telephone company buildings); May N. Stone (hotels); Carol Willis (Western Union Building); Robert Murray (Bankers Trust Building); Luther Harris (620 Broadway); Michele H. Bogert (architectural sculpture); and Deborah Gardner (bibliography).

Among the many who answered questions, offered helpful suggestions, or in other ways assisted us, we are grateful to Adolf K. Placzek, Mosette Broderick, Mardges Bacon, Herbert Mitchell, Sharon Irish, Mark Tomasko, Jane B. Davies, Andrew Saint, Jill Lever, Carol Herselle Krinsky, Barbara L. Michaels, Kayla Stotzky, Stephen M. Raphael, Andrew S. Dolkart, Joy Kestenbaum, Margot Gayle, David Schuyler, Francis R. Kowsky, Timothy Donehoo, Lucy Freeman Sandler, Susan Tunick, Damie Stillman, and members of the Columbia University Seminar on the City and the University of Delaware Seminar in American Art, History, and Material Culture. We also wish to acknowledge, with many thanks, the staff of Yale University Press, especially our editor Judy Metro and our manuscript editor Dan Heaton. Last, and above all, we are indebted to Sidney I. Landau, to whom this book is dedicated, for his patience, missed vacations, and unflagging support over the years.

1

THE URBAN CONTEXT AND THE OFFICE BUILDING, 1850–70

New York City has been the economic capital of the United States since about 1820, but only in the 1850s did it emerge as the nation's preeminent city. And only after that did the tall commercial building become both desirable and feasible. Rapid expansion of transatlantic, coastal, and canal shipping, along with development of a regional rail network in the 1830s and 1840s, marked the beginning of fast growth and internal changes that transformed the port city into the leading metropolitan area in the United States.[1] The panic of 1857 and the Civil War only slowed the process temporarily. By 1860 the city justifiably regarded itself as the national metropolis, even if Boston and Philadelphia disputed the claim.

The decisive factor was the city's foreign trade, which in the middle decades of the nineteenth century constituted a quarter of the total volume in the United States. The urban economy was buoyed by this trade, the value of which more than quadrupled in just twenty years, climbing from $94 million in 1840 to $163 million in 1850 and then to $393 million in 1860.[2] Growth in the city's assessed property value lagged a decade behind commercial expansion, but it revealed the same pattern, expanding from more than a quarter-billion dollars in 1840 to more than half a billion in 1860. By 1875 it exceeded one billion dollars, an increase of more than 90 percent since 1860.

The city's rapid financial and industrial growth continued in the 1860s. The National Bank Act of 1863 made New York the national center for deposits of reserve currency, bringing a steady flow of gold and silver bullion into the city. The establishment of Chicago and St. Louis as reserve centers in 1887 altered the pattern of money movement, but nothing inhibited its increasing concentration in New York and the resulting tie-in to the city of the leading financial centers. The merger in 1869 of two competing organizations with the older New York Stock Exchange, founded as the New York Stock and Exchange Board in 1817, exemplifies this consolidation. The position of the Exchange, already strong, had been solidified by the laying of the Atlantic cable in 1866. Even before the merger more than 90 percent of the stock trading in the nation took place in New York. At the same time, metropolitan New York was becoming the nation's leading industrial center as well, with manufacture expanding as rapidly as trade and finance. Even as late as 1900, more people were employed in industry than worked in financial institutions.

Physical concentration paralleled financial and industrial concentration. The city's population tripled between 1840 and 1870, increasing from 312,710 to 942,292. By 1875 there were more than a million New Yorkers, and in some parts of the city—like the eleventh ward east of Tompkins Square, where by 1880 there were 543 people per acre of land—the congestion had become intolerable. Dense commercial building below Wall Street, stimulated by disastrous fires in 1835 and 1845 as well as by the burgeoning foreign and domestic trades, produced heavily congested traffic. The traffic on lower Broadway, estimated in 1866 at about 18,000 vehicles a day, was described as a "Babel scene of confusion" and the city as a place where "all is intense anxiety"—characterizations that have never grown outdated.[3] Technological, economic, and demographic factors, not to mention the imperative of prestige, contributed to a climate that would by the turn of the century produce the tallest skyscrapers and the heaviest concentration of them anywhere in the world.

By the 1860s New York was also a major intellectual and cultural center. In 1865 the city led the nation in opera, vocal recital, chamber, and general instrumental and orchestral music. It could boast two major institutions of higher learning in New York University and Columbia College, a well-stocked public library (the Astor), and important private libraries, including those of James Lenox and Samuel Tilden, which would later be merged with the Astor to form the New York Public Library. The city was also an editing and publishing center, with about fifteen daily newspapers and some of the oldest and best-known book publishers—Harper, Appleton, John Wiley, and Theodore De Vinne among them. Even before the Metropolitan Museum was incorporated in 1870, New York had a wealth of museums and art galleries, including the National Academy of Design, whose quarters, inspired by the Doge's Palace and designed by the architect Peter B. Wight, were completed in 1865 at Fourth Avenue and 23rd Street. As early as 1857 the Tenth Street Studio Building had been built to the design of Richard Morris Hunt as a unique combination of artists' studios and living quarters. New York already harbored the ballet and the musical revue and would be nationally renowned by 1900 for its cultural assets.

The Shape of the City in 1865

In 1865 the northern limit of paved streets was near 44th Street, and building development in the city extended to about 50th Street in the vicinity of Fifth and Madison avenues. Residential building was spreading uptown. Nearly all of the earliest mansions of the wealthy in the Bowling Green area—among the few, that is, that remained after the downtown fire of 1845—had by now disappeared. Well before the fire most of these had been taken over or replaced by commercial establishments, and their occupants had moved north to Washington Square. In 1865 the square and lower Fifth Avenue still constituted the established residential center for the upper class, but within four years fine brownstones and elegant town houses lined Fifth Avenue from 42nd Street to just below the southern boundary of Central Park at 59th Street. Stuyvesant Square, at Second Avenue and 16th Street, was another fashionable residential center, as was St. John's Park, below Canal Street and west of West Broadway, until it yielded to Commodore Vanderbilt's freight depot for the Hudson River Railroad in 1866. The middle class lived in Greenwich Village between Canal and 14th streets, west of Broadway up to Houston Street, west of Sixth Avenue above Houston, and in Chelsea west of Seventh Avenue between 14th and 34th streets. Shipyard and industrial workers, as well as shopkeepers, lived near their places of work in the triangular area bounded by Chatham Square, East Broadway, Houston, and the Bowery. And recently arrived immigrants lived east of Chatham Square and in the vicinity of the Bowery and lower Third Avenue.

By 1866 twenty-nine omnibus lines served the city with horse-drawn stages, many of which traveled Broadway from South Ferry northward to various terminals, averaging about ten round trips per day. Five streetcar lines, then called rail car lines and drawn by horse or mule, traced fourteen routes as far north as 59th Street. Though most made Broadway stops, none in 1865 ran along Broadway itself. In that year plans were under way to build elevated rail lines. The first of these, begun in 1867 on Greenwich Street and along Ninth Avenue, reached the 30th Street terminal by early 1870.[4] The rail car and elevated lines wrought significant demographic changes in the city, causing the old residential areas in the core to be taken progressively for commercial use and facilitating the migration and residential dispersal of the population. The elevated rail lines at once stimulated and made possible this dispersal because they enabled people to live at greater distances from their workplaces.

Residential Fifth Avenue, built up with fine houses, was New York's pride. But by end of the 1860s, commerce had begun encroaching on its lower end:

> [Fifth Avenue] has been invaded between 12th and 23rd Streets by the aggressive influence of trade. First-class stores have been constructed out of brown-stone palaces and dry-goods, millinery, tailoring, restaurants, and music-stores are beginning to intrude. . . .
>
> Fifth Avenue is sometimes criticized as almost too solemn in its tone. The architecture lacks variety, it is true, and the too-prevailing brown-stone gives it a monotonous appearance. This is far from being the case, however, when filled with promenaders and vehicles.[5]

Broadway, by contrast, was the bustling, commercial spine of the city. A road since the days of New Amsterdam, Broadway became the city's mercantile and residential center in the English colonial period. With its proximity to orchard and garden space and its access to both rivers, it offered important topographic advantages to the early settlers. Then as now, it came the closest to uniting all of Manhattan's streets, running through the city for a length of 14.6 miles and intersecting all the crosstown streets from Bowling Green to 216th and all avenues from Fifth to West End (the continuation of Eleventh Avenue).[6] As a consequence it became the primary axial thoroughfare.

The transformation of Broadway into the prime commercial artery of a metropolis began in about 1850. *Harper's Magazine* described the process in 1862:

> Those who remember the Broadway of twenty years ago can hardly walk the street now without incessant wonder and surprise. For although the transformation is gradually wrought, it is always going on before the eye. Twenty years ago it was a street of three-story red-brick houses. Now it is a highway of stone, and iron, and marble buildings. . . .
>
> And yet, among all the costly and colossal buildings that have of late been erected, how few show any real taste or grace. . . . The fine architectural effects of some streets in Genoa, in Naples, in Rome, in Paris, in Berlin, in Venice, and other great foreign cities, are unknown in New York. There are some exceptions. Some of the new stores in Broadway are almost as imposing as some of the palaces in Italian cities.
>
> [I]n Broadway the cellar and wareroom are invading the boudoir. Great wholesale stores stand where the pretty shops stood, and if you go below Canal Street of an evening there is something ghostly in the gloom of the closed warehouses. . . .
>
> Of course in all these changes the city has lost much of its old town character, and becomes every year more and more a metropolis.[7]

Three themes for the future find early expression in this passage: continuous change, change that alters and may take away the life and variety of the streets, and the problem of finding adequate architectural expression for the new commercial buildings (suggested in the section extolling the street architecture of foreign cities).

The city's commercial establishments were distributed throughout the lower downtown area, with Broadway as the spine. The offices of importers, shipping companies and agents, transportation concerns, financial institutions, and lawyers were housed in buildings mostly four to five stories tall along both sides of Broadway from Bowling Green to Wall Street. Flour, grain, and grocery merchants could be found on Beaver Street, predominantly around the old Produce Exchange. Along Broad Street were the imported wine and fruit merchants and the new Stock Exchange building, completed in 1865 between Exchange and Wall streets. The post office was still on Nassau Street between Liberty and Cedar. The offices of the *Times*, the *Herald*, the *Evening Post*, the *Tribune*, the *Sun* and other newspapers, the American Tract Society, and Harper's publishing and printing plant were at the south end of City Hall Park, in the area known as Printing House Square. On Catherine Street were dry goods, clothing, and millinery establishments, including Lord & Taylor's dry goods store.

From Chambers Street to Canal, Broadway was wholesale dry goods territory; west of Broadway, in the area around Chambers, machinery and tools were manufactured and sold. The large retail stores, notably A. T. Stewart's, were along Broadway between Canal Street and Astor Place and on Broadway and Fourth Avenue between Ninth and Tenth streets. Hotels were scattered, but the largest concentration was along Broadway below 24th Street, including the venerable Astor House near City Hall Park and the famous Fifth Avenue Hotel—the first hotel with a passenger elevator—at 23rd Street. The Fifth Avenue would be joined by other first-class hotels, and the section north and west of Madison Square, close by the city's entertainment center, would remain the city's primary hotel district for many years thereafter.

After 1865 prestigious commercial and fashionable residential quarters moved rapidly north; by 1872, in the area bounded by Madison and Sixth avenues and 42nd and 59th streets, two hundred high-rent buildings were under construction. The relentlessly northward migration is illustrated by successive moves of the Benjamin Altman store: in 1865 it was on Third Avenue between Ninth and Tenth streets; after 1868 it remained nearly four decades in the same neighborhood on Sixth Avenue, first near 21st Street, then at 19th; finally, in 1906, it relocated to Fifth Avenue and 34th Street. The far West Side below 59th Street did not flourish as prime office, retailing, and residential space chiefly because of the docks and the congested traffic, including much nighttime transit of produce into the city, and the presence of Hudson River Railroad tracks.

The Office Building

As office functions became distinct from production, manufacturing, warehousing, transportation, and distribution of foods and raw materials, a need for buildings devoted entirely to offices arose. Manufacturing, service, and railroad industries multiplied and expanded in the nineteenth century, and administrative functions, paper flow, and personnel increased correspondingly. The need to keep records—records of financial transactions, inventories of raw materials and finished goods, manufacturing reports, administrative accounts, itemizations of transported goods, and waybills—required increasingly more personnel and more office space. The proliferation of fixed property and real estate sales; of property, payroll, and income taxes; and of legal transactions expanded the demand for record keeping, as did the need for intramural communications among offices, executives, and sales forces. And every increase in record keeping meant hiring someone to keep those records and providing a place for that person to work.

More office workers in turn created the need for expanded training techniques, added payroll transactions, and more supplies, each requiring still further additions to staff and operations. The coming of the telephone after 1876 ended dependence on the ubiquitous messenger boy, introducing instead telephone operators, instruments, switchboards, and still more office employees, needing much more space. The expansion of corporate headquarters gave rise to the service industry, with its increased emphasis on office functions. All such trends were particularly pronounced in port cities and financial centers; and since it was preeminently both, post–Civil War New York experienced the multiplication of office buildings both as rental investments and as owner-used quarters.

According to the engineer and architect George Hill, office buildings were converted dwellings up to 1858, "except in a few commercial cities like New York."[8] Arising to meet special functional requirements, which in turn demanded new architectural solutions, the special office building type is largely a nineteenth-century invention, if not specifically a New York creation. Its origins can be traced to ancient Rome, where the Tabularium, or Public Record Office (first century B.C.), served as an office building and a repository of official records. European town halls of the twelfth to sixteenth centuries like the Uffizi in Florence (begun 1560) included municipal offices as well as council chambers, courts, and places of public ceremony; another variant was the guildhall of the twelfth to fifteenth centuries, which housed the offices and public spaces of medieval guilds.

1.1

*Schermerhorn Row
(1810–12).
Full row includes
2–18 Fulton Street,
195 Front Street, and
91 and 92 South
Street.
Photograph by
Charles L. Sachs.*

As late as the 1840s in New York, the work of maintaining records, ledgers, and accounts and of meeting with merchants, traders, buyers, and suppliers was done in countinghouses. Originating in England's port and commercial cities, countinghouses nearly always incorporated private dwellings on the upper floors above warehouses and vaults.[9] The buildings were typically houselike in appearance, brick-walled and three or four stories tall, with high-pitched roofs where the hoistways used for loading commodities into the building were stored. One of the best preserved rows of this general type is Schermerhorn Row (1810–12), constructed as twelve adjoining buildings by merchant Peter Schermerhorn on Fulton Street in the South Street Seaport (Fig. 1.1). Apparently built exclusively for warehouse and commercial use, these four-story Federal-style buildings originally had exterior iron stairways leading to the second-floor counting rooms, and in some instances the upper floors were open from one building to the next.[10]

The earliest of New York's specialized bank buildings appeared at the end of the eighteenth century. Although usually only one or two stories high, these banks contained large business halls that anticipated the entrance halls and public business spaces later incorporated in tall office buildings. The same is true of the spacious halls of merchants' exchanges, like that of the first Merchants' Exchange (1825–27), designed by Martin E. Thompson, or the rotunda of its replacement on the same Wall Street site, the second Merchants' Exchange (1836–42), by Isaiah Rogers. The Bank of New York (1797–98) is believed to have been the first building in the city constructed exclusively for banking purposes.[11] Built to the plans of George Doolett, a self-styled architect who apparently came to the city just for this project, the bank was a sophisticated Federal-style block that apparently contained a two-story-high banking hall (Fig. 1.2). Little about its exterior suggested a commercial function, but openings set within inscribed arches on its Wall Street front, which created the effect of arcades, seem in retrospect a prediction of the many arcaded commercial buildings and skyscrapers to come. With the onset of the Greek Revival era around 1820 came the temple-fronted bank. Thompson's Phenix Bank

1.2
View of Wall and William streets with Bank of New York (1797–98; demolished) at left. Drawing by Robertson. Collection of The New-York Historical Society.

(c. 1824; demolished) was the first Wall Street building to adhere to the Greek temple model, but this was not a specifically commercial building type. The temple form and temple portico were adapted to all kinds of large buildings, including domestic, public, and even government buildings dedicated primarily to office functions, like the Patent Office in Washington (1836–40), designed by Robert Mills.

The type of countinghouse represented by Schermerhorn Row was succeeded during the Greek Revival by countinghouses or warehouses with ranges of trabeated granite piers at the ground-story level, usually with severely plain Tuscan capitals. Good examples survive at 207–11 Water Street (1835–36) and at 3 Coenties Slip (1836–37), which was built with five stories. These followed the lead of the Arthur Tappan Store (1826; demolished), said to have been the earliest New York warehouse with such piers (Fig. 1.3). Designed by Ithiel Town and built on Pearl Street, the Tappan Store served as the prototype of the New York warehouse for the next twenty years. The trabeated pier ranges of these buildings, a feature that seems uniquely American but undoubtedly derived some inspiration from abroad, foreshadowed the strongly articulated piers of later warehouses and office buildings. Also interesting in this connection—and in retrospect curiously prophetic of the twentieth-century glass-box skyscraper—is the "Davisean window": a multistoried, near strip window favored by the architect Alexander Jackson Davis for his neoclassical designs after about 1831.[12] Paneled at the floor levels, recessed, and characteristically set between rows of square pillars, such windows appeared in Town & Davis's Lyceum of Natural History on Broadway near Prince Street (1835–36; demolished). Davis's elevation project of 1862 for a domed commercial exchange, in the collection of The New-York Historical Society, features these windows, which rise from base to cornice and create the illusion of a glass wall behind stone piers.

In spite of a style change, which came in the late 1840s with the importation of the palazzo mode from England, the houselike business building did not immediately disappear in New York. The A. T. Stewart "Marble Dry-goods Palace" (1845–46) was the first

American commercial building designed in the newly imported style, but above the distinctly commercial columned and glazed ground floor, and despite the white marble facing, its facades resembled row houses of the type known commonly as "brownstones" then beginning to rise in New York (Fig. 1.4). Peter B. Wight saw the building "as an important link between two styles of store-architecture which have prevailed in New York": the older type, with granite piers at the ground story, and the cast-iron-fronted stores and wholesale houses that immediately followed.[13] Those iron-fronted buildings, typically evocative of the arcaded High Renaissance palazzo—especially those in north Italy with large openings framed by colonnettes—were unmistakably commercial in function.

The styling and construction of storehouses, warehouses, and factories also anticipated the modern office building and the skyscraper. These buildings, distinguished from countinghouses by their requirement of large, undivided expanses of floor area for storage, machinery, or for displaying merchandise, achieved a monumental expression in the nineteenth century both in America and in England, where structures called warehouses have existed at least since the fourteenth century. From about 1840 to 1890, the warehouse and the office building evolved simultaneously, and to a certain extent warehouses influenced skyscraper design. Indeed, the New York City Department of Buildings, which was founded in 1860 and began issuing permits in 1864, did not recognize "office building" as a classification until about 1875, or "warehouse" until 1882. Such buildings were originally defined as "1st class stores and storehouses." The most advanced warehouse structural system of interior cast-iron columns and iron-framed floors was also used in the earliest high-rise office buildings. Merchants, who often had their offices in their

warehouses and received buyers there, wanted their places of business to look impressive, so for a long time the one building type was apparently seen as the equal, or nearly so, of the other. Large dry goods stores like Stewart's "Marble Palace" were simply aggrandized warehouses. They were comparable to midcentury English wholesale warehouses like those in Bristol and Manchester, which had large show rooms or galleried stair halls for the display of goods.

In the second half of the nineteenth century, warehouses, like office buildings and banks, were frequently architect-designed. Several such warehouses, notably Henry Hobson Richardson's renowned Marshall Field Wholesale Store in Chicago (1885–87; demolished) and Babb, Cook & Willard's De Vinne Press Building in New York (1885–86), rank with the best-known skyscrapers as masterpieces of American commercial design. Chicago warehouses, like William Le Baron Jenney's first Leiter building (1879), have long been regarded as signal contributors to that city's emergence as a celebrated city of skyscrapers, and the same is true in New York. Moreover, several New York commercial buildings that figure prominently in the evolution of the skyscraper combined aspects of both warehouse and office building. George B. Post's Produce Exchange built in the early 1880s, for example, devoted most of its interior space to an exchange hall of vast, warehouselike dimensions, but the imposing, ten-story block also contained offices. Warehouses and warehouselike commercial buildings are essential to the early skyscraper story.

English commercial buildings of the 1840s to about 1870, a period when commercial architecture flowered in Britain's urban centers, were a powerful influence on New York buildings. Their palazzo style, strongly articulated piers, and arcaded facades were imi-

1.4
*A. T. Stewart's
"Marble Dry-goods
Palace"
(1845–46, with
later additions),
Trench & Snook,
architects.
Broadway between
Reade and Chambers
streets.
After* New York
Illustrated *(1878).*

The Urban Context and the Office Building 9

tated by New York architects. Henry-Russell Hitchcock emphasized the importance of the palazzo mode as the "first really Victorian formula for the design of monumental commercial buildings" and one that was applied to all types of commercial buildings— from banks and insurance companies to warehouses and even markets—to such an extent that these sometimes appear functionally indistinguishable.[14] The formula was adopted in America in the mid-1840s, and from its early, domestic manifestation in Stewart's "Marble Palace" it remained standard for commercial buildings until the out-break of the Civil War. Although it was afterwards replaced by the Second Empire style, the palazzo mode left its mark on the skyscraper. Hitchcock noticed especially the regular bay treatment, which expressed the regularity of the interior metal skeleton; the unifying, dominant cornice; plastic surface relief; and expansion of the traditional palazzo formula to encompass twice as many stories and windows. The flat roofline, too, was inherited by the skyscraper, though intermittently displaced by such treatments as the Second Empire mansard favored in the 1860s and 1870s and the towered roof popular in the 1870s and 1880s.

The arcaded commercial front came into fashion in New York around 1850, as it had earlier in England, succeeding the trabeated ground stories of Greek Revival commercial buildings. An effective device for unifying the window ranges of the multistory building, arcading can be defined as a series of continuous piers or abutments that frame the windows and are joined at the top by arches. English usage dates from the rise of the palazzo mode in the 1840s, and fully arcaded commercial buildings appeared there around 1850. The Jayne Building in Philadelphia (1849–51; demolished), designed by William L. Johnston and Thomas U. Walter, was a rare commercial building in America in which a (Gothic style) granite arcade spanned fully six stories above the first floor. At a height of seven stories plus an attic and a tower, it was exceptionally tall for the time. Other Philadelphia warehouses and stores from the 1850s had several stories united by arcades.

In England the motif flourished under the influence of Ruskin from the late 1850s through the 1860s. By the mid-1850s arcading had become associated with cast-iron-fronted warehouses in New York, and by 1860 superimposed two-story arcades were commonplace. Even earlier, such predominantly masonry structures as the Chemical Bank (1849–50; demolished) and the Lord & Taylor store (1852–53; demolished), both designed by Thomas & Son, featured floor-to-ceiling windows that were linked vertically as two-story arcades (see Fig. 8.24). Functionally, these admitted much more light into the building; aesthetically, they opened up the facade and affirmed its verticality, and they distinguished the building as having a commercial use. Eventually the rhythmic repetition of arcades became a favorite means of articulating the multistoried New York office building.

France, too, left its mark on the New York office building. In the early 1860s, to some extent via England rather than directly from Paris, the Second Empire mode arrived in America, where it was adapted to all kinds of buildings. Among them was the first elevator office building, the Equitable in New York (completed in 1870). New York office buildings of the 1870s and early 1880s, chiefly those designed by Richard Morris Hunt and his student George Browne Post, preserved aspects of the Second Empire, notably the mansard roof. They were also influenced by such buildings as the Magasins Réunis

1.5
Detail,
Magasins Réunis
(1865–66),
Paris,
Gabriel Davioud,
architect.
After Revue générale
de l'architecture *28*
(1870).

on the Place de la République in Paris (1865–66). Designed by Gabriel Davioud, this warehouselike, structurally expressive building belongs to a type rather confusingly characterized as *Néo-Grec* (Fig. 1.5). Typically, as is true of the Magasins Réunis, the French models employed the highly rational segmental arch, along with low-relief or incised decoration that was subordinated to the basic structural components of the building. These features were adapted to American commercial buildings.

Eugène Emmanuel Viollet-le-Duc's theories of rational construction, which had evolved from his intensive study of Gothic architecture, also impressed New York architects, who had early access to his views in translation. In 1870–71 Peter B. Wight published a translation of Viollet-le-Duc's lectures at the Ecole des Beaux-Arts, and Henry Van Brunt, a former student of Hunt's, began publishing the first English translation of the *Entretiens sur l'architecture* in 1875.[15] Hunt, the first American to study architecture at the Ecole des Beaux-Arts, was an important conduit of French influence in the city, chiefly through his New York atelier conducted in the late 1850s. As a New York architect until 1871, when he moved to Chicago, Wight was exposed to ideas emanating from Hunt's circle.

The *Rundbogenstil*, a German mode of the 1830s and 1840s that was inspired by the pre–High Renaissance round-arched styles, affected midcentury American architecture. German and east European architects and builders who came to America in the 1840s brought the style with them, Alexander Saeltzer and Leopold Eidlitz becoming the two most prominent New York practitioners. In New York the "round-arched style," as it was

The Urban Context and the Office Building 11

frequently designated, hardly challenged the popular palazzo mode but remained, in its several variations, an acceptable option for less expensively detailed commercial structures until past 1860. Especially characteristic was the arcaded brick facade, and often the segmental arch appears on such buildings, typically at the ground floor. Eidlitz's massive Continental Bank (1856–57) on Wall Street was thoroughly *Rundbogenstil*, its arcaded walls nearly as much glass as masonry (Fig. 1.6). Such examples provided a background for the arcaded and pier-articulated exterior walls of skyscrapers.

The influence of the work of Karl Friedrich Schinkel and his pupils, transmitted through German publications available in New York and by the immigrant-architects,

1.7
Detail,
Perspective View of
Bauakademie (1831–
36; demolished),
Berlin,
Karl Friedrich
Schinkel, architect.
After Schinkel,
Sammlung Architek-
tonischer Entwürfe,
1819–40.
Avery Architectural
and Fine Arts Library,
Columbia University
in the City of New
York.

helped shape American commercial design. Schinkel's more utilitarian work, notably his stark, *Rundbogenstil* Packhof warehouses (1829–32) and skeletal-appearing Bauakademie (1831–36) in Berlin, was significant in this regard (Fig. 1.7). With its tall piers, segment-headed ground-floor windows, triple-windows, and polychromatic brick walls, the Bauakademie presaged New York's post–Civil War commercial style. The theoretical treatises of Gottfried Semper, not well known in America until after his death in 1879, had little if any influence on nineteenth-century commercial architects in New York. Semper's views concerning revealed structure apparently impressed Chicago architects, including Louis Sullivan, after 1880, but his impact seems negligible once the New York predecessors of Sullivan's early commercial design—the Marine National Bank project, the Racquet Club, and similar works—are recognized.

The Insurance Company Building

The rise of the office building as a distinctive, specially planned building type is closely associated with the rapid growth of the insurance business in the nineteenth century. All of the factors that necessitated corporate office headquarters were multiplied for insurance companies, which required huge bodies of records for premium and claims payments, investments, and actuarial statistics. But insurance—in the modern sense of a legal and financial instrument by which the insured can recover losses in recognition of payment of premiums to the insurer—was a business device long before the nineteenth century. According to the Florentine historian Giovanni Villani, marine insurance was introduced to the Lombard port cities in 1182. It was adopted in the cities of Flanders and other Low Countries at the end of the fourteenth century. Citations in the first Elizabethan parliament of 1559 and in various literary works throughout the sixteenth century—an allusion in Machiavelli's *Belfagor* (c. 1515–20), for example, to a ship "laden with uninsured merchandise"—suggest that the practice had by then become common.

In 1583 life insurance was introduced in London, and the beginnings of actuarial tables and social-demographic statistics appeared about a century later. The problem of potential loss for the insurer was solved in the late seventeenth century when marine underwriters met at Edward Lloyd's coffee house in London to develop a program of sharing risks by pooling resources and dividing premiums. The mathematical basis of actuarial theory, essential to the accurate establishment of annuities, claims, and premiums, was framed by the Franco-English mathematician Abraham De Moivre in *A Treatise on Annuities* (1725), which remained authoritative into the nineteenth century with numerous revised and corrected editions. Casualty insurance, a by-product of fire insurance, was stimulated by the railroad accidents that accompanied the rapid expansion of rail transit after 1830.

Insurance companies appeared in the American colonies during the eighteenth century and spread to the major commercial centers during the republican period. The Contributionship for the Insurance of Houses from Loss by Fire (1752) and the Mutual Insurance Company for Insuring Homes from Loss by Fire (1784) were established in Philadelphia, where the systematic writing of policies in the American colonies began. Comprehensive life and casualty insurance was made available in 1798 with the founding of the United Insurance Company in New York. In 1840 there were but four life insurance companies in the United States; by 1859 eighteen more were writing policies, and seven of those were in New York City.

The office building as a distinctive architectural type may have originated with the County Fire Office (1819–20), which was designed by Robert Abraham primarily for the insurance business and built as part of John Nash's scheme for the development of Regent Street in London. Modeled on Inigo Jones's Somerset House New Gallery of 1661–62, the palazzo-like facade of the Fire Office, with its open rusticated ground story, heralded the importance of the business going on within. According to Hitchcock, by the 1830s the architecture of banks and insurance company buildings in England was as significant as that of public buildings: "Such financial institutions were the first to have the wealth and the need for prestige that seemed to justify such dignity."[16] Asserting that insurance companies in particular were the architectural leaders, Sir John Summerson explained that "insurance depended, even more than banks, on the wide dissemination of confidence, and, moreover, on the propagation of a sentimental image, the image of upright, prudent men banded together to arrest the cruel hand of fate."[17] For these reasons the architectural image of Medicean wealth and dignity projected by the palazzo mode served well the purposes of insurance companies.

From about 1840 in major English cities, and after the Civil War in New York, large numbers of office buildings began to rise. The widespread construction of buildings specifically to be leased to tenants for office use began in London about 1850, a much earlier instance being a building in Moorgate Street designed by Edward d'Anson (1837). An early New York example, and one of the first buildings in the city that was devoted entirely to offices and had no storefront, was the five-story Trinity Building (1851–53) at 111 Broadway (Fig. 1.8). Its huge size, relative plainness, and ranges of individually arcaded stories—more suggestive of the *Rundbogenstil* than of the English-inspired palazzo mode—marked it as speculatively built and anonymously commercial, rather than domestic in function.

Insurance companies required an open area for doing business with the public, but otherwise their needs were not essentially different from those of other companies occupying office buildings, and insurance-purpose buildings were quickly assimilated into the general commercial type in England. But in New York such buildings were designed

to be especially imposing architecturally until past the turn of the century; a dramatic example is the soaring, Venetianesque Metropolitan Life tower completed in 1909 (see Fig. 11.7). As a highly competitive business in a capitalist country noted for encouraging competition, insurance companies very much needed to be noticed. The first insurance office building in New York of any architectural distinction was probably the palazzo-styled, mansionlike Atlantic and Sun Mutual Insurance Company Building, which was designed by the English-born and -trained Frederic Diaper and built in 1852 on the corner of Wall and William streets (see Fig. 4.29). More monumental examples were built in the 1860s, notably the New York Life and Equitable buildings.

The Hotel and the Apartment House

Some of the earliest large and tall buildings in New York were hotels, and their development must be considered as parallel, if not instrumental, to the rise of the tall office building. The history of the hotel as a public lodging place begins with medieval inns. These accommodations were especially numerous in pilgrimage towns: there were more than a thousand in Rome by the mid-fifteenth century. Inns usually consisted of a common sleeping room, a dining-lounging area, and, by the sixteenth century, a few private rooms as well. The English-language use of the term *hotel* in this sense dates from the eighteenth century, one of the earliest citations occurring in Smollett's *Travels*

1.8
Trinity Building (1851–53; demolished), Richard Upjohn, architect. Museum of the City of New York.

through France and Italy (1766). But at that time such buildings were no more than traditional inns on a larger scale.

Hotels in the modern sense—with private rooms, numerous public spaces, special services, and bathing and toilet facilities—originated at the European spas. The first with a full complement of facilities was probably the grand hotel at Baden-Baden, which was converted from a Capuchin monastery in 1807–9 by Friedrich Weinbrenner.[18] The first comparable hotel in England was the Royal Hotel at Plymouth (1811–19). The first newly built structure in America that qualifies as a hotel, though not in a class with those just named, was probably City Hotel in New York (1794–96). Designed by John McComb, Jr., City Hotel stood on Broadway north of Trinity Churchyard, on the site of the two succeeding Boreel buildings (1849–50, 1878–79) and their successor, the United States Realty building completed in 1907.

Another early New York example was Holt's Hotel (1832), built by Stephen B. Holt at the junction of Fulton, Pearl, and Water streets (Fig. 1.9). Later operated as the United States Hotel, Holt's was one of the first flat-roofed buildings in the northeastern United States. Greek Revival in style, it was six stories tall above the basement and rose 125 feet from the sidewalk to the top of the tower, where there was an observatory. It had 165 rooms, running water on all the floors, and what was likely the first hoisting device in a New York City hotel. This steam-powered baggage lift doubled as a primitive passenger elevator: "The principal operations of the establishment are carried on by means of a small steam-engine, which turns the spit, raises the baggage (and the owner, if he chooses) to the elevation of its destined apartment, pumps the water and conveys the smoking viands from the kitchen to the topmost story."[19] Such luxurious accommodations as a 100-foot-long main dining room, two additional side dining rooms, and twenty-five parlors suggest that Holt's should be deemed the forerunner of the modern hotel in New York City rather than the later, much better known Astor House (1834–36), which is usually accorded that distinction. By the time the 390-room Astor House was completed to the plans of Isaiah Rogers, the nation led the world in the quality of its hotel spaces and facilities, especially in the installation of bathrooms with lavatories and toilets and in the provision of special parlors for ladies and families.

The Astor was followed by such notable New York hotels as the new five-story City Hotel (1851) at 429 Broadway, which was actually two large houses joined. Next came La Farge House on Broadway opposite Bond Street (1852–53; burned 1854; rebuilt 1854–55), designed by James Renwick, Jr.; the sprawling, five-story Metropolitan Hotel on Broadway between Prince and Houston streets (1850–52), designed by Trench & Snook; and its rival, the six-story, 600-room St. Nicholas Hotel by the same firm on Broadway at Spring Street (1851–54). These were followed by the vast, six-story Fifth Avenue Hotel at 23rd Street (1856–59) and by French's Hotel, which opened in 1849 but was renovated and reconstructed in 1859 by John B. Snook. Griffith Thomas of Thomas & Son designed the exterior of the Fifth Avenue, which was the second building in the city to have a passenger elevator. French's, opposite City Hall Park on the corner of Frankfort Street, was fully seven stories tall. By 1866 the city could boast more than thirty first-class hotels, and four years later the number included the huge Grand Central Hotel.[20] None of these early New York hotels is extant.

By 1874 it was estimated that about half of the city's nearly two hundred hotels were

1.9
*United States
(Late Holt's) Hotel
(1832; demolished).
Lithograph by N.
Currier, c. 1839.
Collection of The
New-York Historical
Society.*

occupied by permanent residents.[21] The need for apartment houses was already acute, but few such buildings had yet been built. With the completion of the Stuyvesant Apartments (1869–70), New Yorkers embarked on a new Paris-inspired mode of life: apartment-house living, necessitated by the rising costs of maintaining or renting a private house. The Stuyvesant, generally recognized as the first apartment house proper in the city, was designed by Richard Morris Hunt for the enterprising Rutherfurd Stuyvesant, and it stood at 142 East 18th Street just west of Third Avenue until its demolition in 1959. Five stories high, the building contained twenty units, including four studio apartments on the top floor. Its style, inspired by Viollet-le-Duc, anticipated aspects of Hunt's later commercial work. Following the success of this venture, Hunt's block-long, seven-story Stevens House (1870–72; demolished), which was commissioned by the hotel entrepreneur Paran Stevens and built on 27th Street between Fifth Avenue and Broadway, proved a prototypical if ill-fated experiment in the establishment of the luxury apartment house. In 1879, after several years as an apartment hotel for people of modest means, Stevens House was converted into the Victoria Hotel.[22] In spite of that early failure, the apartment house inevitably took hold among the middle and upper classes after 1880. Before 1885, when a law was passed limiting the height of the apartment house, it left its mark on the city in the form of large, tall buildings that relied on the same construction techniques as office buildings. These, too, must be considered in the skyscraper story.

A combination of geographical, technological, and economic factors made the development of the skyscraper inevitable after 1865. These factors include intensive land use and high land prices, the coming of rapid transit and of the passenger elevator and iron framing, improvement in streets and in public utilities, and the extremely rapid expansion of the American industrial economy after the Civil War, with New York as the financial center.[23] Indefinable psychological factors also played a role, notably the identification of height with prestige, power, and the universe—notions that had helped raise the pyramids of Egypt, the towers of European city halls, and the campaniles and spires of medieval churches. But necessity was the real mother of this invention. The old office buildings were obsolete, many of them associated with the old commercial-residential blocks. There was a need for a new type of specialized building to replace the traditional, small generalized enclosure. Insurance companies and newspapers, especially the Equitable Life Assurance Society and the *Tribune*, pioneered the move to new high-rise buildings. The financial depression of the 1870s inhibited construction, but the office decline was partly offset by the gradual acceptance and spread of apartment buildings, most of them converted from other uses. Hotels had long provided a precedent for the exceptionally tall building divided internally into rooms of more or less uniform dimensions.

Three periods of real estate development in the city can be ascertained in the progress of the skyscraper from inception to maturity: (1) a speculative period lasting from 1868 to about 1873, characterized mostly by the purchase and sale of lots, the major consequences being the construction of the earliest of the tall elevator office buildings and the northward shift of the commercial center of gravity, with the core of retail trade moving from 14th to 23rd Street; (2) a period of fermentation following the panic of 1873, and coincident with the subsequent depression, lasting from about 1874 to 1879; and (3) the period of maturation beginning in 1880.[24] But before turning to that progression, let us examine the technological developments that made the skyscraper possible.

2

TECHNOLOGICAL PREPARATIONS

The skyscraper became practicable only when certain essential technologies had developed to the point that they could sustain the structure and the human activities within it. The most important construction advances were metal framing, wind bracing, secure anchoring, fire protection, and the development of power-operated construction equipment. Once the buildings were standing, worker productivity, comfort, and health required adequate heating, ventilation, plumbing, elevator service, and lighting.

Evolution of the Iron Frame

The high-rise multistory building is theoretically possible with a traditional structural system of masonry piers or walls, small windows, spread-footing stone foundations, piling, and interior bearing partitions, but practicality demanded metal framing. After the Civil War the increase in land values, building costs, and rentals in New York and other cities made the iron frame a necessity in order to maximize interior space and the window area. In addition, iron offered important advantages over masonry: greater intrinsic strength, superior elasticity, and, as a result, high tensile strength.

The chief period of iron construction began with the Industrial Revolution. Cast iron was the first ferrous metal to be used systematically in building construction, from the late eighteenth century. Wrought iron, though it had been used for small structural sections since ancient times, was introduced for primary structural members only about 1830. Modern commercial cast iron is a compound comprising mainly iron and carbon, with some impurities, cast in a mold.[1] Its chief advantage is its compressive strength, which depends on its relatively high carbon content; its shortcoming is excessive hardness and brittleness.

England, France, and Russia were the pioneers in modern metal construction, though the United States soon eclipsed them all. The first use of iron for primary structural members was probably at St. Anne's Church in Liverpool (1770–72), where cast-iron columns supported the gallery. The first cast-iron beams may have been those in the Marble Palace in St. Petersburg, Russia (1768–72), designed by Antonio Rinaldi; and the domed roof of Jean-Victor Louis' Théâtre Français (1786–90), Paris, is supported by a curious and redundant assemblage of open-web cast-iron girders and ribs and wrought-iron hangers and struts. The first cast-iron columns in a factory and the first in a multi-story building appeared in England, in the Calico Mill of Derby (1792–93) and in an exactly contemporary warehouse in Milford, both built by William Strutt. The designer and builder Charles Bage introduced the first cast-iron frame of columns and beams in the Benyon and Marshall Flax Mill (1796–97) in Shrewsbury. Beams with a lower flange and a spreading triangular section in the lower half were introduced by Bage and by the partnership of Matthew Boulton and James Watt in English mills built between 1799 and 1801.

The engineer William Murdock used an iron roof truss in a Soho, London, foundry of 1810. Murdock, the first to recognize the weakness of cast iron in tension and the necessity for wrought iron in tension members, divided the truss elements into cast and wrought iron according to the distribution of stress. In Murdock's king-post truss, the top chord and the struts were cast iron and the bottom chord and hanger wrought iron. The first dome supported on cast-iron ribs and circumferential cast-iron ties was designed by F.-J. Bélanger, assisted by the engineer Brunet, for the Halle au Blé in Paris (1808–13), and Charles Fowler designed the Hungerford Fish Market in London (1835) with the first free-standing iron frame and the first iron frame with wind bracing. In his *Practical Essay on the Strength of Cast Iron* (London, 1822), Thomas Tredgold made the first proposal for a cast-iron beam with an I-section—that is, with top and bottom flanges—the form that would become standard for the metal beam in the subsequent history of iron and steel construction.

In 1831 the mathematician Eton Hodgkinson and the builder William Fairbairn published *Theoretical and Experimental Researches to Ascertain the Strength and Best Form for Iron Beams* (Manchester). Their collaboration established the importance of uniting mathematics and theory with practical building in the service of technical progress. Experiments that they conducted from 1826 to 1830 demonstrated that wrought iron is superior for members subject to deflection and, hence, tension and that the flanged section is the most efficient shape.

Wrought iron, which is composed mostly of iron and glassy slag (iron silicate) and has less than 0.3 percent carbon, is quite different from cast iron.[2] It is shaped, when heated, by hammering or rolling under intense pressure. Wrought iron has greater tensile strength than cast iron, as much as 48,000 pounds per square inch in the direction of the fibers. Because of the strong interest in England in metal framing, the evolution to deep-section wrought-iron girders was concentrated there between 1840 and 1850. Small angles and T-shaped sections had been rolled since 1784, when Henry Cort invented the grooved roller, and were used, for example, in the roof trusses of the Euston Station train shed (1835–39) in London.

The most significant early developments in iron construction began with the introduction of the bowstring or tied arch by Robert Stephenson in the London & Birmingham railway station in Weedon (1835–36). Stephenson used a small cast-iron arch with a malleable iron tie to translate the arch thrust into tension in the tie. About 1840 Stephenson also introduced the built-up plate girder composed of flange plates, web plate, and angles; the design was used for a railroad bridge over the River Wear in 1841. The built-up girder has since been used wherever long spans and heavy loads require depths greater than can be rolled. After about 1890 it was commonly used for the massive transfer and distributing girders in skyscrapers.

Reinforced castings originated in 1849, when J. N. Rastrick proposed riveting wrought-iron plates to the lower flange of cast-iron beams to take the tension in a simple member. Late in the same year Peter W. Barlow introduced the technique of inserting wrought-iron bars in the lower flange of the cast-iron beam or girder as a means of increasing the tensile strength. According to the American structural engineer Corydon T. Purdy, the wrought-iron girder appeared about 1840 in America at Sedgwick Hall in Lenox, Massachusetts. Each girder of Sedgwick Hall was built up with an arched top flange and a horizontal bottom flange, both connected by bolts set about twenty inches center to center, with a corrugated web plate multiply curved so as to lie on alternate sides of the bolts.[3]

Other milestones in iron construction include William Fairbairn's London flour mill of 1839, which was all cast-iron construction with masonry piers, and the Crystal Palace of 1851. That vast, 1,848-foot-long exhibition hall, designed as a modular, prefabricated, and demountable construction by Joseph Paxton in association with the engineering firm of Fox & Henderson, was built with cast-iron columns, cast- and wrought-iron girders and beams, trussed girders, and with protoportal and full diagonal bracing. The first wrought-iron plate floor arches are described in Fairbairn, *On the Application of Cast and Wrought Iron to Building Purposes* (1854), and the first H-columns and full portal bracing were used in the Royal Navy Boat Store (1858–60) in Sheerness, England, which was designed by Godfrey Greene.

The first multistory, iron-framed, fireproof, and curtain-walled building in the world was the St. Ouen Docks warehouse, designed by Hippolyte Fontaine and built in Paris in 1864–65. The walls, which were made of brick panels, were carried story by story on cast-iron spandrel beams, and cast-iron columns were used throughout the interior and in the wall. The primary girders were built-up wrought iron, with a span of twenty-six feet and a depth of twenty inches, and the cast-iron beams that supported the brick arches of the floor had a span of thirteen feet between the wrought-iron girders. The unprotected iron, however, although incombustible, could be weakened to the point of collapse should the contents catch fire. The floors were leveled up with concrete that had a loading factor of 600 pounds per square foot, far above the usual maximum for warehouses of 300. All the components to be used in skyscraper construction were in place, though the skyscraper itself was still several years away and would be developed on the other side of the Atlantic.

A number of interesting experiments in reinforcing masonry buildings with iron were carried out in San Francisco following the earthquake of 1868; however, the use of iron to supplement masonry was not new. It was done in classical antiquity and from time to time in post-Renaissance buildings. The Minoans, moreover, had reinforced masonry against earthquake forces with an elastic material—wood—in the early second millennium B.C.

Although its form is a mystery, the iron roof used in Benjamin Latrobe's reconstruction of Nassau Hall at Princeton University in 1803 was probably the first important development in the American chronology of iron construction. Cast-iron columns were probably first used in American buildings soon afterward. We know that iron columns supported the balcony of the reconstructed Park Theatre in New York, completed in 1821, and that Latrobe's pupil William Strickland designed the Chestnut Street Theater in Philadelphia, which opened in 1822, with such columns. A wrought-iron truss of multi-panel king-post construction, its members angles and bars, supported the roof of the Philadelphia Gas Works (1835–37). The girder at Sedgwick Hall in Lenox appeared in c. 1840, followed in 1842 by a storefront on Washington Street in Boston that was fabricated of cast-iron columns and lintels manufactured by Daniel D. Badger. The Travers Library in Paterson, New Jersey (1846), employed cast-iron columns and beams, although these were actually primitive by that date, the beams being cruciform rather than I-section. The first use of brick-arch, iron-beam floor construction occurred in the ground floor of the Smithsonian Institution (1847–55), designed by James Renwick, Jr.[4] Seven-inch-deep wrought-iron deck beams, the first wrought-iron beams rolled successfully in the United States, were manufactured by Peter Cooper's Trenton Iron Company in New Jersey in 1854.[5] These framed the brick-arch floors of Harper & Brothers printing plant of 1854 in New York. By 1855 the floors of customhouses designed by the supervising architect of the Treasury, Ammi B. Young, were being fabricated with brick arches and wrought-iron beams and girders, a type of construction at that time still considered "wholly new."[6]

By 1868 a number of engineering treatises important to construction in iron and concrete were circulating. These include the seminal *Skeleton Structures, Especially in Their Application to the Building of Steel and Iron Bridges* by the German-born and -trained Olaus Magnus Friedrich Erdmann Henrici, who had migrated to England. Published in the United States by Van Nostrand in 1867 with a preface dated "Westminster 1866," the book specifically applies to truss bridges of iron and steel and contains the first use of the expression "skeleton structure," applied only in that context. Henrici's treatise was useful to all builders because it provided accurate descriptions of truss action, of the geometric basis of rigidity of the triangulated truss, and of the distribution of stresses in the deflected simple beam. It also offered a method of calculating forces and deflections in truss members and girders. It probably superseded similar earlier treatises by Squire Whipple (1847) and Hermann Haupt (1851), and the concept of truss rigidity that it presented was later useful in understanding the need for and the behavior of wind bracing. The titles of other treatises published between 1854 and 1870, when the Equitable Building was completed, reveal the concerns of the time: Fairbairn, *On the Application of Cast and Wrought Iron to Building Purposes* (London and New York, 1854); François Coignet, *Bétons agglomérés appliqués à l'art de construire, notamment: à l'état monolithe, . . . et l'état de pierres artificielles* (Paris, 1861); Quincy A. Gillmore, *A Practical Treatise on Limes, Hydraulic Cements, and Mortars* (New York, 1863); James B. Francis, *On the Strength of Cast Iron Pillars* (New York, 1865); Robert G. Hatfield, *Fire-proof Floors for Banks, Insurance Companies, Office Buildings, and Dwellings* (New York, 1868); Francis Herbert Joynson, *The Metals Used in Construction* (New York, 1868); William Humber, *Strains in Girders* (New York, 1869); Julius Weisbach, *A Manual of the*

Mechanics of Engineering and of the Construction of Machines (translation from the 4th German edition, New York, 1870).

Wind Bracing

Wind bracing is a crucial component of fully developed skyscraper construction. The problem of the action of wind on structures resolves itself into two fundamental questions: (1) what is the relation between the movement of air and the pressure on any object in its path, and (2) what can be done to counteract the force and avoid its possible destructive effects?

The phenomenon is an aspect of the science of hydrodynamics, which begins with Newton's *Principia*, Book II (1687). The English physicist and inventor Robert Hooke conducted the original experiments on the interrelations of wind velocity and pressure in 1664, laying the foundations for an important branch of meteorology. The experiments were continued by the French military engineer Bernard Forest de Belidor, whose attempts to measure the wind pressure on surfaces, described in his *Architecture Hydraulique* (1737, 1739), led to the establishment of a formula to describe the relation between velocity and pressure. Belidor's formula proved to be incorrect and excessively restricted in its limits, but it marked the first attempt to calculate empirically the required wall thickness of lighthouses. Similar experiments by John Smeaton, who used the rotational or angular velocity of windmill sails to correlate wind velocity and pressure, became the basis for a table of wind pressures that was submitted to the Royal Society in England in 1759. These formulas, refined by increasingly accurate measurements over the years, became the basis of empirical formulas for the design of wind bracing in the 1880s.

The form of the modern formula is the work of the French physicist and mathematician Jean-Charles Borda and resulted from experiments begun in 1763, using flat plates fixed to a rotating arm that was calibrated to record the revolutions per minute and the pressure necessary to propel the arm at a given speed.[7] In 1832 Léonor Fresnel, the director of lighthouses for the French government, calculated the wind pressure on the prismatic surfaces of a sixty-meter-high masonry lighthouse planned for Belle Isle. Although all of Fresnel's figures for wind load and bending moment are substantially higher than those used today, he created the method by which total loads and moments are calculated, and these in turn have formed the basis for calculating forces, moments, and dimensions in the members of an iron or steel frame.[8] Fresnel's formulas were refined and used by Gustave Eiffel in calculating the bending moment of the wind load on the Eiffel Tower (1887–89). The formulas derived from Smeaton, Borda, Fresnel, and Eiffel, supplemented by the assumption that a high building is a vertical cantilever with the maximum bending moment under the wind at grade level, were being employed in New York by 1890 in the calculation of the wind loads and the bracing necessary for skyscrapers.

Foundations and Manhattan's Geology

Suitable foundation techniques had to be developed for the New York skyscraper. Roman Imperial, medieval, and Renaissance buildings had contributed such technologies as foundation piers and footings of stone and brick, spread footings of stone, the consolidation of soil with layers of crude concrete (not high-grade Roman concrete but rubble in mortar), piling, and cofferdams for construction in streams or marshy areas.[9] The peculiar geology of Manhattan Island, however, as well as the great heights to which its skyscrapers ultimately rose, dictated pile and, later, caisson foundations.

Although limited to buildings of fewer than twenty stories—and only in the mid-1890s did higher skyscrapers begin to rise with frequency—pile foundations presented problems. Because of the water, quicksand, and boulders through which the piles had to be driven, the pneumatic caisson was seen to be essential for the protection of the workers. The technique of sealing the footing area, excavating under air pressure equal to the surrounding fluid pressure, and then laying up masonry in the excavated space had been invented in 1830 by Thomas Cochrane in England and was first used for bridges. It was introduced in the United States in 1852 and employed on a large scale for the Eads Bridge (1868–74) in St. Louis and the Brooklyn Bridge (1869–83), and the first pneumatic caisson for office buildings was used in the construction of the Manhattan Life Insurance Company Building in New York in 1893. The first caisson foundation for a building in the United States, that of the Kansas City, Missouri, City Hall (1888–90), utilized the well-type or open caisson, not the pneumatic; the same is true of all caisson foundations in Chicago.

In theory, the geology of Manhattan Island is ideal for skyscrapers. The island's sunken, glaciated bedrock system, made up of the metamorphic rock that constitutes the Manhattan Prong of the New England Province, is for the most part good bearing rock. The overburden is glacial materials, chiefly quicksand, dry sand, clay, gravel, and drift that includes pebbles, cobbles, and the boulders that protrude aboveground in the upper part of Central Park. The bedrock of the island is divided into the Fordham, Inwood, and Manhattan formations, each of which has distinctive characteristics. The Fordham formation, which is considered the oldest, covers a very small area in the shape of a narrow tongue along the Harlem River around 155th Street. It consists chiefly of gneiss that is derived from sedimentary rock and various other metamorphic rocks. The Inwood formation, which encompasses the northerly district bounded roughly by Central Park West, 96th and 110th streets, and the East and Harlem rivers, plus the eastward bulge of the island between 23rd Street and the west end of the Brooklyn Bridge, is predominantly dolomitic marble. Covering the remainder of the island from Spuyten Duyvil to the Battery—about three-quarters of its total area—is the Manhattan formation. The youngest of the three, and thus the uppermost layer, it consists chiefly of a micaceous schist known as Manhattan schist.

Except in the softer joints and areas of intense shattering where decay has occurred, Manhattan schist is well suited for supporting skyscrapers. Its distribution, however, is far from consistent; the level dips far below street surface in the area between downtown and midtown—plunging hundreds of feet on the north side of Washington Square, rising again to about minus 100 feet at Chambers Street, and dropping to minus 178 feet or lower at the site of the Municipal Building. Along the commercial spine of Broadway the bedrock level from Madison Square (23rd Street) to 14th Street remains consistently close to the street surface. Between 14th and Chambers streets the level drops, reaching a low point of about minus 134 feet at Canal Street. At Duane Street, according to William

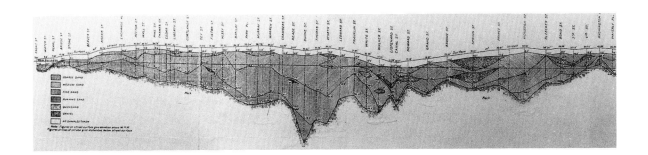

Herbert Hobbs's 1905 map of the rock basement along Broadway from the Battery to 23rd Street, the level drops to minus 183 feet, or about 153 feet below mean high-water level (Fig. 2.1).[10] The rock basement rises sharply at Chambers Street and then gradually ascends toward the tip of the island. On the site of the Hudson Terminal, however, it again drops, to levels from minus 85 to minus 110 feet.

This plunge area has been cited as the major factor in the distribution of Manhattan's skyscrapers; it has been alleged that the bedrock between midtown and downtown lies too deep even for caisson foundations. According to the journalist and popular nature writer John Kieran, writing in the late 1950s, the bedrock between midtown and downtown "is, for all practical purposes, unavailable under current construction methods as a foundation for a modern skyscraper."[11] It is true that minus 144 feet was the lowest point to which pneumatic caissons were sunk, due to a provision in the city's building code, yet it is also a fact that the well-type caissons used for the Union Terminal Tower in Cleveland (1925–28) went down 243 feet before reaching the Niagara dolomite that underlies the area. Geologist Christopher J. Schuberth is more cautious: "It is readily seen how clearly the accessibility of the bedrock has, *to some degree*, controlled the architectural planning of the city"[12] (emphasis added).

Taking into consideration the pattern of Manhattan's development, it is obvious that other factors helped determine the location of the city's skyscrapers. The area between Houston and Canal streets known today as SoHo, for example, was becoming a manufacturing and mercantile center before the Civil War, and although its more prominent businesses had begun to move uptown by the turn of the century, SoHo remained the stronghold of such marginal industries as textiles and paper waste for decades thereafter. Even though the district has been a gallery and artists' center since the 1960s, some light manufacturing still goes on there. The city's zoning laws have helped keep SoHo architecturally intact, and in 1973 a large section west of Broadway was designated a historic district.

Long before the skyscraper era, Greenwich Village was an established residential center. It, too, has been protected to some extent from high buildings by the zoning laws and, since 1969, by historic district designation. The area around and north of Union Square, the heart of the Ladies' Mile, functioned as the city's retail shopping center and amusement district from the 1870s until the first decade of the present century, when tall office buildings began to rise in the area. Geologically that section could well support buildings of forty or more stories, yet the early, relatively low skyscrapers of sixteen to twenty stories have not yet been superseded. Provisions in the zoning law have protected a large part of the area from the office towers and tall apartment buildings that would

2.1
From William Herbert Hobbs, "Section of the Rock Basement of Manhattan along the Line of Broadway from the Battery to Thirty-third Street," 1905.
Detail extends from Fourth Street to Front Street, with lowest point at Duane Street. After Gratacap, Geology of the City of New York *(1909 edition).*

have brought high rents and thus driven out small manufacturers, and in 1989 a large section of the area was accorded city landmark status as a historic district. Preestablished land use, then, was a major factor, and since the enactment of the first zoning law in 1916, zoning has played a major role in curtailing high-rise development in the area between lower Manhattan and midtown. Property ownership and land values have undoubtedly contributed as well. One other condition may also be significant: the concentrations above 37th Street and below Canal Street of the bridges and tunnels that link Manhattan to the outer boroughs and New Jersey.

Fireproof Construction

Although fireproof construction is chiefly associated with the growth of the modern city, its history can be traced to ancient Rome. Attempts to minimize fire damage and reduce the volume of combustible materials began with a building code that was enacted after the Rome fire of A.D. 64 (*Lex Neronis de Aedificatoria* . . .). The code regulated heights and minimum spacing of buildings; it required that upper stories have platforms or balconies for fighting fires; and it called for concrete and brick construction rather than wood. At the same time the Romans introduced hollow brick in concrete vaulting, presumably to lighten the load; it is not known whether they recognized that this construction also impedes the transmission of heat. In later centuries other cities—London after the fire of 1666, for example—implemented building codes to limit fire damage. After repeated fires since the settlement of New Amsterdam by the Dutch in the 1620s, Peter Stuyvesant in 1648 appointed fire wardens and prohibited wood chimneys between Fort Amsterdam and the Collect Pond, and in 1657 he prohibited thatch roofs.[13] These were the first steps toward a fire code.

The modern history of fireproof and fire-resistant construction begins at the end of the eighteenth century with the earliest French patents for fireproof flooring and the first experiments with reinforced concrete. In 1782 an architect known as Ango invented a composite floor of unflanged wrought-iron beams of rectangular section that spanned wall to wall and were set in plaster in which hollow terra-cotta pots were embedded. The beams were set in pairs in a vertical plane, the upper pair arched upward, the lower pair level. Because plaster has no bearing strength, the floor must be regarded as an iron frame protected from heat by the plaster and the pots. For the sake of fireproofing and reducing the weight, Sir John Soane vaulted the offices of his Bank of England with hollow earthenware cones, beginning with the Bank Stock Office of 1792. In 1845 the French government tested a "metallic floor" that a builder named Vaux constructed of unflanged wrought-iron I-beams anchored in masonry walls and tied by wrought-iron bars running transversely and bent or arched up to lap over the beams, with the whole structure then set in plaster. At the Paris Exposition of 1849 the iron contractor Baudrit exhibited a floor construction of wrought-iron I-beams that were tied by paired rods at the top and bottom, the whole set in plaster with embedded hollow pots. By the next decade concrete had superseded plaster. Concrete was thought of as a fireproof as well as a structural material; for example, François Hennebique, one of the early developers of ferro-concrete, advertised his product with the slogan, "Plus d'incendies désastreux."

Beginning in 1866 the French took out a great number of patents for hollow-tile construction. In 1867 patents were granted for perforated terra-cotta blocks; for hollow tiles that were aligned between wrought-iron I-beams and incorporated internal transverse diaphragms that formed an arched surface; for hollow-tile blocks with the inner ends shaped to form a herringbone pattern when properly aligned; and for a hollow-tile arch that sprang between adjacent beams. Another patent was taken out in 1868 for hollow blocks of various shapes that formed a flat arch between beams.[14]

The first English patent for the technology was secured by Joseph Bunnett in 1858 for his large hollow-tile floor arches—actually vaults—that spanned between brick walls or partitions. In 1862 William S. Hogg patented a cast-iron column that consisted of an inner cast-iron cylinder surrounded by brick that was recessed from the column surface to leave a thin insulating air space between iron and masonry. In the floor arch that Joseph Gilbert patented in 1865, corrugated sheet iron spanned between wrought-iron I-beams, was leveled up with concrete, and was enclosed by a wood subfloor and a wood finished floor. A similar construction, probably used in 1845, is described in Fairbairn's *On the Application of Cast and Wrought Iron . . .* (1854).

In the United States the Prussian-born architect and civil engineer Frederick A. Petersen was issued a patent in 1855 for a fireproof floor in which hollow pots or tubes were set in the vertical space between the plaster ceiling and the finished wood floor, nearly filling the space between the floor I-beams. He used this construction in the Cooper Union building (1853–59) in New York City. In 1860 the New York iron manufacturer John B. Cornell patented a fireproof column that consisted of two concentric cylindrical columns of cast iron, the space between filled with a fire-resistant baked clay. In the same year New York City enacted the first building law in the country to set up a separate Department of Buildings as the means of enforcing standards of fire prevention and safety in new construction. The model for similar laws in other cities, this legislation also prohibited the construction of frame or wood buildings below 52nd Street, river to river; subsequent amendments extended that ban. At the federal level, Alfred B. Mullett, supervising architect of the United States Treasury from 1866 to 1874, advocated the use of fireproof and fire-resistant materials and urged that buildings be surrounded by open spaces, broad streets and landscaped grounds.

The beginning of a mature understanding of the fire-resistant construction of iron-framed buildings can be traced to a paper by Peter B. Wight, "Remarks on Fireproof Construction," which was read before the New York Chapter of the American Institute of Architects on 6 April 1869. Wight advocated solid floor-to-ceiling brick partition walls to vertically compartmentalize buildings in which volatile combustibles that required ventilation were stored. He also warned against the danger of using combustible materials in iron-framed buildings. He admired the modern iron construction of the Harper & Brothers building in New York City, but he criticized the interior woodwork of the printing plant, which contained such highly inflammable materials as printing inks and solvents.

Wight was the first to understand fully that iron, though incombustible, loses strength so rapidly with a rise in temperature that it is no better than wood in a fire. In a paper read before the annual convention of the American Institute of Architects immediately following the Chicago fire of 8–9 October 1871, Wight proposed that the undersides of iron beams be protected with cement mortar, concrete, or terra-cotta. The patent that he and his partner William H. Drake took out in 1874 called for a cruciform cast- or wrought-iron column with gores of oak or some other insulating material fitted into the quadrants between the adjacent flanges or arms and apparently held in place by thin metal strips screwed to the flanges. Experiments conducted by the architects had clearly demonstrated the danger of unprotected metal and had established that the slow-burning oak, with its low thermal conductivity, would protect the iron from buckling under heat or from cracking under a jet of cold water—though for how long was not clear. Wight never used the oak-gore column but instead adopted Sanford E. Loring's invention of porous terra-cotta, a fire-resistant material also patented in 1874.[15] The Drake & Wight column was used first in the Chicago Club, completed in 1876, and its first use in New York was in the Orient Mutual Insurance Company Building of 1877–78.

A succession of catastrophic fires at the beginning of the 1870s had spurred Wight and his contemporaries to develop better methods of fireproofing. The Chicago fire resulted in losses of $196 million, the Boston fire of 9–10 November 1872 did $80 million worth of damage, and twenty-two people died in the Fifth Avenue Hotel fire of 10 December 1872 in New York. But even before those disasters, Americans had begun to address the problem. In 1869 George H. Johnson, an architect associated with Daniel Badger, patented a wall for grain elevators that was composed of hollow prismatic tiles laid with staggered masonrylike joints and held in place by internal terra-cotta clamps. This wall was readily adaptable to internal partitions. In 1871 Johnson and the Staten Island firebrick manufacturer Balthazar Kreischer were granted a patent for a hollow-tile floor system much like Petersen's of 1855: thick terra-cotta tubes were set between floor beams, with the flanges of the beams protected by plaster-covered wood strips. A concrete layer on top was covered by the finished floor.

Another patent for a similar plan was granted on the same day in 1871 to Kreischer alone. In this system the tubes were formed of three wedge-shaped hollow blocks, suggesting that Kreischer understood that reducing the volume of trapped dead air further diminished convection currents. As in the Johnson-Kreischer system, the end blocks were shaped to abut snugly against the I-beams of the floor and to surround the ends and the top and bottom of the lower flanges of the beams to provide a flush surface with the top of the tiles. The Kreischer patent was reissued in 1872 with some changes: each flat arch now comprised a number of small prismatic hollow blocks, minimizing convection currents (Fig. 2.2). In 1872–73 Kreischer's hollow-tile flat arches were introduced simultaneously in New York and Chicago—in the New York Post Office (1869–75), built during Mullett's tenure as supervising architect, and in the Kendall Building, designed by John Van Osdel, with floors executed by George H. Johnson. Another manufacturer, Leonard F. Beckwith of New York, who had studied engineering in France, founded the Fire-proof Building Company in 1873 to produce hollow-block flooring based on French precedents. His company's flooring was used in the Tribune Building and other New York buildings designed by Richard Morris Hunt in the early 1870s.

2.2
Flat arch from circular of Heuvelman, Haven & Co., N.Y., 1873 (manufacturers of Kreischer patent of 3 December 1872). After Brickbuilder (1897).

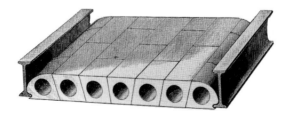

Hollow-tile fireproofing was used consistently in New York after about 1874 and in Chicago after 1878. Its use was widespread by 1882 and continued into the twentieth century. By the end of 1881 the P. B. Wight Fireproofing Company in Chicago was operating at full capacity; six years later it had subsidiary offices in New York, Cincinnati, and St. Louis. Wight's porous terra-cotta-clad columns were employed in the construction of the Mutual Life building in New York (1883–84), and another of his inventions—floor beams protected by hollow tiles under the bottom flange—was used for the first time in that project.

By the late 1870s fireproof construction reflected a clear understanding by designers of the comparative behaviors of common building materials under intense heat. Brick survives best under fire; stone is inferior, although rock of volcanic origin, such as basalt, offers high resistance. Other igneous rock, however, is less reliable—granite, for example, is subject to cracking, splintering, and exfoliation. Limestone, marble, sandstone, and lime plaster disintegrate; iron loses strength as the temperature rises, and wood in thick sections, treated with various chemicals or coated with plaster, is slow-burning and may under certain circumstances be as fire resistant as iron. By the end of the decade, at least two patented processes for the treatment of wood were available.

The number of papers on fireproofing read at the annual conventions of the American Institute of Architects throughout the 1870s attests to the continuing attention to the problem. Wight repeatedly stressed the importance of protecting the metal structural elements of buildings with fireproof and fire-resistant material. The detail in which architects addressed the topic is evident in a paper read in 1873 by the Baltimore architect N. H. Hutton. Hutton proposed the following: (1) walls capable of standing independently after the collapse of floors; (2) joists rested on continuous corbeling, not inserted into masonry of walls; (3) walls ending in parapets above the roof, with openings for fire hoses; (4) use of hydraulic concrete for the main mass of walls; (5) use of incombustible material for floors and vaulting, and support for floor arches with beams of lambda or Y-section; (6) iron, masonry, or concrete construction of stairways; (7) masonry or concrete construction of stairwells and elevator shafts; (8) enclosure of skylight glass in an iron armature; (9) fireproof and fire-resistant cladding of iron; and (10) use of only the heavy, hard varieties of plaster. In a paper read in 1877, the architect and engineer Robert G. Hatfield recommended brick for interior partitions as well as for exterior walls, stairwells with brick or stone walls, fireproof cladding of iron, and large flues.[16]

Experiments on the relative strength of iron and steel when exposed to rising temperatures had begun before midcentury. Observations by Eton Hodgkinson in England in 1846 were augmented by William Fairbairn in England in 1871, by C. Huston in the United States in 1878, and by J. Kollman in Germany in 1880. The general conclusion of all these experiments was that ferrous metals gained strength when moderately heated—to about 900 degrees Fahrenheit—but lost strength rapidly when the temperature was further increased.[17]

The proliferation of papers, tests, inventions, experiments, and quantitative data since Wight's pioneering essay of 1869 attests to the thoroughgoing, scientific approach to the problem of making the high building fireproof and fire resistant. Architects and engineers recognized that iron, though incombustible, loses its working capacity to bear loads as the temperature rises, and extraordinary precautions had to be taken to guarantee the safety of occupants. That disastrous fires still sometimes occur indicates that the problem has never finally been solved.

Heating

The mechanism of central heating was essential to making the skyscraper feasible. The first significant developments in centralized steam heating came in England in the mid-eighteenth century. In a paper for the Royal Society of London's *Philosophical Transactions* in 1745, William Cook proposed to heat a three-story building with a single pipe that extended from a boiler and bent in numerous U-turns throughout the structure to a discharge point. The inventor James Watt heated the writing room of his house in 1784–85 by adopting Cook's technique, and in 1799 the team of Watt and Matthew Boulton used hollow cast-iron columns as steam pipes in their seven-story Twist Mill at Salford, England.

At almost the same time, a central hot-air heating system was introduced by William Strutt at the Belper Mill, Derby (1792), and by Oliver Evans in the United States (1795). Use of the system spread gradually in the early nineteenth century, and it became the usual means of heating small buildings before the twentieth century. Hot-water heating appears to have followed steam. An early system, possibly the first, was introduced in the orangery of Windsor Palace and described by Joseph Bramah in 1836. Authoritative texts by Charles Hood, Charles Richardson, and Thomas Tredgold on hot-water and other forms of central heating appeared in England in 1836 and 1837, thus marking the general acceptance of the method.

Between 1802 and 1810 Boulton and Watt installed steam-heating systems in a number of mills and warehouses, in a castle, and in the Covent Garden Theatre. The essential elements were a boiler, a header, and a series of parallel four-inch cast-iron pipes laid horizontally along the walls and connected with a return line to the boiler feedwater. All of the elements were arranged in a large prismatic envelope to fit into the rectangular enclosure of the building. The first use of exhaust steam from a boiler to generate steam for steam engines to provide heat occurred in Middletown, Connecticut, in 1811. After the turn of the century several British treatises addressed steam and other heating techniques, among them Robertson Buchanan, *An Essay on the Warming of Mills and Other Buildings by Steam* (Glasgow, 1807) and *A Treatise on the Economy of Fuel* (Glasgow, 1815), as well as Thomas Tredgold, *Principles of Warming and Ventilating* (London, 1824). Tredgold, who made numerous contributions to the building art, may have been the first to produce a systematic work on ventilation.

Jacob Perkins pioneered in the development of central heating in the United States. Perkins, born about 1765 in Newburyport, Massachusetts, was a prolific inventor, known primarily for his nail-making machine, fire-engine pump, and printing and engraving techniques. He went to Philadelphia in 1815 and to London in 1819. He and his son Angier Marsh Perkins were granted an English patent in 1831 for a high-pressure hot-water system, the chief elements of which were a furnace, a small pipe three-quarters of an inch in diameter, a coil inside the furnace, supply and return lines, and coils to act as radiators in the rooms. The system had no valves and operated on pure gravity flow. It was closed and sealed so the water temperature could be raised far above the boiling point.

The danger of the Perkins system was that a rupture of the pipe would cause water to flash instantaneously into steam, resulting in a disastrous explosion. Although the low-pressure system was safer, Perkins's was widely accepted. It was installed in at least ten buildings in England by 1840, and it was used in the New York Custom House in 1841. The Boston-born Joseph Nason, said by one source to have gone to London in 1815 to work with Angier Perkins and by another to have begun as an apprentice to Jacob Perkins in 1837, developed a high-capacity steam-heating system by 1855.[18]

When Nason obtained a contract to install steam-heating and ventilating systems in the United States Capitol between 1855 and 1861, he became the recognized authority. His system, which was tested in the winter of 1857–58, included a steam-generating boiler and coils of wrought-iron pipe that carried steam at low pressure. Air was blown over the coils by two steam-operated fans and then conveyed to the rooms by ducts. In that way the building was simultaneously heated and ventilated. By 1861, judging from the catalogue and price list of Morris, Tasker and Company in Philadelphia, all the parts needed for a complete steam-heating system were available. And by the decade of the 1880s heating techniques were the subject of numerous articles in the engineering press; for example, an author called "Thermos" published a long series on steam-heating equipment, piping, fittings, and valves in various issues of the *Sanitary Engineer* of 1882–83. Hot-water heating received similar attention in *Engineering and Building Record*, 1887–89.

The typical elements of a steam-heating system in the 1880s are evident from a description of the system used in the Manhattan Company and Merchants' Bank building (1883–85). The nine-story Wall Street building was designed by the architect William Wheeler Smith and constructed with the assistance of mechanical engineer W. J. Baldwin, master plumber James Muir, and engineering contractor Bates & Johnson. The heating system comprised the following parts, listed according to the direction of steam flow: one or more boilers; regulating valves, to reduce pressure from the usual range of 15 to 20 pounds per square inch to a safer level of 2 pounds; a low-pressure supply main; main risers; distributing pipes and risers; radiator coils; return risers or pipes; a receiving tank for condensate; returns to the boilers; pumps, valves, seals, traps, and sump pumps.[19] By 1885 steam heating had been developed to the state of a mature technology and was to remain standard throughout the subsequent history of large-scale commercial and public buildings.

Ventilation

Although ventilation was given little attention before the eighteenth century, a description of fans and bellows used for ventilating mines appears in the sixteenth-century treatise *De Re Metallica* (1556) by the German scientist Georgius Agricola. In 1736 John Theophilus Desaguliers introduced a hand-cranked centrifugal fan to bring fresh air to the lower decks of ships and into the British House of Commons. Lavoisier's oxygen hypothesis in 1777 led to recognition of the chemical bond between carbon and oxygen in carbon dioxide. That knowledge, in turn, explained the vitiation and pollution of air and the need for fresh air. Further insight was gained through the slow evolution of the theory of pathogenic organisms after 1837.

Such ventilation as existed in houses and other buildings before the modern era depended on using a fire to create a convection current that caused a reduction of the pressure in the immediate vicinity and stimulated the movement of fresh air from an outside source into the room. This unstable and unpredictable method created drafts and temperature stratification. The first system deliberately designed to use heat for moving currents of air was David B. Reid's for the House of Commons in 1835. Reid also originated mechanical ventilation: he used steam-driven fans to move warmed and filtered air at St. George's Hall in Liverpool (1841–54).

The need for an adequate supply of fresh air became acute in the nineteenth century, particularly in densely built urban areas, with the the increasing use of gas for illumination and wood and coal as fuel. John Simon reported to Parliament in 1863 that the death rate from pulmonary diseases was higher in cities than in rural areas, and research by the pathologist and Yorkshire College professor Ernest Jacob beginning in 1870 confirmed that finding. Jacob stressed the need for the regular replacement of vitiated air with fresh air in public buildings, and he particularly attacked architects for their indifference to the problem. Some designers, however, were already giving priority to adequate ventilation. In 1860 J. J. Drysdale designed his house in Liverpool on the principle of a continuous exchange of interior and outside air. John Hayward followed in 1867 with the design of his Liverpool house, and the two collaborated on the pioneer treatise *Health and Comfort in House Building* (Liverpool, 1872).

Parallel developments in America include the recommendations of Catharine E. Beecher in a book that she wrote with Harriet Beecher Stowe, *The American Woman's Home* (1869). She recommended that all household utilities be centralized, that a continuous supply of fresh air be provided, and that outlets for polluted and hot air be incorporated into the design of houses. She advocated a spread plan with narrow wings that would allow the maximum amount of sunlight to enter the house. Earlier in the decade, the squalid conditions of tenement houses in New York had provoked discussion in the press and elicited proposals from architects. E. T. Potter, for example, in an article published in the *New-York Daily Tribune* (3 December 1866), called for smaller buildings with air passages between them and specified that housing should be designed without interior corridors to permit cross ventilation. The city's first tenement law, passed in 1867, reflected the growing concern for adequate ventilation though it established only minimal regulations: halls had to be ventilated, and inner bedrooms had to be ventilated through outer rooms.

From a practical standpoint, modern forced-draft ventilation in the United States began with the steam-driven centrifugal fan and the associated steam supply introduced by Benjamin Franklin Sturtevant, whose company was established in 1860 to manufacture the necessary parts. Drawbacks of the Sturtevant system included the large space required for the steam engine and the early fans and the inefficient location of the fan in the basement. Fan speed could be increased and the fan moved from its position adjacent to the source of power to one near the fresh-air supply only in about 1890, after various refinements in the electric motor. But by 1870 reasonably reliable forced ventilation was being used in multistory buildings.

Attempts to establish a mathematico-scientific basis for ventilation and the fresh-air requirement began about 1880. The fundamental constants were published in August

1885 in the *Journal of the Association of Engineering Societies.* These primary data then had to be related to the capacity and efficiency of fans and blowers, to the pressure loss through friction in ducts and other passages, and to the amount of leakage.[20] By about 1890 the art of forced ventilation had attained a state of considerable sophistication. Until air conditioning was sufficiently developed after World War I, the technology, although increasingly refined, would remain essentially the same.

Plumbing

Like central heating and forced ventilation, plumbing was well developed by the mid-nineteenth century; and because steam and hot-water heating relied on plumbing equipment, those two areas of technology overlap extensively. The essential plumbing components include a pressure water supply; piping and multidirectional pipe fittings; control devices, such as valves, seals, and traps; and fixtures. All were available by 1858 in a form sufficient to the needs of a tall building.

By the end of the eighteenth century, chiefly due to the efforts of English engineers, the standard plumbing fixtures—flush toilet with flap valve and trap, bathtub, and lavatory with valve-controlled water supply—were being refined. The fertile genius of Benjamin Latrobe brought these devices to the United States. Latrobe proposed a second-floor flush toilet in his project of 1799 for the John Tayloe house, Washington, D.C., and was the first to put a toilet and tub in the same room, at his Markoe house in Philadelphia of 1808—the first step in the centralizing of plumbing equipment and the source of the American usage of the word *bathroom.* Further evolution addressed basic elements of the plumbing system—separation of waste and supply lines and of hot and cold supply lines, a citywide pressure supply, and sewage disposal.

The most sophisticated plumbing techniques were found in American hotels. Tremont House (1828–29) in Boston, widely regarded as the first modern hotel in the country, was a plumbing landmark. The architect Isaiah Rogers installed eight flush toilets in a row on the first floor and baths in separate enclosures in the basement below. At Astor House in New York, Rogers first adopted the consolidation and large-scale use of plumbing equipment appropriate to the multistory hotel or office building. Capitalizing on Latrobe's innovations, Rogers centralized the toilets, lavatories, and baths at the same location on each floor so that all of the pipes could be contained in stacks or utility shafts.

By the mid-nineteenth century, the traditional gravity water supply was outmoded for municipal requirements. The first pressure system—water supplied by power-operated pumps—was installed at York, England, in 1712, when the Buildings Waterworks Company used pumps to lift water that was propelled by Savery steam engines. New York was provided with a pressure system by means of extensive aqueducts and siphons when the Croton system was constructed under the direction of John B. Jervis in 1837–42. The main parts of the system were Croton Dam, Croton Reservoir, Croton Aqueduct, Aqueduct Bridge, and a distributing reservoir at Fifth Avenue and 42nd Street, now the site of the New York Public Library. The system lessened but did not eliminate the danger of wholesale destruction by fire, and much of lower Manhattan below Wall Street burned in 1845.[21]

The developments of plumbing and heating pipe are necessarily parallel. The earliest water pipe was made of cast iron, but its low tensile strength and its lack of adaptability to small diameters made that material unsuitable. By 1835 the Messrs. Russell of Wednesbury, Staffordshire, had developed the lap-welded wrought-iron pipe that Perkins used in his high-pressure hot-water heating system. Cast-iron pipe was introduced in the United States in 1825, and the first wrought-iron pipe in the country—rolled pipe of a diameter and strength recommended for gas, steam, and water—was manufactured by Morris, Tasker and Company of Philadelphia in 1848. The company's catalogue of 1858 listed all of the necessary pipe, valves, fittings, fixtures, and traps that were essential to a high-quality plumbing system in a first-class, multistory building. By the Civil War years, plumbing seems to have been more advanced than any other realm of building technology. Not long afterward, metal bathroom fixtures began to be replaced with porcelain-glazed or porcelain-enamel ceramic ware. The all-porcelain siphon-jet toilet appears to have been invented by William Smith of San Francisco in about 1880. Although expensive, its use began to spread after it was recommended in 1881 by the authoritative sanitary engineer George E. Waring, Jr.

In New York the manufacture of plumbing equipment was apparently pioneered by the Jordan L. Mott Iron Works, a company whose name may have been immortalized—if obscurely—by Marcel Duchamp's notorious sculpture "Fountain," a porcelain urinal signed "R. Mutt" that was rejected for exhibition in 1917. (Duchamp said that the two American achievements he most admired were its plumbing and its bridges.) In 1860 the Mott company introduced cast-iron soil pipe, high quality wrought-iron pipe especially for hot water, and the porcelain-lined cast-iron bathtub; by the early 1870s the company manufactured a comprehensive line of modern equipment.

The establishment of the Citizens' Association of New York in 1863 reflected a concern with public health that encouraged the spread of modern plumbing. The aims of this organization were to reform the municipal government, expose the evil of the slums, and replace tenements with adequate housing. The Association published a revealing sanitary survey of the city in 1865 under the title *Report of the Council of Hygiene and Public Health of the Citizens' Association of New York upon the Sanitary Conditions of the City.* The Metropolitan Health Law was passed in 1866, and the city's Board of Health was established in 1870. In 1879 state legislation expanded the board's authority to oversee construction of tenement housing. The New York State Board of Health was established in 1880.

By 1870 the theory of pathogenic organisms was superseding the older zymotic or miasmatic theory of contagious disease, mainly through the work of Pasteur in the 1860s. By the time Robert Koch demonstrated conclusively the relation between specific organism and specific disease in 1876–80, sanitary engineering had become a recognized profession and George E. Waring, Jr., had become its chief figure in the United States. Waring's first major work was *The Sanitary Drainage of Houses and Towns* (1876). He analyzed plumbing equipment, piping, and valves and prescribed their proper installation in various articles published from 1878 to 1880 in the *Sanitary Engineer* and the *American Architect*. By the time the Cotton Exchange was completed in 1885, the problems of plumbing had been largely solved (see Fig. 5.14).

Elevators

Two contradictory arguments have overstated the connection between elevators and tall buildings: on the one hand, that the invention and maturity of the elevator followed from the high-rise building, and, on the other, that the skyscraper was entirely a consequence of the elevator. In fact, the power-operated elevator antedated any of the protoskyscrapers, and as we have seen, many other factors contributed to the rise of skyscrapers. But the elevator was unquestionably among the essential factors in the evolution of high buildings, and a skyscraper design with the elevator as a primary determinant—the Equitable Building—emerged by 1868.

The elevator went through similar evolutions in Europe and in the United States. Yet Europe had few buildings above five to six stories at the start of the twentieth century and no really tall buildings until after World War II. In contrast, the skyscraper was both essential and desirable for the port of New York, on its narrow island site, and to America's midwestern industrial cities, which were rapidly being built up—or rebuilt, as in the case of Chicago—in the late nineteenth century. The concentration in the United States of administrative and mercantile operations into small inner-city areas, along with the emphasis on providing as many urban functions and services as possible in a single building, fostered the development and spread of the skyscraper and encouraged higher and higher buildings. The same forces that increased building heights powerfully stimulated elevator techniques and competition among elevator manufacturers.

The power-operated elevator called a teagle was being used in English factories and warehouses by 1835. The teagle was a cage whose platform was open or walled in at the sides. It was hoisted in brick-walled shafts by ropes passing through sheaves enclosed within the pulley block. The sheaves were turned by means of a geared connection with the belted shafting that activated all of the factory's machinery. Depending on the source of power in use for the particular factory, the shafting was rotated by steam-engine or water power. The baggage lift in Holt's Hotel was probably similarly designed. Hand-operated variants provided power in warehouses. These early elevators, used for both freight and passengers, were subject to breaks in the hoisting rope, resulting in the free fall of the cage. Henry Waterman of New York City has been credited as the first American manufacturer of the platform freight elevator, in use by 1850, and Otis Tufts, a Boston civil engineer, as the designer of the first closed car.[22]

Elisha Graves Otis of Yonkers, New York, invented the safety brake in 1851. That such a device was necessary indicates that the power-operated elevator was introduced into the United States before midcentury, but the first to receive widespread attention was the steam-operated passenger elevator in the observation tower of the New York Crystal Palace exhibition of 1853. Otis dramatically exhibited his brake at the second season of the fair in 1854, allowing himself to be raised in the elevator cage and then cutting the hoisting rope. Otis's brake involved a leaf spring, as in wagons, which was fixed to the car frame and constrained by the tension in the hoisting rope. If the hoist ruptured, the spring was released, driving lugs fixed to the back of the spring into racks extending along the elevator guides in the shaft. Though the design was crude and the stop abrupt, the Otis brake functioned before the car began to accelerate noticeably.

Otis recognized the need for an independent source of power to free the elevator car from the continuously running factory shafting. In 1855 he invented a steam-engine drive that at first was restricted to passenger elevators. The first practical and also first commercial application was the elevator his company installed in the five-story Haughwout Building at 488 Broadway (1856–57).[23] The next passenger elevator in New York seems to have been the one installed by Otis Tufts in the Fifth Avenue Hotel in 1859. The hotel's experimental "perpendicular railway" operated by means of an immense vertical screw. This hollow screw, which was made of iron cylinders joined together, extended from the cellar to the attic right through the elevator car and was revolved by a belt from a steam engine. The car formed the "nut of the screw . . . so that as the screw revolves to the right or left, the car ascends or descends. A guide-way at one corner of the well prevents the car from turning around with the screw."[24] But this elevator was expensive, slow, and clumsy; only two were ever installed, and the one in the Fifth Avenue Hotel was replaced in 1875.

By around 1870 the technology of the steam-powered elevator engine was fully developed, though further refinements in controls and safety devices continued to the end of the century. But the critical defect of the technique appeared as buildings rose in height: the engine-and-car system could operate only by winding the hoisting cable around a rotating drum; as the length of the shaft increased, the diameter of the drum grew to unmanageable size.

The next step was the vertical hydraulic elevator, invented in 1870 by Cyrus W. Baldwin of Boston and refined by William E. Hale of Chicago, who produced its final, practical form in 1873. The hydraulic elevator was operated entirely by water acting under the force of gravity. Running over pulley sheaves, the hoisting cable was attached to a large bucket of water that served as a counterweight. To move the car upwards the operator opened a valve that filled the bucket, causing it to descend and thus raise the car. Another valve emptied the bucket, causing it to rise while simultaneously allowing the car to descend under its own weight. When the car reached the bottom floor, pumps filled the bucket for the next trip. Movement up and down was smooth, fast, and economical, but dangerous: the car was controlled only by its brake, which could (and sometimes did) fail.

A contemporary British system replaced the Baldwin-Hale elevator. In 1846 the English engineer William Armstrong had invented the hydraulic crane. Water under pressure was introduced into a cylinder to move a piston and a connecting rod, which rotated sheaves that carried a loop of chain fixed to the arm of a crane. In effect, this was a power-operated tackle (of which the teagle is a variant): water raised the load through the movement of the chain. The Armstrong crane was introduced into the United States in 1867. With the substitution of a car for the crane boom and the provision of a lifting hook and control valves—connected to a continuous rope passing through the car and accessible to the operator—the essentials of the hydraulic elevator were all present; these were adapted to the elevator in nearly fully developed form by 1876.

The rapid increase in building heights was a powerful stimulus to the development of the hydraulic elevator, which by 1880 was being widely manufactured. Its advantages over the steam elevator included greater speed of movement, a more economical use of space, and increased safety. The cylinder, piston, and valves were now located within the elevator shaft because of the premium on space in high-cost, high-rent buildings; the pulley sheaves were at the top and bottom of the shaft, clear of the car; the operator had

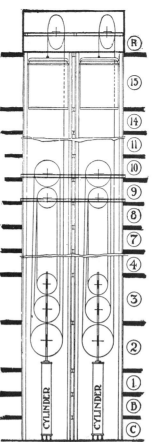

2.3
*Section through
elevator shaft showing
equipment for
hydraulic elevators,
Central Bank
Building
(1896–97).
After Birkmire,*
Planning and
Construction of High
Office Buildings.

good hand-control, supplemented by an automatic brake. As the height of buildings increased, the car could be made to travel longer distances by multiplying the hoisting cables and the sheaves without significantly enlarging the cylinder and piston, the sources of power (Fig. 2.3). With the appropriate number, size and arrangement of the sheaves, the ratio of car speed to piston speed could be increased to 12 to 1. That the hydraulic elevator could be used in the highest skyscraper was powerfully demonstrated by the Eiffel Tower, whose cars reached a height of three hundred meters, or 984 feet.[25] But by the time the tower opened in 1889, the far superior mode of electrical operation was approaching maturity.

Lighting

The last of the utilities to be developed into a form both effective enough and safe enough for use in the high-rise building was lighting. The eighteenth century had brought improvements in efficiency and candlepower over the earliest lamps, fueled by animal or vegetable oils; Pierre Argand, in particular, developed the double-glass lamp chimney in 1784. But the major defect of early lamps was that each unit was discrete, with its own supply of illuminant, so lighting was limited to small areas of small buildings.

Gas lighting made it possible to supply many units from a common source of fuel. William Murdock anticipated such a network in 1779, when he piped coal gas into his home at Redruth, England, through small, branched iron tubes. But Murdock's technique was an extremely inefficient method of lighting. He improved efficiency by welding the end of the tube shut and drilling small holes in the sides, but the air supply was still inadequate at the point of combustion. Murdock installed the first multiunit system with branching tubes and a single reservoir of gas in 1807 in the Phillips and Lee Mill at Manchester. Thereafter, the use of coal gas as an illuminant spread to other European cities and to the American seaboard.

In 1825 the New York Gas Light Company brought illuminating gas to New York City. Pipes were laid under Broadway from the Battery to Canal Street, and in 1830 the Manhattan Gas Light Company was established to supply the streets above Canal. The Philadelphia Gas Works introduced the expandable gas holder in the iron guide-frame, useful for maintaining a large supply, in 1835–37. Incandescent gas lighting evolved from various experiments in England, France, and Germany, leading to the discovery in 1826 that various salts, oxides, and lime could be brought to incandescence by being heated in an open flame. Austrian chemist C. A. von Welsbach found that a mantle of cotton gauze soaked in a solution of oxides of thorium and cerium produced brilliant light with high efficiency; he patented his system in 1885 and 1886. Gas lighting was problematic in the large public or commercial building, where a gas holder under pressure supplied a network of tubes that distributed gas to single- or multiunit fixtures in the building's various enclosures.[26] The system could provide an adequate level of illumination for most activities, but it also generated heat and consumed oxygen, unwelcome side effects in large spaces occupied by a large number of people—theatres, for example. Then, too, gas lighting presented the ever-present danger of fire and explosion. Electric lighting offered the only reliable solution.

A variety of studies in the eighteenth and nineteenth centuries established the experimental and theoretical background of electric lighting. After Luigi Galvani and Alessandro Volta posited their theories of current in 1791–1800, Humphry Davy discovered the thermo-optical power of electricity early in the nineteenth century, and Jean Bernard Léon Foucault (1840s) and Charles Francis Brush (1870s) investigated arc light. Lighting by means of incandescent filaments began with Davy's experiments and was taken further by Joseph W. Swan in England in 1860 and afterward. Edison experimented with a succession of filament lamps between 1879 and 1884. The filament lamp required a filament of carbon or other less fragile material, an evacuated glass bulb, and a continuous electric current that entered the filament circuit and returned by a second wire.

The United States Electric Lighting Company began in 1878 placing arc lights in New York on an experimental basis—in the main Post Office at the tip of City Hall Park, in the Park Avenue Hotel, and in the corridors of the Equitable building. The Edison Electric Light Company was established in the same year to manufacture Edison-Swan incandescent lamps. In 1879 the Board of Aldermen asked the Municipal Gas Commission to investigate the feasibility of illuminating streets with electric arc lights. In 1882 central power generation was established in Edison's Pearl Street plant, and within a year power was supplied for 2,323 lamps; by 1884, 11,272 lamps in five hundred buildings relied on the plant. Until around World War I, however, most large hotel and office buildings had their own generating plants, and the same was true for the newly electrified railroads serving New York City.[27]

Power-Operated Construction Equipment

Power came to construction in 1836, when William S. Otis of Canton, Massachusetts, patented the steam shovel, or excavator, an implement whose form survives today. Hand-operated building devices dated to the Romans, who used both a hoisting wheel with tackle and a crane, which, as described by Vitruvius, also incorporated a tackle. The medieval construction hoist was a large operator-turned wheel attached to a drum wound with a hoisting rope, and a crane with a swivel base was used in the Renaissance. The hand-operated pile driver was used from Roman times, and the crank was a late medieval device. Until the Renaissance, when animal power was substituted, human beings supplied the power for operating all of these devices.

The huge crane built by Montgomery C. Meigs for the construction for the U.S. Capitol dome (1855–65) was hand operated, although Meigs had recommended steam operation. The Washington Monument, begun in 1848, was also raised with a hand-operated crane, but after 1880 the machinery of the Otis steam elevator was adapted to the operating hoist for raising stone blocks. The actual beginning of steam operation came with the construction of the Jayne Building in Philadelphia in 1849–51, where building superintendent S. K. Hoxie used a steam hoist for lifting granite blocks. Isolated instances of the technology appeared even earlier, as in raising the capstone for the Bunker Hill monument in 1842. The first systematic large-scale use of steam-powered equipment in North America was the construction of the Grand Trunk Railway Victoria Bridge over the St. Lawrence River at Montreal in 1854–59. All the cofferdam pumps, hoists, excavators, dredges, and pile drivers in that project were operated by steam. In 1866 compressed-air rock drills were introduced in the construction of the Hoosac Tunnel in Massachusetts.

In New York, steam-operated derricks were used for the first time in 1870 by the builder Jeremiah T. Smith in the construction of the foundations of the United States Post Office. In 1878 the Brooklyn-based iron contractor Post & McCord first used steam-powered derricks to raise iron in constructing the Morse Building.[28]

In spite of the availability and reliability of power-operated equipment, its use spread very slowly. The high initial cost of such machines as the Otis steam excavator weighed against the technology, particularly in the United States before the Civil War, when capital was scarce. Dependence on steam as a power source also meant that every piece of large equipment had to have its own power supply or that some means had to be found to distribute power over the building site. Not only was this costly but the presence of shafting or piping or both would have blocked access to parts of the site, an especially troublesome impediment on New York's narrow, hemmed-in lots. Although labor costs were high, gangs of men had long been organized into efficient work units, following the precedent of organized section gangs used in the construction of railroads. But by 1890 costs had risen to the point where the builder had no alternative but to use power. At the same time—and largely because of the construction advantages afforded by the change-over—the height, size, and number of high-rise buildings constructed in New York began to increase at unprecedented rates.

3

TOWARD THE SKYSCRAPER: ARCHITECTURAL AND TECHNICAL ACHIEVEMENT IN NEW YORK BEFORE 1870

Both the evolution of the office building that we summarized in the first chapter and the technical advances that we reviewed in the second were essential to the evolution of the high-rise building, but they do not by themselves explain how the skyscraper came into existence. The iron frame, the necessary utilities, and the elevator had to be brought together in association with a new kind of architecture before the new building type could attain a mature form.

Winston Weisman has proposed a series of seven phases in the evolution of skyscraper form. In his sequence techniques and architectural forms appear in an irregular progress that finally culminates in a new union of all lines of development.[1] Our own assessment of skyscraper development recognizes no such neat schema, and although Weisman's identification of a preskyscraper phase—lasting from about 1849 to about 1870 and largely concentrated in New York—is more or less accurate with respect to purely architectural form, it fails to account adequately for technology. Iron construction, too, was essential. It had appeared in New York by 1820, and likely earlier, antedating the crystalizing of the office building type and the development of appropriate architectural modes.

Early Iron Framing

The early history of iron construction in New York is difficult to reconstruct as much of its documentation is limited to newspaper descriptions and to old engravings and watercolors that must be visually interpreted for structural techniques. Theatres and other buildings that required large, covered spaces and minimally obstructed views of a stage or dais were early candidates for iron construction. The first Park Theatre on Park Row may have started the trend. When the theatre was built in 1795–98 to the design of the brothers Joseph and Charles Mangin, the boxes or galleries were constructed without vertical supports, but that element was added in 1807 when the theatre interior was extensively altered by the Englishman John Joseph Holland. These supports were probably wood: when the building burned in 1820, the interior was reportedly destroyed, and only the exterior walls were left standing. But the theatre was immediately rebuilt, and the new interior did include iron supports. According to newspaper accounts published at the time of the reopening on 1 September 1821 and confirmed by a print made that year, four balconies arranged on the horseshoe plan were supported by extremely slender, widely spaced iron columns—so widely spaced as to suggest that the balcony floors had iron beams.[2] (If, by chance, the construction of the prefire building was the same, then it may have been the first of its kind in the country.) The Chatham Garden Theatre (1824–25), on Chatham Street (now Park Row) between Duane and Pearl streets, apparently was similarly constructed, with thin iron columns carrying balconies.

The commercial facade, less encumbered by tradition than other building types, provided further opportunities for early iron construction. Iron columns were being used in New York commercial facades by 1837, when the Lorillard Building—where these columns were continuous through the first two stories of the facade wall—was completed on Gold Street. By 1835 Jordan L. Mott had built a foundry on Water Street for fabricating iron storefronts; in 1836 he obtained a patent for casting iron columns, and in 1837 he displayed his iron storefront at the American Institute in New York.[3]

One of the earliest iron roof frames in the city, if not the first, may have been that of the Broadway Tabernacle (1835–36) at 340–44 Broadway. The building, which survived only until 1857, was constructed by the Congregational Church of New England. As shown in *Frank Leslie's Illustrated Newspaper* (15 March 1856), the interior was a circular enclosure with a horseshoe-shaped balcony on columns; a flattened dome over the main floor was reinforced by a ring beam that was supported by six giant columns. These columns appear large in section, but their small number and the long spans of the ring beam suggest iron construction.

Pictures, however, can be deceiving. Castle Garden, originally constructed after the design of John McComb, Jr., as West Battery Fort (1807–11) and known today as Castle Clinton, was provided with a roof in 1845 when its interior was remodeled by the architect-builder Calvin Pollard as a theatre for opera and concerts.[4] The building gave the appearance of iron construction; a Nathaniel Currier lithograph commemorating Jenny Lind's American debut there on 11 September 1850 shows a multidomed and circular clerestory-lighted ceiling, supported by exterior masonry walls and two concentric rings of tall, slender columns that spread into lotus-flower capitals. Although the low conical roof and circular-roofed oculus at the center seem to be supported by some kind of iron frame, the carpenter's contract for Pollard's interior, preserved in The New-York Historical Society, clearly specifies wood construction for the ceiling and the columns. The only iron elements in the structure were wrought-iron bolts, nuts, plates measuring eight inches square and one-half inch thick, and straps used to brace the ceiling timbers.

The masonry-walled Niblo's Garden Opera House (1849–50; demolished), designed by Trench & Snook and built at Broadway and Prince Street, had a balcony that rested on iron beams spanning radially between piers at the outer ends and cast-iron columns at the inner ends, and its horseshoe-shaped gallery may have been supported on iron brackets cantilevered from the piers. The flat-edged ceiling with its low center dome may have been hung from iron roof trusses.

Public buildings that were designed to accommodate large numbers of people in large spaces also employed iron construction. The oldest (southernmost) section of the Astor Library (1849–53), designed by the important but little-studied German-born and -trained architect Alexander Saeltzer, utilized interior iron framing. Saeltzer's design was influenced by Friedrich von Gärtner's *Rundbogenstil* Staatsbibliothek in Munich, completed in 1843. A contemporary source describes the New York library as unusual for being "formed to so large an extent of iron" and describes the iron floor beams, the iron galleries over the aisles surrounding the two-story-high, skylighted reading room, and the iron spiral staircases leading up to the galleries (Fig. 3.1).[5] The galleries and the grand staircase from the raised ground floor to the second level disappeared around 1920, when the space was split to accommodate another floor, but the fourteen piers that originally divided the aisles from the library nave remained intact. These incorporated cast-iron columns inside brick casings. Giorgio Cavaglieri, who discovered the cast-iron cores while removing one row of the ground-floor brick piers during his restoration of the building in 1967, suggests that they may have embodied "a completely new structural concept of reinforced masonry, probably considered to increase the bearing capacity of the smaller brick piers, rather than as a fireproofing of the cast-iron columns."[6] The coved, skylighted ceiling is of mixed iron and timber construction, with the primary iron supports resting on the iron-reinforced brick piers. Certainly the Astor's interior framing foreshadowed metal cage construction in New York.

3.1
Interior, Astor Library
(1849–54),
Alexander Saeltzer,
architect.
425 Lafayette Street.
Collection of The
New-York Historical
Society.

By the mid-1850s, the city's new theatres were extensively iron framed. Saeltzer's Academy of Music (1853–54) at 14th Street and Irving Place, another of his *Rundbogenstil* designs, must have incorporated iron roof trusses, girders, and balcony frames, although wood columns supported at least the second tier. With 4,550 seats, the opera auditorium had the largest seating capacity of any in the world, but the stage could not be seen from a great many of the seats due to the horseshoe plan.[7] Completed a year later, the Volksgarten (1854–55) at 45 Bowery—often called the German Winter Garden—may well have made the most extensive use of iron to date. Circular in plan, the central dance, concert, and general assembly floor was surrounded by a balcony on brackets cantilevered from the ends of a ring of haunched iron beams that were supported by slender iron columns. Light emanated from a clerestory that rested on a similar arrangement of iron beams carried by slender iron columns, and the roof was a dome on iron ribs radiating from an iron-framed oculus.

The "Commercial Palace" and Iron Framing

Beginning about 1845, as the use of iron as a primary structural material was increasing, a new commercial architecture emerged, promising an age of commercial splendor. The new buildings, aptly described as "commercial palaces," were designed in the newly imported palazzo mode.[8] The building that announced the new style, Alexander Turney Stewart's so-called Marble Dry-Goods Palace, was designed by Trench & Snook, with the Italian emigré Ottaviano Gori as the marble-cutter (see Fig. 1.4). Constructed in 1845–46 as the first luxury dry goods store, extended in the early 1850s, and still standing in a much altered condition on Broadway between Reade and Chambers streets, the four-story, marble-clad A. T. Stewart Store excited great enthusiasm and much praise. It attracted attention because of its height, which was increased to five stories in 1850–51, and consequent visibility—considered unambiguous virtues at midcentury:

> A few years ago when a man returned from Europe, his eye full of the lofty buildings of the Continent, our cities seemed insignificant and mean.... But the moment Stewart's fine building was erected ... [it] was a key-note, a model. There had been other high buildings, but none so stately and simple. And even now there is, in its way, no finer street effect than the view of Stewart's building seen on a clear, blue, brilliant day, from a point low on Broadway.... It rises out of the sea of green foliage in the Park, a white marble cliff, sharply drawn against the sky.[9]

John Butler Snook was one of the architects most responsible for popularizing the version of the palazzo mode—borrowed from Charles Barry's London clubs—that his firm used for the Stewart Store. Trench & Snook's Boreel building (1849–50) and Metropolitan Hotel were in the same style.

The interior of the Marble Palace's oblong rotunda also excited comment. The springing ring and ribs of the dome structure were apparently not iron, and no evidence has come to light concerning the material of the columns that supported the ring, but it is likely that the columns were cast iron. A bridgelike iron gallery encircled the springing ring. The east wall of the rotunda was mirrored to make the oblong space appear twice the actual size, and frescoes painted by the Italian artist-craftsman Mario Bragaldi decorated the ceiling and side walls. Surely derived in concept from European and American shopping arcades—and perhaps indebted to the rotundas of City Hall and the second Merchants' Exchange, as well—this dramatic space recalled the resplendent display halls of the wholesale dry goods warehouses Stewart could have visited in Manchester and other English mercantile cities while on buying trips abroad. The Stewart store's rotunda started a vogue in New York: the Lord & Taylor Store, completed by Thomas & Son in 1853 on the corner of Grand and Chrystie Streets, incorporated an iron and glass dome that was visible on the exterior.

Architects were expressing height through vertical design well before the appearance of the skyscraper—in the "Davisean window," for example, the Jayne building, and the two-story arcades that appeared on New York commercial facades as early as 1850. One of the earliest with two-story arcades was the Lord & Taylor store, and the Moffat Building (1847–48) represented one more step—both in verticality and in technology—toward the skyscraper (Fig. 3.2). The English-born architect Thomas Thomas and his son Griffith Thomas were responsible for the Fifth Avenue Hotel and for many of the city's commercial structures built between 1845 and 1880, including the Moffat, on the northwest corner of Broadway and Anthony (now Worth) Street. At six stories the Moffat Building was essentially a slab, its narrow main front given vertical emphasis by the window treatment. The narrow windows of the four upper stories were combined vertically to suggest two very tall stories rather than four. The effect was achieved by introducing recessed spandrels between the windows within each pair and by crowning the uppermost window of each pair with an elaborately foliated cast-iron hood molding of a type or style sometimes described as "Anglo-Italianate" but actually a variant on the palazzo mode.

Much iron was used in the Moffat Building: cast-iron columns at the Broadway ground floor framed large plate-glass store windows; the iron roof utilized a new technique of iron plates in ridges; door and window shutters were iron, and the vaults below street level were lighted by fanlights and by cast-iron illuminators, patented by Thaddeus Hyatt in 1845.[10] Though intended principally to house Dr. William B. Moffat's patent-medicine business, the Moffat Building also included offices for rental, a cost-effective measure later adopted by skyscraper builders.

New York had no commercial structure by 1850 as vertically expressive as the seven-story Jayne Building in Philadelphia. The Jayne was also quite advanced technologically, equipped with its own water supply for fire protection and with flush toilets on every floor. But the arcaded white marble front of the Bowen & McNamee Silk Warehouse at 112–13 Broadway (1849–50; demolished) was at least comparable to the Jayne's in its openness and its recognizably commercial design (see Fig. 4.4). The flamboyant Venetianizing facade of this combination store and warehouse designed by Joseph C. Wells provided an eye-catching contrast to Stewart's somber palazzo. Although specific information on its structure has not come to light, the interior iron-framing of the Bowen & McNamee building was far ahead of the Jayne's combination of all-wood floors and interior iron columns. Wrought-iron floor beams with a clear span of about thirty-three feet wall to wall eliminated the need for interior columns and permitted unencumbered, open areas of nearly five thousand square feet on every level.[11]

A proposal for a truly high-rise building in New York was made in about 1849 by

Calvin Pollard for Dr. Benjamin Brandreth. Though unbuilt, Pollard's design forecasts the future. Intended for 241 Broadway—the address of Dr. Brandreth's flourishing Universal Vegetable Pills business since the late 1830s—this narrow, eighty-foot-high building would have encompassed eight stories. The story heights were to have diminished gradually from twelve feet at the ground level to just under eight feet for each of the three uppermost floors—which apparently were meant to be reached without an elevator. All that survives of the project is an undated drawing in the collection of The New-York Historical Society, which shows an all-masonry front except for some ground-floor cast-iron elements. Most likely, brick walls would have enclosed a massive "slow-burning" timber frame.[12]

Two other buildings of the midcentury, both masonry walled, featured facade designs that seem especially forward-looking: the Bank of the Republic at the northeast corner of Broadway and Wall Street (1851–52) and the Trinity Building erected just north of Trinity

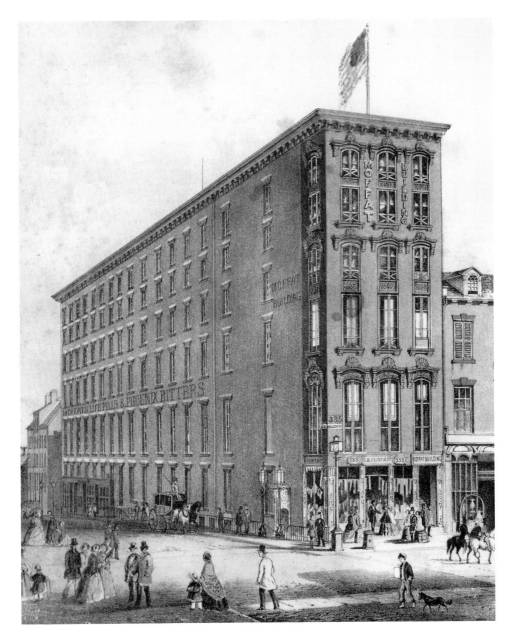

3.2
Moffat Building (1847–48; demolished), Thomas & Son, architects. Lithograph by G. Hayward, c. 1860. Collection of The New-York Historical Society.

Churchyard at 111 Broadway (1851–53), which also anticipated the sheer size of the skyscraper. The five-story bank building, designed by Hurry & Rogers, heralded the tripartite or column formula that would later dominate skyscraper design: base, in this case arcaded; strongly vertical shaft; and capital, here formed by an attic story above the cornice (Fig. 3.3). Massive segmental pediments over the entrances and stone quoins framing the rounded corner contributed elegance and monumentality to this latest and most elaborate representative of the prevailing palazzo mode.

Trinity Building—or Trinity Buildings as it was termed in the 1850s to indicate its huge size—has been cited as one of the city's first structures intended exclusively for offices (see Fig. 1.8). It was the work of Richard Upjohn, the architect of Trinity Church and the most renowned American church designer of his day. Upjohn moved his office into the building when it was completed and also took other rooms, which he then leased out. In 1857 Upjohn was one of the founders of the American Institute of Architects, which was established in Trinity Building and rented space there. The first office of Henry Hobson Richardson was in this building, and other well-known architects shared the address, but throughout its existence, the building was mainly occupied by lawyers and insurance companies. In 1904 it was demolished to make way for the new Trinity Building. The first Trinity Building, a veritable slab only about 40 feet wide on Broadway, was five stories high and stretched through the block from Broadway to Church Street—nearly 263 feet. The clearly defined story levels and unvaryingly regular disposition of the arch-topped office windows set the pattern for future office buildings, and so did the terra-cotta cornice and exterior ornamentation, an important early architectural use of that material in New York. Lion's heads cast after a design by the sculptor Henry Kirke Brown decorated the keystones of the lintels. According to the proprietor of the company that supplied the lion's heads, the original design was more exactly reproducible in terra-cotta than in stone, and he also observed that "the advantages of 'Terra Cotta' are best seen when we produce duplicates of the *highest order* of *artistic design, equally durable* with *stone*, and at *one half* the price."[13] Also unusual was the facade facing material: yellow unpressed brick from Buffalo, New York, rather than the stone or marble then preferred for masonry-walled commercial buildings.

It is reasonable to assume that the structure of Trinity Building was as advanced for its time as that of the Upjohn firm's Mechanics' Bank on Wall Street (1855–56; demolished). Begun two years after Trinity Building was completed, the bank building made extensive use of iron. Its brick-arch floors, leveled with concrete, rested on an iron frame that utilized Cooper's rolled beams, and the window frames and folding shutters were iron.

In retrospect the Gilsey Building, designed by John W. Ritch and built at the southwest corner of Broadway and Cortlandt Street (c. 1854), seems a striking cast-iron predecessor of the skyscraper (see Fig. 10.17). Topped by a bracketed cornice in turn surmounted by small pediments, the facades of this six-story block comprised seven adjoining units marked by two heavy belt courses—thick moldings that effectively segmented the building's vertical planes. One separated the arcaded ground story from the two-story section immediately above, and the other set off the second and third stories from those above. Such apparently arbitrary "shaft" divisions were later criticized in New York skyscrapers, but the verticality established by the continuous pilasters in each division of the street elevations made the Gilsey noteworthy for the time.[14] The iron fabricator was Daniel D.

3.3
*Bank of the
Republic (1851–52;
demolished),
Hurry & Rogers,
architects.
Eno Collection,
Miriam and Ira D.
Wallach Division of
Art, Prints and
Photographs, the
New York Public
Library, Astor, Lenox
and Tilden
Foundations.*

Badger, who in 1846 had established a business that was later known as the Architectural Iron Works of New York, which became one of the country's major iron foundries. Badger was also responsible for the ground floor exterior ironwork of the section added to the A. T. Stewart Store in 1852–53, as well as the iron fabrication of the elegantly Venetian-esque Haughwout Building.

Though it may have contained some offices, the Gilsey was not primarily an office building; it housed the business of its owner, the tobacco merchant Peter Gilsey. All-iron facades quickly became identified with stores or warehouses, where an ornate exterior functioned as an added selling point, and with factories, where large windows were needed to admit maximum light. A fancy cast-iron exterior like the Gilsey Building's could be produced at a cost considerably lower than that of comparable stonework, because iron parts could be prefabricated and assembled rapidly. Windows could be large because the iron facades were self-supporting frameworks rather than bearing-wall construction.

The Harper & Brothers printing plant (1854), which was designed by John B. Corlies, with James Bogardus as engineer, presented both a strongly vertical, arcaded cast-iron front on Franklin Place and a noteworthy interior structural frame. Actually the Harper plant was two buildings linked to a common staircase tower by iron bridges across an open court. The only cast-iron front—constructed by Bogardus—was the one on Franklin Square; all the other walls were brick. But the court wall of the Franklin Square building was punctuated by big iron-framed and iron-sashed windows. Thus Corlies's building was almost a glass shell supported by a frame made chiefly of iron. This frame consisted of fluted Corinthian cast-iron columns manufactured by James L. Jackson, concrete subflooring on brick arches, composite cast-iron bowstring girders with wrought-iron ties, and seven-inch wrought-iron rail or deck beams with wide flanged bottoms to support the brick arches. The floors were finished in pine plank (Fig. 3.4).

The wrought-iron beams used in the Harper building came from the first lot to be rolled in the United States, produced by Peter Cooper's Trenton Iron Company. The iron construction of the Astor Library and the Bowen & McNamee store, and probably that of the Academy of Music, was also fabricated by this famous ironworks. In order to roll the beams for the Cooper Union building, Peter Cooper had a set of rolls specially made to

3.4

Floor construction at a typical bay, Harper & Brothers printing plant (1854; demolished), John B. Corlies, architect.
After Abbott, The Harper Establishment; or How the Story Books Are Made.

turn out complete iron girders. After 1852 Cooper's ironworks rapidly developed the true I-beam of single rolled section, progressing from the seven-inch rail beam of bulb section (rolled in 1854) to the compound beam in 1853 and the eight-inch I-section beam in 1854 or 1855.[15]

The Harper & Brothers plant was by far the most important construction of the mechanical and structural inventor Bogardus. In 1850 he had been granted a patent for an all-iron building, and his most notable cast-iron-fronted works include his Laing Stores (1848; demolished), which had a unified cast-iron front, and his Duane Street factory, known as the Eccentric Mill (1848–49; demolished), both of which employed timber girders and likely also timber flooring on brick arches rather than the comparable iron elements in his patent description. Possibly more prophetic than his iron-framed and iron-fronted buildings were his project for the New York Crystal Palace and his series of iron-framed fire and shot towers designed between 1851 and 1855. His Richard McCullough Shot Tower, built at 63–65 Centre Street in only three months (1855; demolished), rose to an impressive 175 feet, with eleven stories above ground and one below. Its structure comprised brick curtain walls carried bay by bay in a cast-iron frame below grade as well as above.[16] The importance of the McCullough Shot Tower in the development of skyscraper construction, however, has been overrated: its structure was anticipated by the cast-iron framework of the gas holder of the Philadelphia Gas Works, and its simplicity offered few lessons for the builder of the high-rise office building.

The iron beams of the Bogardus system were exposed and thus vulnerable to fire and surface oxidation, and the unbraced frame, with its crude, hand-bolted connections, was lacking in rigidity. Peter B. Wight took a rather dim view of Bogardus's achievements as a builder of iron structures, but today Bogardus is revered as a pioneer in that field. It has been suggested that the cast- and wrought-iron construction of the Astor Library and the Bowen & McNamee Store may owe something to the experiments of Bogardus and others in the late 1840s.[17]

The most important building fabricated by Daniel D. Badger, Bogardus's chief rival, was the I. M. Singer and Company sewing machine factory (1857). Isaac Merritt Singer's business had grown rapidly since 1851, when he established it in New York in partnership with Edward Clark. The company's new quarters, designed by George H. Johnson work-

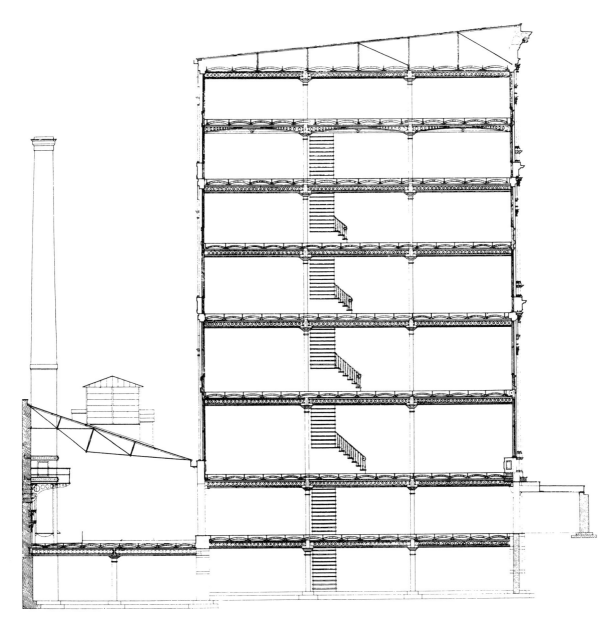

3.5

*Transverse section,
I. M. Singer Factory
(1857; demolished),
George H. Johnson,
architect.
After Badger,*
Illustrations of Iron
Architecture.

ing for Badger, were erected on Mott Street by Architectural Iron Works. Unparalleled expansion of sales followed; and the Singer Manufacturing Company, as it was known after its reincorporation in 1863, eventually dominated the world market in sewing machines. The elegant Mott Street front of the Singer factory was all cast iron, its six stories expressed as pairs by means of three tiers of two-story arcades separated by strong belt courses. The interior construction comprised wood flooring on brick arches that spanned between wrought-iron beams of inverted Y-section, which were carried by deep cast-iron girders of modified T-section, assisted by wrought-iron tension rods on their undersides (Fig. 3.5). The origins of the Y-beam date back to the cast-iron beams of flared section that Charles Bage used in the Shewsbury flax mill, a design to which Boulton and Watt added a bottom flange for their Salford cotton mill. Badger's Y-beam was a great advance over Bage's primitive, heavy, solid forms.

The first rolled-iron, eight-inch I-beams had been designed by Peter Cooper's ironworks specifically for use in the new Cooper Union building on Astor Place (1853–59), but circumstances dictated that except for some compound beams that supported sections of the first, second, and third floors, the only beams used there were the same seven-inch bulb-section beams as those used in the Harper & Brothers plant.[18] The walls of the new Cooper Union building were bearing stone masonry with brick interior partitions, and the auditorium floor and the floor immediately above the auditorium each comprised a series of two-way, solid-spandrel brick arches that carried the floor load directly to the interior cast-iron columns. The arches and columns of the two floors were aligned. The building included two mechanical innovations: a cylindrical shaft intended to house a future elevator and a large steam-driven exhaust fan for forced-draft ventilation. The fireproof floor construction, from a design patented by the building's architect, Frederick A. Petersen, was discussed in the previous chapter. All of the cast-iron work was produced by Badger's Architectural Iron Works. Although Cooper Union is an institutional building, the exterior articulation of its five stories, especially the incorporation of third- and fourth-story windows in a two-story arcade, paralleled the most advanced commercial design of the time.

Some architects, notably those influenced by John Ruskin's strictures against using iron to imitate stone, openly scorned the cast-iron front. By the late 1850s, however, iron components were being introduced into the masonry facades of prestigious office buildings. One of these was the much-admired New York Times Building (1857–58), designed by Thomas R. Jackson and constructed at the intersection of Park Row and Spruce and Nassau streets (Fig. 3.6).[19] Its light olive–colored Nova Scotia freestone walls were embellished at the ground story with delicate iron arches that were carried on iron columns and enframed doors and windows. Attenuated, superimposed two-story arcades—probably of stone rather than iron—differentiated the pedimented center of the long Park Row front above the ground story. As a reporter for the *Times* boasted, "The architectural appearance . . . is singularly bold and striking, and though designed with a total disregard of classical models and artistic rules, the two principal facades display great inventive genius and a most harmonious combination of apparently incongruous elements."[20] The floors were constructed of brick arches carried on wrought-iron beams that had been rolled at the Trenton Iron Company. Any interior supports on the ground floor, which was treated as one large space, were probably cast-iron columns. Proudly cited by the *Times* as being thoroughly fireproof, the five-story building did in fact survive a terrible fire in 1882 that destroyed the old New York World Building next door. The floors of the Times Building were considered so solid that they were reused in the still-extant building later erected for the newspaper on the same site.

The New York Times Building helped set the standard for floor use: the heavy printing presses were in vaults below street level; the publication office occupied the entire ground floor, which was the most richly decorated space in the building; the offices on the next two floors were rented out; the editorial offices were on the fourth floor; and the typesetting and composing operations were on the fifth (top) floor where the light conditions, and the view, were optimal. There was no elevator; rather, a wide iron staircase provided access to all floors.

By the end of the 1850s the cast-iron-fronted store had become such a convention of design that Stewart chose to build his uptown store at Broadway and Tenth Street (1859–62) with rhythmically articulated cast-iron facades. (The "Marble Palace," until it was

3.6
*New York Times
Building
(1857–58; largely
demolished),
Thomas R. Jackson,
architect.
Collection of The
New-York Historical
Society.*

sold in 1884, continued to serve as Stewart's wholesale store.) The new store was designed by the prolific John Kellum in partnership with his son, and in 1868 Kellum & Son
enlarged it to extend all the way to Ninth Street. With wrought-iron beams manufactured
by the Trenton Iron Company and ironwork fabricated by the J. B. and W. W. Cornell Iron
Works, the extended five-story emporium, with its vast 325,000-square-foot floor area,
was the largest iron-framed building in the world aside from the London Crystal Palace.
The floor construction was the standard plank made of timber joists between wrought-
iron beams that spanned between cylindrical cast-iron columns. But the vast central
court with domical skylight had an unusual structural feature: deep wrought-iron girders—actually built-up I-beams—spanned between cast-iron columns of rectangular or
box section with richly ornamented surfaces. This was a very early use of the box column.

The deep I-beams were necessitated by the long, clear span between the corner columns of the light court on the long dimension; shallow wrought-iron beams could be used over the rest of the floor area because of the close spacing of the columns.[21] The skylights rested on triangular wrought-iron trusses, and the surrounding floors that overlooked the court resembled tiers of iron galleries. A fire destroyed all of the combustible materials in 1956, and the whole structure was subsequently demolished, though the frame apparently suffered little damage.

Wight, writing in 1876—by which time the cast-iron front was generally considered somewhat déclassé for high-quality commercial establishments—denigrated the uptown Stewart store as "a perfect mine of wasted iron" marked all over by cheapness, "a cheapness which comes from the desire to save pattern-making." Guessing that no more than six patterns were used in casting the entire wall surface, he pointed out that all the interior cast-iron columns were molded from but a single pattern. Wight, who had always abhorred cast-iron-fronted buildings for both aesthetic and practical reasons, blamed the uptown Stewart store for having "done more to retard architectural progress in New York than any other dozen buildings of the worst possible design."[22] Yet the cheapness of its standardized, prefabricated parts, which enabled rapid, on-site construction, was the very quality that helped raise cast-iron fronts in New York for yet another decade and more, even if not on the "best" buildings. Cast-iron construction is an exact, if primitive, forerunner of the curtain-wall construction associated with the skeleton frame.

Midcentury Banks and the Maturing of the Iron Frame

As a result of New York's increasing importance as the financial center of a flourishing national economy, bank buildings proliferated in the mid-1850s, and they displayed ever-increasing sophistication in both construction and architectural design. Early in 1855 *Bankers' Magazine* stressed the importance of marking the bank building "externally, internally, and throughout, by *stability* as its leading feature." Fireproofing was a particular concern:

> The best fire-proof buildings in this country are constructed either wholly of iron, or of brick or stone, with iron beams and columns, properly framed and held together by rods built into the walls; with brick arches for the floors; which arches are supported by, and spring from, the lower flanches [flanges] of each beam, and are thus extended in succession on each floor, from one end of the building to the other. The floors should be laid with stone flags, or tiles, upon the arches, after they are properly levelled, and filled up in the interstices by a concrete of lime, sand, and ashes. . . . This description of building, when properly constructed, and supported by an iron roof, is perfectly impervious to fire. . . .
>
> The external doors should be of the strongest character; and if wood be used, it should be lined with iron, or thickly studded with rivets of the same material. The shutters should always be of iron.[23]

Virtually every bank of that time was built to those specifications, and many, if not all, that were more than three stories high incorporated Cooper's iron beams.

The construction of the Bank of the State of New York, which was built on the

northwest corner of William Street and Exchange Place in 1855–56, has been documented in considerable detail (Fig. 3.7). The architect was James Renwick, Jr., known primarily for his churches but also one of the great constructive architects of his time.[24] Like many other banks built since 1850, Renwick's handsome five-story building evoked the Roman Renaissance palazzo. The light color of its Westchester marble–faced exterior was similarly conventional: white marble and cream-colored stone were regularly used for commercial facades of the time. Renwick's bank building could be readily identified as commercial by the treatment of its stories; it could be identified as a bank by the presence over the entrance of the sculpted head of Mercury–"the god of thieves and money-dealers before . . . the two professions were separated."[25] Strong moldings divided the facades into three distinct sections: an arcaded first story (the banking room floor), second and third floors with columned and pedimented windows joined to suggest a single tall story, and the top two stories beneath a heavy bracketed marble cornice. Although all the floors above the first were used for offices, Renwick, in the manner of his time, chose design unity over the cell-like expression of individual offices that would only come into widespread use when buildings grew to three times this height.

Within its brick bearing walls, the Bank of the State of New York was fully iron framed and had no interior columns.[26] The primary floor framing elements included riveted

3.7
Bank of the State of New York (1855–56; demolished), James Renwick, Jr., architect. Collection of The New-York Historical Society.

wrought-iron built-up plate girders that spanned thirty-five feet clear wall to wall and ten-inch-wide built-up floor beams.[27] The girders were eighteen inches deep, possibly the deepest to date in the United States, and spaced about eight and one-half feet center to center. The concrete floor, anticipating late nineteenth- and early twentieth-century techniques, was set into thin corrugated sheet metal plates and laid in twenty-four-inch widths with corrugations running parallel to the girders from beam to beam. (Typically, bank building roofs of this time were covered with galvanized, corrugated sheet iron.) The maximum floor depth was eight inches, the minimum two inches; the ceilings were lath and plaster.

This construction offered an imaginative technical strategy for supporting floor loads over a wide span before the mills could roll a beam larger than eight inches. The floor framing system had serious defects, however: the connections between beams and girders were weak, and the load of the beams fell entirely on the bottom flange of the girder, resulting in extreme shear in the rivets and increasing the normal tension in the girder web. As a consequence, these crude connections were an invitation to failure, especially under the concrete floor's total load of about sixteen thousand pounds. Still, the system had great web strength, and the boxlike form of the web provided resistance to lateral bending and torsion. The built-up girder with angles uniting the web and flange plates followed the form that was developed by Stephenson in 1840 and is still in use today.

As a group, four buildings, all produced in the 1850s and none still standing, revealed the strong current of German influence in midcentury commercial architecture: Richard Upjohn's Trinity Building on Broadway, his Corn Exchange Bank on the northwest corner of William and Beaver streets (1853–54), Leopold Eidlitz's Continental Bank on the west side of Nassau Street between Wall and Pine streets (1856–57), and Eidlitz's American Exchange Bank on the northeast corner of Broadway and Cedar Street (1857–58). The Prague-born, technically trained Eidlitz had worked in Upjohn's firm in the mid-1840s and later designed such major structures as the New York Produce Exchange —another *Rundbogenstil* work—and the Brooklyn Academy of Music.

Eidlitz knew the latest construction techniques and was fully cognizant of the need for adequate fireproofing. The floors of both of his banks were made of stone slabs carried on rolled iron beams and iron pillars, and the interior doorjambs of the American Exchange Bank—and presumably the Continental Bank as well—were iron and the architraves concrete. The Continental Bank owed some of its appearance of strength to the concerns of the fire warden (see Fig. 1.6). To convince him that the heavy stone cornice was adequately supported, Eidlitz included deep reveals that enhanced the sculptured quality of the wall. The ceiling of the Continental Bank's main banking room was richly frescoed to harmonize with the "German-Byzantine" style of the exterior, and the banking room ceiling of the American Exchange Bank, its "flat surfaces all worked in slabs of stone supported by iron beams," simulated German Gothic tracery in keeping with the medievalizing *Rundbogenstil* exterior.[28] The exceptionally large windows of both buildings served to heighten the apparent massiveness of their light-colored, freestone-faced walls.

The period of rapid financial growth that produced this plethora of new bank buildings ultimately resulted in an overexpanded national economy, mass unemployment, depression, and the crisis known as the panic of 1857. There was hardly time for full recovery before the Civil War broke out in 1861, yet several architecturally important buildings rose in the interim. One was Ball, Black & Company's five-story, white marble palazzo—still standing, although in altered form—on the southwest corner of Broadway and Prince Street (1859–60). By surmounting an open, arcaded base with walls articulated by pedimented windows, the architect, John Kellum, effectively combined forms associated with the cast-iron fronted store and the marble palazzo to achieve an appropriately dignified image for a company that dealt in fine jewelry and silverware.[29] Another impressive work of the pre–Civil War era was Eidlitz's fortresslike New York Produce Exchange, which stood on a site just north of the battery (1860–61). Massive brick walls trimmed in New Brunswick olive stone and pierced by tall arch-topped windows enclosed an impressive two-story-high exchange room. The only iron used in the framing construction may have been the floor beams and the exposed iron bowstring girders that supported the clerestory walls; four brownstone piers supported the hall's open-timber ceiling. Eidlitz's building was superseded in function by Post's Produce Exchange and replaced by the United States Army Building in the 1880s.

The Second Empire Commercial Building

The hiatus in construction during the Civil War years prolonged the life of the discreetly plain marble palazzo, which remained the preferred high-class commercial image until the late 1860s. John Kellum's New York Stock Exchange building on Broad Street (1865; demolished) was a near copy of his Ball Black & Company Building, suggesting the limitations of the style—and perhaps those of the architect—and its waning vigor. But the removal of the Stock Exchange into these new and larger quarters signaled the end of economic stagnation in New York and the beginning of another building boom.

The Brown Brothers Bank Building at 59 Wall Street (1864–65), described as the "finest private banking house in the world" and said to have cost a million dollars, represented the baroque phase or final efflorescence of the marble palazzo.[30] The architect, Edward T. Potter, substituted a series of tall, square-headed openings with inset Corinthian columns for the more usual ground-floor arched openings flanked by piers or half-columns (Fig. 3.8). Potter avoided the palazzo's ubiquitous quoins, instead articulating the elevations in a more sculptural manner than was usual for the mode: pavilionlike projections at the corners and at the center of the side elevation were defined by a giant pilaster order with richly foliated Corinthian capitals that bore the winged caduceus of Mercury. On the advice of the real estate brokers, who pointed out that only the first two floors would bring remunerative rents, the building was planned with only four stories and without the usual raised basement–ground story. The introduction of a low-ceiled banking (first) floor made it possible to reduce the number of stair treads normally needed to reach the second floor, and low stair risers further facilitated the upward climb. With the elevator office building only two years away, these accommodations may soon have seemed less than farsighted. But the Brown Brothers Banking House remained as built until 1885, when it received a three-story mansard addition. The architect responsible for this alteration, Charles W. Clinton, had been Potter's associate on the original building and would later emerge as one of the city's leading skyscraper designers.

More significant, perhaps, than the style and decoration of this banking house was the iron framing within its brick bearing walls. Here in one of its earliest uses appeared the

3.8

*Brown Brothers &
Company Banking
House
(1864–65;
demolished),
Potter & Clinton,
architects.
Museum of the City
of New York.*

popular Phoenix column, manufactured by the Phoenix Iron Company of Phoenixville, Pennsylvania: a rolled wrought-iron column of hollow circular section built up of either four, six, or eight segments riveted together. Invented about 1861 by the Baltimore and Ohio Railroad engineer Wendel Bollman and patented in 1862 by Samuel Reeves of the Phoenix Iron Company, the Phoenix column was then considered so experimental that, according to one of the banking firm's partners, "neither the architect nor the builder was willing to assume the responsibility, and the owners had to be content with the guarantee of the makers."[31] Advantages over the cast-iron column, the manufacturer contended, included greater rigidity derived from its flanges and a more even load distribution achieved by its circular section. Thoroughly convinced of the superiority of wrought over cast iron, the Phoenix company claimed that its column supplied a maximum of strength with a minimum of weight. The details are vague, but because the Brown Brothers Bank Building was designed to be "thoroughly" fireproof, it can be safely assumed that the floor construction also comprised wrought-iron floor beams, the usual brick arches, and stone flooring on concrete. The roof was carried on wrought-iron trusses, and windows and door were trimmed in cast iron.

Wind bracing was not a serious concern for the four- to six-story buildings typical of the mid-1860s, but the introduction of the wrought-iron Phoenix column was an important precursor. The earliest unambiguous record so far uncovered of a provision for wind bracing is the sole surviving drawing of the frame and bracing for the Tower Building of

1888–89. Henry H. Quimby, an authority on the subject, wrote in 1892 that bracing was considered unnecessary, or at least unimportant, until the introduction of the wrought-iron column: though it has greater tensile strength, the wrought-iron column is theoretically less able to withstand compression than the cast-iron column. The architect and historian Alan Burnham, on the other hand, writing in 1959, maintained that the great advantage of the Phoenix column over the cast-iron column was not realized until the mid-1880s, when the need for wind bracing became more important with the rise of taller, narrower buildings. Because wrought iron can be riveted, Burnham pointed out, the wrought-iron column has greater effective rigidity than cast-iron column. According to Burnham, the riveted column-beam connections of wrought-iron columns were rigid enough to allow simpler methods of windbracing than would have been possible with the less rigid, hand-bolted connections required by the cast-iron column. Cheaper than other iron columns because of its simpler construction, the Phoenix column was widely used into the 1890s, when the Z-bar and rolled H-column—structural elements that facilitated connections and more efficient distribution of loads—began to replace it and other cylindrical iron columns.[32] But in the 1880s and 1890s many high buildings in New York and Chicago were constructed with Phoenix columns, among them the enlarged Equitable Building, Madison Square Garden, and the World, Union Trust, Commercial Cable, and Dun buildings. Typically, these columns were used where floor loads were greatest, in the center and innermost parts of buildings.

Griffith Thomas's six-story Continental Insurance Company Building at 100–102 Broadway (1862–63; demolished) was the first New York commercial building in the Second Empire style. A high, boldly silhouetted mansard roof, the hallmark of the style, crowned a cast-iron front. Elaborately profiled moldings, greatly attenuated vertical members, and projecting window enframements and balconies contributed a plasticity unusual to the cast-iron front without sacrificing its characteristic openness. As Continental was a fire insurance company, one suspects that cast iron was selected for the facade because the directors considered the material thoroughly fireproof. Indeed, the building stood until replaced by the American Surety Building thirty years later.

Formal as well as economic and technical factors made the new style seem appropriate to the newly tall elevator building of about 1870. As building heights increased, the essential horizontality of the flat-roofed palazzo no longer served. Architects were compelled to find forms with vertical emphasis or at least neutral expression, a need intensified by the narrow sites available in lower Manhattan. Moreover, the delicate scale of the ornament associated with the palazzo style was inappropriate to the great size of the new buildings, especially because the tops of buildings were now so far above eye level. And, perhaps most important, the association of the new style with the regime of Napoleon III and his massive reconstruction of Paris appealed to enterprising organizations and individuals seeking visibility, prestige, and financial profits from their new buildings. Long after the demise of the Second Empire mode, insurance company buildings would preserve the high roof image, although in other forms.

Without doubt, Griffith Thomas's imposing National Park Bank on Broadway just below Ann Street (1867–68) helped more than any other structure in the city to establish the Second Empire mode as the tall building style (see Fig. 8.2).[33] Established in 1856, the Park Bank was reorganized ten years later as a national bank, and its directors obviously wanted their new building to advertise the importance of their expanded organization. Previous so-called Second Empire examples in New York, including the New York Herald building (1865–67) by Kellum & Son, which adjoined the National Park Bank, were little more than older-style palazzos under fashionable mansard roofs. By contrast the richly embellished, axially symmetrical front of the National Park Bank called to mind the New Louvre in Paris. Approximately 59 feet wide on Broadway and 159 feet deep, with a 9.5-foot el on Ann Street, the lot alone cost the then-astronomical sum of $350,000; and, judging from contemporary accounts, no expense was spared in the construction of the 104-foot-high, six-story building. While it was going up, "crowds of people pause[d] by the railing of St. Paul's to stare up at its elaborate and massive Westchester marble front, its colossal features, and its columns and pediments."[34] It must have seemed unusually tall, standing more than 25 feet higher than the typical palazzo bank—Renwick's Bank of the State of New York, for example. Inside, a ribbed iron and glass dome of elliptical shape in the "Roman Corinthian" style crowned a well-appointed 40-foot-high banking room. Architecturally as well as technologically, the stage was set for the first elevator-office building, the Equitable, and by early 1871 a steam elevator manufactured by Otis Brothers & Company had been installed in the Park Bank building.[35]

The Second Empire Hotel

For many years hotels had been the tallest buildings on the New York skyline, and post–Civil War hotels contributed both to the popularity of the Second Empire as a tall building style and to the phenomenon of increasing building heights. The Fifth Avenue Hotel had incorporated a passenger elevator a decade before these were included in office buildings, and the hotel as a building type presented a challenge to the designer because it required complex utilities combined with diverse interior spaces and an inviting visual expression on the street. The expanding city as port and entrepôt required an unprecedented number of such buildings, and construction took off at the end of the Civil War.

Exemplified by La Farge House and the famous Fifth Avenue Hotel, the marble palazzo was the reigning hotel style of the 1850s and early 1860s, but it, too, yielded to the Second Empire in the late 1860s. An early example is the Grand Hotel (1868–69), a mansarded, marble-sheathed block articulated by quoins and a champfered corner and still standing at the southeast corner of Broadway and West 31st Street. Its sophisticated design, created by the German-born architect Henry Engelbert for the carpet merchant and manufacturer Elias S. Higgins, recalls the simpler styling of the new *hôtels particuliers* lining the side streets of Second Empire Paris rather than the high style of the New Louvre. The total number of stories is eight, counting the two within the pavilioned mansard roof, and in the tradition of the French apartment house, a cast-iron ground-floor front initially provided large display windows for stores. The building was first intended to function as a family hotel—or, to apply the later term, an apartment hotel—essentially an apartment house without private kitchens and where meals are taken communally. But the location of the site in an emergent hotel district and entertainment center dictated that it become a transient hotel instead. Apparently the Grand did not have an elevator at the time of completion, although it had a steam engine in its basement. Reportedly, it later incorporated the first electric elevator in the city.[36]

The same architect-builder team next created the marble-fronted Broadway Central Hotel (1869–70), known originally as the Grand Central Hotel (Fig. 3.9). Said to have cost $2 million, including the land under it, this mansarded "monster hotel" at 667–77 Broadway opposite Bond Street occupied the former site of the Winter Garden theatre and La Farge House. In 1867 a fire had destroyed the theatre but had spared the front of the hotel, which Higgins and Engelbert retained. Thus the older Renwick-designed hotel shaped the rather old-fashioned palazzo front of the Broadway Central. But Higgins and Engelbert added three stories to the La Farge's five-story front, two under a high, pavilioned mansard, and they extended the 175-foot-wide building through to Mercer Street, making it 200 feet deep. Two passenger elevators served the first six floors, and five staircases led from the sixth to the seventh and eighth floors, where there were single rooms for gentlemen. The pavilions at the center and ends of the mansard included a ninth story that was probably used as storage or utility space. When the hotel opened, observers pronounced the view from the highest rooms "superb," well worth "the trouble of ascending, which trouble is rendered infinitesimal in quantity by the use of the handsomely inlaid, gas-lighted, mirror-decked elevator."[37] With 650 rooms the hotel could accommodate 1,500 guests, and as late as 1893 it was still reckoned the largest in the city. In its heyday, the Broadway Central was popular with theatre people and big spenders like Diamond Jim Brady and the railroad tycoon Jim Fisk, who was shot on the grand marble staircase in 1872 by a rival for the attentions of a well-known actress of the day.

3.9
Broadway Central Hotel (1869–70; demolished), Henry Engelbert, architect. Collection of S. B. Landau.

With its passenger elevators and its exceptional height of 149 feet—197 feet to the top of the flagpole!—the Broadway Central could be considered one of the first skyscrapers. It was 7 feet taller than the Equitable Building, which was begun a year earlier but also completed in 1870. But in the construction of both the Broadway Central and the Grand Hotel, no iron seems to have been used beyond the inclusion of iron floor beams and interior columns, the latter probably only at the store-front and lobby levels. Both were built with brick bearing walls and brick partition walls. According to their building permits, the Grand utilized 3-by-12-inch iron floor beams, and the Broadway Central employed iron floor girders in its newly built rear portion.[38] The mansard roofs of both hotels rested on heavy galvanized iron cornices, but apparently neither was iron framed, as was the Equitable Building's. The Grand Hotel survived many years of second-rate residential hotel status in the present century to become an official city landmark in 1979, but the deterioration of age combined with many years of neglect and poor maintenance brought a sudden and tragic end to the Broadway Central. On 3 August 1973 its historic Broadway front collapsed, killing four people.[39] The building was not reconstructed.

Other tall Second Empire hotels followed, notably Gilsey House at the corner of Broadway and West 29th Street (1869–71) and A. T. Stewart's vast Park Avenue Hotel, built as the Working Women's Hotel on Fourth Avenue between 32nd and 33rd streets (1869–78). Another of Peter Gilsey's real estate ventures, Gilsey House was designed by Stephen Decatur Hatch, who afterwards achieved some reputation as a commercial architect. Hatch was responsible for the second Boreel Building (1878–79), an eight-story brick-fronted office building with fully iron-framed floors. Inspired by the New Louvre and painted gleaming white to simulate marble, Gilsey House's column-bedecked iron facades were cast at Badger's Architectural Iron Works. When it was completed, the eight-story building was considered exceptionally tall.[40]

Stewart's Working Women's Hotel was conceived as a benevolent enterprise and intended to house one thousand women at low rents. Said to have cost $3 million to build, it took nearly a decade to complete, due in part to hard times following on the 1873 financial panic and in part to Stewart's poor health—both he and Kellum died before it opened. The hotel was doomed to failure because of the financial impracticality of operating it as a philanthropic venture. It closed within three months of its opening, then reopened a few weeks later as a luxury hotel for men and women.

The Park Avenue Hotel, reflecting the courtyard plan established for hotels back in 1836 by the Astor, was designed as a hollow square. Its inner court became a popular outdoor dining area. The elaborately ornamented, cast-iron street fronts were somewhat retardataire in style, recalling Kellum's earlier buildings in the palazzo mode, but a pavilioned mansard roof contributed the required touch of modernity. Most of the hotel was seven stories high, including the mansard story, with an eighth story at the central section of each front—the same as the Equitable Building's floor count. Elevators and staircases served all floors. The need for fireproof construction was satisfied by interior wall-bearing partitions and court walls of brick, as well as brick-arched floors that utilized 9-by-12-inch wrought-iron beams, supported on iron columns and girders and finished in concrete and wood. State-of-the-art tiled ventilating shafts passed from the basement through every room in the building to supply fresh air. The building's most novel feature may have been the massive trough-shaped castings filled with brick at the top of each wall section, designed to carry the wall section next above. Early electric lighting was installed in 1878, and the building survived until 1926.[41]

The Second Empire was not a long-lived style. By 1880 no ranking architect was still using it, although the mansard roof in modified forms held on for many years. It nonetheless left an indelible mark on the New York hotel, bequeathing its pomp and majesty to the Beaux-Arts hotels of the 1890s and 1900s. On the whole, American Second Empire buildings have fared poorly. Tainted by their association with the many federal buildings in the style undertaken during Ulysses S. Grant's scandal-ridden tenure as president, the larger examples were soon heartily despised, and many have been demolished—the New York Post Office, for example, razed in 1939. Therefore, the survival of the Grand Hotel and Gilsey House—both now apartment buildings and the latter carefully restored and renovated—seems remarkable. Two large cast-iron-fronted stores on Broadway just north of Union Square—the former Arnold Constable & Company Store designed by Griffith Thomas (1868; with later additions), and the former Lord & Taylor store by James H. Giles (1869–70)—have also survived. To some degree their location in areas still preponderantly given over to the mercantile and garment trades helped preserve these buildings, and today all are protected by official New York City landmark designation. Unfortunately, the three mansarded elevator buildings that opened the skyscraper era—the Equitable, the Western Union, and the Tribune Building—have all vanished.

4

THE "FIRST SKYSCRAPERS": INNOVATION IN THE 1870S

Although there may be some justification for denying the term "skyscraper" to wall-bearing structures or to office buildings no more than ten stories tall, several of the most assiduous students of the building type have proclaimed three such buildings the "first skyscrapers." Winston Weisman bestowed the title on the Equitable Life Assurance Society Building (1868–70) because it was "the first business building in which the possibilities of the elevator were realized."[1] In 1899 Montgomery Schuyler traced the beginning of the skyscraper to the ten-story Western Union (1872–75) and Tribune (1873–75) buildings. Others since then, notably Henry-Russell Hitchcock and Weisman, have designated that ten-story pair as either "first skyscrapers" or next in sequence after the Equitable because of their marked height increase.[2] Writers who wished to be less controversial—and conveniently noncommittal—have called the trio and other elevator buildings of the 1870s and early 1880s "protoskyscrapers" or "preskyscrapers." We risk "first skyscrapers" for the purpose of emphasizing their importance, and our investigation of the Equitable's architectural and structural character confirms that it did indeed initiate the skyscraper building type (Fig. 4.1).

The Equitable Life Assurance Society Building

The Equitable Life Assurance Society of the United States was organized in 1859 with a small capital investment of $100,000. By 1870 its assets were worth more than $11 million, rivaling those of the longer established New York Life Insurance Company. In an article describing the history and features of the new building in detail, the *Sun* speculated that the company's volume of new business for the year 1868, more than $6 million, had not been

4.1
Equitable Building (1868–70; demolished),
Gilman & Kendall, architects, and G. B. Post.
After Robert Blackall, Photographs of the U.S.
Courtesy of the Rotch Visual Collections, MIT.

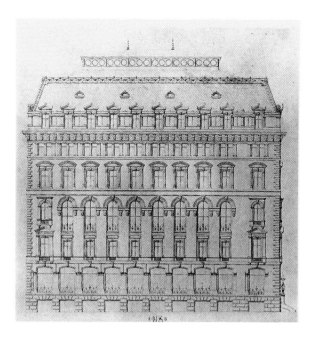

surpassed in any single year by any company in the world. Since its founding, Equitable had rented space in adjoining buildings on lower Broadway. In 1864 company directors initiated plans to build suitable headquarters for Equitable's increasingly successful business, and in 1865 the company started assembling its new site at the southeast corner of Broadway and Cedar Street. Over the next two years the company acquired properties encompassing nearly eight thousand square feet at a cost considered quite reasonable for the time—an average of $59.62 per square foot.[3]

In 1867 the building committee visited the larger American cities to look at plans and buildings and get cost figures; it also examined designs submitted by eleven architects, eight of whom had been invited to compete in October of that year. The known projects include submissions by H. H. Richardson, Richard Morris Hunt, and George B. Post (Figs. 4.2–4). The accepted design of Arthur Delavan Gilman and Edward Hale Kendall, published in the company's promotional brochures, corresponds closely to the building as executed. All of the surviving designs share certain features, evidence that the building committee issued explicit instructions concerning the plan, number of stories, and appearance of the new headquarters. All follow to some degree the canons of the heavy Second Empire mode that had become popular since the Civil War, especially for buildings serving public and institutional functions. Characteristically, all display a high mansard with dormers, a rusticated basement or ground story, walls strongly articulated with emphasis on the separate stories or layers, and orders liberally applied (though less so in Richardson's case). The story count is difficult to determine. Several of the many extant variations of Hunt's proposal appear to project seven, including the raised basement or ground floor. Apparently Post's would have had eight. Richardson seems to have proposed six or six and a half stories above a half-raised basement. The building as executed had a partly raised basement, seven stories above that, and an additional story in the mansard pavilions, for a total of eight stories above the sidewalk. The eighth was probably not full height.

It is evident from the competing designs and photographs of the building as completed that the committee specified a tall lobby floor and above that a two-story-high, galleried hall to be used for the company's business transactions. Richardson's plan for the business-hall floor, in the collection of the Houghton Library, Harvard University, shows iron columns, iron-framed skylights, and iron window mullions, indicating that the building committee expected a certain amount of iron construction. All known versions of the building make use of an intriguing and prophetic feature for future commercial design, one that would later serve Richardson and Post particularly well: two stories are made to look like one tall story in a manner that acknowledges the two-story-high space but conceals the actual number of stories within. Richardson and Hunt expressed the double story as a tall arcade, and Hunt even included the fourth story within a pair of giant arched windows on his Broadway facade. Post treated the double story as tall, arched windows within aedicular enframements. In the actual building, where the two normal-height floors below the cornice were also treated as if a single floor, Gilman & Kendall expressed the double story as segmental arched windows framed by paired half-columns. So deceptive was this "architectural legerdemain"[4] that the Equitable has frequently been described as having only five stories. Reports differ, but its height was probably about 142 feet from the curb to the roof at its highest point. The building's huge windows, which measured 9 by 17 feet and were said to have been the largest in America, were a particular point of pride.

The competitors were doubtless attempting to follow instructions yet adhere to the requisite horizontal, or layered, expression of the Second Empire mode. Those critics who later denigrated New York architects for failing to express the height of these early tall buildings in a "rational" or straightforward manner have disregarded the imagery

4.3

Perspective project for Equitable Building, 1867, R. M. Hunt, architect. Prints and Drawings Collection, the Octagon Museum, American Architectural Foundation.

4.4

Perspective project for Equitable Building, 1867, G. B. Post, architect, showing Bowen & McNamee Store (1849–50) at right. Collection of The New-York Historical Society.

The "First Skyscrapers" 65

associated with architectural style and the operative rules of style. The image projected by the Second Empire–style "commercial palace"—the wealth and cosmopolitan distinction of Napoleon III and Baron Haussmann's Paris—was incompatible with the simplicity of rational design. In this era only warehouses and inexpensively built commercial structures were apt to be "rational." In the years after 1840, when the American economy entered a period of rapid expansion, the life insurance business boomed. Insurance companies were eager to convey the impression of established wealth and absolute security. The new Equitable Building was instrumental in promoting the image of prosperity that would characterize insurance company buildings for at least a half-century and also inform the richness of style associated with the mature New York skyscraper.

Unable to decide between two designs, the building committee awarded the commission to Gilman & Kendall—probably on the basis of style—and appointed Post consulting architect in charge of ironwork, elevators, and vaults. Post also functioned as supervising architect. It is likely that Gilman, the oldest and most experienced among those architects identified as having submitted designs, was responsible for the choice of the Second Empire style for the building, although Kendall had actually studied architecture in Paris.[5] In addition to having studied with Hunt, Post had a degree in civil engineering from New York University and was apparently already an expert in the use of structural iron. Nowhere can this be better appreciated than in his Troy (New York) Savings Bank–Music Hall Building (1871–75), where rolled iron trusses support the roof and the music hall's plaster ceiling is attached to an iron grid hung from iron bars that extend from the roof trusses.[6] By 1890 Post had become one of the nation's leading designers of business buildings. Daniel Burnham once called him "father of the tall building in New York," but that title could be conferred on Post without the qualification of city, for it was only in the late 1870s that Chicago began building elevator office buildings of more than six or seven stories, and Post designed the earliest ten-story office building, the Western Union.[7]

Credit for incorporating two steam-powered elevators has traditionally been given to Henry Baldwin Hyde. Hyde was the founder of Equitable, its vice president at the time of the building's construction and, from 1874 until his death in 1899, company president. The only member of the building committee in favor of elevators, Hyde supposedly convinced his colleagues of their value. (Richardson's plan does not appear to include one, which suggests that the decision was made after the architect was selected.) Post, however, promised the building committee that "if they would build the building six or more stories high and put elevators in, he would be personally responsible for renting the upper floors if there was any difficulty in doing so."[8]

The two elevator shafts, said to rise 130 feet, were the highest yet built anywhere. Manufactured not by the famed Otis elevator company but by Otis Tufts, who was responsible for the peculiar (and unsuccessful) elevator in the Fifth Avenue Hotel, the elevators were expected to enhance the building's prestige. Roomy enough to provide seating, they were described as the "largest, most complete, and comfortable ever constructed . . . in constant but noiseless motion . . . rendering the grand stairway of the building almost an ornamental superfluity."[9] Situated at either side of the lobby's grand staircase, they made it commercially feasible for the Equitable to be nearly double the height of previous business buildings. Their placement at the court wall of the building, where they would

4.5
*Wrought-iron beam
fastened to cast-iron
column by wrought-
iron straps passing
through column;
wrought-iron box
column C: Equitable
Building at light shaft
N. As damaged by the
fire of 9 January 1912.
After New York Board
of Fire Underwriters,
Report on Fire in the
Equitable Building.
The Equitable Life
Assurance Society of
the United States
Archives.*

not usurp desirable rental space, presaged the arrangement that characterized the mature New York skyscraper.

The Equitable's internal iron framing is of particular interest because it was so extensive. All the exterior walls were bearing masonry (granite lined with brick), and the primary bearing partitions were brick. Inside, cylindrical cast-iron columns sixteen inches in diameter helped carry floors composed of segmental brick arches springing from wrought-iron I-beams that spanned between brick partitions or wrought-iron girders. Supported at either end by bluestone templates in the brick walls, the I-beams were anchored by wrought-iron straps to pins set in the brickwork, a method still used as late as 1912.[10] Wrought-iron beams were fastened to cast-iron columns by wrought-iron straps passing through the column (Fig. 4.5). Above the third floor, box columns built of wrought-iron channels and plates were used instead of cylindrical cast-iron columns. The studding and the lathing were all iron, the roof was completely iron framed, and there were iron rolling shutters as well. Most interesting is the construction of the inner court walls. The engineer and architect William Harvey Birkmire, suggesting that the Equitable anticipated skeleton construction, observed that the walls of the inner court were supported on cast-iron columns.[11] He may have been stretching the point, but it is worth considering.

At the time of its completion, the Equitable Building was considered thoroughly fireproof because of its granite, brick, and iron construction, yet it was the section most severely damaged in the fire that devastated the enlarged building on 9 January 1912. Its deficiencies included the lack of fire-resistant covering on the bottom flanges of the floor framing members and on the columns (except those in the business hall). The vast underground vaults, however, which extended halfway across Broadway and Cedar Street, were so well constructed that they withstood the fire, contents undamaged.

The building also incorporated an innovative system of forced draft ventilation designed by the Philadelphia engineer Lewis W. Leeds. A complex arrangement of flues moved the air by means of heated shafts, as indicated on his plan (Fig. 4.6), rather than by steam-driven fans used in other systems at this time. Leeds received a good deal of publicity for his system; but Post later criticized it, saying that he thought not one of the "entire collection of shafts carried off one cubic foot per hour of foul air."[12]

As completed in 1870, the Equitable's stately gray granite facade on Broadway was crowned by a high pavilion roof, and in the fall of 1871, an allegorical sculpture group called "Protection" was placed over the entrance portico. Designed by the famous sculptor J. Q. A. Ward, this Carrara-marble group represented the Society's emblem: the Guardian Angel of Life Assurance protecting the widow and the orphan. The building was trapezoidal in plan, and except for a light court in the form of a shallow recess on the south side and two light shafts above the business hall floor, it covered the whole of its site. The Equitable company occupied the entire second-third floor, which contained the most remarkable interior in the building: a 35-foot-wide, 105-foot-long galleried hall where business with the public was transacted (Fig. 4.7). The 26-foot-high ceiling was climaxed by two raised skylights that added 7 feet more to the height of the hall; and twelve scagliola-covered iron columns divided the central space, where the clerks' desks and a long marble counter were located, from the side aisles. Forty offices on two levels surrounded this hall; the five at the Broadway end that were used by the company officers were separated by sliding doors so they could be opened up to each other. A private spiral staircase ascended from the vice president's office to the gallery, from which every desk in the hall below was visible; and dining facilities for the officers and employees were located in adjoining space on the third floor. The arrangement of the business hall was a direct source for Post's Produce Exchange, built a decade later, and it anticipated the galleried light courts of early Chicago skyscrapers.

By renting out the rest of the building, Equitable was able to get its own space "rent-free."[13] It deliberately took the least desirable floors, now made conveniently accessible by the elevator, for its own quarters. These were the two that neither accommodated off-the-street traffic (as the ground and first floors did) nor were sufficiently high enough above the street to offer insulation from street noise and provide "pure" air—selling points for the upper floors. The raised basement and entrance-hall floors were planned for occupancy by banks and corporations that required money exchange and needed ready access from the street. Three of the banking suites, as well as the entrance hall and the company's quarters, were fitted with marble floors and wainscoting of various rare marbles. The fourth, fifth, and sixth floors, laid out around the light shafts above the business hall, accommodated fifty offices. Most of these, as planned, were immediately leased to lawyers who apparently agreed with the *Evening Post* that the location would be highly advantageous: "If you call on a lawyer—instead (as now) of throwing away time, rupturing blood vessels, and losing your wind by clambering up dark staircases—you

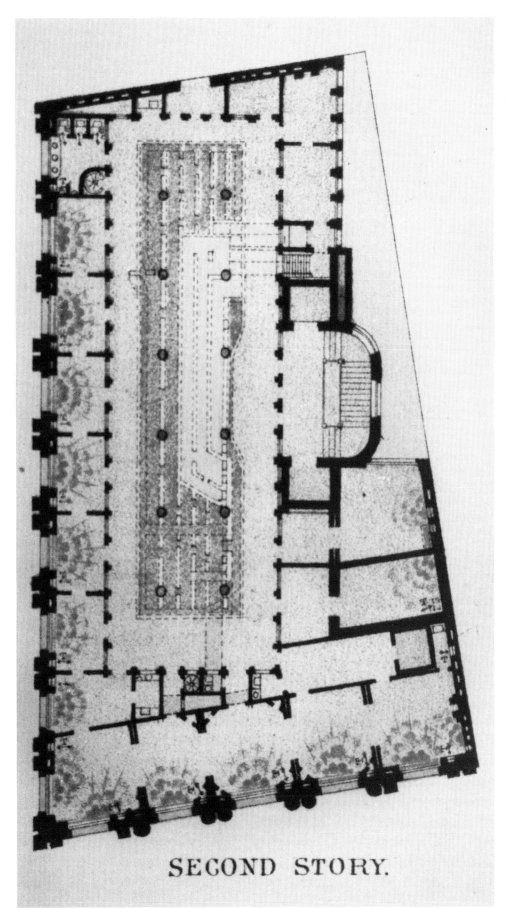

SECOND STORY.

4.6
*Plan of the second
story, Equitable
Building
(1868–70).
After Leeds, A*
Treatise on
Ventilation.

4.7
*Equitable Business
Hall as it appeared
after 1889.
The Equitable Life
Assurance Society of
the United States
Archives.*

walk directly from the street into one of the handsome vertical steam cars (which will always be in readiness, one ascending while the other descends), and taking a seat on the comfortably-cushioned seats, will be almost instantaneously lifted to the sixth floor, where, apart from the world, and undisturbed by the noises of the street, you can consult your advisers in seclusion and repose."[14] The seventh floor, in the mansard roof, contained apartments for the janitor and his helpers.

Apparently there was no difficulty finding tenants for the highest rental floor. According to M. A. Brooks, Post himself offered to take the top suite on the Broadway side at the appraised (and presumably quite reasonable) rental. " 'No,' declared Mr. Hyde, 'you will take the suite at twice that figure,' to which Mr. Post agreed. The judgment of both these pioneers was later vindicated when Mr. Post was offered a bonus of $6,000 for his lease within six months after the building was opened."[15] The view from the top was truly panoramic, and thousands of people were said to have come to ride in the elevators: "Before us is spread the most exciting, wonderful, and instructive view to be had on our continent. . . . East and North Rivers and the bay appear as if at our feet, with their myriad flotillas of the navigable world. Suburban Brooklyn, Jersey City, Hoboken, Hudson City, and Harlem are all plainly before us. Certainly not elsewhere in all New York can such another unobstructed bird's-eye view be had as from the open pavilions of the Equitable Life Assurance Society's building."[16]

The Equitable company's cost-effective real estate enterprise set an example for future skyscraper builders to follow. It proved an immediate financial success. By 1871 rental quarters in the building were yielding about $136,000 annually, and more than four hundred people were regularly in occupancy. Other corporations were considering adding stories (and elevators) to their existing buildings, and buildings under construction were said to be "introducing the same plan and building to a much greater height than formerly."[17] All the exceptional features of the Equitable Building—its elevator-predicated height, "fireproof" construction, extensive iron framing, large window area, and rent-free owner quarters—justify the title "first skyscraper." The building also helped establish the importance of achieving an architectural expression appropriate to an urban setting, in this case Parisian splendor.[18]

The subsequent history of the first Equitable Building is one of gradual expansion until it covered its city block. The number and nature of extensions to the building were a measure of the ever-increasing prosperity of its owner. As early as 1875–76, with Kendall as architect, assisted by Theodore Weston, the building was extended along its Cedar Street side towards Nassau, and the business hall was lengthened accordingly. The mansard was then raised to accommodate at least one more story, which resulted in a more commanding corporate image (cf. Figs. 4.1 and 4.8). In 1878 electric lighting was introduced on an experimental basis in the Equitable's corridors, making it one of the earliest buildings to be electrified. By 1885 Equitable owned most of its block, and by the time of the 1912 fire, its headquarters was a composite structure of five buildings. Overall, Post was responsible for at least eight alterations, the most extensive undertaken in 1886–87 and completed in 1889. At that time the building was doubled in width along Broadway so that it took in the entire block from Cedar to Pine streets and extended along its center axis from Broadway to Nassau Street (Figs. 4.9 and 4.10). Two stories were added under a new mansard roof.[19]

In order to accomplish this extensive work successfully, Post had to anticipate various structural problems. His ingenuity in solving them placed him in the front rank of engineer-architects working at the time. On one occasion, in order to prevent unequal settlement of the building, especially over a quicksand bed on the Cedar Street side near Nassau, he introduced wedge-shaped plates, or shims, to raise the cast-iron columns. In another instance a bearing wall at the third floor had to be moved outward by 12 feet to increase floor area. Post lengthened the existing beams by clamping deeper, 14-foot sections on either side with a 2-foot lap joint. He also substituted lighter-weight, hollow-tile floor arches for brick, and all his additions reflected the latest improvements in construction.[20]

Post's most spectacular feat of new construction, and the most impressive architec-

4.8
*Equitable Building
as altered 1875–76.
Collection of The
New-York Historical
Society.*

4.9
*Equitable Building
as it appeared after
1889. Demolished.
The Equitable Life
Assurance Society of
the United States
Archives.*

4.10

*Ground floor plan of
Equitable Building as
enlarged
1886–89.
After Alexander,*
Description of the
New Equitable
Building.

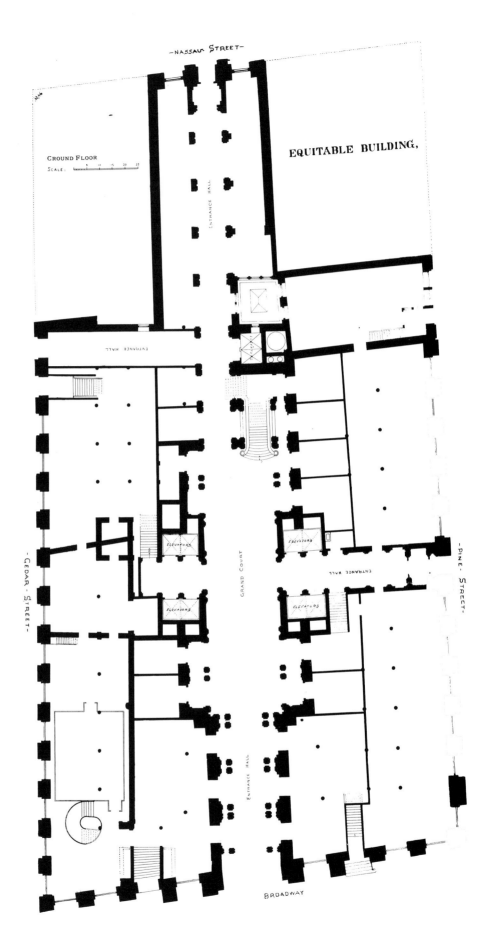

EQUITABLE BUILDING,

GROUND FLOOR

SCALE:

NASSAU STREET

ENTRANCE HALL

ENTRANCE HALL

CEDAR STREET

GRAND COURT

ELEVATORS

ELEVATORS

ELEVATORS

ELEVATORS

ENTRANCE HALL

PINE STREET

ENTRANCE HALL

BROADWAY

4.11
Entrance Floor
Arcade of Equitable
Building as it
appeared after 1889.
The Equitable Life
Assurance Society of
the United States
Archives.

tural feature of the enlarged Equitable, was the new lobby introduced when the building was widened in the 1880s. At that time, the main entrance became a broad archway at the midpoint of the newly expanded Broadway facade. This entrance opened into a vaulted corridor that led to a magnificent 100-foot-long, 44-foot-wide arcade covered by a stained glass skylighted barrel vault and featuring a mosaic supplied by the Herter Brothers (Fig. 4.11).[21] The glass was set in a wrought-iron armature on marble-sheathed cast-iron arches. Above this vault an enclosed court—spanned by a bridge that linked the two halves of Equitable's floors—lighted the inner offices of the building. The newly built court walls were iron framed with brick panels supported on girders—the same skeletal construction that Post used for the interior walls of the Produce Exchange completed in 1884.

Along either side of the arcade were booths where such necessities as railway tickets, telegraph service, candy, and umbrellas were sold. There were also post office boxes to be used in conjunction with the innovative Cutler patent letter drop, a mail chute that served every floor of the building; stock exchange tickers; a restaurant; barber shops; and a guard station. Said to be a "novelty in this country" and "in respect to its size and imposing appearance [to] eclipse most of the similar structures of Europe," the arcade was thought to have supplanted the A. T. Stewart Store's rotunda as a "marvel of the architect's and builder's art." It could be entered from each of the surrounding streets like the *passages* of Paris and the Galleria Vittorio Emmanuele in Milan that inspired it. Because of its proximity to the Wall Street financial center, this arcade was heavily used, and the building functioned as a "little city in itself."[22] As such, the expanded Equitable might be considered a forerunner of the twentieth-century "micro-city" skyscraper.

Equitable was a relative newcomer in the life insurance business; it was founded in competition with the older Mutual and New York Life Insurance companies. By 1870 rivalry among insurance companies was intense. The rapid growth of the industry was evidenced by the spate of new and costly insurance company buildings that rose in the city after 1868. To a considerable extent the ornate insurance company style with rich, classically inspired details was set in the Mutual Life Insurance Company Building, designed by John Kellum (1863–65; demolished). Just a block north of the new Equitable Building on Broadway, Mutual's elegant marble palazzo covered a larger area than the first Equitable Building but adhered to the conventional commercial height limit of four stories. Founded in 1842, Mutual had been the first American insurance company to offer life insurance on the mutual plan to the general public. As of 1870 it had the largest income of any life insurance company in the United States.[23] Henry Baldwin Hyde started his career as a salesman with Mutual. Setting the example for Equitable, Mutual helped carry its costs by including space in its building for rental tenants. And in 1870, imitating the new Equitable, Mutual added two stories (and an elevator) to its old building under a new, towered mansard roof.

Moving ahead architecturally, Mutual completed a new eight-story building in 1884 that was roundly criticized as being too tall and massive for the narrow streets (Nassau, Cedar, and Liberty) bounding its site. Two years later Equitable began its mammoth expansion, thoroughly outstripping the Mutual in building size. So fiercely competitive were the two companies, by this time recognized as the most important of their kind in the country, that Equitable was rumored to have purchased the property behind Mutual's building to prevent further expansion of the building on that site.[24] But Mutual subsequently completed huge additions to its building, and the resulting behemoth of 1904 overtopped the Equitable Building and rivaled it for sheer ground coverage (see Fig. 10.1).

Much of the Equitable Building's grandeur and modernity doubtless resulted from its owner's rivalry with the New York Life Insurance Company. Founded in 1841, New York Life began writing policies in 1845, two years after Mutual had actually opened business. It also built new headquarters on the east side of Broadway between Leonard Street and Catharine Lane in 1868–70 (Fig. 4.12). Plans for its new building were filed in the city's buildings department in April 1868, seven months before Equitable's, but the official opening date for both buildings was 1 May 1870, surely no accident. Griffith Thomas, the city's leading commercial architect until Post came on the scene, won the New York Life commission in a limited competition. Thomas had been one of the first American architects—perhaps the very first—to adapt the Second Empire mode to the commercial building, starting with his Continental Insurance Company Building. But his building for New York Life was essentially an old-style marble palazzo with a flat roof, though the pilasters that adorned the facades and the monumental entrance portal betokened Second Empire modernity.

Equitable's choice of the fully developed Second Empire style over New York Life's hybrid style was surely conscious; so was the erection of taller quarters. The center portion of the New York Life Building rose only three stories above the basement, the

4.12
*New York Life
Insurance Company
Building
(1868–70; de-
molished),
Griffith Thomas,
architect.
After* New York
Illustrated *(1878), 19.*

ends only four above; but because of the sloping site, the basement was entirely above ground at the rear of the building, giving the appearance of five stories on that side. Prominent belt courses divided New York Life's arcaded stories; cast iron was used extensively at the street level; and, in keeping with the general style, ornamental detail was comparatively restrained. Each company prominently displayed its insignia in the form of a sculpted group over its entrance pediment; New York Life's is an eagle feeding its young.

According to New York City Department of Buildings records, the New York Life Building's foundation walls and piers were laid on fourteen-inch-thick concrete beds. The building was iron roofed and internally iron framed, using cast-iron columns, rolled-iron floor and roof beams, and heavy built-up wrought-iron girders similar to those in the Bank of the State of New York (Fig. 4.13).[25] The frame was far from fully rigid, however, and although the details of the Equitable's construction are less certain, its framing was apparently lighter, more rigid, and generally more advanced. New York Life also had an elevator, placed inside the well-hole of the grand staircase and apparently planned from the beginning, but not installed until several months after the building opened—and after those of the Equitable Building were put in. The company's quarters were on the first floor behind the marble-floored, black walnut–finished entrance hall and on part of the second floor. The business hall on the first floor was larger in area than Equitable's and similarly laid out but only one story high. The remainder of the building was rented out for stores and offices.[26]

The race was on. In 1879 two stories were added to the New York Life Building. In the 1890s the company replaced its old building with a new skyscraper on the same (enlarged) site. By 1907 Equitable was planning a new building that would be realized after the fire of 1912 and that would far exceed New York Life's in both height and bulk. In 1886 Equitable surpassed Mutual, becoming for a time the largest life insurance company in the world. By 1892 Mutual was represented as the largest life insurance company in the world, and in 1908 it was evaluated as the richest in assets, with New York Life a close

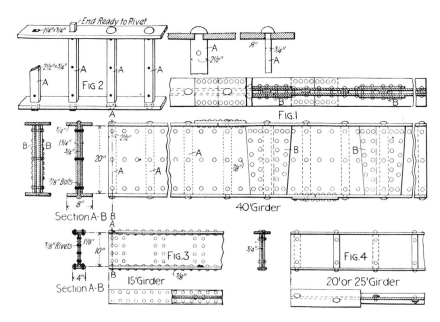

4.13

Details of girders in New York Life and National Bank of Commerce buildings. After Engineering Record (1896).

second. The rivalry has continued. Ranked by assets, Metropolitan Life is today the largest New York life insurance company and the second largest in the country. New York Life is number four in the United States; Equitable is ranked seventh and Mutual twenty-third.[27] Equitable raised yet another new skyscraper in New York in 1986.

The Western Union Building

When the Western Union Telegraph Company and the *Tribune* began building new quarters in the early 1870s, the development of the skyscraper was clearly under way. Just as life insurance had become a thriving industry in the nation's largest city and principal port, the business of communication by telegraph and newspaper had also flourished in New York. By 1870 several of the city's daily papers were quartered in Printing House Square. Post's Western Union Building, which rose nearby on the northwest corner of Broadway and Dey Street, was built because the telegraph industry had experienced phenomenal growth since Morse constructed the first practical recording instrument in 1835 (Fig. 4.14). Fifty American telegraph companies already existed by the time Western Union incorporated in Rochester, New York, in 1851, but in the 1860s the new company began its ascent to the position of virtual monopoly it attained in the 1940s. In 1861 it constructed the nation's first transcontinental telegraph line; in 1866 it relocated to New York City, and by early August of 1872 Post's design for the company's new building had been selected from among several submitted in an invited competition. Excavations for the foundations began shortly afterward.

Judging from the surviving competitive projects by Hunt, Napoleon LeBrun, and George Hathorne, as well as an albumin photograph of a preliminary perspective by Post, the new building was initially planned to incorporate only nine stories.[28] It was built with ten, however, counting the ground story (actually a fully raised basement) as the first and the two lowest rows of dormers under its mansard as nine and ten; it was just over half again as large in cubic volume as the Equitable.[29] If the attic is included, the building

4.14
Western Union Building
(1872–75; demolished),
G. B. Post, architect.
Collection of The New-York Historical Society.

could be described as having ten and a half or even eleven stories. It rose 230 feet from the sidewalk to the top of its clock tower, overtopping all other structures in the city except the spire of Trinity Church, the almost contemporary Tribune Building, and, by 1876, the towers of the Brooklyn Bridge. Its prominence on the skyline was reinforced by an iron time ball mounted on a flagstaff at the top of the tower: each day at noon a signal telegraphed from Washington would cause the ball to slide down its staff, and "people on ships, in New Jersey, on Long Island and far north on Manhattan Island set their time pieces daily by it."[30] This ball was a precursor of the lighted globe that since 1908 has slid down from the top of the Times Building in Times Square at the stroke of midnight on New Year's Eve.

In general, the construction of the Western Union differed little from that of the Equitable. Post had planned to use iron in the facades, probably for the lintels, but the client insisted that no iron be used on the exterior. The interior frame comprised the usual cylindrical cast-iron columns, fifteen-inch-deep wrought-iron floor girders, and ten-inch-deep floor beams with brick jack arches springing from their bottom flanges. The floor finish was mostly tile on a concrete bed, the partitions chiefly plaster blocks, and the ceilings either plastered soffits of arches or plaster on lath carried by iron Ts and angles suspended from the floor beams. Although the Chicago fire of 1871 had alerted architects that iron columns could collapse under intense heat and would fail when suddenly chilled by the water from the firemen's hoses, the cast-iron columns as well as the lower flanges of the floor beams were left exposed rather than covered with fireproof material. The system of flat, hollow tile arches that by the end of the decade would come into general use was just being introduced in America when the Western Union was being built. But when the upper stories of the building caught fire in 1890, the ironwork and the flooring suffered little damage nonetheless.

Perhaps the Western Union Building's most impressive construction was its tall mansard roof. Like the Equitable's, it was iron framed with wrought-iron rafters and king-post trusses, its iron-trussed beams spanning sixty-five feet (Fig. 4.15). This "roof" construction made it possible to build taller without necessitating enormously thick, space-consuming masonry walls below. By the mid-1880s the operators' lunchrooms (ninth floor) and the kitchen, as well as bedrooms for the engineer and the steward (all on the tenth floor) and storage space in the attic, were located in this area. Some of the building's mechanical equipment was housed there as well. Thus, the mansard roofs of these early skyscrapers, so often criticized by modernist historians as ungainly disguises of height, served a practical as well as an image-making function.

The same can be said for the large windows and arcaded treatment of the Western Union's eighth-floor exterior walls: these were undoubtedly calculated to lighten the load as well as to admit as much natural light as possible into the interior. Occupied by the company's vast main operating room, where telegraph operators sat at tables arranged in neat rows and attended to their transmitters and receivers, the entire 23-foot-high space of this floor was unobstructed by walls or columns except for the four iron pillars that supported the iron clock tower. There was surely some kind of special overhead framing—built-up girders or trusses—which makes this building all the more important, as does the presence of what must have been the most elaborate electrical circuitry of the time. And the exterior iron-railed balcony above the seventh floor, as frivolously decorative as

BROADWAY FROM ASTOR HOUSE LOOKING DOWN.

it may appear in photographs, was in fact designed to serve a practical purpose. Initially it bristled with hundreds of telegraph wires entering the building at this high point in order to avoid the inconvenience of having them pass through the building. Inlaid around the inside of the balcony base, these wires were distributed onto the seventh-floor ceiling, and from there they were carried to the eighth-floor operating department. And yet Post surely realized that this part of the building would be in a sense the center of the world and sought to distinguish it on the exterior by treating it differently from the other floors. Appropriately, the ceiling of the operating room depicted the sky above.

Among the more progressive features of the Western Union Building were its system of fire extinction and its early hydraulic-gravity elevator. On the assumption that the Croton water supply in lower Manhattan might not provide adequate fire protection, tubular wells were dug in the cellar to a depth of seventy feet below street level. From there iron water mains were passed through the building, with taps on each floor, up to the roof deck, where heavy streams of water could be pumped up by powerful steam pumps in the cellar and projected onto surrounding buildings if need be. The steam that heated the building was also used to operate its small freight elevator and two of its three passenger elevators. The third passenger elevator, designed especially for the company's employees, was one of the earliest hydraulic-gravity elevators.[31] This elevator caused numerous difficulties, including some injuries, because the operator's control was limited, and in 1891 it was replaced by a steam elevator. Initially, the passenger elevators ran only as far as the sixth floor, but the freight hoist rose to the tenth floor, where the kitchen was located.

The Western Union's facade was more or less tripartite in organization. Its heavily rusticated granite base was articulated by two heavy belt courses, and its alternately striped brick and granite shaft was terminated by a low seventh story beneath the balcony. The "capital," or third part of the composition, comprised the arcaded eighth story and the high roof. At the base paired columns and pilasters of amber-spotted Quincy granite flanked the main entrance, and two bronze statues, one of Morse, the other of Franklin, stood on the stone balcony overhead.[32] Yet despite the rich ornamentation and

4.15
View down Broadway from Astor House to Wall Street,
c. 1874.
Center: Western Union Building under construction, with Trinity Church in the distance. Right: Astor House (demolished) and St. Paul's Chapel. Left: New York Herald Building (demolished). Collection of Herbert Mitchell.

much-criticized striping of the walls, the design emphasis fell on the piers and hence on the structural system. The street elevations were more strongly articulated and more unified than photographs suggest: massive, as they needed to be, yet vigorous and kinetic through continuous piers and recessed spandrels above the base. Of the six piers across the Broadway facade, the second and fifth were enlarged to support the mansard pavilion and tower above, and the same was done at strategic points on the Dey Street side. The stone courses at the sill levels provided a secondary horizontal element that was intensified by the segmental arches over the sixth-story windows and by the brick and stone striping.

The resulting bony, gridlike wall treatment represented a new style that would have far-reaching effects on commercial design. In part this treatment was dictated by the city's building code, which mandated thick walls for structures classified as "store" buildings. That requirement could be met by piers or buttresses, and the wall between the piers could be thinner. But the functional appearance and details of the Western Union's exterior walls were also indebted to French utilitarian architecture of the 1850s and 1860s in the style known as *Néo-Grec*. The Beaux-Arts-trained Hunt (and his students) transmitted the style in altered form to the United States, where it flourished in New York and Boston in the 1870s and 1880s and spread to other cities as well. The Western Union Building was frequently described in the 1870s as "French Renaissance" or "modern Renaissance" in deference to its high, pavilioned roof with round lucarnes and classically inspired ornament, but a more accurately Americanized description of its style would be "commercial Neo-Grec."

Inspired by French design, Post restated the functional-structural approach growing since midcentury in effective, if somewhat busy, architectural terms. As assessed by Weisman, "Post seems to have understood the basic principle involved as one dictated by function and even realized the great flexibility of such a system where forms of great variety could exist in harmony so long as they were shaped by the same fundamental principle. This, of course, is the essence of all great architecture. What Post did then was to state the principle architecturally in refined form and in an exceptionally tall building where its message could not be missed."[33] Weisman's principle is oversimplified: a key factor in all great architecture is the effective manipulation of nonfunctional detail, and it is on that ground that the Western Union has been faulted from the beginning. Post's contemporary, A. J. Bloor, who appreciated the building as "a bold and towering performance in Renaissance of the modern type, which he [Post] has done so much to extend, and of the sub-type partially suggestive of an engineering standpoint, which has become peculiar to him," criticized the design of the shaft and also the roof, which he thought was "rendered picturesque at the cost of repose" and "not without a suspicion of coarseness."[34] Bloor also regretted that Post had had to substitute a less expensive and lighter-colored banding stone for the one that he had initially selected, a substitution that may explain the exaggerated striped effect. Somehow it is comforting to discover that what the twentieth-century eye finds disturbing also bothered Post's contemporaries.

Aside from the executive offices and board and dining rooms on the fourth story, the ground story where the public was received was the most impressive space in the building. Here encaustic tiling in mosaic covered the floor. The receiving and delivery departments were located on this floor as well. Presumably, the rental floors above were simply decorated. Much of the second floor and all of the third were rented out, but by 1886 the company had taken over all of the second and much of the fourth, and the fifth floor was at least partly rented to concerns that did business with Western Union. The sixth floor was fully rented; the seventh housed the batteries and dynamo engines; and the operating facilities were on the floors above. The telegraph wires essential to the operation of the company dictated to a great extent the functional aspects of the building.[35]

The first large fire to occur in a tall, theoretically fireproof structure struck the Western Union Building on 18 July 1890, when a short circuit in the seventh-floor battery room started a fire in the upper stories. Filled with flammable material—insulation on telegraph wires, tons of paper, battery coverings—and lacking satisfactory means of escape, these floors were a firetrap, and it was only by luck that there were no casualties. The company carried no insurance on the building because it was thought to be thoroughly fireproof.[36] Post's building suffered subsequently at the hands of Henry J. Hardenbergh, who designed the four-story, flat-roofed replacement for the burned upper stories that was completed in 1891 (see Fig. 7.15). By this date the mansard roof was thoroughly outmoded; Hardenbergh, who was also responsible for the company's new building (1890–91) adjoining the old one, was attempting to reconcile old and new styles, but he had to take structural difficulties and commercial requirements into consideration as well. The *Real Estate Record and Builders' Guide* accused him of ignoring what it perceived to be the controlling idea of Post's design, the deliberate lessening of the apparent height of the building through heavy horizontal divisions that minimize the verticality of the piers: "One is at a loss whether to regard the piece of work as a freak or the most notable of those hybrid monstrosities which the conjunction of strong commercial instincts with weaker artistic ones produce so prolifically in New York. . . . As it is the reconstructed building is an incongruous piling of one structure upon another."[37] And how often that has happened since.

Without question Post was one of the great innovators of American architecture. Although he never restricted himself to a single design scheme, the articulated continuous-pier wall was a recurrent theme in his work. It began with his remarkable project of about 1870 for the arcaded Marine National Bank and appeared in the well-unified structural forms and classical detail of his six-story Smith Building at 3–7 Cortlandt Street (1879–80). He was equally innovative in mechanical utilities. His New York Hospital (1875–77) incorporated an advanced hot-air heating system within the architectural fabric of the building, and the wards were vertically planned so as to unify the mechanical equipment in vertical enclosures. The architect's other accomplishments include the popularizing of terra-cotta trim as used on his Henry M. Braem townhouse and on the Long Island Historical Society building (both 1878–80).[38] All of this was preparation for the Produce Exchange.

The Tribune Building

By mid-1873, when its new building was begun, the thirty-two-year-old New York *Tribune* had become a major American newspaper and the focus of national attention. This achievement was due in large measure to the efforts of its founder and first editor, Horace Greeley, whose political activism and responsible journalism had brought him the Liberal Republican and Democratic parties' nominations for the United States presidency in 1872. Greeley died in late November of 1872, living long enough to lose the election and, presumably, to have selected Hunt as the architect for the newspaper's new quarters. Although the *Tribune*'s circulation plummeted due to Greeley's unsuccessful campaign, plans for construction went forward. The new building was meant to be a sensational monument to the newspaper, its founder, and the city of New York.

At least one other architect made a design for the building: Josiah Cleaveland Cady, who is best known for the south wing of the American Museum of Natural History (1891–1908). Published in 1874, Cady's rejected design may actually have had even more influence on the developing design scheme of the tall commercial building than did Hunt's accepted design and the completed structure (Fig. 4.16). Proposing what appears to be a nine-story building, Cady's perspective shows the facades articulated by four tiers of arcades, the tallest spanning and unifying three stories. The rhythms, round-arched form, and bichromatic banding of these arcades surely influenced the powerful commercial work of Richardson, who was to be appreciated as the greatest architect of his day. Moreover, the strong, campanile-like corner tower seems a prediction of the Metropolitan Life tower and generally prophetic of the tower-skyscrapers of the future.

Hunt's drawings for this and for the Equitable, Western Union, and Coal and Iron Exchange buildings disclose his experiments with different rhythms of arcading. They presage the design scheme made famous by Richardson's Marshall Field Wholesale Store in the mid 1880s: a quickening rhythm utilizing several tiers of arcades. Hunt's arcades,

4.16
Project for the
Tribune Building,
1872,
J. C. Cady, architect.
After New-York
Sketch-Book of
Architecture *(1874)*.

however, are not round-arched but segmental, after the work of his French contemporaries; and his penultimate design for the Tribune Building, as well as the building as completed, features the wide, triple-window bay usually associated exclusively with Chicago work (Fig. 4.17).[39] As on the Western Union Building, heavy supporting piers are a prominent element of the exterior structure, and their upward movement is similarly inhibited by strong horizontal divisions, especially the massive relieving arches midway up that were included to strengthen the building walls. Hunt reportedly asserted that "the exigencies of the case demanded a new style of architecture—a style which was at once an outgrowth of the country and the demands of the time."[40] He was describing the commercial Neo-Grec.

Nobody has ever had much good to say about the architectural features of the Tribune Building's exterior. Even Bloor, who thought highly of Hunt's work, disliked the "violent" color contrast of the dark red and black–patterned brick with the light-colored granite trim and criticized the "extravagant" form of the building. But he also pointed out that the lack of "repose" could in part be attributed to Hunt's difficulties with the oddly contoured site at the northeast corner of Nassau and Spruce streets, specifically with the obtuse angle at the main front (Fig. 4.18).[41] Attempting to resolve the problem, Hunt positioned the main entrance and the tower at the point of the angle. Endeavoring to unify the front, he began articulating the tower midway up, although the four heavy piers that supported it—visible at each of its corners, and the two on the front expressed all the way down to the first floor—originated in the basement. He increased the thickness of the south wall of the tower from four to four and a half feet because the "bend" in the long elevation north of the tower threw the outer wall faces out of parallel. From the beginning the newspaper expected someday to enlarge its new building according to Hunt's plans. Eventually, when Hunt's addition was accomplished in 1881–83, the plan took on a more regular, L-shaped contour, with the building extending back along Spruce Street for one hundred feet, twice as far as it does in the first-story plan illustrated in Figure 4.18, and spanning all the way across from Spruce to Frankfort streets.

The least successful aspects of the executed design, namely the heavy proportions of the mansard in respect to the low height of the base and the resulting "compression" of the shaft, were due entirely to circumstances beyond Hunt's control. Comparison of the preliminary designs and the actual structure reveals that the Tribune Building's height was gradually increased from eight to ten stories, with the tenth story apparently settled on after construction had begun. One suspects that the belated decision to increase the height of the building was motivated by a desire to overtop the Western Union. At 260 feet from the sidewalk to the top of its finial (which accounted for at least 10 feet of that dimension), the Tribune Building reached that goal and also managed to overpower the tiny Sun Building next door. It is usually described as ten stories tall but can be considered so only with the inclusion of either the attic—7 feet high at its highest point and used to house elevator machinery, water tanks, and ventilating apparatus—or the basement. The attic was hardly more than a half-story both here and in the Western Union; thus, in effect, the two buildings had the same number of stories above their cellars, the chief difference being that the Western Union's basement story was entirely above ground and could be entered from the street. The tower of the Tribune Building had additional rooms on three levels that were used for storage.[42]

4.17
*Tribune Building
(1873–75; de-
molished),
R. M. Hunt, architect.
Prints and Drawings
Collection, the
Octagon Museum,
American Architec-
tural Foundation.*

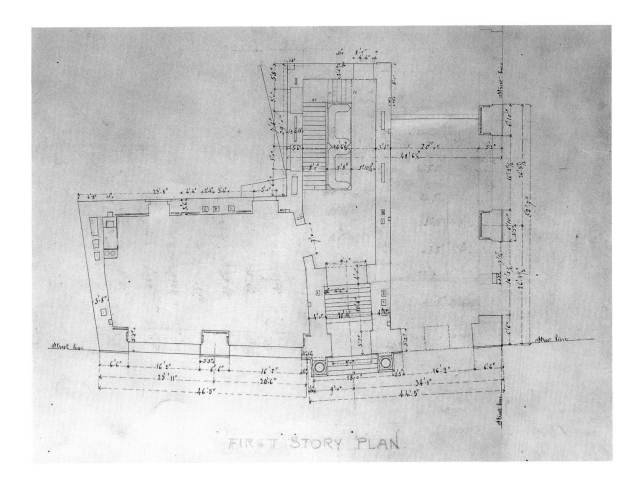

FIRST STORY PLAN

4.18

First story plan of the Tribune Building, c. 1873, R. M. Hunt, architect. Prints and Drawings Collection, the Octagon Museum, American Architectural Foundation.

The Tribune offers a striking demonstration of the great amount of potentially usable floor area that was usurped by the supporting structure of the high masonry building. The brick piers of the exterior walls had to be enormously thick in the lower part of the building to bear the weight of the stories above. Irregularly trapezoidal in form, these piers, as well as the rear wall, diminished in thickness as the building rose in height and the number of floors being supported correspondingly decreased. According to a section drawing of the building that was made in Hunt's office when only nine stories were planned, all of the piers were 6.5 feet deep at the basement level and 5 feet, 2 inches deep at grade level, thereafter diminishing in thickness at a rate of 4 inches per floor, to a depth of only 3 feet, 2 inches at the seventh and eighth floors (Fig. 4.19). As constructed, the thickness of the walls tapered to 2 feet, 4 inches at the top of the building. Floor heights decreased as well, ranging from 17 feet, 10 inches in the cellar and 15 feet, 7 inches in the main floor hall to 12 feet on the eighth floor. In the floor plan illustrated in Figure 4.18, the total area of the first floor, within the outside perimeter of the piers and walls, equals 376.5 square feet. Nearly half of this space, more than 187 square feet, is taken up by solid masonry. And the windows of the building were set near the outer face of the piers, leaving deep reveals inside wherever they occurred. Awkward as this arrangement may appear, Hunt's plan did provide at least one outside window for every room in the building, making light shafts unnecessary.

The composition of the 18-inch-thick concrete bed under the building's granite foundation walls—Portland cement, sand, gravel, and stone—was new to the city at the time

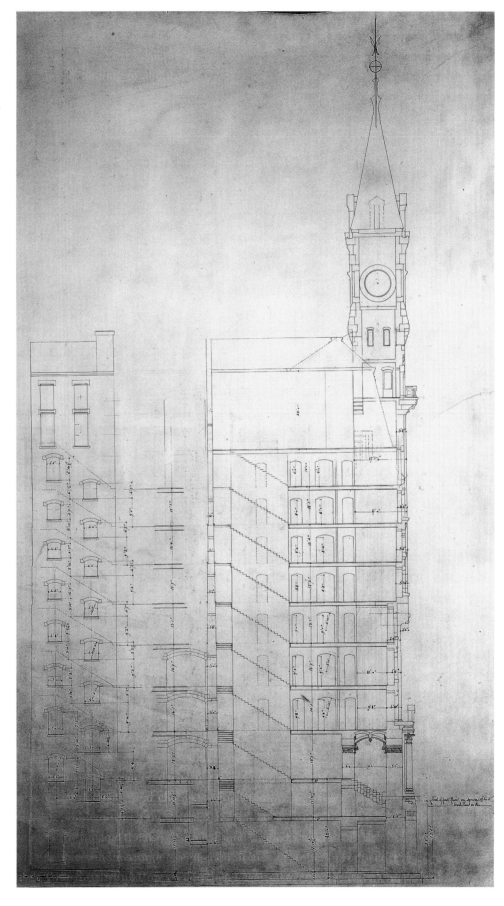

4.19
*Section through
entrance, tower, and
stairway wing,
Tribune Building,
c. 1873,
R. M. Hunt, architect.
Prints and Drawings
Collection, the
Octagon Museum,
American Architec-
tural Foundation.*

and had the advantage of hardening quickly and solidly. All the foundation piers were on spread footings, apparently on sand at 30 feet below grade; bedrock lies deep below grade in this vicinity, at minus 86.5 feet. Also exceptional were the massive segmental arches bonding through the entire thickness of the wall at the first- and fifth-floor levels, as well as the flat hollow-tile arches used in the floors. The floor arches, molded to fit as voussoirs between beams that were uniformly 12¾ inches deep, with spans under the tower that varied from 10 feet, 4 inches to 14 feet, were manufactured by Leonard Beckwith's Fireproof Building Company of New York according to a system recently patented in France. These were a decided improvement over the heavy brick arches used in the Equitable and Western Union buildings. Hunt is credited with having recommended to the company the substitution of hollow tile blocks for the heavier hollow concrete blocks normally used in the French method; his were among the earliest American buildings with these arches.[43] As added protection against fire damage, no upright iron supports were used in the building; the iron floor beams were protected by fireproof material, and wherever possible pressed Baltimore brick was incorporated in the walls.

At the time of completion at least two rooms of the basement were expected to be rented out; some of the *Tribune*'s presses and its paper stock were in the basement as well. On the first floor, the public entrance on Nassau Street opened into a vestibule that was covered by a distinctive groined, marble-ribbed brick ceiling. From there a short flight of steps led up to the main hall, which, like the halls on every floor, was paved with colorful Mettlach mosaic tiles and wainscoted with blue-gray Vermont marble. Two passenger elevators flanked the iron staircase at the rear of this hall, and to the left of the hall was a large banking room planned as a rental space. The *Tribune*'s counting room—the most sumptuously decorated space in the building—and its publication office were also on this floor but could be entered only from Spruce Street. The counter in the counting room, made of black Belgian and varicolored Italian marbles, extended nearly the full length of the 46-foot-long, 21-foot-tall space and was topped by an elaborately carved ash screen with ground-glass panels. In many respects this room was similar to the business hall of the Equitable.

The second through the seventh stories were planned as offices, typically numbering eight per floor. With lawyers in mind as potential tenants, some of the offices were joined as suites. The editorial rooms were on the eighth floor, including the office of the chief editor, then Whitelaw Reid. The tower room served as Reid's study and was accessible to his office below by a spiral staircase, and the rest of the ninth floor functioned as the composing room. This huge, 23-foot-tall space resembled the operating room of the Western Union in its size and openness, but, according to the *Tribune*'s long article on the day that the building opened (10 April 1875), its decoration was more interesting. Oiled to bring out the red color, bare brick walls were surmounted by a geometrically patterned red and black brick cornice. The partly exposed iron framework of the mansard, built into the walls of the composing room but actually supported by the piers below the story, was decoratively detailed and painted in a "lilac tint."

According to the British architectural press, the building was at first "hailed as a piece of folly," and people said that "tenants would never be found who would risk their lives in it."[44] Its solid, fireproof construction, however, allayed these fears, and the top floors were rented first. People appreciated the quality of light and air available high above the street and the freedom from noise and dust. Indeed, the building proved so successful that by 1883 it was said to be paying between six and seven percent on the initial investment in annual rental income; the percentage includes the rental value of the newspaper offices had they not been occupied cost-free by the owner.[45] The financial success of the Tribune Building inspired other such ventures.

In spite of its aesthetic flaws and functional defects—chiefly the irregular and constricted plan and the extreme sacrifice of space dictated by masonry construction—Hunt's Tribune Building demonstrated the skills of its architect in skyscraper engineering and design. With its extraordinarily high corbeled clock tower and its almost overbearing facade, the building, along with the Western Union, signified a transition from the modesty and urbanity of the earlier commercial building, whether of the palazzo or Second Empire variety, to a new proclamation: the building as skyscraper. Weisman said it very well:

> The total effect of the design is not elegant. It is structural. Sensuousness gives way to logic. Magnificence is replaced by massiveness. Brick is substituted for marble and iron. Color turns from white and gold to bright red. . . . Stylistic evidence and other reasons indicate that it belongs to a new breed of building, namely, the skyscraper.[46]

The Coal and Iron Exchange and Evening Post Buildings

The Tribune was consciously planned as a sensational new type of building, but Hunt's rather less ambitious Delaware and Hudson Canal Company Building, better known as the Coal and Iron Exchange (1873–76), was a much superior work of architecture (Fig. 4.20). Chartered in 1823, the Delaware and Hudson Canal Company had completed a canal in 1828 to connect the Delaware Valley anthracite fields with the Hudson River at Kingston, New York. By 1860, the company had expanded to include common-carrier rail operations, and eventually its rail lines extended to Albany and Montreal. The canal was abandoned in 1899, but the railroad, once a vital link in the network of canals and rail lines that supplied coal to New York City, still survives. The company's main objective in building its new quarters was to centralize the coal business by providing offices for all the large coal companies under one roof.[47]

The new building, constructed on the southeast corner of Cortlandt and Church streets, occupied a larger site than the Tribune Building and contained twice as much floor area. Though it was at first planned to be nine stories tall (counting the ground or raised basement story as the first), it was built with seven stories on the main Cortlandt Street side and eight, including the attic, on the rear side, with an additional story in the pavilion roofs (Fig. 4.21). The exterior was functional to the point of severity, though restrained formal details were used with great skill—the monumental main entrance with Neo-Grec pediment and polished granite columns, for example, and the incised sandstone pediments of the dormers. Pressed Baltimore brick trimmed in Nova Scotia sandstone produced a more subtly colored exterior than the Tribune's, although here, too, the bricks were laid in black mortar. As built, the rhythm of the superimposed arcades, which linked two and three stories on the facades and bracketed double and triple windows,

4.20
Delaware and Hudson Canal Company Building (1873–76; de-molished),
also known as the Coal and Iron Exchange,
R. M. Hunt, architect.
After King's Photo-graphic Views.

prefigured that of Post's Produce Exchange. In contrast to the horizontally restrained piers of the Tribune, those of the Coal and Iron Exchange rose with strong continuity above the rusticated sandstone base. As befits a carrier of essential commodities—and one not threatened by competitors—Hunt's building projected an image of sobriety rather than flamboyance.

The structure was considerably more advanced than the Tribune's, though essentially it followed the same system (Fig. 4.22). Spread foundations were bedded in solid concrete like those of the Tribune, the footings at about minus twenty feet. The foundation piers were joined by inverted arches built up with four deep courses of stone, a very early—possibly the first—use of these arches. The aim was to counteract the unequal settlement of footings by making an entire row act as a unit, with the bending force exerted by the downward push of any one pier counteracted by the built-in rigidity of the curved arch. Comprising widely spaced masonry piers and solid brick rear and party walls, the exterior walls decreased in thickness from forty to twenty inches, a considerable improvement over those of the Tribune. The slate-covered mansard was entirely iron framed, like the Tribune's, and the floor structure was the same as the Tribune's. The internal structure of the Coal and Iron Exchange included an irregular distribution of brick piers, partitions, and, unlike the Tribune, iron columns. The entire floor area was much more open than in the cramped Tribune plan. Two factors had handicapped Hunt in designing the Tribune: the narrow, oddly shaped lot and the need to support the heavy machinery used in the composing room on the ninth floor.

4.21

*Elevation, Coal
and Iron Exchange,
c. 1873,
R. M. Hunt, architect.
Prints and Drawings
Collection, the
Octagon Museum,
American Architec-
tural Foundation.*

The first floor of the Coal and Iron Exchange, its layout recalling the Tribune's main floor, accommodated the Delaware and Hudson Canal Company's offices in a large, open room to the right of the entrance (Fig. 4.23). This space was approached through an anteroom under a cross-arched ceiling of segmental section. The rest of the building was arranged as offices for rental, all, according to a *Tribune* article, with outside windows; the plan, however, shows one area looking onto a large light shaft that separated the lavatory area at the rear from the rest of the building. As in the Tribune Building the floors were tiled, the halls marble-wainscoted, and the gas fixtures and bronze hardware architect designed, all as usual for the time.[48] In 1906 the company sold the building, moving its main offices to Albany, and the huge City Investing Building replaced it.

During the same period that Hunt was involved with the Tribune and Coal and Iron Exchange commissions, he also designed such interesting commercial structures as the Royal Phelps store and office building at 25 Union Square (1872) and the adjacent, cast-iron-fronted Van Rensselaer (1871–72) and Roosevelt (1873–74) buildings on Broadway, all five stories tall. Only the Roosevelt at 478–82 Broadway survives. The Roosevelt and Van Rensselaer buildings successfully exploited the extreme attenuation of columns and mullions made possible by cast iron. Although both of these warehouse-and-store buildings were initially painted bright colors, the so-called Moorish front of the Van Rensselaer stood out for its exotic, multicolored detailing. Louis Sullivan surely learned much about the aesthetic merits of both tripartite design and the arcaded, amply glazed mid-

4.22
*Longitudinal section,
Coal and Iron
Exchange,
c. 1873,
R. M. Hunt, architect.
Prints and Drawings
Collection, the
Octagon Museum,
American Architec-
tural Foundation.*

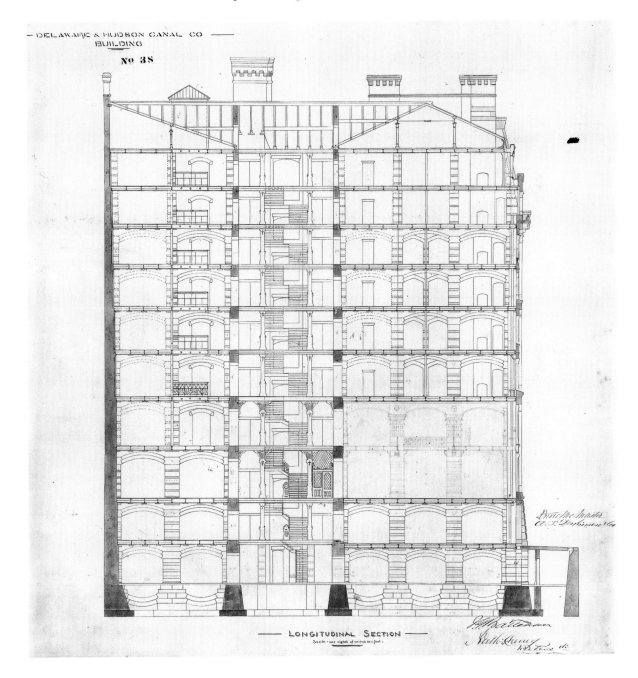

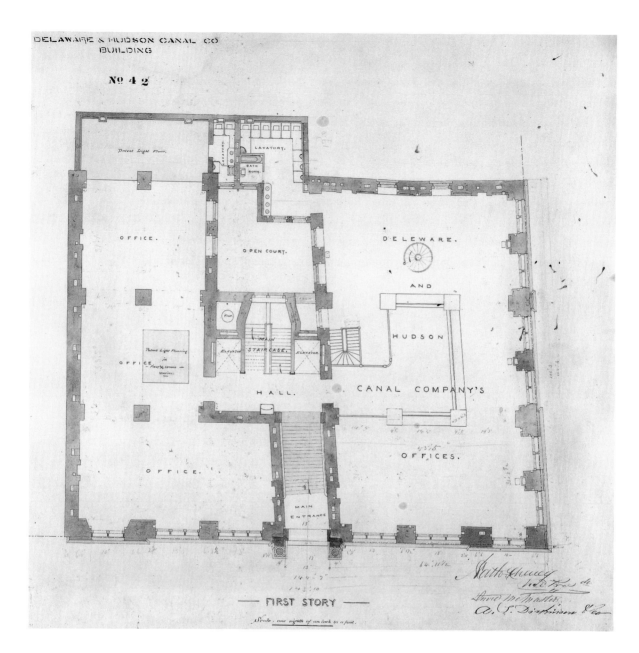

— FIRST STORY —

Scale : one eighth of an inch to a foot.

4.23

*Main floor plan,
Coal and Iron
Exchange,
c. 1873,
R. M. Hunt, architect.
Prints and Drawings
Collection, the
Octagon Museum,
American Architectural Foundation.*

section from the example of the Phelps and Roosevelt buildings. The seven-story Guernsey Building (1881–82; demolished) at 160–64 Broadway, another of Hunt's commercial Neo-Grec designs, seems to have been the last of his office buildings. Its bichromatic brick-and-stone front, though well unified and functional, was out of style by that date. Hunt himself was by this time thoroughly engaged in designing mansions for New York's millionaires.

One other structure belongs in the earliest group of New York skyscrapers: the ten-story Evening Post Building (1874–75; Fig. 4.24). The new-building docket (6 July 1874), which is based on the original buildings department permit, lists Charles F. Mengelson as the architect. Normally that would be unimpeachable evidence, but two other names are firmly associated with the design. George Hathorne won the competition for the commission with a project that included a mansard roof, but he was dismissed, according to one account, after he failed to remove that roof and bring the building up by two more stories as instructed. Mengelson was then engaged but was replaced by Thomas Stent. In Octo-

4.24
*Evening Post
Building (1874–75;
demolished).
After King's
Handbook
of New York City
(1893 edition).*

ber 1875 Hathorne sued the newspaper for damages, claiming that the building as completed was his design "except the hideous additions and alterations made by new hands."[49] But Bloor, who disparages the facades of the completed building as "thin slice[s] of *pseudo*-Victorian Gothic work," refers to Hathorne's greatly superior unused design.[50] The *Evening Post* names Thomas Stent as the architect and alludes to Stent's education in England, his authorship of numerous churches, and his Singer Sewing Machine Company buildings then under construction in Chicago and St. Louis.[51]

The most unusual feature of the Evening Post Building, possibly the client's idea, was its flat-topped roof, exclusive of the octagonal cupola. This roof signified the demise of the commercial mansard and foretold the future. If the raised basement is counted as the first story—the publication office and rental offices were on that floor—the story count is ten; the cupola room added another half-story. Severely handsome pressed brick and stone—trimmed elevations followed the general commercial style of the time. Verticality was achieved by piers that divided the main front into three bays and by projecting sections of wall that produced a complex bay rhythm along the Fulton Street side. Restrained belt courses supplied the secondary horizontal emphasis, and arched lintels performed effectively as transitional elements between the vertical and the horizontal. The newspaper was proud of the flat roof and "purely conventional" style of its new quarters and in so characterizing its style seems to criticize the Tribune Building implicitly: its own building, the *Evening Post* declared, "is simple in style, and will be admired more for its massiveness and substantiality, and for its complete adaptation to the uses for which it was constructed, than for anything peculiar or striking in its outlines or extravagant in the treatment of its interior."[52]

The round, banded lintels over the windows, to which Bloor's criticism undoubtedly referred, were somewhat exceptional in New York and represented the latest variant of the High Victorian Gothic. They call to mind Cady's round-arched project for the Tribune and suggest that the building committee leaned towards Ruskinian ideals. In fact, William Cullen Bryant, the editor and part-owner of the *Evening Post*, was closely associated with several artists of the Hudson River School, a group known to have admired Ruskin's writings. The preferences of Bryant, an extraordinarily learned editor, undoubtedly influenced the building's style.

The Evening Post Building was only 140 feet tall. Its bearing walls diminished in thickness from about 3 feet at the bottom to 2 feet at the top, an improvement over the Tribune Building facilitated by the flat, towerless roof. The Evening Post's interior construction, of a type well established by this time, differed from the Tribune's in that cylindrical cast-iron columns carried the wrought-iron beams that supported the concrete-covered brick floor arches. The floor uses were nearly identical to the Tribune's: the deep cellar housed the presses; the newspaper's publication office was on the ground floor; all the floors from the second (main) through the ninth were partitioned as offices for rental—here, too, most of the tenants were lawyers—and the editorial offices and composing room were on the tenth floor. Following the example of the Western Union, the building had hydraulic pressure elevators, but these were a special kind of "telescopic elevator": a pump in the basement forced water into iron tubes that were suspended from below the car to raise it, and the tubes telescoped into themselves when the water was drawn out and the elevator descended.[53] Though a workable system, these elevators proved unsatisfactory and were replaced within three years.

The high rate of return on the Evening Post Building in less than a decade after its completion—reported as ten percent on the initial investment—may be taken as evidence of the overall financial success of the early skyscraper.[54] The *Evening Post* remained in these quarters at 202–8 Broadway until it moved to its new and larger building completed in 1906 on Vesey Street.

Other Innovative Work of the Decade

The buildings discussed above were the outstanding commercial structures of the decade, but others also contributed to the evolving technology and design of the new, taller building in the transitional 1870s. One of these, although only six stories high above its shallow basement, utilized extraordinary construction features. The Seamen's Bank for Savings (1870–71) stood at 74–76 Wall Street on the northwest corner of Pearl Street. The architect was Robert G. Hatfield, one of the more innovative constructionists of the time, and the building contractor was Marc Eidlitz, a prominent mason-builder in New York from about 1854 until 1888, when he accepted the presidency of the Germania Bank. After that, his sons Otto M. and R. J. Eidlitz took over the business, which continued as one of the city's most active builders well into the 1930s, constructing such major skyscrapers as the Empire and Bankers Trust Company buildings. Marc Eidlitz routinely acted as builder for his brother Leopold Eidlitz.[55]

Hatfield's reputation had been established by his Sun Building (1850–51) in Baltimore, for which Bogardus had manufactured the cast-iron facades and interior columns. Hatfield was a member of the American Society of Civil Engineers and a founding member of the American Institute of Architects, and his foremost achievement was the structural and architectural design of the Grand Central Depot train shed (completed 1871), which he modeled after the roof of St. Pancras Station in London. For a busy architect, Hatfield was also a prolific and influential writer. Among his most important works were *Fire-proof Floors for Banks, Insurance Companies, Office Buildings, and Dwellings . . .* , a pamphlet published by the New York Chapter of the American Institute of Architects in 1868 as a pioneer work, and his widely acclaimed and much needed *Theory of Transverse Strains and Its Application to the Construction of Buildings*, published first in 1877 and in a second edition in 1880.[56]

Emulating the exterior design of the Equitable Building, but only about two-thirds as large and with cast-iron facades, the Seamen's Bank was unremarkable architecturally. The *Record and Guide* particularly disliked the exterior because the iron simulated granite—even including fake chisel marks—but praised the "fine frontispiece" on Wall Street, a Corinthian portico surmounted by the figures of a seaman and an Indian supporting a shield that depicted the bank's arms.[57] A convenience was the provision of direct access to the building's two elevators by way of the street-level Pearl Street entrance. From there, anyone wanting to go only to the higher floors could reach the elevators by walking down a few steps into the shallow basement and thus avoid having to climb the staircase of the main, Wall Street entrance.

The great constructive innovation of this building was the iron trusswork that Hatfield used inside. He had to devise a way to carry four floors of offices over a skylighted banking room that was forty feet wide, fifty-nine feet deep, thirty feet high, and ringed by a gallery. His solution was to introduce iron trusses, described as "bridge trusses," to span the full forty-foot distance between the interior brick side walls of the banking room (Fig. 4.25). Two parallel tiers of trusses were set in vertical planes, one above the other, along the lines of the brick partition walls at either side of a central corridor. These were extended in depth at right angles to Wall Street and parallel to Pearl, and the three trusses in each tier carried the floor frames of the third, fourth, and fifth floors, as well as the

Seamen's Bank
for Savings
(1870–71; de-
molished),
R. G. Hatfield,
architect.
Trusses supporting
floors over the
banking room,
exposed during
demolition.
After Engineering
News-Record *(1925).*

ceiling of the banking room. Each truss comprised a cast-iron top chord, cast-iron inclined end posts, and wrought-iron angles for diagonals. In its form and distribution of forces, this construction mimicked the Pratt web system developed in 1844: Hatfield relied on one of the great basic inventions in bridge design. All compression members were cast iron and tubular in form; the tension members were wrought-iron hangers in the form of rods and wrought-iron bottom chords; and the horizontal tie of each truss consisted of two rolled wrought-iron I-beams that ran the full length of the truss to support the ends of iron floor joists.[58] This construction may have been the first use of trusses to carry superimposed floor loads.

The Seamen's Bank contrasts with the Bennett Building (1872–73) at 93–99 Nassau Street, which is more interesting architecturally but less innovative structurally. Its construction is of the fireproof type standard for large office buildings of the time.[59] Designed by Arthur Gilman, it was built by James Gordon Bennett, Jr., the owner of the *New York Herald*, near the Herald Building. At seven stories, the Bennett was initially a long, low, mansard-roofed block before it was enlarged by the addition of several stories in the 1890s. Above the cast-iron-fronted ground story, the exterior walls are brick bearing, with the three exposed to view sheathed in cast iron. Undoubtedly, the cast iron was intended to imitate the stonework characteristic of more costly Second Empire work but at a much lower cost. It is also possible that the iron sheathing was introduced as additional fireproofing.

Although the mansard roof identified the Bennett Building's style as Second Empire and its facades display classically derived architectural details commonly associated with masonry, Gilman's wall treatment was highly original. He designed the castings to take full advantage of the impressionable, moldable character of iron; and the result is so successful that even Ruskin might have found this treatment suited to the material (Fig. 4.26). The Bennett's large windows are enframed by sharp-edged iron jambs articulated by scrolled corbels under simply ornamented impost blocks that adjoin crisply profiled segmental heads; the glazing in the corner rows of windows creates smooth curves that initially contributed to the illusion of corner tourelles under pyramidal, corner roof pavilions. As if to suggest the "nature" of iron, quoins with recessed panels displaying a molten lavalike image originally adorned the ground-story piers. Between 1890 and 1894, with James M. Farnsworth as architect, the Bennett was enlarged by its new owner,

4.26

*Detail, cast-iron
facade of Bennett
Building
(1872–73),
Nassau Street side.
Arthur D. Gilman,
architect,
with addition by
James M. Farnsworth
(c. 1894).
Nassau Street
between Ann and
Fulton streets.
Photograph by Becket
Logan.*

John Pettit. Its height was increased to ten stories, with twelve in the narrow, westernmost section of the building on Ann Street, under a new, flat roof. Fortunately, the iron-reinforced, brick-walled addition at the top was clad in castings identical to those of the lower stories.[60]

From the beginning the Bennett had steam heating, and it added its own generating plant after electric lighting became available. The original structure likely had elevator service; the hydraulic elevators put in at the time of the addition in the early 1890s were said to allow passengers to ride "in the light of day, with fresh air and a panoramic view" of shipping, the Brooklyn Bridge, the East River, and lower Manhattan, at an unsurpassed speed of "500 feet per minute," but it is not clear just where these were situated in the building.[61] Judging from the description, they were on the Spruce or Fulton Street side.

Few commercial buildings were constructed between 1874 and 1880, during the economic depression that followed the "Jay Cooke panic of 1873." By 1877 the value of all building, in constant dollars, had declined to just over 40 percent of the 1871 total.[62] Several among those that were built, however, including one not primarily commercial in function, helped further the use of multistory arcading and the tripartite composition that would identify New York commercial work for the next two decades. As demonstrated by the designs of Hunt, Richardson, and others discussed above, arcading was immediately applied to the new, taller buildings that began to rise around 1870. In this regard, George B. Post's unexecuted project for the Marine National Bank (c. 1870), which was intended for the northwest corner of Wall and Pearl streets, seems especially precocious (Fig. 4.27).[63] Apparently never published but certainly known to those working in Post's office—and likely to others in the profession—this French-influenced, Neo-Renaissance design features a clear three-part division of the facades, continuous piers or pilasters that span the full height of the building, and bounding wide bays infilled with great areas of glass. Inevitably, one thinks ahead to Louis Sullivan's mature work and the "column skyscrapers" that proliferated in New York in the 1890s.

The former Racquet Club Building on the northeast corner of Sixth Avenue and 26th Street (1875–76) is a rare surviving example of 1870s avant-garde commercial design in New York (Fig. 4.28). Better known as the Coogan Building after a later owner, it was designed by Alfred H. Thorp, one of the first Americans to study architecture at the Ecole des Beaux-Arts in Paris. It was built with a commercial ground story and housed club facilities above. On the outside it appears to include six floors, but as originally constructed, the combined forty-foot height of the two topmost floors was given over to the indoor courts. The building's tripartite composition comprises a one-story cast-iron-columned and brick-arched base (as it appeared before a shingled canopy was added), an arcaded midsection where continuous pilasters terminated by arches join four stories, and a narrow attic story of small windows in doubled rhythm. Once again, the design scheme is in advance of Sullivan's skyscrapers and seems to forecast the commercial formula prescribed in his famous essay of 1896, "The Tall Office Building Artistically Considered." The strong brick piers suggest the commercial Neo-Grec styling of Hunt's and Post's buildings; the minimal brickwork ornament seems affiliated with the High

4.28
*Racquet Club
Building
(1875–76),
also known as the
Coogan Building,
A. H. Thorp, architect.
776–782 Sixth
Avenue.
Photograph by S. B.
Landau.*

Victorian Gothic; and the repeated round arches, overhanging eaves, and general block-like form presage the Neo-Renaissance that would become high fashion in the 1880s.[64]

Thorp did relatively little in the city, but he was also architect of the seven-story Orient Mutual Insurance Company Building at 41–43 Wall Street (1877–78), which adjoined the exactly contemporary six-story Queen Insurance Company Building by Charles W. Clinton and James W. Pirsson at 37–39 Wall (Fig. 4.29). The two companies had purchased the property with the intention of constructing a common building, but they were unable to agree on various matters and instead divided the land and built independently. Each building had only a 30.5-foot frontage, the two separated by a party wall and utterly different in style. Thorp's severely reductive, marble-sheathed facade with large square-headed windows seems a prediction of twentieth-century modernism, whereas Clinton & Pirsson's red and black–brick front trimmed in brownstone and bluestone had all the trappings of the High Victorian Gothic. Indeed, to the *Record and Guide* Thorp's building seemed without stylistic precedent:

> If there is any style of architecture on the building at all, it may safely be termed the nineteenth century style, as it is progressible in conception and progressive in execution. The architect . . . seems apparently to have understood that the problem of erecting an office building today is quite different from that which had to be solved by the builders of the Greek or even the middle ages, and that archaeology is not architecture. . . .

Second from right:
Orient Mutual
Insurance Company
Building
(1877–78),
as later enlarged,
A. H. Thorp, architect.
Right: Queen
Insurance Company
Building (1877),
Clinton & Pirsson,
architects.
Far left: Atlantic and
Sun Mutual Insurance
Company Building
(1852),
Frederick Diaper,
architect.
Second from left:
United States Trust
Company Building
(1888–89),
R. W. Gibson,
architect.
All demolished.
After King's
Handbook of New
York City *(1893*
edition).

In the Orient Building all superfluity has been evaded and right down honest, practical work stamps it all over, from cellar to roof.

With light and air as a primary objective, the facade ornament in the so-called "Queen Anne" style just then coming into fashion in America was kept to a minimum. There being no need for artificial light, none was provided. Nor did the building have the usual narrow air shafts "compelling parties on one floor to breathe the air of their neighbors on another."[65]

The Orient Building was constructed with the latest and best methods of fireproofing. All the interior iron framing members were coated with cement or terra-cotta, which was separated from the metal by air spaces; floors were constructed with iron beams and girders and flat hollow-block arches. On the two lower stories, the floors were marble tiled; on the upper stories, they were finished in wood. The roof was protected by a layer of Portland cement covered by layers of felt and gravel. And the Orient was one of the first structures to make use of the Drake & Wight patent fireproof column. The plumbing, considered the best available, incorporated a "novel" patented trap, said to prevent completely the escape of sewer gas; Fuller Meyer patent self-closing cocks, guaranteed for three years, were used over the basins. A "simple contrivance" known as Weaver's patent basin waste emptied the bowls instead of the usual plug and chains.[66] The Queen Insurance Building and the Orient Building had two elevators each, by this time common practice.

The Morse Building (1878–80), still standing at the northeast corner of Beekman and Nassau streets, concludes the major work of the decade (Fig. 4.30; see also Fig. 7.26). It was speculatively built by the cousins Sidney E. Morse and G. Livingston Morse on the site where their fathers had for many years published a religious newspaper known as *The New York Observer* and where their uncle, Samuel F. B. Morse, had first experimented with his telegraph. The Morse Building was one of two early skyscrapers produced by the young architectural firm of Silliman & Farnsworth, the other being Temple Court. One of the partners, Benjamin Silliman, Jr., was the grandson and namesake of the eminent professor and scientist with whom Samuel Morse had studied at Yale.[67] The building was designed as a *Rundbogenstil* variant of the polychromatic High Victorian Gothic, with facades somewhat resembling those of the similarly proportioned Evening Post Building. But the red and black brick of the Morse's exterior walls, the continuous fluted piers defining the corners and central bays, and the segmental arches over the windows of several floors recall those features of Hunt's Tribune Building. Integrated to form a distinctive style, this mix of German, Victorian Gothic, and Neo-Grec elements was epitomized in the original terra-cotta-framed entrance portal on Nassau Street.

The ten-story Morse Building was the wave of the future: 85 feet wide, 70 feet deep, and 165 feet high, it was a flat-roofed slab close to a tower in form. Those very attributes prompted Thomas S. Hines to claim that the Montauk Block (1881–82), Chicago's first ten-story building and one of the earliest structures to be called by the name *skyscraper*, foreshadowed "much of the later aesthetic of the Chicago School and of the modern movement in general."[68] The same could be said of the still earlier Morse Building. Certainly, the Morse's height and controlled variety of formal elements impressed observers during its construction. According to the *American Architect*, "Many who watched

the uprising walls wondered whether they would ever cease growing sky-wards.... There is contrast, diversity, and change, a great remove from monotony and a solution of a difficult problem which must strike all as a most satisfactory one."[69] Subtle changes in window rhythm and the use of single round-arched windows on certain floors alternating with double windows under segmental arches on others produced this diversity, and midway up the rhythm stopped and then began all over again as if identical buildings had been set one on top of another. But the continuous piers and relative simplicity and

104 *The "First Skyscrapers"*

regularity of the facade treatment imparted a quality of wholeness not typical of early skyscrapers.

Two years later the *American Architect* offered a thorough analysis, recognizing the Morse as a pioneer prestige office building in brick but also lamenting the aspects that make it seem so modern today:

> The first of the noteworthy attempts to build in brick alone, and to discard stone, even in the positions in which stone had been accepted as indispensable, was . . . the Morse Building, which remains one of the most interesting and successful of these attempts. The manufacture of terra-cotta has been much improved in the interval, but there has been no example of brick-work built since in which moulded brick and colored brick have been used with more fitness and sobriety, nor in which a more agreeable and satisfactory result has been attained. The flat roof over a tower building of which the area is so small compared with the height, is of course the misfortune of the building, and not the fault of the architects.

And the article noted with approval that in Temple Court, slated to rise on the corner diagonally opposite the Morse, the architects had "attempted to supply that animation in the skyline the lack of which is the chief defect of their older building."[70]

The Morse Building was considered thoroughly fireproof. It had unusually thick, brick bearing walls, 4 feet at the cellar level and 3.5 feet at the first floor. The roof was iron beamed, and the floors were constructed with $15\frac{1}{4}$-inch wrought-iron beams that were spanned with corrugated iron arches and filled in with concrete according to Hoyt's patent fireproof construction to produce a curbed ceiling that was finished in flat, glazed tile. As additional protection, all partitions were covered with iron laths and plaster by Smith & Prodgers, who were the mason builders as well as the plasterers.[71] This firm had worked on the Equitable and Western Union buildings and was one of the best in the business. It was in the construction of the Morse that the iron contractor Post & McCord used steam-powered derricks to hoist iron beams and girders for the first time.

The building immediately proved a good investment. By mid-January of 1879, fourteen months before it was completed, the three topmost floors had been rented. Clearly, high floors were desirable, as was the building's convenient location hard by City Hall, the post office, and Printing House Square in the heart of the city's fast-developing, first skyscraper district. As reported in 1883, the owners claimed the Morse—then paying over ten percent on their initial investment—as "the tallest straight wall building in the world."[72] The Morse was later known as the Nassau-Beekman Building; in 1901, under new ownership, it was increased in height to twelve full stories, and its two lower stories were refaced. These changes were probably made to cash in on the popularity of Cass Gilbert's columnlike Broadway Chambers Building nearby. The resulting heavily emphasized base and four-story capital with large square-headed windows produced a structure grossly inferior to the original.

By the end of the decade all of the more prestigious buildings—including the Morse and Hatch's Boreel Building—were employing iron extensively for interior columns and floor frames. Iron was still used on occasion for street elevations, but high-quality pressed brick was increasingly favored as an inexpensive, fireproof facing. Much of the technology employed in floor framing rested on pragmatic and empirical views that derived from the cumulative experience of practical builders, but theoretical publications with tables and mathematical analyses began to multiply. Of signal importance were Hatfield's books, especially his *Theory of Transverse Strains*, which focuses on the specific aspect of building in iron. The first comprehensive book on iron construction for architects was William J. Fryer's *Architectural Iron-Work* (1876), which included numerous tables and formulas, but these were often unreliable or inadequate or both, and many were borrowed without acknowledgment.[73]

The fundamental principles and characteristics of iron framing were well established by 1879:

1. Uniform quality and uniform strength of cast and wrought iron is needed throughout the body of metal.

2. The weight of the iron girder increases directly in relation to its depth; its strength increases directly with the square of its depth and is inversely proportional to its length. The problem, therefore, is to determine not only the depth and sectional area for a given load and deflection, but also the optimum dimensions for economy and manageability.

3. All girders and roof trusses should ideally bear directly on the walls. If the span is too great, they should bear on columns by means of shoulders; the beams then span between girders.

4. The strongest and most efficient form for the cast- or wrought-iron column is that of a hollow cylinder; the octagonal hollow prism is about equivalent.

5. The strongest and most efficient form for horizontal framing members is the I-section.

6. The most economical depth of the built-up plate girder is one-tenth of the span.

7. The most economical shape of the roof is a segmental vault on arched trusses with ties, like a railroad train shed, but this shape is seldom adaptable to a building. The next alternative is a gable roof on trusses. The fashionable mansard usually required a system of primary girders, rafters, and purlins less economical to construct than the gable roof, but it had the advantage of being capable of incorporating fully usable additional stories at lighter loads than would be the case with masonry walls. The flat roof, however, used on several of the latest buildings discussed here, was already beginning to displace the mansard.

So far, building heights relative to floor areas had necessitated no wind bracing other than that afforded by the massive masonry envelope. But if buildings were to rise higher and utilize available floor space to the fullest—and clearly that was desired—a system of wind bracing incorporated in the floor construction would be essential. In that regard the chief limitations of 1870s floor framing, to be gradually corrected in the next decade, were the insecurity of bolted connections, although these were rapidly giving way to riveting in large buildings; the presence of exposed ironwork; and the problem of indeterminacy of arches, continuous forms, and floor framing members fixed in masonry.

The architectural forms and style of the 1880s were heralded in such examples as the Western Union, Racquet Club, and Morse buildings. Though usually equipped with towers, and sometimes even disguised as mansards, flat or gabled roofs would predominate; the long block and the vertical slab would coexist side by side; and the gridlike brick wall, ornamented with cast terra-cotta and articulated with continuous piers and arcades of Renaissance or Romanesque derivation, would be further exploited. As buildings rose ever higher, the search for appropriate architectural and structural form would continue unabated.

THE FUTURE REVEALED: TECHNICAL DEVELOPMENTS AND FORMAL SOLUTIONS IN THE 1880S

If ever there was a time when the city revealed the form it would assume in its maturity—electrified, steel-framed, high-rise, architecturally sophisticated, ethnically diverse, socially and civically aware, an international center for the performing, literary, visual, and building arts—it was the halcyon decade of the 1880s. This was the time when the essential technological and architectural—as well as sociopolitical—foundations were set.

The City in 1880

At the close of the 1870s the new metropolis was starting to show the signs of its coming shape (Fig. 5.1).[1] Commercial docks lined the North River waterfront from the Battery to Eighth Street and the East River waterfront from the Battery to Gouverneur Lane. Smaller docks for local cargo vessels and pleasure craft extended as far north as 66th Street on the North River just above the New York Central & Hudson River Railroad yard, and along the East River to 34th Street, although above Houston Street they were increasingly scattered. Commercial building with a high proportion of office blocks walled both sides of Broadway, filling two-block corridors on either side all the way up to Canal Street. In the area bounded by South Ferry, William Street, the East River, and the approach to the still unfinished Brooklyn Bridge, there was solid commercial, industrial, and warehouse development with some residential mix. High-density residential coverage still characterized the rest of the "old city" up to the traditional boundary of Houston Street, Sixth Avenue, Greenwich Avenue, and 14th Street. The greatest building density, mainly commercial with some residential intermingled, occurred east and west of Broadway between Canal and Houston streets and in the rectangle and

THE CITY·T

5.1
*Detail,
1879 map of lower
Manhattan below City
Hall.
After Taylor, The City
of New York.
Library of Congress.*

adjoining triangle bounded by Houston, the East River, Grand Street, Lafayette Street, and Fourth Avenue.

Development in solidly built insulae, mainly residential, crossed the island up to an irregular line between 55th and 59th streets. East of Central Park and Fifth Avenue as far north as 96th Street there were occasional small residential enclaves with small shops; but north and west of Central Park from 60th Street to Inwood Hill and Spuyten Duyvil, there were just a few scattered houses. The section of that area north of Harlem lacked passenger service on the Hudson River Railroad line, but the Ninth Avenue elevated line, which reached 83rd Street in mid-1879, guaranteed active residential development to the west and north of Central Park.

But the shape of the city was also undergoing change and would soon be radically transformed. The economic downturn occasioned by the panic of 1873 was over. Recovery had been rapid in 1878, and by 1880 the total value of all new building, in constant dollars, nearly reached that of 1871. The upward climb continued—reaching by the end of the 1880s a volume of two and one-third times that of 1880—until the next depression struck in 1893. In 1880 downtown residential spaces up to and including 14th Street were rapidly disappearing. Twenty-third Street between Third and Seventh avenues had become almost exclusively retail trade; 42nd Street was starting to become commercial, although Broadway was still the major shopping artery, with Sixth Avenue between 14th

The Future Revealed 109

and 23rd streets in second place. Along the same latitudes, Fifth Avenue was lined with office buildings and bookstores, and the central avenues, Third to Seventh, between 23rd and 59th streets, had progressively lost their low-rise dwellings to stores, office buildings, hotels, apartments, and other building types. All these changes, especially the outward movement of the residential areas, were being accelerated by improved public transportation.

Wall Street and lower Broadway in 1880 were more than ever the great financial arteries. Trinity Church, the height of its spire as yet unchallenged, stood sentinel at the top of Wall, which was still a street of four- and five-story structures. Lower Broadway appeared much the same, although its uniform rhythm was violently interrupted at the corner of Dey Street by the bulk of the mansarded and towered Western Union Building. By mid-June, the United Bank Building (1880–81; demolished) designed by the Boston firm of Peabody & Stearns had begun to rise at the northeast corner of Wall and Broadway (see Figs. 7.20, 7.28). It would house the Bank of the Republic and the First National Bank. Continuing the commercial style and construction technology that had evolved by the late 1870s, this nine-story, flat-roofed slab anticipated the early skyscrapers of such Chicago architects as Burnham & Root. Its brick and brownstone facades of tripartite design were articulated by continuous piers reaching to the eighth story, four-story arcades, and a trabeated attic story and corbeled cornice reminiscent of Post's and H. H. Richardson's commercial work and indicative of much that was to come in the next few years.

Around 1880, with a variety of factors in the mix, a revolution was brewing. The Bell Telephone Company had incorporated in 1878, and its first exchange opened at 82 Nassau Street in 1879. On 20 December 1880, lower Broadway between 14th and 26th streets became the first of the city's thoroughfares to be electrically lighted. The first central generating plant, established by the Edison Electric Light Company, and the one that powered the first area-wide commercial electric lighting in the section bounded by Nassau, Pearl, Spruce, and Wall streets, began operation at 257 Pearl Street in 1882. In 1880 the Third, Sixth, and Ninth Avenue elevated railroad lines reached the Harlem River, and the Second Avenue elevated line extended to 129th Street. At long last, the Brooklyn Bridge opened in May of 1883, and the first cable cars went into service in 1885. The advent of rapid transit, more than any other single factor, promoted the increase in real estate activity and the rise in property values that began around 1880. By this time the elevator was standard equipment; without it, commerce would have been quickly paralyzed. This dependence is underscored by a journalist's record of a day in the late summer of 1881 when he had to make twelve office visits, eleven of which required an elevator. He calculated that he was lifted a total of sixty-two stories, an average of more than five-and-a-half stories for each trip.[2]

In the realm of culture, two leading metropolitan institutions were entrenched by 1880: the American Museum of Natural History and the Metropolitan Museum of Art. Each had established a permanent location; the former completed its building on Manhattan Square west of Central Park in 1877, and the latter finished its first building in Central Park near Fifth Avenue and 82nd Street in 1880. In 1883, yet another venerable institution, the new Metropolitan Opera house, America's first permanent home for grand opera, would open at the corner of Broadway and 39th Street.

A Fear of Heights

The great height of the new office buildings attracted attention that ran the gamut from enthusiasm to hostility. In the late 1870s many marveled at the new structures. The *Cincinnati Gazette* recorded a positive midwestern reaction in 1879:

> The stranger who approaches New York by the harbor sees now an imposing array of lofty buildings where there used to be very few. The Tribune towers above them all, but there are, besides the new buildings on Nassau Street, the Evening Post and Western Union Telegraph buildings on Broadway; the Mutual and Equitable insurance buildings; the Coal and Iron Exchange; the Boreel building, and half a dozen others, which give to a bird's eye view of the city a look of real grandeur. What with the elevated roads and the nine-story buildings, New York will soon assume the appearance of a city built in several stories, and only needing a mansard roof.[3]

So rapidly did office buildings both proliferate and grow taller in the affluent eighties that by 1883 the city was perceived as being in the throes of the "High-Building Epoch":

> The present . . . is likely to be known in the history of New York as the High-Building Epoch. Seven or eight years ago, after struggling in vain to pack the lower or business end of the city more closely with buildings, in order to supply the insatiable demand for office room, real estate capitalists suddenly discovered that there was plenty of room in the air, and that by doubling the height of its buildings the same result would be reached as if the island had been stretched to twice its present width.[4]

Others, however, anticipated dire consequences if heights went unchecked. The *Record and Guide* expressed its fear that the major thoroughfares below City Hall would soon be choked with traffic from the new Brooklyn Bridge and that the old narrow streets would be deprived of light and air by nine- and ten-story buildings. Observing that Paris had a law regulating the heights of buildings according to the widths of the streets, the publication warned: "The self-interest of owners will be enlightened after a few elevator buildings have been put up fronting each other across lanes, and will impose on them the same restrictions elsewhere imposed by law. . . . Now this height [the old five-story standard] is to be doubled, and the narrow streets are to become mere slits between towering masses of masonry." As a solution to the problem, the widening of Nassau and other narrow streets was recommended, and in a subsequent issue of the same journal a "conservative builder" called for a law, modeled on one in Berlin, that would limit the height of buildings to 100 feet.[5] Robert Kerr, a visiting English architect, was dismayed by what he saw on his tour in the winter of 1883–84 and immediately recommended legislation for height limitation.[6] His was an early expression of a British antipathy toward the skyscraper that would long endure.

What galvanized New Yorkers to action was not high office buildings—their height was unregulated until 1916—but the danger of devastating fires in the "enormous" new apartment houses that were rapidly rising in the early 1880s. In response to this concern, a specially appointed committee of city officials met in February 1883; in a report dated 1 July the committee urged that apartment-house heights be determined by the width of the street and that the limit be 65 feet. The fire department's chief engineer had told the committee that even in buildings 65 feet tall, fire was difficult to control on the upper floors. The report pointed out that between 11 July 1881 and 15 March 1883 the buildings department had issued permits for the construction of more than one hundred buildings exceeding 80 feet in height. Fifteen were for buildings between 130 and 160 feet tall; more than 80 percent of the permits were for residential structures, and—most newsworthy—plans and specifications had been filed for a fifteen-story flat house on the northwest corner of 57th Street and Seventh Avenue! The Osborne Apartments, which would house thirty-eight families and rise 182 feet, with a cupola 40 feet higher, was expected to be the highest building in the city, perhaps in the nation. The Osborne (1883–85), designed by James E. Ware, was built with eleven stories in front and fourteen in the rear, the difference owing to the fact that the apartments were duplexed with rear mezzanine floors. The projected cupola was not built (see Fig. 5.18).[7]

In March 1883, in response to a proposed new building law regulating the construction of dwelling houses, a committee of architects and builders urged a height limit of 60 feet. No action was taken. At a meeting at City Hall on 23 January 1884, citizens urged a height limitation for residential buildings to improve fire protection and ensure adequate sanitary facilities. The following April, spurred by a fire in the seven-story St. George's Flats on East 17th Street, the *Scientific American* attacked high buildings without adequate fire protection and urged a similar limitation. (By 1890, that journal would have nothing but enthusiasm for the new skyscrapers.) The *Record and Guide* urged the same, but it also foresaw the future: "New York is destined to become a city of monster buildings, and no legislation will avail against the inevitable."[8]

At last, in the winter of 1884–85, a bill to limit the height of apartment buildings to 80 feet above the sidewalk level was introduced in the New York State legislature. The arguments in favor of the bill cited the evils that would be eliminated with its adoption: the shadowed streets and contiguous buildings, the liability of tenants in high buildings to "zymotic diseases" due to leaking joints in drain pipes, the ready spread of contagious diseases because of the difficulty of isolation, and interior darkness and inadequate ventilation. Those arguing on the other side countered that a good site and good architectural planning could provide light and air to interiors regardless of the building's height and that in fact high buildings, being taller than their neighbors, would have more of both. Elevators were cited as safer, more comfortable, and less tiring than stairs, and the contemporary fireproof construction used in high buildings was judged superior to the standard for low buildings.

As signed into law on 9 June 1885, the bill limited the overall building height of "dwelling houses" on streets less than 60 feet wide to 70 feet—the same height specified in the Roman *Lex neronis* of A.D. 64. On streets wider than 60 feet, the height was limited to 80 feet.[9] An 1897 amendment to this law permitted a maximum height of 150 feet but no more than twelve stories for fireproof apartment buildings that contained one or more passenger elevators on streets wider than 79 feet, and the 1901 Tenement House Act limited the height of a multiple dwelling to one-third more than the width of the widest street on which it fronted. These regulations caused apartment houses to lag behind office buildings and hotels in the height race. Apartment hotels were also exempt; these as well as transient hotels were considered commercial structures. This exemption encouraged the proliferation of apartment hotels from about 1889 until 1929, when the

Multiple Dwelling Law limited the height of all high-rise apartment buildings. Some developers complained that no exception was made in the 1885 law for apartment houses fronting on parks or public squares or filling an entire block. The only regulation on the height of commercial buildings, meanwhile, was the section in the 1885 building code stipulating that any building over 70 feet high had to be of fireproof construction.

In an editorial of 8 January 1887, the *Sanitary Engineer* became the first engineering journal to attack high buildings. The editors found nothing good to say about sky-scrapers, opposing them on a variety of grounds: darkness of the lower floors (actually a factor of density of buildings rather than height of individual structures), absence of sunlight and dependence on artificial light, difficulty of providing adequate ventilation (also a factor of density), the hazard of turbulent winds and downdrafts, the nuisance of shadows cast on adjoining property, and the danger of fire. The intersection of Nassau and Beekman streets was declared the worst corner in the city.[10] Indeed, as had been predicted by the *Record and Guide*, New York's first skyscraper district was now con-gested, its narrow streets cast in deep overshadow by ten- and eleven-story buildings. The controversy would not end.

Another challenge associated with the height and bulk of buildings prompted dan-gerous practices in the 1880s. Excavations for deep foundations required that contiguous walls of older, adjacent buildings be shored, and because existing statutes were inade-quate and easily circumvented, the reinforcement was often inadequate. The problem, in fact, led to a disaster on Grand Street, where a number of large commercial blocks, chiefly stores, were constructed in a setting of jerry-built tenements. One such tenement col-lapsed in 1882 because of improper shoring around the excavation, killing and injuring a number of the residents; another similar accident in 1884 caused three deaths.[11]

All of the problems associated with great height and density, whether real or imagined, could be properly addressed only through the united skills and knowledge of all the professionals concerned: the architect, the engineer, the contractors, city officials. Build-ing was no longer a craft tradition but rather a scientific technology. As early as the summer of 1878, the *American Architect* editorially urged a closer union of the talents and education of architects and engineers. Too much building was being done without concern for the building's formal character, and too much architecture was divorced from structure. In an effort to overcome the problem, the editors recommended more joint meetings of the American Institute of Architects and the engineering societies.[12]

The First Mammoth Office Buildings: The Post, the Mills, Temple Court

With the Post (1880–81) and Mills (1881–83) buildings, neither of which is extant, George B. Post introduced the U-shaped commercial block (Fig. 5.2). This innovative plan, in which the stories above a two-story base are recessed so as to leave projecting wings, afforded more natural light and better ventilation to the interior offices of large commercial blocks than the usual enclosed light courts provided. Ordinarily reserved for buildings of blocklike dimensions covering large areas, the plan was used for commercial buildings and apartment houses until well past the turn of the century and can be considered the forerunner of the skyscraper H-plan that came into use around 1907. Writing in 1888, the architect William B. Tuthill observed that the modern office building "by surprisingly rapid steps has reached its present elaborate and nearly perfected condition." He recognized the U-plan as the "most frequent form of interior court," which held great potential "for an effective business architecture."[13]

Financed by Post's father and uncle, J. B. and J. A. Post, the eight-and-a-half-story Post Building was constructed on an oddly angular site at the juncture of Exchange Place, Beaver Street, and Hanover Street. Particularly striking features were the near-tripartite organization of its facades, a development in avant-garde New York commercial work of the 1870s and 1880s that is especially notable in Post's designs; its single-tone coloring of pale yellow brick and terra-cotta; and its extremely open, two-story base. This base was predominantly glass with piers so narrow and so thoroughly suppressed between corners as to suggest metal framing.

The nine-and-a-half-story Mills Building, considered "the first modern office building" by Winston Weisman, was one of the largest—and, at a cost of $1,430,000, most expensive—commercial structures yet built in the city.[14] It introduced a series of "Mills buildings" constructed by the California gold rush millionaire, banker, and philanthropist Darius Ogden Mills.[15] It attracted considerable notice because of its huge size, about 23,000 square feet in ground area, with a gross floor area of nearly 200,000 square feet; its prominent location on the corner of Broad Street and Exchange Place (it also had an entrance on Wall Street); and the speed of its construction—facilitated by the new "calcium lights" (limelights) on Broad Street, work went on at night as well as in the daytime.

The geology of the site presented difficulties that were overcome by a combination of luck and ingenuity. In the process of preparing for the foundations, a test-pit inside sheet piling was sunk through the top layer of dry sand down into the subsoil. Suddenly, the pit began filling up so rapidly with quicksand that the surrounding buildings seemed threatened. Fortunately, there was plenty of concrete on the site, and it was immediately used to infill the pit, solving the problem. Because the water level was at minus 17 feet—bedrock is at minus 65 feet—a brick foundation wall was carried to various depths from about 13 to 18 feet. The sectional shape of this wall was unusual: the thickness at grade was 3.5 feet; then the wall stepped outward and downward on a uniform taper to just over 5 feet, terminating in very broad footings over 8 feet wide. The interior supporting columns were mounted on individual spread footings. In February of 1882, cracks perceived in the unfinished superstructure caused great excitement, attracting "thousands of bankers, brokers, and merchants" to the site.[16] Post explained the cracks as the result of normal settling, but the source was traced to a defective casting in the basement.

The interior framing was iron, and the bearing-wall piers were so narrow as to suggest cage construction. As additional fireproofing, the partitions were hollow tile, and in all likelihood the ironwork was tile clad for the same reason. The impressive entrance lobby was roofed by a skylight on an iron armature, and the flat roof was brick on iron beams.

Contemporary sources describe the style of the Mills Building as "Renaissance." In fact, the gridlike exterior walls, where glass nearly filled the bays, recalled the commercial Neo-Grec of the Western Union Building, but the Mills Building's flat roof, striking proportions, and somewhat more reticient color arrangement created a clearer, more comprehensible pattern than that of the earlier building. The elevations were divided into four horizontal sections of two or three stories each; the base was chiefly New Jersey brownstone; the piers of the second layer comprised alternating courses of brownstone and red brick; and the piers of the two uppermost layers were brick. The color scheme was completed by an elaborate brownstone cornice (which hid the topmost floor), brownstone trim, and ornamental red terra-cotta panels below the windows of several stories. A wrought-iron portcullis operated by hydraulic power closed the main entrance. Both the coloring and the overall design were much criticized in the early 1880s. The *Record and Guide* considered the recess between the wings too narrow for its depth, calling it "a

5.2

Mills Building (1881–83; demolished), G. B. Post, architect. Collection of The New-York Historical Society.

mere slit," and attributed the faults of the building to "slap-dash" design and hasty construction.[17]

According to C. M. Ripley, the Mills was the first office building in the city, and likely the first in the world, to have its own electricity-generating plant.[18] Installed in 1883, this plant powered the circuits for 5,588 lights. Six hydraulic elevators, said to move at a rate of 300 feet per minute, carried eleven thousand people up and down each day. The offices, which were intended for rental to bankers, brokers, and railway and insurance companies, were finished in cherry wood, and the halls were tile-floored and marble-wainscoted. A well-equipped restaurant on the topmost floor was large enough to serve all the occupants. Mr. Mills's investment must have paid off, for an addition, also designed by Post, was quickly made to the Exchange Place side.[19]

The mansarded Temple Court building (1881–83), although not especially innovative in plan, merged ideas of commercial style developed in the 1870s with a new emphasis on verticality (Fig. 5.3). Designed by Silliman & Farnsworth, it stands on the southwest corner of Beekman and Nassau streets, diagonally across from the same firm's Morse Building. As intended by the builder, banker Eugene Kelly, most of the offices were initially let by lawyers—hence the name. At nine stories, or ten if the top story of the two towers is counted, Temple Court had no more usable floors than the Mills Building and would shortly be outstripped by the adjacent Potter Building. Yet its twin pyramid-roofed towers have continued to preside, cathedral-like, over the tight thatch of surrounding tall buildings that make up the city's first skyscraper district. Contemporary criticism was harsh. *Building News* considered the new brick-and-granite-walled structure architecturally "nondescript" and compared its towers to "donkey's ears." But because of its height and bulk, Temple Court was recognized in 1895 as "the pioneer among the great office buildings."[20] It was originally about 100 feet wide by 105 feet deep with a 212-foot-square interior light court. It could be considered the grandfather of the twin-towered apartment-skyscrapers that rose on Central Park West in the 1930s.

The New York Produce Exchange

Although few nine- and ten-story office buildings survive today, they were fairly common in New York by the early 1880s. One such was the conservatively "French Renaissance" Welles Building (1881–83), designed by Walden Pell Anderson and constructed at 14–20 Broadway just above Bowling Green (see Fig. 5.16, building at right).[21] The New York Produce Exchange (1881–84) was therefore not unusual for its height, which was equivalent to ten stories exclusive of the tower (Fig. 5.4). But its architectural design and construction technology made the Exchange one of the great buildings of the decade, George B. Post's masterpiece. The site of the building, at 2 Broadway facing Bowling Green, had been the location of the weekly "Monday market" established by Pieter Stuyvesant in the seventeenth century. The New-York Commercial Association had been founded in 1861 and renamed the New York Produce Exchange in 1868; its origins were in the Produce-Exchange Building Company and the Corn Exchange. The new building was intended to replace the smaller Eidlitz-designed Produce Exchange, which by 1880 was no longer adequate to its purpose.

5.3
Temple Court
(1881–83),
Silliman & Farnsworth, architects.
Southwest corner Beekman and Nassau streets.
Collection of The New-York Historical Society.

In October 1880, a committee of the members invited ten established architects to compete for the commission, and seven more apparently submitted designs voluntarily. The competitors so far identified are the winner, George Post; the runner-up, E. T. Mix of Milwaukee; Frederick C. Withers; Leopold Eidlitz; Richard M. Upjohn (the son of Richard Upjohn); and Charles B. Atwood. In response to the building committee's instructions, all of the entries projected a 50-foot-wide light court over a skylighted exchange room 300 feet long by 100 feet wide and 45 feet high; and in all the projects, the court walls were supported on iron columns. Although no particular style was specified by the committee, the competitors were requested to express in their designs the public function of the building and to cause the exchange room to "harmonize" with the exterior. As a result, in every submission the tall windows of the exchange room were continuous across the main front (Fig. 5.5). Post's "Renaissance" arcaded treatment, which gave "a sense of the value of repeated openings," was judged the most successful.[22] He had prepared three alternate designs, two with mansard roofs and the other with a flat roof. One of his mansard-roofed projects was selected, but for the building as executed he increased the number of stories, replaced the mansard with a flat roof, and, for practical reasons, added a clock tower on the New Street side. The staircase and two elevators inside this campanile-like tower provided additional access to the upper floors. Adjoining the tower was a terrace under which the boilers were located.

Although slightly at variance with one another, several contemporary sources provide the impressive facts and figures of the new building. The total cost, including the land and the interior fittings, was just over $3 million; the building alone cost about $2 million. The dimensions of its slightly irregular, rhomboidal plan were about 308 by 150 feet. This area, plus that of the tower and the terrace, yielded a vast ground coverage of 53,779 square feet. The exchange room encompassed nearly 29,000 square feet—215 feet long, 134 feet wide, and, beneath the skylight, 64 feet high (Fig. 5.6). At a height of 123 feet from the sidewalk to the top of the coping, the building incorporated ten stories, or levels, above the basement. Rising to about 224 feet, the tower added four more. Inside, the building was far more complex than its facades suggested. There was an intermediate story between the first floor and the second (exchange room) floor; and at the north end of the exchange floor there were two intermediate stories and a mezzanine level below the first office story. These functioned as executive offices and accommodated an amphitheatre-like "call room" as well as a galleried members' library. Finally, four floors of offices surrounded the open court above the exchange room skylight. Nine hydraulic elevators manufactured by Otis Brothers served 190 offices, which were by 1886 said to be renting for $180,000 annually, a return of about six percent net on the full investment.[23]

Constructed with some difficulty through numerous beds of quicksand, the building's foundations utilized more than fifteen thousand spruce and pine piles. These were driven to hardpan—probably to a depth of about minus 35 feet—and cut off at minus 16.5 feet, a little below tide level. Many years later Post's grandson, Everett Post, witnessed the underpinning of the footings after the building had settled due to lowering of the ground water when the subway was built nearby. He remembered "sharing the amazement of all concerned that the damage was so slight and paying tribute to the engineering prowess of my grandfather who had built so staunchly."[24] Brick was the material of the walls, piers,

5.4
*New York Produce
Exchange
(1881–84; de-
molished),
G. B. Post, architect.
Broadway front.
Collection of The
New-York Historical
Society.*

footings, and roof, with granite used for the lower walls, porches, and terrace. The decorative work and the copings were of terra-cotta. In his commentary on the building, Post pointed out that the iron lintels of the basement windows were faced in terra-cotta for fire protection and that the only exposed iron on the exterior was in the window mullions and transoms, "which carry no weight whatsoever in any case." The exchange membership was proud that its new building was among the first to benefit from a recently developed speaking tube system and that its tower was to be lighted electrically at night, "forming a blazing beacon visible miles away."[25]

Except for the great open area of the exchange room, the interior structural system of the Produce Exchange consisted of rows of cast-iron columns uniformly spaced in both directions, wrought-iron girders said to have weighed twelve tons each, beams, arch ribs, and trusses (Figs. 5.6 and 5.7). Surviving working drawings indicate that the outer walls were bearing masonry, although detail drawings showing the connections between the girders and piers are missing. The wall piers were granite at the lowest levels and brick above, with the possible exception of the row of columns at the attic story. It is conceivable that these were cast iron, clad in terra-cotta, but Post does not say so. In response to the diminished load they had to carry, the wall piers decreased in size as the building rose

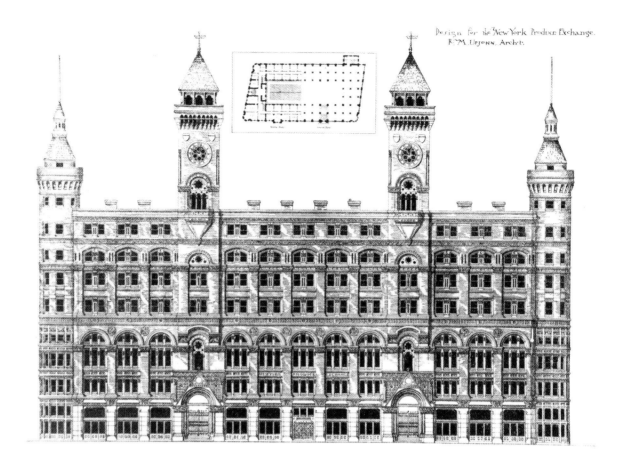

5.5

*Competition Design
for New York Produce
Exchange,
R. M. Upjohn,
architect.
Broadway and
Whitehall Street
elevation.
After American
Architect and
Building News
(1883).*

higher; for example, at the basement level they were nearly 11 feet thick, but at the first office story level (the seventh floor), they were about 4 feet thick.

The most important technological advance by far of the Produce Exchange was the early use of skeleton, or skyscraper, construction in its inner court walls (Figs. 5.7 and 5.8). Post later said that these walls were the "first adopting a metal cage for exterior wall construction," and the *Evening Post* recognized that Post "built for the central courtyard wall a cage of cast and wrought iron, with panels of brickwork; the precursor of the present steel cage."[26] By this time, many architects and builders had claimed that distinction, chief among them William LeBaron Jenney. Jenney claimed it for his ten-story Home Insurance Building in Chicago, which was begun two years after the Produce Exchange was started and completed a year later in 1885. Indeed, the partially metal-framed Chicago building is widely regarded as the first instance of skyscraper construction, although recent scholarship has established that the building's ironwork was primitive and based on already established principles.[27]

The use of the term *cage* to describe the construction of the Produce Exchange's court walls is confusing. As William J. Fryer wrote in 1898, *steel-cage construction* was the term first used to describe skeleton construction; Fryer said that *skeleton construction* was introduced into the written language in 1892 by the *Real Estate Record and Builders'*

New York Produce Exchange.

SET 2
H

TRANSVERSE·SECTION·ON·LINE·C—D

SCALE·FOUR·FEET·TO·THE·INCH·
Geo.B.Post·Architect
87·COURTLANDT·ST·N·Y·CITY

5.6

Transverse section drawing of Produce Exchange, G. B. Post, architect. Collection of The New-York Historical Society.

Guide, which used the term as a heading in its edition of the New York City building code adopted in April 1892. But, as Fryer also explained, there was a fundamental difference between cage and skeleton construction.[28] The distinction was brought into focus by the Tower Building of 1888–89. Cage construction describes a framework of iron or steel columns and girders that carry the floors only and not the exterior walls. The outer walls are independent and completely self-supporting; they can be thin because they are not bearing. In skeleton construction, an iron or steel framework carries the outer walls as well as the floors. Thus the outer walls are chiefly infill, "curtain walls." Mid-nineteenth century cast-iron-fronted buildings that were predominantly iron framed on the interior—for example, the Harper & Brothers plant—might be described as iron cage framed. The outer walls of the Home Insurance Building could be considered cage framed, but the point has been much debated. Unlike their Chicago counterparts, many New York architects and engineers preferred cage to skeleton framing, notably Post, who believed cage was safer than skeleton primarily because it afforded better protection to the easily oxidized and rapidly heated metal.

Masonry may also have been applied to the curtain walls of the Produce Exchange court, which differed markedly in appearance from the row of piers along the main facade. The framing of the skylighted trading room and the support of the court walls

The Future Revealed 121

above posed the most difficult problems, and Post's solutions showed him to be at the top of his profession. The court walls were realized as true skeleton construction: wrought-iron girders carried the infill panels and fenestration floor by floor, and the whole column-and-girder frame of each wall was carried downward to the columns on the periphery of the trading room floor by Pratt trusses. The skylight framework was on shallow Warren trusses, and, when the framing system was completed, the only visible elements were the arched trusses that spanned between the columns around the trading room (Fig. 5.9).

5.8
*Produce Exchange,
view of skylight and
court walls under
construction,
1883.
Collection of The
New-York Historical
Society.*

The exterior of the Exchange was extraordinarily well designed. On three sides of the building, the entrances were formed as triple arches and framed by paired columns; on New Street a columnless entrance was approached from the terrace. Above a deliberately suppressed base, two arcades, one above the other, spanned the full length of the Broadway, Beaver Street, and Stone Street facades and extended to meet the tower on the New Street side. The more monumental of these spanned the four-story height of the huge exchange room within; the other, doubling the rhythm, united two of the office floors above. The narrow story with rectangular openings just below the cornice doubled the rhythm yet again; and, set back from the edge of the roof as if it were an afterthought, the attic with a much-reduced arcade kept to the quick rhythm of the rectangular windows below. Although bearing masonry, the strongly articulated wall-pier system seemed to announce the interior iron construction and thus fulfill Viollet-le-Duc's prophecy: "A practical architect might not unnaturally conceive the idea of erecting a vast edifice whose frame should be entirely of iron, . . . preserving the frame by means of a casing of stone."[29]

In general the towered aspect of the building was inspired by European town halls, and Post was certainly indebted to Henri Labrouste's great Bibliothèque Sainte-Geneviève in Paris for the design scheme of the facades. However, the Exchange's arcaded red-brick walls, strong horizontal divisions, and blocklike form also call to mind German *Rundbogenstil* work, for example, the Berlin Rathaus (1859–70) by H. F. Waesemann. Indeed, the generic resemblance to that prominent building is so striking, even to the red-brick walls and terra-cotta ornament, that one wonders whether Post might not have had it in mind. Post described the style of the Produce Exchange as "modified Italian Renaissance, with strongly developed horizontal cornices." He asserted rather immodestly, but accurately, that his design, "with its long, simple, and strongly marked cornices and unbroken rows of arches, is in marked contrast to the prevalent fashion of minute

5.9
*Produce Exchange,
interior of exchange
room.
After* King's
Handbook of New
York City *(1893
edition).*

moldings, small window panes, and irregularly broken sky lines. What is lost in pictur-esque effect is certainly gained in dignity and repose."[30]

Contemporary appraisal of the building was generally positive, but the architecture critic Mariana Griswold Van Rensselaer thought that it had some serious defects—the "untruthful" relationship of the exterior openings to the interior arrangement and an-other, the "utterly superfluous and disturbing tower." The *Record and Guide* called it a "box" among other boxes that had no relation to each other and suggested that "if the architect . . . ever takes the South Ferry to Brooklyn, . . . he must be considerably disgusted with the effect of his own work from that point of view, unless he is satisfied with mere bigness and redness." But a German visitor had high praise for the building, comparing its situation to that of the Palazzo Farnese in Rome: "The [Produce Ex-change] appears to me even more impressive than the [Palazzo Farnese], through the addition of the proud tower, which, with its calm and beautiful contour and effective composition, forms a far-visible characteristic feature of New York. . . . In this simple work you do not find any weak results, no playful divisions, no meaningless ornaments; but you find grave and grand wall spaces in noble proportions, and decisive contrasts in the various stories."[31] Other tributes to the Exchange included Theodore Wenzlik's "New York Produce Exchange Galop," which was performed at the opening ceremonies on 6 May 1884. Richardson and Sullivan undoubtedly admired the Exchange, for it influenced the former's famous Marshall Field Wholesale Store (1885–87) and the latter's much-admired Auditorium Building (1887–89).

That this great building should have been demolished in 1957, apparently without protest, for the glass-walled monstrosity that replaced it now seems unforgivably venal. Not one piece of the richly symbolic terra-cotta relief ornament was saved, although an offer of purchase was made at the time of demolition.[32] The most notable decorative motifs were the roundels enframing the seals of the states and set between the arches over the exchange-floor windows, the reliefs of ships' prows in the soffits, and the frieze above the exchange-room arcade, where heads of animals projecting from a field of conventionalized cereal grains served to symbolize the produce traded inside.

The Washington Building and Other Notable Office Buildings of the Early 1880s

The Washington Building (1882–85), or the Field Building as it was sometimes called after its builder, was erected on the opposite side of Bowling Green from the Produce Exchange and overlooking the Battery (Figs. 5.10 and 5.11). The two opposing buildings, which together anchored Broadway at the Battery, compared in bulk and materials but were otherwise a study in contrasts. The name "Washington Building" commemorated the historic building previously on the site, the Archibald Kennedy house, which, according to legend, had served as George Washington's headquarters and, since 1848, as the Washington Hotel. The principal builder, Cyrus W. Field, is remembered as the person responsible for laying the Atlantic Cable.

In September 1881 Field invited six well-known architects to submit designs in a limited competition: Cady, Kendall, Post, Richard M. Upjohn, Thomas Stent, and Silliman & Farnsworth. Apparently Charles B. Atwood also submitted a design, for it was published in the *American Architect* (Fig. 5.12). As advertised, the commission was for a narrow trapezoidal site running back to a depth of only 54 feet on Broadway and 64 feet on Greenwich Street, with a frontage on Battery Place of about 172 feet. Field stipulated that the exterior masonry be Milwaukee or light-colored brick with stone trimmings, the interior framing iron, the height ten stories, and the construction fireproof; and, likely with a particular tenant in mind, he asked that the design accommodate a composing room on the upper floor, vaults for printing presses under sidewalks along each of the bounding streets, and large office rooms for rental.[33] In fact several prominent steamship lines were expected to rent space in the building, and the Postal Telegraph-Cable Company was there for several years before its own building was completed farther up Broadway.

Atwood's interesting project is extremely open, with highly articulated walls on the street elevations, to provide maximum light for the compositors. It calls for granite piers at the first two stories with the requisite brick and freestone above and two massive, interior transverse brick walls to provide lateral stability because of the narrow plan and near-150-foot height. These are an early form of the shear wall and possibly its first use for a tall building. Elsewhere on the interior Atwood proposed iron columns, girders, beams, and freestanding movable partitions. He planned a restaurant for the tenth floor. This was a prophetic design at the beginning of Atwood's career; in the 1890s, as the designing partner in Daniel Burnham's firm, he was responsible for several major skyscrapers. But Edward Kendall won this competition.

Evidently, Field was able to add to his site before construction began, for the Broadway and Greenwich Street facades of the building as executed were roughly twice as long as initially proposed. The foundations of the new building went to bedrock except at one point where the bottom of a cleft could not be reached; the gap was spanned by a brick arch 15 feet wide, which carried the walls above it. Above a limestone base, the exterior walls and piers were load-bearing brick faced with hard red brick—not light-colored as

By W. J. Roege N.Y.

stipulated in the competition instructions—and trimmed in New Jersey brownstone. As specified, the interior framing was iron, and flat hollow-tile arches spanned between the floor beams. The oriels at the chamfered corners were supported on wrought-iron cantilever frames. For several years after it was occupied, the building had a balustraded flat roof and only ten stories, but the decision to add two more had been made by mid-1883. Characterizing the building as a "honeycomb of offices, singly and *en suite*, after the manner of the Post and Mills Buildings," *The Churchman* (15 September 1883) regretted the seeming incompleteness and lack of a "Hotel de Ville" roof. That lack was remedied in 1886–87, when Kendall increased the height to twelve stories, with one more in the tower and pavilions of his new mansard roof. At its ultimate height, 258 feet from the sidewalk to the top of the lighthouselike cupola, the Washington Building surpassed even the Produce Exchange tower. Indeed, the views it afforded were said to be spectacular from all directions.

The elevations featured the strong vertical piers that characterized the early skyscraper, but their five horizontal divisions and two-tone coloring, the high dormered mansard, oriels, corner entrance, and tall cupola contributed those qualities of picturesqueness that Post had avoided in the Produce Exchange. Van Rensselaer was highly critical; she found the tall pilasters ineffectual compositionally and the detail, which was inspired by the recently imported Queen Anne style, "too delicate and too small in scale, and . . . distributed too impartially." Another writer, however, appreciated the fact that "no long monotonous lines meet the eye."[34] In essence the old Washington Building belonged to the early and evolving skyscraper style: its somewhat forbidding appearance was the inevitable consequence of great height and masonry piers. But the building looks entirely different today. In 1919–21, under the influence of the then popular, quasimodern version of Beaux-Arts classicism, the architect Walter B. Chambers drastically altered it for the International Mercantile Marine Company, later the United States Lines and Panama-Pacific Lines.[35] The result of this alteration, a severely classical decor in bland Roman-white limestone veneer with mosaic ornamental details, covers over the original dark red, heavy, and strongly rhythmic facades.

The commission for the New York Cotton Exchange (1883–85) was won by Post in 1883 in an invited competition (Fig. 5.13). The exchange had been organized in 1870 with a hundred members and incorporated in the following year. Taking full advantage of the oddly shaped site at the conjunction of Hanover Square and William and Beaver streets, and demonstrating that he could summon a picturesque treatment when it was called for, Post designed an asymmetrical nine-story structure organized around a shallow, U-shaped light court. At its most conspicuous corner at Beaver and William streets, the building was rounded and topped by a high, cone-shaped roof to suggest a tower. Contemporary sources described the style as "French Renaissance." The two-story base was faced with a light-colored, quarry-faced Kentucky oolite (limestone) and the stories above with cream-colored brick and matching terra-cotta trim; the roof was covered in red slate. The galleried exchange room on the second floor had a plaster ceiling supported by an iron framework that hung from the iron beams above—a construction that Post favored—and was embellished by a triple window infilled with Tiffany stained glass. Weisman, judging it by modernist standards, considered the building one of Post's least successful, but it deserves more notice than he gave it.[36]

The sophisticated plumbing and water supply system of the Cotton Exchange attracted the attention of the professional journals. In many respects it approximated systems still used today, except that the pipes were made of galvanized wrought iron, cast iron, and lead. Receiving and distributing tanks for the hot- and cold-water supply were in the basement (Fig. 5.14). Fresh water was drawn in from Hanover Square, and the sewage was piped out partly toward Hanover Square and partly through the wall on the opposite side of the building. Pipes that had to pass through walls ran through larger pipe sleeves so that repairs or alterations could be easily made. Where the pressure was adequate, as it was on the lower floors, water could be brought in from the street mains; a tank on the roof, filled by pumping, supplied water for the upper floors, and both systems could serve the intermediate floors.

Also in the basement were sixteen water closets, paired back-to-back, and seven urinals. Special pipes that vented the traps of each closet ran above the roof in order to prevent filling or overflowing. The urinals, "No. 1 Bedfordshire 'flat back'" models, were similarly vented and included "step-traps" under the platforms that could be washed through stopcocks. All the floors above also had water closets and toilets, and the janitor's apartment in the topmost story received its water supply from a smaller tank set above the large water tank to provide the necessary pressure. An additional roof tank held the fifteen thousand gallons of water needed to operate the Otis hydraulic elevators. The

5.12
*Competition design for Washington Building,
Charles B. Atwood, architect.
After* American Architect and Building News
(1883).

steam-fitting system, meanwhile, employed a pipe system to dispose of the steam conden-sate produced by the building's radiators; the pipes returned the water to a steam-operated pump, which automatically sent it through a discharge pipe to the boiler.[37]

The exactly contemporary Manhattan Company and Merchants' Bank Building at 40–42 Wall Street, the central heating system of which has already been discussed, offered a very different commercial design solution that would prove both influential and enduring (Fig. 5.15). It was designed by William Wheeler Smith, who used advanced technology in his buildings and who would later design the Syms Operating Theatre (1890–92) of Roosevelt Hospital. Although the bank was of the usual masonry-iron construction and enclosed by other buildings, the combination of extraordinary openness with classical detail and a quadripartite organization of the facade made a powerful statement. Stylis-tically, it offered a classicizing variation on Hunt's and Post's commercial Neo-Grec, though in Smith's building heavy, extruded moldings separated the story groupings and the facing material was mainly a light-colored granite. A contrasting darker granite was used at the lower floors, and the roof was flat except for the raised, temple-like center section. Smith's design seems to have been appreciated. It was nominated with twenty-three other New York buildings in a contest held by the *American Architect* in 1885 to select the ten best American buildings.[38]

In 1884, *Engineering News* reported the construction of the "finest office building in the world," a thirteen-story skyscraper of tower dimensions that was rising at Liberty and Nassau streets. Although the building was not identified in the report, it was probably the second Mutual Life Building (1883–84), designed by Charles W. Clinton and then under construction at 34 Nassau Street between Cedar and Liberty streets. As completed,

5.13
New York Cotton Exchange (1883–85; demolished), G. B. Post, architect. Collection of The New-York Historical Society.

5.14
"Plumbing work in the New York Cotton Exchange–view in water-room, engraved from a photograph." After Carpentry and Building (1885). A: hot-water tank; B: tank for distributing cold water under pres-sure derived from tank on roof; C: cold-water distributing tank under street pressure; D: re-ceiving tank communi-cating with roof pump and the boilers in the boiler-room under side-walk; E: water meter; F: steam trap connected with the hot-water tank A; G: water indicator; nos. 1–26: gate valves.

however, that building was slablike and only eight stories high. Perhaps the complaints about its projected height and massiveness relative to narrow Nassau Street influenced the builder to reduce the number of stories. According to the report, the new building was to have all utilities available, from steam heat to electricity, a complete plumbing installation, and elevators capable of reaching the thirteenth floor in one minute—probably an exaggeration, for that would have required a speed of about 30 feet per second. Most interesting were the projected accommodations. In addition to banking facilities on the first floor and nearly two hundred offices, the building would include a "complete hotel" on the top floor: a restaurant equipped to serve the building's tenants, a reading and writing room, a library complete with librarian, a telegraph office, a telephone exchange, and—for the first time in an office building—many bedrooms "for men detained down town all night."[39] Had it been so constructed, the new Mutual Life Building would have been a more complete "micro-city" than the enlarged Equitable Building—and the first on such a grand scale.

The first Standard Oil Building (1884–86), which would serve as home to the powerful Standard Oil Trust that John D. Rockefeller formed in 1882, went up at 24–26 Broadway next door to the Welles Building (Fig. 5.16). Its rather obscure architect was Ebenezer L. Roberts, who had his office in the building from the time it was finished until he died in 1890. Judging from the design of the Broadway front, Roberts had taken a good look at the Manhattan Company and Merchants' Bank, which was still under construction in 1884. The ten-story Standard Oil Building also had a flat roof and a towerlike, one-story-high center bay. Its uniformly light-colored granite front, however, must have seemed radically different from the bank, as well as from its own immediate neighbors. This

5.16
Center:
Standard Oil
Building
(1884–86),
E. L. Roberts,
architect.
24–26 Broadway.
Right:
Welles Building
(1881–83;
demolished),
W. Pell Anderson,
architect.
Photograph c. 1888.
Museum of the City of
New York.

5.17

*Dakota Apartments
(1880–84),
H. J. Hardenbergh,
architect.
West side Eighth
Avenue (Central Park
West) from 72nd to
73rd Street.
Collection of The
New-York Historical
Society.*

coloring, in retrospect, seems well ahead of its time. In 1895 six skeleton-framed stories were added by Kimball & Thompson, who at the same time built an extension that utilized caisson foundations; in 1910–11 yet another floor was added. In 1922, at a time when lower Broadway was being heavily rebuilt, the old Standard Oil Building was refronted and heavily reconstructed to meld with an addition, designed by Carrère & Hastings and Shreve, Lamb, & Blake, that extends all the way to Beaver Street (1921–26; 1928). The addition incorporated the site of the Welles Building, which was demolished in 1922.[40]

Mammoth Apartment Houses of the Early 1880s

Before 1885, when the law was passed that regulated the height of dwelling houses, large apartment buildings had been constructed that not only competed with contemporary office buildings in their ground coverage but exceeded them in height. The Dakota (1880–84), which spans the blockfront between 72nd and 73rd streets on Central Park

West (then Eighth Avenue), was the first of New York's large, luxury apartment houses (Fig. 5.17). It was designed by Henry J. Hardenbergh for the enterprising real estate developer and Singer Sewing Machine Company president Edward Severin Clark. In building this far north, Clark cleverly anticipated, and in fact stimulated, the development of the upper west side as a desirable residential neighborhood.

Roughly 200 feet square, the nine-story Dakota was exceptionally large, and its plan was both extraordinary and precedent setting. Instead of the usual light court, the architect provided an interior courtyard large enough to accommodate a carriage turn-around and offer a garden view to the Dakota's tenants. Hardenbergh's choice of a baronial, German chateau mode, for which he used yellow brick trimmed in rusticated olive sandstone, set a domestic tone and created a highly picturesque silhouette that was meant to be appreciated from a distance as well as close up. The building's fifty-eight suites were originally provided with hotel-like amenities, including a wine cellar and a large dining room for private parties; eight hydraulic elevators with hand-carved cabs fitted with plush velvet seats served the occupants. Solid 3- to 4-foot-thick foundations supported the upper walls, which decreased in thickness from 28 inches at the second story to 16 inches above the sixth story, and 9-inch layers of dirt and concrete packed in the spaces between the iron-framed floors and the ceilings of the apartments below insulated thoroughly against sound and contributed additional fireproofing. The building had its own electric plant as well as central heating.[41] No office building of the time was more solidly constructed.

The Central Park Apartments (1882–85; demolished), also called the Spanish Flats or the Navarro Flats, after the builder Jose F. de Navarro, comprised eight ten-story buildings styled in a quasi-Moorish manner. Intended to be offered as cooperatively owned apartments, the complex was designed by Hubert, Pirsson & Company, who are credited with having introduced co-op apartments to the city, as well as duplexes or split-level apartments in the early 1880s. The buildings overlooked Central Park between Sixth and Seventh Avenues, ran through the block from 58th Street to 59th, and flanked a 350-foot-long rectangular garden court beneath which a passageway functioned as an underground mews lane for service vehicles. Each building was expected to accommodate sixteen shareholders in large, luxury apartments. Due to financial difficulties, however, the complex failed as a co-op. The Navarro's failure, along with the new dwelling-house height law, temporarily suppressed the co-op movement and served to inhibit the building of large apartment houses until the turn of the century.[42]

Hubert, Pirsson & Company's Hubert Home Club (1882–83) was eleven stories high. Still standing on the northeast corner of Madison Avenue and 30th Street, it was designed as a co-op and is the earliest such building surviving in the city. In characterizing this building as the highest apartment house yet completed, the *Record and Guide* observed that it was technically possible to build much higher: "Living at the top of an absolutely fire-proof building is as safe as living at the bottom; the air is better: the prospect is wider. . . . Why not go on as high as the strength of materials will permit, or until the tenants of the upper stories begin to suffer, like Humboldt in the Andes, from nose-bleed and ringing in the ears. . . . When two fifteen-story buildings confront each other across a sixty-foot street, we may begin to have trouble, but there is no immediate occasion for borrowing it on that score."[43]

The same firm's famous Chelsea Hotel (1883–85) on West 23rd Street near Seventh Avenue was another very large apartment house of the time. It began as a co-op apartment house but became a hotel in 1905. In style a cross between the High Victorian Gothic and the Queen Anne, this long, red-brick building has twelve stories, including the attic story in the pavilions, which originally served as studio apartments for artists. At 180 feet, the Chelsea rises twice the limit set by the new law of 1885. The Osborne Apartments utilized the U-shaped plan, but its light court opens, dumbbell-like, toward the rear of the building rather than toward the front. (The Osborne's architect, Ware, had in fact originated the "dumb-bell" tenement plan that flourished in the city from 1879 until the 1901 Tenement House Act.) The building's rusticated brownstone masonry, cornices, flat roof, and uniform brown color were meant to evoke the Renaissance palazzo and probably also the facades of the city's many brownstone-fronted houses (Fig. 5.18).[44]

Like the office buildings of the time, these apartment houses were bearing-wall construction with iron floor beams and girders and iron roof rafters. Undoubtedly, more that were taller—and larger—would have gone up had the 1885 law not been enacted; the new height limit made it unprofitable to build large apartment houses because large sites were needed to justify the investment.

5.18

Osborne Apartments (1883–85), James E. Ware, architect. Northwest corner 57th Street and Seventh Avenue. Photograph c. 1886. Collection of The New-York Historical Society.

The Potter Building: A Thoroughly Fireproof Creation

The Potter Building (1883–86) at Park Row, Beekman, and Nassau streets is distinguished above all by its ruggedly picturesque red brick and cast-iron-clad outer walls abundantly trimmed with terra-cotta (Figs. 5.19 and 5.20). Its builder, Orlando Bronson Potter, was a shrewd and active real estate developer who served as a Democratic congressman from 1883 to 1884. Its architect was Norris G. Starkweather, who had previously collaborated with Potter in the construction of a seven-story building (1881–83) at the northeast corner of Broadway and Astor Place. Also extant, the Astor Place building is similar in style and materials to the Potter but less elaborately detailed; though intended to house a hotel in the upper stories, it seems to have had only commercial tenants.

In his early career, Starkweather's primary work was Gothic Revival churches, seminary buildings, and houses in the *Rundbogenstil* and Italian Villa modes. His expertise in iron construction can be appreciated in his First Presbyterian Church in Baltimore (1855–74), which was said to utilize the "most massive and scientifically arranged [interior] iron framework ever done in this country, or any other."[45] The church's tall, slender spire, completed in 1873–74 according to Starkweather's original plans, is also intricately iron framed. If one had to guess what sort of skyscraper the designer of an iron-framed, Gothic Revival church endowed with an impressive pendant-vaulted ceiling would produce thirty years later, the pinnacled Potter Building might well come to mind.

With eleven stories above ground, two basement stories, and space within for at least two hundred offices, the Potter Building was one of the largest office buildings yet constructed. Planned with a deeply indented U opening and dimensions that corresponded exactly to its irregularly shaped site, the Potter's principal front on Beekman Street measures about 145 feet across. Its Park Row and Nassau Street fronts are, respec-

tively, 97 and 90 feet wide, and its rear wall adjoining the old Times Building is 104 feet in width (Fig. 5.21). The height of the building is 165 feet from the sidewalk to the roof, and the highest terra-cotta finial projects another 30 feet above that. Because of the thickness of the walls and the heavily clad interior columns, however, the space inside the Potter is less than the generous outside dimensions of the building might lead one to expect.

The old World Building, which formerly stood on the site, was devastated by a fire in 1882 that was "heralded as the quickest one on record"; many people died.[46] Potter, who had owned that building, resolved that his new building would be thoroughly fireproof. As a result, it employed state-of-the-art techniques of fireproof construction.[47] The exterior walls are divided into brick piers, which are bearing members and also contain flues that carried the furnace gases to chimneys concealed by the terra-cotta finials. These piers gradually diminish in thickness from 40 inches at the first floor to 20 inches at the top (Fig. 5.22). Cast iron clads the piers and lintels of the lower two floors, and the first-floor piers are 4.5 feet wide—apparently the pier width all the way to the top of the building. Although not visible because of the terra-cotta facing, the lintels in the upper street walls are iron comprising four parallel wrought-iron beams with the out-to-out width across the outermost flanges ranging from about 21 inches to 32 inches. The architect's plans indicate clearly how the iron and the masonry are united: the lintel

5.19
Potter Building (1883–86),
N. G. Starkweather, architect.
Northeast corner of Park Row and Beekman Street.
After King's Photographic Views of New York.

5.20
Detail, first and second stories, Potter Building.
After King's Photographic Views of New York.

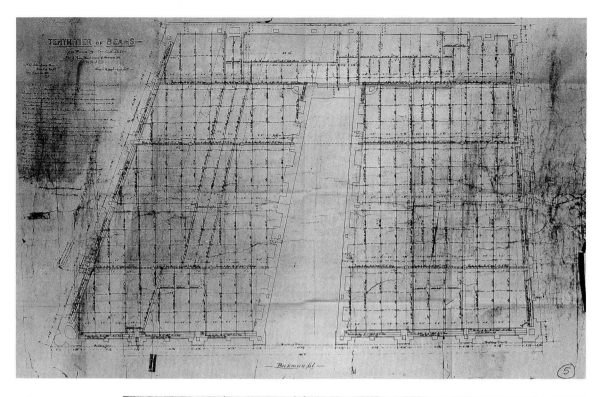

5.21

Framing plan of a typical floor (tenth tier of beams), Potter Building. Drawing by office of N. G. Starkweather. Whereabouts unknown.

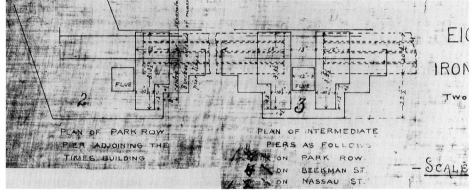

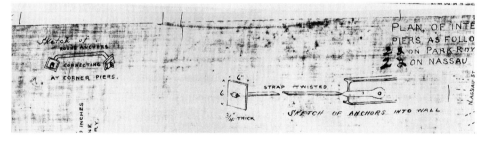

5.22

Horizontal section of piers at base, Potter Building. Left: Park Row pier adjoining the old New York Times Building. Right: typical intermediate pier. Drawing by office of N. G. Starkweather. Whereabouts unknown.

5.23

Sketch of iron anchors, Potter Building. Left: anchor joining corner piers (see Fig. 5.22). Right: anchor joining wall girder to wall masonry. Drawing by office of N. G. Starkweather. Whereabouts unknown.

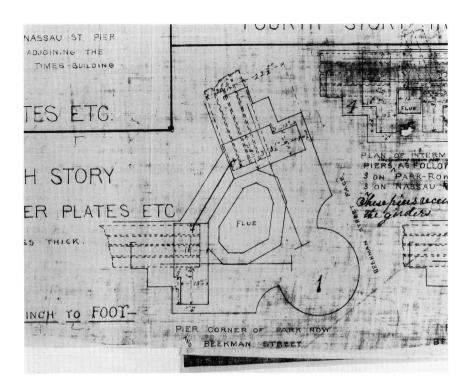

5.24

Potter Building: horizontal section of corner pier of typical upper story, corner of Park Row and Beekman Street. Drawing by office of N. G. Starkweather. Whereabouts unknown.

beams rest on iron plates that are set in the pier masonry and anchored by means of a twisted iron strap; the strap is riveted to the beam web through an eye at one end and fixed to a plate that is set at right angles to the strap and embedded in masonry at the other (Fig. 5.23). Special round anchors tie the beam groups together at the corners where the axes of two groups of lintel beams lie nearly at right angles (Fig. 5.24). On the court the lintels are stone. Iron trimmings appear at some of the upper stories; and the original windows were kalamein (iron-clad wood), new at the time and considered fireproof.

The interior framing was all iron comprising cast-iron columns, 15-inch wrought-iron girders, and 10.5-inch wrought-iron floor beams (see Fig. 5.21).[48] Beams and girders are set into the brick along the walls, and the court walls are tied by transverse girders that support beams. For the sake of fireproofing, the supporting cast-iron columns were surrounded by wire-net lath covered with lime and, leaving a narrow air space between, encased in a cylindrical covering of radial firebrick that was plastered on the outer surface. The floor construction was typical for the time: flat hollow-tile arches spanning between the floor beams, the tile covering the underside of the bottom flanges (Fig. 5.25). The upper surface was filled in and leveled with concrete that contained a coarse aggregate of broken stone and brick; the floor finish was wood, and plaster on the underside of the floor arches formed the ceiling of the story below. The partition walls were brick. Completed at a cost of $1.2 million—58 percent higher than the initial estimate—the Potter Building was as fireproof as could be built at the time.

The building's plan, tripartite design, and wall-pier system were influenced by the Post and Mills buildings. But its rich ornamentation—especially the ebulliently foliated giant capitals above the eighth story, the heavily molded cornice above the ninth, and the massive finials that culminate the round corner piers—is in a class by itself. The architec-

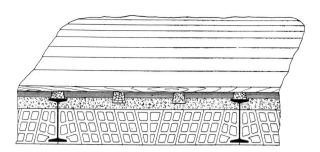

Section through floor construction showing typical fireproof floor arches used c. 1875 et seq., as in the Potter Building.
After A History of Real Estate, Building and Architecture in New York City.

tural style is not easy to name. For want of anything better, developer's advertisements and brochures called it Queen Anne, but the Potter Building belongs to the same commercial style phase as the Mills and Washington buildings. Most of the professional journals deplored it. Especially harsh criticism came from the *Record and Guide*, which blamed the owner for the addition of an eleventh story and the elaboration of the pediments and pinnacles after the design was completed. The journal also castigated the architect: "All the good work that has been done in recent architecture has been thrown away on the designer of the Potter Building which is coarse, pretentious, overloaded and intensely vulgar." Moreover, the *Record and Guide* wondered, why were "square castings of iron" used on the lower stories when no space was saved by using them? Instead, the hollow castings, which are "presumably filled with masonry, or possibly with concrete," act as a "mere frame to keep the contents in place."[49]

The criticisms notwithstanding, the Potter Building is a remarkable confection. In its proportions, vertical design, and emphasis on a picturesque skyline it fits within its own time and also foreshadows the skyscrapers to come. It stands out not only because it has survived relatively intact but for its extreme emphasis on a vertical continuity that somewhat paradoxically combines openness, a kinetic rhythm of piers, and rich sculptural detail conveying mass and power. The building's early commercial occupants included two newspapers; the New-York Architectural Terra Cotta Company, which Potter himself founded in 1886; the elevator manufacturer Otis Brothers & Company, and a leading assessment insurance company. In 1980 the Potter Building was renovated as cooperative apartments with ground-floor commercial space.

Prominent Low-Rise Commercial Buildings of the Decade

Among the best-designed commercial structures of this prosperous decade were the low-rise office, warehouse, and press buildings—structures of eight stories or less. Where great height and the technology necessary to sustain that height were not the overriding considerations, the architect could more easily rely on the canons of traditional architecture: unity, repetition of elements, and the classic tripartite scheme. Or he could turn to one or another of the more picturesque styles of the time without fear of overloading the exterior elevations.

Among the noteworthy smaller office buildings of the time are two that were early to break out of the downtown triangle. One is O. B. Potter's Astor Place building. The other, built for the Western Union Telegraph Company on the southwest corner of Fifth Avenue and 23rd Street (1883–84), was one of the earliest office buildings on Fifth Avenue (Fig.

5.26
*Western Union
Building
(1883–84),
H. J. Hardenbergh,
architect.
Southwest corner
Fifth Avenue and
23rd Street.
After* Architectural
Record *(1897).*

5.26). By the new high-rise standards it was modest at six stories, with a seventh under the roof. The architect, Hardenbergh, employed a restrained picturesque style paralleling the contemporary Queen Anne but perhaps directly inspired by Dutch and German Renaissance brick architecture. Montgomery Schuyler considered it one of the most successful office buildings in the city, and Hardenbergh's office was there for many years.[50]

New York's handsomest surviving commercial structure of the 1880s, and one of the nation's outstanding architectural monuments, is the De Vinne Press Building (1885–86) on the northeast corner of Lafayette and East Fourth streets (Fig. 5.27). The great architectural historian Henry-Russell Hitchcock deemed it worthy of comparison to H. H. Richardson's Marshall Field Wholesale Store. Critically acclaimed in its day, it was commissioned by Theodore Low De Vinne, a famous printer and the publisher of *Century Magazine* (until 1881 known as *Scribner's Monthly*) and the *Century Dictionary*, both of which were produced in this building; it is the masterwork of Babb, Cook & Willard. The chief designer was probably Walter Cook, who had studied in Paris and in Munich, where he surely admired the round-arched buildings of Gärtner and Klenze.[51] Inexpensively built and discreetly ornamented, the press building belongs to a New York genre of arcaded brick-walled buildings that originated in the 1850s but found its finest expression in the 1880s. Even this late, the style is derived from the *Rundbogenstil*. It calls to mind such examples as the former municipal building in Geneva, Switzerland (as altered in 1841–42), now occupied by Crédit Lyonnais.

Seemingly elemental, the design scheme is in fact highly sophisticated and is intended to signify the printing trade. The building's massive brick walls are deliberately empha-

5.27

De Vinne Press Building (1885–86), Babb, Cook & Willard, architects. Northeast corner Lafayette and Fourth streets. Private collection.

sized by segmental and round-arched openings with deep reveals and spare but well-placed terra-cotta ornament. This ornament comprises long, narrow quoins rounding the corners, interlace-filled spandrels in the central doorway, a pair of roundels—displaying the date of construction and De Vinne's initials—at either side of that entrance, and thin horizontal bands bearing raised motifs between the stories. The abstract patterns suggest individual blocks of type, and the initials are evocative of elaborate medievalizing initial letters. From one facade to the other, the window rhythms vary subtly, and each of the two exterior walls is framed by vertical rows of windows and by the quoins. The enlarged bold scale speaks of simplicity, severity, power, and hard work, but with the plastic-sensuous quality of fine masonry. On the main front a shallow, arcaded gable that recalls North European Romanesque gables effectively completes the composition.

The building is a warehouse in plan and construction. It has the usual interior iron frame, iron-trussed roof, and brick bearing walls—except for the glazed court wall. That

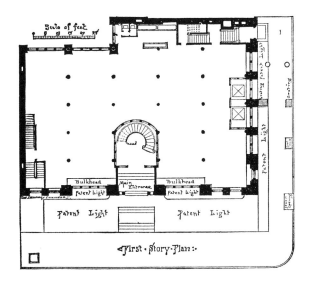

5.28
*First floor plan,
De Vinne Press
Building.
After* Sanitary
Engineer *(1886).*

wall is a curtain wall supported by rolled-iron girders, one at the level of each floor; thus the De Vinne Press Building is another early example of partial skeleton construction (Figs. 5.28, 5.29). The interior cast-iron columns were brick clad. In an account in *The Century*, De Vinne mentions solid 5-foot-thick piers in the plate room on the sixth floor. Rock asphalt flooring on top of the brick floor arches absorbed the press vibrations, and the heaviest presses were situated under the sidewalk on the Lafayette Street front in a vault lighted by an iron-and-glass bulkhead. If the basement is counted—and the basement windows are above the sidewalk level—the building can be considered eight stories tall. By that reckoning, the main entrance is on the second floor up a flight of steps, in the usual New York City manner, and originally it opened into a glazed vestibule partly enclosed by a spiral iron staircase. More presses and possibly offices as well were on this floor. Two of the upper floors were devoted to type storage, and a full floor seems to have been reserved for typesetting, or composition, which was done for the magazines by young women "whose work is as accurate and acceptable as that done by men."[52] The electrotype foundry, where the plates were made, was on the sixth floor; the seventh served as the gathering floor, where women also worked and where the dry presses and part of the bindery were located. The bindery proper, the mailroom, and a storeroom were on the top floor. In 1890–91 a compatible, eight-story addition was made to the building on the Fourth Street side by the original architect.

McKim, Mead & White's Goelet Building (1886–87), located farther uptown at 894–900 Broadway and constructed to serve as a store building, is another well-designed smaller commercial structure of the decade. As it appeared before receiving a five-story addition in 1905–6, it had unified street elevations comprising a tall and heavy arcaded base, continuous piers, and windows grouped within a tripartite arrangement (Fig. 5.30). Smoothly rounding the corner, its tan brick walls were trimmed with contrasting colors of brick and terra-cotta, and exposed iron elements were visible in the arcaded base. The Archer & Pancoast Manufacturing Company, which made gas fixtures and metal work, was an early tenant.[53]

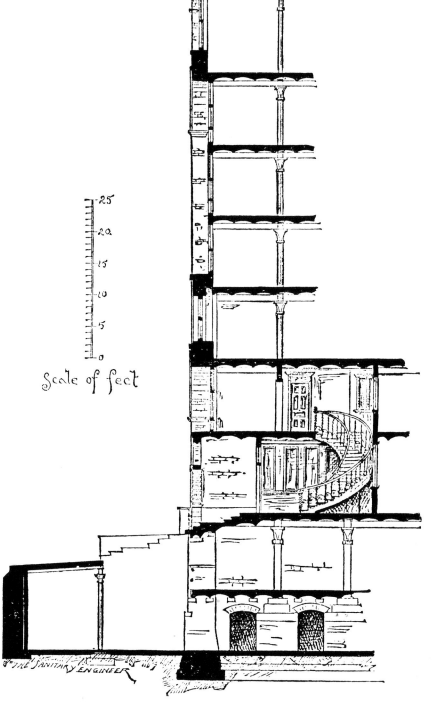

Scale of feet

Steel Construction

None of the buildings so far discussed seems to have utilized steel framing members, but it is difficult to determine exactly when steel came into common use because the terms *iron* and *steel* were often used interchangeably in the nineteenth century, just as they are today. Still, the probability is that iron remained the preferred metal throughout the

1880s. Steelmaking was not a local industry as iron was, and the tendency was to stay with local interests. Moreover, even though steel's advantages over iron—greater homogeneity, strength, and ductility—had been well established by the 1870s, variations in its quality caused it to be mistrusted even after steel beams began to be rolled on a large scale in the 1880s.

Steel had been known for centuries, but its inexpensive, bulk manufacture was a nineteenth-century achievement made possible chiefly by discoveries of Sir Henry Bes-

5.30

Goelet Building (1885–86), McKim, Mead & White, architects. Southeast corner Broadway and 20th Street. After Building *(1888).*

semer in England in 1855, William Kelly in the United States in 1847 and 1857, and Siemens-Martin in Germany by 1868. Produced by means of a rolling process in a molten bath, structural steel is an alloy of iron with a low percentage of carbon and small amounts of other elements; it can be made from either cast or wrought iron.[54] By 1870, steel was being used in bridges: chrome-steel arches and bracing were used in the Eads Bridge, and the suspension cables of the Brooklyn Bridge were carbon-steel wire. Trusses of plain carbon steel (high-grade structural steel) were employed in the construction of the Chicago & Alton Railroad bridge (1878–79) over the Missouri River in Glasgow, Missouri, and Bessemer steel beams rolled by the Carnegie-Phipps Steel Company were used above the sixth floor in the Home Insurance Building in Chicago.

In New York, a stable with 15-inch steel "timbers" (beams), designed by Paul F. Schoen for the Third Avenue Railroad Company, was constructed on Tenth Avenue at 128th Street (1884–85). Steel girders carry the floors and cast-iron front of a former dry goods store designed by John A. Wood for iron merchant Albert Tower and still standing at 691 Broadway (1885–86). This imposing six-story building, which runs through the block to Mercer Street for a depth of 200 feet, was subsequently enlarged by the addition of an identical adjoining structure at 687–89 Broadway (1887–88), designed by the same architect for the same client and also extant.[55] The use of steel girders in 691 Broadway, a low-rise, cast-iron-fronted mercantile building, suggests that by 1885 steel framing members were not a novelty in New York. At least partial skeleton framing was apparently also common, because the standard application form for a new-building permit included this request: "If the front, rear or side walls are to be supported, in whole or in part, by iron girders or lintels, give definite particulars."

In 1885 a steel pier shed was built at Pier 13 on the Hudson River. In 1886 the Cyclorama Building, said to have been "of special steel construction," with a diameter of 126 feet and about 100 feet high, was erected in Brooklyn, then reerected in Manhattan and later at other sites for the purpose of exhibiting a large painting.[56] Steel beams were used in the Science Hall at the University of Wisconsin (1885–87), designed by H. C. Koch & Company, assisted by Allen Conover, professor of Civil and Mechanical Engineering at the university. Such instances are apparently sporadic and certainly hard to document, but it is clear that by the mid-1880s, steel was being used in the construction of low-rise utilitarian and mercantile buildings in New York City. The significant trend, however, was not steel's replacement of iron, but the development of the full metal frame.

Transitional Skyscrapers: Aldrich Court, the Times Building, and Others

Meanwhile, along Wall Street taller bank buildings were rapidly replacing the old four- and five-story structures. At 36 Wall Street, between Nassau and William streets and adjoining the old Assay Office, the nine-story Gallatin National Bank (1886–87) presented quite an open facade, perhaps inspired by the Manhattan Company and Merchants' Bank Building two doors away (see Fig. 5.15). The architect, J. C. Cady & Son, opted for a horizontally as well as a vertically tripartite organization of the facade; for red sandstone as the masonry material; and for the round arches, thick columns, and Byzantine leaf ornament associated with the currently fashionable neo-Romanesque style. This was a style that H. H. Richardson had introduced and Cady had helped to establish. The bank was named for statesman Albert Gallatin, who had served as its president from its founding in 1829 until 1838.[57]

At ten stories, Aldrich Court (1886–87) at 41–45 Broadway was the first tall building to break the lineup of low structures along the west side of Broadway between the Washington Building and Trinity Church (Fig. 5.31). Built by the estate of Herman D. Aldrich and designed by Youngs & Cable (Henry Walmsley Youngs and William Arthur Cable), it was a large building running through the block to Trinity Place with a light court at the center. Open enough to suggest metal framing, the arcaded, neo-Romanesque Broadway facade was colorful; it had quarry-faced Oxford bluestone at the basement level, a lighter-colored Wyoming bluestone facing the next two stories, and red brick and red terra-cotta trim laid in red mortar above. Culminating in a tall gable, the two northernmost bays gave the impression of a tower. Perhaps the architect of the Tower Building, shortly to rise across Broadway, found some inspiration in this portion of Aldrich Court.

The building permit for Aldrich Court specifies pile foundations sunk to a depth of 20 feet and states the builder's intention to use as the lower side walls the old party walls of the adjoining five-story buildings on the north and south, which went through to Trinity Place. The interior was iron framed in the usual manner, and the front and rear walls were to diminish in thickness as they rose, from 44 to 28 inches, which suggests that they were bearing walls. The party walls also diminished in thickness, from 24 to 12 inches. According to the permit, "No girders besides [the floor girders] used except a safety lintel over the 2nd story-front on Broadway."[58] This specification is open to interpretation, but it does suggest that Aldrich Court may have been partially skeleton framed. Moreover, a few years later, again working for the Aldrich estate, Youngs & Cable designed the Columbia, said to have been the third skeleton-framed building erected in the city.

Addressing "The Question of Overbuilding," the *Record and Guide* pointed out that between 1 January and 1 September of 1887, a total of 2,334 buildings had been completed in the city; and at the end of that period 3,110 more were under construction. Most were residential, with a great many going up in the fast-developing section west of Central Park, but numerous office buildings were either completed or enlarged during the year, and new ones were begun. With respect to size and architectural design, the most impressive downtown structure rising in 1887 was probably the fortresslike eight-story United States Army Building (1886–87). Stephen D. Hatch was the architect of this freestanding granite and red-brick building, which rose on the foundations of the old Eidlitz-designed Produce Exchange on Whitehall Street and had a four-story-high court at its center, lighted by a stained-glass dome (Fig. 5.32).[59] The mid-1880s were boom years not only for new construction but also for additions to the tall commercial buildings of the 1860s and 1870s. For example, in 1885 three stories were added to the Brown Brothers Bank; in 1886–87 two were added to the Washington Building; and between 1886 and 1889 the Equitable Building was raised by two stories and also doubled in width.

In 1888 the *New York Times* undertook a reconstruction of its 1857 building. Although filed in the city's buildings department as an alteration, the result was in effect a brand new building (1888–89) designed by George B. Post (Figs. 5.33 and 5.34). In response to the client's stipulation that as much of the old building be used as possible and that the newspaper's operations not be interrupted, the new building literally went up around the

5.31
Aldrich Court
(1886–87;
later Hamburg-
American Building;
demolished),
Youngs & Cable,
architects.
With later alterations
to top story of left
portion.
After King's Views of
New York *(c. 1908).*

5.32

*United States Army
Building
(1886–87),
S. D. Hatch, architect.
39 Whitehall Street.
After King's Hand-
book of New York
(1893 edition).*

old one while making use of the old floor framing (Fig. 5.35). The work of publishing the newspaper continued throughout the early phase of construction. The *New York Herald* (12 June 1888) described the result as "the old Times building with a new stone overcoat on, a mansard roof for a high hat and a practically new interior." Only Post could have handled this feat, although *Harper's Weekly* attributed the methodology to the builder, David H. King, Jr.[60] New foundations had to be put in, and in some places these were fused with the old ones. The stone walls of the old building were removed "bit by bit"; the floors were shored up and new iron columns were put through them. When the outside demolition was finished, the new walls were erected, and it was all done "without disturbing traffic at all," in part because work went on at night and on weekends as well as during the week. This miracle was possible because

> the iron floor beams of the old building did not rest on either the Nassau Street or the Park Row walls, being supported on the south by the party wall of the adjoining [Potter] building and in the interior by partition walls, resting on an outer wall only at the Spruce Street front. The removal of the side walls, therefore . . . did not immediately endanger the stability of the building. . . . The interior of the old building was thus for a time supported by the partition walls, themselves shored up by vertical lines of shoring from the basement up, and by the party wall on the south, independent of its three former outside walls.[61]

As a result, the first five floors of the new thirteen-story building corresponded in height to those of the old, and the two basement levels remained virtually the same.

5.33

*New York Times
Building
(1888–89),
G. B. Post, architect.
41 Park Row.
After* A History of
Real Estate, Building,
and Architecture in
New York City.

Besides the unusual method of construction, the most advanced features of the new building were its strong foundations, which enabled the walls to be much lighter than would otherwise have been the case, and its iron framing. The underlying soil is a natural sand bed extending to about minus 103 feet; thus the new foundations were separate brick piers that supported the building's masonry piers and iron columns. These were carried to minus 22 feet, set in thick beds of concrete, and joined by inverted brick arches laid in a chain, as in the Coal and Iron Exchange building, with the lowermost point of the underside 27 feet above the mean waterline. The building's load-bearing walls are

5.34
*View of New York
Times Building
(foreground) and
American Tract
Society Building
(1894–95),
as seen from the
northwest,
c. 1900.
Photograph by
George P. Hall.
Collection of The
New-York Historical
Society.*

chiefly masonry; but above the second story, and opposite the old partition walls on the Nassau Street and Park Row fronts, the piers are reinforced by Phoenix columns within the masonry. The resulting thick piers form anchorages in the side walls, to which cross-girders of the iron floor framing are secured. The interior framing was entirely wrought iron to the eleventh floor, consisting of rows of Phoenix columns supporting iron girders, and beams spanned by flat hollow-tile arches. Above the eleventh floor the interior columns were relatively light cast iron.[62]

Modern viewers brought up on Louis Sullivan's formula for skyscraper design are likely to agree with Montgomery Schuyler that the Times Building was typical of New York's early skyscrapers: confused in conception, with too many indistinct divisions in the facades. But the extent to which their design was constrained by functional, structural, and code requirements has not been properly appreciated. Clearly, the proportions of the old Times Building and the technology required to achieve the new, much taller building while retaining parts of the old one influenced the organization of Post's facades. The first five floors became the base of a complex tripartite composition, and the thick, iron-reinforced masonry piers dictated the four-part vertical division of the Nassau Street and Park Row facades. As the load lightened toward the top of the building, the piers diminished in thickness, and Post had to make adjustments in his design. He did so by bracketing the stories in groups and by introducing moldings at strategic points.

Contemporary reviews of the new building, including the *Times'* own detailed and self-congratulatory account, recognized Richardson's work as the source of Post's newly adopted neo-Romanesque style. The extensive publication of Richardson's buildings after his death in 1886 greatly influenced American architectural design. Post was by no means alone in realizing the potential of Richardson's style for the skyscraper. An exactly contemporary, classic example, the United States Trust Company Building at 45–47 Wall Street (1888–89; demolished), designed by Robert W. Gibson, combined the polychromatic detailing of Richardson's Trinity Church in Boston with the arcaded treatment of his Cheney Block (1875–76) in Hartford (see Fig. 4.29). There are certainly similarities between Post's dormered mansard and that of Richardson's Cincinnati Chamber of Commerce (1885–88). Post, who had competed for that commission, would certainly have been interested in the outcome. Following the example of Richardson's monochromatic, light-colored late work, he chose a light Maine granite for the first two stories and a matching Indiana oolite for the walls above. Aspects of Post's previous arcaded neo-Renaissance style also informed his interpretation.

The *Times* bragged that its new building overtopped the adjacent Potter Building by 23 feet[63]—exactly the height of the top-floor composing room. The space of the reconstructed building was occupied essentially as it had been in the old building, except that ten office-rental floors, instead of two, now separated the publication offices on the ground floor from the editorial offices and city rooms on the twelfth floor. In 1904–5, when the newspaper shifted operations to 42nd Street, the Park Row structure was converted entirely to office use and its height was raised (Fig. 5.36). The top two stories were removed and four more were added, for a total of fifteen. The original Phoenix columns were judged capable of carrying the additional load, but the light cast-iron columns above the eleventh floor were replaced by steel members. These and other necessary structural changes were made for the new owner, the Park Company, by the German-born architect Robert Maynicke of Maynicke & Franke. Maynicke had earlier been in Post's employ and had supervised the construction of the Times Building as well as the Mills, Equitable, Pulitzer, Union Trust, and Havemeyer buildings. The Times Building was eventually acquired by Pace University.

The Corbin Building (1888–89) is remarkable not for its construction technology or its height—only eight stories, with one more in the pavilions—but for its fine detail and slablike proportions (Fig. 5.37). The building occupies an extraordinarily long and narrow site at the northeast corner of John Street and Broadway. At 20 feet, the main front on Broadway is the width of a standard row house, but along John Street the building is 161 feet long. It was commissioned by the banker and railroad president Austin Corbin, and for many years the Chatham National Bank occupied the ground floor. Although the architect of record is Stephen D. Hatch, reliable contemporary sources dating from the time of the building's completion name Francis Hatch Kimball as the designer, indicating a change early on.[64] Schooled in the English High Victorian Gothic of William Burges, for whom he served as supervising architect of Trinity College in Hartford (1875–83), Kimball was in 1888 approaching the midpoint of a distinguished career that would culminate in the

5.36

Panorama of City Hall Park and Park Row. Left to right: City Hall; Brooklyn Bridge Terminal; and World, Tribune (as enlarged), and Times buildings. The American Tract Society Building can be seen above the Times Building. Collection of The New-York Historical Society.

production of some of the largest and most artistically ornamented skyscrapers of his time. For the Corbin Building he was able to call on his extensive experience with terra-cotta ornament in such works as his Moorish-styled Casino Theatre on Broadway at 39th Street (1881–82; demolished), designed in association with Thomas Wisedell.

Schuyler deplored the irrational horizontal division of the Corbin Building's facades into two equal parts of four stories each. But he admitted that the unequal distribution of materials, tawny brick and brown terra-cotta in the upper five stories and dark brownstone in the first three helped tie the two halves together. He also recognized that "at the Broadway end, the pavilion works out naturally and effectively into a tower, and the tall arcade is a very impressive feature."[65] Constructed on the eve of the skeleton-framed skyscraper era, this long neglected building is in many respects worthy of notice, not least for the studied rhythms of its arcades, its rich, reddish coloration (today blackened by a patina of dirt), and its intricate terra-cotta and iron ornament. By adapting the François I style of contemporary Fifth Avenue mansions to a commercial structure, Kimball was able to embellish round arches with Gothic detail. The Corbin Building is the stylistic forerunner of later Gothic skyscrapers by Kimball and Cass Gilbert.

The ten-story Western Electric Building still standing at the southeast corner of Greenwich and Thames streets (1888–89), itself neither exceptionally tall nor structurally progressive, deserves notice for its architectural character and its designer (Fig. 5.38). The architect was Cyrus Lazelle Warner Eidlitz, the son of Leopold Eidlitz and chiefly remembered as the designer of the third Times Building. The Western Electric was constructed by Marc Eidlitz & Son, the firm of Cyrus's uncle, and is stylistically descended from his father's Produce Exchange. C. L. W. Eidlitz was also responsible for New York's earliest consolidated telephone exchange buildings, the Metropolitan Telephone and Telegraph Company buildings on Cortlandt Street (1886–87; eight stories), West 38th Street (c. 1890; seven stories), Broad Street (c. 1890; seven stories), and 140 Spring Street (1889–90; six stories), of which only his Spring Street building survives. In style (neo-Romanesque) as well as function, this early group was kin to the Western Electric Building, where telephone instruments were manufactured for the Bell Company. All were necessarily of thoroughly fireproof construction.[66] Essentially tripartite in design, the Western Electric has tawny brick walls, a castellated top story, and large, unmolded, iron-framed windows.

Technical Progress and the Tower Building

In 1888, the year the Tower Building was begun, the city's architecture was exciting favorable comment. The *New York Times* quoted a "prominent city official" on the improvement in design and style of the city's commercial architecture in the 1880s:

> Until recently the real estate proprietors have not felt justified by the outlook in investing much in the higher forms of artistic structures. There was not that reliable promise of satisfactory returns upon the money invested in making their buildings artistically beautiful and harmonious in design that is now perfectly apparent. . . .
>
> But the change has come at last, and in response to the increased demand for more room that has come with the rapid increase in population and to the popular conviction that New York City is destined to become the most beautiful city in the Western Continent, if not the whole world, the owners of property have begun the redemption of the city from its reproach of ugly monotony, and older buildings are gradually giving way to the construction of more imposing edifices, many of them expressive of a higher order of architectural beauty than the world has ever before seen and which, although not departing in a pronounced manner from the ancient and established precedents, yet combines them with new departures in such effective and novel designs as to indicate a peculiarly American origin and to establish the American order of architecture.[67]

Concomitant with these "new departures" in design was a technological revolution in skyscraper construction. By the time of the Produce Exchange the iron frame had been developed to the point where skeletal construction was feasible, but wind loads and the consequences of wind action required further investigation. Stimulated by the Tay Bridge disaster of December 1879 in Dundee, Scotland, in which ninety lives were lost when the bridge collapsed during a storm, the necessary experiments were performed in the 1880s. These were carried out by British and American engineers, with the first papers on the

5.37
*Corbin Building
(1888–89),
S. D. Hatch and F. H.
Kimball, architects.
Northeast corner John
Street and Broadway.
Collection of The
New-York Historical
Society.*

5.38
*Western Electric
Building (1888–89),
C. L. W. Eidlitz,
architect.
Southeast corner
Greenwich and
Thames streets.
After* King's
Handbook of New
York City *(1893
edition).*

subject appearing in 1881. By 1886 the United States Weather Service had devised a formula for determining the pounds of pressure per square foot of exposed surface exerted by wind velocities calculated in miles per hour, and by 1889 the Royal Meteorological Society in England had determined the constant in the formula, which was close to the currently accepted value.[68]

At the same time leading engineers like Gustave Eiffel developed techniques for translating wind pressure into the total bending moment on a structure treated as a vertical cantilever and, hence, for calculating shear, tensile, and compressive stresses in the framing members. If a building is treated as a vertical cantilever, then the bending moment induced by the wind load would have these effects independent of the compression in the columns and the tension and compression in the floor framing members generated by gravity loads. On the windward side of the vertical centroidal axis columns are subject to tension, increasing from the minimum in those columns nearest the center line to the maximum in the columns at the outer edge. The shear would vary from the minimum in the peripheral columns to the maximum in those closest to the center line. The compression from wind loads would be in addition to the compression resulting from gravity loads. The tension would be subtracted from the compression under gravity loads, and in extreme cases might result in an uplifting force in place of the downward gravitational force. These findings influenced the development of skeleton framing.

Some of the most important technical advances of the 1880s occurred in large public monuments. The most spectacular was the Statue of Liberty (1884–86), designed by the sculptor Frédéric Auguste Bartholdi with a stone base by Richard Morris Hunt and an internal steel and wrought-iron armature engineered by Eiffel. Likely assisted by engineers on the staff of the Keystone Bridge Company, which fabricated the iron- and steelwork, Eiffel created a framework capable of withstanding a wind-load factor of 58 pounds per square foot. Liberty's overall height, about 151 feet, is equivalent to a twelve-story skyscraper of the time, and its copper envelope and internal framework are carried on heavy steel girders placed on top of the stone pedestal. Eiffel's iron frame consists of four inward leaning posts rising from the supporting girders to the neck, and an envelope of angles supports struts that carry the copper sheathing. There are horizontal ties between the posts, double diagonal wind bracing in the panels formed by the ties and posts, and single diagonals outside the vertical bents. The copper envelope is stiffened by horizontal and vertical wrought-iron straps that are separated from the sheath by asbestos strips to prevent the generation of electric current from the junction of dissimilar metals. (The technique was imperfect, and resulting electrical action led to damage that required repair work by 1982). The framing of the head and the arm are small-scale variations of that of the body. As Eiffel was a leading authority on the aerodynamic stability of high, framed structures, the statue conveyed important lessons for builders of the iron-framed skyscraper.

Fireproofing technology also progressed, mainly due to experiments conducted in 1880–81 under the sponsorship of the Franklin Institute in Philadelphia. The results, published in architectural and engineering journals, evaluated the relative ultimate tensile strength, elastic limit, and elongation percent of ferrous metals—fibrous wrought iron, fine-grained wrought iron, and Bessemer steel—as well as the strength of ferrous metals at increasingly elevated temperatures. The experiments demonstrated the increasing loss of strength of ferrous metals as temperatures rose. In the case of fine-grained wrought iron and Bessemer steel, for example, the metals lost 95 percent of their tensile strength between the temperatures of 400 and 2,000 degrees Fahrenheit. The lesson was obvious: to withstand fires generated by combustible contents in a building, all structural metals had to be covered with a fire-resistant material, preferably cement plaster, plaster and lime, or firebrick with interior hollows. In 1885, the comparative thermal conductivity of various structural materials was determined by J. C. Buckle and

A. E. Woodruff. Because cement plaster and plaster particles and lime were determined to have the lowest coefficients, these investigators recommended that terra-cotta or fire-brick tile, which has a higher coefficient even with interior hollows, be covered with a layer of plaster.[69]

In many respects the Tower Building (1888–89) was the beneficiary of the technological experiments conducted in the 1880s (Fig. 5.39). It embodied the most fully developed wind-braced iron framing to date. Commissioned by the silk manufacturer John Noble Stearns, this intriguing office building was designed by Bradford Lee Gilbert, already an experienced railway station architect.[70] The eleven-story structure was not in actuality a tower but an extremely long, narrow slab extending from Broadway through to New Street. Its Broadway front was a mere 21.5 feet wide; its New Street front measured 39 feet, 4 inches; and the full depth was 159 feet, 7 inches, with the narrow portion 108 feet deep. On Broadway the building was 145 feet high; on New Street, where it incorporated at least one more story, 158 feet. Its plan was partly dictated by the shape and size of the lot and partly by the owner's desire to have an entrance on New Street.

Gilbert decided independently on skeleton construction for compelling reasons dictated by the dimensions. As specified by the building code, the wall thickness at grade for a bearing wall 145 feet high was 36 inches, leaving a maximum clear interior width through the first 50 feet (four stories) of 15.5 feet, of which the stairs and elevators would have taken half (see Fig. 6.3). At the first basement level the specified thickness was 44 inches, leaving 14 feet, 2 inches in the clear. Even if the narrow interior space had been manageable—as it evidently was in the case of the Corbin Building, where the building expanded to a width of 46 feet at the rear—the estimated loss of rental income with bearing-wall construction was $10,000 a year. The wall thickness had to be reduced if the property were to generate a reasonable income.

Gilbert's decision was immediately attacked by architects, engineers, newspapers, and public officials. Wind bracing was enough of a novelty to be objectionable, and the extreme narrowness and great height and depth of the building intensified the hostility. In spite of the objections, the Board of Examiners and the Department of Buildings granted the building permit on 17 April 1888. The application for the permit had to be referred to the Board of Examiners because the building code made no provision for composite brick and iron construction. Various board members had strong prejudices against iron and in favor of solid masonry, but they yielded eventually to the majority. Gilbert gave an account of his troubles in a *New York Times* interview:

> When the actual construction of the building began, my troubles increased tenfold. The mere suggestion of a building 21½ feet wide, rising to the height of 160 feet above its footings, filled everybody who had no particular concern in the matter, with alarm. Finally an engineer with whom I had worked for many years came to me with a protest. When I paid no attention to him, he wrote to the owner. The owner came to me with the letter. He was afraid the building would blow over and that he would be subject to heavy damages. My personal position in the matter and that of the Building Department that had given me the permit, never seemed to strike him at all. Finally I drew out my strain sheets, showing the wind bracings from cellar to roof, and demonstrated by analysis that the harder the wind blew the safer the building would be; as under one

5.39
*Tower Building
(1888–89; de-
molished),
Bradford Gilbert,
architect.
Museum of the City of
New York.*

hundred tons, under hurricane pressure, while the wind was blowing seventy miles an hour, the structure was cared for by its footings and was safest. . . .

This seemed to satisfy him and we went ahead. One Sunday morning, when the walls of the building were ready for the roof, I awoke to find the wind blowing a hurricane. That gale is a matter of record in the Weather Bureau. . . . I went down town to the sky-scraper. A crowd of persons who expected it to blow over stood at a respectful distance to watch the crash. . . . I secured a plumb-line and began to climb the ladders that the workmen had left in place when they quit work the previous evening. . . . When I reached the thirteenth story, the gale was so fierce I could not stand upright. I crawled on my hands and knees along the scaffolding and dropped the plumb-line. There was not the slightest vibration. The building stood as steady as a rock in the sea.[71]

Gilbert was a little free with the word "hurricane"—a gale of 70 miles per hour would not quite qualify—and his statement that the building would be safest at the maximum wind velocity and cared for by its footings is misleading. He probably meant that all the loads would be safely transmitted to the footings.

When the building was being demolished in 1914, its fabric was given a detailed examination by the Department of Buildings' engineer-inspector. His report, extracts from which were published in *Engineering News*, must be taken as the last and most reliable word.[72] Although the framework purportedly included steel members, the report mentions only iron components and specifies cast-iron columns of hollow square section measuring 20 inches on the side. The caption "floor steel" accompanying a photograph in the report probably refers to wrought iron; we can assume that the framework was mostly if not all iron. For the sake of fireproofing, the columns were encased in cast-iron shells three-eighths of an inch thick with some air space left between. Without the air space, the technique would be useless. Wrought-iron floor beams that spanned between wall girders were spaced 4.5 feet apart and, judging from a poor-quality plate reproduced with the report, were about 15 inches deep. The beam-column connection was made by resting the end of the beam on a shelf in the form of a small channel, probably cast integral with the column, and riveting the web of the beam to the column face, although this is not clear in the photograph. The foundation consisted of timber piles in double rows 18 inches apart and driven to refusal in hardpan. Estimated roughly from the data available for the second Equitable Building at 120 Broadway, the upper surface of the hardpan is at about minus 40 to minus 45 feet. The heads of the piles were embedded in a raft of concrete to a depth of 18 inches, and granite caps on the concrete carried the cast-iron bases of the columns.

The floor construction comprised the usual flat terra-cotta arches springing between beams, but the terra-cotta did not cover the bottom flanges. Instead—and this was an important factor in preserving the beams from corrosion—cement mortar completely filled the joints between the arch skewbacks and the beams. At the time of demolition, the ironwork was discovered to be in sound condition. Corrosion of the ironwork, potentially a serious problem, was said to be negligible except at points of contact, where it illustrated "the fact that corrosion takes place readily at connections where two surfaces come in contact."[73] But because the building was only twenty-five years old when it was razed, there was no opportunity to observe the condition of the iron members after long use.

As shown in a drawing published in 1909, the wind bracing consisted of a single diagonal in each bay, each diagonal composed of two angles (Fig. 5.40). All the field connections were riveted, although a photograph in the *Engineering News* report is labeled "bolted windbrace connection at foot of column." For the lower six stories the walls were carried on paired wall girders, the outer to carry the outer half of the brick wall load, the inner to carry the inner half of the wall load and the peripheral floor load. A curious feature of the building was that it had 12-inch curtain walls for the first six stories and a bearing wall resting on peripheral wall girders for the upper five, the wall thickness varying from 20 inches for the first three stories to 16 inches for the remaining two. The floor beams must have been inserted into the masonry of this wall. The columns terminated at the sixth floor except for two on each of the long elevations, which were continued to the roof level. The bearing wall must have been introduced to add weight to the upper stories, thus increasing weight on the columns and hence resistance to wind.

The *Engineering News* correspondent speculated that the wind-bracing diagonals were an "afterthought," but Gilbert's testimony suggests otherwise. A close examination of the drawing that shows the bracing members reveals that the bracing consists of two parts: a line of vertical elements, for which the section cannot be determined, set in partitions along a corridor at about the one-third point in from the north wall and rising from the New Street level to the top; and floor-to-floor diagonals in the pattern of the Warren truss on end, set between vertical bars or suspension rods along the corridor and the south line of columns. The reason for this odd arrangement was to provide full diagonal bracing while leaving adequate space for an access corridor along the offices. In addition, there were two diagonals in the basement floor up to the New Street level.[74] The structural engineer Henry M. Quimby, who was the authority on wind bracing at the time, and the bridge engineer Theodore Cooper regarded the bracing as unstable and the connections as insecure. The weight of the masonry was probably the chief factor in preserving the stability of the building, and the heavy, self-sustaining brick walls above the seventh floor acted as a surcharge on the columns below, contributing further to the stability.

The architectural style of the Tower was neo-Romanesque, with marked vertical emphasis achieved by continuous shafts that were realized as a five-story arcade above a rather cavernous and deliberately overscaled entrance. Gilbert ingeniously minimized the narrow slab by treating it as though it were a separate element and handled the Broadway end as if it were a square-prismatic tower. As an anonymous commentator observed: "Here was made an attempt worthy of future development, to treat the principal front of a deep and very narrow building in an architectural way without making it a mere facade. The front on the street is returned on either side so as to make a veritable tower, four square in plan with four pinnacles at the corners and a pyramidal roof; and the body of the structure is continued behind it without architectural treatment of any sort."[75] The top two stories and high, tiled roof were treated as the topmost segment of a powerful tripartite composition.

The building quickly attracted praise and generated controversy. Partly for his achievement in the Tower Building, Gilbert was awarded the Gold Medal of the World's

5.40
Partial transverse section showing wind bracing of Tower Building.
After Scribner's Magazine *(1909).*

DIAGRAM · OF · WIND · BRACING
IN · PARTITIONS · FROM · FOUNDATION · UP
· ON · LINE · 'D'D' ·

Columbian Exposition in Chicago in 1893, "for a new type of American architecture." William J. Fryer, who was a distinguished engineer and builder as well as writer, and also a member of the New York City Board of Examiners, claimed that the Tower was an original work of skeleton construction. Gilbert, he said, had "thought out a better method, and to him belongs the credit of being the first in the world to construct a building in which the weight of the walls, as well as the floors, is transmitted through girders and columns to the footings, and New York City has the honor of being the birthplace of what is in effect a new method of building."[76]

On 9 August 1899 the Society of Architectural Iron Manufacturers, New York, affixed a bronze plaque to the building that read as follows:

> This tablet placed in 1899 by the Society of Architectural Iron Manufacturers of New York, commemorates the erection during 1888–89, in this, the Tower Building, of the earliest example of the skeleton construction, in which the entire weight of the walls and floors is borne and transmitted to the foundation by a framework of metallic posts and beams. Originated and designed by Bradford Lee Gilbert, architect. Jackson Architectural Iron Works, contractors for the steel and iron work.[77]

But controversy over both the definition of skeleton construction and the true inventor of the technique had already begun.

William Harvey Birkmire asserted that he, not Gilbert, was the author of the Tower's structural system. Birkmire, an authority on iron and steel construction, was in charge of the construction department of the iron supplier for the Tower's frame, the Jackson Iron Works, at the time of the building's construction. In the 1890s he produced important books and articles on construction technology that have served as major resources for this study.[78] Birkmire contended that Jenney had originated skeleton framing in the Home Insurance Building and that Gilbert had adopted that technology in order to reduce the wall thickness on a narrow lot. Gilbert responded that "the Chicago plan used prior to the erection of the Tower Building was what is known as 'cage construction,' not 'skeleton construction,'" and he took full credit for the latter, saying that plans had been filed with the buildings department before the association with Birkmire. Others, prominently the Minneapolis architect Leroy S. Buffington, who had patented a system for skeleton construction in 1888 but never applied it, argued that the Tower's framing was not a true skeleton.[79] The only fair conclusion to be drawn is that architects, engineers, and builders in New York, Chicago, and Minneapolis were simultaneously and independently developing the iron skeleton system.

What can be stated with assurance is that the Tower Building was the first complete skeletal structure built without masonry adjuncts. It was very likely the first building with a complete system of wind bracing, and it was certainly the first for which a drawing of the bracing survives.[80]

New York was a rich city in 1889. By the end of the decade it was far in the lead among American cities in total dollar value of all building. According to *Scientific American*, the city's share of the total for the nation's five leading cities in 1889 was 41.1 percent, or $75,912,816. This figure was more than double that of Boston, which came in a poor second.[81] At $537,082,467, the aggregate capital and other resources of its national banks amounted to more than 19 percent of the total of all national banks in the country. The New York Maritime Exchange, which had been chartered by the state in 1874 to promote the city's maritime interests, had expanded greatly during the eighties, and the Real Estate Exchange, founded in 1883, had grown rapidly in influence.[82] The Real Estate Exchange aimed to provide a properly designed space and a systematic order in the conduct of transactions instead of the traditional chaotic and primitive auctioneering scattered over the city—at times held in open lots and on the street—and to establish committees on state and municipal legislation and city improvements. It would also lobby for legislation favorable to real estate interests and operations. The market value of the city's real estate had passed the two-billion-dollar mark in 1888. Times were ripe for undertaking more, and taller, skyscrapers.

STATE OF THE SKYSCRAPER ART, 1889 TO THE MID-1890S

The proliferation of skyscrapers in the 1890s completely changed the appearance of Manhattan's central business district, still largely confined to a small triangle below Wall Street. By the middle of the decade no other city even remotely approached New York in its concentration of sheer commercial splendor. Not everyone would have agreed at the time, but to us, looking back from the vantage point of a century, William Birkmire's enthusiasm seems fully justified:

> Indeed it is a beautiful sight. Looked at from any point in the upper bay south of the Battery, there can hardly be a more beautiful city in the world than New York is at the present time [1896].
>
> Where Broadway stretches away directly in front, as the centre of the picture, is there a more perfectly carried skyline, a more harmonious blending of color, or a nobler appearance of the useful and the beautiful combined than these buildings that reach from river to river?[1]

By 1890, just as the descriptive appellation "sky-scraper" was coming into common parlance, the New York high-rise commercial building was rapidly approaching maturity. The final technical components were being developed, the steel frame, fireproof covering of all framing members, wind bracing, the curtain wall, electrically operated elevators, central heating, incandescent electric lighting throughout the building, forced-draft ventilation in all enclosures, and automatic controls. And the New York skyscraper's distinctive towerlike form, with heavy masonry cladding and classical detailing, was evolving.

Utilities: Lighting, Plumbing, Elevators

Exclusive of structure and enclosure, the utilities necessary to render the tall building safe, habitable, and comfortable had become numerous and highly sophisticated by 1890. Individual items might range from a minimum of one—as in the case of boilers—to the many thousand components of the plumbing or lighting systems. Indeed, this vast complex of equipment placed the architect in an extremely circumscribed position. The opportunity to achieve any architectural distinction worthy of the new metropolis was limited to whatever richness and expressive power he was able to give to the street elevations and interior public spaces.

As developed by 1890, electric lighting included relatively few separate kinds of equipment—light fixtures, circuits, switches, outlets, insulation, and protective devices—although in complexity of installation and sheer numbers of individual components it was the most extensive and costly of utility equipment. Plumbing equipment had diversified markedly in the twenty-five years since the Civil War, as the demand grew for comfort, cleanliness, and sanitation—the last energized by the great triumphs of public medicine and public health in the latter half of the century. An important stimulus to these improvements was the rapidly growing number of women in the office force. A listing of the components of a plumbing system by 1890 gives an idea of the space consumed by utilities and of their complexity: supply lines for lavatories, toilets, drinking fountains, slop sinks, boilers, fire-hose connections, feedwater, fire, domestic supply, and sump pumps; drain and wastewater lines from all fixtures and basement floors; and valves, seals, traps, vents, storage and receiving tanks. A moderately tall office building of the time, the ten-story Bank of America Building (1888–89; demolished), which was designed by Charles W. Clinton and constructed on the northwest corner of Wall and William streets, contained fifty lavatories, forty toilets, twenty urinals, and six slop sinks. Its two janitor apartments were also supplied with plumbing fixtures.[2]

Elevator transportation improved rapidly in the years around 1890, with Otis Brothers & Company in the lead. The successful adaptation of the electric motor to street railway operations promised similar advantages in using electric power for elevators. Ernst Werner von Siemens, the European pioneer in electric traction, had conducted the initial experiment in the use of an electrically driven elevator car in 1880. But because difficulties remained in adapting electric power to the direct rotation of the elevator cable drum, the hydraulic elevator had no competition throughout the 1880s. It was given great public display in the Eiffel Tower, and it would continue to be used in high buildings until past the turn of the century.

In 1889 Otis Brothers began experiments with the new form of power, using a worm-geared drum powered by an electric motor. Late that year two such elevators were installed in the Demarest Carriage Company building on Fifth Avenue at 33rd Street.[3] Then the Otis company began manufacturing the first successful, generally applicable, electrically driven elevator, and the first lot was placed on the market in the spring of 1890. Besides the car itself, the new elevator's essential features were hoisting cables; a drum, with its surface grooved in the form of a worm gear, attached to the motor; gearing; switches; operator's controls; a counterweight; a brake applied to the motor shaft; and circuitry. The armature of the motor was directly connected to the drum, around which

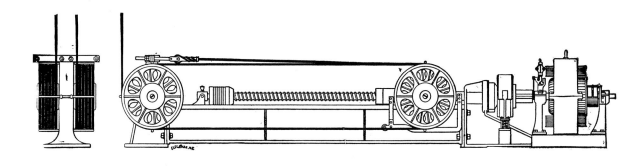

6.1

Sprague-Pratt electric elevator equipment, as in Lord's Court Building (1895–96).
After Birkmire, Planning and Construction of High Office-Buildings.

the hoisting cable wound. The operating equipment was usually located in the attic story, later on in a penthouse above the roof plane. The operator started the elevator on its trip up or down by pulling a hand rope inside the car. This released the brake and closed a switch, allowing current to flow to the motor. Otis's secret was a system of controls by which the flow of current was increased slowly and continuously, accelerating the motor smoothly rather than intermittently.[4]

At the same time an alternative form of elevator was being developed. In 1888 Charles L. Pratt, a specialist in elevator technology from Montclair, New Jersey, invented an electrical variation on a type of hydraulic elevator that used a horizontal rather than a vertical cylinder. The essential features of the Pratt technique were a Sprague electric motor, initially set with its armature axis horizontal, and a drive that consisted of an extremely long screw engaged with a traveling nut at the free end (Fig. 6.1). The rotation of the screw moved the nut in such a way as to draw together or separate two sets of traveling sheaves connected to the elevator car by hoisting cables. A smooth operation was made possible by the controls, and in the event of current failure or excessive speed, the brake set immediately, stopping the rotation of the screw and the motion of the car.

The Sprague-Pratt elevator was patented in 1888 and installed after 1893 in a number of prestigious office buildings, including the Postal Telegraph-Cable, Lord's Court, and Park Row buildings. By the time of the Park Row Building (1896–99), the system was being mounted vertically (Fig. 6.2). It worked well enough, but had serious defects. The motor-screw assemblage and generating plant required a great volume of space, and the working elements were subject to excessive wear, especially the screw and the so-called frictionless nut. By 1893 many of the drum-type electric elevators were in use; these had the advantage of a compact arrangement, without long horizontal or vertical screws.[5] In all respects the drum-type system as manufactured by Otis Brothers was superior, though it did not wholly supplant the Sprague-Pratt until after the turn of the century.

Iron and Steel Framing

The city's building code made some provisions for skeleton framing for the first time in 1892. Throughout the 1890s, whether in cage or skeleton construction, iron or steel framing exhibited the characteristics expected of an early stage in technical evolution. The forms and arrangement of the members as well as the methods of bracing them and the types of connections were highly diverse, and the merits and defects of the various structural systems were earnestly debated.

Cast iron was rapidly being eclipsed by wrought iron for all structural elements,

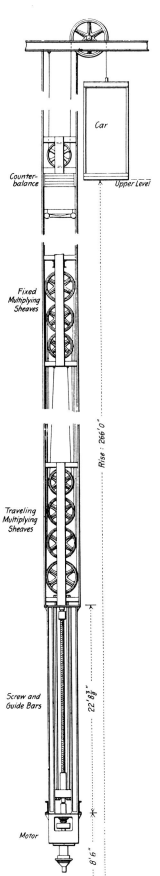

6.2
Drawing showing essential parts of the Sprague electric elevator with armature axis set vertically as used in Park Row Building (1896–99). After Engineering News *(1899).*

Car

Counter-balance

Upper Level

Fixed Multiplying Sheaves

Traveling Multiplying Sheaves

Rise : 266'0"

Screw and Guide Bars

22'8⅜"

Motor

8'6"

Basement Floor

although it continued to be used for columns until after the turn of the century. In the 1890s there were six different column sections in regular use, with the H, the hollow square or rectangle, and the hollow cylinder dominant. Although cast iron has a high compressive strength, is very hard, and oxidizes at a relatively low rate, its defects as a structural metal had been known since the Fairbairn-Hodgkinson experiments of 1826–30. Its tensile strength, coefficient of elasticity, stiffness, and uniformity of internal structure are less than for wrought iron and substantially less than for steel. According to the engineer Corydon T. Purdy, writing in 1891, wind bracing with cast-iron members presents almost insurmountable difficulties. These and other defects caused the decline and ultimate abandonment of cast iron.[6]

By 1890 wrought iron was used for all floor and framing members and its use for columns was spreading rapidly. During the 1890s eight different sections were available, but the Phoenix and the hollow box were dominant. Wrought-iron columns were nearly always built up of separate elements; these were longitudinal, stave-like quarter sections in the case of the Phoenix column, plates and channels for the box type. Steel columns were also built up of plates, angles, and channels, although H-columns could be rolled; the H, box, and Z-bar were dominant for use in high buildings.[7] Very large sections had internal diaphragms to increase the resistance to buckling, a particular advantage of the Z-bar type, especially when used with plates. In all cases the shapes were designed to carry not only the compressive or gravity loads of the floors, roof, and contents of the building but also the bending and torsional forces induced by the wind.

Beginning with Eton Hodgkinson's tests on cast-iron columns in 1840, numerous load tests were made on the various types of columns to determine their ultimate strength.[8] Based on the results as accepted in 1890, the New York Building Code of 1892 specified a safety factor of 4:1; that is, a column must be able to carry four times a given load. The safe load for wrought-iron columns at common lengths, 14, 15, and 16 feet, ranged from 8,420 to 10,326 pounds per square inch. The allowable safe fiber stress in wrought-iron beams was 12,000 pounds per square inch and in steel beams 16,000 pounds per square inch.[9] The floor loading factor for apartments and hotels was 70 pounds per square foot; for offices, 100 pounds per square foot; and for warehouses, 150 pounds per square foot and upward. It was the usual practice to make the upper floors of office buildings carry the minimum load, and the factor increased to 150 pounds per square foot on the first floor.

Two forms of skeleton construction were used in early framed skyscrapers. In one, the primary or wind girders were set in the wall envelope, and these carried both the curtain wall and the ends of the floor and roof beams for a given bay. In the second form, two girders of equal section were used, one in the wall, which carried the curtain wall of the bay and also supported the end of the second girder, which was the primary floor girder and extended at right angles from the wall. The floor girder carried the ends of the floor beams, which ran parallel to the wall.

In the early 1890s enthusiasm for iron or steel skeletal framing was by no means universal. Even as more such buildings were constructed, distrust of its reliability increased. Of particular concern was the vulnerability of metal framing members to the corrosion that could result from dampness within the masonry walls; although steel was generally recognized as being more resistant to strains, it was considered more vulnerable than cast iron to corrosion. At the American Institute of Architects convention held in New York on 16 October 1894, George Post spoke on the subject of the rapid oxidation of iron and steel, observing that no known paint or asphalt could protect ferrous metals from rusting. He cited in particular the old Times Building; his reconstruction in 1888 had disclosed that many iron beams in the ceiling of the old press room had been rendered useless by rust through the action of steam, even though they had been encased in brick and the floors had been leveled with concrete. Post, therefore, preferred cage construction and recommended its use with cast-iron columns because cast iron rusts more slowly than wrought iron and does not split off in laminae (as in the foliation of igneous rock). He recommended that the cast-iron columns be incorporated with cast-iron girders "locked" into the columns. In the discussion that followed, the New York architect Robert Henderson Robertson agreed with Post, but Jenney, D. H. Burnham, and the bridge engineer William H. Burr tended to disagree. Their chief objection, on good grounds, was to Post's recommendation of cast iron in place of steel. No conclusion was reached, however.[10]

Later, the New York civil engineer and architect Howard Constable challenged the accepted fireproof framed construction, citing numerous fires. He emphasized the lack of scientific knowledge of the properties of iron and masonry, the lack of established principles, and the extreme variations in techniques, with safety factors ranging from less than 1 to 20. He seems to have been unaware of extensive investigations of the effects of heat on metal, of thermal conductivity of materials, and of techniques of uniting metal and masonry cladding, as well as evidence of fires in which the contents of the building were destroyed but the structure itself was undamaged. Although his views were strictly functionalist, he saw no reason why architecture should be in conflict with engineering:

It is to be remembered that Michael Angelo, Leonardo da Vinci, Sir Christopher Wren, and Viollet-le-Duc showed the highest order of engineering skill. . . . I would also call attention to the fact that in the true and practical application of mathematics and exact science to materials, whereby any construction is well-proportioned to its purpose, with its strength of materials and factor of safety properly distributed, it is not necessarily antagonistic to or conflicting with good art. A great battleship, the liner *New York*, the Brooklyn and Washington Bridges, the locomotive 999, on the New York Central, the Pyramids and the Parthenon, are examples of a close approach to this principle, and of which must always be said that they are either beautiful, magnificent, or impressive and stimulating to the imagination.[11]

Nevertheless, high-rise iron frames were still novel enough and posed enough engineering and architectural difficulties to make many architects and builders reluctant to embrace full skeleton construction in spite of the plain fact that bearing-wall, cage-wall, and even curtain-wall thicknesses for high buildings were becoming unmanageable and compelling a costly sacrifice of space. The New York building code of 1892 was conservative on wall thicknesses. For example, the typical bearing-wall section specified for a 250-foot-high building was 52 inches at the base (Fig. 6.3). For the same size building, though much reduced, the curtain-wall dimension was required to be 28 inches at the base (Fig. 6.4). The prescribed thickness, of course, gradually decreased as the building rose to its full height. For lower buildings, the cost of masonry construction was less than that of

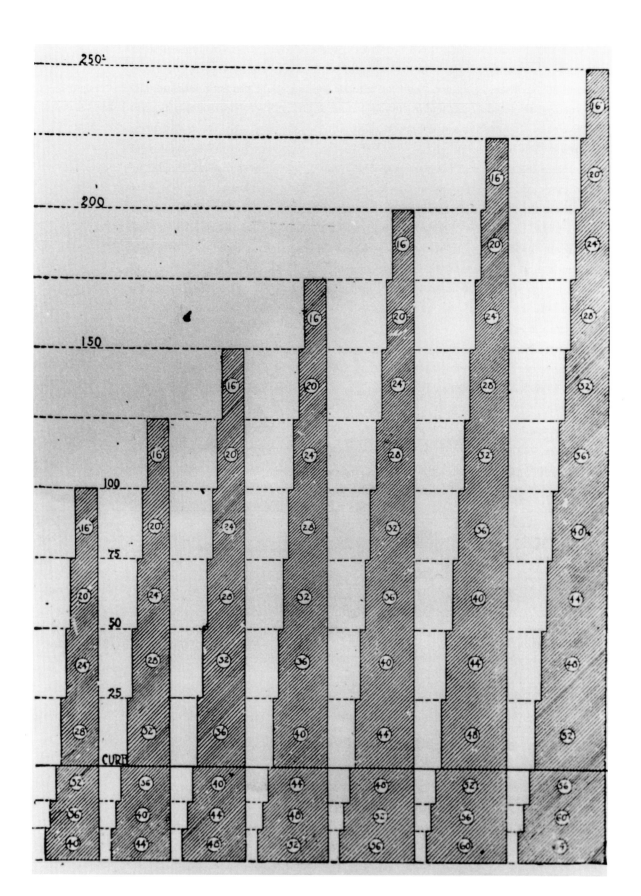

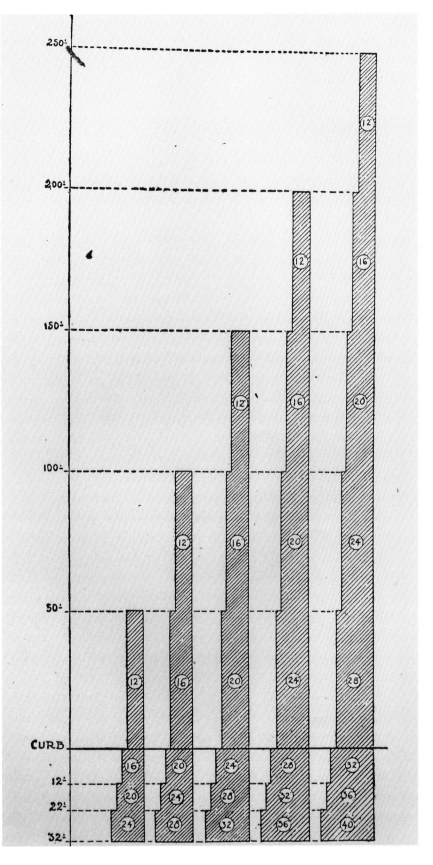

6.3
Typical bearing-wall thickness specifications, New York Building Code (1892).
After Birkmire, Planning and Construction of High Office-Buildings.

6.4
Curtain Wall thickness specifications, New York Building Code (1892).
After Birkmire, Planning and Construction of High Office-Buildings.

steel framing, and masonry was still preferred for those despite the sacrifice in floor space. Such authorities as the engineer and architect George Hill regarded cage construction as a waste of space to no purpose. Others, like Post, thought it the best solution to all structural problems.

Principles and Criteria of Functional Design

In 1893 Hill published his assessment of the guiding principles and criteria that governed functionally designed skyscrapers. Aside from the need to adhere to zoning regulations—which were nonexistent or virtually so in the mid-1890s—these principles were much the same as they are today, though they might not be ranked in the same order of importance. First on his list is easy elevator access: elevators must be directly accessible from the street and no more than a few steps above or below grade level. Moreover, they should stand contiguous to each other in one public lobby and be visible from a single focal point. A U-shaped or circular-segmental arrangement of elevators allowed easiest access and visibility, and they should be located equidistant from the offices at the furthest extremes of the building. In the best-designed buildings of the mid-1890s the interval between cars was forty seconds and the speed of travel 6.67 feet per second, or 400 feet per minute. The number and capacity of elevators required for a given building were calculated according to the number of floors, offices, offices per floor, and the amount of public traffic, with the optimum floor area of an elevator for large structures—more than ten stories—specified as 6 by 6 feet.[12]

Secondly, consistent with protection, safety, strength, and other factors, the high building should be designed so as to receive the maximum amount of natural light and to provide some sunlight for offices facing every direction. For maximum solar penetration, the court axis should lie on a bearing of 21.5 to 22.5 degrees—that is, parallel to the chief longitudinal arteries of Manhattan. For the maximum noon sunlight a court on this bearing should be rectangular in plan with its opening to the south (for Manhattan, a bearing of 158 degrees). The court width should be 6 to 25 feet, depending on the area of the building, its plan dimensions, and the depth of the offices. If the south light is to be dominant, the optimum location is the northeast corner of the street intersection; if the north light is dominant, the southwest corner. The optimum office area is 9 by 15 feet, with at least one window measuring 4 by 6 feet and the top of the window no more than one foot below the ceiling.

Utilities were the third concern for Hill, who advised that a well-designed high building include the following: one toilet for every five offices; one wash basin with hot and cold water for every two toilets; and one urinal for every two toilets. Ideally, every office should have a wash basin as well. Each of these units should be connected by a separate drain line to the central drainage system in the central stack. He recommended that the plumbing equipment include a coagulant, filters, and refrigeration for a drinking water supply. Heat should be generated by radiators fed by steam or hot water in all the offices and public spaces. Forced-draft ventilation was needed primarily to exhaust air, as open windows would provide a sufficient supply of incoming air (leaving aside the problem of cold weather and drafts). And a system of electric lighting would be supplied, as well as some gas fixtures and a gas supply for emergencies.[13]

"Pleasing environment and approaches," fourth in Hill's list, are the province of the owner and his architect, and Hill has no specific prescription. A critically important fifth principle, however, was the need to maximize the rental area in ways that were economical and consistent with the required equipment and the easy flow of traffic. The building should be planned to accommodate elevator stops, stair entrances, access corridors, service space, and plumbing facilities on each floor. In the interests of providing as much office space as possible, the areas these utilities occupied should be minimized, but without loss of safety, comfort, or ease of movement. Offices should normally be no more than 16 feet deep; and all dimensions should be determined by the number of offices, the number of tenants, the amount of public traffic, and the area of the plan. The optimum area of the building's ground plan seems to have been 50 by 100 feet, with a corner location.[14]

In addition to the building's plan, the method of construction was a major factor in economically maximizing the rental area. The alternatives were a full skeleton frame or masonry bearing walls with an interior iron frame, and the relative cost was a concern. As we have seen, cage construction was controversial. The unit cost of wall construction—the cost per linear foot of wall for skeleton and bearing-masonry construction—was computed according to height:

	Cost for Brick	Cost for Steel	Excess for Steel	Percent Excess
1 story (12.5 ft.)	$ 4.00	$ 6.25	$ 2.25	56.25
10 stories (125 ft.)	80.00	193.73	113.73	142.16
20 stories (250 ft.)	221.32	697.00	475.68	215.00

But for a twenty-story building the higher construction cost was offset by a 26 percent reduction in the area per linear foot that was occupied by structural elements (wall versus frame and bracing). Another variable was the cost of the lot. In fact, there were many variables, making a single resolution impossible.[15] The general principle, however, can be stated as follows: if the number of offices for a given area of lot is to be maximized, the total floor area within the envelope must be maximized. High buildings up to the twenty-story maximum of the time were a necessity, which in turn mandated skeleton construction as the best means of providing adequate light and floor area. The skyscraper and skeleton construction were thus symbiotic.

To achieve "ease of rearrangement to suit tenants," listed as the sixth guiding principle, movable partitions permitted the most efficient and convenient method of handling interior enclosures. Perhaps the most important consideration of all was the seventh and last condition, the need to minimize the costs and yet maintain the maximum quality. In order to achieve this relationship, the optimum ratio of height to width was set at 5:1 for safety and comfort. Thus, the recommended height for a 50-by-100-foot building was 250 feet, or twenty stories. The recommended materials that would best achieve durability and economy were the steel frame, brick and terra-cotta sheathing, hollow-tile floor construction and fire-clay tiles for column cladding, marble floors in the halls and toilets, Georgia yellow-pine floors in the offices, hard-finish rock-plaster, white-oak trim, and polished plate-glass windows.[16]

Constructing the High Office Building

The procedures followed in building a skyscraper in the mid-1890s were much the same as they are today. Once the property was purchased, an accurate survey had to be made. Architectural and engineering plans and specifications were prepared next, and these had to be approved by the Department of Buildings before work could go forward. Then followed the advertising for bids, letting of contracts, and demolition of any preexisting structures on the site. Preparation of the site involved excavation, shoring, and sheet-pile walling; dewatering the excavated area; and shoring and bracing the surrounding earth, streets, walkways, and buildings. Enclosures and covered walkways had to be provided as protection for people and any property and public utilities that might be affected by the construction.

Then the piling of the foundation began. The length of the piles depended on the soil conditions at the site, but their diameter was 8 to 12 inches at the large (lower) end and, as prescribed by the building code, 5 inches at the small (upper) end. They were spaced at 24 to 30 inches in both directions, and the ends were cut off at one foot below low-water level and covered with a continuous mat of concrete. For buildings twenty stories or higher, caissons became a necessity; pneumatic caissons were used in New York after their introduction in the Manhattan Life Building, because the city's peculiar geology required complex excavation techniques. After the concrete footings were poured, an 18-inch-thick granite cover slab and steel column base plate were set in place on top of them.

Once the foundation was in, the iron or steel frame could be constructed, comprising columns, girders, beams, connections (angles and gussets), and bracing. Then the hollow-tile floor arches were set out and the concrete floor-slab poured up to the finish level of the frame. After that the wall and partition masonry was laid up, although the installation of interior utilities could begin before this process. At this point the plumber began laying the vent and waste pipes in the basement; the building was enclosed by attic walls and a roof; and the carpenters and ironworkers installed the doors, window frames, elevator shafts and doors, and the sleepers that underlie the rough wood subflooring. The plumbing, heating, and electrical contractors' crews worked progressively on the interior utilities. Next the ceilings were plastered, as well as the interior surfaces of the walls and the partitions, unless movable and freestanding. Then the glazing was done; and the gas and electrical fixtures, basement utility equipment, fire pumps, hoses, and storage tanks were installed.

Throughout the process materials and equipment had to be delivered to the site when needed, with large items such as caissons and massive girders often coming at night. It was no small matter getting the necessary equipment to the site and finding a place to store it, especially in lower Manhattan, where the streets are narrow. For example, during construction of the Manhattan Life Building, which fronted on both Broadway and New Street, no materials could be stored on Broadway, because it was a major thoroughfare; the stone for that front had to be lifted directly out of wagons from that side. And New Street is too narrow for the storage of reserve materials, although certain exceptions reportedly were made for the Manhattan Life Building. The excavated matter, meanwhile, had to be removed from the site immediately because a cleared space was essential for the work to progress. After the foundations were finished, some thirty thousand tons of material, averaging about one thousand tons per week—but certainly more in the early months of construction—had to be brought to the Manhattan Life site. To overcome the storage problem, work had to proceed so rapidly that a large workforce was kept constantly on the job. Near the end of the Manhattan Life's construction, more than a thousand men were employed.[17]

The rates at which the various processes were completed depended on a systems program invented by Imperial Roman builders and carried to a highly efficient state by the end of the nineteenth century. In the 1890s, extraordinary feats of large-scale construction were performed. Many large buildings and building groups were completed in a year or less, and this was accomplished by a combination of power-operated hoisting, excavating, and pile-driving equipment, as well as by large gangs of workers. Ordinary masonry and concrete foundations were usually completed in about two months, and during that period the superstructure contractors got together their subcontracts and materials. If caisson foundations were used, however, as for the Manhattan Life Building, then the foundation construction phase lasted longer. This gave the contractors ample time to get ready, but in order to keep to the expected schedule of about a year, the time for building the superstructure was proportionately reduced. Once the building was finished, the final step in the process was the cleaning and restoration of the surrounding areas.

A great step forward in the rapid and efficient construction of high buildings was the establishment of the office of general contractor, who took responsibility for the entire construction process, including the organization and control of the operations of the subcontractors. George A. Fuller, whose company was founded in Chicago in 1882 and incorporated in New York in 1896, was instrumental in this development and in distinguishing the contractor's role from that of the architect.[18] The most important mechanism of control exercised by the general contractor, and the one that led to the rationalization of the whole process, was the comprehensive time schedule. In documentary form, this schedule ensured the systematic flow of all building materials to the site and correlated that flow with the stages of building construction. The time schedule would reach its most sophisticated level with the construction of the Empire State Building nearly fifty years after the Fuller Company was founded.

Outstanding Problems and Some Solutions

Foundation piling presented serious problems in lower Manhattan, where the lowering of the groundwater level over the years exposed piling to rot above water level. The peril was particularly acute within the area of the Collect Pond, whose centroid was almost exactly at the intersection of Centre and Leonard streets and close to the area of the Brooklyn Bridge subway loop. There the soil consisted of mud, sand, peat, and miscellaneous soft materials. Up to about 1890 the groundwater level was 8 to 10 feet below grade, so the piling was cut off at minus 10 feet in the water. Construction involving heavy pumpage of water in the excavation area as well as drainage from the buildings and subways directly into the sewer system progressively lowered the water level through the 1890s and past the turn of the century until it was minus 15 to minus 20 feet. Thus the upper ends of the piles were exposed and subjected to rot. Shortly after the turn of the century buildings began to settle noticeably, by 1908 reaching a minimum of one inch per year. The solution for many buildings, notably the Havemeyer, was to cut off the piles well below the existing groundwater level and to extend brick or concrete foundation walls and column footings down to the new level of the pile-heads—a technique that was both elaborate and costly.[19]

Many variations on traditional foundation techniques were developed in the 1890s, notably the pneumatic caissons used for the Manhattan Life Building. An alternative technique of underpinning foundations, invented by Jules Breuchaud of Arthur McMullen & Company and patented in 1896, it involved using hydraulic jacks of sixty-ton capacity to force successive lengths of cast-iron pipe into the overburden until bedrock was reached. Equal to a multitude of small hollow caisson foundations, this technique was first used in the foundation wall of the Commercial Cable Building and also for the support of the adjacent Western Union Building.[20]

If receding groundwater was a new difficulty, the threat of fire persisted—and persists today—as a painfully familiar concern. The nature of fire damage in the early 1890s at the same time indicates the gravity of the problem and illustrates the effectiveness of hollow-tile fireproof cladding on iron members. For example, at 6 A.M. on 2 April 1893 a fire in the Temple Court Building decimated the contents of about thirty-five offices, causing extensive cracking and spalling of the building's stone sills and destroying the plaster in many rooms. But the hollow-tile flooring, the tile covering of the beams and the columns, and the brickwork were undamaged. The cast- and wrought-iron framing elements survived intact, with only small pieces of the tile covering the columns stripped away. Water was the main cause of damage to the tile partitions, not the fire itself.[21]

In November 1895 intense heat from a fire in a building across the street cracked the windows of the eight-story Manhattan Savings Bank (1889–90) at the northeast corner of Broadway and Bleecker streets and set fire to the wood floors and furnishings of its interior. The building was considered fireproof because it had masonry bearing walls and an interior iron frame, but its frame collapsed because a section at the bottom of its wrought-iron box girders had been left exposed below the tile cladding and plaster, and the heat elongated the lower flanges of these girders to the point of severe buckling. The building also had another defect: its shallow floor arches between I-beams had an air space between the extrados and the wood flooring that exposed the underside of the flooring to the heat.[22]

The Cable Building (1892–94), the handsome steel-framed structure designed by McKim, Mead & White as the power station of the Broadway Cable Railroad Company, was struck by fire on 22 April 1896. The fire destroyed the contents of rooms that were exposed to heat sufficient to melt the tips of the gas and electrical fixtures, causing pipes and conduits to buckle, but the hollow-tile partitions and plastering on the walls and ceilings remained intact.[23] Indeed, the hollow-tile cladding was recognized as having protected the ironwork from damage and as having prevented the spread of fire through conduction of heat in iron members.

The subject of fire continued to be discussed in the professional press with undiminished vigor. Henry Goetz and Edward Atkinson, in the March and May 1892 issues of *Engineering Magazine*, repeated warnings about the dangers of fire in high buildings, the difficulty of preventing contents fires and the spread of fire from neighboring buildings, and the problem of control. In the October 1892 issue, the architect John Merven Carrère of Carrère & Hastings considered at length design, interior plan, disposition of utilities, and the location and protection of elevator shafts and stairwells with regard to maximizing fire protection and minimizing the spread of fire. In the December 1896 number of the same journal, A. S. Himmelwright reviewed six leading systems of hollow-tile and concrete protection in light of recent tests.[24]

The New York Building Code

The city's successive building codes addressed the issues of fire and wind, problems relating to soil conditions, the behavior of structural systems, and the reliability of utilities, prescribing responses in accordance with the state of the art. As the codes grew in complexity, they became increasingly controversial.

Before 1860 the regulation of building in New York was the responsibility of the fire wardens. Acting as inspectors who monitored compliance with such meager regulations as existed, they served chiefly to prevent the construction of wooden buildings in the narrow streets of lower Manhattan and to eliminate wooden chimneys. The enactment of a building law in 1860 signaled a new order, providing for a municipal Department of Buildings and a superintendent of buildings. The department's first responsibility was curtailing the construction of new wooden buildings, and eliminating existing ones, below 52nd Street. As amended in 1862, the law required the superintendent and all department officers to pass an examination before a committee of the American Institute of Architects as a prerequisite for appointment; as amended again in 1866, it pushed the boundary below which wooden buildings were proscribed to 86th Street and stipulated that the walls of buildings used for storage had to be 4 inches thicker than the thickest walls required for other structures. A professional fire department with paid fire fighters was also established in 1866.[25]

Further amendments and additions of 1871 restricted the width of buildings that had combustible interior construction, but no height limit was specified. Another useful step was the requirement that all iron beams be tested before use, but the only material or performance specification in the law appears to have been the prohibition of combustibility. A board of examiners was created to represent all of the special interests in the building profession, undoubtedly to ensure flexibility of interpretation. The board was empowered to act only when interpretation of the law allowed discretionary action.[26] An amendment to the building law that passed in 1874 divided the Department of Buildings into three separate bureaus: inspection, violations, and fire escapes and ironwork. In 1880, however, because of corruption at City Hall, the entire department was made a bureau of the fire department.

William P. Esterbrook, appointed head of the bureau in 1880, tried repeatedly to get a new code through the legislature and finally succeeded in 1885. Its most important features were the requirements that all buildings over 70 feet tall be built completely fireproof and incombustible—a provision that in 1887 would be amended to 80 feet, in 1892 to 85 feet, and in 1897 reduced to 75 feet—and that the construction of theatres and other public buildings meet standards of safety. In addition, the new code specified that foundation walls had to be carried at least 4 feet below grade and to a "good solid bottom"; as had been the practice since Roman times, these had to be thicker than the walls above by a stated amount. Piles had to be driven or laid below the waterline and had to conform to diameter specifications. Footings had to be stone or concrete, and foundation walls stone or brick. The code also delegated adequate powers of enforcement.[27]

The first attempt at structuring a national code came in 1891. Although neither this nor any national code was ever adopted, the effort was noteworthy. In April of that year a joint committee composed of representatives of the American Institute of Architects, the national associations of Master-Builders, Building Inspectors, and Fire Engineers, and the National Board of Underwriters met to prepare a model building law intended for nationwide adoption. Based on the codes of France and Italy, where fire losses were markedly less than in the United States, it was conceived as a set of general principles of safe and durable construction that could serve as the basis for specific codes to be drawn up by individual cities. It recommended, for example, that all buildings over 70 feet high be fireproof and that all interior structural iron and steel be covered with fireproof material of low thermal conductivity. Going beyond the New York code, the model recommended a height limit for all buildings: a building could be no taller than two-and-one-half times the width of the principal street on which it stood; and no building, excepting a church spire, could rise higher than 125 feet unless authorized by special permit.[28] Without a doubt, special permits would have been freely disbursed in New York City had its code included such a requirement.

On 9 April 1892, the general assembly reestablished an independent New York City Department of Buildings under the direction of the superintendent of buildings. Armed with a new building code, the Department of Buildings, in addition to its previous functions, took over matters pertaining to light, ventilation, plumbing, and drainage that had previously been under the jurisdiction of the board of health. The 1892 code also legitimized the skeleton frame—the ruling for which it is most often cited—and set forth precise specifications for foundations, piling, walls, floor loads, and framing. "Good, solid, natural earth," for example, was judged capable of safely carrying 4 tons per square foot. The maximum spacing for piles was set at 30 inches, with the tops to be cut off below the lowest low-water line. The maximum load for a single pile was set at 40,000 pounds, and the range of bearing capacity at 5,000 pounds minimum for piling in alluvial soils to 28,000 maximum for penetration into firm earth above sand or gravel.[29] Most important, for the first time, the new code prescribed curtain-wall dimensions. These, of course, were much less than for bearing walls (see Figs. 6.3, 6.4): "Curtain walls of brick built in between iron or steel columns, and supported wholly or in part on iron or steel girders, shall not be less than twelve inches thick for fifty feet of the uppermost height thereof, or to the nearest tier of beams to that measurement, in any building so constructed, and every lower section of fifty feet or to the nearest tier of beams to such vertical measurement, or part therof, shall have a thickness of four inches more than is required for the section next above it, down to the tier of beams nearest to the curb level."[30]

As we have seen, the code also established loading factors for specific building types, based on a maximum wind-load factor of 30 pounds per square foot along with a maximum column length/radius ratio. No wrought-iron or steel column could have an unsupported length more than 30 times its diameter or narrowest transverse dimension. All columns for high buildings were assumed to be built up of H-sections, channels, plates, Z-bars, and angles. Aside from portal bracing (not identified as such), wind bracing seems to have received little attention. All connections were to be made by angles that were riveted to the webs of the members. The code also designated allowable stresses for beams, girders, lintels, and rivets, and it required that all iron or steel below the low-water level be coated to prevent rust.[31]

The provisions that mandated fireproof construction were more detailed in the new law than ever before. All theatres, schools, and institutional buildings taller than 35 feet and all other buildings more than 85 feet tall had to be of fireproof construction, and refractory tile cladding was required for all ironwork and for lining flues, furnaces, and elevator shafts.

The continuing use of cast iron for columns is indicated by the difference in the code-mandated safety factors for columns and floor-framing members. Beams and girders, which were subject to transverse loads and hence deflection, were allowed a safety factor of 3, half the factor for columns and other compressive members. Yet beams and girders under deflection are subject to both tension and compression, whereas columns are subject to compression only, except when under wind pressure—to which the code pays no attention. The reason for the difference in factors must be the unpredictable quality of cast iron. The increasing use of steel made such artificial distinctions unnecessary.

Although the building code may have at least temporarily resolved several critical issues, primarily regarding foundations and piling, other matters required continuing attention. As the heights of buildings steadily increased, so did column and wind loads. There was an ongoing need to determine accurately the quality, strength, and physical properties of ferrous metals and to translate knowledge acquired through experiment into steel-manufacturing technology. Addressing these issues, an authoritative paper read by A. E. Hunt before a meeting of the American Society of Mining Engineers in 1891 presented a survey of extensive tests for determining the tensile, compressive, and impact strength, and the elasticity, hardness, ductility, and malleability of wrought iron and steel. The range of the maximum ultimate tensile strength of wrought iron was found to be 48,000–52,000 pounds per square inch, for steel 60,000–64,000 pounds per square inch.[32]

With regard to fireproof construction, reliable data were still needed on the strength of steel relative to temperature change. Experiments carried on by a Professor Martens at the Royal Technical Laboratories, Berlin, in the summer of 1891 showed that steel with a tensile range of 46,000–60,000 pounds per square inch lost strength through a rise of temperature from 20 to 50 degrees Celsius; it gained strength and reached its maximum at 200 to 250; and thereafter, with a continuing rise in temperature, it lost strength at an increasingly rapid rate.[33] This information indicated precisely what load-bearing protection was necessary to resist the damaging effects of high temperatures.

By the mid-1890s various types of fireproof and heat-resistant floor construction were in use, the best of which offered full coverage of metal members with a material (terracotta or concrete) of low thermal conductivity.[34] Eventually, the costly system of laying hollow-tile arches would be superseded by cladding steel members with a thick coating of porous vermiculite concrete.

The additional costs to developers brought on by the new code requirements did not force them to the suburbs, as one source predicted, but within three years after the 1892 municipal code was adopted its revision was being actively promoted by redrafting committees representing building tradesmen and the professional societies. Due to developments in the iron and steel construction of skyscrapers that went well beyond the general knowledge of most architects, the engineering profession had achieved a new prominence and now raised its voice to effect changes in the building laws and to ensure that engineers played a greater role in the construction of high buildings. H. Waller Brinckerhoff, for example, urged that the buildings department "require that the structural work of all buildings of a certain class, in regard to height, weight, and foundation . . . be designed and superintended by a civil engineer approved by the Department."[35]

By the early 1890s professionally trained engineers, more often than not employed in the architect's office, were in fact actively involved in the process, but Corydon T. Purdy recalled that when he opened his New York office in 1894, "he was told that there was no chance for an engineer in that city; that excepting a few who regularly employed engineers in their office-force, the architects depended upon one of three or four of the great iron manufacturers of New York for their steel designing, and that that arrangement was a fixed one in the architectural practice of the city."[36] Purdy's subsequent success as a consulting engineer in the city suggests that the situation may have been more fluid than he was led to believe.

By and large the laws were considered too conservative. Particular effort on the part of the redrafting committees went into evaluating and reevaluating working-stress and compression factors for all framing and floor elements, including ferrous metals, wood, concrete, mortar, and rivets and bolts. But the Department of Buildings preferred to adopt modifications of the existing code rather than accept these proposals. Further attempts by the professional groups at getting the city to undertake a radical code revision were made in response to the establishment on 1 January 1898 of Greater New York, a momentous event that created new conditions for builders and regulators to take into account. Although it adopted some recommendations, however, the city was still unwilling to enact a drastically revised code.

Skyscraper Style

The decade saw a profound change in the architectural style as well as the height of New York skyscrapers. Partly in response to Richardson's late work, the preference for light-colored exterior masonry was apparent by the end of the 1880s, and when the budget allowed, stone sheathing was preferred over brick. A neo-Renaissance mode had caught on by the mid-1880s, and by 1895 many of the leading commercial architects had given up the eclectic modes and pre-Renaissance arcaded styles fashionable in the late 1880s in favor of the revived classicism popularized by the 1893 Columbian Exposition in Chicago. The new style of the 1890s, which in fact embraced many varieties of classicism, including that of the Italian Renaissance, is today often called Beaux-Arts in acknowledgment of the French orientation and training of architects in this period. Although arcading remained a favorite means of articulating the midsections of commercial facades, it was now thoroughly transformed by the substitution of Roman or Beaux-Arts detailing for the fast-waning Richardsonian Romanesque, as in the case of the Cable Building or the Manhattan Life Insurance Building. Some of the American-trained architects, notably Post, clung to their earlier styles, but by the end of the decade virtually all had yielded to the change.

Characteristically, the ornament of the new skyscrapers was derived from classical and Renaissance precedents, although usually much modified. The stone sheathing was richly textured, often as diamond-faced ashlar, and frequently of marble or granite, but sometimes gneiss or sandstone. Other visual arts were incorporated to a greater degree than previously, notably figural sculpture used on the facades, but also murals, mosaic work, and stained glass in the lobbies. The ornament itself veered between boldly abstract machine-cut forms, influenced by the steam-powered tools used for cutting, and intricate, often realistically detailed ornament in cast terra-cotta, which since about 1880 had been used in increasing amounts on commercial facades. By the early 1890s large sections of facades, and later entire skyscraper exteriors, would be sheathed in terracotta, which added a richness of texture and color that would have been impractical and prohibitively expensive in stone. As for the principles of symmetry, axiality, and sequential spaces fundamental to the Beaux-Arts aesthetic, except in those rare cases of the freestanding tower, these were confined almost entirely to the architectural treatment of the main elevation and to the entrance and elevator lobby. The *promenade marché*, or sequence of spaces incorporating a grand staircase that led up to an elevated space, was possible only when there was sufficient space to spare, which was not often. The neo-Renaissance, white-marble Metropolitan Life Building of 1890–93 had such a lobby.

Long a dominant feature of New York commercial buildings, and with an architectural history reaching back at least to classical Greece, the three-part-facade composition was commonplace in New York skyscrapers by the mid-1890s. It remained for Louis Sullivan to provide it with a modern aesthetic and a functional basis in his famous essay "The Tall Building Artistically Considered" (1896), and his own skyscrapers of the 1890s eloquently expressed his beliefs. The essay appealed to the New York professionals—Birkmire, for example, quoted from it liberally[37]—but Sullivan's influence on the *appearance* of the New York skyscraper was barely, if at all, perceptible. As Sullivan himself observed, the critics had been recommending the classical column with base-shaft-capital schema as the aesthetic model for the tall building well before his essay was published. The study of the orders was, after all, fundamental to the Ecole des Beaux-Arts curriculum, which by the 1890s was being followed by numerous Americans studying in Paris and was also influencing the programs of American architecture schools. In a city where the tower-skyscraper was coming to the fore, and where the building law required thick curtain walls, the resulting masonry expression and weighty appearance justified a traditional aesthetic.

Even Montgomery Schuyler, who early on admired Sullivan's work and who helped to shape the conventional interpretation of the Chicago School, remained committed to tripartite design on aesthetic rather than functional grounds, often citing the column analogy. Schuyler cited Post's Union Trust Building (1889–90) in New York as the first to "powerfully" enforce the tripartite composition, and also acknowledged the American Surety Building (1894–95) as a serious, though flawed, attempt at utilizing the column aesthetic.[38] George Ashdown Audsley of the firm responsible for the tripartite Bowling Green Building (1895–98) also quoted Sullivan on tripartite design, but, like Schuyler, endorsed the scheme purely on its aesthetic merits. Given the situation in New York, not even the example of Sullivan's Bayard Building could stimulate Sullivanesque designs.

Sullivan articulates the central problem posed by the new building type: how to "impart to this sterile pile . . . the graciousness of those higher forms of sensibility and culture?"[39] The design of the tall office building, he argues, must be derived from the necessary character of the building: "Form ever follows function." Ostensibly, his only strictly aesthetic theory is the celebration of "soaring" height, although the architect was allowed considerable scope in the treatment of details.[40] As for Sullivan's belief that loftiness should be the "dominant chord" in the design, a counterargument was already in evidence in New York: because the skyscraper comprises many stories layered one above the other, the architect should indicate its essential horizontal structure in the detailing of the exterior wall surface and in doing so preserve some sense of human scale. Moreover, the code requirement for diminishing wall thicknesses encouraged a horizontal emphasis.

The column/tripartite aesthetic predominated, but conflicting attitudes toward the skyscraper on the part of both laymen and architects indicated that a solution to the problem of design was far from settled. Although willing to find an aesthetic solution, Sullivan thought that the skyscraper grew from immoral and even sinister propensities in American capitalism. True to his Ruskinian heritage, the critic Russell Sturgis saw a nearly absolute antithesis between art and commerce. R. H. Robertson baldly acknowledged that "the principal object of the high building is to get above your neighbors for light and air. . . . They are uninteresting architecturally" because of all the restrictions placed on them.[41] Bruce Price, designer of the American Surety Building, believed that only when the building was treated as an isolated tower with all four sides fully designed could valid and expressive form follow.

Thomas Hastings of Carrère & Hastings stated the argument eloquently:

From the artistic standpoint . . . the limitations are almost insurmountable. The extreme height, tending to the treatment of every building as a tower; . . . the exaggerated demand for light, which destroys all possibility of wall surfaces, which are requisite to the design of a beautiful tower; and the impossibility, owing to fire laws and other regulations, of using even the structural features of the building to accentuate the design, have resolved the problem into vain attempts resulting either in absolute monotony, expressive only by its size, or absolute decoration of wall surfaces.

A tower has always been intended as an isolated feature. The grouping together, side by side, of towers on both sides of the street cannot possibly produce under any circumstances an artistic result.[42]

Hastings specifically addressed the impact of the building laws on facade design, calling for their revision so that architects would have the capability of "honestly showing the iron and steel on the facade, with a filling in of terra-cotta, brick, or faience, with projections constructed in apparent iron and terra-cotta." Once the laws were revised, "we could only wait for some one capable to experiment in this direction."[43]

And yet, despite all that was said, it is the density of these early "towers," compounded by their diversity of silhouette, ornamentation, and massing, that appeals to present-day sensibilities. The eminent architectural historian Vincent Scully rhapsodized on the lower Manhattan skyline as it appeared around 1914: "Even the unique massing of skyscrapers which became the glory of New York and, indeed, the major symbol of America as a whole, occurred because the street pattern was followed. . . . Precisely that passionate density made the group splendid, so that later, obsessed schemes to thin it out according to the principles of Le Corbusier could only have destroyed it."[44] We would add that the visual competitiveness of these high buildings, which Scully also appreciated, intentionally expressed the underlying business competition and importance of business in the city and the nation as a whole.

Opposition to the High Building

At the beginning of the 1890s, as the number, height, and cost of buildings grew, public and professional opposition to the unrestricted height of skyscrapers began to gather force. Even builders were opposed. In its peculiarly American aspect this aversion paralleled the growing popular antagonism toward the buccaneering methods of finance and business competition in the last decade of the century.

Public health was an issue for the British architect Robert Kerr. Voicing an early concern with atmospheric pollution, he again launched an attack on high buildings, strenuously opposing them on the ground that they prevent the dissipation of noxious effluvia (which he called the *sweat* of the city) from building and roadway surfaces, animals, humans, standing water, factories, chimneys, and locomotives.[45] He argued that the foul and noxious air trapped by an excessive concentration of buildings over 150 feet high in New York would foster endemic disease and a high death rate.

In America, doubts on the part of real estate firms, building managers, architects, and engineers about the feasibility and safety of skyscrapers can be summarized by four essential arguments, all arising from financial concerns: (1) On densely built streets inadequate light to the lower stories affects their rentability; such space rents slowly, at low rates, or not at all. (2) The risk of damage or destruction from earthquakes (said to occur at serious magnitude in New York every twenty years) makes tenants of upper stories unwilling to pay higher rents. (3) The difficulty of maintaining adequate water pressure on the upper floors makes it impossible to extinguish rapidly spreading fires. (4) The building designed exclusively as office space results in low-unit floor loadings, making it impossible to convert to other purposes such as warehouse, library, or public use. Obviously, all of these problems could be solved technically, but not if the hesitant owner was unwilling to spend the money in the face of possible rental difficulties.

The problem was exacerbated by the pressure that owners of low buildings adjacent to the new skyscrapers felt to redevelop their properties in order to recapture light, air, and prestige, and to take advantage of the opportunity for financial gain. Noting that legal restrictions on height were not likely to come anytime soon and that at present "the attractiveness of the high building depends upon its isolation," the *Record and Guide* predicted that "if the whole commercial quarter were built up with high buildings it would be a very terrible region for all but the occupants of the topmost stories, a region of Cimmerian gloom. . . . The tenants who now have pure air and a wide outlook would face other tenants across a well."[46]

Concerned about the dangers and economic risks of high buildings, architects took the lead in advocating a height limit. At a meeting of the Architectural League of New

York on 1 August 1894, George B. Post confronted the problem, and over the next ten years he and Hastings were in the forefront of other such efforts.[47] Russell Sturgis and the editors of *Engineering Record* also favored height limits.

By 1895 antiskyscraper sentiment had spread beyond the professions. As reported by the *American Architect*, "Public opinion in New York appears to be taking definite form in opposition to allowing the erection of the enormously lofty buildings which have lately sprung up in such numbers in the lower part of the city."[48] This opposition was strong enough to compel business organizations and public bodies to propose remedies. The New York Chamber of Commerce appointed a committee to study the matter and, in late 1895, endorsed the committee's report urging laws to restrict the height of buildings. Then, in January 1896, this organization proposed a law that included a provision aimed at increasing light on the street and lower floors. It called for buildings over 80 feet high to cover no more than 80 percent of the lot. This was a timid beginning, but it undoubtedly influenced the inclusion of a section in the 1899 building code stipulating that "office buildings when not erected on a corner shall not cover more than 90 per cent. of the lot area, at and above the second story floor level."[49] Weak as these restrictions were, they were the forerunners of the setback and floor-area-ratio principles of the 1916 and 1961 zoning laws. Other cities already had height restrictions in place: in Berlin, the height could be equal to the width of the street (a concept traceable to the Roman architect Vitruvius of the first century B.C.), in Paris the height could be 50 percent higher than the street width, and in Boston two-and-a-half times the street width. In 1893 Chicago had passed a law limiting the height to 130 feet.[50]

With the able assistance of George Post, the City Club of New York proposed an alternative law that was taken up in the state senate of the general assembly in February 1896. Presented as the Pavey bill, also known as "An Act to Limit the Height of Buildings in New York City," its main provisions were as follows: (1) The height of a building could be no more than fifteen times the square root of the street width (Post's formula); but, if the street should be wider than 100 feet, the height was limited to 100 feet. (2) If the building is set back from the lot line, its height may be raised by an addition equal to twice the depth of the setback. (3) On squares, corners, avenues wider than 100 feet, the height may be raised above the limit on approval of the superintendent of buildings, the Department of Public Health, and a member of the Council of Fine Arts Federation.[51]

The New York Chapter of the American Institute of Architects discussed the issue of height limitation at a meeting on 30 March 1896 and went on record as favoring the height restriction embodied in the Pavey bill. Members voiced their opposition to high buildings, Post at length and persuasively:

> I have built many of the high buildings in New York, and have on my table, at the present time, plans for several proposed new buildings in which my clients demand that they should be, in my opinion, abnormally high. I, nevertheless, believe it my duty as a citizen . . . to advocate as strongly as possible the passage of a law restricting the height of buildings. . . .
>
> The objections to very tall buildings are serious. . . . [Their] construction can be stopped now by legislation before the city is irreparably damaged. If it is not stopped the consequence must be disastrous, and redress will be almost impossible. The

results of bacteriological investigation show that the evil microbes flourish and increase in damp, dark places, but that sunlight destroys their life. Our narrow streets, when lined with tall structures, will become unhealthy alleys with an inadequate capacity for the passage of the crowds which will flow from these tall buildings if occupied, for the capacity of the streets is already severely taxed at certain times of day.

Post went on to argue that height limitation is also artistically justified, for even if the facade is well designed, the sides and the rear "will always form a hideous mass." Buildings, he maintained, should always be treated as separate towers, but their continuous facades along the street rendered this impossible. Howard Constable agreed with Post, adding that damp dark places encourage the spread of typhoid fever and tuberculosis, and that the sewer system would be overwhelmed and the water mains and fire department overtaxed. Even if the building is fireproof, he averred, there is a risk of death or serious injury from panic and smoke inhalation guaranteed by the presence of narrow stairs and too few elevators. John Carrère concurred, arguing that the rights of property owners take second place to the good of the city: "As an investment high buildings do not justify their construction, and are mainly built as advertisements, by corporations. . . . The streets being practically public courts, the height of the buildings should, therefore, be regulated by a public Act, so as to make the courts healthy, beautiful, and useful." Walter Cook, Thomas Hastings, and Henry Hardenbergh agreed, adding detailed points.[52]

But the approval of the New York chapter was not enough to carry the day. Some architects opposed the Pavey bill, along with real estate interests and the building material industries, all arguing that the narrow streets made the proposed limits impractical and arbitrary and that the street system of lower Manhattan necessitated high buildings and density for the transaction of business in adequate proximity to the financial and commercial centers. These opponents also insisted that the city's fire-fighting equipment, supplemented by fire-fighting apparatus in the buildings, was sufficient to overcome even fires on the highest floors of tall buildings, and that high buildings as well as low could be heated, ventilated, and rendered sanitary. And so the bill died in the legislature.

In December 1896 the New York Board of Trade and Transportation held meetings on the question of height limitation. The meetings opened with a report submitted by the president of the New York City Department of Health, Charles W. Wilson, on height regulations in various European cities. (Here is an early suggestion of the attitude that would develop with the Progressive Movement later on: that European cities were superior to American cities in regard to public health and services.) The board proposed a limit of 165 feet for hotels and apartment buildings and 200 feet for office buildings. This 200-foot limit—which had already been exceeded—and other recommendations were submitted to the general assembly in January 1897. But no bill was passed to restrict height, in part because the Greater New York Charter was pending in 1897 and would empower the city to decide the matter. The Board of Trade temporarily suspended its efforts due to "the enormous labor involved in arranging and harmonizing the affairs of the consolidated territory."[53]

In editorials published in 1896, *Scribner's Magazine* joined the New York Chapter of the American Institute of Architects in opposing skyscrapers primarily on the grounds of fire hazards, loss of light and air, and traffic beyond the capacity of the streets. The architect Ernest Flagg held that tenants on the lower floors of high buildings as well as the public are robbed of light and air. The public authority, he believed, should place the comfort and health of the community first and impose building height control. He recommended the Paris law, which required mansard roofs as well as height limitation to minimize the shading of the street.[54]

Throughout the 1890s the concern with the skyscraper as a threat to public health and safety added to the burdens of the architect who was trying to cope with the technical and ecological aspects of design. By mid-decade he was required to prepare four sets of plans in addition to those required by the building contractor. A copy had to be filed with the inspector of buildings at City Hall, one each with the Bureau of Light and Ventilation and the Bureau of Plumbing and Drainage, both at the Department of Health, and a fourth with the insurance underwriters. Architects regarded these requirements as an unnecessary and expensive nuisance. The vigor of their opposition suggests that the various bureaus required original tracings rather than prints; this was certainly the case in the Department of Buildings. This annoyance may account at least in part for the architects' negative reaction to high buildings.

One of the few authoritative voices raised in favor of high buildings was that of the architect C. H. Blackall. He believed there was a business need for skyscrapers, and he saw no reason why they should not rise to thirty stories if economically justified. The problem, as he saw it, was to find the appropriate architectural design and solution to the environmental problems: "Very few of our tall office buildings are in accord with their locations and surroundings, but this is more due to the selfishness of the owners of high cost land than real lack of appreciation by the architects. We do not need to reduce the height of buildings, but rather, we want to reform the public tastes and the greed of capitalists, so that we will design our tall buildings as ornaments and not as mere money mills."[55] As the buildings themselves confirm, the architects tried hard to do that.

7 MONUMENTS TO COMMERCIAL POWER AND CORPORATE PRESTIGE, 1889–95

The city entered the last decade of the century with an unassailable lead in building and in the nation's economy. Though flattened for a year or so by the economic depression of 1893, the upward curve of real estate development continued relentlessly. The confidence, power, and wealth of business, especially insurance and banking, increasingly found expression in high-rise commercial buildings. Along with the imposing new civic and public architecture of the period, skyscrapers reflected the ruling features of the commercial city as they approached maturity under the combined influences of Beaux-Arts principles and the mastery of high-building technology.

Madison Square Garden and Transitional Structures of c. 1890

The public and the commercial coalesced with art and entertainment to create a famous showpiece that ushered in the "gay Nineties": Madison Square Garden (1889–90). Although not a skyscraper in the usual sense of the term, the Garden warrants consideration here for its mixed but daring construction and its soaring tower (Fig. 7.1). The property it was built on was formerly owned by the New York & Harlem Railroad and had been the site since 1873 of several entertainment centers housed successively in the old railroad passenger station. The most recent of these had been known as Madison Square Garden, hence the name.

Stanford White of McKim, Mead & White was a shareholder in the Madison Square Garden Company that owned the property and paid for the new Garden; it therefore comes as no surprise that he won the competition for the new building in 1887. But his design fully deserved to win. White's dramatic creation was in-

spired by Renaissance architecture. Its buff-colored brick walls were richly trimmed in buff and brown terra-cotta, and the whole was topped off by a graceful tower derived from the Giralda of Seville Cathedral and crowned by Augustus Saint-Gaudens' famous weathervane sculpture of Diana. The architect's exuberant genius was fully expressed in the Garden's combination of perfectly controlled ornament, sophisticated elegance, and playful use of color and decorative detail. (There can be no greater irony than the retention of the name Madison Square Garden for the present concrete vacuity on the site of Pennsylvania Station.)

Newspapers all over the country carried reports of the new building. It covered the entire block between Fourth and Madison avenues and 26th and 27th streets, encompassing an area of 93,000 square feet, making it the largest amusement place in the country. As the press pointed out, the arena could accommodate more patrons than London's Albert Hall, the Paris Opera House, the Chicago Auditorium Building, and the Salt Lake City Mormon Temple. Reports vary, but the oval-shaped amphitheatre could seat at least eight thousand people, with standing room for another six thousand. The *Sun* waxed enthusiastic about the arena's exposed Pratt trusses and interior metal framing, describing the trusswork as "wonderful steel-truss arches of 186 feet span, said to be the largest and lightest ever constructed" and also commenting on the large skylight at the center of the roof, which could be mechanically opened in warm weather, "making the amphitheatre an open-air affair." The truss arches were supported by two rows of "light steel columns," actually built-up Phoenix columns, one row flanking each of the long walls to leave the arena wide open.[1] Much attention was given to the hundreds of incandescent lights mounted on the overhead arches and powered by the building's own generating plant.

The 304-foot-high observation tower, touted as "the highest sightseeing point on the Island" and said to have been exceeded in height only by the contemporary World Building downtown, could almost qualify as a skyscraper.[2] The seven floors below its first observation-deck level contained private concert and ballrooms as well as studio apartments. White himself kept a tower apartment where he entertained his friends. For a fee of twenty-five cents, two elevators took passengers up as far as the lowest observation deck; thereafter one could climb all the way up to Diana's feet via a spiral staircase. Thirty-eight feet wide at the sidewalk level, the tower tapered to 34.5 feet at the steel-and-iron-framed loggia levels, and the 18-inch bearing walls of its apartments were described as "so thick the window seats will be deep enough for a bed."[3] Alas, this gem was too expensive a luxury. After the bankrupt Garden was sold at foreclosure by the New York Life Insurance Company, it was demolished in 1925.

The reworking of the Giralda was to be repeated in other buildings. The three most notable examples are all extant: the Municipal Building (1909–14), also a McKim, Mead & White product; the Wrigley Building (1919–21) in Chicago, which is nearly as good as the original adaptation; and Terminal Tower (1925–28) in Cleveland, a grossly inflated version of the model. Designed by Graham, Anderson, Probst & White, the Chicago and Cleveland skyscrapers are indebted to the Municipal Building.

The transitional architectural and technological status of the skyscraper in the late 1880s was epitomized by the nine-story Lincoln Building (1889–90), still standing on the northwest corner of Union Square West and 14th Street (Fig. 7.2). The construction of a

7.1
Madison Square Garden (1889–90; demolished), Stanford White, architect. *After McKim, Mead & White,* A Monograph of the Work of McKim, Mead & White *1879–1915. Avery Architectural and Fine Arts Library, Columbia University in the City of New York.*

commercial building as tall as this one so far uptown was made possible by the transformation of Union Square, which before c. 1860 had been exclusively residential. Since that time it had become a theatre, hotel, and mercantile center, and by the late 1880s it was heavily given over to retail, manufacturing, and publishing. Indeed, the Lincoln Building accommodated a range of businesses from architects' offices and ground-floor stores to a company that manufactured buttonhole sewing attachments. Its name may have been inspired by the proximity of Lincoln's statue (1868) in the Square; its builder was one William Crawford.

The Lincoln was the first tall commercial building designed by Robert Henderson Robertson. R. H. Robertson was an apprentice-trained architect who had worked briefly in the offices of George B. Post and Edward T. Potter before joining in partnership with William A. Potter in 1875. Since 1881, when that partnership was terminated, Robertson had established himself as a successful New York practitioner and would go on to produce some of the city's most impressive skyscrapers, including two of its most conspicuous pre-twentieth century examples, the American Tract Society and Park Row buildings.

Like Aldrich Court, the Lincoln Building followed the Richardsonian style, but unlike the earlier building, which adopted a darker color scheme, it featured the light-colored brick and limestone walls characteristic of Richardson's late work. It was of mixed construction that combined an interior metal frame of steel beams and girders and cast-iron columns with metal-reinforced, load-bearing walls. The Lincoln's arcaded facades exhibit numerous horizontal divisions, a design feature that would characterize all of Robertson's skyscrapers—and for which he endured Montgomery Schuyler's criticism. Schuyler maintained that, in the Lincoln, "the subordinate division is carried so far as to confuse the principal division." Instead, Robertson's "power of design is shown in the parts, rather than in the whole, in the picturesque features in which his . . . work abounds."[4] Indeed, the building displays fine carved-stone and terra-cotta ornament of the Romanesque type associated with the Richardsonian style. And, assuming that the divisions correspond to the shifts in bearing-wall thickness mandated by the 1885 building code, as is apparently the case, the horizontal emphasis could be considered structurally expressive.

George B. Post's contemporary Union Trust Company Building (1889–90) at 78–82 Broadway was also a transitional skyscraper, but, in contrast to the Lincoln Building, it was critically acclaimed (Fig. 7.3; see also Figs. 7.20, 7.21). It replaced two small buildings opposite Trinity Churchyard and for a few years towered over its immediate neighbors, surpassing even the nearby Tower Building by more than 40 feet. Including its double-height banking floor and two attic stories, the Union Trust had eleven and a half stories. Like the Tower Building and others on this side of Broadway, it extended through the block to New Street, where its entrance was conveniently located opposite the Stock Exchange. The bank itself, which had immense resources estimated at more than $35 million in 1892, occupied the galleried banking floor at the second/third-story level. The rest of the building was largely rented to Wall Street brokers. The accessibility of sunlight and air to the office floors, owing to the presence of low structures on all sides and a 20-by-50-foot interior court above the banking room skylight, was cited as a major selling point, and the building was characterized as "enormous."[5]

7.2
*Lincoln Building
(1889–90),
R. H. Robertson,
architect.
Northwest corner
Union Square and
14th Street.
After Architectural
Record (1896).*

In its architectural style and light coloration the Union Trust resembled the Lincoln Building. On Broadway its walls were light-colored granite with iron components, and on New Street buff-colored brick and terra-cotta. It was also bearing-wall construction, with floors framed with steel beams and supported by wrought-iron columns clad in fireproof terra-cotta. However, it featured a steep, pyramidal roof recalling that of the Tower Building. This and the verticality of its design anticipated the tower-skyscrapers that would soon dominate the area. Well before Schuyler praised the building's tripartite scheme, the *Record and Guide* pointed out that the Union Trust's "coherence and unity"

were owing to its well-proportioned tripartite facade configuration; in 1898 Russell Sturgis recognized the facade as "one of the best fronts that has yet been achieved."[6]

The World Building: A Monument to Success

At the other end of the architectural spectrum, erected at the same time as the Union Trust and also designed by Post, a huge, overbearing, and controversial work—the New York World Building, also called the Pulitzer Building, on the northeast corner of Park Row at Frankfort Street—compelled attention in a multitude of ways by its inescapably powerful image (Fig. 7.4). The cornerstone was laid ceremoniously on 10 October 1889, and the new building opened on 10 December 1890. The *World* reported all the details of its new building in a well-illustrated souvenir issue on the day the building opened. The World Building demonstrated even more conspicuously than Post's earlier Times Building the important role played by newspapers in the development of skyscraper structure and image, a role that was at the end of the century second only to that of the insurance industry. The owner of the *World*, Joseph Pulitzer, regarded his formidable record-high skyscraper as an expression of the highest ideals of American journalism: dedication to liberty, justice, democracy, and "true Americanism."[7] The building was also intended to broadcast the supremacy of the *World* over all of its competitors. Internally, it housed facilities for the publication of a morning and an evening newspaper and also included rental space.

Founded in 1860, the newspaper had been purchased by Pulitzer in 1883 and since then had prospered greatly, its average daily circulation swelling from more than 33,500 copies in 1883 to nearly 341,000 in 1889. It had thoroughly outgrown its previous quarters at 32 Park Row. According to Pulitzer's biographer, W. A. Swanberg, in 1888 Pulitzer bought up Park Row property directly across from the Herald Building with the idea of diminishing the newspaper of his archrival James Gordon Bennett, Jr. He was not able to get enough land there, however; instead, he bought a site three blocks to the north that he valued for its historic associations and that he thought deserved a "monument," or so the *World* reported. (To make way for this monument, French's Hotel was demolished.) Thus it happened that instead of dwarfing the Herald Building, Pulitzer's new building thoroughly overwhelmed the tiny Sun Building, occupied by another archrival. An architectural competition was held, for which Richard Morris Hunt served as professional adviser. It was reported that Post bested his competitors by making three bold moves: he called on Pulitzer just after submitting his plans; he "annexed" the approach to the Brooklyn Bridge by "throwing his building out over it"; and, instead of guaranteeing Pulitzer that he could stay within the budgeted $1 million, he bet $20,000 against the publisher's $10,000 that the cost would not exceed that figure. The same source states that the cost had since escalated to $2 million.[8]

In plan the World Building was a parallelogram with a large rectangular space cut out of the inner corner along the Brooklyn Bridge approach; its main entrance was on Park Row. Towerlike in form and dimensions, it measured 115 feet across its Park Row front and 136 feet on the Frankfort Street side. Because of the steep grade of Frankfort Street, the basement on that side was only two steps below grade, and on that side the building was said to rise 309 feet from the sidewalk to the base of the lantern on top of the dome

7.3

Lower Broadway looking south. Left: Union Trust Building (1889–90; demolished), G. B. Post, architect. Center: Manhattan Life Building as widened in 1903–4. Right foreground: Empire Building. Collection of The New-York Historical Society.

and 349 feet to the top of flagstaff. The story count varies from one report to another; eighteen is a number often cited in contemporary accounts. The *World*, however, stretched the count to twenty-six, which included two below-grade levels, fourteen full stories in the tower, three above-ground mezzanine stories, six stories in the dome, and the lantern observatory level. Whatever the number, the World was the tallest building yet constructed in the city and easily overtopped the spire of Trinity Church.

True to Post's belief in the necessity of masonry or cage construction to guarantee the integrity and reliability of the inner iron frame, which had to be protected from fire and moisture, the structure was massive, solid, conservative, and cage-framed. The walls were thick, diminishing from about 88 inches at the curb line to 24 inches at the top; but, as the *World* correctly observed, they would have taken up virtually all the ground-floor space had the building been constructed according to "old-fashioned methods" (Fig. 7.5). Inside the masonry envelope, built-up wrought-iron columns supported steel girders and steel beams said to be "the largest pieces of steel ever made in this country." The floor arches were hollow tile, as were the partitions, and the floors were concrete. Of this construction, the *World* boasted, "Knock away the massive walls, and the structure still would stand. Build a fire on any floor, and the edifice could not burn. . . . This is a mighty skeleton, and the walls are but as clothing."[9] The ribbed, copper-clad dome was framed in wrought iron braced with double diagonals between alternate pairs of columns and with its ribs sprung from iron columns that extended down through the building to independent foundations. This framing, especially the independent columns, suggests that the dome, which was 52 feet in diameter at its base, was treated as an independent structure (Fig. 7.6). The building's mat-type foundation incorporated brick and concrete piers that rested on a continuous footing of concrete carried down to a bed of firm gravel; bedrock in this area exists at least 100 feet below grade.[10]

The basement was reserved for the machinery required to operate the building's eighteen elevators and for the steam and plumbing lines. The subbasement had two levels, one for the presses, the other for the boiler and engine room. The building was fully electrified, with all of its wires, including telephone and cable, contained within a central shaft and routed underground. The ground floor served the *World*, as did the first mezzanine floor and a total of seventy-nine offices located on all the floors from the eleventh up. In addition to those offices and an eleventh-floor, two-bedroom apartment created for the use of the newspaper "on special occasions," there were 149 rentable offices, all in the shaft of the tower. Three of the building's four hydraulic passenger elevators served the lower eleven floors; the fourth, a circular elevator just inside the main entrance, was reserved for the use of the newspaper's editors and staff. It ran up to the top of the dome and was said to be "the highest business elevator in existence."[11] Along with the rest of the editorial offices, Joseph Pulitzer's private office was on the second level of the dome where he could overlook the nearby Sun, Tribune, Times, and Potter buildings and survey the panorama of the surrounding area (see Fig. 5.36).

The architectural image of the new building, that of a multitiered palazzo crowned by a domed temple, was surely intended to suggest the cosmopolitan nature of the newspaper and its publisher; the gilded dome was certainly meant to attract attention and to triumph over every other building in the vicinity. Described by the *World* as being "of the Renaissance order with a tendency to Venetian detail," the building's style, general

7.4

World (Pulitzer) Building (1889–90; demolished), G. B. Post, architect. Collection of The New-York Historical Society.

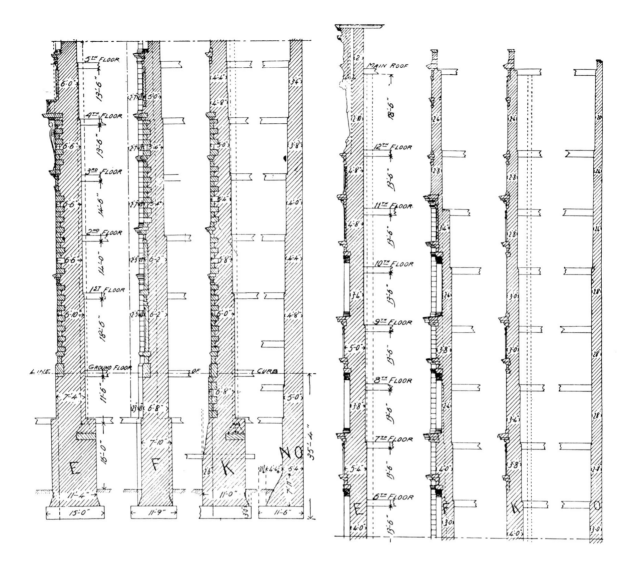

7.5

Wall sections, World (Pulitzer) Building. After Engineering and Building Record *(1890).*

features, and record-breaking height were heavily influenced by Pulitzer's preferences. Not surprisingly, the dome was "entirely his conception." So, apparently, was the rounded corner and the publication office's special entrance within that corner, for this feature also appears in R. H. Robertson's competition design published in the *American Architect* (9 February 1889). And so was the three-storied entrance archway on Park Row, which, the *World* reported, "necessarily involved the sacrifice of valuable renting space in three stories." According to the same source, Post at first considered this entrance "well-nigh an impossibility," but "after repeated efforts all architectural and engineering difficulties were overcome."[12]

The building was more colorful than photographs suggest; its walls were red sandstone up to the fourth story and buff-colored brick and darker buff terra-cotta above, and the columns and spandrel panels of the base were red and gray granite, respectively. Classically inspired figural sculpture liberally embellished the facades, notably four bronze female torchbearers above the porch to symbolize the arts and four "black copper" caryatids beneath the pediment at the top to represent the four human races. Karl Bitter, later to become one of the nation's best-known sculptors, modeled the torchbearers. Post had a penchant for such sculpture; similar figures appear on many of his skyscrapers. Just inside the publication office entrance, heralded by appropriate symbolic figures in the spandels of the archway, an elegantly appointed rotunda-vestibule opened into the publication office.

Yet all of this was heavily criticized. "The World building is a monstrosity in vari-colored brick and stone," wrote one detractor, "with hideous bronze figures projected from its front, and an incongruous dome perched upon the summit of thirteen stories of ugliness." The lack of transition between dome and tower and resulting "high-shoul-dered look" were especially faulted by the *Record and Guide*, which hinted that the architect was not entirely to blame.[13] The newspaper prospered greatly during its sensa-tional era of "yellow journalism," and so in 1907–8 the building was remodeled and given a thirteen-story addition designed by Horace Trumbauer. A conservative period followed, but by the late 1920s the *World* was in decline. It died in 1931, and its domed memorial became "merely another office building—a relic of New York's Newspaper Row."[14] In 1955 the building was demolished, and its site was utilized for the widening of the Brooklyn Bridge approach.

About the time the World Building was completed, the *Sun* was apparently consider-ing building new quarters. If it had constructed the stunning tower illustrated and de-scribed in its issue of 8 February 1891, where the caption reads "If the Sun Should Try It!" (Fig. 7.7), a new height record would have been set, relegating the World Building to second place. The designer of this project was Bruce Price, an American- and office-trained architect who had previously concentrated on domestic work, but who was also

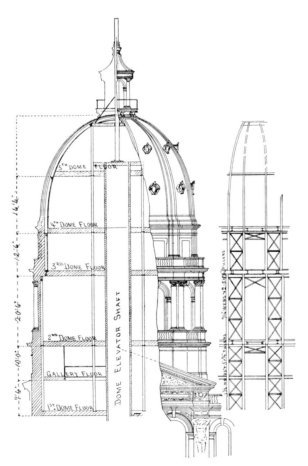

7.6
Left: section through dome of World (Pulitzer) Building. Right: part of dome framing.
After Engineering and Building Record *(1890).*

*Project for Sun
Building,
1890,
Bruce Price, architect.
After* Architectural
Record *(1891).*

responsible for such large-scale structures as Windsor Station (1888–89) in Montreal.[15] Price's project, his first-known skyscraper essay, called for a building 442 feet tall and 75 feet square with thirty-two stories. It was inspired by the Campanile of San Marco in Venice and may therefore be considered the forerunner of the Metropolitan Life tower as well as the architect's own American Surety Building. The campanile image was thought to embody expressions of both the civic and the business worlds. The *Sun*'s interest in Price's design may have resulted from an inferiority complex. Already overwhelmed by the adjoining Tribune Building, its diminutive mansarded quarters were now reduced to utter insignificance by the new World Building just across Frankfort Street. If bedrock were available, the foundation would go down to it; and the intention was to use cage construction, with a steel frame inside masonry walls. As matters transpired, however, the *Sun* chose not to attempt this daring tower because, according to Price, "the plot was not adapted to the design."[16]

Skeleton-Framed Skyscrapers Number Two and Number Three

The immediate followers of the innovator rarely get any notice unless they are otherwise meritorious, but in the case of the skeleton frame, it took courage to follow the leader— courage, or the impetus of a narrow site. The city's second and third skeleton-framed buildings rose on such sites.

Around the time the Tower Building was finished, in the fall of 1889, plans were filed for the city's second skeleton-framed building: the Lancashire Insurance Building (1889–90; demolished), the New York office of a fire insurance company based in Manchester, England. Designed by J. C. Cady & Company and constructed by Marc Eidlitz, it stood at 25 Pine Street, next door to the old United States Sub-Treasury Building (Federal Hall Memorial). A 25-foot-wide site militated in favor of skeleton framing, and the building was ten stories tall and 74 feet deep. Its only visual distinctions were its narrow proportions and the vertical row of large bay windows—made possible by its framing—in the arcaded, tripartite front. Clearly the Tower Building had set a precedent for handling both the design and the construction of the narrow, slab building. According to buildings department records, 8-inch steel beams were used in the Lancashire Building's floors, and iron girders in the side and rear walls; steel Z-bar columns were utilized.[17] As was usual in the case of infill buildings that loomed above neighboring structures, the exposed side walls were left as plain brick, with small conventional windows—an economy measure usually undertaken with the expectation that those walls would someday be hidden from view by adjoining tall structures.

The city's third skeleton-framed building was the twelve-story Columbia Building at 29 Broadway on the northwest corner of Morris Street (1890–91), a narrow, L-shaped slab with a rounded corner (Fig. 7.8; visible also in Fig. 5.11). Built by Spencer Aldrich, representing the Herman D. Aldrich estate, the Columbia was designed by Youngs & Cable; the drawings for its iron skeleton were prepared by the president of the Union Iron Works, P. Minturn Smith, who was said to have convinced the owner of the safety of skeleton construction. The frame consisted of cast-iron columns of hollow rectangular section, wrought-iron girders and beams with the standard hollow-brick floor arches, and full diagonal bracing in which two angles were set back-to-back and bolted to a column

*View of Bowling
Green,
c. 1891.
In background:
Columbia Building
(1890–91;
demolished),
Youngs & Cable,
architects.
Collection of The
New-York Historical
Society.*

by triangular gusset plates and angles set against the column face (Fig. 7.9).[18] Made prominent by its high, chateauesque roof and narrow, 30-foot front on Broadway, the Columbia spanned the full distance of 184 feet from Broadway to Trinity Place. The Columbia, with its style, odd proportions and form, and facade materials of stone, brick, iron, and terra-cotta, somewhat resembled the smaller Corbin Building. Its electricity was partly supplied by an underground connection to Aldrich Court, which was just up the block. As an inducement to potential occupants, the agents initially proposed that the tenants of the building's 273 offices not be charged for electric lighting, steam heating, or janitor's service. An early tenant, the Provident Savings Life Assurance Society, was perhaps attracted by this benefit.[19]

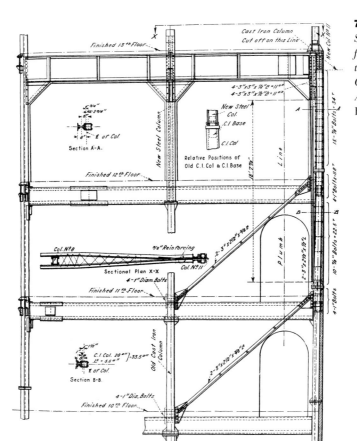

7.9

Section showing iron framing at tenth through twelfth floors, Columbia Building. After Engineering Record *(1910).*

The Havemeyer Building: "An Organic Idea"

The Havemeyer Building (1891–93), unfortunately no longer extant, was one of Post's finest works (Fig. 7.10). It was built on speculation by Theodore A. Havemeyer of the New York family that had made its fortune in sugar refining. Given a conspicuous, if oddly dimensioned, site across the street and to the north of Hunt's Coal and Iron Exchange, Post was said to have taken "manifest delight in the task that lay before him."[20] The resulting fifteen-story, irregularly shaped slab covered the entire 214-foot-long block-front on the east side of Church Street between Dey and Cortlandt streets (Fig. 7.11).

Post acted as engineer as well as architect, and he apparently planned the Havemeyer's foundations to overcome the unstable subgrade condition of the site. Spruce piles, cut off at minus 22 feet, 7 inches, were driven to minus 42 feet, 7 inches at the Dey Street curb and covered with a timber raft of two-way planking. Around 1903, when there were plans to add stories to the building, the foundation was renewed with piles cut off at minus 27 feet, 7 inches; at that time the plank raft was removed and the remaining 6 feet of vertical space filled with a solid raft (or mat) of concrete reinforced with a grid of wrought-iron I-beams.[21] Above grade, the Havemeyer was cage framed, with iron columns inside its masonry wall piers. Apparently adhering to the code requirements for bearing-wall thicknesses, but further thickened by the iron columns, the piers diminished from 56 inches at the basement level to 20 inches at the top. Post had consistently recommended and defended cage construction for its protection from moisture and the attendant corrosion, for its superior fireproofing, including protection from fire in adjacent buildings, for the

*Havemeyer Building
(1891–93; de-
molished),
G. B. Post, architect.
Rendering by
Hughson Hawley.
Collection of The
New-York Historical
Society.*

accessibility of wall columns and column-girder connections for inspection and maintenance, and for its direct connections to the floor-framing system, which avoided the
eccentric loading of wall columns, as well as awkward connections with excessive shear.

The interior framing was designed to support 200 pounds per square foot, an unusually
high floor loading factor for an office building. Half was dead load, that is, the structure
and fixed contents, and half live load, or traffic and wind. The base plates were cast iron,
and the box columns, box girders, and I-section beams and girders were wrought iron and

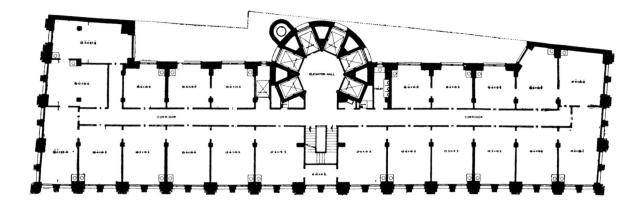

7.11

*Typical floor plan,
Havemeyer Building.
After Birkmire,*
Skeleton
Construction in
Buildings.

steel. The floor girders were double channels connected to the outer lateral faces of the freestanding box columns. In the case of the peripheral columns, the girders were cantilevered beyond the outside faces of the columns into the masonry of the piers and attached to the columns by means of triangular gusset plates above and below the girder flanges. The lintels were cast iron. The double-diagonal wind bracing comprised wrought-iron rods of varying dimensions (Fig. 7.12).[22]

In the spring of 1892 an accident occurred during construction. The plasterers had prepared a pile of wet plaster that covered an area on one floor of about 14 by 15 feet and weighed about 240,000 pounds. The weight of the plaster raised the floor load to about 1,000 pounds per square foot, causing a girder under the area to fracture as a result of shear failure across the entire section. The resulting collapse dropped the heavy load of plaster to the floor below, killing two workers. Such accidents occurred with some frequency.[23]

Of necessity, the interior of the building was planned around the elevators, the adjacent stairway, and the plumbing shafts (see Fig. 7.11). To avoid taking any more of the floor space than necessary, the passenger elevators were arranged in a three-quarter circle that projected outside the building envelope, and the corridor was reduced to a narrow aisle. The rest of the building's vascular system of conduits, wires, and junction boxes had to be made to fit into the walls, floors, and partitions. Clearly, the architect's opportunity to design the interior with any kind of style was severely restricted. An arcade of stores on the ground floor, reached from the Church Street entrance, and more stores on the basement level serviced the building's occupants and visitors. Perhaps following the example of Madison Square Garden, the Havemeyer featured a large roof garden with restaurant facilities and a promenade.

The Havemeyer's utilities and appointments were state-of-the-art for the time. At their capacity of 2,500 pounds, the six Otis hydraulic passenger elevators moved at a rate of 25 feet per minute, and for the first time in New York two cars ran express, with the first stop at the seventh story. A service elevator, also of the Otis hydraulic type and located to one side of the elevator hall, could move at the same rate while carrying its maximum load of 5,000 pounds. The building was steam-heated, with radiators regulated for a temperature of 70 degrees. Forced-draft ventilating equipment was confined to the basement and toilet rooms, of which the building contained fifty-four, in addition to forty-eight urinals and 315 wash basins. Telephone and messenger service equipment was provided, as well as gas, electricity, and all the necessary fixtures.[24]

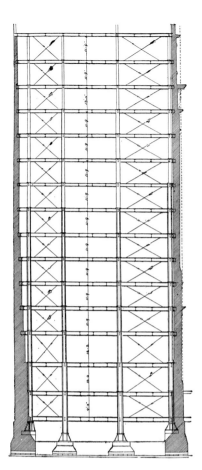

7.12
*Transverse section
showing wind
bracing, Havemeyer
Building.
After Birkmire,
Skeleton Construc-
tion in Buildings.*

The exterior permitted Post the freedom to perfect the continuous-pier wall treatment
that he had long favored for his institutional and commercial buildings, and which had
served him to such advantage in the Produce Exchange. An arcaded base beneath a
transitional story, a seven-story arcade of thirteen bays on the shaft, and a high, double-
tiered crown combined to form a satisfyingly proportioned facade that wrapped around
the Havemeyer Building, unifying all three fronts. Although the *Record and Guide* found
some fault with the design—the "capped on" appearance of the attic stories, for example—it warmly praised the definition and legibility of Post's design and recognized that
the Havemeyer represented a new type, "an organic idea," that went far toward "the
beginning of a style."[25] The wall piers, continuous from the sidewalk level to the thirteenth story, and the strongly molded sills recessed between them evinced a thoroughly
rational approach to design, so rational that much of Sullivan's design theory seems to be
anticipated here. Indeed, the Havemeyer raises the question of whether Sullivan's buildings might have influenced Post, but in view of Post's previous work, there is no reason to
assume that. Light in color, the walls were brick with limestone and terra-cotta trim.
Creamy-white terra-cotta Atlantes supporting a heavy classical cornice enriched the
uppermost segment of the exterior. No trace of the Richardsonian remained; Post had
instead rejuvenated his earlier neo-Renaissance style by adding neoclassical proportions
and details.

Maturity of Design: Some Extraordinary Office Buildings of 1892–95

A series of high office buildings erected from 1892 to 1895 affirms the skyscraper's rapid evolution to stylistic and technological maturity. During these years, the adaptation of academic-classical and Beaux-Arts design principles produced one of the outstanding solutions to the problem of formal design: the dignified, classicizing image that would prevail for at least two decades. This accomplishment, along with the innovation of the pneumatic-caisson foundation, distinguishes the New York skyscrapers designed in this period.

The new Postal Telegraph-Cable Company (1892–94) and Home Life Insurance Company (1892–94) buildings at 253 and 256 Broadway, under construction simultaneously, sited cheek by jowl, and highly visible because of their proximity to City Hall Park, excited critical comment from the real estate and architectural press (Fig. 7.13). The *Record and Guide* perceived "an irrepressible conflict": "The two buildings war violently with one another. . . . The two designs are antagonistic not in spirit only, but even the materials selected in each case were chosen apparently upon the principle of opposition. One would say, were not the idea unwarranted, that the architects of the two buildings were bitter rivals and desired to declare publicly, by their works, that positively no connection existed with the 'shop next door.' " Although admitting a similarity in their fenestration patterns, the same source contrasted the "daintiness" and "feminine prettiness" of the Home Life to the marked "vigor" of its neighbor, which was said to have a "structuresque" character. The Home Life, on the other hand, displayed "a quantity of applied carving . . . forming no more an organic part of the edifice than so much sgraffitto." The Postal Telegraph-Cable exuded the "obstreperousness of commerce" whereas the Home Life, to its credit, had "a certain *rieuse* air that contradicts the grim commercialism of the actuary." Of the two, the Home Life came off better; it was described as "one of the most picturesque bits of architecture in the city." Their incompatibility was perceived as indicative of a more serious problem: "The artistic obtuseness which the conflict bears witness to testifies to the strength of the Philistine in the land."[26]

Today, when the slightest semblance of compatibility between adjacent new buildings is a welcome surprise, it is hard to understand what seemed in 1894 so egregious. True, the roofs and certain other features are dissimilar, but on the whole the two seem amazingly compatible, and the gender difference that the *Record and Guide* described is appealing. Both are faced in light-colored materials, even if the Home Life's white Tuckahoe marble is rather lighter than the Postal Telegraph-Cable's gray Indiana limestone and brick. Both adhere to the principles of Renaissance classicism; both are tripartite in facade composition; and—even if the floor levels do just miss lining up—the compatibility of their window arrangements is remarkable and was surely intentional. On both fronts centrally grouped windows are framed by rows of windows, and both have bull's eye windows at the third-story level. The only jarring discordance is the result of an alteration that harshly modernized the base of the Postal Telegraph's main front in the late 1930s. The Home Life Insurance Company acquired the Postal Telegraph Building in 1947, and both buildings now serve as its headquarters.

The product of a merger of several telegraph plants, the Postal Telegraph-Cable Company had by 1892 become a formidable rival to the Western Union Telegraph Company. It

now required more spacious quarters and to that end leased a site at the northwest corner of Broadway and Murray Street from Trinity Church Corporation. Its new fourteen-story building was designed by the partnership of George Edward Harding and William Tyson Gooch, who won the commission in a competition. During Harding & Gooch's five-year tenure from 1891 to 1896, the firm produced several New York skyscrapers. Harding had been trained as an engineer, and his specialty was commercial buildings. In 1887 the young, Pennsylvania-born Frederick P. Dinkelberg was his junior partner; years later, while working for Daniel Burnham in Chicago, Dinkelberg would serve as the principal designer of the Flatiron Building. Because of Dinkelberg's early association, the Flatiron, its Chicago affiliations notwithstanding, could be said to owe something to Harding's New York commercial style.

The Postal Telegraph-Cable Company Building is of steel-cage construction. Its two exposed facades are distinguished by an emphatic horizontality provided by a flaring cornice and narrow unobtrusive belt courses at the sill line of every story. As originally executed, a three-story glazed entrance bay imparted great openness to the Broadway front. According to the electrical engineer Reginald Pelham Bolton, the first Sprague-Pratt electric elevators were installed here, and city directories confirm that the Sprague Elevator Company rented space in the building at the time of its completion and for several years thereafter.[27] The Postal Telegraph-Cable Company itself occupied the top three floors, part of the basement, and a corner office on the lobby floor.

Napoleon LeBrun & Sons won the commission for the Home Life Insurance Company Building in an invited competition that was judged by William R. Ware, professor of architecture at Columbia University. Harding & Gooch was also one of the invited competitors.[28] The Home Life Company had been founded in 1860 in Brooklyn, where its main office was located, and its Manhattan branch had previously occupied the company's five-story building on the site of the new building. That building was demolished and additional property was obtained in order to accommodate the new building. The son of French immigrants, Napoleon LeBrun had practiced architecture in Philadelphia before coming to New York in 1864. Since 1870 his firm name had twice been changed to reflect the partnership of his sons, first Pierre L. LeBrun and later Michel M. LeBrun. The Home Life commission was an early skyscraper for this firm, which was better known for its churches and firehouses, though it was also responsible for the Metropolitan Life Company's elegantly appointed, eleven-story building (1890–93) then under construction on Madison Square. In light of the father's age, and the firm's shifts in style and technology in the late 1880s, it seems likely that Pierre LeBrun was the partner responsible for the Home Life Insurance Building.[29]

The Home Life broke no records, but at a height of 256 feet from sidewalk to roof crest, and with sixteen floors, including the mezzanine and tower stories in the count, it was on the frontier. The framing elements are steel; and the construction is primarily skeleton, with only the street wall adhering to the cage formula. Birkmire describes the construction as "entirely fireproof and of the composite description, as provided for in the New York Building Law, passed April, 1892," and he states that "the marble of the front extends through the full thickness of the wall from base to cornice."[30] Stylistically, the building is stamped with the mix of traditional and innovative characteristic of much high-style commercial architecture. Contemporary sources, including Birkmire, describe

7.13
*View of Broadway and Murray Street, c. 1910.
Center:
Postal Telegraph-Cable Company Building (1892–94), Harding & Gooch, architects.
Right:
Home Insurance Company Building (1892–94), Napoleon LeBrun & Sons, architects. City Hall in right foreground. Collection of The New-York Historical Society.*

7.14

Detail, facade of
Home Life Insurance
Company Building.
Photograph by Carl
Forster.
New York City
Landmarks
Preservation
Commission.

its style as early Italian Renaissance, but its steep pyramid-roof and delicate ornamentation contribute more than a touch of the French Renaissance (Fig. 7.14). Indeed, considering the Second Empire style of the earliest insurance buildings, the French details of the Home Life Building may have served to identify the nature of the owner's business. Once again the insurance industry had demonstrated its premier role in fixing the character of the early skyscraper.

On 4 December 1898 the building was struck by the worst fire to date in a New York skyscraper. It started in the adjacent Rogers, Peet & Company clothing store, and from there penetrated the windows of the Home Life and ignited the office furniture inside. The fire moved up the air shaft, which acted like a chimney, and ignited the contents of the upper floors. Protected by hollow-tile cladding, all the steelwork and most of the partitions survived virtually untouched, but the contents and wood finishes of the interiors, especially the wood floors, fed the spreading fire and were destroyed. The front of the building above the seventh story was sufficiently damaged that it had to be reconstructed. The steam engine used by the firemen could not throw water as high as the eleventh floor, where the damage was most severe; that problem was remedied in 1908, when a high-pressure fire system was put into service. The Postal Telegraph-Cable Building was believed to have survived virtually untouched because of its cement-finished floors; only the top floor was damaged.[31]

Other lesser-known skyscrapers under construction in these same years were noteworthy in one way or another. One such building was the Mail and Express (1891–92), designed by Carrère & Hastings and built by the newspaper's owner, Elliott F. Shepard. It stood at the southwest corner of Broadway and Fulton Street opposite St. Paul's Chapel churchyard and two doors up from the Western Union Building (Fig. 7.15). Said to have the highest front in the world on so narrow a lot, this T-shaped building was 25 feet wide on Broadway and 211 feet deep. It rose to a height of sixteen stories on its Broadway side; on Fulton it dropped to eleven. The Paris-trained architects, inspired by such French

7.15
*View of Broadway at
southwest corner of
Fulton Street.
Center: Mail and
Express Building
(1891–92),
Carrère & Hastings,
architects.
Left: Western Union
Building as altered by
H. J. Hardenbergh in
1890–91.
Both demolished.
After* King's
Handbook
of New York City
(1893 edition).

Renaissance landmarks as the sixteenth-century Château d'Anet, did everything possible to call attention to their building. From the caryatid-framed portico to the double-tiered lantern on the steep roof, they loaded the Broadway front with orders and pediments and ornamental sculpture.[32] As usual, the side walls were left as plain brick. As we have seen, Hastings criticized just this kind of building two years later.

Although the *Record and Guide* recognized that sixteen-story buildings represented a benchmark in the history of commercial architecture, it was overly optimistic concerning their longevity: "They are necessarily pretentious, aggressive and permanent . . . it is scarcely conceivable that they will ever be replaced by thirty-story buildings."[33] The Mail and Express, in fact, lasted only until 1920, when it, along with everything else on its blockfront, yielded to the twenty-seven-story American Telephone and Telegraph Building (1913–22).

Fortunately, the eleven-story Decker Building at 33 Union Square (1892–93), later the Union Building, survives (Fig. 7.16). In this sliver building Chicago and New York joined forces. It was built for the Decker Brothers Piano Company and replaced their previous Leopold Eidlitz–designed quarters of c. 1870 on the same site. The polychromatic, Venetianesque arcading of the earlier building's High Victorian Gothic facade had stood out from its sober neighbors, and the designer of the new building obviously sought a similar artistic effect. The Decker's Moorish tower with onion dome was the most exotic crowning feature of any New York office building of the time. The architect of record is the German-born and -trained Alfred Zucker, who specialized in mercantile buildings, but the actual designer was likely John H. Edelmann, the mentor and friend of Louis Sullivan. Edelmann worked for Zucker off and on between 1891 and 1893; on the grounds of the Decker Building's wildly eclectic and Sullivanesque ornament, which also appears on other "Zucker" buildings of those years, several scholars have not only identified Edelmann as the designer but declared this his most important extant building.[34] The terracotta ornamentation of the tripartite, brick-faced facade presents a medley of the Moorish and the Venetian, with Islamic motifs predominating.

Constructed as an appraisers' warehouse, the building later known as the Federal Archives (1892–94; 1896–98) barely qualifies as a skyscraper by the height standards of the mid-1890s (Fig. 7.17). Only ten stories tall, it adheres to the warehouse block form characteristic of the 1880s, but its physical prominence, its marked formal relationship to the Produce Exchange, and its fine design place it among the extraordinary tall buildings of its time. Henry-Russell Hitchcock judged it, "after the long-demolished Marshall Field [by H. H. Richardson], the finest arcaded building"—reason enough to include it here.[35] It was begun in 1892 to the design of the Chicago-born Willoughby J. Edbrooke in his capacity as supervising architect of the United States Treasury, and it was constructed in two stages. According to plan, the lower two stories were completed and enclosed in 1894. The upper eight were constructed from 1896 to 1898 during W. Martin Aikin's tenure as supervising architect; Aiken preserved Edbrooke's arcaded exterior walls, though he modified their articulation. With deep-red brick facades curving at the corners, the building completely fills its large trapezoidal site bounded by Christopher, Greenwich, Barrow, and Washington streets in west Greenwich Village. Construction is wall bearing with an interior iron and steel frame; the frame of the later portion is all steel and comprises Z-bar columns and rolled beams with riveted connections. Hollow-tile fireproofing encases the interior columns and the girders, except for the bottom flanges. Initially, an open court in the center afforded light and air to the interior.[36]

Comparison of Robertson's Corn Exchange Bank building (1893–94) with his Lincoln Building reveals a marked change of style for this architect (cf. Figs. 7.18 and 7.2).

7.16
*View of west side
of Union Square
at 16th Street.
Center: Decker
Building (1892–93),
John Edelmann,
architect.
Photograph by
George P. Hall.
Collection of The
New-York Historical
Society.*

7.17
*Federal Archives
Building
(1892–94; 1896–98),
W. J. Edbrooke et al.,
architects.
666 Greenwich Street.
Photograph by
S. B. Landau.*

Under a shallow hipped roof with projecting cornice, the arcaded facades of the eleven-story bank building displayed a striking verticality and openness of design made possible by—indeed inspired by—the use of a full steel-and-iron skeleton frame. Designed to replace the bank's four-story, Richard Upjohn–designed quarters on the same site at the northwest corner of Beaver and William streets, the new building appeared to be a discrete slab; in reality it was L-shaped with the longest and widest portion hidden from view. A two-tiered limestone shaft defined by piers forming arcades and by a large window area contributed the vertical emphasis, offset by what Schuyler considered an excessive number of horizontal divisions.[37] Two of those divisions, one above the two-story red-granite base and the other—to which Schuyler most objected—dividing the shaft, appear to correspond to the specified 50-foot curtain wall segments. Thanks chiefly to Schuyler's prejudices and his indifference to building code requirements, the degree to which New York skyscrapers were "structurally expressive" has never been appreciated.

Eight years later, in partnership with Robert Burnside Potter as Robertson & Potter, Robertson created a compatible steel-framed twenty-story addition (1902–4) in the same Richardsonian-cum-Renaissance style, with its lower divisions exactly corresponding to those of the earlier building (see Fig. 8.1 for the plan as enlarged). Together the two affirmed the upward climb of the New York skyscraper and the solidity of a great banking establishment. Regrettably, both were demolished in 1989, victims of an inflated economy. In early 1995 the property was still undeveloped.

Sheer audacity distinguished the twelve-story John Wolfe Building (1894–95), named for the man whose estate built it on speculation. Not especially tall by mid-decade

7.18
*Corn Exchange Bank
building
(1893–94; de-
molished),
R. H. Robertson,
architect.
Photograph by
George P. Hall.
Collection of The
New-York Historical
Society.*

standards, but nonetheless towering over its Federal-era neighbors, the building received notice for the highly decorative, almost playful treatment of its street elevations (Fig. 7.19). Always predisposed to the Dutch and German Renaissance styles, the architect, Henry J. Hardenbergh, looked to the early seventeenth-century Meat Market Hall in Haarlem as the inspiration for this, his first true skyscraper. The choice was appropriate to the building's narrow trapezoidal site at the juncture of Maiden Lane and William Street, for the site owed its odd shape to the original Dutch street plan. The building's high peaked roof, with stepped and richly ornamented gables and dormer windows, as well as its red brick facades activated by a lively pattern of light-colored stone and terra-cotta ornament, won it high praise from the *Architectural Record*, which designated it a "picturesque sky-scraper" and hailed its "character, freshness, and charm."[38] The corner configuration was especially felicitous; its acute angle was chamfered, with the chamfer widened at the sixth floor above a six-story bay. The building obviously gained interior space by its use of a steel frame.

Flamboyance vs. Respectability: Manhattan Life and New York Life Buildings

One of the most important skyscrapers of the decade was constructed at 64–66 Broadway with an entrance at 17–19 New Street: the Manhattan Life Insurance Company Building (1893–95), headquarters of a major company founded in 1850 (Fig. 7.20). Like its formidable rivals, Equitable, New York Life, Mutual, and Metropolitan Life, Manhattan Life has continued to the present, though it has been a subsidiary of the Union Central Life Insurance Company of Cincinnati since 1986. Assembled in several transactions at a total cost of $1,225,000, the site of the new building was just three doors south of the Union Trust Building. The Union Trust is visible in George B. Post's finely proportioned and well-designed competition project, which, had it been realized, would have nicely complemented his earlier building (Fig. 7.21).

The commission was won by Kimball & Thompson in a two-stage, invited competition. The instructions to the competitors specified the site dimensions—approximately 67 feet on both Broadway and New Street with depths of about 120 feet on one line and 125 feet on the other—and called for sixteen stories on Broadway, seventeen on New Street, and "absolute fireproof construction." The new building was expected to be the tallest east of Chicago, and work was not scheduled to begin until the following year because some of the tenants in the existing buildings on the site had not yet agreed to give up their offices.[39] As completed, rising above the sidewalk to about 348 feet at the tip of the lantern on its six-story dome, the Manhattan Life did indeed set a record; its height was said to have been exceeded only by the spires of St. Patrick's Cathedral. (Taking advantage of the situation, a weather forecaster stationed his meteorological equipment high up in the building). In plan the Manhattan Life Building was shaped as a wide U around a deep light court that was open above the seventh floor (Fig. 7.22).

The partnership of Francis H. Kimball and George Kramer Thompson was formed in 1892 and lasted until 1898, long enough to produce several major lower Manhattan skyscrapers. According to Fryer, Kimball had used ordinary caisson foundations for his Fifth Avenue Theatre on West 28th Street (1891–92; demolished), possibly the first building in the city to employ that technology. Another source reports that it was Thomp-

7.19
*John Wolfe Building
(1894–95; de-
molished),
H. J. Hardenbergh,
architect.
After* Architectural
Record *(1897).*

COPYRIGHT 1895.
BY J.S. JOHNSTON, N.Y.

7.20
*Manhattan Life
Insurance Company
Building
(1893–94; de-
molished),
Kimball & Thompson,
architects.
From left: American
Surety Building
(1894–96)
under construction,
Bruce Price, architect;
United Bank Building
(1880–81; de-
molished),
Peabody & Stearns,
architects;
Union Trust Company
Building
(1889–90; de-
molished),
G. B. Post, architect.
At right: Consolidated
Stock and Petroleum
Exchange
(1887–88; de-
molished),
E. D. Lindsay,
architect.
Photograph by
J. S. Johnston, 1895.
Collection of The
New-York Historical
Society.*

7.21
*Competition Design
for Manhattan Life
Building,
G. B. Post, architect.
At far left: Post's
Union Trust Building.
Collection of The
New-York Historical
Society.*

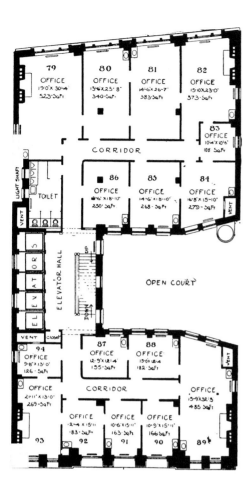

7.22
*Typical floor plan,
Manhattan Life
Building.
After Birkmire,
Skeleton Construc-
tion in Buildings.*

son who, after considerable effort, finally convinced the Department of Buildings and the tenants of nearby buildings that the innovative pneumatic-caisson foundation proposed for the building was a safe type of construction.[40]

The construction timetable for this huge skyscraper is as impressive as its structure: the foundation was laid in less than six months and the superstructure took eight more, for a total of thirteen months and twenty-one days.[41] Certainly the foundation was the building's most innovative feature. Bedrock at the site is minus 57 feet on the average and is overlaid primarily by saturated mud and sand (quicksand), with some glacial till. The complex mix of overburden and fine materials under hydraulic pressure made pile driving inadmissible and the excavation hazardous. If the piles had been spaced as closely as the building code allowed, the required number would have been 1,323 over the foundation area for a total superimposed load of 30,000 tons, yielding an average of 45,300 pounds per pile, far above the code limit of 40,000 pounds. The well-type caisson was thought to be hazardous because of the possible collapse of adjacent building walls so Charles Sooysmith, the foundation consultant and a respected engineer, recommended the pneumatic caisson technique, never before used in the construction of an office building.[42]

Fifteen caissons were used, eleven rectangular and four circular. The largest measured 25.5 feet by 21.5 feet in plan, was 11.5 feet high, and weighed over 32 tons. Stiffened by brackets made of steel angles and strengthened by I-beams, the sides and roofs of the caissons were built up of light steel plates, and the bottoms were left open. Within the working chambers air locks allowed a faster, more efficient, and less hazardous removal of spoil—*muck*, in engineering argot. A special wagon and team brought the prefabricated caissons through the downtown streets to the site.

Operations began with compressed air being forced into the airtight enclosure at the top of the box to counteract the water pressure while the workmen excavated material inside the working chamber. As the excavation was carried to greater depth, the masons built up brick footings on top of the caisson, increasing the weight of the masonry and forcing the cutting edge of the caisson deeper into the soil. When the edge reached bedrock—or hardpan, as was later determined to be the case of the Manhattan Life—the surface was leveled for tight bearing, and the caisson was then filled solidly with concrete.[43] A brick pier was then laid up on top of the concrete, carrying in turn a granite cap and a cast-steel shoe (Fig. 7.23). The height of the pier added to the depth of the caisson brought the top of the pier to minus 32 feet, which was the bottom of the excavation and also the level of the subbasement floor. There were three caissons along each column line, one for the shoe to carry the fulcrum of the party-wall cantilever, one for the interior or intermediate column, and one of almost double width for the second interior column plus the fulcrum for the cantilever of the opposite party wall. The editors of the *American Architect* raised questions about the structural soundness of the technique, but Sooysmith defended it.[44] As for the safety of the workers, although the pressure was much lower, there was no evidence of caisson disease—the bends—as had occurred in the construction of the Eads and Brooklyn bridges.

The cantilever girders at the basement floor level had been adopted for two reasons: because the peripheral columns of Manhattan Life's frame were too close to the walls of the adjacent buildings to be put in place, and because any position between the inner and the peripheral columns would have placed an eccentric load on the brick foundation

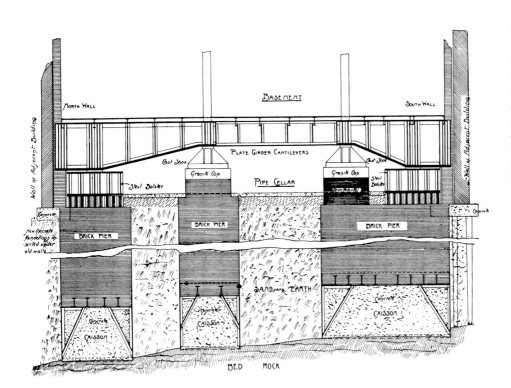

7.23
Transverse section through foundation showing brick and concrete caisson piers, Manhattan Life Building.
After A History of Real Estate, Building and Architecture in New York City.

pier. The weight of the light curtain side walls of the skeleton frame was therefore transmitted to the inner piers by the massive cantilever girder.

The frame of the Manhattan Life Building was steel-skeleton construction with two exceptions: the front wall on Broadway, which was bearing masonry that carried only its own weight, as in cage construction, and the primary columns, which were cast iron to the sixth floor. The wind bracing comprised angle-iron knee braces between the columns and, above the fifth floor, spandrel girders; longitudinal trusses at the fourteenth floor carried offset columns for the three floors above because of changes in the outline of those upper floors. There were additional trusses in the seventeenth story to take the load of the 100-foot tower and to distribute the weight and wind loads in the columns over the frame below. The tower and dome frame comprised ribs and supporting columns of open-web or lattice-web box forms, and the same was true of the peripheral girders disposed to lie along the oval plan of the tower. The sixth-floor rotunda was vaulted, using the extremely strong thin-shell, laminated tile vault system introduced in this country in the 1880s by Rafael Guastavino, and Guastavino tile arches between steel beams carried the basement floor. Elsewhere floor construction comprised the usual hollow-brick arches spanning between steel beams.[45]

The building's electric light and power plant, said to be the most efficient available, was designed to support about 3,500 lights, four engines and four dynamos, and all the elevators and pumps were electrically powered. The extensive wiring required was "ingeniously" concealed from view, yet every inch of it was accessible if repairs should be needed. Electric blower fans generated the building's ventilation system, which aired the cellar directly and caused stale air in the offices above to be drawn through "hang-down" ceilings into vertical shafts that led to large exhaust fans on the roof. Simultaneously, fresh air entered each room via sash ventilators; in cold weather, this air supply was automatically warmed because it passed directly over the radiators.[46]

The Manhattan Life's architectural design was criticized for unclear tripartite division, specifically the base, which could be read as either two or seven stories, and the shaft, which was divided into two parts. Schuyler believed that in departing from the tripartite scheme the building lacked "the unity in variety that comes from an assemblage of related and independent parts."[47] Examination of a longitudinal section drawing of the building reveals that the vaulted ceilings of the company's and director's rooms corresponded to the horizontal division above the seventh floor (Fig. 7.24). Moreover, this floor culminated the company-occupied floors, which were the lower seven; it appears that Kimball was attempting to distinguish those from the upper, rental floors. Above the fourteenth floor, the elevation of the Broadway shaft was active in the flamboyant manner of Kimball's theatre designs, but it was on the whole well composed, and the tower effectively integrated with the main block. The details appear to be derived from the French Renaissance style that Kimball was using at the same time, although with far greater restraint, for the Reading Terminal office building (1891–93) in Philadelphia.

The Broadway front was granite, and terra-cotta was the dominant material of the New Street front. Although the side walls were the usual blank brick, the continuation of moldings from the front around the sides and the presence of the copper-clad iron bridge and gallery over the open court lent some interest to the secondary south elevation. But whatever its faults may have been, the building certainly proclaimed to an extravagant

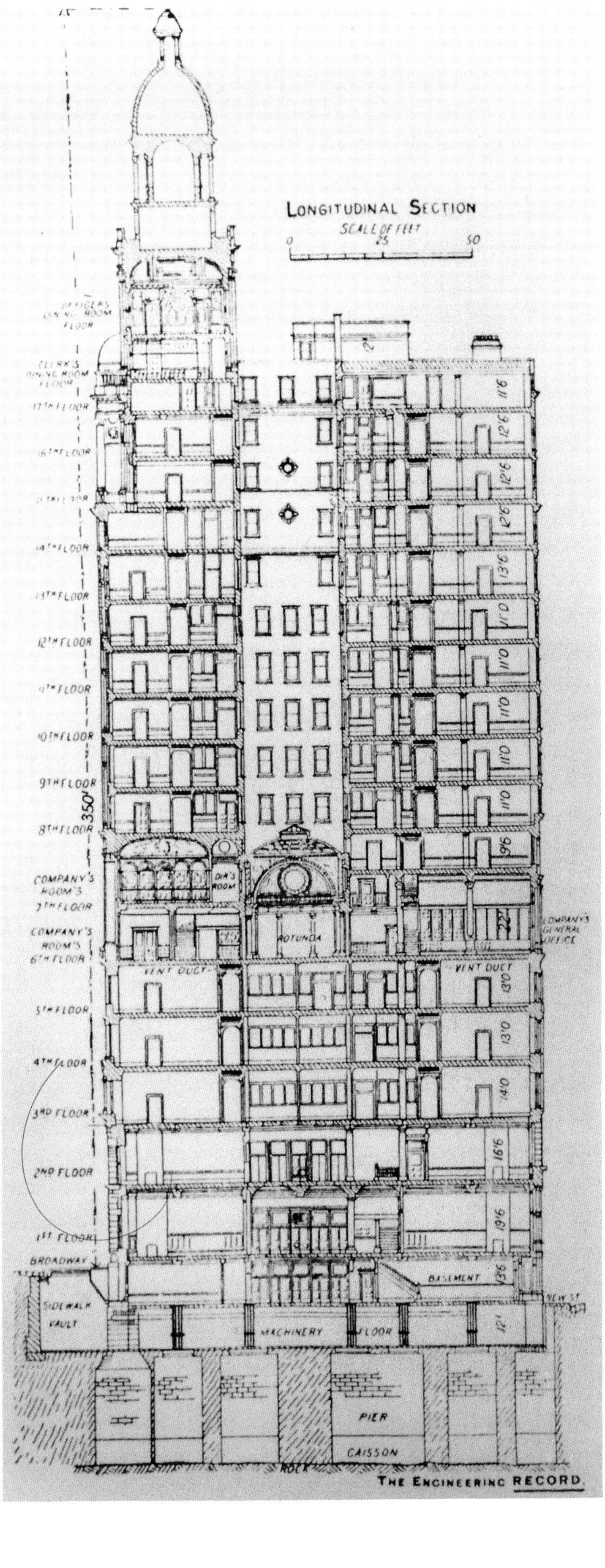

LONGITUDINAL SECTION

SCALE OF FEET
0   25   50

OFFICERS DINING ROOM FLOOR

CLERK'S DINING ROOM FLOOR

12TH FLOOR

16TH FLOOR

15TH FLOOR

14TH FLOOR

13TH FLOOR

12TH FLOOR

11TH FLOOR

10TH FLOOR

9TH FLOOR

8TH FLOOR

COMPANY'S ROOMS 7TH FLOOR

COMPANY'S ROOMS 6TH FLOOR

5TH FLOOR

4TH FLOOR

3RD FLOOR

2ND FLOOR

1ST FLOOR

BROADWAY

SIDEWALK VAULT

350'

VENT DUCT

VENT DUCT

DIR'S ROOM

ROTUNDA

COMPANY'S GENERAL OFFICE

BASEMENT

MACHINERY FLOOR

NEW ST.

PIER

CAISSON

ROCK

THE ENGINEERING RECORD

7.24
*Longitudinal section,
Manhattan Life
Building.
After* Engineering
Record *(1894).*

degree the authority and importance claimed by the insurance company in its own right and in its urban image. In 1903–4, the company having acquired a lot on the north side, the main shaft and tower were widened by two bays; the new frame was spliced to the old, with Kimball as architect (see Fig. 7.3).[48]

In contrast, New York Life's new steel-framed headquarters (1894–96; 1896–98) projects a conservative image (cf. Figs. 7.25 and 7.20). The building's style resulted chiefly from the company's initial plan to add to its old five-story quarters a new thirteen-story structure that would extend to Elm (now Lafayette) Street on property the company had over the years acquired for the purpose. With that end in mind, the company in 1893 invited Stephen D. Hatch; McKim, Mead & White; George B. Post; Babb, Cook & Willard; and Daniel H. Burnham of Chicago to submit plans for the addition. Hatch won the commission with a rather retardataire design that complemented the Italianate style of the original building (cf. Fig. 4.12).[49] Construction had been under way for several months when in August 1894 Hatch suddenly died. New York Life retained McKim, Mead & White, which, aside from some minor changes in the design, completed the stone-, marble-, and brick-clad addition according to Hatch's design.

In the meantime, New York Life decided to replace its old building with one that would provide additional space and a more stylish image. The young Henry Bacon, then working for McKim, Mead & White and later to achieve fame as the architect of the Lincoln Memorial in Washington, was the designer. The new building continues the exterior design of Hatch's addition and merges with it imperceptibly, but in the pavilion fronting on Broadway, Hatch's Italianate is transformed into the fashionable neo-Renaissance style that McKim, Mead & White had introduced and on which its reputation as an innovative firm in part rests. In contrast to the relentlessly layered, 400-foot-long side elevations, the twelve-story pavilion features a more distinct tripartite scheme, and the giant Ionic order at the entrance contributes breadth to the 60-foot width of the front. A clock tower, surmounted by Atlantes supporting an open globe topped by an eagle, consummated the pavilion in a appropriately civic and cosmopolitan manner. The image of stability, longevity, and worldwide standing, the New York Life Building was at once reactionary and in step with the style trend of its time.[50]

Twenty Stories and Up: American Tract Society and American Surety Buildings

By mid-decade the New York skyscraper had pushed past the twenty-story mark, with the architect R. H. Robertson in the ascendant. Chicago had already achieved this feat. Burnham & Root's Masonic Temple (1891–92) held the record at twenty-two stories, or 302 feet, but a city ordinance in 1893 limited building height to 130 feet. By the end of the decade New York surpassed Chicago's tallest skyscrapers. The years 1894 and 1895, affected by a financial panic in 1893, were generally dull for real estate development, but a number of large office buildings were begun nonetheless in 1894. Immediately after Robertson's Corn Exchange Bank was completed, his American Tract Society Building (1894–95) went under construction on the southeast corner of Nassau and Spruce streets (Fig. 7.26; see also Fig. 5.34). With twenty full stories and three more in its arcaded tower, rising 291 feet from sidewalk to tower top, this huge building dwarfed the adjoining Morse Building. It was commissioned by an organization that published and distributed

7.25
*New York Life
Building
(1894–96; 1896–98),
S. D. Hatch and
McKim, Mead &
White, architects.
346 Broadway.
Photograph c. 1900.
Collection of The
New-York Historical
Society.*

nationwide and at foreign mission stations low-cost Bibles, religious books, pamphlets, and periodicals in many languages. The aim of the organization, which directed much of its effort toward recent immigrants, was to preempt sectarian doctrine and propagate a generalized nondenominational Protestantism. The ultimate goal was to create a Christian America that lived according to sound moral principles derived from Scripture and, presumably, common to all the major sects. The income generated from sales was used to aid the poor and to support missionary activities at home and abroad.[51]

The new building, which replaced one on the same site that had been occupied by the society since its founding in 1825, was financed by mortgaging the property. It was built on speculation, with George R. Read, a prominent real estate broker, serving as adviser and agent, in the expectation that its very desirable location—close to the post office and to city and federal offices—would yield the society a substantial endowment from office rentals. Each floor had thirty-six offices, and all told there were approximately seven hundred, which could be let individually or in suites. Real estate lawyers, architects, and dealers in building materials, supplies, and fittings were targeted as potential tenants, and by early 1896 the Department of Public Works had taken the entire seventeenth floor, as well as space on the ground floor and in the basement.[52] The success of the enterprise is physically embodied in this huge New York building, which powerfully represented the association of money with popular religion in the United States.

Appearing towerlike due to its roughly square ground dimensions of about 100 by 94 feet, the building in plan is a slightly irregular parallelogram, with wings forming a deeply indented U-shaped light court (Fig. 7.27). A peculiarity is the arrangement of the building's six Otis hydraulic elevators in a wide arc at the inner corner of the longer wing; this was the only place where the Society allowed Robertson to be generous with space.

7.26
*American Tract Society Building (1894–95),
R. H. Robertson, architect.
Southeast corner Nassau and Spruce streets.
After* American Architect and Building News *(1894).*

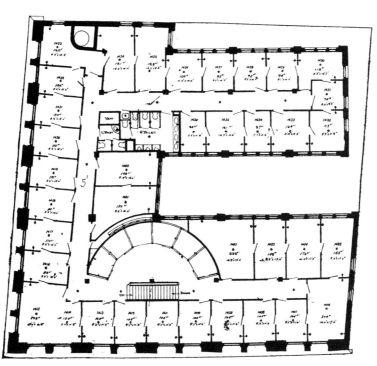

NASSAU STREET

7.27
Typical floor plan, American Tract Society Building. After Birkmire, Planning and Construction of High Office Buildings.

Elsewhere the public areas are narrow, tunnel-like corridors that lie along the central axes of the main block and wings. Structurally, the building is a steel skeleton with footings on piling driven to firm sand at minus 36 feet; bedrock here is below minus 100 feet. The piles are capped by a continuous raft of concrete topped by granite slabs that carry stepped footings. An unusual feature of the frame is that the cantilevers that carry peripheral columns along the party walls are inverted triangular trusses. In other aspects the construction was typical of the period. There is no record of any bracing, and the massive masonry envelope probably made it unnecessary.[53]

From the beginning the formal design was controversial, with detractors objecting to the breaking up of the street elevations into six horizontal divisions and to the considerable diversity of treatment from top to bottom. Again, the divisions appear to correspond to the 50-foot segments of the curtain wall as specified in the building code, but without question the design also affirms the architect's preference for a layered, horizontal appearance in contrast with Sullivan's soaring verticality. It is also worth recalling that horizontal divisions were common in large Gothic cathedrals—most conspicuously Notre Dame in Paris—and so, of course, were towers. The intention may have been to symbolize the religious interests of the American Tract Society; certainly the winged-victory caryatids that originally supported orbs at the corners of the navelike tower presented a celestial image, albeit a compromise with the pagan classical. That compromise is also evident in the overall styling of the gray granite and buff-colored brick facades. Schuyler criticized the layered design, finding it inconsistent with the underlying steel construction. Barr Ferree was harsh: "There is no structural significance in the design—simply a using up of space, and a fear of long, uninterrupted lines."[54] Despite what Ferree says, however, there is sufficent design unity so that the facades do not suggest six separate and discordant buildings. One of the few favorable comments came early on from *Engineering News*, which admired the "pleasing" appearance achieved by "breaking up the surface by bold belt lines and by a bold treatment of details."[55] Today, though deserted by its flamboyant neighbors, the Tribune and World Buildings, and challenged by the enlarged Times Building, the American Tract still reigns as the flagship of its fleet of early skyscrapers.

The religious purpose underlying the construction of the American Tract Society Building did not preserve it from calamities. Two similar elevator accidents occurred within a year of each other, both when controls failed. The first, a free-fall over a number of stories on 14 November 1896, resulted in damage but no casualties. The second, on 10 September 1897, was much worse. The elevator car stalled on its rise between the first and second floors because the safety clutches were engaged. The night engineer took over from the elevator boy and released the clutches, whereupon the car rose to the nineteenth floor but then suddenly dropped to the bottom of the shaft, killing both occupants when the compressed air under the car failed to form an adequate cushion. The coroner's jury blamed the deaths on the release of the safety clutches together with a failure to operate the valves that should have regulated the outflow of water from the master cylinder; as a result, the car rose fast to the top and then fell free. No blame was fixed, but the jury emphasized the need to have a competent engineer for maintenance and the emergency operation of high-speed elevators.[56] Such accidents underscored the necessity of employing highly trained technical personnel in the maintenance of big office buildings, as well as in their design and construction. Indeed, though elevator accidents of this kind no longer occur, the technical problems of high-rise buildings—notably fire and collapses of structural elements—have never been completely solved.

Meanwhile, one of the city's finest early skyscrapers was completed: the American Surety Building (1894–96; Fig. 7.28; see also Figs. 7.20 and 8.11). Recognized as the classic realization of the three-part composition and as the first of the city's isolated towers, it was characterized as "a highly successful application of Greek detail to a modern office building" and as the first of the city's pure, "simplified" skyscrapers—an honor often claimed for the later Broadway Chambers Building.[57] Organized in 1884, the fast-growing bond insurance company that commissioned the building conducted an invited competition in 1893. A fifteen- to twenty-story building was projected, to be about 85 feet square and 300 feet high and to rise on a site at the southeast corner of Broadway and Pine Street that was approximately 85 feet wide by 100 feet deep. The nine competitors—among them such accomplished architects as Carrère & Hastings; Napoleon LeBrun & Sons; McKim, Mead & White; and George Post—were said to have been stimulated by the opportunity to design a tower. Their priorities were first to plan the building so as to give "the greatest possible amount of renting area . . . on each floor, and then to give an outward form in keeping with the importance and height of the structure."[58]

Bruce Price won the competition with a design derived from his earlier Sun Building project. It was the simplest and severest scheme of all those submitted, and apparently also exceptional in having a flat roof. Because of the high cost of the site—reportedly $1,435,000, or $198.62 per square foot, considerably more than Manhattan Life's $157.02—and the estimated $1,250,000 cost of construction, the building had to be sufficiently tall if it was to be cost-effective. When completed, it had twenty-one stories, the twenty-first having been included in a late revision, and Price later said that he had wanted a tall, pyramidal roof capping five more stories. Apparently it was he who convinced the client that the building's visibility from all sides required four designed facades, which increased the cost considerably.[59]

The American Surety Building is of steel-skeleton construction, and its street walls are curtain walls. From the first to the eighth floor, the east and south walls were bearing-brick; above that, they were curtain walls. As completed, the building rose to a height of 312 feet, although some sources give 308 feet. Its granite sheath provides a powerful demonstration of the great advantages in weight and open interior area offered by the curtain wall compared with bearing-wall construction. As Birkmire pointed out, for a building of this size a maximum bearing-wall thickness of 84 inches would have been required, with a consequent weight on the foundation of 150,000 pounds per linear foot. As built, with the maximum curtain-wall thickness of 32 inches at the base as specified in the 1892 code, the weight was only 80,000 pounds per linear foot. And if the maximum thickness were reduced to 16 inches, which Birkmire recommended, the weight would have been reduced to 54,000 pounds per linear foot.[60] The gain in rentable area between the 32-inch and the 84-inch wall for the typical twenty-foot-wide bay was close to 87 square feet, which might have been worth as much as $2,000 per bay per year in rents along Broadway. The cost of the foundation was also greatly reduced, though that reduction was partly offset by the increased cost of steel over masonry.

The column footings and foundation piers were sunk by pneumatic caissons to bed-

AMERICAN SURETY BUILDING.

rock at minus 71 feet (some sources give minus 79 feet). From the bedrock up, the foundation structure consisted of concrete-filled caissons, brick piers, a two-way steel grillage, a course of 4-inch-square steel billets, and column base plates that receive the lower ends of the columns (see Figs. 7.29 and 7.30). The intention was to spread the high, concentrated column loads over the broad area of the brick pier tops. The outermost line of columns along the wall contiguous to the adjacent building rested on the ends of massive cantilevers supported at fulcrum points by similar grillage and billets but more than double in width.[61] The foundations and substructure took eight or nine months to complete, at least 40 percent of the total twenty-month construction period.

The wind bracing was of portal construction with triangular gusset plates at the column-girder connections and full double-diagonal rods in some bays (Fig. 7.30). In January of 1896, five months before the building was officially completed, it was subject to a wind of 82 miles per hour; tests made with a transit and level showed no evidence of oscillation or wind drift.[62] In the interests of fire protection, all columns, girders, and beams were covered with 3.5-inch fireproof tile, and the floor arches between the 15-foot I-beams were composed of 10-inch-thick firebrick. The floors comprised brick arches, concrete with ash aggregate (for lightness and porosity), and 4-inch steel joists; the finish-flooring was marble. Granite sheathed the exterior; the south wall, adjacent to the 110-foot-high Schermerhorn Building, was solid brick, 4 feet thick, up to a height of 100 feet to block any fire that might issue from its neighbor. Each floor was supplied with a fire-hose, and water was supplied by two tanks with a combined capacity of 50,000 gallons, one on the tenth floor, the other on the twenty-first, which was entirely given over to utilities. Throughout, this was a high-quality, high-cost, high-prestige building.

The American Surety represented the column-skyscraper at its pinnacle. Some observers, however, claimed to recognize the spirit of Chicago in its tripartite design. The building was remarkably well proportioned, its height approaching four times its width, and its shaft was articulated only by rows of windows and projecting horizontal courses of granite. As explained by Price, "The idea is a campanile with four pilaster faces, the seven flutes being represented by seven rows of windows." Price also described a novel feature: the windows were progressively recessed behind the plane of the wall, one inch per story, to a maximum depth of 20 inches.[63] The recession accomplished two purposes: architecturally it took advantage of the curtain-wall code dimensions to impart the illusion of entasis appropriate to the column image; functionally it admitted light most readily where light was less plentiful, at the lower stories, where the windows were placed closest to the plane of the wall. Although the resulting screenlike appearance of the shaft may not have expressed the underlying steel construction, it certainly suggested the nonsupporting nature of the curtain wall. The main entrance, on Broadway, is heralded by a two-story-high Ionic colonnade that supports a one-story "porch," inspired by the famous Porch of the Maidens of the Erechtheum on the Athenian Acropolis and embellished by six caryatidlike figures that symbolized such reassuring virtues as Fidelity, Fortitude, and Surety. A competition was held in 1894 for their design, and the fine classical figures created by the winner, John Massey Rhind, contribute greatly to the character of this handsome building.[64]

In October of 1895 a suit brought against the American Surety Company charged that the cornice on the south side of the building projected over the Schermerhorn Building

7.29

Principal elevation, American Surety Building.
Drawing shows the caisson piers supporting the columns and the cantilever girder that carries extreme right-hand line of columns.
After Scientific American *(1894).*

7.30

Longitudinal section showing frame and foundations, American Surety Building.
After Engineering Record *(1896).*

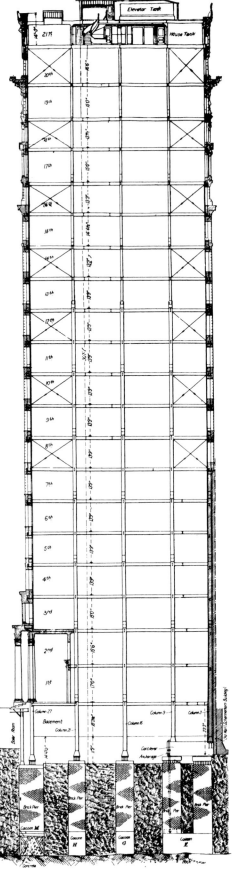

next door, obstructing its light and air. The Astors, who owned the Schermerhorn, at one point threatened to build a twenty-two-story skyscraper on their site that would in turn usurp the American Surety's light and air. The matter was resolved when the American Surety leased the Schermerhorn property for ninety-nine years at $75,000 a year.[65] This was an early instance of legal complications arising from building at excessive density, and it demonstrated the need for some kind of control. In this pre–zoning law era, the only means of protecting one's light and air were to purchase or lease adjacent lots or voluntarily leave open part of the site. The clearance provided by several low buildings on Pine Street was hardly enough to ensure such protection to the American Surety Building, which by 1903 would be confronted on that side by the twenty-two-story Hanover National Bank Building (1901–3; architect: James B. Baker). Narrow Pine Street proved to be no protection at all from the enormous bulk of the second Equitable Life Building completed in 1915.

In 1921, as if attempting to regain its former dominance, the American Surety Company widened its building by four window bays on the Broadway and Pine Street sides, taking in the Schermerhorn site, and also increased the number of stories to twenty-six, raising the height to 338 feet by the addition of another layer. The architect Herman Lee Meader skillfully performed this feat, using what buildings department records describe as "reerected old windows," presumably taken from the rear of the building. The enlargement is perceptible only if one is aware of the stoutened proportions of the building. The Ionic colonnade at the entrance was lengthened by two columns, and the maiden porch above was extended to include two more figures—perhaps also taken from another part of the building—that perfectly complement the originals. The relief sculpture at the level of the capital was similarly augmented. In 1975, the Bank of Tokyo altered the ground-floor entrance to incorporate a glass-fronted arcade—fortunately, without obscuring the portico.[66] Regrettably, the original windows have been replaced by windows set flush with the exterior walls.

The twenty-plus-story, skeleton-framed skyscraper was firmly established in New York City with the completion of the American Tract and American Surety buildings. Alarmed by the prospect of such buildings lining the streets of lower Manhattan, professionals and laymen alike worried that these streets would be unsanitary and unsafe. The skyscraper builders, however, were undaunted by such fears and reacted by extending their reach still higher.

THE
SYNDICATE-BUILT
SKYSCRAPER,
TECHNICAL ADVANCES,
CONTINUING DEBATE,
1895–1900

Interest in skyscraper building was undiminished in the year 1895, although some construction planned in that year seems to have been delayed by the vestigial financial depression. By this time, the skeleton frame was ubiquitous, but efforts continued toward improving that technology and others that affected the efficiency, safety, and cost of skyscrapers. As far as the real estate speculator was concerned, the skyscraper had no limit. On the first day of July a permit was granted to Henry Osborne Havemeyer for the construction of one twenty-six stories high. Completed three years later, this would be the St. Paul, one of many speculatively built office buildings that were constructed in the second half of the decade. Often these investment skyscrapers were anonymously financed by individuals or companies—or by syndicates formed for the purpose. At least two such syndicate-built structures were actually known by the name Syndicate Building. Although the speculatively built high-rise building was by no means a new phenomenon, so many colossal and/or striking examples were undertaken in the second half of the 1890s as to eclipse, at least for a time, the corporation-built skyscraper.

Lord's Court (1895–96), for example, still standing on the southwest corner of the intersection of William Street and Exchange Place, was built as an investment skyscraper by the civil engineer, architect, and capitalist John Townsend Williams, who served as his own architect and contractor. William Birkmire was his collaborator on this project and also on the Central Bank Building begun a year later. Today Lord's Court fades into its skyscraper background, but in 1896 this fifteen-story steel-framed office building must have seemed an overwhelming presence in the financial district. Although not especially distinguished architecturally, its rather plain facades adhere to the standard tripartite

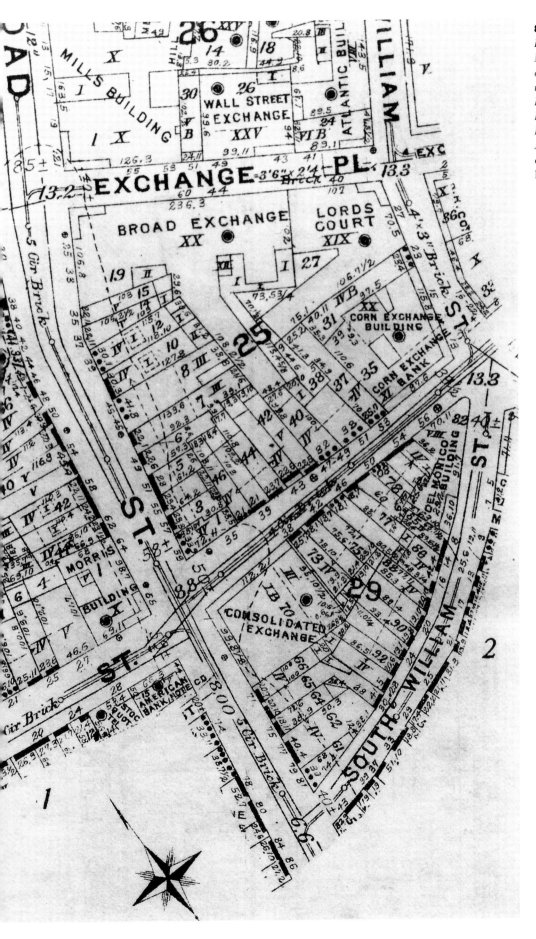

8.1
Block 25, lower Manhattan, showing dense build-up and unusual plans of Lord's Court, Broad-Exchange, and Corn Exchange buildings. After Miniature Atlas of the Borough of Manhattan *(1912).*

8.2

*St. Paul Building
(1895–98; de-
molished),
G. B. Post, architect.
At left across Ann
Street: Park Row
Building
(1896–99);
at right:
National Park Bank
(1867–68; de-
molished).
Collection of The
New-York Historical
Society.*

composition, materials, and monochromatic color scheme of the period. Above a light-colored granite base, the walls are pale brick with window surrounds and ornamentation in a matching, light-colored terra-cotta. The building's peculiar doglegged plan, however, is unusually irregular, even for lower Manhattan, where oddly shaped plans were and still are the norm (Fig. 8.1).[1]

Artful Investments: The St. Paul Building and Bowling Green Offices

Of greater architectural interest, the St. Paul Building at the juncture of Broadway, Park Row, and Ann Street (1895–98) was the tallest skyscraper yet built (Fig. 8.2). Designed by George B. Post and named after the historic St. Paul's Chapel just across Broadway, it rose to a height of 315 feet, with no cupolas, pointed roofs, or flagpoles added on to swell that number. Including the topmost utility floor on the main block, it was twenty-six stories high. Because it was commissioned by the brother of the builder of the Havemeyer Building, the choice of Post as architect comes as no surprise. In February of 1895, preparatory to construction, the site was cleared of the old New York Herald Building, but work on the foundations of the new building began only in July. The steelwork for its modified skeleton construction was supplied by J. B. & J. M. Cornell, and Post apparently served as his own engineer. For the foundations, however, a consulting engineer was called in, likely employed by the general contractor, Robinson & Wallace. Sculptor Karl Bitter was responsible for the four atlantes above the main entrance, on Broadway.

In order to lay a steel grillage-type foundation on a site where bedrock exists at minus 86.5 feet, the excavation was carried to sand at minus 31.5 feet, which was to be the underside of the subbasement floor.[2] The initial plan for founding the southern wall, expected to be a party wall, was to insert hydraulic jacks under the column base plates to lift the columns, then insert plates, should it become necessary, to counteract unequal or excessive settlement arising from contiguous high buildings. The technique had been used in the construction of the Eiffel Tower. But this costly and time-consuming "movable foundation" was abandoned in favor of cantilevers when the neighboring property owner decided not to build.

The St. Paul Building's steel frame introduced an unusual variation on skeleton construction. Box columns were placed well inside the inner pier faces; the masonry and window area of each bay was supported on a parallel channel and an I-beam that was carried in turn by the projecting or cantilevered ends of the floor girders. The technique was adopted for several reasons: to facilitate the inspection and replacement of corroded steelwork (Post's persistent concern), to avoid the transmission of moisture through the wall to the primary steel framing members, and to prevent heat from fire in adjacent buildings from raising the temperature of the framing members to the danger point. Wind bracing was achieved by portal-arch bracing and knee bracing in the form of solid triangular gusset plates at the projecting ends of the beams (Fig. 8.3).[3] There was a special problem in framing the canted corners where all the column and girder lines through the depth of one bay had to turn through a 45-degree angle (Fig. 8.4).

The plumbing and elevator systems were designed for the utmost efficiency. The elaborate plumbing systems required by tall buildings were continually being modified to accommodate greater heights and meet ever more exacting requirements. In the Manhat-

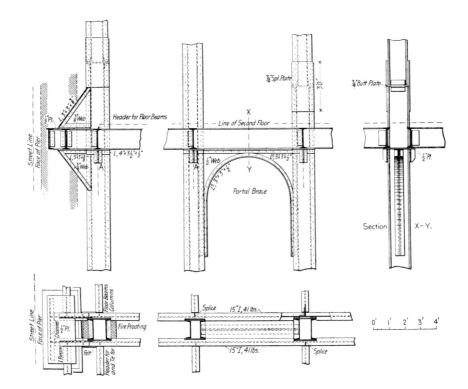

8.3

Forms of wind bracing, St. Paul Building. After Engineering News *(1896).*

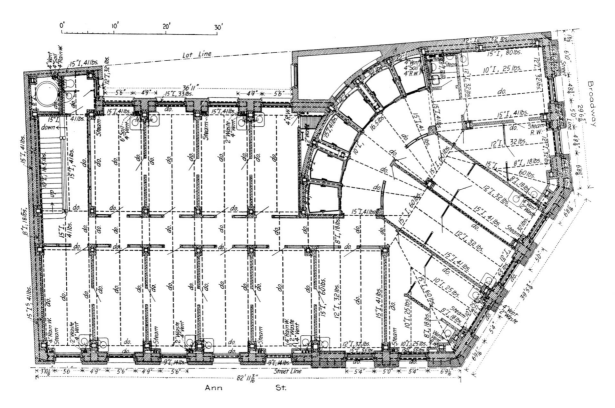

8.4

Typical floor plan, St. Paul Building. After Engineering News *(1896).*

tan Life and American Surety buildings, auxiliary intermediate supply tanks had been installed midway between the roof and the street as a means of reducing the maximum water pressure. The St. Paul's system was designed to accept the highest pressure with only a single high-pressure water tank, which was housed on the twenty-sixth floor. To accommodate the maximum pressure head produced by this tank, about 333 feet—equal to the highest possible pressure of about 156 pounds on the lowest point of the connected system—extra-heavy pipe was used throughout; high-grade valves, cocks, and associated items were specified; and valve openings were throttled so as to diminish the discharge pressure at the fixtures.[4] Six high-pressure hydraulic elevators arranged in a quadrant circle were deployed so that two made stops to the eighth story, two ran express to the eighth and from there made stops up to the sixteenth, and the remaining two ran direct to the sixteenth floor and served all the floors above.

To a relentless degree the St. Paul belonged to the horizontal mode of skyscraper design, with some variation among the divisions and an overall adherence to a tripartite organization of stories. The Indiana limestone–faced main block was treated as a relatively slender five-sided tower comprising a four-story base, a sixteen-story shaft layered as eight two-story segments bounded by strong belt courses, a transitional story beneath a massive cornice-like belt, and a five-story capital that introduced a vertical accent via engaged columns and relief-carved corner piers. Except on the undeveloped south side of the building, the fifth story of the capital was hidden from view by the crowning parapet. The five-bay rear portion of the building was twenty-two stories high and set back about twenty feet at the nineteenth story on the Ann Street side. On that side, the building gave the appearance of a mounted tower, anticipating—even if modestly—the Woolworth Building and the setbacks mandated by the 1916 zoning law (Fig. 8.5).[5]

Critics were merciless, one journal calling it "perhaps the least attractive in design of all New York's skyscrapers."[6] The layering of the shaft drew Schuyler's criticism on the ground that the natural similarity of its stories was denied by this treatment. In an attempt at justification, Weisman suggested that Post was probably looking for a rectangular unit with suitable proportions to organize and unify each of the three disparate street elevations (seven bays on Ann Street, three on Park Row, two on Broadway). It should also be pointed out that any planning or formal solution would have been hampered by the irregular pentagonal lot and the need to use every inch of a restricted site. But regardless of these difficulties, Post's neoclassical solution certainly complemented the pilastraded and columned facades of City Hall, the nearby Post Office, and the adjacent National Park Bank. In turn, the layered and columned American Telephone and Telegraph Building later erected across Broadway responded to the delicacy and elaboration of the St. Paul's Roman Composite order, asserting instead the strength and purity of the Greek Ionic.

Ironically, Post was the architect who had done the most to organize opposition to skyscrapers of unlimited height. Noting that the St. Paul had given him "the occasion to say 'I told you so' at his own expense," the *Record and Guide* paid tribute to "the public spirit of the architect who urges that he shall be cut off from one of the most tempting avenues of professional employment." The same source pointed out that Post was fortunate in having the "unobstructed outlook" of St. Paul's churchyard; observing that the construction of so high a building on an ordinary street would abrogate the

8.5

*Lower New York and
Bay, looking south
from Woolworth
Building with St. Paul
Building in left
foreground.
After New York
Illustrated (1914).*

ability of adjacent property owners to realize the value of their own investments, it urged that "some limitations upon private greed [be] imposed by public authority."[7] The twenty-foot setback and the lower height of the rear portion of the building, features that reduced the loss of light and air on the narrow Ann Street side, apparently went unnoticed.

The almost exactly contemporary Bowling Green Offices at 5–11 Broadway (1895–98) stands out as a major work of the period in both design and size (Fig. 8.6; see also Fig. 5.11). Perhaps because it was completed in a boom building period or because its "Hellenic Renaissance" style was considered so peculiar, it received only scant notice in the professional press. The builder was the Broadway Realty Company, formed for the purpose of constructing and managing the building. The New York investment banker Spencer Trask, who for some years would maintain a special suite on the top floor, was that company's president and largest stockholder.

The architect was the Scottish-born George Ashdown Audsley, working in association with his older brother William James Audsley under the firm name W. & G. Audsley. This

firm is not known to have designed other skyscrapers or even other office buildings, but, rather, produced churches, synagogues, and an American art museum. The Audsleys, who had practiced first in Liverpool and then in London, were also leading organ builders and had published numerous pattern and ornament books. Aside from Bowling Green Offices, their best-known American work is the Layton Art Gallery in Milwaukee (1885–88; demolished 1957), commissioned by the English-born Milwaukee meat packer Frederick Layton.[8] A local architect supervised construction of the art gallery, and

8.6
Bowling Green Offices (1895–98),
W. & G. Audsley,
architects.
5–11 Broadway.
After Real Estate Record and Builders' Guide *(1898).*

Syndicates, Technical Advances, Debate 243

G. A. Audsley settled in America only in 1892, when his firm's New York office opened. Just how he got the Bowling Green Offices commission has not come to light, but the connection may have been through Trask's principal partner, George Foster Peabody.[9] Intentional or not, the choice of a British architect to design a monumental building that overlooks, and is named for, Bowling Green—the historic site where in 1776 rebels toppled and mutilated a statue of King George III—seems an act of reconcilation.

Noting with approval that all the main lines of the Bowling Green Offices building are vertical, one source observed that its English architects planned to "abandon the effort, hallowed though it is from time immemorial, to conceal height"; and, as was done in Chicago, would "boldly admit and even . . . accentuate height."[10] G. A. Audsley, in fact, adhered to Sullivan's aesthetic ideals. Quoting at some length from Sullivan's "The Tall Building Artistically Considered" in an article on the design of tall office buildings, Audsley emphasized the importance of considering the points of view from which such a building would be seen as well as the proportion of its height to the width of the street. He stressed the need to "judiciously" and "sparingly" apply ornament to the structural features. Further, he criticized the fashion for treating the lower division as "simply a base or pedestal to the upper stories," especially when realized in "intensely vulgar, rock-faced, cyclopean masonry," maintaining that this section of the building should be "refined and beautiful" and treated "in perfect accord with the main lines and general vertical feeling of the design." Moreover, Audsley advised, "sculpture should be within easy range of the eye . . . and used sparely in the high portions," which are farthest from view. In order to achieve the proper effect, the architect should "prepare silhouettes of the portion which rises above the surrounding buildings."[11]

Constructed with a steel skeleton and built to a height of seventeen stories, Bowling Green Offices is impressively broad in its proportions. On Broadway the building rose to a height of 235 feet, and on that side it is 162 feet wide. On Greenwich Street it is 152 feet wide, and its depth averages about 190 feet. Its plan forms an irregular U-shape with an unusually large light court, measuring about 110 by 60 feet, and open above the first floor (Fig. 8.7). The rental brochure boasted that this court, together with that of the adjacent Washington Building to the south, formed the largest light court of any office building in the city.[12] Just as Audsley prescribed, the horizontal design element is apparent in the rows of windows lighting the stories of the white brick-clad shaft but is subordinate to the vertical element, which dominates by means of projecting bays articulated by tall piers at either end of the Broadway facade.

The crisply incised Grecian ornament concentrated at the building's smooth white granite base and its white terra-cotta capital looks like a translation in stone of the Greek ornament plates in the Audsleys' ornament books (Fig. 8.8). This ornament, as well as the liberally applied piers and columns and the battered antae of the Broadway entrance porticos, which reminded the *Record and Guide* of Egyptian pylons, call to mind Alexander "Greek" Thomson's work in Glasgow. Thomson's distinctive churches, terrace houses, and commercial buildings, which date from the third quarter of the nineteenth century, undoubtedly inspired the Scottish-born Audsleys. Distinguishing their Hellenic Renaissance from the Neo-Grec—which they characterized as "the common and impure French treatment"—the Audsleys maintained that their style was "free but pure."[13] Too free for the tastes of contemporary critics, who found little that was "pure" about it. Time,

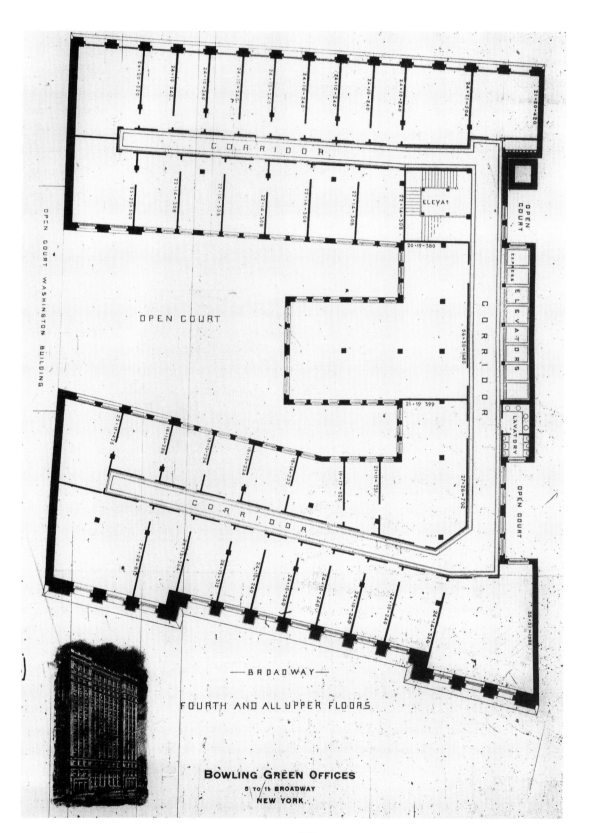

8.7
Plan of fourth and all upper floors, Bowling Green Offices.
After Spencer Trask & Company, Bowling Green Offices *(1896).*
Art and Architecture Collection, Miriam and Ira D. Wallach Division of Art,
Prints and Photographs, the New York Public Library, Astor Lenox and
Tilden Foundations.

8.8

*Detail showing south
entrance, Bowling
Green Offices.
Photograph by
S. B. Landau.*

however, has been good to the Bowling Green Offices building—and alterations, fortunately, discreet. The entrance hall and main corridor retain their fine marble floor and
revetement, and an original stained-glass mural depicting the historic sport of bowling on
the green still graces the corridor.

As for the utilities, the fire-fighting system in particular was advertised in the rental
prospectus as being new and unique, and as having been approved by the New York
Board of Fire Underwriters and "commended" by the chief of the fire department.
Instead of the usual tanks on the roof, a system of standpipes and drums for compressed
air was installed. These could sustain a pressure of 200 pounds per square inch and
would permit a three-quarter-inch-thick stream of water to be projected at the top of the
building for 66 feet at a rate of 160 gallons per minute. If necessary, the drums could be
connected at the street to fire engines, in which case, according to the rental prospectus,
"streams of water sufficient to flood the building in a short time could, at the above
pressure, be distributed at any part of the building."

Selling points noted in the prospectus include a large passenger-and-freight elevator
under the staircase on the Greenwich Street side. Said to be capable of lifting 7,000
pounds—clearly an advantage for any shipping concerns that might be based in the

building—this elevator supplemented the eight passenger elevators that were concentrated at the center of the northern edge of the building. The sashes of the large office windows could be swung open, and access to direct natural light (and fresh air) was said to be so good that artificial lighting would not be needed on sunny days. The building apparently did not have its own electric power plant; the rental brochure states that it was to be connected directly to the mains of the Edison Electric Illuminating Company. Heating, lighting, and janitor service were offered free to prospective tenants, and a particular advantage was the easy accessibility of public transportation: the Battery Place station of the elevated railroad behind the building on Greenwich Street, the Broadway Cable Lines, and the forthcoming subway station. The subway had been in the planning stage for several years, and in 1900 construction would begin.

Bowling Green Offices was completed in two phases, with the Broadway section ready for occupancy by mid-1896. On that side of the building, two entrances (in addition to the main entrance at the north end) permit private access to large sections of the ground floor that were designed to serve major tenants. The building's 512 offices were rented to concerns related to steamship lines and shipping interests, to lawyers—seemingly in unlimited supply—and to financial and industrial companies. In 1920 the building's height was increased, but fortunately the additions are not obtrusive.[14]

Efficiency and Early Obsolescence: Central Bank and Gillender Buildings

The Central National Bank Building, erected on the northeast corner of Broadway and Pearl Street (1896–97), went virtually unnoticed in the architectural and real estate press (Fig. 8.9). Little about it was extraordinary, except perhaps its efficient and highly professional execution, nor did any problems arise that might have made it newsworthy. The building itself gave way to the extension of Federal Plaza, completed in 1976. But thanks to Birkmire, a detailed record of its construction survives. Erected by the largest banking institution in the surrounding dry goods district, the fifteen-story structure replaced an Italianate "palazzo" previously occupied by the bank. The builder of record was the Central Syndicate Building Company, and the architect of record was John T. Williams—although he gets no credit from Birkmire, who, if not the actual designer, participated actively in its construction. Birkmire's account presents evidence that the building took only seven months to construct. Building department records, however, indicate a much longer period.[15]

Every detail of the steel framework was precisely specified, down to the diameter of the rivets, and the contract agreement contained a clause that claimed the right of the owner's representative to inspect the steelwork at the mill during construction and to reject any parts that did not measure up to the requirements. Construction seems to have been standard: a portal-braced steel skeleton that utilized columns of H-section reinforced by plates and angles, hollow-tile encased floor beams of the Kreischer type as patented in 1871–72, and marble-finished floors in the lobby and all public rooms. The five passenger elevators were hydraulic, and the freight elevator was steam powered.[16] Cost may have been a factor in the choice of hydraulic and steam power over electric, but speed, too, was likely a consideration.

By this time functional and utilitarian-mechanical space exceeded 75 percent of the

floor area, which left little opportunity for architectural design. In that respect, the Central Bank Building typified the standards of its time. It was treated as a tripartite tower and featured a giant Doric order that united the second and third stories of the base. Twice as deep as it was wide, the E-shaped building spanned 75 feet on Broadway and 150 on Pearl Street. It incorporated two interior light courts, 350 offices with an average area of 300 square feet, and an 8-foot-wide main corridor (Fig. 8.10). In justification of the style adopted, Birkmire observed that "the conditions and spirit of modernity must necessarily be recognized in the application of a style of such antiquity" to a high-rise commercial structure of the late nineteenth century.[17] He also noted that the Doric order was especially suited both to heavy structures and to the image of a metropolitan national bank. The temple-fronted bank was in fact undergoing a revival at this time.

Almost the exact contemporary of the Central Bank Building, the Gillender Building (1896–97) was an elegantly handsome nineteen-story office building (Fig. 8.11). But looks alone could not save it for posterity. It had perhaps the shortest life span of any skyscraper on record, a mere thirteen years. Charles I. Berg of Berg & (Edward H.) Clark was the architect.[18] The consulting engineer was Henry Post, and the general contractor Charles T. Wills. Wills was a leading New York City builder who began his career by working on the foundation of the Sixth Avenue Elevated Railway and who was also in charge of the construction of the American Surety and Mail and Express buildings, as well as New York Life's new quarters.

A narrow and exuberantly crowned slab, the Gillender filled a tiny site—only about 26 feet wide by 74 feet deep—at the northwest corner of Wall and Nassau streets. Tripartite in facade composition and enriched by a three-tiered "capital," it rose about 273 feet from the curb to the top of the cupola lantern. It was clad in granite at the base, limestone at the shaft, and brick at the upper stories, and trimmed with terra-cotta. On the main, Nassau Street, side, the shaft was articulated by tall arcades that embraced bay windows in the manner of contemporary Chicago skyscrapers. The framing corners of this facade and the narrow-end elevations of the building included windows that opened onto small balconies. The plans were said to have been drawn up and filed in time to evade an expected—but unenacted—law to limit the height of buildings, and construction did not officially begin until four months after the filing. Rising from a pneumatic-caisson foundation, necessary because of the loose, wet sand below it, the Gillender had a wind-braced steel skeleton that included no interior columns. The floor construction incorporated the standard hollow-tile floor arches, and the interior partitions were cement mortar on wire lath, probably supported by a framework of light steel angles.[19]

The Gillender was demolished in 1910, and its site is today still occupied by its replacement, the venerable Bankers Trust Building. By 1909 the land under the Gillender had so appreciated in value that the owner evidently could not resist selling. Indeed, the phenomenal escalation of the property's value since midcentury epitomizes the financial history of Wall Street and the city during that period. In 1849, the property had been purchased at a cost of $55,000 by George Lovett, and a structure known as the Union Building had been erected on the site. By 1896, the value of the land had increased to $625,000, and the owner at that time, Lovett's granddaughter Helena Lovett Gillender, undertook the construction of the Gillender at a cost of $500,000. Less than thirteen years after its completion in 1897, she sold the property to the Manhattan Trust Company,

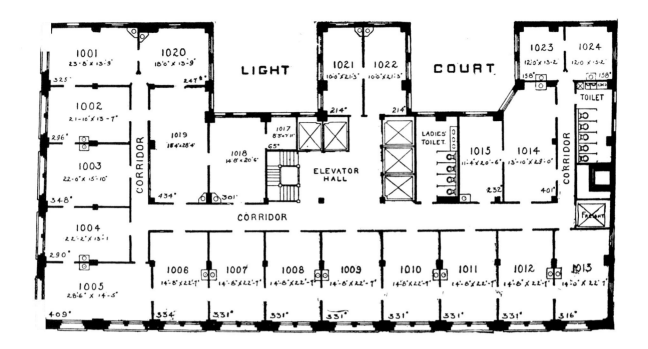

8.10

*Typical floor plan,
Central Bank
Building.
After Birkmire,*
Planning and Construction of High
Office-Buildings.

which had been a primary tenant of the Gillender, for a sum reported as between $600 and $700 per square foot, a record price for New York City. Some sources quote sums of more than $800.[20] The facts are unclear; Manhattan Trust may have acted on behalf of another buyer. In any case, the property wound up in the hands of Adele Livingston Sampson, who owned the adjoining Stevens Building. She leased the entire site, including that of the Stevens Building, to the Bankers Trust Company; Bankers Trust then proceeded to construct a thirty-seven-story skyscraper, probably in association with Manhattan Trust.

So many new and larger skyscrapers were going up at the time of the Gillender's completion that it received relatively little notice when it was constructed, but the demolition of a building so tall and so recently constructed attracted the attention of the engineering press. The wrecking process—which in Imperial Rome had been organized on a systematic basis, into a *collegium*—had become a science by 1910. As protection to pedestrians and traffic, demolition workers constructed a shed comprising massive plank decking and wide walls that were supported by a heavy timber frame of posts and transverse beams; under that, as further protection, heavy steel netting was stretched across the adjoining sidewalks and roadways. The system was much the same as that used today. The Gillender's windows, doors, trim, fittings, pipes, and copper sheathing were removed carefully enough to be salvaged intact, and the walls were taken down in such a way as to preserve the stone, brick, and terra-cotta for reuse. The operation was labor-intensive, with a hundred men on the day shift and forty working at night. Ten trucks were used in the process, but only at night, so as not to encumber the street in daylight hours. The entire process was completed in forty-five days.[21]

The only useful aspect of the Gillender's demolition was that it provided the opportunity for direct inspection of the steelwork, the condition of steel in high buildings of cage or skeleton construction having been a subject of continuing debate since 1890. The

GILLENDER BUILDING

8.11
*Gillender Building
(1896–97; de-
molished),
Berg & Clark,
architects.
American Surety
Building at left and
behind.
After Freitag,* Archi-
tectural Engineering.

Gillender's steel proved to be in an excellent state; it had been protected from oxidation mainly by terra-cotta fireproof cladding and, to a limited degree, by the inferior paint that was applied when it was shipped. The heat of the building had thoroughly dried the cladding, evaporating any moisture that might have caused oxidation. The same was true for the structural steel embedded in concrete and for the reinforcing steel. The only rust on the steel occurred where the outer face of the outer column plate was close to the exterior wall. At those points the porosity of the stone and brick had allowed rainwater to enter. (The code had permitted the column-to-wall distance to be as little as five inches.) Elsewhere, oxidation occurred in the bay-window framework, where the T-bar supports between the sills and the floor were not enclosed in masonry and thus were exposed to intermittent wetting.[22]

A New Record: The Park Row Building

At first known as the Ivins Syndicate Building, or just as the Syndicate Building, the enormous Park Row Building (1896–99) was nearly three years in construction (Figs. 8.12 and 8.13). This formidable, twin-towered office building fills an oddly shaped, octopus-tentacled site bounded by Park Row, Ann Street, and Theatre Alley and hard by the group that makes up the city's earliest skyscraper district. Still a powerful presence at the foot of City Hall Park, the Park Row replaced several low commercial structures and in doing so rudely interrupted the low scale of this part of Newspaper Row. Clearly, had the corner property been available, it would have been included in the site. The builder of record was William Mills Ivins, a prominent lawyer and former judge advocate general for New York State; evidently he headed a syndicate of investors. The architect was R. H. Robertson, and Nathaniel Roberts served as structural engineer. With thirty stories, counting the four within its towers, and reaching a height of 391 feet from curb to lantern tops, this was the tallest building in the world until the Singer Tower was completed in 1908. It cost $2,750,000 to construct, contained between 950 and 1,000 offices, and could accommodate up to four thousand people.[23]

The resources and techniques of experimental and theoretical science were used throughout the Park Row's design and construction. The building is supported by a pile and steel-grillage foundation, for which the excavation was taken down to about the same depth as that of the neighboring St. Paul Building, where subsoil and bedrock conditions are much the same.[24] The Park Row's all-steel skeleton includes open-web lattice floor girders and bracing of the standard portal type comprising lattice girders riveted to the columns through the depth of the web, full double diagonals (probably tie rods), and portal arches that span the light court at various floor levels (Fig. 8.14). The steel specifications were exacting, and sample sections of steel bars manufactured by the Carnegie Steel Company were thoroughly tested for ultimate tensile strength and elastic limit before being accepted.[25]

For purposes of fireproofing, the original specifications for the floors called for either the Roebling concrete-arch system or the hollow-tile arch system. The former, manufactured in Trenton, New Jersey, by John A. Roebling's Sons—the company owned by the Roeblings of Brooklyn Bridge fame—consisted of a stiff perforated rolled-iron or steel sheet curved into a vault form and covered with fire-resistant concrete. Both the architect

8.12
*Park Row Building
(1896–99),
R. H. Robertson,
architect.
15 Park Row.
Photograph c. 1905.
Collection of The
New-York Historical
Society.*

POST OFFICE

ASTOR HOUSE

AM. TRACT SOCIETY BLDG.

PARK ROW BUILDING.

ST. PAUL BUILDING

ST. PAUL CHAPEL

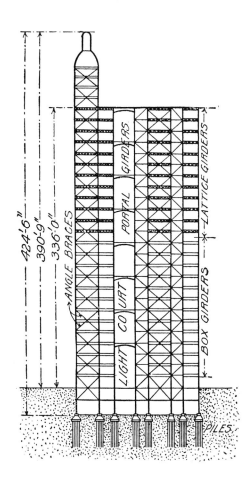

and the engineer of the Park Row preferred the Roebling technique because it cost less and weighed 30 percent less than hollow tile, enough to reduce the load on the piling by 4,500 tons. But New York City is notorious for resisting concrete for large buildings, and for no apparent reason the board of examiners of the Department of Buildings three times refused to accept the Roebling system, thus compelling the use of hollow tile. The owner and the architect, however, went to court and obtained a favorable ruling; the superintendent of buildings finally approved the Roebling system in December of 1897, but only after much tile had already been installed. The ironies then multiplied, for the tile work turned out to be radically defective, and investigation revealed bad workmanship in its handling and placing. Why, then, had it been accepted by the Department of Buildings inspectors? Defective construction of tile arches apparently was common and was accepted because tile work functioned as a protective, rather than a structural or bearing, element. The danger lay in the exposure of the steel framing members. In the Park Row, the worst instance occurred in the tower flooring, where there was a patchwork of broken tile, crude mortaring, and jagged holes. Much had to be redone.[26]

Except for the towers, the Park Row's formal design is rigorously frontal and confined to the 104-foot-wide main facade and the 20-foot-wide Ann Street front. The elevation is vertically divided, with the emphasis on solidity and mass at the corner bays in contrast to the more open central section. Numerous horizontal divisions also mark the front, with the base comprising either two or five stories, depending on how it is perceived, and the capital encompassing the five stories at the top and the domed and turreted corner

8.13
Park Row and St. Paul buildings with St. Paul's Chapel and churchyard in foreground. Photograph by Underhill. Collection of The New-York Historical Society.

8.14
Steel frame and wind bracing, Park Row Building. After Freitag, Architectural Engineering.

towers—or, again depending on one's perception, just the towers. Expressing the hope that "no more [such] monsters will be allowed to rear themselvse [sic] in New York," the *Record and Guide* characterized the Park Row's facade as "capricious" and "without rhyme or reason" and its highly visible blank side walls as "inexpressive and vacuous." (Could it be that the developer, knowing of the American Surety's difficulties over the projection of its cornice, opted to forgo projecting ornament?) Inevitably, the building was compared to the St. Paul: "two domineering structures [that] stand and swear at each other." The "stiff archaic treatment" of the Park Row's freestanding figural sculpture, modeled by J. Massey Rhind, was adjudged more successful than the "impossible 'realism' of the St. Paul figures, where it has been attempted to show what would happen to a giant if he really tried to hold up a twenty-story wall." On the other hand, compared with the St. Paul's well-proportioned capital, the Park Row's copper-roofed cupolas were deemed "ineffectual and insignificant terminations which add nothing."[27]

By mid-1899 the building was owned by the investment banker and subway sponsor August Belmont under the name Park Row Realty Company. The first headquarters of the Interborough Rapid Transit (IRT) subway were here. In 1905–6 Belmont constructed an eight-story office building nearby, designed by Robertson & Potter, with an L through to Ann Street. The new building was separated from the Park Row Building by a lot that Joseph Pulitzer owned and on which a four-story building stood. On its south side, Belmont's new building adjoined the eight-story Clark Building at the corner of Ann Street, also on Pulitzer-owned property. Belmont was said to have obtained his site as a means of protecting the Park Row's natural light. Doubtless afraid that if all three properties were to come under one ownership, a mammoth skyscraper would rise on the assembled lots, he took the only preventive means available in the pre–zoning law era. No tall building has yet been built on either the north or south side of the Park Row Building, nor is one likely to be under the current zoning law, and Belmont's 1906 building and the Clark Building are still standing.[28] The Clark building, however, was threatened with destruction as of early 1995.

The building's Sprague electric elevators were a vertically assembled variant of the type used in the Lord's Court Building (see Fig. 6.2). Arranged in a curve next to the north wall were ten passenger elevators, two of which served only the towers, and one slow-speed freight elevator.[29] Again, the system worked well enough except for the wear of the screw and nut, which required frequent maintenance and replacement of bearings. After the Park Row installation, the Sprague elevator in both its horizontal and vertical forms rapidly lost favor. For example, the builders of the Broadway Chambers, completed in 1900, preferred the Otis hydraulic elevator. Meanwhile, the Otis company's engineers had been busy concentrating on simplifying the machinery of its electric elevator through the elimination of the drum and gears. In 1903 the company produced a drumless and gearless machine by running cables over the sheaves and attaching them directly to counterweights. There were two mechanical advantages: the kinetic energy of the falling counterweight reduced the load on the motor in the lifting car, with a lower consumption of current; and fully developed motor controls successfully and smoothly controlled the start, speed, and stop of ascending and descending movement.[30]

Vertically Designed and Technically Advanced Skyscrapers

In the mid-1890s, the formal treatment of skyscraper street elevations was settling into three variations on the tripartite scheme: vertical emphasis (Bowling Green Offices), horizontal emphasis (St. Paul Building), and a neutral window pattern in the shaft (American Surety Building). The roof could be flat, usually with some projecting decorative details or an overhanging cornice, or it could be picturesquely high and even domed or towered, as in the case of the Park Row Building.

With few exceptions those office buildings designed with vertical emphasis tended not to be very tall, and for that reason attracted little attention from the professional press. It may well be that shorter buildings, because they required fewer increments of wall thickness, were better candidates for vertical expression. One truly aberrant example was the fifteen-story Syndicate Building (1895–96) on the southwest corner of Liberty and Nassau streets (obliquely visible in Fig. 8.15), a rare skyscraper designed by the partnership of Hugh Lamb and Charles A. Rich. The Lamb & Rich firm was known primarily for its houses and institutional buildings, but in this instance the developer of record was one of the architects, Hugh Lamb. In fact, the partners maintained an office in the building for several years after it was completed. The concentration of continuous curved bay windows framed by vertical rows of windows at the corners introduced unusually large areas of glass into the building's cream-colored brick facades.[31] By 1899 the Syndicate Building was known as the German-American Building, after its primary tenant at that time, the German American Insurance Company. By 1908 it was the Provident Life Building.

The nineteen-story National Bank of Commerce Building (1896–97), erected on the northwest corner of Cedar and Nassau streets next to the Syndicate Building, was an exceptionally tall, if somewhat more conventional, example of vertical design (Fig. 8.15). The architect was James B. Baker, today remembered primarily for the old Chamber of Commerce Building on Liberty Street (1901). Stemming from the city's long tradition of arcaded commercial buildings, the bank's boldly articulated, brick-clad shaft featured wide multistory window bays topped by arches.[32] The Bank of Commerce and Syndicate buildings both gave way to Skidmore, Owings & Merrill's Marine Midland Bank in the late 1960s. Numerous other moderately tall office buildings of the time were designed with arcaded midsections, for example, Clinton & Russell's twelve-story, U-shaped Exchange Court (1897–98), which stood on the southeast corner of Broadway and Exchange Place until 1981.

Before the Park Row Building was finished, three technologically innovative office buildings produced by Harding & Gooch had been completed. All were essentially tripartite in facade design, although each had a strongly horizontal emphasis. None is extant. The first was the twenty-one-story Commercial Cable Building at 20–22 Broad Street (1896–97), with an entrance on New Street as well (Fig. 8.16). The corporate sponsor, in the business of transmitting messages to Europe via submarine cables, was allied through common ownership to the Postal Telegraph-Cable Company. That company, for which Harding & Gooch had earlier designed headquarters, provided an overland system of communication.

As noted earlier, the Commercial Cable's foundation was unusual in having concrete-

8.15

View of Cedar Street between Nassau Street and Broadway, with National Bank of Commerce Building
(1896–97), J. B. Baker, architect, on the right. Oblique view at right and adjacent to Bank of Commerce:
Syndicate Building (1895–96), Lamb & Rich, architects. Both demolished. At far right in distance:
Liberty Tower. At left: American Exchange Bank (1901; demolished), Clinton & Russell, architects, and
Singer Tower behind it. Center: New York Clearing House (1896; demolished), R. W. Gibson, architect.
Collection of The New-York Historical Society.

8.16
*Commercial
Cable Building
(1896–97;
demolished),
Harding & Gooch,
architects,
as seen from court
of Mills Building.
Photograph by
Wurts, 1897.
Museum of the
City of New York.*

filled cast-iron cylinders under the column footings. The technique likely was adopted as a means of overcoming the danger posed by the presence of quicksand in this area. Utilizing Phoenix columns, an all-steel cage frame supported cement-finished floors of the same type that proved so effective against fire in the Postal Telegraph-Cable Building. A constricted, interior-block site dictated a multiangled plan, shaped like an irregular dumbbell. Following the example set by the Mail and Express and Manhattan Life buildings, the architects endowed the resulting tall, thin slab with tremendous presence by adapting motifs from the Renaissance and Baroque eras. The base was configured as a giant, rusticated version of the classic Serlian, or Palladian, motif, and the shaft was terminated by baroque domes on both street fronts. But none of this was appreciated. In reaction to its form and height, the Commercial Cable was harshly characterized as "the pushing shoulder and brazen terminal bulb" and condemned as "about the most obstreperous structure to which the new construction has given rise."[33]

Harding & Gooch's towerlike Queen Insurance Company Building (1896–97), constructed on the northwest corner of William and Cedar streets, had a more regular rectangular plan than that of the Commercial Cable. With the exception of its curved corner, the formal treatment of this seventeen-story building resembled that of the Postal Telegraph-Cable. It was the second building constructed by this insurance company, replacing the one at 37–39 Wall Street. Its steel skeleton rested on a grid of I-beams embedded in concrete, mostly on piling. Offset columns and a party-wall problem required a number of large distributing girders of box section, the largest weighing 37 tons. The problem arose from the need to protect the adjacent eleven-story Stokes Building (1890–91; Charles W. Clinton, architect). The risk of collapse was considered so great that the entire east wall of the Stokes was underpinned with a new foundation. The technique involved a process known as needling: the insertion of steel I-beams into the lower part of the old wall by drilling three feet into the brick mass. The beams were paired one above the other and the space between them infilled with steel-reinforced brickwork. Each such brick-and-beam assemblage was then set on a cast-iron cylinder fitted with a hardened steel cutting ring to facilitate driving through the overburden.[34]

Harding & Gooch's Dun Building (1897–99), erected on the northeast corner of Broadway and Reade Street a block below the Central Bank Building, was similar in architectural design to the Queen Insurance and also rectangular in plan. It was flat-roofed, its stone- and brick-clad facades layered in design, and it had a high, four-story base matched by an equally tall capital. The builder and chief occupant of the Dun Building was the R. G. Dun & Company Mercantile Agency, which would in 1933 merge with the Bradstreet Company to become the world-famous financial-communications corporation Dun & Bradstreet. At first a twenty-three-story building was planned, but the Dun company reconsidered and instead built a fifteen-story structure—a rare exception to the practice of building higher than first projected. Construction was similar to that of the Queen Insurance, with steel Phoenix columns used in the steel skeleton.[35]

Apparently the Dun Building incorporated a state-of-the-art fireproofing technique; the Electric Fireproofing Company claimed that its patent process for fireproofing interior wood finishes enabled the building to withstand a fire virtually intact. On a Saturday afternoon in 1900 a fire that started in a wastebasket in one of the offices was said to have "burnt itself out as harmlessly as a fire in a grate," leaving the woodwork virtually unscathed and requiring only "a few hours of carpenter work and a little varnish."[36] By that date other companies were marketing similar processes, all of which involved the use of a chemical coating, in response to the municipal building code of 1899, which mandated that only fireproofed wood could be used in buildings more than 150 feet high.

Speculation Downtown and Uptown: Empire and St. James Buildings

The Empire Building (1897–98), still standing on the southwest corner of Broadway and Rector Street, where it overlooks the Trinity Church graveyard, shares so many formal characteristics with the Queen Insurance and Dun Buildings that it might have been designed by the same architect (Fig. 8.17). It is similarly tripartite with horizontal emphasis; its ornamentation is also classically inspired, and it too is flat-roofed. The architect, however, was Kimball & Thompson, which illustrates how widely accepted this architectural treatment was by the end of the decade. Little about the Empire—not even the four eagles perched on orbs atop the columns that flank the Broadway entrance—would suggest the Kimball whose previous New York work had tended toward the flamboyant. In contrast to the ebullience of his Manhattan Life Building, the Empire possesses a quiet dignity and an assured elegance. The buff-colored stone-clad walls of this clifflike slab are relieved by a subtle pattern that, though predominantly horizontal in character, includes as a vertical component the rows of windows accented by balconies and terminating in arched and pedimented windows at the top.

The Empire was speculatively built by the O. B. Potter estate. It was named after an earlier building on the site, where in 1891 an unsuccessful attempt had been made on the life of financier Russell Sage. Recalling that the St. Paul Building had benefited similarly from its proximity to the St. Paul's Chapel churchyard, Schuyler quipped that the Empire owners "owe an obligation to the piety which has . . . [excluded] from secular uses the churchyards of Trinity parish."[37] A permit to build was obtained on 31 December 1895, but for reasons unknown construction of the twenty-story building began only in May of 1897. Before the steel skeleton of the new building could rise, the old Empire Building had to be removed and a caisson foundation laid to a depth of minus 50 feet. The new Empire's elongated and somewhat distorted plan, with shallow indentations for light courts, offers a good example of the exigencies that influenced skyscraper design (Fig. 8.18). The long, narrow lot dictated the attenuated plan, and the engineer designed the frame and especially the wind bracing to cope with the resulting narrow frontage and long side exposure (Fig. 8.19). As Kimball explained, in order to accommodate the bracing required in such situations, "there must be an adjustment of the architectural composition" (Fig. 8.20).[38] The long, streetlike entrance hall of the Empire, treated as a shopping arcade, gave access to the Rector Street station of the elevated railroad; the building also incorporates entrances to the Broadway-Lexington IRT subway. Within a decade of its completion the Empire would find its neo-Gothic complement in Kimball's Trinity and U.S. Realty buildings, erected on the north side of Trinity's churchyard.

The recent accidents in the American Tract Society Building made elevator safety a matter of paramount concern in the Empire Building, and various techniques were developed to assure it. Ten high-speed hydraulic elevators installed by Otis served the building, and the lower part of each elevator shaft was designed to provide an Ellithorpe

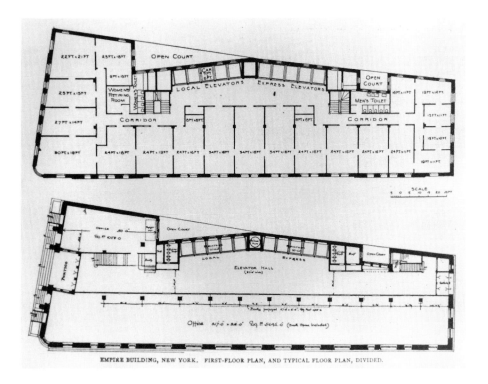

EMPIRE BUILDING, NEW YORK.   FIRST-FLOOR PLAN, AND TYPICAL FLOOR PLAN, DIVIDED.

8.18

Plans of first floor and typical floor, Empire Building.
After Engineering Magazine *(1897).*

air cushion (named for its inventor, F. T. Ellithorpe of New York City) that would slow the car should it fall. From the third floor to the basement floor, for a distance of 50 feet, each shaft was treated as an air-tight, steel-plated well. In actual construction, except for the bronze elevator doors, each shaft was independently enclosed in solid masonry walls. The shaft walls were battered from the third floor down, and within the 50-foot depth below the third floor they were wider at the top by 10 inches in order to allow some air to escape and thus avoid an excessively rapid deceleration of car speed in the compressing air. To prevent a vacuum from forming under the ascending car, a suction valve that opened inward was incorporated in the lowest slab of the shaft, and a safety valve opened to the atmosphere as a means of reducing excessive pressure. In the event that a car were to fall from the top of the shaft, which was 287 feet high, the pressure of the air cushion was calculated to equal 3.5 pounds per square inch above atmospheric pressure. On 18 July 1898, a test was performed in an experimental drop. Allowed to fall free from the top of the shaft, a car weighing 2,000 pounds passed the third floor at a speed of 120 feet per second, or about 82 miles per hour, but the cargo of eggs and incandescent light bulbs survived the descent intact. The test was not considered conclusive for human beings, but this was a technological advance toward ultimate elevator safety.[39]

Bruce Price's St. James Building (1896–98), another anonymously financed office tower and still standing on the southwest corner of Broadway and 26th Street, rivals his American Surety Building in sheer architectural grandeur and fine design (Fig. 8.21). As an "uptown" skyscraper, it joined other tall buildings that in the 1890s began to transform the low-rise theatre and shopping section around Madison Square and Madison Square Garden into the medium-rise, mercantile district that it has remained. Russell Sturgis noted the "singular classification of occupants" in the new uptown skyscrapers and identified the tenants of the St. James as architects, "nearly all [of whom] . . . have left the commercial and banking centre of the city"; engineers; agencies associated with the

8.19

Elevations of steel frame, Empire Building. Left: section parallel to Trinity Place. Right: section parallel to Broadway. After Engineering Magazine (1897).

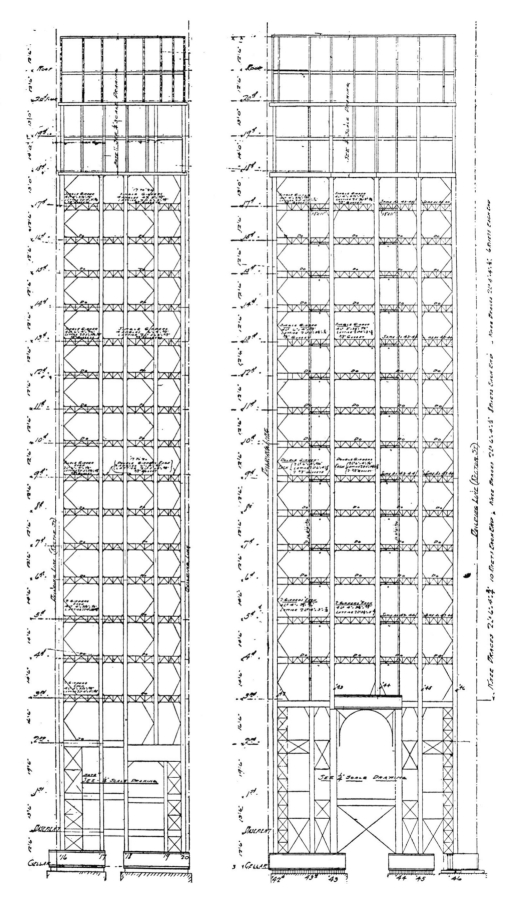

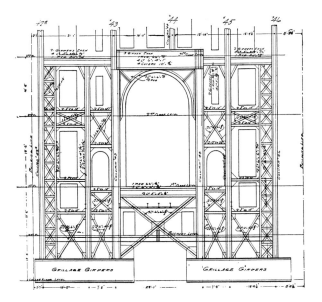

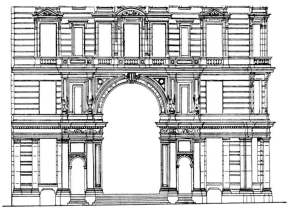

8.20

Left: section showing lower part of Empire Building frame at Broadway entrance. Right: corresponding facade elevation at Broadway entrance. After Engineering Magazine *(1897).*

entertainment industry; and small tradesmen.[40] The building takes its name from a hotel formerly on its site, and its builders—recorded mysteriously in the building permit as the St. James Company—were Joseph and Abraham Pennock of Philadelphia.[41] The names of these syndicate- and anonymously financed structures often alluded to the history of the site or its immediate vicinity, the intention usually being to lend prestige to a building lacking a corporate identity.

Although more ornate and more colorful than the American Surety, in keeping with the relaxed and recreational atmosphere of its surroundings, the St. James also adheres to the column formula and can also be characterized as a "rusticated pillar." Its shaft, however, is heavily clad in red brick and light terra-cotta, in marked contrast to the sedate, light-toned skin of the American Surety and other downtown skyscrapers. Its luxuriantly sculptural four-story capital is far more elaborately articulated than the American Surety's, having large, iron-framed oriel windows surmounted by arches, an attic story, and a heavy copper cornice. Stone-carved owls roost on top of the oriels, and open-mouthed gargoyles adorn the two-story base. Although well-proportioned with respect to its sixteen-story height and facade widths, about 90 feet on Broadway and 110 feet on 26th Street, the St. James communicates an impression of breadth and mass rather than soaring height. This is partly because it is hemmed in by narrow streets. Another noticeable distinction from the typical downtown skyscraper is that the St. James has large show windows in the ground story, intended to serve a different sort of tenant. The main entrance lobby on Broadway has fortunately been preserved, with its impressive barrel-vaulted ceiling, marble revetement and floors, an "Aesthetic Movement" mural with lounging classical muses, and a fine spiral staircase at the rear.

8.21
*St. James Building
(1896–98),
Bruce Price, architect.
Southwest corner
Broadway and 26th
Street.
After* One Hundred
and Sixty Glimpses of
Greater New York.

Revival of the Insurance Company Image: The Washington Life Building

Although the new insurance company quarters undertaken in the 1890s were neither as tall nor as ostentatious as some of the speculatively built skyscrapers discussed above, some, notably the Washington Life Building (1897–98), were exceptionally well designed (Fig. 8.22). Founded in 1860, the Washington Life Insurance Company of New York had over the years conservatively invested its capital in real estate securities. Said to be worth $14 million in 1895, the company's assets had more than doubled since 1880. Its offices had been in the Coal and Iron Exchange building before its new building was completed at the southwest corner of Broadway and Liberty Street. The architect was C. L. W. Eidlitz, the builder Marc Eidlitz & Son.

8.22
*Washington
Life Building
(1897–98;
demolished),
C. L. W. Eidlitz,
architect.
Museum of the
City of New York.*

A series of photographs documenting the construction process over the course of a year reveals that the Washington Life replaced two midcentury commercial buildings. The photographs also establish that the excavation and laying of its caisson foundation took five months and that application of its exterior cladding began at the bottom while the upper part of the steel frame was still under construction. (By this date such photographic documentation was not unusual.) A creative means of solving a foundation problem was adopted for the building. The surrounding buildings could not be easily underpinned or shored because the caissons occupied almost the whole site. If the usual needling and bracing had been applied, the construction work would have been greatly hampered. Instead, using hydraulic pressure, steel tubes were driven down to the bedrock beneath the adjoining walls and then filled with concrete. Remarkably, this was done before the two old buildings on the site were removed.[42]

The ordinarily critical *Record and Guide* characterized the Washington Life as "perhaps the most popular of all the sky-scrapers down town" and (rightly) declared it "one of the few that are positively attractive, and in which allowances do not have to be made."[43] Treated as a column with respect to its tripartite facade configuration and 50-foot Broadway front, but in actual ground dimensions an irregular slab, the new building extended 150 feet along Liberty Street and rose to a height of seventeen stories. Piers and columns defined its three-story, pink granite–clad base. Above that, the shaft was quite plain, its smooth-surfaced limestone-clad walls regularly punctuated by minimally enframed windows. Two-story arches framed by pilasters enriched the capital, and the crowning glory of the building was its high wedge roof, picturesquely embellished by crested "German Renaissance" dormers and tiled in gleaming bronze. Long associated with the insurance company building, the high roof helped to identify the corporate sponsor. Only the south wall was left blank, and the *Record and Guide* was pleased to note that even it was articulated sufficiently to suggest a continuity of design with the rest.

Sullivan in New York: The Bayard Building

At thirteen stories, the Bayard (1897–99) may not have measured up to the skyscraper heights of its city and time, but it is an exquisitely beautiful tall building and a masterwork of its famous creator, Louis Sullivan (Fig. 8.23). It is also Sullivan's only New York building and, according to Frank Lloyd Wright, his favorite. Hidden away on Bleecker Street in an area given over in the late nineteenth century to assorted manufacturing, publishing, and mercantile interests, the Bayard was designed as loft space that could be partitioned to accommodate stores and other uses as well as offices. Its cream-colored terra-cotta-sheathed facade embodies Sullivan's predilections for functional tripartite design, for piers that reveal the skeleton frame, and for lush, fluidly handled ornament.

The Bayard's importance within Sullivan's oeuvre and with respect to his design theory—especially its rationally differentiated pier and mullion system—has long been recognized. From the time the building was completed, however, critics and scholars expressed reservations about the density and character of the ornament, particularly the six winged female figures beneath the cornice. For many years these were believed to have been included at the behest of Silas Alden Condict, the Bayard's second owner, and to have embodied a special meaning as requested by him. That myth has been thoroughly

8.23
*Bayard Building
(1897–99),
Louis Sullivan,
architect,
with L. P. Smith.
65 Bleecker Street.
Wurts Collection.
Museum of the City of
New York.*

debunked; Narciso Menocal discusses the quasi-medieval iconography and feminine principle embodied in the facade as a whole and in the figures, tracing their immediate inspiration to angels included in the decoration of a room in the Louvre.[44] Sullivan, of course, had already used winged figures on his Transportation Building at the Chicago World's Fair of 1893, and the Bayard's angels have an affinity with the classically inspired allegorical figures on native New York skyscrapers, owing to a shared Beaux-Arts background.

Like many commercial structures built on speculation, the Bayard was given a historic name associated with its site. Originally part of the Bayard family farm, the property had been occupied since the 1850s by the building of the Bank for Savings in the City of New York, the state's oldest savings bank. The Bayard's name specifically commemorates William Bayard, the bank's first president and the scion of one of New York City's most distinguished Dutch Colonial families. As the seller and the holder of a mortgage on the property, which it recalled before the construction was completed, the bank itself may have selected the name. In 1897, having recently moved its business to new quarters further uptown, the bank transferred its Bleecker Street property to the United Loan & Investment Company, which then demolished the old building and began construction of the Bayard.[45]

The supervising architect was Lyndon P. Smith, who is listed in the rental prospectus as Sullivan's associate and on the building permit as the builder (contractor). It was Sullivan's practice to work with a local architect on buildings constructed outside of his home city of Chicago, and in this case there seems to have been a direct connection. In 1889–90 Smith had been the partner of John H. Edelmann (Edelmann & Smith). Edelmann was close to Sullivan, who may have known Smith before their association on the Bayard. Smith was also likely to have been present at Sullivan's lecture to the New York chapter of the American Institute of Architects in 1895, and he would later publish articles on Sullivan's buildings.[46]

Much has been published in recent years concerning the aesthetic and formal character of the Bayard, but its construction history is less well known and has a good deal more to do with the history of the New York skyscraper. The building's genesis spawned a clash with the city's building laws and practice. United Loan unsuccessfully petitioned the buildings department to allow the use of uniform 12-inch-thick curtain walls for the full height of the building. United Loan was also denied permission to employ a structural system of columns known as the Gray system, which had been used for Adler & Sullivan's Guaranty Building in Buffalo. Often applied in bridge construction, this system involved the use of 14-inch-square columns set on cast bases and connected vertically to columns above and below by plates and an angle seat. The resulting vertical steel structure needed no additional support from walls or partitions, could carry the entire weight of the building, and allowed the maximum usable floor space. In its petition regarding the curtain walls the owner asserted: "Circumstances are such that while this building must be substantially constructed, it must be built with the utmost economy. . . . The strength and stiffness of the structure will lie in its skeleton frame."[47] As it happened, the added costs and loss of usable floor space occasioned by the construction requirements resulted in financial difficulties for United Loan, and in mid-1899 the Bayard came into the possession of Silas and Emmeline Condict.[48]

Alien though the Bayard may appear on the surface, its infrastructure is thoroughgoing New York City. The foundations involve superposed steel grillages resting on a thick concrete bed and encased in concrete, a type of construction that was then being used for other New York skyscrapers. Filling its rectangular interior lot, the building is approximately 83 feet wide by 100 feet deep, the latter representing the depth of a standard New York lot, and it is 162 feet tall.[49] The curtain wall thicknesses adhere to the New York building law: 20 inches between the sidewalk level and the fifth floor, 16 inches from the fifth to the ninth floor, and 12 inches above that. At the ground-floor level the structural columns are 24 inches in diameter, and they gradually diminish to 13 on the top two floors. Floor-to-ceiling heights also diminish from 15 feet on the first floor to 13 on the second, 12 on the third, 11 on the fourth and fifth, 10 from the sixth through the eleventh, and 9.5 feet on the twelfth, before returning to 14.5 feet under the cornice on the thirteenth floor.

Faithful to Sullivan's rationale, the Bayard Building's top two stories are merged on the exterior to appear as one, because as originally constructed they incorporated a two-story-high, skylighted room surrounded by a gallery. Design-merged stories, however, were not out of character in a New York commercial building. Yet despite its generic relationship to the tripartite, arcaded facades of other New York buildings and its structural adherence to the city's building code, the Bayard was, and remained, a Manhattan anomaly. The hope of the intransigent Schuyler—that the Bayard's "promising starting point" would alter the look of the city's skyscrapers—went unfulfilled. New York had already arrived at its own solution "to the problem of the skyscraper."[50]

A Model of Its Kind: The Broadway Chambers Building

The Broadway Chambers (1899–1900) epitomizes that solution (Fig. 8.24). Named for its site opposite City Hall Park on the northwest corner of Broadway and Chambers Street, this eighteen-story, 235-foot-high tower was commissioned by Edward Reynolds Andrews, who represented the principal property owner, the Sarah A. Andrews Estate of Boston. The George A. Fuller Company was also an investor in the project. It was the first in a series of stunning New York skyscrapers designed by Cass Gilbert, the finest being the Woolworth Building. The opportunity to design the Broadway Chambers brought the Ohio-born architect permanently to New York, where he opened an office in 1899. After several months of travel abroad, following his graduation from the Massachusetts Institute of Technology, he had worked from 1880 to 1882 in the office of McKim, Mead & White. Since then he had practiced in St. Paul, and in 1895 he had won the competition for the Minnesota State Capitol. His first skyscraper was the twelve-story Brazer Building (1896–97) in Boston, which was also constructed by the Fuller Company. Following on the Broadway Chambers commission, in late 1899 he won the competition for the United States Custom House in New York City over some of the nation's leading architects.

The columnlike proportions and rusticated surface treatment of the Broadway Chambers recall the American Surety Building. In classic tripartite form, and with all four facades fully designed, Gilbert's tower rises from a three-story rusticated granite base that is pale red in color and defined by strong piers. Above, a multihued red-brick shaft comprising eleven stories is articulated horizontally by recessed courses and vertically by paired windows in each bay. The four uppermost stories, faced in cream-colored terra-cotta accented by colorful glazed terra-cotta motifs, form the capital. Banded with brick, the transitional fifteenth story is enriched by a festoon that is accented by red and green medallions. The sixteenth and seventeenth stories are united by arcaded loggias flanked by red and yellow-green panels, and the attic story features projecting Hermes' and lions' heads between the windows. A substantial copper cornice with acroteria terminates the composition. The variegated coloring was unusual for the time and made the building more revealing of its steel skeleton than most of the city's skyscrapers. Montgomery Schuyler recognized its polychromy as "the next advance in the execution of the accepted scheme [the tripartite scheme]" and as its "architectural novelty and distinction."[51]

At the International Universal Exposition held in Paris in 1900, the Broadway Chambers was the focus of an ambitious exhibit mounted by its construction contractor and major promoter, the George A. Fuller Company. The display featured two eleven-foot-tall models of the building, one a replica in brass of its steel skeleton, incorporating all the mechanical parts, and the other a plaster model that Gilbert contributed, showing the exterior. The Fuller company published an informative sixty-page pamphlet on the building for use as a souvenir giveaway and promotional piece. The various companies that had furnished the building's utilities—the Kenney Company, for example, which supplied the innovative "flushometers" for the water closets—also contributed models of their products to the exhibit. As a result of the display, Gilbert won two awards: a gold medal for the models and a silver medal in the category of civil engineering. The Fuller company and the consulting engineer, Corydon T. Purdy of Purdy & Henderson, were also awarded medals. Soon after completion, the building itself attracted the attention of the German government, which, investigating the construction and planning of high steel-framed buildings in the United States, ordered a model of the Broadway Chambers that could be disassembled to allow analysis of the construction.[52] This appears to be the first such recognition of the advanced state of American architecture by Europeans, deputations of whom would come to study American buildings before World War I.

The foundation of the Broadway Chambers was laid and the superstructure completed with economical rapidity. The slowest part of the construction process, beginning in May of 1899 and taking about four months, was the placing of new foundations under the adjacent buildings to ensure their stability; this involved sinking and securing new piles close to the existing walls. Once the adjacent buildings were supported in this manner, new brick foundation walls on concrete footings were installed beneath them. The concrete-bedded steel grillage foundation of the Broadway Chambers went in rapidly, and by early December the steelwork for seventeen stories was complete. By February of 1900 the superstructure was virtually finished. As of May 1 some of the tenants had moved in, and all but the final touches had been completed, despite such difficulties as strikes by workers at the site and at the factories that supplied the materials. As Gilbert explained about skyscraper building in general, "Rapid construction is not undertaken merely for the purpose of making a record. It is a necessity arising from economic conditions." The less time spent building, the less rent is lost and the less unrecoupable interest is paid on the investment. At the going interest rate of 4 percent, Gilbert observed, the mortage payments on a land value of $1.5 million would be $120,000 for two years; hence the need for rapid construction. Noting also that "architectural beauty" affected a building's income, Gilbert aptly characterized the skyscraper as "the machine that makes the land pay." He believed that it "should represent about two-thirds of the land value under normal conditions."[53]

Assessments at the End of the Century

In the last years of the nineteenth century, skyscraper construction, as well as other forms of building, was obviously flourishing. Cass Gilbert, in fact, commented on the difficulty

8.24
*At right: Broadway
Chambers Building
(1899–1900),
Cass Gilbert,
architect.
Northwest corner
Broadway and
Chambers Street.
At far left: Chemical
Bank Building
(1849–50; de-
molished),
Thomas & Son,
architects.
Collection of The
New-York Historical
Society.*

of getting building supplies for the Broadway Chambers because of the high demand for such materials in 1899, a peak year for construction in Manhattan.[54] Although many architects regarded skyscraper commissions as the plums of the profession, issues relating to their design, form, and height were debated on into the new century. Matters of functional design proved just as refractory due to the overwhelming technical presence of foundations, framing, fireproofing, and mechanical and electrical utilities.

In the July 1897 number of *Engineering Magazine*, Kimball sought to lay down an authoritative guide to the functional and structural parameters within which the architect had to maneuver, and at the same time to suggest a scope for decisions that were independent of engineering necessities. He addressed many of the planning principles that George Hill had discussed four years earlier, but in contrast to the latter's prescriptive and thoroughly pragmatic approach, he focused on the difficulties encountered by the architect. First of all, in formulating his design, the architect had to consider the conditions imposed by the site, above all the light sources. (Usually he had to depend on a court for sufficient light, unless the building was a freestanding tower of small dimensions.) Next, he had to consider the placement of the entrance and its relationship to the elevators; that is, the need for an easy flow of traffic had to be balanced against the formal composition of the principal elevation and public spaces. The accessibility of the elevators, a major consideration, had to be balanced against the need to place them in the area of least rental value. (Accordingly, the Empire Building's elevators are lined up midway along the south wall; see Fig. 8.18).

The placement of the supporting columns, wall columns, and wall girders, Kimball explained, are influenced by a number of factors. In order to determine the location of the supporting columns—obviously a major parameter governing functional design—the architect had to take into account structural necessity, the need for maximum economy in the use of steel, and the need for the greatest possible openness and flexibility of space on every floor. Irregularities often mandated that columns be offset rather than uniformly spaced, and that made it all the more difficult to find the optimum resolution of space use versus cost. Likewise, the location and depth of the girders had to meet structural requirements, to achieve the minimum floor-to-ceiling depth, to provide adequate space for utilities and a ceiling height appropriate for the size of the enclosure, and, finally, to effect a harmonious relation between the external and internal compositions. Similar considerations had to be taken into account in determining the location and spacing of wall columns. Here the controlling condition was likely to be the size and spacing of windows in the external wall, but structural necessities could turn the relationship around. Comparable determinants apply to the placement of wall girders. In the case of a stone front, Kimball advised that the girders be located "where cornices or band courses occur, so that the heavy stone forming these features may run through the wall and be borne on the girders, thus acting as corbels on which the walls above may be carried up to the next horizontal line of girders."[55] This suggests that by the late 1890s New York skyscraper architects had developed a "form follows function" design rationale, expressed as horizontal layers.

After all of the above challenges had been resolved, the architect's final chore, Kimball wrote, was to decide what kind of foundation was required. The nature of the soil, the depth of the bedrock, and the loads to be supported were all determining factors, but, insofar as possible, the distribution of elements must be adjusted by the engineer to leave the maximum unobstructed cellar space for the arrangement of the mechanical systems. These, in turn, had to be arranged for the most efficient interdependent operation.[56] Shackled by so many functional requirements, the skyscraper architect was left with a narrow scope for independent decisions of any kind.

Following a visit in 1896, a British journalist offered a commentary that recognized the essence of the American spirit: "Never have I seen a city more hideous or more splendid. Uncouth, formless, piebald, chaotic, it yet stamps itself upon you as the most magnificent embodiment of Titanic energy and force. . . . The very buildings cry aloud of struggling, almost savage, unregulated strength. It is the outward expression of the freest, fiercest individualism."[57]

The same point was made—but in a thoroughly negative sense—in an exchange between British and American critics published in *Engineering Magazine* in late 1897. The English critic S. Henbest Capper led off. Decrying the "huckstering spirit" in the United States, he alleged that Americans boasted of constantly breaking height records and of surpassing Europeans in building height. He recognized that skyscrapers constitute part of the American contribution to modern architecture, but he submitted that tallness in itself is no guarantee of artistic success. Although the problems of skyscraper construction had been solved with characteristic American audacity, formal solutions remained elusive. In New York, architectural design was so diverse and extravagant that it suggested a trial-and-error approach aimed at advertising value. Complex and extensive technology, Capper observed, put the architect last and made him subservient to the owner, the engineers, the manufacturers, and the tenants. The only satisfactory aesthetic expression was the treatment of the high building as an isolated tower, in the round.

Recognizing that great height, *de facto*, was regarded as an inescapable necessity in the United States, Capper recommended (contra Sullivan) that it be deemphasized in the design. He advocated the use of terra-cotta—a more plastic material preferable to stone sheathing—as a means of interpreting and expressing the steel skeleton. Lavish exterior ornament, he warned, was not only out of place but went unnoticed, and was unnoticeable. The repetition of a single motif, however, could have a potent visual effect. Acknowledging the aesthetic value of the three-part composition, he pointed out that the cornice was problematic; that typically it either had too much overhang or too little. Another problem he identified was that tall buildings in mass tended to submerge well-designed low buildings, but he admitted that the great massing of tall buildings downtown, as seen from the harbor, produced a potent visual effect and made up for the absence of natural heights at the lower end of Manhattan Island.[58]

A. D. F. Hamlin answered Capper, not by arguing with him but by expanding on his comments. Asserting that the high building was an inevitable consequence of economic factors, Hamlin maintained that the essential cause of great height is not the cost of the land, which was just as expensive in London and Paris, but the value derived from concentrating many economic and urbanistic activities in a minimum of space. Great height, Hamlin said, is a consequence of American hurry, of not wasting time. It does not result from the love of height or bigness for its own sake, because the ambition to surpass is found in all cultures. Although maximum return was important, saving time and effort in the pursuit of business seemed paramount:

The "sky-scraper" is a huge labor-saving and time-saving device. Not only does it make possible the concentration within a small geographical area of an amount and variety of business which otherwise would be spread over five or six times the same extent of territory, but it gathers into a single edifice an extraordinary number of activities, which otherwise would be widely separated. Each building is almost a complete city, often comprising within its walls banks and insurance offices, post office and telegraph office, business exchanges, restaurants, club-rooms, and shops. The business man can provide himself with clothes, shoes, cigars, stationery, and baths; receive and dispatch his mail and his telegrams; speculate on 'change [the exchange], consult his lawyer and his architect in their offices; and transact his own business,—all without leaving the building in which his office is located. The express elevator which shoots him up to the sixteenth story or drops him with breathless speed to the basement is a product of this same American haste and economy, and without the elevator the tall office building would be an impossibility. It is the triumphant success of the "sky-scraper" as a time-saving invention which has made it so conspicuous and insistent an element in our American architecture.[59]

Hamlin, then, viewed the skyscraper as a technical and utilitarian triumph, but he concurred with Capper that the formal aspect presented great difficulties. Reiterating a point already made by many others, he acknowledged that the difficulties occurred because the architect had no freedom but had to work within the exigencies of structure and utilities. He contended that these exigencies compelled a union of technical and artistic design, drawing a parallel with the medieval Gothic. In defense of the New York skyscraper, he observed that the close association of sculptor, decorator, mosaic artist, and architect had been especially fruitful. He reaffirmed the aesthetic validity of the base-shaft-crown composition, with corners treated as broad piers, a plain shaft in which the windows are the main emphasis, and a crown of three or four stories where richness of detail is magnified by strong contrasts of light and shade and an increase in scale because of the distance from the eye. And he cited the need for scale, above all, as well as unity.[60]

Also in 1897, *Scribner's Magazine* began publishing a series of articles and editorials on the state of architecture, the skyscraper, and New York City. The perceived dismal state of architecture provoked editorial comment in the June 1897 issue. Especially lamented were the indiscriminate use of cheap machine-made materials, the absence of handicraft work, and the unfamiliarity of untrained workers with both new and old uses of materials. Also faulted were the contract system, which dictated that every component be designed and manufactured in advance; the commission system, under which the architect was paid on the basis of how much money the client was willing to invest; and the system of supervision under which the architect became an agent charged with spending his client's money. Each architect went his own way, the editorial bemoaned, mixing traditions to suit his taste or whim rather than seeking to develop a steel-skeleton style that followed the example of Chicago. Dismayed by the ascendance of Beaux-Arts classicism in the East, the Chicago-based architect and critic Peter B. Wight later argued that the architect must drop his "individuality" for "mutuality."[61]

In the July 1897 issue of *Scribner's*, J. Lincoln Steffens followed the theme by condemning the every-man-for-himself attitude that had failed to place the urban common-wealth first. He explained that capital, high land prices, and the elevator had made the high building a functional and investment success for business. Moreover, iron and steel framing (the "Chicago method"), which had reduced the building cost from $5.00 to $0.37 per cubic foot, had facilitated the achievement of unlimited heights and financial returns. A successful business technique that had been developed for handling the process of design and building involved the appropriate organization of architect, engineer, rental agent, contractor, suppliers, and others, who were to a great extent selected or recommended by the sponsoring financial institution or developer to work as a team in producing a remunerative building. Steffens went into great detail on financial techniques and returns and identified as a major goal the search for tenants who would give the maximum status to the building: established, respectable firms. Steffens' article represents big-time architecture as seen in the light of a new Progressive spirit, but does not spare the formal character of the New York skyscraper: "To have a light, airy, all-supporting steel cage veneered with a stone that suggests enormous weight and massive walls, is an ugly lie."[62]

For some time the *Record and Guide* had been pessimistic about the future of the high building. In 1897 it questioned whether or not the skyscraper actually paid off as an investment, noting that its novelty as a corporate prestige-booster had worn off. With some assurance, it ventured that "the big insurance company and the profitable daily newspaper cannot go on building much longer."[63] Indeed, for the moment the major newspapers, as well as most of the large insurance companies, seemed to be well en-sconced in their own high buildings, or about to be: New York Life's new quarters and those of the Queen Insurance and Washington Life companies would soon be completed. But the prediction would nonetheless prove to be inaccurate within just a few years. In 1898 the same publication, pointing out that skyscrapers taller than any so far constructed were structurally possible, observed that "the limiting factors now coming into operation are of an aesthetic, sanitary and financial nature." The effort to achieve control over the first two through the passage of state legislation had thus far failed; the financial factor, however, was "working more silently, but perhaps more effectively." In particular, the elevator—the very invention "which years ago made the tall building possible"—would restrain any major height increase.[64] Increased height would require increased elevator service, and the additional space needed for more elevator shafts would reduce the rentable area, thus making it unprofitable to build higher. Certainly this was a limiting factor, but it alone would not end the race to the sky.

At least from the artist's perspective, a more cheerful view had emerged by 1899:

Behind a foreground of tall masts . . . looms . . . the towering white city of 1900, a cluster of modern high buildings which, notwithstanding the perspective of a dozen blocks, are still high, enormously, alarmingly high—symbols of modern capital, per-haps, and its far-reaching possiblities, or they may remind you, in their massive grouping, of a cluster of mountains, with their bright peaks glistening in the sun far above the dark shadows of the valleys in which the streams of business flow, down to the wharves and so out over the world.

Now, separately they may be impossible, these high buildings of ours—these vulgar, impertinent "sky-scrapers"; but, as a group, and in perspective, they are fine, with a strong manly beauty all their own.[65]

By this time Schuyler, too, was reasonably satisfied that the commercial building had come of age, even if all of its formal problems had not been resolved to his satisfaction. American architects, he felt, were too much disposed to be original, though he acknowledged that the skyscraper, which had risen from five to twenty-five stories in just a quarter of a century, demanded originality. By the mid-1890s experimentation had given way to a skyscraper style "nearly as distinct . . . as the Greek temple or the Gothic cathedral" but that preserved the indispensable tripartite or column composition.[66] For quite some time to come, the several variations on the tripartite that had ruled since the mid-1890s would prevail; yet another variation, the campanile-skyscraper as projected first by Bruce Price and later by George Post, would find expression in the first decade of the twentieth century.[67]

Controversy over the skyscraper's height, density, and urban consequences as well as its formal character would continue with increasing vigor in the new century as the high building passed 500, 600, and even 700 feet. Fostered by the Progressive Movement, critical insights into the urban process would bring into focus the elemental difficulty: the inability of the municipality to control these processes. Although eventually the instrument of zoning would achieve some results, the problem would not disappear.

9
SKYSCRAPERS AND THE URBAN SCENE AT THE TURN OF THE CENTURY

At the turn of the century New York City had established itself as a world metropolis through the continuing growth of its leadership and authority and the expanding vitality of its artistic and intellectual life. Imbued with the ideals of the City Beautiful and Progressive movements, the city was becoming increasingly conscious of its shortcomings and began efforts to correct them through planning, zoning, and building and housing codes, as well as such public improvements as an expanded transportation system. The new subway was opened in 1904; Grand Central was electrified in 1906; the Manhattan, Williamsburg, and Queensboro bridges and Pennsylvania Station were completed by 1910. The affluence and prosperity of the city were derived from manufacturing as well as shipping, finance, wholesale and retail trade, and building construction. In the fifteen years preceding World War I, the number of employees in manufacturing increased by 65 percent, and salaries and wages, along with the monetary value of the manufactured product, nearly doubled. But the city's economic strength lay in the large number and diversity of its separate establishments, and its status as an international metropolis was in part founded on its small industries, each with comparatively few employees.

Building Costs, Land Costs, and Related Statistics

The annual rate of building was subject to extreme vicissitudes resulting from sensitivity to changing economic conditions. A summary of the dollar volume of building between 1870 and 1905, as published in the *American Architect*, reveals that the annual number of new buildings in the city remained relatively constant around an average of 2,694, ranging from a low of 1,311 in 1873 (the year of the "Jay Cooke panic") to a high of 4,894 in 1899. The dollar values, however, varied to the extreme, from a low of $13,365,114 in 1877 to a high of nearly $163 million in 1905—an indication of the increasing size, complexity, and cost of buildings.[1]

At the end of the century, the engineer Reginald P. Bolton reported that the cost of a typical high-quality building—a sixteen-story, steel-framed, fully fireproof structure, including all utilities and with "a moderate amount" of exterior ornament—was between 36 and 40 cents per cubic foot. For higher buildings, the unit cost was proportionately higher. The proportion of the mechanical and electrical utilities was said to equal 14 to 15 percent of that.[2] According to the *American Architect*, the estimated $3.25 million value of the new, and enormous, Broad-Exchange Building was the highest in 1901 of any office building in the city, with the Produce Exchange coming in second at $3 million. The most valuable insurance company building was the Equitable, said to be worth $6.35 million. The new Waldorf-Astoria Hotel outstripped all the major hotels at $6 million. As reported by the same source in 1905, the highest land prices in the city were as follows:

1. Southeast corner of Wall Street and Broadway (One Wall Street): 1,138 square feet; sold June 1905 for $700,000 ($615 per square foot);
2. Southwest corner of Wall and Broad streets: sold for $400 per square foot; and
3. Northwest corner of 34th Street and Broadway: sold for $348 per square foot.[3]

As of 1900 fifteen office buildings appear to have exceeded the height of 250 feet, if floors in mansards, domes, and other types of high roofs are included. Not surprisingly, measurements and story calculations vary from one account to another, sometimes taking in unusable space in domes and cupolas; these appear to be the most accurate figures:

	Number of Stories	Height in Feet[4]
American Surety	21	312
American Tract Society	23	291
Bank of Commerce	19	270
Bowling Green Offices	17	273
Commercial Cable	21	255
Empire	20/21	293
Gillender	19	273
Home Life Insurance	16	256
Manhattan Life Insurance	16/17	348
New York Life	12/13	270
Park Row	30	391
St. Paul	26	315
Standard Oil (remodeled 1895)	17	263
Washington Life	17	278
World Building	20?	309

At the end of 1902, sixty-six skyscrapers were under construction in the city, with heights ranging from nine to twenty-five stories. Forty-three of these reached or exceeded twelve stories, compared with fifteen in 1900. Along with increasing height, there was a trend toward increasing breadth wherever the land was available.[5] In response to a growing demand for office space and economic building management, the trend toward higher and broader buildings would continue throughout the first decade of the new century, although many architects and engineers would vigorously, and with mounting intensity, oppose unrestricted height and bulk.

Status of the Metropolis: Critical Views

The status of the metropolis as a whole and the quality of life that it offered also aroused criticism, especially from those intellectuals dedicated to Progressive ideals. These critics questioned whether the city could be considered an American equivalent of Paris—or even a real metropolis like Paris and London. Herbert Croly, later the editor of the *New Republic*, explored the issue in 1903. In his opinion, the city was approaching a metropolitan character, but the existence of too many other urban centers in the United States, some older, prevented it from becoming the Paris of the United States. Although there was no question of New York's industrial, commercial, and financial leadership or of its status as a world port, the dense influx of people from the rural hinterlands, plus immigration from abroad, had resulted in the rapid increase of a population with great ethnic and economic diversity and lacking in social cohesion. New York, therefore, was not yet a social and intellectual center comparable to Paris and London, although its intellectual and artistic activity was strengthening. Part of the difficulty was that the upper strata of the city's population were divided into disparate groups: big-money, political, intellectual, and artistic "sets." Because of this social fragmentation, as well as widespread poverty, civic ideals and public support and demand for civic excellence were lacking, as was concern for the appearance of the city. According to Croly, "the streets have been made a gift to real estate speculators and builders to deform [the city's appearance] as suited their interests; and they have done, and are still doing, their worst." If New York were truly a "social metropolis" it would have standards even higher than those of Boston and Chicago; instead, the standards were lower, with no other height restriction than that inflicted by "the amount of elevator service, which it pays to provide."[6]

The view of New York as the leading center of uninhibited and uncontrolled rapacity had long been widely held by Europeans, among them Balzac: "New York [is] a place where speculation and individualism are carried to the very highest level, where the brutality of self-interest reaches the point of cynicism and where a man, fundamentally isolated from the rest of mankind, finds himself compelled to rely upon his own strength and at every instant to be the self-appointed judge of his own actions, a city where politeness does not exist."[7] Some Americans were of a similar opinion. In 1904 Henry Adams saw the city as verging on madness:

> As he came up the bay again, . . . he found the approach more striking than ever— wonderful—unlike anything man had ever seen—and like nothing he had ever much cared to see. The outline of the city became frantic in its effort to explain something that defied meaning. Power seemed to have outgrown its servitude and to have asserted its freedom. The cylinder had exploded and thrown great masses of stone and steam against the sky. The city had the air and movement of hysteria, and the citizens were crying, in every accent of anger and alarm, that the new forces must at any cost be brought under control.[8]

If the forces could not be controlled, and obviously they never have been, there were many at an influential level of municipal life and politics who believed that something not only should but could be done about the city's appearance. And architects genuinely wanted to create both a great commercial architecture and a more beautiful city. In 1893 the Municipal Art Society was founded by a group of influential citizens, art lovers, artists, and architects, among them Edward Kendall, Henry Hardenbergh, and the group's founding president, Richard Morris Hunt. The intention was to provide sculptural and pictorial embellishments for the city's public buildings and parks. This was the first of a swelling number of civic attempts at establishing order, harmony, and aesthetic excellence in the place of chaos, squalor, and conflict.

The problem was inspiring the necessary favorable public opinion in the face of American individualism and the absence of civic spirit. What Sam Bass Warner called *privatism* had gained permanent ascendancy in the United States. Charles H. Caffin expressed the Progressive view of individualism, which, "in selfish indifference to everything which does not concern its immediate interests, trades its birthright to a boss, and leaves to anybody or nobody the control of public issues. . . . Buildings are erected with reference to no other consideration but the personal interest of their promoters. . . . [Municipal governments] have left the individual to his own devices, and neglected their own duty of tackling the municipal problems."[9] Art societies at least encouraged legal recognition of the artistic responsibilities of municipal government. Caffin argued for height restriction as the primary means of control in New York, and he called for the construction of fountains, statuary, and plazas as the appropriate foreground for monumental public or high commercial buildings.

Yet in all fairness, Manhattan showed much evidence of civic spirit at the turn of the century. It had parks and public spaces, large and small; it could boast institutions of all kinds and such civilized and cultural amenities as fine hotels, restaurants, theatres, opera houses, music and concert halls, museums, and libraries—the greatest of which was the newly created New York Public Library—and it had all of these in quantity. There were in the city, moreover, at least a dozen private art collections that were open to the public on suitable application with credentials.

Status of New York Architecture: More Criticism

Contemporary criticism of the city's architecture as it had developed between the Civil War and the turn of the century continued to be largely negative, much of it aimed at "superficial" and historicist design and cheap, fast construction. The voluble adverse commentary of nineteenth-century observers deserves a major share of the blame for the negative attitude toward post-1850 architecture that persisted until the 1960s.

As perceived by an anonymous critic writing in the late 1890s, the problem arose because American architects were unprepared to cope with the great volume of work that came to them after the war. In the thirty-year period between 1868 and 1897, more than seventy-five thousand buildings had been constructed—at a cost of well over a billion dollars. Pressed for time and forced to operate as efficiently as possible, architects were "obliged to borrow and adapt instead of creating and developing" and had to accept the "easiest and speediest processes." Undeniably, the innovations that had to be introduced into the city's architecture, including "the elevator, the . . . apartment house, fireproofing, skeleton-construction, the sky-scraper, electric lighting" and more, constituted a "revolutionary force" that added to the complex challenges of architecture.[10]

The same source also pointed out that much of what people attributed to architecture was actually engineering. The skyscraper was a feat of engineering and not of architecture. Some few architects "whose ability and training were far stronger on the mechanical side than the artistic" had helped to conceive the skeleton frame, but the engineer had developed that technology and had taken full charge of it. Increasingly, the architect had concerned himself only "with the superficial side of design," leaving to others not just mechanical problems but such essential architectural matters as the tenement plan and the city house plan, which were passed to the contractor and the contractor's draftsman for resolution.

> The modern building is a product of many brains, and the architect's contribution
> consists in the main of administration, the general plan, and the exterior design. . . . He
> has preferred the role of dillettante [sic], which in architecture runs invariably to
> history and studies in the externals of "styles." Its practical result is draughtsmanship
> and paper designing. Logical, organic, substantial architecture requires more solid
> foundation. . . . The architect has produced his pictures and stylistic essays, and these
> have been built as facades devoid of radical correspondence with the internal disposi-
> tion, and construction of the buildings they enclose.

To make matters worse, the architect's studio had become a veritable "workshop" due to the press of work; the business of architecture had become highly competitive and thoroughly commercialized. As a result, novelty of style had become a primary concern. "The mercantile spirit has conquered the studio, and 'Art' there has become a commodity."[11]

Numerous themes and implications may be distilled from the stimulating essay summarized above. To begin with, two concerns that would continue to plague twentieth-century design were already being articulated at the close of the nineteenth: the prospect of architecture as social failure and the reduction of architecture to a fashionable commodity for sale. Another theme that would persist in various forms was the aesthetic problem: the perceived lack of relationship between utility and form and the need to establish such a relationship as a fundamental principle. Always overlooked in articulations of this principle is the fact that the steel frame is a rigid rectilinear pattern of horizontal and vertical lines. If form must always express this structure, the result may end up at best monotonously repetitious, as in the work of Mies van der Rohe's imitators, at worst poverty stricken and sterile.

The architect of the early skyscraper, despite the criticisms leveled at him and within his shrinking role, had produced designs that were both good and interesting. The treatment of the tall building as a slender isolated tower—the form preferred at the end of the century—compelled the architect to draw on historical forms, notably the column and the campanile, but in virtually all cases these forms were translated into modern designs. The transformation was accomplished through change of scale, from functional necessity, and by means of ingenious combinations that were needed to give variety to the exteriors of buildings that comprised an endless repetition of floors committed to an identical use. And the architect's abdication of responsibility to the engineer and others is easily overstated. If the Equitable Building of c. 1870 is taken as the beginning of the skyscraper, then it is fairer to say that the owner and the architects created the form, but the engineer and the manufacturers made possible its realization. The same is true for the Equitable's successors.

Everyone had something to say about the skyscraper, most of it negative. Yet in spite of all the carping over novelty of style, simplicity was not necessarily what was wanted either. The editors of the *Architectural Record* suggested in 1901 that the exteriors of the latest tall buildings were ornamentally impoverished because their builders—who were not the owners but "some company organized especially to 'finance' such big undertakings"—refused to spend money on anything but the essentials and whatever special features might be demanded by prospective tenants. The new skyscraper was "a severe, four-squared, flat-roofed, many-windowed thing, presenting to the gazer from without as little splendor—as little sumptuosity—as may go with fine material and good building, and that in spite of the millions spent upon them."[12] The editors of the *Record and Guide*, however, simultaneously expressed a dissenting view. In their opinion, the new "plainly utilitarian" structures, although created by economic necessity, were "really more impressive than were the older buildings overloaded as they were with 'architecture.' . . . We have apparently developed a type which in future will be adhered to closely."[13] Both journals adduced the example of Clinton & Russell's recent work in support of their arguments, a coincidence that may reflect the different constituencies of the two publications.

A few months later the municipality showed official concern with the state of architecture in the city. P. M. Stewart, who had been appointed building commissioner in the fall of 1900, asked the American Institute of Architects to cooperate with his department in an effort to raise the standard of New York's architecture to that of European cities. The editors of the *American Architect* were dubious because of the status of property rights in the United States. As they pointed out, the city's building laws permitted the property owner to construct just about anything he wanted so long as it met the fireproofing requirements, whereas "regulations like those in force in Europe, where Governments exercise their police power in regulating the heights of cornices and string courses, while admirable in their effect on the artistic beauty of cities, would hardly be suited to our notions of individual liberty."[14] The same could be said with regard to height control, where no restriction would come until the commercial powers themselves were ready to support it.

Foreign criticism at the turn of the century centered on the aesthetic shortcomings of architecture in New York. The French critic Jean Schopfer, for one, criticized the heterogeneous quality of high-rise commercial architecture in the city, where "hostile forces" and "deplorable conditions" beyond the control of the architect had prevented the creation of a "genuine commercial style." New York architecture was severely constrained by the rectangular shape and arrangement of the lots, he said, as well as by apathy on the part of the state and city governments, by tremendous rivalry among the developers, by the practice of replacing houses rather than reusing them, by a want of taste on the part of the middle and upper classes, and, "on the other hand, [by] a perpetual desire for change and a disinclination to wait."[15] Like Schuyler, Schopfer perceived the promise of the

Bayard Building, citing it as the city's best commercial structure because its formal character was related to its steel frame.

An English visitor saw the problem as the triumph of utility and money over aesthetic values: "When the novelty has worn off . . . there comes the sense of having sacrificed to false gods, and the city resolves itself into nothing more than a triumph of mechanics, of iron, steel, bricks, and electricity, built by the Titans, laid out by Euclid, and furnished by Edison. . . . It is this undisguised triumph of mechanics over aesthetics, of the new and useful over the old, that after a time makes New York for an Englishman, rather a deadening city to live in. . . . There is too much machinery in New York, and it is too inhumanly good of its kind."[16] Yet the same utilities had made the city's living arrangements, in his estimation, vastly superior to those of London. Ironically, this visitor overlooked the greatness of New York's best commercial architecture.

The British engineer E. Kilburn Scott saw the same dichotomy between the mechanical and the spiritual. He perceived that the city had no regard for its skyline because any individual or corporation could build to any limit. Nor was there any concern for the common-law doctrine of "ancient lights"—that is, for protection against obstruction of windows that had been in use twenty years or more. There was no aesthetic control in the building code as there was in European cities, and the church spires were either hidden or omitted, so that nothing in the city reminded one of spiritual values. Engineering, on the other hand, was a feature of the city that he, like most foreigners, greatly admired.[17] Never mind the inconsistency.

The last word on the subject, for the time being, goes to Henry James. After his return to New York in 1904 following an absence of twenty-one years, his view of the skyscraper was wholly negative. Comprehension of any aesthetic quality was impossible because of the absolute tyranny of money: "Window upon window, at any cost, is a condition never to be reconciled with any grace of building. . . . The building can only afford lights, each light having a superlative value as an aid to the transaction of business and the conclusion of sharp bargains. . . . It is easy to conceive that, after all, with this origin and nature stamped upon their foreheads, the last word of the mercenary monsters should not be their address to our sense of formal beauty."[18] Two years later, James characterized the skyscraper in more poetic terms as an expression of power within the most extravagant of cities:

> The "tall buildings," which have so promptly usurped a glory that affects you as rather surprised, as yet, at itself, the multitudinous sky-scrapers standing up to the view, from the water like extravagant pins in a cushion already overplanted, and stuck in as in the dark, anywhere and anyhow, have at least the felicity of carrying out the fairness of tone, of taking the sun and the shade in the manner of towers of marble. . . . They are independently new and still more independently "novel"—this in common with so many other terrible things in America—and they are triumphant payers of dividends; all of which uncontested and unabashed pride, with flash of innumerable windows and flicker of subordinate gilt attributions, is like the flare up and down their long, narrow faces, of the lamps of some general permanent "celebration."[19]

The city's older buildings held beauty, but in James's estimation skyscrapers defied traditional evaluation. That certainly seems an accurate assessment.

If nothing else, the criticism reviewed above illuminates the degree to which the quality of city life and the state of the urban fabric had become paramount concerns by the turn of the century. Those concerns, as well as the desire to improve amenities and municipal housekeeping, fostered a number of ambitious city-planning efforts that can best be examined against the background of metropolitanism. The first attempts at organizing the city on a metropolitan scale date back to the 1850s. In 1857 the general assembly in Albany established a metropolitan police district that covered New York City (Manhattan), Kings County (including Brooklyn), Richmond County (Staten Island), and Westchester County. A similar metropolitan fire district was instituted in 1865 for New York and Brooklyn. In the following year a metropolitan health district was established for New York, Kings, Richmond, and Westchester counties. These efforts were promising, but subsequently all three districts were killed by New York aldermen who opposed any external control over their fiefs. Indeed, the history of planning in New York is primarily one of ambitious schemes that were never realized due to political controversy.

Eventually, with the creation of Greater New York on 1 January 1898, the damage was partly repaired. Preparation for that event had begun in 1890 with the establishment of the Consolidated Inquiry Commission, which was authorized by the city and state to consider the question of metropolitan government and the merger of New York City with the surrounding suburbs. The commission proposed unification of New York (which already included Bronx County and Borough) with Queens, Kings, and Richmond counties under a single all-embracing municipal government. Under the charter of union granted by the state general assembly in 1897, the respective borough governments (coextensive with the counties) were to be responsible for local affairs, leaving common needs and responsibilities to the central government.

Not until late in the nineteenth century were any potentially effective government agencies set up to oversee public improvement in the city. In 1891 the city appointed a commissioner of street improvements to be responsible only for uptown Manhattan and the Bronx. The major objective was to widen existing streets and to determine the necessary property acquisitions for the task. In 1898, with the establishment of the enlarged municipality, a citywide Bureau of Streets was established to plan an adequate system of streets, boulevards, and city parks. Later in the year the more potent and far-reaching board of public improvements was instituted, comprising directors of the departments of water supply, sewers, bridges, streets, street-cleaning, and public buildings. This was to be a model municipal agency which could have inaugurated a comprehensive program, developed cooperative relations among city departments, and guided them in the realization of plans and the carrying out of public works. The board, however, was abolished in 1901, principally because the boroughs demanded autonomy in public improvements, even those that were interborough in nature.

The broad powers of the new board during its brief existence raised hopes for implementing a comprehensive city plan. Several were put forward, notably one that the architect Julius F. Harder first proposed in 1898 in the journal of the Reform Club, *Municipal Affairs*. To some degree his plan was a response to the City Beautiful movement that had swept the country after the Chicago World's Fair of 1893 so impressively demonstrated the aesthetic of Beaux-Arts planning. Harder was inspired by the existing major urban plans, especially L'Enfant's Washington and Haussmann's Paris, and his plan would have introduced the vistas and axially sited monuments favored by City Beautiful planners. It would have ended the dominance of the 1811 gridiron, superimposing on it a system of diagonal avenues radiating from a civic center that would embrace and surround Union Square. The intersections of the diagonals and the main gridiron arteries were to be marked by genuine squares and public monuments. Aesthetic reform, however, was not Harder's major goal. Recognizing the importance of the urban economy, he recommended relocations and improvements for the most efficient use of the city's street system, railroad lines, bridges, ferries, docks, manufacturing centers, warehouses, markets, and parks. In the interest of accessibility and maximum benefit to the users, he also proposed optimum locations for the city's commercial and public buildings and residential areas.[20]

Harder showed foresight in his understanding of the metropolitan character of the urban agglomeration and the interdependency of city and surrounding region. He regarded the New York tributary area as lying within a radius of fifty miles from downtown Manhattan and as taking in 7,854 square miles. (As currently defined, the metropolitan area comprises twenty-two counties and 6,914 square miles.) Informed by the new Progressive spirit, Harder's scheme would have curtailed individual rights and liberties in the interest of a planned, rebuilt city aimed at the good of the commonwealth—and thus, ultimately, at the good of all individuals. The plan, however, was purposely forgotten by the new metropolitan government. Instead New York City was allowed to explode outward to its periphery and inward to a skyscraper core in the usual haphazard way.

Charles Mulford Robinson, planning theorist of the Progressive Era and author of *Modern Civic Art; or, The City Made Beautiful* (1903), saw both the enormous potentiality and the dismal reality of the city's development. Marshaling a quotation taken from a contemporary newspaper comment, he provided *Atlantic Monthly* readers with a neat summary of the problem: "We are plodding along on village lines, with village methods, marring with patchwork improvements that disfigure. . . . We are laying out the new districts of the Greater New York, not as the ideal city or the city beautiful, or even as the city of common sense. We are merely permitting it to grow under the stimulus of private greed and real estate speculation."[21] Today those words seem more a prophecy of the future than history.

Efforts to improve and beautify the city continued against this tide. In 1898, under the new city charter, a municipal art commission was founded that still exists. Its mandate, initially limited to beautifying the city through the installation of public art, had by 1907 been expanded to embrace the review of all works of art and architecture built on city-owned property. In July of 1903 a plan calling for a new civic center on Chambers Street was brought before the city's Board of Estimate and Apportionment by Henry F. Hornbostel, designer of the Williamsburg and Queensboro bridges (both 1905), and by George B. Post under the auspices of the city's bridge commissioner, Gustav Lindenthal. This long-range scheme, which was also supported by the Municipal Art Society, had been initiated by Mayor Seth Low. Along with a proposal to empty City Hall Park of all structures but City Hall itself and another that specified the configuration of the Manhattan terminal of the Brooklyn Bridge, it called for a forty-five-story municipal office building in the form of a campanile to be sited at the intersection of Chambers and Centre streets.[22] A site near that location had in fact been proposed in 1890 for a new municipal office building. Although the civic center project fell by the wayside, the city did undertake the construction of Hornbostel's bridge terminal and, in 1907, the colossal white skyscraper known as the Municipal Building and designed by McKim, Mead & White. The axial situation, embracing form, and Beaux-Arts style of that monumental structure would represent the municipality's most conspicuous response to City Beautiful planning ideals.

Supported by the Municipal Art Society and inspired by the Macmillan Senate Park Commission in Washington, D.C., a city improvement commission was established in December 1903 by ordinance of the board of aldermen, approved by Mayor George B. McClellan. The commission, which comprised prominent professionals and laymen, issued a preliminary report in 1905 and a final report in 1907 that proposed extensive changes: setting aside land for waterfront parks, constructing parkways and a continuous waterfront route, and widening Fifth Avenue and other commercial streets.[23] Although the commission's recommendations were useful, they did not go to the heart of the city's problems, as Harder's plan did. All of the proposals were ignored, except for improvements to the waterfront in the Chelsea district and the widening of Fifth Avenue and some peripheral interconnecting streets.

In 1904 the Paris-trained architect Ernest Flagg came up with a plan intended to improve the Commissioners' Map of 1811. Flagg, whose best-known building would be the record-high Singer Tower, recommended the creation of broad arterial ways along the waterfronts and in the central area of Manhattan. The most radical aspect of his plan was the redesign of Central Park as a more extensive series of small formal parks that would provide a foreground for large commercial and public buildings and break up the existing barrier to easy movement of crosstown and north-south traffic. Contrary to Olmsted's ideal of the park as a naturalistic refuge from the built-up city, the park grounds as modified by Flagg would provide settings for buildings, which in turn would serve as ornaments to the parks. If Flagg's plan had been implemented, Manhattan would have incorporated open squares, trees and other landscaping, and also parkways, including a grand, centrally located artery connecting to the Bronx by means of a Harlem River bridge at its northern end and joining his proposed Varick Street parkway at its lower end. This Grand Parkway would have served as the ideal foreground for skyscrapers of modest height set at varying depths along the margins. The cost of Flagg's Haussmannian scheme would have been offset by the sale of city-owned lands, some in the areas left after the breaking up of Central Park; the plan would have been realized in forty to fifty years.[24]

Fortunately, Flagg's plan, too, was ignored; for, like Harder's scheme, it would have resulted in the destruction of some of today's cherished buildings, as well as Central Park. Yet if ever there was a time for change, this was it. Flagg's proposal to make Varick Street a major artery was partially realized around World War I, when that street was widened and extended, cruelly scarring Greenwich Village in the process, to become Seventh Avenue South.

Skyscraper Economy and Technology

By the turn of the century the art of skyscraper design had reached a state such that all of the demands of the owners and the urban economy could be technically satisfied. The problems of structural design and construction, however, had by no means ceased to exist. On the contrary, they had been aggravated by the continuing concentration of tall office buildings in the downtown area. At first it had been possible to contain the demand for office space within a "walking area" below Wall Street, leaving the residential blocks to extend northward to the foot of Fifth Avenue, but the demand for both office and residential space had since increased to the point that residential areas had been pushed north along Fifth Avenue to 42nd Street. Because travel from 42nd to Wall Street took an hour, commercial development began moving northward. But the extension of the elevated rail lines in the late nineteenth century cut that travel time to fifteen minutes and prompted office construction to move back downtown, abetted by the peculiar gregarious compulsion of corporations to locate within a quarter-mile radius of the Stock Exchange. Ironically, instead of relieving the density of tall buildings, the elevated lines had intensified that situation.

Density of construction in the downtown business area, high construction costs, and urban economic expansion—which brought with it demands for office space, solutions to technical problems, and architectural mastery within ever more stringent financial necessities—these describe the problems and the architectural possibilities of skyscraper building at the turn of the century. The economy of the office building was discussed at some length—and apparently for the first time—by George Hill in the April 1904 *Architectural Record*. Considering first the length of the skyscraper's economic life, Hill noted that because the high office building was ordinarily too large and costly to be occupied by one company, part of the floor area had to be rented, and that the only index by which the building's financial success could be assessed was its average net return from rentals over a period of about fifteen years. From the economic standpoint, purely aesthetic additions that required costly materials had become more difficult to justify, especially those affecting the building's exterior. Building design, therefore, had become increasingly an engineering problem, with engineers responsible for structure, utilities, planning, and the construction process. In Hill's opinion, all the space below Chambers Street would soon be occupied exclusively by office buildings; therefore, skyscrapers in that area should be built to last at least fifty years.[25] A good many have in fact proved useful for a considerably longer time, and several historic churches and a few other structures have somehow withstood the predicted onslaught of office building.

The most important technical improvements in Hill's estimation in the decade between 1893 and 1903 were a "very slight" increase in net elevator speeds due to more precise controls, especially with electric power; the replacement of gas by electric lighting; and the increased use of automatic heat regulation. He might have added that wind bracing had become more scientific. Theoretically, there was no structural height limit, but as a general rule, sixteen to twenty stories would remain the favored height. The average height, and the maximum for an acceptable return on the investment, was in Hill's opinion likely to be twenty-five stories. (In 1893, it will be recalled, it was twenty.) He seems to have anticipated further improvement of the elevator through the incorporation of better mechanical controls, including the automatic safety stop, but he did not expect electric elevators "in any of their present forms" ever to replace hydraulic service in office buildings.[26] (At the turn of the century the hydraulic elevator was still nearly universal; the major shift to electrically powered elevators occurred after 1904.)

The existing techniques of heating and ventilation, as well as the use of coal for fuel, were deemed unsatisfactory on various counts and certainly ineffcent. Ideally, in Hill's judgment, in the future a fixed quantity of warmed fresh air would be introduced into each office at regular intervals to maintain a comfortable temperature range and keep the carbon dioxide at a minimum. Electricity would be the best means of operating heaters, fans, and controls, with filtering screens to be used for all incoming air, but this, too, was an aim to be realized later. Windows, Hill wrote, were best divided into three parts, one sash to be clear glass to admit light and accommodate the view, the other two to be wire glass for fire resistance. To further reduce combustibility, metals and other nonflammable materials should replace wood. That improvement was starting to occur and should be encouraged by architects, as should the use of fireproof partitions. Lighting was progressing in the direction of continuous illuminated surfaces (indirect lighting), as opposed to direct point-source lighting.

Although the quantity of steel used in frames for direct loads had been decreasing, the increasing elaboration of wind bracing had resulted in an increase in the total weight of the frame per unit of floor area. As a means of increasing fire resistance and reducing the weight, thickness, and cost of floor construction, Hill predicted—and recommended—the reduction of structural steel in floors in favor of reinforced concrete. That material, he believed, should eventually replace all steel in horizontal frames. (There was still the question, however, of adequate wind resistance.) In order to increase the fire and corrosion resistance of steel, metallurgy would have to be improved.

Addressing the question of fire insurance, Hill alleged that it was too easy to build badly, then suffer destruction—causing damage to neighboring property in the process—and yet recover losses through insurance. The difference in the premiums for safe and unsafe construction was much less than the difference in the cost of the interest on the respective investments; insurance companies thus effectively placed a premium on inferior building, especially by their refusal to insist on total incombustibility. Hill recommended that actuarial statistics and the associated premium charge rest on a scientific inquiry into the relationship between inferior construction and fire losses, with the amount of the damage payment related as closely as possible to the quality and, hence, the cost of construction.[27]

On the subject of power plant design, Hill pointed out that while the operation of boilers, engines, and generators had become more efficient, much fuel was being wasted in all such installations, which were operated under improper conditions. Moreover, the coal in common use, mainly large-lump Pocahontas, did not produce the best combustion. Hill implied that many of the defects endured because architects, engineers, and contractors were unfamiliar with the technologies in use, because their training and education lagged behind improvements in technology. In planning the basement area, for example, the architect rarely provided sufficient space for the utilities; and so Hill offered specific recommendations for the number, type, and arrangement of these.[28]

As Hill explained in some detail, the height of a skyscraper is determined by a number of factors. For buildings no higher than sixteen stories, footings on piles or timber grillages with rafts were acceptable for any soil conditions, no matter how poor. Bedrock caissons, however, were necessary for buildings above that height, and in order to meet the added expense of the caissons, the building would have to be still higher. The number of elevators required was a major factor. For sites encompassing between 7,500 and 12,500 square feet, five elevator cars were necessary up to a height of twelve stories. Beyond that, one car was needed for each additional three stories, and each car would result in a loss of 100 square feet per floor. Hence, the height would again have to be upped to meet the loss—obviously a serious consideration. As for the cost of additional stories beyond the sixteen-story optimum, a seventeenth story would add 6.25 percent of the original building cost, plus 5 percent of the increment, for a total increase of 6.5625 percent. The initial percentage increase for the eighteenth story would be the same as for the seventeenth, but the supplemental increment would be 10 percent for a total increase of 6.875 percent. So if the original cost of the sixteen-story building was $500,000, then the seventeenth story would cost $32,812.50 and the eighteenth $34,375.00.

Another factor that influenced the height of a building was the cost of heating, which, if live steam heat was used, increased rapidly with height. The expense of heating one story above the tenth floor, for example, equaled that of heating the two lower stories. Two conditions accounted for the added cost: first, the higher the building rose, the greater the volume to be heated and the greater the surface of radiation loss; second, the higher the elevation above grade level, the lower the circumambient air temperature. The same differential was advantageous in the summer, if the building was cooled by forced draft.

By averaging all of the variables involved in a number of specific examples, Hill was able to draw several conclusions regarding the ratio of increased rental income to additional height. First, assuming that the sixteen-story building yields a gross return of 10 percent, a thirty-two-story building would yield 11 percent under similar conditions and lot size. In a hypothetical example, the cost of the lot of the sixteen-story building might be $1 million. Add that to the cost of the building itself, $1 million, and the total cost becomes $2 million, which could be expected to yield a return of $200,000. For a thirty-two-story building, the lot, again $1 million, plus the cost of the building, $2,240,000, equals $3,240,000, with a return of $376,200. Therefore an additional expenditure of $1,420,000 would yield an additional return of $176,200, or 12.41 percent of the increment. Hill's analysis offered abundant evidence that it paid to build as high as the technology and the financial resources allowed.[29]

Although Hill gave little attention to wind bracing, that technological challenge was explored by Robert M. Neilson in *Engineering Magazine* in January 1903. Reviewing European experiments from Borda in the eighteenth century to date, Neilson covered all types of wind effects: of direct frontal pressure, pressure on surfaces inclined or in other ways not normal to the wind vector, turbulence (a discovery of the late nineteenth century), and back and negative pressure on the leeward side of the building, as well as the effect of overall size on the total pressure and stability.[30] As was known at the time—though Neilson did not address the issue—the building acts as a vertical cantilever, with the bending moment induced by wind at its theoretical maximum at grade level. On the windward side, the bending is negative, hence under tension; on the leeward side, the bending is positive, hence under compression. The distribution of the shear was probably not known at the turn of the century, nor was, in all likelihood, the factor of oscillation or wind drift, although the existence of that factor was known.

The problem of protecting iron framing members from the corrosive action of moisture continued to be a matter of concern, and with the widespread use of all-steel framing after the turn of the century the concern became acute. The oxidation of steel, as well as other forms of corrosive action, arose from three factors: direct penetration of atmospheric moisture; the penetration of ground water into the footings; and direct electrolytic action causing corrosion—the passage of electric current from moisture to metal, from one metal to another, and from metal to masonry or concrete. The extent of the problem was not known, although it turned out to be exaggerated. When an important building that had been completed before 1905 was found to have suffered from penetration of groundwater into the subbasement through the foundation slab and footings, the subject again attracted attention. An editorial in the October 1907 issue of *Architecture* sensibly pointed out that the architect must be trained to recognize this and other technical difficulties, and that the engineer must know the fundamental laws of physics and chemistry as well as the practicalities of structure and utilities.[31]

One more problem remained at the turn of the century with regard to iron and steel construction: fatigue stress, the reduction in the strength of metal that resulted from stress under the prolonged application of load. Such overstress was known to exist, although an examination of iron columns loaded for more than thirty years revealed no deflections resulting from a loss of strength. And investigations undertaken mainly by German engineers during the second half of the 1890s showed that iron and steel under working stresses specified by code in a properly designed structure would retain their strength indefinitely.[32]

At the turn of the century the importance of good foundation work was not widely accepted; indeed, many contractors held that ragged masonry and irregular concrete work were acceptable because footings and foundation walls are invisible. Events, however, proved otherwise. On 19–20 March 1905, eight new brick buildings erected in New York City by various hands collapsed. Investigation revealed poor foundation work, voids in the walls, and irregular masonry work, with courses inadequately bonded and improperly bedded.[33] As witnessed by the near-disastrous failure in the 1960s of the caissons in the John Hancock and 500 North Michigan buildings in Chicago, the problem still exists.

The possibilities of reinforced concrete construction, meanwhile, were slow to be realized in New York. The Manhattan Bureau of Buildings, as it had been constituted under the new charter, did not permit employment of the technology until 1903. What may have been its first use in the city occurred in a private residence built in 1903, the permit having been issued in December 1902, where reinforced "cement" floors were built on the system patented by François Hennebique. The permit was granted because fireproofing was not required, and the material "promised something better than wood."[34] New York builders believed that this construction was promising for the future, but there was no unanimity as to whether any system of reinforcing was adequate for modern urban requirements. Apparently they were unaware of, or indifferent to, Ernest L. Ransome's extremely important reinforced concrete warehouse buildings across the river in New Jersey, early East Coast examples close to home. Multistory building in reinforced concrete appears to have been delayed until the construction of the eleven-story McGraw Building on West 39th Street and a building called the Monolith on 24th Street near Broadway, both of which were completed in 1907.

Although it had been slow to gain acceptance, construction with power-operated equipment was standard by the turn of the century. By 1900 the steel used in high buildings was being erected by steam-powered cranes or boom derricks with a reach of from 40 to 70 feet and a capacity of 6 to 15 tons. In the case of buildings no higher than eighteen stories, a single derrick, centrally located, was usually sufficient for the purpose; the largest derricks could emplace up to 1,000 tons per month. Higher buildings with unusually large floor areas required one or more supplementary derricks. As the work rose, usually two to three floors at a lift, the large derricks hoisted themselves from floor to floor. A high capacity and relatively lightweight derrick, with its boom and mast built up with latticework sides and angles at the corners, was designed and built by Levering & Garrigues for the steel erection of Clinton & Russell's ten-story Farmers' Loan and Trust Company Building at 22 William Street (1908–9; demolished). The Levering & Garrigues firm also developed a similar stiff-leg derrick as a supplement. By 1902 compressed air was coming into use as a means of powering construction machinery, and the pneumatic riveting hammer and ratcheting drill were greatly facilitating steel-frame construction.[35]

Besetting Questions of Architectural Form and Height Limitation

As the technical problems were solved and the innovations incorporated into design and construction, the whole process was progressively rationalized, taking on a quasi-scientific character. The perceived danger was that the architectural aspect would take on a similar character as it steadily yielded to function, technique, and economy. Asserting that "the artistic expression, the form, the covering, the outer aspects [of the high building], are of supreme public importance," the critic Barr Ferree assessed the periods of skyscraper design and its state in 1904. He suggested that during the introductory decade of the 1870s the possibilities of high-building design were beyond the architect, and in support of that contention he cited the examples of the Western Union and Tribune buildings. Although architects had grappled bravely with the problem, the results, according to Ferree, had provided no future direction.[36] What he failed to realize, possibly because he was too close in time to that era, was that the tall buildings of Hunt, Post, and their confreres had in fact anticipated virtually every feature of turn-of-the-century design from the distinctive and costly-appearing corporate image to the tower and columnar forms. With regard to architectural design, it was primarily the *language* of style and form, and the height, of course, that had changed.

The skyscraper was made to appear "showy" during the second phase, which Ferree designated the "advertising period." The well-designed, extravagant building of the late 1880s and early 1890s had appealed to the high-rent tenant because it attracted favorable attention through its sumptuosity, splendor, and richness and had enjoyed a high status with the community. The architect had been given a great opportunity, but had failed because he had misunderstood the problem. Instead of recognizing his own incompetence, he had faulted the "problem"—the high building itself. As for the third phase,

Ferree's own time and the period of the skyscraper's maturity, the solution was ever more the reduction, even elimination, of artistic detail. As buildings became higher, wider, more strictly prismatic in outline, and costlier, the design elements of pattern, movement, accent, rhythm, and ornament were progressively reduced to the bare minimum, leaving little means of adding aesthetic splendor. Form had taken the place of ornament, and, in Ferree's opinion, the skyscraper had become "a frigidly severe edifice, a sheer brick wall, lit with numberless windows," and a "featureless high building." In other words, it had become a box with windows for light, air, and the view. The outlook was thoroughly pessimistic: "There is no standard of artistic excellence. . . . There is plenty of haphazard effort, a good deal of well meant effort, and occasional success. We had as much ten years ago; and we have today a vast quantity of uninteresting building which harms through its negativeness."[37]

Thomas Hastings was a bit more optimistic because he believed that the problem of satisfactory design could be solved with admirable results and that there were guides to point the way. In his view, the successful designer in the mode of the "modern Renaissance" (his term for the prevalent "modern French" or what now would be called Beaux-Arts style)−that is, the designer who will respond to all the requirements and produce vital and expressive form−should welcome the new problems and conditions before him. He should design honestly in terms of practical requirements, and use the new structural techniques. Hastings, who regarded Les Halles Centrales in Paris as the first important complex in which iron was used honestly and artistically, thought the way to design in terms of modern demands was to begin with a thoroughly developed floor plan that would then "determine the entire structure of the building, both external and internal."[38] The architect of 1900 could use the classical and Renaissance forms as guides and precedents. Hastings, however, did not quite come to terms with the refractory nature of the skyscraper; its floor plan was so much controlled by function and utilities that the architect had little latitude in what he could do in the way of design.

The issue of skyscraper form drew attention whenever anyone sufficiently interested discussed the subject in the public journals, but the question of skyscraper height limitation remained a matter of endless debate, with the architects usually speaking in favor of such limitation. A signal event was the passage in 1898 of a Massachusetts state law that restricted building heights in Boston, for this law ultimately brought the issue before the courts. Real estate and building interests fought it on the grounds that it infringed on private property rights and that the state had no right to pass legislation affecting local building regulations. Eventually, litigation brought the case to the Supreme Court, which ruled in the spring of 1909 (*Welch v. Swasey*) that the state had the right to limit the height of buildings and to allow variations of height in different zoning districts, as in the Massachusetts law.[39] Height restrictions on dwellings and apartment houses in New York City had by then been passed by the state legislature and could have been cited as a precedent for office building height restriction, although the restrictions had never been tested in the courts.

In 1896 the New York Chamber of Commerce called for legislation restricting height, but no action was taken; efforts by other groups were also unsuccessful, including a bill proposed by the New York Board of Trade to the New York Board of Aldermen in 1899, which would have limited the height of commercial buildings to 200 feet.[40] The consensus of American engineers, as expressed at a joint meeting in London in July 1900 of the American Society of Civil Engineers and the British Institution of Civil Engineers, opposed such limitation. The undesirable and dangerous consequences of great height had been exaggerated, the engineers contended, and excessive height would in any case be controlled by technical, utilitarian, and economic conditions. The arguments were advanced principally by Corydon T. Purdy and Reginald P. Bolton, outstanding spokesmen of the profession who had worked on the Broadway Chambers Building. Not surprisingly, the British engineers were mostly in favor of height controls, recommending that the width of the street should be the governing factor. The *Engineering Record* called for "a comprehensive and intelligent survey" of the whole problem, so that all interests would be served.[41]

The *Record and Guide*, commenting on the increasing trend to protect an existing skyscraper's light, air, and rentability through the purchase of adjacent lots, put the question in practical terms: "Why build twenty-story structures, when space as great as that which the structure occupies itself has to be reserved for low and unremunerative buildings?"[42] Not only the American Surety and Park Row buildings but also the Washington Life, Mills, Havemeyer, and others had been so protected by their owners. The question of height restriction was thrown into bolder relief in late 1900 when the Aetna Real Estate Company bought a lot at Broadway and 33rd Street measuring 98 by 118.5 feet and announced a plan to erect a thirty-story, 455-foot-high building. Had it been constructed, it would have been the highest in New York, overtopping the Park Row by 64 feet, but only with the inclusion of some kind of towerlike extension above the top floor.[43]

New York architects then mustered their resources. In 1903 George Post and Charles D. Purroy, the city's acting fire chief at the time, publicly demanded that building heights be regulated by law, and various architects proposed an amendment to the city's building code that would limit building height to 150 feet. The editor of the *American Architect* was a particularly strong advocate:

> A uniform limit of one hundred and fifty feet would allow very comfortably of twelve stories, and this is not an unreasonable number for such a city as New York, but it would prevent the future erection of office buildings three hundred feet high, which shade the streets, darken other buildings, and inflict damage of various kinds upon a whole neighborhood. While even one hundred and fifty feet is too liberal a limit for a city which aspires to be beautiful, the lower part of New York is too far gone in ugliness for reclamation, so that this consideration need not count for much; but darkness, dampness and chilling winds are also to be thought of, and common prudence suggests that lower Broadway and the adjacent streets, with a few more additions to the "sky-scrapers" with which they are lined, would become intolerable.[44]

In 1904, along with Thomas Hastings, the artist-planner Charles Rollinson Lamb recommended a number of improvements for Fifth Avenue, including height limitation. As early as 1898, Lamb had envisioned the setback skyscraper, and for Fifth Avenue he proposed that the height of building cornices be restricted as was done in Paris, leaving the rear portion of the building to rise unrestricted, as long as it did not project above the angle of view from across the street.[45] Lamb's ideas were too far in advance of his time to be taken seriously. Architects, however, kept up the agitation, with Ernest Flagg coming to the forefront in 1908.

Had it been enacted, the architects' proposed amendment of 1903 would have affected the building code that had been adopted by the City Council in late 1899 and ratified in 1901 by the state legislature. At the same time, the legislature had abolished the Department of Buildings and had established instead a bureau of buildings in each of the five boroughs. In a weak attempt at guaranteeing light and air for the occupants, the code mandated that office buildings not on a corner could cover no more than 90 percent of the lot above the second story level, but it set no height limit for these buildings. It did contain an improved section on the physical properties and performance of brick, stone, sand, lime, cement, concrete, wood, and metal, as well as a section precisely specifying the allowable stresses in metals.[46] The standards for foundation construction were based on the assumption that the materials would be brick, stone, iron, steel, or concrete, or two or more of these together, and floor loads for office buildings were now set at 75 pounds per square foot minimum, a change from the 1892 code, where the loading factor was 100 pounds per square foot.[47]

The code also contained specifications for two types of curtain walls enclosing skeleton-framed structures: "inclosure walls for skeleton structures," meaning walls "of brick built in between iron or steel columns, and supported wholly or in part on iron or steel girders"; and "curtain walls," also infill but unsupported by steel or iron girders. For inclosure walls, the code specified a minimum thickness of 12 inches for the topmost 75 feet of the building and required an increase of 4 inches for every additional 60 feet below.[48] In the 1892 law such walls, there described as curtain walls, were required to be 12 inches thick for the top 50 feet and increased by 4 inches for every 50-foot section below. The new dimensions were still conservative, but improved.

The 1899 code, the city's first enacted municipally, was adopted over considerable opposition from the American Institute of Architects, who complained that it had been drawn up without consulting their membership and that it granted too much power to the building commissioner to waive or modify its provisions, thus creating the potential for corruption. Although the code would not be extensively revised until 1915, by September 1903 it incorporated the first regulations on the use of reinforced concrete adopted by any city in the country. These cautiously detailed regulations included a provision stating that such construction would be approved for buildings required to be fireproof by the code only if a sample of the material passed fire and water tests conducted under the supervision of the Bureau of Buildings.[49]

By the early years of the new century the stage was set for the great skyscraper boom that would reach its culmination in the Singer, Metropolitan Life, Municipal, Bankers Trust, and Woolworth buildings. Plans for ninety-three buildings more than nine stories tall were filed in 1902; eleven of those were projected to rise more than fifteen stories, and sixty-three were to be sited north of 14th Street. High-rise construction was spreading into midtown, with tall buildings going up along Fifth Avenue, along the spine of Broadway, near Madison Square, on 34th and 42nd streets, and a new thatch of office buildings was being planned for the lower West Street and Hudson and Battery tunnel area.[50] Simultaneously, the earliest tall buildings were being transformed—sometimes deformed

—through height additions, as in the case of the Tribune Building, where nine stories were added (1903–5); the Morse, raised to twelve full stories (1901); Aldrich Court, extended to fourteen (1906); and the former Times Building, raised to fifteen (1905). And a new type of high-rise building, the hotel, was fast populating the Greeley and Longacre (Times) Square sections, Fifth Avenue above 42nd Street, and the vicinity of 72nd Street and Broadway. The skyscraper had come of age, but whether it was acceptable as it stood in the urban milieu remained a subject of controversy.

10 THE SKYSCRAPER COMES OF AGE, 1900–1910

Skyscraper office building boomed in the first decade of the new century, at the same time achieving technical maturity, architectural confidence, and unprecedented heights. In their exterior design the new works predominantly represented variations on three themes that had emerged in the 1890s. The first was the simplified classical three-part elevation. The second was vertical continuity achieved through continuous pilasters that defined bays, which became increasingly more open to the point that the shaft dissolved into a screen, the vertical emphasis and screenlike quality becoming more pronounced in the Gothic skyscraper that appeared in 1905. The third was the isolated tower treated as a campanile or other towerlike form. Most of the new buildings were light in color, although occasionally brightened with colorful terra-cotta accents, and their architectural expression was informed by the desire to impart a sense of enduring, Old World monumentality to this innovative New World building type. At the beginning of the decade the flat-roofed skyscraper predominated, but by 1907 towered or otherwise picturesque roofs were again activating the skyline as builders endeavored to produce office buildings that would attract attention and tenants. The mounted tower also made its debut, before the advent of the Woolworth Building, with the new Times Building in 1904.

First Skyscrapers of the New Century: Mutual Life, Atlantic Mutual, Broad-Exchange, and Flatiron Buildings

The sober classical form particularly marked the work of Clinton & Russell (Charles W. Clinton and William Hamilton Russell). Formed in 1894, by 1900 this partnership was fast becoming one of the city's leading skyscraper producers. It opened the century

298

with major essays that pointed the way to future work. Undoubtedly, Clinton's long association with the Mutual Life Insurance Company had enhanced his reputation and accounted at least in part for his firm's success as commercial architects. Since designing Mutual Life's second building, completed in 1884, Clinton had served steadily as that company's architect. He was independently responsible for two additions to the 1884 building, the first an eight-story enlargement completed in 1888, the second a fifteen-story addition finished in 1892, and in 1899 his firm designed yet another fifteen-story addition that was completed in 1904 (Fig. 10.1).[1] All the additions harmonized with the neo-Renaissance style of Clinton's initial building.

The proportions of base, midsection, and capital, if not the uniform light-colored masonry, of the same firm's Atlantic Mutual Insurance Company Building (1900–1901; demolished) recalled Cass Gilbert's Broadway Chambers. The headquarters of a company founded in 1842 to insure cargo-ship owners and also importers and exporters, this eighteen-story, flat-topped, L-shaped slab replaced the company's previous building on the southwest corner of Wall and William streets. More interesting than its formal design, however, was the Atlantic Building's pneumatic caisson foundation work. In spite of such problems as a high water level and the need to shore up the walls of surrounding buildings, the foundation was completed in only five weeks and ahead of schedule. In the interest of saving time and money, the walls of the adjoining U.S. Trust Company Building, which rested on quicksand, were left virtually unshored. Instead, the outermost row of caissons was sunk against the Trust Company walls to a depth of about 40 feet below the foundations. Invented by the building's engineer, John F. O'Rourke, the caisson used

10.1
Mutual Life Insurance Company Building (1883–84; 1888; 1892; 1900–4; demolished), C. W. Clinton and Clinton & Russell, architects. Collection of The New-York Historical Society.

was made of wood staves and had an unusual oblique cutting edge and a removable steel-plated cover to its air chamber, which permitted additional concreting.[2]

The Broad-Exchange Building (1900–1902), another Clinton & Russell product, was the largest office building yet constructed. With 326,500 square feet of rentable floor area, it was nearly one and a half times larger than its closest rivals, the Equitable, Bowling Green, and Forty-two Broadway buildings.[3] This vast, twenty-story monolith, still standing on the southeast corner of Broad Street and Exchange Place, fills a site as peculiarly shaped as that of its immediate neighbor, Lord's Court. The main portion of the light-colored brick and stone-clad building is 107 feet wide on Broad Street and 236 feet wide on Exchange Place, where it literally walls in that narrow street. From this main section of the building a long "tail" extends deep into the center of the block (see Fig. 8.1). Aptly characterized as a "town under a single roof," the skeleton-framed, conservatively neo-classical structure was built with marble-clad lobby walls and eighteen "high-speed" elevators.[4] The owner of record was P. J. Merrick, who seems to have represented a syndicate known as the Alliance Realty Company. The George A. Fuller Company, which for the time being had captured the construction field, built the Broad-Exchange.

In 1903, when the Fuller, or Flatiron, Building was completed (1901–1903), it was the tallest skyscraper north of the financial district (Fig. 10.2). The product of a contractor-developer who had earlier been based in Chicago, a Chicago architectural firm, and an engineering firm that had begun its practice in Chicago, this elegantly slender building fills its triangular site just below Madison Square at the intersection of Broadway, Fifth Avenue, and 23rd Street (Fig. 10.3). It takes its distinctive shape from the site, which not only molded it from the ground up—in itself not unusual in New York—but inspired the architect to finish off the building with a heavy, projecting cornice and flat balustraded top. The continuity of the horizontal divisions between the floors was emphasized as a means of unifying the building's aggressive form (Fig. 10.4). Including the narrow attic story, the story count is twenty-one, and the height was reported as 307 feet. Above the first story the width of the Broadway front is 190 feet; the Fifth Avenue front is 173 feet

10.2
Flatiron Building (1901–3), D. H. Burnham & Company, architects. Bounded by Broadway, Fifth Avenue, and 22nd and 23rd streets. *After* De Leeuw, Both Sides of Broadway.

10.3
Plan of typical floor, Flatiron Building. After *Architecture (1902).*

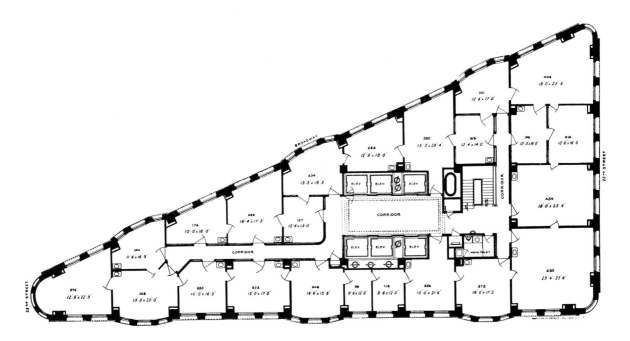

10.4
*Detail,
Broadway facade of
Flatiron Building.
Photograph by
S. B. Landau.*

wide, and the building is nearly 87 feet wide on its 22nd Street side. Its north end is a mere one-bay point, prompting a description of the Flatiron as the slenderest building in the city.[5] In 1902, while it was under construction, the decision was made to add a one-story, metal-framed, glass-enclosed "prow" for show-window purposes at the point; that addition further reinforces the Flatiron's striking form.

The first public announcement of the building, which came in November 1900, projected a structure of twelve to fifteen stories. But a building permit filed in August 1901 called for twenty stories; it also specified the architect as D. H. Burnham of Chicago and listed the owner as the Cumberland Realty Company, a name inspired by the Cumberland Hotel, which had previously stood at the southern end of the site. In actuality, the Flatiron was developed by its builder, the George A. Fuller Company, and for a time was called the Fuller Building until its popular nickname took over. It was financed by a syndicate that included Samuel and Mott Newhouse and also Fuller's son-in-law Harry S. Black, who had succeeded Fuller upon his death in 1900 as head of the company. In 1901 Black established the United States Realty and Construction Company, which acquired a major share of the George A. Fuller Company and went on to finance the construction of such important skyscrapers in the city as the Trinity and U.S. Realty buildings, with the Fuller Company as contractor. By 1904 the U.S. Realty and Construction Company was listed as the owner of the Flatiron Building. The Fuller Company took space on an upper floor and remained in the building until 1929, when it completed new headquarters farther uptown. It was responsible for the construction of numerous important buildings in the city, including the old Pennsylvania Station, the Plaza Hotel, Lever House, and the Seagram Building, as well as major buildings in other American cities and in Europe. It remained active until 1994, although its business began to decline in the 1970s.[6]

By this time, the firm of Daniel Hudson Burnham had achieved prominence as one of the leading architectural and urban planning firms in the nation. Burnham himself did no architectural designing, and it is difficult to know who in his large office actually designed the Flatiron. Signed drawings in the collection of the Art Institute of Chicago, however, indicate that the design and detailing owe heavily to Frederick P. Dinkelberg.[7] For some unknown reason, in its 5 October 1901 issue the *Record and Guide* published a view of the building labeled "The Cumberland," with Bruce Price named as the architect. Assuming this to have been a case of mistaken identity and not a change of architect, the error may be significant because the published perspective, which is virtually identical to the building as executed, evokes the rustication and columnar aspect of Price's American Surety Building.

The site afforded visual and functional advantages, chiefly light and air, and all offices would have outside, wide-view exposure. The building would stand clear and at a considerable distance from its neighbors, but its narrow triangular-prismatic form created planning and framing problems that had to be resolved. Fortunately, bedrock depth in the immediate vicinity ranged from about minus 30 to minus 37 feet, close enough to the excavation floor that very little cutting into solid rock was required for the concrete footings with granite caps that would support the cast-iron column bases. Engineered by the skilled firm of Purdy & Henderson, who had worked with the Fuller Company on the Broadway Chambers, the steel skeleton frame was constructed to withstand a heavy load and a maximum working stress and to provide the wind bracing necessary for an exposed structure of this peculiar form.[8] The wall bays were braced by triangular gusset plates (or solid-web knee braces) above and below the girder at all column-and-girder connections (Fig. 10.5). On the transverse, at the inner bays, large knee braces above and below the girders extended to the center points of the columns in the form of K-trusses. In the intermediate bays there were only knee braces below the girders. Because of the extreme angle of the walls at the northern end, the wind loads presented a special problem, but the building's triangular form helped offset the difficulty, offering superior wind resistance to that of a rectangular prism. The bracing of the narrow north end of the building, where the walls meet at an unusually sharp angle, was resolved by using built-up wall girders of two elliptical segments spanning between the end wall columns and the apex column. None of this prevented wind gusts exacerbated by the shape of the building from affecting passersby. In 1903 wind reportedly forced a messenger boy into Fifth Avenue, where he was killed by an automobile, and women were inconveniently blown about and paper money lost from their pocketbooks.[9]

The shallow eight-story-high oriels above the seventh floor on the Broadway and Fifth Avenue sides were not common in New York office buildings, but many Chicago sky-

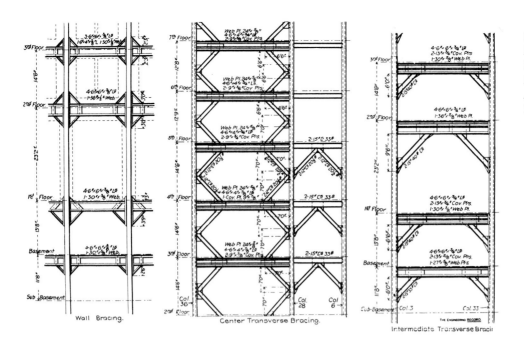

10.5
Forms of wind
bracing,
Flatiron Building.
After Engineering
Record (1902).

Wall Bracing.

Center Transverse Bracing.

Intermediate Transverse Bracing

scrapers, including the Burnham firm's Fisher Building (1895–96), had utilized them as windbreakers. Otherwise the elevations follow the standard New York tripartite division, with five-story base, twelve-story shaft, and four-story attic. The subtle swelling of the oriels gives the walls an undulating character, and the rustication and unified warm color of the sheathing, pale buff-gray limestone at the base and pale buff-colored terra-cotta and brick above, add to the general unity of treatment. Openings, moldings, ornamental details in high and low relief, and unusual copper-clad, wood-framed (kalamein) windows contribute a rich texture to the surface and heighten the screenlike character of the wall.

The Flatiron joined Hardenbergh's Western Union Building across Fifth Avenue and the Metropolitan Life Building and Madison Square Garden on the east and north sides of Madison Square (see Fig. 11.7). It was the object of great interest during and after construction. Soon after it was finished the photographer Alfred Stieglitz captured it as it loomed above the snowladen trees in Madison Square, giving it the appearance of floating free in space like a weightless screen. He was quite taken with the building: "With the trees of Madison Square covered with fresh snow, the Flat Iron impressed me as never before. It appeared to be moving toward me like the bow of a monster ocean steamer—a picture of new America still in the making. . . . The Flat Iron is to the United States what the Parthenon was to Greece."[10] Within the decade, the immediate area, which had earlier been part of the city's fashionable hotel and entertainment district, became a major business district. Today, freshly cleaned with its prow restored (1991), the Flatiron is the flagship of the historic Ladies' Mile shopping district, where Arnold Constable, Lord & Taylor, Siegel-Cooper, and many other dry goods stores flourished before the turn of the century.

Meanwhile the Fuller Company had completed construction of the Bank of the Metropolis building (1902–3) on the corner of Union Square West and East 16th Street and adjoining the Decker Building (Fig. 10.6). Established in 1871 primarily to serve local businesses, the bank had previously occupied several buildings on the Square, and its new sixteen-story building rose on the site of its first headquarters.[11] Steel framed with brick curtain walls, the limestone-clad bank and office building is L-shaped but presents a narrow slab to the street. The architect of this well-proportioned, exquisitely detailed skyscraper was Bruce Price. Once again, as with his American Surety Building, he employed to good effect the column design formula and the classical vocabulary traditionally associated with bank architecture. A subtly curving Ionic portico at the center of the narrow Union Square front was intended to signal the bank's principal entrance, and the building's smooth, screenlike shaft, where rows of windows clearly indicate the tiers of offices, is topped by a four-story capital featuring carved lion's heads and crowned by a heavy copper-clad cornice.

The Blair Building (1902), which stood on the northwest corner of Broad Street and Exchange Place next door to the Commercial Cable Building, was another sixteen-story design success (Fig. 10.7). It was described in the engineering press as the first skyscraper executed by architects trained at the Ecole des Beaux-Arts, but that assertion overlooks the work of Richard Morris Hunt in the 1870s. The partners of the designing firm, John M. Carrère and Thomas Hastings, had met as students in Paris, and both had worked in the McKim, Mead & White office in the early 1880s. Founded in 1885, Carrère & Hastings had executed such major commissions as the Ponce de León Hotel in St. Augustine, Florida (1888), and the New York Public Library (1902–11). The owner of the Blair Building, listed on the building permit as the Sussex Realty Company, but in fact a company whose principal member was the Blair & Company investment banking firm, was said to have given the architect a free hand.[12]

The architectural treatment of the Blair's two street fronts was another essay in vertical continuity. The marble envelope was pure veneer, unrelated to the underlying structural geometry, but only steel framing would allow this surface manipulation. Above a sculpturally treated base shallow central pilasters rose through ten stories. Recessed areas of continuous glazing between the pilasters intensified the vertical continuity. The corner bays were "strengthened" by the use of rusticated masonry and vertical rows of individual windows in such a way as to carry out the superficial, screenlike character of the wall. The shaft, terminated by a balcony with wrought-iron decorative details, was topped by a three-story capital that was treated sculpturally in harmony with the base.

Clinton & Russell abandoned its usual sobriety in the design of Sixty Wall Building (1903–5), which was constructed as a two-part, setback skyscraper by the International Banking Corporation, alias the Sixty Wall Street Company (Fig. 10.8).[13] Built with its fourteen-story lower portion on Wall Street and its twenty-six-story part on Pine Street, Sixty Wall was developed on all four sides because of its prominent siting and visibility from the East River and the bay. It may deserve recognition for its voluntary setback design that at least respected Wall Street, but the two-part form was also the means of gaining light and air and a view of the bay—hence, higher rentals—for more of the

10.7
*Blair Building
(1902; demolished),
Carrère & Hastings,
architects.
At right: Commercial
Cable Building.
Museum of the City of
New York.*

10.8
*Sixty Wall Street
Building
(1903–5; de-
molished),
Clinton & Russell,
architects.
After* King's Views of
New York *(1915)*, 27.

building's offices. Sixty Wall's four-story attic sections, almost whimsically classical, were topped by parapets shaped like pediments at the sides and sporting escutcheons and urns. The Wall Street front displayed above a columned base four sculpted female figures that were reminiscent of the American Surety Building's caryatids. While Sixty Wall was under construction, Leroy S. Buffington alleged that this and other buildings infringed on his patent for a twenty-eight-story skeleton-framed skyscraper. Sixty Wall's builders denied the allegation.[14]

The Times Building: "City's Tallest Structure from Base to Top"

In a minutely detailed, lavishly illustrated supplement published on 1 January 1905, the *New York Times* proudly described every aspect of its new, nearly complete, skyscraper-headquarters (1903–5), from the excavation of its foundations to the modernity of the machinery it housed and its electrically powered vacuum sweeping system (Figs. 10.9 and 10.10). Entitled "City's Tallest Structure from Base to Top," the opening article begins with the following summary of the new building's most extraordinary features:

> It touches Higher Clouds Than Anything Within Twelve Miles—Extreme Height of 476 Feet—Nearly Half of the Work and Its Most Wonderful Part is Under Ground—A Pumping Plant, 61 Feet Below the Curb—The Sub-structure on a Base More than Three Times the Size of the Building Lot—New Record in Structural Steel Tonnage—A Larger Percentage of Steel to Cubical Contents Than Any Other Office Building—Comparative Statistics of Recent Erections—The Stongest and Stiffest Steel Frame Structure of Similar Dimensions Ever Erected—Floor Space that is 21 Times the Area of the Building Lot.[15]

The article goes on to explain that the "extreme height of 476 feet" is measured from the floor of the lowest basement to the top to the flagpole; but that by the usual standard, measuring from curb to top of building, the height was only 362 feet, 8¾ inches. Therefore, by the accepted standard, the new building ranked second to the Park Row Building. Measured by the *Times'* standard, however—and it should be noted that the height given for the Park Row, 380 feet from curb to top, is a good ten feet less than that cited elsewhere—it was taller by 66 feet and could therefore be considered the highest building in the city. The floor count was twenty-five stories from street to observatory.

For its new quarters the newspaper had deliberately selected an uptown location and a trapezoidal site open on all sides, one of four such sites below Central Park formed by the intersection of Broadway with another major avenue. (The Flatiron Building occupied the one at 23rd Street and the Herald Building the one at 34th.)[16] This was Longacre Square, where Broadway and Seventh Avenue intersect at 43rd Street. The ongoing construction of hotels, office buildings, club buildings, theatres, and especially the Broadway IRT subway, to open in 1904, ensured that the section would prosper and long remain a major uptown nexus. In its supplement the *Times* referred to the area as "Times Square"—a name that had already been given to the subway station—and it has been so called ever since. The subway meant that newspaper operations need no longer be confined to the vicinity of City Hall, and the subway tracks and 42nd Street subway station located directly beneath the new building rendered the *Times'* new site central to

10.9

*Times Building
(1903–5),
Eidlitz & McKenzie,
architects.
View from southeast
on Broadway at
42nd Street.
Photograph by
George P. Hall & Son,
c. 1905.
Collection of The
New-York Historical
Society.*

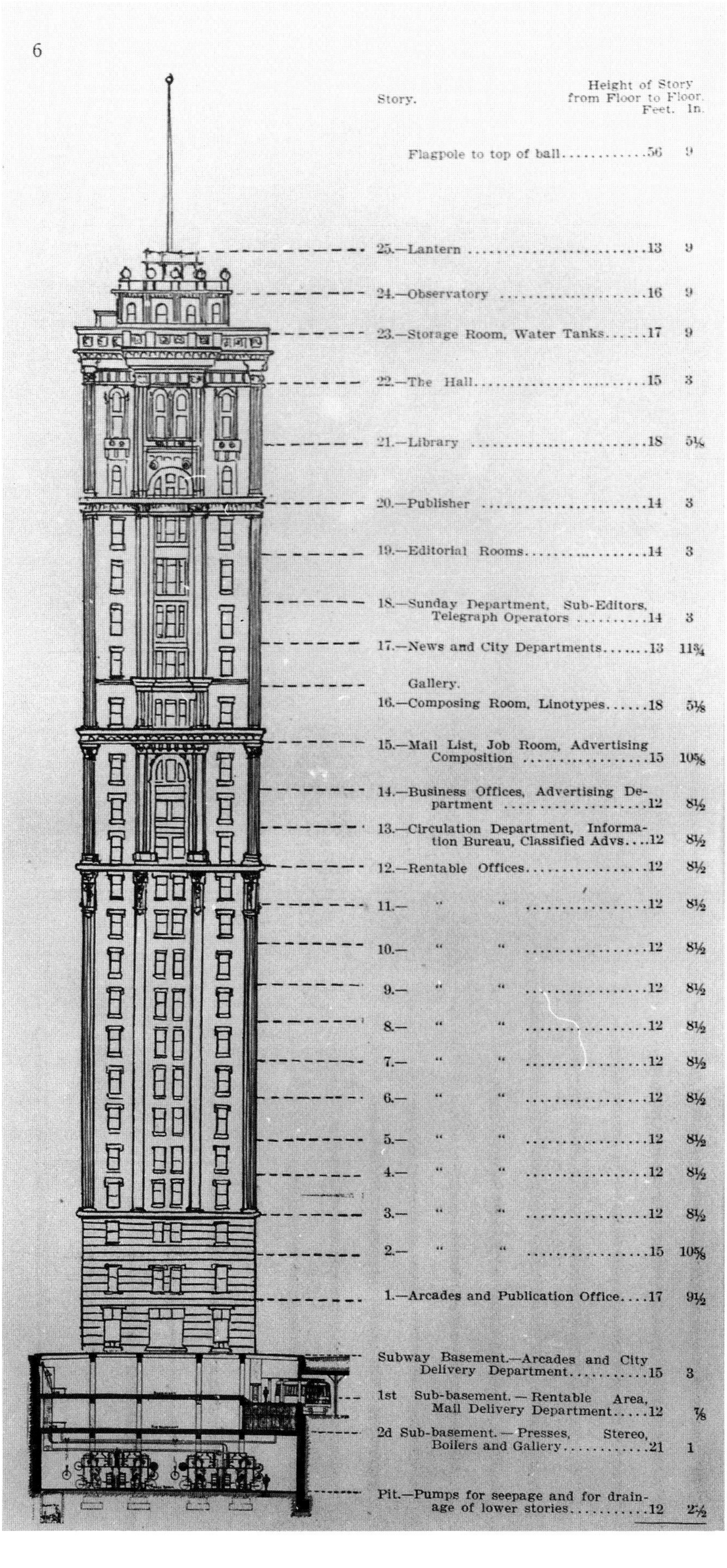
6
Story.
Height of Story from Floor to Floor. Feet. In.
Flagpole to top of ball............56 9
25.—Lantern..........................13 9
24.—Observatory.....................16 9
23.—Storage Room, Water Tanks......17 9
22.—The Hall..........................15 3
21.—Library...........................18 5⅛
20.—Publisher.........................14 3
19.—Editorial Rooms...................14 3
18.—Sunday Department, Sub-Editors, Telegraph Operators..........14 3
17.—News and City Departments.......13 11¾
Gallery.
16.—Composing Room, Linotypes......18 5⅛
15.—Mail List, Job Room, Advertising Composition..................15 10⅝
14.—Business Offices, Advertising Department...................12 8½
13.—Circulation Department, Information Bureau, Classified Advs....12 8½
12.—Rentable Offices.................12 8½
11.— " " 12 8½
10.— " " 12 8½
9.— " " 12 8½
8.— " " 12 8½
7.— " " 12 8½
6.— " " 12 8½
5.— " " 12 8½
4.— " " 12 8½
3.— " " 12 8½
2.— " " 15 10⅝
1.—Arcades and Publication Office....17 9½
Subway Basement.—Arcades and City Delivery Department..........15 3
1st Sub-basement. — Rentable Area, Mail Delivery Department.....12 ⅞
2d Sub-basement. — Presses, Stereo, Boilers and Gallery............21 1
Pit.—Pumps for seepage and for drainage of lower stories...........12 2½

10.10

Elevation of Times Building with data on floor heights, uses, utilities, and construction.
After New York Times Building Supplement (1905).
United States History, Local History & Genealogy Division, the New York Public Library, Astor, Lenox and Tilden Foundations.

the distribution of newspapers throughout the city for many years to come. Indeed, the newspaper still operates in the area, though not in this building.

The architect was Eidlitz & McKenzie (C. L. W. Eidlitz and Andrew C. McKenzie); the general contractor was the George A. Fuller Company, and Purdy & Henderson served as structural engineers. The irregular site dimensions, 58 feet at the southern end, 20 feet at the northern end, and 138 and 143 feet on the long sides, created a distorted trapezoidal lot, a difficulty that prompted exhaustive architectural studies, which were carried out entirely for determining visual effect. The architects, having decided against building to the limit in the manner of the Flatiron but instead to make one section of the building higher than the other, began with the idea of making the building taller at the broader southern end than at the narrow northern point.[17] This arrangement, essentially that of a mounted tower, would accommodate the rentable portion in the lower part and the editorial offices and composing room in the tower, and thus visibly express the double purpose of the building.

The Gothic style was said to have been chosen because the irregular dimensions of the site and towered form precluded the use of the classical or Renaissance styles. Giotto's Florence Cathedral campanile inspired the tower's design and allowed the arcade of the main block to be exaggerated and stretched out so that the irregularity of the quadrilateral prism was made to appear rectangular. The building's form could be said to express its structure because "slight projections along the sides indicate the places of the steel uprights which form the real skeleton of the structure."[18] However, in true New York fashion, and well within the tradition of the Beaux-Arts skyscraper, the design scheme was tripartite, and the walls at the base and the capital appeared massively thick and sculpturally rich. The *Times* explained that the effect of massiveness was possible at the lower level because the window openings could be smaller than usual, there being no lack of light. In the upper section, strongly projecting ornamental elements created the appearance of deep reveals. Overall, the coloring was uniformly light, with a light-toned limestone at the base and creamy brick and terra-cotta cladding the superstructure. Contrary to what has often been alleged, it was the Times Building and not Cass Gilbert's Woolworth Building, or even his West Street Building, that inaugurated the Skyscraper Gothic. This is easy to forget because in 1966 the Times Building—also known as Times Tower—was reclad in marble in a modernist and thoroughly insensitive manner by Eidlitz & McKenzie's successor firm, Smith, Smith, Haines, Lundberg & Waehler. Today it attracts attention only for its electronic sign band and series of huge signs mounted one above the other on its north facade.

The excavation, foundations, and framework of the Times Building presented special problems due to the irregularity of the site and asymmetry of the building mass, the presence of bedrock near the ground surface and of many water pockets in the broken and fissured schist, and the need to build the subway tunnel at the same time as the new building. The foundations were carried to bedrock with the pressroom subbasement at about minus 55 feet, enabling the *Times* to report that its building was truly "founded upon a rock."[19] It was decided to make the foundations and steel framework of the subway independent of the building's, and to build the subway within the envelope of the building's two basements. In order to give the subway its "supreme" right-of-way, as mandated by legislative act in 1904, many of the building's most important steel columns had to start from the subway roof, necessitating the use of cantilevers. According to the *Times*, the 30-ton built-up plate girder that carried the building's north wall was one of the heaviest ever used in an office building; the girder was essential to prevent train vibrations from jarring the building. This construction was accomplished by embedding the subway's supporting columns, which extended below the subbasement floor, in sand cushions, used here for the first time in building. The wind bracing, similar to that of the Flatiron, involved triangular gusset plates above and below the wall girders at the column-girder connections. Full-bay doubled diagonals were used in the north wall bays, inverted K-trusses in other bays.[20]

Among many claims for the superiority of its building, the *Times* boasted that one of the four Otis electric drum-type elevators rose higher than any electric elevator in any office building in the world: 326 feet, 1¾ inches from the subway level to the twenty-third floor. The *Times* also noted proudly that every office had light and air, that there were no inside rooms and no "well holes" (light shafts), and that no point in any office was more than 23 feet from a window.[21]

Gothic Neighbors: Trinity and U.S. Realty Buildings, One Wall Street

The construction of investment skyscrapers continued unabated, with the U.S. Realty and Construction Company functioning as a major developer in the early years of the new century. Aside from the Flatiron, twin freestanding skyscrapers designed by Francis Hatch Kimball and known as the Trinity (1904–5; addition, 1906–7) and U.S. Realty (1906–7) buildings represented this company's most picturesque venture (Figs. 10.11 and 10.12). These Gothic-styled, Indiana limestone–clad slabs extend all the way from Broadway to Trinity Place, for lengths of from 260 to 275 feet. The Trinity Building occupies the site of Upjohn's Trinity Building at 111 Broadway, and the U.S. Realty, intended to serve as the headquarters of its sponsor, that of the Boreel Building at 115 Broadway. Each is twenty-one stories tall on Broadway and twenty-two on Trinity Place, where the land slopes downward by about 11 feet. The builders intended to construct the two simultaneously, but because of delays in procuring the sites they were built two years apart and with some differences. In 1912 a steel-framed footbridge with decorative panels designed by Kimball was built over Thames Street, joining the two buildings at the roof.[22]

Given the odd shape and location of the two buildings, long, narrow slabs separated by narrow Thames Street, the architect maximized the amount of rentable floor area. Additional width was gained for the Trinity Building when the city granted permission for Thames Street to be moved 28 feet to the north. The addition that resulted from this decision, made in 1907, increased the building's width on Broadway to about 68 feet and on Trinity Place to 75 feet, making Trinity the wider of the two skyscrapers by about seven feet in front and fourteen in the rear. Permission was also granted to close Temple Street, which bisected the site of the U.S. Realty Building. In return for these favors the city required that Thames Street be widened by 5 feet, but the added width did little to alleviate the darkness caused by two tall slabs separated by only about 35 feet. Fortunately, the Trinity Building's proximity to Trinity Churchyard permitted a full exposure of its southern facade, and the U.S. Realty's long Cedar Street side was also afforded ample access to light and air.

10.11
Trinity (1904–5;
1906–7)
and U.S. Realty
(1906–7) buildings,
F. H. Kimball,
architect.
111 and 115
Broadway.
View looking north
with Trinity Church-
yard in foreground, c.
1912.
Collection of The
New-York Historical
Society.

10.12
View of Broadway
looking south from
Cedar Street, showing
Trinity Building (left)
and U.S. Realty
Building (center),
with Trinity Church
and Empire Building
in the distance.
Photograph by
George P. Hall, 1908.
Collection of The
New-York Historical
Society.

The foundations for the two steel-framed buildings involved the sinking of pneumatic caissons, which, as we have seen, were first used for buildings in the construction of Kimball & Thompson's Manhattan Life Building just down the street. Bedrock in this location was on average at minus 80 to minus 85 feet, nearly 30 feet deeper than at the site of the Manhattan Life Building, prompting speculation that "these will probably be the deepest foundations ever put down in New York."[23] The engineering of the foundations by the Foundation & Contracting Company involved several new features—removal of the forms used to mold the concrete columns on top of the caissons before actually sinking the caissons, for example, and the use of innovative types of caisson shafting. Yet construction time for both buildings set a new record; each, not counting the addition to the Trinity Building, was constructed in a year.

As for the interior arrangement of the two buildings, for obvious reasons the elevators and a minimum number of offices were located along their Thames Street sides (Fig. 10.13). Flanked by the elevators, the buildings' marble-walled, rib-vaulted "lobbies" are actually corridors that run through from Broadway to Trinity Place and occupy space with little or no rental value due to the lack of light. The elevators were of the plunge type, an expensive form of hydraulic elevator that involved a plunger and a cylinder sunk into the ground to a depth equal to the height of the elevator rise. These had for some years been used for freight. This elevator was likely selected over other types not just because it was fast but because its workings occupied less space in the basement; in the end, however, the electric elevator would prevail as the choice for long runs and high speeds.[24]

Kimball's training and experience as a Gothicist served him well in these commissions. He was, in fact, engaged to design the Trinity Building because the client "wished to have a building in harmony with the architecture of Trinity Church."[25] As completed, these nicely scaled fraternal twins form a most sympathetic backdrop to the church and churchyard. Their Gothic aspects are limited chiefly to door and window enframements, some of which feature bronze tracery and stained glass in their transoms, and to the decorative sculptural details that occur mainly in the base and capital zones. There is also a Gothic openness in the design of the base and the capital that is achieved by wide window bays within two-story arcades. Vertical rows of Gothic-enframed windows occur

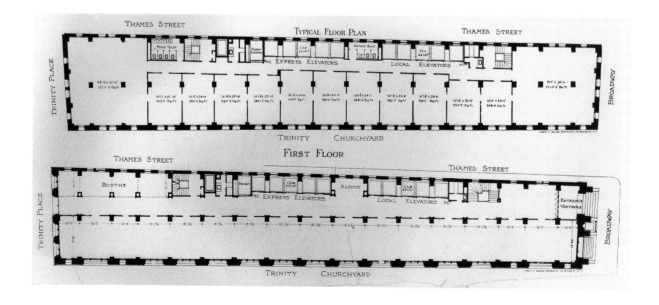

at regular intervals on the shaft, alternating with simply framed square-headed windows. There are no such vertical projections as on the Times Building; rather, moldings divide the shaft horizontally. This feature, as well as the generally smooth-surfaced shaft treatment and tripartite design scheme, relates to the classically styled skyscrapers of the era. The 1907 addition to the Trinity Building, which is not readily apparent, forms a canted corner on Broadway and is marked at the roofline by an asymmetrically placed, copper-roofed cupola, a modified version of the domed towers that were initially planned to crown the building at the ends. Crenellated parapets at either end of the U.S. Realty Building on its Cedar Street side give the impression of low towers, a difference from the Trinity Building's roofline.

Times were prosperous, and well before the Trinity Building was finished the *Record and Guide* could report the names of twenty-three incoming tenants, among them such diverse interests as the United States Guarantee Company, the Midvale Steel Company, the Diamond Match Company, the renamed U.S. Realty and Improvement Company, the Westinghouse Manufacturing Company, and the American Locomotive Company. The U.S. Realty Building also rented readily, with 70 percent of its space taken by the time of completion. Initially, the ground floor tenants were the Carnegie Trust Company and the new National Copper Bank.[26] As of May 1907 the average annual rental cost per square foot in the Trinity Building was said to be $3.00, while the average in the U.S. Realty Building was computed at $2.75, with space on the ground floor renting at $10 per square foot, considered quite a goodly sum. But, good as it was, this amount pales in comparison with the rental income from the ground-floor store in the new One Wall Street Building across the way.

Until it was replaced by the Irving Trust Building in the early 1930s, a slender tower known as One Wall Street (1906–7) occupied a site described in 1906 as "probably the most valuable piece of real estate in the world"[27] (Fig. 10.14; see also Fig. 11.17). This was a 30-by-40-foot plot on the southeast corner of Wall and Broadway opposite Trinity Church, formerly the site of a historic, four-story building and purchased for $700,000, or about $615 per square foot. Taking full advantage of its costly address, the new building incorporated eighteen stories above ground and rose to a height of 217 feet. A structure of such attenuated proportions was made possible by steel construction, with particular attention given to the wind bracing, a column-free interior, and especially compact elevators. Architecturally, the shaft of One Wall was treated as a plain brick screen penetrated by minimally framed windows; perhaps in deference to Trinity Church, the flat roof was crowned by a crested bronze cornice featuring tall, obelisk-like finials at the four corners. With a wild stretch of the imagination, this treatment might be labeled late Gothic or Jacobean; it was the only feature anyone ever noticed. One Wall was financed, designed, and constructed by St. Louis companies. The architect was Barnett, Haynes & Barnett of St. Louis, also responsible for the new St. Louis Cathedral and Chicago's Cook County Courthouse.[28]

The investment paid off. The first floor and basement were rented for $40,000 per year to the United Cigar Stores Company, which had been in the previous building on the site. At $51.02 per square foot per year—more than five times that of the U.S. Realty Building's first floor, which was neither storefront space nor located on a prime corner—the rental for the first-floor store was believed to be the highest on record.[29] This figure gives an

10.14
*View of Broadway
with One Wall Street
Building
(1906–7)
at center.
After* King's Views of
New York *(1915).*

idea of storefront rents in prominent locations, as well as the flourishing state of the retail tobacco business.

Giants West of Broadway: U.S. Express, West Street, City Investing Company, Hudson Terminal, and Whitehall Buildings

Generally, real estate activity was prodigious during 1905, exceeding that of any previous year in the city's history. Although new construction in the financial district was more active than it had been since 1902, the *Record and Guide* noted a "sensible tendency . . .

to erect new skyscrapers on the cheaper land to the west of Broadway."[30] One such sensible developer was the U.S. Express Company, which in late 1904 commissioned Clinton & Russell to design a twenty-three-story building (1905–7) for a site west of Trinity churchyard between Greenwich Street and Trinity Place at 2 Rector Street (Fig. 10.15). Among the earliest companies in the express business, having incorporated in New York in 1854, the U.S. Express Company worked in cooperation with railroads. Its original contracts had been confined to roads terminating on the New Jersey side of the New York harbor, and in Philadelphia and Baltimore, but by the turn of the century its contracts extended to a number of midwestern companies. Eventually the U.S. Express Company merged with the Railway Express Agency, as did all such early competitors.

The caisson foundations for this spread-U-plan building were engineered by the highly reputable Foundation and Contracting Company, which had executed similar foundations for the nearby American Surety, Empire, Trinity, and U.S. Realty buildings. In the case of the U.S. Express Building, which would cover an area of approximately 17,800 square feet, the situation was complicated by several factors. One difficulty was that the supporting posts of elevated railroad tracks bordered the excavation site on three sides. The special shoring required for these posts was accomplished by building a wood frame on piling at the center of the site from which braces extended outward to meet the posts. The north side of the site was flanked by an older building, but the space between was so narrow—only about 2 inches—that the existing building had to be supported by means of six 8-inch pipes jacked to solid footings, filled with concrete, and capped with granite. Another block of granite was placed on top of the cap, and wedges were driven between them to form a solid support for the old building. Such problems offer insight into the many exigencies involved in the construction process and the innovations that were introduced to deal with them. Because the tenant of that building would not permit the contractor to come inside, all the shoring had to be done from the outside. A combination of well-type and pneumatic caissons supported the sixty-four columns that carried the steel skeleton of the building. Edging the site on all four sides, seventeen pneumatic caissons were joined so as to form a solid concrete wall that was carried down to bedrock at an average depth of minus 55 feet.[31]

If somewhat formulaic in design, the U.S. Express Building is nonetheless elegantly and minimally styled in a Renaissance-inspired mode. Its sheltering ground-floor arcade on the downward sloping Rector Street side, the principal front, is perhaps its most unusual feature. The exterior walls are clad in white terra-cotta, with the five-story base made to appear rusticated. The fifth and nineteenth stories, set off by heavy belt courses, are treated as transitional floors, and the smooth-surfaced shaft is unornamented and marked only by rows of simply molded windows rising from the sixth to the eighteenth floors. Before the addition of three stories sometime after 1911, the capital included a three-story arcade, topped by an attic with small round windows. Modest, closely ranked acroteria edged the heavy cornice. The design was handled with an easy assurance, as though size and rhythmic patterns need little embellishment.

Early in 1906 it was obvious that even more skyscraper construction would be undertaken that year than in 1905 and that the new buildings would be taller than ever. In its 30 June issue, the *Record and Guide* reported that nine buildings close by one another and ranging in height from eighteen to forty stories seemed to be in a "race" for comple-

10.15

View of Trinity Church showing United States Express Building (1905–7), Clinton & Russell, architects, at left. West Street Building in center distance.
After King's Views of New York *(1915).*

tion: the U.S. Express, West Street, Trinity addition, U.S. Realty, Hudson Terminal (two buildings), Singer, City Investing Company, and new Evening Post buildings.[32] With some trepidation, the same journal later regretted the lack of any persuasive demand to limit the height of office and hotel buildings, observing that "the tendency is to build, on the average, higher and higher."[33]

Not only were the new skyscrapers higher, they were larger in floor area than had been the norm in previous years. Their sites were carefully selected with an eye to the continuing availability of light to the offices within, and their architectural design took on new significance in this regard. Big new skyscrapers like the U.S. Express Building in the still underdeveloped area west of Broadway below Vesey Street took advantage of the light afforded by the narrow streets bounding their sites. The mounted tower form could permanently guarantee light from all sides to the prestigious and highly remunerative upper stories. Kimball's enormous City Investing Building, completed in 1908, featured such a tower. Perspicaciously, the *Record and Guide* considered these towers "the best device as yet invented to obtain good light, and an economical plan for the upper floors of a lofty office building."[34]

The West Street Building (1906–7)—known at first as the Coal and Iron Building or the Railroad and Iron Exchange Building in recognition of its tenants—was realized as the most successful expression yet of the evolving Skyscraper Gothic (Fig. 10.16; see also Fig. 10.15). It effectively revitalized the tripartite form, and its late Gothic details of French and Belgian inspiration set a new standard of opulence for the most prestigious skyscrapers. Moreover, it confirmed the trend toward a picturesque skyline. Designed by Cass Gilbert, this extraordinarily beautiful, lavishly ornamented tower was commissioned by General Howard Carroll, who was the vice president of a company which specialized in river transportation. Carroll controlled a syndicate known as the West Street Improvement Company, which also included as one of the investors the West Street Building's general contractor, the John Peirce Company.[35] On the east side of West Street between Cedar and Albany streets, the site was selected for the virtually unobstructed river view it offered, for the accessibility of light and air to offices on all sides, and for its location in a section devoted to the transportation business. Around it were freight and ferry stations, warehouses, and longshoremen's hotels.

Although plans were filed in September of 1905 and specifications were completed before the end of December, construction began only in April of 1906, after Gilbert's office had put forward a proposal to mount a five-story tower on a twenty-three-story building. The proposed tower, which anticipated the Woolworth Building's mounted-tower form, was ultimately rejected by the client, but as completed, the West Street presaged many aspects of the Woolworth, to which it is often compared. The structurally expressive vertical projections seen in embryo on the shaft of the Times Building were more fully developed in the West Street Building, as was the arcaded treatment of the base and capital of the Trinity and U.S. Realty Buildings. A white granite base and matching white terra-cotta-clad upper walls are subtly relieved by polychrome tiles and marble diamonds inlaid around the arched entrances and below the moldings that set off the third story; by red granite columns that frame the entrances; and by dark green, copper-clad window frames high up in the capital. Pier clusters on the shaft of the West Street Building rise uninterrupted through twelve stories, and, reinforced by thin non-structural piers, rows of windows between the pier clusters form nearly continuous vertical strips of glazing. Thus the eye is drawn rapidly upward to feast on the mansarded, dormered, and pinnacled six-story capital that is the West Street's crowning glory.

In plan the building comes close to being a parallelogram with a deep right-angled indentation in the rear that functions as a light court. Along West Street the main front was originally about 300 feet from the Hudson River bulkhead line. (The landfill under Battery Park City has considerably increased that distance.) Although bedrock lies about 50 feet below the ground surface, the contractor and the structural engineer Gunvald Aus decided that caisson foundations were unnecessary. Their decision was based on the perception that bedrock in this area is fairly level and covered by a thick layer of hardpan

10.16
*West Street Building
(1906–7),
Cass Gilbert,
architect.
90 West Street.
Museum of the City
of New York.*

clay. The piles were driven to refusal through layers of sandy soil, mud, and the hardpan, and areas of "soft ground" where the hardpan was thin or missing were reinforced by sheet piling and collaring.[36] In the standard manner, footings on the piling carried a two-way grillage of steel I-beams and column base plates. At the extreme dimensions of the site, the floor of the excavation was covered with a 6-foot-thick concrete raft to resist the upward-acting hydraulic pressure, and the boiler room floor and enclosing basement walls were heavily reinforced for additional water-pressure resistance.

Completed at a cost of $2 million, the West Street Building immediately attracted favorable attention. As expected, important railroad and ferry organizations took space in the building, among them the Delaware, Lackawanna & Western Railroad Company, which occupied three of the upper floors. Frank Winfield Woolworth was one of the building's early admirers. The "5 and 10 Cent Store" business that he had founded in 1879 at Lancaster, Pennsylvania, had flourished to the point that he was prepared to make a grand gesture in New York City, and Gilbert was equally prepared to give that gesture reality. The result was the Woolworth Building, which Montgomery Schuyler characterized as "a 'higher power' of the West Street Building." Ever the apostle of Sullivan, Schuyler admired the West Street's confession of "its actual construction by the substitution of continuous reeded uprights for the blank brick piers of the Broadway Chambers."[37]

In the opinion of Guy Kirkham, offered at the time of Gilbert's death in 1934, the West Street Building "showed a consistent and logical and distinctly pleasing handling of structure and material in mass, proportion, color, and detail. It stands today as one of the most satisfying buildings in New York, antedating the zoning laws."[38] Certainly, in his treatment of its structure and mass, Gilbert combined a sense of strength and stability with openness and movement, qualities to be characteristic of the best skyscrapers in the great creative period announced by the Woolworth Building and lasting until 1930. Although it is today physically diminished by the proximity of Battery Park City, the World Financial Center, and the World Trade Center, the West Street Building is as distinctive today as it was when it opened in 1907; its architectural qualities shine for all who have eyes to see.[39]

The City Investing Company Building, also known as the Broadway-Cortlandt Building (1906–9), demonstrated the extent of its architect Francis Kimball's tendency to extravagant theatrical flamboyance, in absolute contrast to Clinton & Russell's sobriety (Fig. 10.17). Although inferior to it in height and design quality, through sheer mass this clifflike, thirty-three-story skyscraper held its own against its soaring next-door neighbor and contemporary, the Singer Tower. The City Investing Building was the largest office building yet constructed, with 500,000 square feet of floor area; its depth from Broadway to Church was 313 feet, its width on Cortlandt 209 feet, and its frontage on Trinity Place about 109 feet. A monument to pure greed, the building's distorted F-shaped plan in part resulted from a holdout, the former Gilsey Building, at this date known as the Wessells Building, on the southwest corner of Broadway and Cortlandt Street. Other factors influencing the plan were the client's determination to have Broadway frontage, even if only 37.5 feet wide, and the need for a light court on the building's main Cortlandt Street side.

City Investing had incorporated in late 1904 as what would later be called a conglomerate—a diversified holding company that controlled manufacturing, printing, transpor-

10.17

*City Investing
Company Building
(1906–8),
F. H. Kimball,
architect.
At left corner,
Gilsey Building
(c. 1854; demolished),
J. W. Ritch, architect.
After* Scientific
American *(1907).*

tation, mining enterprises, and, above all, real estate. The company was founded as the result of a split within U.S. Realty, and Robert E. Dowling, formerly a vice president of U.S. Realty, became its president.[40] Kimball, the recognized master of vast, through-block skyscrapers, whose reputation was founded, so to speak, on pneumatic caissons, was the obvious choice for architect. In this instance, he and his client figured out a way to protect the light and air of the building's tenants and thus increase the rental value of seven stories of office space by putting them inside a mounted tower at the center of the building. As light and air protection for the north-facing offices in the Broadway wing, the client was able to obtain a long-term lease on the old Gilsey Building and eventually would replace it with a harmoniously styled addition.

Yet with all the consideration given to maximizing rental space and cost return, the building incorporated a feature that was even then considered a waste of space: a grand, two-story-high lobby-arcade that extended the full length of the building from Broadway to Church Street. According to Kimball, Dowling had instructed him to provide a "thoroughfare . . . with an elevated railroad connection, and . . . twenty-one elevators for the use of the tenants."[41] Moreover, the irregular shape of the building had afforded a generous arcade, its 32-foot width determined by the width of the Broadway front and large enough for the elevators to be put in a passage off to one side, where they would not interfere with pedestrian traffic to and from the elevated rail station on Church Street. A good deal of attention was given to the lobby's marble work and elaborate plaster-relief and fresco ceiling decoration. Although the architect Donn Barber admitted that the building's exterior was "somewhat showy both in design and material," he considered the lobby-arcade "the finest piece of commercial designing and execution that we have yet seen downtown. The rationalist may find it over-gorgeous, but then he never concedes to the architect any right to the 'joy of design.'"[42] Grand skyscraper lobbies had existed since the 1880s, of course, but in the early years of the new century public spaces in skyscrapers reached a pinnacle of elegance. Judging from the magnificent lobbies of the contemporary Singer Tower and the later Woolworth Building, the owners of City Investing were not alone in believing that the image of corporate wealth and success was worth the cost of an impressive lobby.

This huge edifice was constructed by a highly organized labor force of 3,000 men in only twenty-two months, a record surpassed only on projects with direct rail delivery of supplies, like the Sears Roebuck merchandising center in Chicago (1905–6). Much work had to be carried on at night because of the heavy traffic on the adjacent streets and the unusual nature of the site. In the manner of other skyscraper construction in the vicinity, the columns and footings of the City Investing Building's steel skeleton were founded on rectangular caissons that were sunk to bedrock at minus 80 feet. The framing columns rested on steel pedestal bases, grillages, and distributing girders that were cantilevered at the peripheral bays in order to reduce and equalize the loads to the allowable pressures. To oppose the upward-acting hydrostatic pressure as well as to distribute the loads, the subbasement floor was constructed as a monolithic 6-foot-thick raft of reinforced concrete. Wind resistance resulted from the sheer weight of the building, including its heavy masonry veneer and transverse interior walls, from the use of curved knee braces in parts of the frame, and from portal bracing. The total weight, encompassing both dead and live loads and including the building's concrete-slab floors on flat terra-cotta arches, terra-cotta partitions, limestone and terra-cotta exterior cladding, and interior marble work, was said to be 86,000 tons. One account speculated that if "placed end to end," the 3,000 tons of terra-cotta used in the building "would reach from City Hall up Broadway to Times Square."[43]

Kimball described the light color scheme of City Investing's imposing exterior, the result of white glazed-brick facing and white terra-cotta trim above a limestone base, as "an unusual and distinctive treatment for an office building in the locality, where the buildings are mostly of stone and dark brick, red and yellow prevailing, rendering them darker and more sombre in appearance."[44] Indeed, the contemporary Hudson Terminal and Singer Tower buildings were predominantly clad in red brick. Essentially tripartite and vertical in design, City Investing started from a rusticated, heavily ornamented base of almost baroque character and concluded with a picturesquely profiled, medievalizing top capped by a high, steeply pitched roof. This was Kimball's most exuberant essay in his eclectic Skyscraper Gothic, and it is no exaggeration to say that he turned the prestige skyscraper into a grand stage setting for the street and made it into a spectacle inside. The skyscraper had now fully entered a phase that would reach its finest expression in the Woolworth Building and resurface in the great Art Deco skyscrapers of about 1930, a phase for which Kimball should be given considerable credit: the skyscraper as theatre. Some were interested in preserving the building, primarily for the sake of the sculpture at the entrances, but few complained when the City Investing Building was demolished in 1968, along with the Singer Tower, to make way for Skidmore, Owings & Merrill's hulking United States Steel Building. Taste had changed radically with the onset of Modernism.

Other "giants" constructed west of Broadway in these years were the buildings constituting the Hudson Terminal (1907–9), a pair of twenty-two-story structures designed by James Hollis Wells of the Clinton & Russell firm and erected by the George A. Fuller Company for the Hudson & Manhattan Railroad Company (Fig. 10.18). Fronting on Church, Cortlandt, Fulton, and Dey streets, and separated by Dey Street, which the city would not allow to be closed, the two formed the largest office building complex yet constructed; they took in a ground area of 70,000 square feet, with the out-to-out area at the station level (below ground) measuring 210 by 435 feet. They belonged to a small category of multistory commercial buildings that incorporated rail terminals, a special type in which New York City pioneered. Indeed, the Hudson Terminal was the first of its kind and an engineering masterpiece. It was also handsomely designed in the formal Renaissance manner typical of the designing firm's best work. Although the below-ground terminal was completed only in 1909, the offices in the two skyscrapers were occupied by mid-1908.[45]

Construction of the first Hudson River tunnel between Morton Street in Manhattan and 15th Street in Jersey City had begun in 1874, but financial difficulties, engineering problems, litigation, and disaster—a blowout in 1880 took twenty lives—had caused the project to drag on for a quarter of a century. In 1901 William G. McAdoo acquired control of the company that had begun the construction, the Hudson River Tunnel Company. He reorganized it by incorporating the New York and Jersey Railroad Company in 1901 and the Hudson & Manhattan Railroad Company in 1903. Construction of the tunnel system was resumed in 1904; the first tunnel was completed in 1908, and in 1906 contracts were let out on the new terminal buildings. In 1909 the second tunnel was completed; in 1910 rail lines were extended to Newark, New Jersey, and to 33rd Street in Manhattan, and the Hudson & Manhattan Company quickly achieved an unparalleled success in urban transport.[46]

The Terminal's two steel-framed buildings were identical except in floor area, the southernmost being the larger. Joined by tunnels below ground, the two were connected by a bridge above. Each building was composed of twin nineteen-story slabs connected above ground by the lower three stories of the base, an arrangement that provided access

10.18
*Hudson Terminal
Buildings
(1907–9; de-
molished),
Clinton & Russell,
architects.
After New York
Illustrated (1914).*

to light and air for the interior offices. The plan of each was H-shaped, an innovation for office buildings that was borrowed from public school buildings and large apartment houses for the purpose of giving light to the interior offices.[47] A street-level glass-enclosed arcade with shops and booths, described as "much larger than the famous European arcades," swept through buildings served by thirty-nine Otis electric elevators, and each building had a "dining club" on the roof.[48] The rail terminal occupied three levels, all below grade, the first given over to the concourse, waiting rooms, ticket offices, service facilities, and shops (Fig. 10.19). The tracks and associated platforms were on the second level, and the lowest was reserved for the boiler, generating plant, electrical substation, and baggage-handling facilities. Curving tracks at the ends of the station loop under Fulton and Cortlandt Streets, respectively, and the subway station at Broadway and Fulton Street was accessible by a passageway under Dey Street.

Because of the tracks, the framing of the station had to be irregular, and because the area of watery subsoil that had to be covered was so vast, the buildings were constructed within a concrete cofferdam said to be five times the size of any previously built. The pneumatic caissons supporting the box columns of the steel frame were sunk to depths varying from minus 75 to minus 98 feet, for an average of about minus 80 feet. According to the real estate prospectus, "every building in the vicinity had to be underpinned to keep them from sliding into the chasm."[49] The cost of construction, covering the whole of this micro-city, was the then enormous sum of $8 million.

Perhaps the most outstanding feature of the formal design of the two buildings was the tripartite composition emphasized by their red brick–clad shafts. The four-story base of each, clad in polished granite and limestone, was distinguished by an unusually open treatment of the first and second stories. At the ground story, glass completely filled the bays. The six-story capital was clad in light-colored terra-cotta, and light terra-cotta strips defined the corners and vertically articulated the Church and Cortlandt Street facades. Tall arches linked three stories of the capital; and, on the Cortlandt Street side, towerlike projections rising part way up the shafts and similar projections with pitched roofs relieved an aspect that might otherwise have appeared monotonously blocklike. The ornament was restrained and generally restricted to base and capital. On the whole, this

10.19

Plan of station concourse, one story below grade level, Hudson Terminal Buildings.
After Droege, Passenger Terminals and Trains.

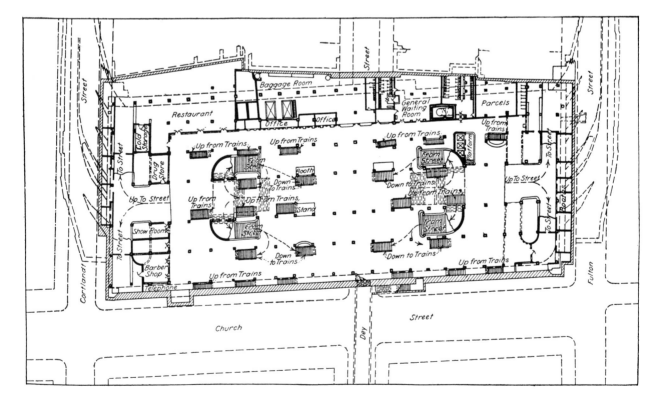

was an impressive pair of buildings, however much they may have darkened the surrounding streets. Along with many other structures, they gave way to the World Trade Center.

Also west of Broadway, but well below the congested Hudson Terminal area, the Whitehall buildings (1902–3; 1909–11) form an assertive and harmoniously styled ensemble that overlooks Battery Park between Washington and West streets (Fig. 10.20; see also Fig. 11.27). (The name Whitehall commemorates the seventeenth-century governor's house, known as White Hall, which stood close to the site.) The initial nineteen-story building fronting on Battery Place was designed by the hotel and apartment house architect Henry J. Hardenbergh in a style designated as Italian Renaissance. In 1911 a thirty-one-story addition—the "Greater Whitehall"—was completed to the plans of J. Hollis Wells of Clinton & Russell. The builder of both structures was the Battery Place Realty Company, representing the interests of William H. Chesebrough of the Vaseline manufacturing family.[50] In 1909, during the early phase of the Greater Whitehall's construction, the Battery Place Company became a subsidiary of the U.S. Realty and Improvement Company.

To make room for the Greater Whitehall, seventeen older structures had to be demolished, and the total area coverage with the addition was estimated at 20,000 square feet more than that of the huge City Investing Building.[51] Owing to the adjacency of Battery Park and the Hudson River, the Whitehall was virtually guaranteed unencumbered views and light on the west and south, and it still has those despite the intervention of Battery Park City. By 1911, it could be reported that although rents were lower here than on Broadway, "averaging only about $1.70 a square foot, . . . the building is proving to be one of the best investments of its kind in the city."[52]

The steel frame of the Greater Whitehall was conventional for the time, and the hollow-tile floor arches and partitions, concrete subfloor, and exterior walls of pressed brick and terra-cotta were also standard. The foundations, however, are of interest because they occur at the tip of Manhattan Island, just above the Battery Park landfill, where the depth of the bearing materials varies, with hardpan at minus 27 to minus 36 feet and rock at minus 33 to minus 65 feet. Constructed by the O'Rourke Engineering Construction Company, which had similarly handled the Hudson Terminal foundations, the footings were mostly on timber-lined pneumatic caissons sunk to hardpan. In a few places footings on steel-lined pneumatic caissons were sunk to rock. The enclosure for the boilers and the generating plant, which was below water level and as deep as minus 10 feet in places, was constructed of reinforced concrete with a 2-foot-thick floor and continuous 7-foot-thick walls. In the form of a floored cofferdam, these walls were extended 33 to 40 feet below the basement floor into hardpan and rock, where they could act as a retaining wall and seal against hydrostatic pressure. Otherwise, the foundation includes the usual I-beam grillages in the footings and distributing girders.[53]

Linked visually as well as physically at the lowest sections of their bases, which are uniform in height and styling, the two buildings give the appearance of two slabs set at right angles to one another when seen from Battery Park. The taller building, however, is irregularly shaped and somewhat overwhelming in aspect; a wing not visible from the Battery Park side intersects the lower building in the courtyard. Both buildings are balustraded and pedimented, the arched form of the Greater Whitehall's pediment com-

plementing the elaborately embellished ocular opening of the Lesser Whitehall's pediment. And the older building's red-and-buff-colored brick shaft and horizontally organized stories and masonry stand out against the deferential monochromy and vertical
articulation of the later structure. Decorative stone swags and ornaments such as caducei
and lion and human heads enhance the six-story, rusticated-stone base and three-story
top of Hardenbergh's building.

While steel-framed behemoths were taking shape, more modest works were at last bringing concrete construction to maturity in New York City. The first reinforced concrete office building to rise in the city was the eleven-story McGraw Building (1906–8) erected for the McGraw Publishing Company and still standing at 231–241 West 39th Street (Fig. 10.21). The McGraw Company, a leading publisher of technical journals, had incorporated in 1899; the Hill Publishing Company followed in 1902, and in 1917 the two merged to become the McGraw-Hill Publishing Company.[54] Radcliffe & Kelley (R. D. Radcliffe and Frederick P. Kelley) served as architects; perhaps more important with regard to the construction technology, the consulting engineer was the distinguished bridge engineer William H. Burr. In 1910–11 the building was extended by 66 feet to take in the site at 243–249 West 39th Street, with the firm of Jackson & Rosencrans serving as architects.

With its column footings on solid rock about 20 feet below the ground surface, the building was designed to handle the heavy loads and vibrations of printing presses. As originally constructed, it measured 126 feet across its front and was about 98 feet deep; its floor loads were rated at 250 and 200 pounds per square foot on the first and second floors, respectively, and at 125 pounds per square foot on every level above that. Before the McGraw Building was designed, the New York code allowed only 350 pounds per square inch maximum for concrete in direct compression, which meant that many columns had to be used, requiring a prohibitive sacrifice of floor space. The McGraw's columns were heavier than usual and simpler in design; they were steel box columns with latticework sides entirely encased in concrete. The municipal Bureau of Buildings accepted the new design, thereby increasing the allowable compressive stress to 750 pounds per square inch. No brick was used in the construction. The primary girders, floor beams, floor slabs, and columns were cast monolithic; and even the facade facing, characterized as "an honest expression of the construction of the building," is concrete.[55] Wide, open bays separated by heavy continuous piers and spare but powerful neoclassical ornamentation dignify the long industrial-looking front. The construction, which involved girders reinforced for tension at the top and bottom, with diagonal segments for the shear at the ends, was apparently Burr's variation on Ernest L. Ransome's pioneering system. Construction of the formwork and the pouring of the concrete were accomplished by means of a central steel-framed tower with derricks attached.[56]

A lavishly ornamented, terra-cotta-clad loft building still extant at 15 West 38th Street (1908–9) marks another development in reinforced concrete construction. This was one of the early works of the subsequently well-known architecture firm of Delano & Aldrich (William Adams Delano and Chester Holmes Aldrich). Because the columns and column footings of this twelve-story steel-frame building had to be kept outside the property lines of adjacent buildings with contiguous walls, various columns had to be supported on cantilevers; three of them, closely spaced on a diagonal line, had to be carried on a continuous girder. All these distributing members were reinforced concrete supplied by the Hennebique Construction Company, and the girders not only embodied Hennebique's system of reinforcing—tension bars, bent bars for shear, stirrups—but also represent the only time the construction firm of the leading French pioneer in reinforced concrete was used for an American building. Considering that Ransome's system was

10.21
McGraw Building
(1906–8; 1910–11),
Radcliffe & Kelley
and Jackson &
Rosencrans,
architects.
231–249 West 39th
Street.
After American
Architect and
Building News *(1915).*

homegrown and virtually the equivalent of Hennebique's in all respects, the mystery is why the owner went to the French contractor. Likely it was because concrete was still a novelty in New York, and perhaps the Beaux-Arts training of the designing partners disposed them in favor of Hennebique.[57]

The German-American Insurance Building (1907–8), nicknamed the Downtown Flatiron, was shaped by its odd, trapezoidal site in the heart of the insurance district east of William Street at the intersection of Maiden Lane and Liberty Street (Fig. 10.22). Established in 1872, the German American Company had for many years been a tenant in

10.22
German-American Insurance Building (1907–8; demolished), Hill & Stout, architects. After King's Views of New York *(1915).*

the second Boreel Building. The company occupied the first, third, fourth, and fifth stories of the new building and rented the remaining floors as offices. The firm of Hill & Stout (Frederick P. Hill and Edmund C. Stout) designed the well-proportioned, twenty-one-story structure to take full advantage of the exposed site, crowning its tripartite, white granite and white terra-cotta-clad walls with groined, strongly flaring eaves faced in colored glazed terra-cotta and edged in copper. The vaulted marble lobby was correspondingly grand. For want of a better term, the building's style might be described as neo-English Baroque.

Noting the difficulties of the site, which on its widest side measured about 137 feet and on its narrowest only 19, the architect (Hill) regretted that the windows and panels were not more deeply recessed and the columns of the base larger to give still greater vertical emphasis to the design. He explained that the resulting loss of light and floor space would not have yielded "a proper return on the investment," hinting at a disagreement with the client. Regarding the building's bold treatment at the top, which omitted "any form of cornice," he argued that "the idea that a cornice, whether Classic, Gothic or any other style, can be exaggerated or enlarged to such a degree as to be discernible hundreds of feet above the ground, appears to us entirely wrong and is far from the solution of the problem of treatments of these high buildings."[58] The designers of such picturesquely roofed skyscrapers as the City Investing Building and Singer and Liberty towers would doubtless have agreed with his statement.

Because of the odd shape of the lot, some of the pneumatic caissons used were the largest yet made for a New York City building. They carried the foundations down to hardpan at about 25 feet below tide level and about 50 feet below curb, where they were then keyed to fabricate an unbroken cofferdam around the site. The general contractor, the Whitney-Steen Company, had to resort to innovative techniques in order to keep to a tight schedule, which it was apparently able to do despite the heavy traffic around this very exposed site.[59] Remarkably, the building was completed in about thirteen months and stood until about 1971, when it was demolished by the city in order to widen the street and accommodate the traffic flow.

Along the way, a cavalcade of skyscrapers was rising on sites scattered from the Battery to 42nd Street, many embodying special features and serving to set off the climactic works: the Singer, Metropolitan Life, Municipal, Bankers Trust, and Woolworth buildings. Indeed, the advantages of the skyscraper were such that fraternal and professional organizations were building them as supporting enterprises; Burnham & Root's record-setting twenty-two-story Masonic Temple (1891–92) in Chicago is probably the best-known example. The eighteen-story, Beaux-Arts-style Masonic Hall (1907–9) at 46–54 West 24th Street between Fifth and Sixth avenues is a handsome, moderately tall sky-scraper that was intended to serve the needs of the Free and Accepted Masons of the State of New York (Fig. 10.23). The architect, Harry P. Knowles, was a Master Mason who had been the LeBrun firm's head draftsman.[60]

Masonic Hall's richly detailed, limestone, granite, and diamond-patterned red brick facade encloses both a series of impressive double-height meeting rooms, decorated according to Masonic tradition in such historic styles as Egyptian, Gothic, Grecian Doric, and French Ionic, and a remarkable three-story-high auditorium capable of seating twelve hundred people.[61] Masonic Hall was built as an extension of Napoleon LeBrun's

10.23
*Masonic Hall
(1907–9),
H. P. Knowles,
architect.
After* Real Estate
Record and Builders'
Guide *(1908).*

10.24
Liberty Tower
(1909–10),
Henry Ives Cobb,
architect.
55 Liberty Street.
After King's Views of
New York *(1915).*

Masonic Temple (1870–c. 1875) on 23rd Street, but in 1911 the temple was demolished and replaced by another Knowles-designed building (1911–13), this one nineteen stories tall. Constructed to generate supporting income for the order, and about ninety percent rental in 1995, that building was largely given over to Masonic lodge rooms and executive offices in the early 1930s.

Not long after the Singer Tower was completed, construction began just a block away on the slender, thirty-three-story Liberty Tower (1909–10; Fig. 10.24). For many years these two picturesquely roofed skyscrapers stood in striking juxtaposition. The site of Liberty Tower, on the northwest corner of Liberty and Nassau streets and bounded on the west by Liberty Place, had been occupied by the *Evening Post*'s headquarters until 1875. That building was succeeded by the Bryant Building (1882), named for the newspaper's famous editor, William Cullen Bryant; at the very beginning of its construction, Liberty Tower was also called the Bryant Building. It was built by the C. L. Gray Construction Company, a St. Louis company, for a group that included St. Louis investors and was organized under the name Liberty-Nassau Building Company. (Recalling that One Wall Street Building was also the speculation of a St. Louis company, one can only wonder at the extent of midwestern financial investment properties in the city.) The architect was Henry Ives Cobb, who also had midwestern connections.

Unusual construction techniques were required to address the structural problems that were presented by Liberty Tower's small, irregular site, where no sides are parallel, and the building's great height. Pneumatic caisson foundations were sunk through quicksand and hardpan to bedrock at about minus 95 feet, a depth said to have exceeded that of any other building in the city except for the nearby Mutual Life Building, where the caissons were at the same depth. The steel frame's wind bracing, crucial in a relatively slender tower, utilized spandrel girders 36 inches deep to the fifth floor and 24 inches deep above, portal-brace connections, and solid triangular gusset plates at all the column-girder connections. An unusual framing feature occurs at the narrow, three-bay front on Liberty Street. In order to accommodate a raised ceiling height at the first and second floors, the primary girder across the center bay was raised above the level of those in flanking bays, which resulted in eccentric horizontal column-girder connections. These connections were braced by the portal technique and extremely deep gussets below the girders.[62]

Liberty Tower should be counted among its architect's major works; moreover, with respect to its Gothic styling, copper-clad pyramidal roof, and white terra-cotta cladding, it was a precursor of the Woolworth Building. Cobb, a specialist in the neo-Gothic among other styles, and trained as both architect and engineer, had for many years practiced in Chicago, where he was responsible for major buildings of all types. These included the thirteen-story Owings Building (c. 1888) and many neo-Gothic buildings on the University of Chicago campus. He had moved his practice to Washington in 1896; in 1902 he came to New York, and Forty-two Broadway (1902–3) was one of his early commissions in the city. He conceived Liberty Tower as "a tower rising from a solid base and growing lighter toward the top. This effect is reached by keeping the wall up to the sixth floor a plain surface, at the sixth it breaks into large bays, extending through seventeen floors, to where it is again broken into smaller bays, until finally large dormers break into the roof. Thus we have the solid base, the shaft, and the cap or crowning motive."[63] In spite of its English Gothic detailing, which includes pinnacles, finials, gargoyles, Tudor-arched en-

10.25

*Waldorf-Astoria Hotel
(1891–93; 1895–97;
demolished),
H. J. Hardenbergh,
architect.
Photograph, c. 1900.
Collection of The
New-York Historical
Society.*

trances, and continuous, alternating thick and thin piers on the shaft, Liberty Tower makes use of the tripartite formula that had long been standard in the city. A contemporary journal applauded the choice of the Gothic for its vertical lines, also pointing out that the Home Life had begun the trend for distinctive roofs, and that the Singer, West Street, and Liberty Tower buildings had set the new fashion.[64] Indeed, for the time being, the flat-roofed skyscraper had been eclipsed.

The Liberty-Nassau Building Company, asserting that the new building was "unique in its Gothic design" and offered "perfect light and ventilation," claimed in its real estate brochure that Liberty Tower "was not erected as a speculation, but as a permanent investment." No expense had been spared, and the company offered to divide the floors to suit the needs of the tenants, who were to be restricted to "stockbrokers, financial institutions, large corporations, and lawyers." The Chamber of Commerce building next door would, the company promised, protect "for all times the building's location as central."[65] A full description of the building was provided, including the lobby, which featured two mural paintings, one on either side of the staircase, representing Autumn and Spring and with Bryant as the central figure. From the beginning there were stores on the ground story. No one could have predicted that less than seventy years after its completion Liberty Tower would be converted to cooperative apartments (1979)—or that the Chamber of Commerce building would be the headquarters of the New York branch of a Japanese bank in the 1990s.

The Skyscraper Hotel

A last word about hotels. Although the term *skyscraper* is usually reserved for office buildings, by the turn of the twentieth century there was some justification for extending its application to hotels. Early on, hotels had played a precedent-setting role in the development of the high-rise building, with the eight-story Broadway Central Hotel of 1869–70 worthy of "early skyscraper," if not "first skyscraper," designation. In 1890 the official hotel directory listed 128 hotels in the city; twenty or so were said to have been constructed since 1880, and hotel construction had entered a boom period. City directories list 183 in 1895, and by 1912 there were 222 that had fifty rooms or more. Although London and Paris had more hotel buildings, New York City could accommodate more people in its hotels than any other city in the world.[66]

By 1893, iron and steel framing was being used routinely for hotels as well as office buildings, but hotels posed problems in engineering design that required special solutions, particularly in regard to fireproofing, fire prevention, and fire control techniques. Additionally, the incorporation of extensive open interior spaces like ballrooms and dining rooms required unusual and unprecedented forms of wide-span framing with massive girders or trusses to carry the overhead columns, and the range and quality of the mechanical utilities, mainly plumbing, lighting, and heating, exceeded those of the office block. Hotels should be studied independently and are here considered only to indicate the extent to which their upward climb, technology, and architectural style paralleled the development of the office skyscraper.

Like office buildings, hotels were not subject to a height restriction. However, during the period covered by this study, for practical and economic reasons their height did not

keep pace once office buildings reached twenty stories in the mid-1890s. By 1905 the high-rise hotel had for the time being settled on a standard height of about seventeen stories; at the end of 1913, only ten hotels were taller, compared with seventy-one office buildings.[67] Instead, hotels tended to sprawl over large areas of ground and assume heavy, blocklike dimensions, as epitomized by the merged Waldorf and Astoria hotels. Joined as one block in 1897, the luxuriously appointed Waldorf-Astoria on Fifth Avenue between 33rd and 34th streets (1891–93; 1895–97) covered an area of nearly 70,000 square feet (Fig. 10.25). The earlier twelve-story portion of this German Renaissance–inspired pile was designed by Henry Hardenbergh for William Waldorf Astor, and Hardenbergh was also responsible for the sixteen-story Astoria addition, commissioned by John Jacob Astor.[68] (The Empire State Building stands on the site today.) As exemplified by this impressive mansard-roofed hotel, luxury hotels as a rule tended to be more exhibitionist in style than office buildings, especially at the roofline, in an attempt to evoke historic residential structures.

Other notable skyscraper hotels from the 1890s include two that overlooked Central Park at the intersection of Fifth Avenue and 59th Street. The twelve-story Hotel Savoy on the southeast corner (1891–92), designed by Ralph S. Townsend and distinguished by its continuous vertical rows of bay windows, was one of the city's early metal-framed buildings (Fig. 10.26). It utilized rolled steel columns supplied by the Carnegie Steel Company and may have employed skeleton rather than cage construction, judging from the great area of windows and narrow piers. The Hotel New Netherland (1892–93), designed by William Hume and situated on the northeast corner of the intersection, was cage framed (Fig. 10.27). This ebulliently neo-Romanesque structure rose to a height of seventeen stories and 234 feet, causing it to be touted as the "tallest hotel structure in the world."[69] It was known as the Hotel Netherland after 1908, and in 1927 it was replaced on the same site by the towering Sherry Netherland Hotel. Another Henry Hardenbergh design, the Hotel Manhattan (1895–96; demolished), on the northwest corner of Madison Avenue and 42nd Street, soon claimed the record at a height reported as 250 feet; it had sixteen-and-a half stories, including three levels of dormers in its high, chateauesque roof. Hotels were always avant-garde in regard to elevators; the Hotel Manhattan incorporated four Sprague Electric passenger elevators at the same time that the contemporary Lord's Court did.[70]

In the first decade of the twentieth century some of the city's finest hotels were constructed, among them the St. Regis (1901–4) on the southeast corner of Fifth Avenue and 55th Street (Fig. 10.28). Designed by the firm of Trowbridge & Livingston for John Jacob Astor and built to a height of eighteen stories, this lavishly ornamented, Beaux-Arts-styled hotel is steel-skeleton framed, with limestone curtain walls, and is topped by a high mansard roof. Its four-story capital is nicely set off by a continuous balcony that is supported by heavy decorative brackets. Fitted with the latest and best of mechanical utilities, especially its heating and ventilating system, the St. Regis testified to the fact that the big modern hotel is the most complex type of structure ever invented.[71] The Gotham Hotel (1902–5), sited directly across Fifth Avenue from the St. Regis, was built nineteen stories high and styled in a more restrained Beaux-Arts manner to harmonize with the University Club next door.[72] Both the St. Regis and the Gotham were cited as "offensive" in the 1913 report of the city's Heights of Building Commission because of their Fifth Avenue location.

No sooner had the St. Regis been completed than a hotel erected opposite Grand Central Terminal on Park Avenue between 41st and 42nd streets established a hotel height record. This was the Hotel Belmont (1904–8; demolished), designed for the August Belmont Hotel Company by Warren & Wetmore, a firm noted for its work on Grand Central Terminal and, later, for the design of other hotels in the terminal vicinity

(Fig. 10.29). Described in the company's promotional literature as "the giant among New-York hotels," the steel-framed, Beaux-Arts-styled building measured 368 feet from its foundation to its rooftop and had twenty-two above-ground stories and five more below street level. Excavation for the below-ground stories and foundations involved blasting to depths from 35 to 60 feet through solid rock, which is near street surface in this area, and entailed other difficulties due to construction of the subway going on simultaneously under part of the site and adjacent to it.[73] Like other luxury hotels of the time, the Belmont had a sumptuously decorated two-story-high lobby.

10.26
Hotel Savoy (1891–92; demolished), Ralph S. Townsend, architect. After King's Photographic Views of New York.

10.27

*Hotel New
Netherland
(1892–93;
demolished),
architect.
After King's
Photographic Views
of New York.*

Two other grand hotels, neither especially tall by skyscraper standards of the time but both distinctive presences in the urbanscape, deserve notice. The earlier is Henry Hardenbergh's finest work, the majestic Plaza Hotel (1905–7), which stands on the west side of Fifth Avenue between 58th and 59th streets, where it overlooks the Grand Army Plaza and Central Park (Fig. 10.30). This eighteen-story, French Renaissance–inspired monument was crafted by the same financial interests, engineers, and builders who produced

10.28
St. Regis Hotel (1901–4), Trowbridge & Livingston, architects. 2 East 55th Street. Museum of the City of New York.

many of the great office towers of the era: a syndicate headed by Harry S. Black of the U.S. Realty Company, the engineers Purdy & Henderson, and the Fuller company. Technologically, the steel-skeleton framed structure was state-of-the-art, and its heating and ventilating system was the largest that had yet been installed. Taking full advantage of one of the nation's great urban vistas, the Plaza's limestone facade and picturesquely massed mansard roof can be seen from deep inside Central Park.[74] In stark contrast, the exterior of the sixteen-story Ritz-Carlton (1908–10; demolished) was deliberately unpretentious. Designed by Warren & Wetmore for Robert W. Goelet, this flat-roofed hotel with severely tripartite elevations stood on the west side of Madison Avenue, filling the block

10.29
Hotel Belmont
(1904–8; demolished),
Warren & Wetmore, architects.
After Architecture *(1905).*

10.30
Plaza Hotel
(1905–7),
H. J. Hardenbergh, architect.
West side of Fifth Avenue, 58th to 59th Street.
Photograph by Brown Brothers, New York, c. 1929.
Collection of The New-York Historical Society.

front from 46th to 47th Street, until it was razed in 1951. At the time of completion, it was considered the finest hotel yet constructed and also the best designed, especially its base, defined by a two-story Ionic colonnade at the second and third stories.[75]

A full study of the high-rise hotel would examine others constructed before 1913, especially two built in the Times Square area: the mansarded, fourteen-story Knickerbocker Hotel (1902–4; 1905–6), still standing on the southeast corner of 42nd Street and Broadway, and the similarly styled but more restrained sixteen-story Hotel Rector on the southeast corner of Broadway and 44th Street (1910–11; demolished).[76] But the skeleton-framed, triple-towered McAlpin Hotel near Herald Square on the east side of Broadway between 33rd and 34th streets (1911–12) was the largest hotel of the period and came closer to office skyscraper heights of the time (Fig. 10.31). It reportedly had more rooms than any hotel in the world, and its twenty-five stories required elevator runs higher than any before installed in a hotel (350 feet). The architect, F. M. Andrews & Company, designed it for the heirs of the D. H. McAlpin estate as a businessmen's hotel, not as a luxury accommodation, and accordingly dispensed with the more costly residential imagery. One source described the exterior as " 'new,' of no specific style, but very effective in its use of textured brick and modelled terra-cotta ornament—essentially a modern expression of design."[77] Styles were changing, and the conservative mode of the McAlpin Hotel would define apartment houses and hotels throughout the 1920s. The McAlpin was immediately rivaled by Warren & Wetmore's twenty-four-story Biltmore Hotel in the Grand Central Terminal area (1912–13). Skyscraper hotels were starting to soar.

The apartment hotel also began to increase in both numbers and height at the end of the 1880s, but it never reached the heights of the transient hotel, much less the office building. By the turn of the century, economy dictated a maximum of eleven stories plus a penthouse, effectively twelve stories. Code regulations regarding woodwork fireproofing, wall thicknesses for skeleton framing, and area coverage were inhibiting factors.[78] To some degree the same regulations also affected transient hotel heights. A notable exception was the magnificent, Paris-inspired Ansonia Hotel (1899–1904) on Broadway between 73rd and 74th streets, which was eighteen stories tall, including the tower.[79] Ninety apartment hotels rose in the city between 1900 and 1902. As a result of the influx of these and other high-rise buildings into midtown and uptown streets, lots were bought up and deeds drawn up to incorporate restrictions as the means of protecting uptown properties from the loss of light and air caused by tall buildings. In 1902 the *Record and Guide* perceptively anticipated "a renewal of former effects to restrict the height of fireproof buildings—at least in certain parts of the city."[80] Permits to build no fewer than twenty-one steel-framed, twelve-story apartment hotels in the midtown area were granted in 1902; but by mid-1905, construction of apartment hotels had dwindled. This was due in part to the increasing preference for housekeeping apartments and the overbuilding of apartment hotels, but it was also substantially affected by the cost of implementing code regulations for large buildings. Although apartment hotels continued to rise through the 1920s, their heyday was over after 1910.

10.31
*McAlpin Hotel
(1911–12),
F. M. Andrews &
Company, architects.
East side of
Broadway, 33rd to
34th streets.
After King's Views of
New York (1915).*

Physical Growth and Mounting Problems in the First Decade

Throughout the first decade of the century the city's hopes and achievements, as well as its doubts, questions, and problems, continued to multiply along with its skyscrapers. From the standpoint of the builder and the investor, everything appeared to be flourishing. The number and the height of commercial buildings seemed limitless. Later studies confirmed in quantitative detail that up to a certain limit the rate of return from an office building increased with its height. The upper limit in 1910 was fifty stories. Investigation in 1928–29 indicated that the rate of return more than doubled between the eight-story and the fifty-story height.[81]

While skyscrapers achieved new and staggering records, both in height and sheer number, the city was enormously expanding its peripheral and interborough circulatory system. The IRT subway, the several East River bridges, the Hudson & Manhattan tunnels, and the East River Tunnel, connecting Bowling Green to Borough Hall in Brooklyn (1908), were completed in the years between 1900 and 1910. The new tunnels and bridges took the pressure off the ferries and improved the circulation between New York and New Jersey and the eastern boroughs, but they also contributed to congestion, especially in lower Manhattan, where all but the Queensboro Bridge converged. And they intensified certain technical problems that accompanied the increasing number and size of buildings. The most serious of these problems arose from the need for large sewers to serve the high buildings, for subway lines adjacent to these buildings, for the pumping of ground water from excavations, and for the sealing of foundation areas—all of which resulted in the lowering of the water table and the consequent increasing exposure of piling to rot, with the result of unequal and sometimes dangerous settlement. True, hardpan- or rock-caisson foundations offered a solution, but only the owners of the largest buildings could afford the cost.

Combined with the excessive density of building and heavy traffic congestion, such problems led to the renewal of endless—and mostly fruitless—discussions of planning controls, provision of adequate municipal services, and height limitations. The need for planning controls—to cover land use, density, building height, and the reservation of space for future public use, parks, and housing—was being openly asserted and debated by 1907, which was a banner year for new construction despite a minor financial panic that affected the real estate market. Discussion centered around the report of the New York City Improvement Commission and the establishment of the Russell Sage Foundation that year, with authoritative voices arguing for some kind of metropolitan, or at least citywide, planning. The Fifth Avenue Association was organized in 1907, comprising real estate owners, brokers, retail merchants, and businessmen who were determined to sustain and promote the section between 32nd and 59th streets as a premier shopping district. Distressed by the increasing presence of the garment industry in that area and by the resulting construction of increasingly taller manufacturing buildings, this group, represented by the officially appointed Fifth Avenue Commission, recommended in 1912 a height limit of 125 feet for buildings on the avenue and within 300 feet of it on the adjoining side streets. Although the proposal was rejected by the Board of Estimate and Apportionment, the Fifth Avenue Association would be a powerful force in the passage of the 1916 zoning law.[82]

In 1908, Robert W. de Forest, at various times president of the New York Art Commission, the New York Charity Organization Society, and the new Russell Sage Foundation, argued for the creation of a permanent central municipal authority to control and to assess the optimum future locations of parks and public buildings and the street layout. Continuity of control was essential. Frederick S. Lamb, secretary of the Municipal Art Society, lent a supporting voice, recommending in a review of the city improvement commission's report of 1907 that a permanent planning commission with a metropolitan authority be established.

Benjamin C. Marsh, secretary of the Committee on Congestion of Population in New York, formed in 1907, thought that proper housing was more important than parks, drives, and architecture. He urged, instead, comprehensive planning for the removal of slums, relief of overcrowding, control of overinflated land values and rents, and prevention of land usurpation by powerful financial interests for private gain. Any qualified plan commission, he argued, should concern itself with housing, transit, industry, and land use in place of monumental buildings and civic embellishment. Marsh represented the most radical voice to emerge from the Progressive Movement, which understood that indiscriminate building for commercial gain could produce results contrary to the good of the commonwealth. He outlined what he believed should be the six principal aims of a municipal planning commission: the precise delimitation of areas reserved for industrial development; adequate freight transportation facilities; zoning regulations to control building height and density; street and transit patterns that facilitate access between housing and places of work; the provision of open space, parks, and playgrounds adequate for future needs; and the authority to condemn areas large enough to serve future needs as well. In 1908 Marsh's committee sponsored an exhibit held at the American Museum of Natural History on the bad effects of building and population congestion.[83]

These were private voices, but those in authority were not oblivious to the city's growing problems, especially the consequences of the excessive density of high buildings on the overloaded circulatory and sewer systems. In his annual messages to the board of aldermen in 1907 and 1908, Mayor George B. McClellan stressed the inadequacy and overtaxing of the sewers in areas of densely built-up office blocks where there was "no permeable area which will absorb storm water." Calling attention to the constant need for digging up the streets to repair and replace the ever more elaborate underground facilities required by these aboveground structures, he observed that "a second street beneath the roadway used for traffic will be required to accommodate them." Noting that "an army of working men and women" rely on public transportation, he also cautioned that "the transportation problem of each section of the city must be worked out in relation to that portion of the traffic which will begin or end in the office district of . . . Manhattan."[84]

McClellan might well have added that there was a need to limit height and density, especially in the downtown area, and that eventually it would be necessary to disperse high-rise construction, for it was in this context of broad urbanistic concern that the question of height limitation was discussed with renewed vigor. The events of the time reinforced that concern: construction technology had progressed to the point that buildings could reach seemingly unlimited heights, and the outlook of building interests was aggressive. Indeed, in 1908 the potential began to be realized in many forms: the completion of the 612-foot-high Singer Tower; construction of the 700-foot-high Metropolitan Life Tower, which would be completed in 1909; the announcement—premature by six years, as it happened—that a thirty-eight-story skyscraper with six underground stories would replace the Tower Building at 50 Broadway; the report that the Equitable Life Assurance Society was planning a 909-foot-high, sixty-two-story skyscraper to replace its old building; and a rumor circulated that Ernest Flagg was planning a 1,000-foot-high office tower for the corner of Broad and Wall streets on part of the Mills Building site. The last-mentioned building, whether actually planned or not, was never built.[85]

As had previously been the case, the need for height limitation was recognized mainly by those professionals who acknowledged some responsibility: architects, engineers, and bureaucrats. Early in 1906 the *Record and Guide* had reported that presently "there is practically no influential demand from any quarter that the height of hotels and business buildings in Manhattan should be restricted," but less than a year later the author of a letter to the editor urged that height limitations be set.[86] In May 1907 the same source offered a succinct statement of the problem: "The average skyscraper of to-day is erected in self defense, for the man whose property is made almost valueless by the proximity of tall buildings, has no alternative but to erect a taller building. Where this sort of thing will lead is hard to predict."[87]

At a meeting on 14 September 1907, George W. Babb, president of the New York Board of Fire Underwriters, urged a height limit, invoking the danger of fires on the upper floors of high buildings in narrow streets. Combustible materials inside these buildings could ignite the contents of adjacent buildings and thus start a conflagration, even if all the buildings concerned were of fireproof construction. Babb recommended conservative height and area limits: for combustible buildings, 55 feet and 5,000 square feet; for fireproof buildings, 125 feet and 30,000 square feet. At the same meeting architect John Carrère spoke against a uniform height limit, later explaining that the resulting "monotonous cornice line" would leave "the artist no opportunity to vary the skyline or to design buildings to extend into the air and silhouette against the sky in contrast with the lower buildings which surround them." Instead, he suggested building in a pyramidal form—the original setback proposal—and taxing skyscrapers on the basis of height and floor area, because such buildings require the costliest municipal services.[88]

In the fall of 1907, the New York Board of Trade also recommended building in a pyramidal or setback form, or "stepped offsets," as the Board called it, with appropriate legislation to include the recommendation in the mandatory provisions of the building code. The editor of *Architectural Review* approved: the form "would incontestably admit more light and air to the streets and the lower outer stories of these city structures. The violent street gales and unpleasant dampness now so evident might, in a measure, disappear; roof-garden restaurants, bar-rooms, and vaudeville performances in the open air would probably become the rule—and the millennium be near at hand."[89]

In 1908 the city government, heeding the new proposals, established within the building code revision commission a special committee on the limitation of height and area. Ernest Flagg presented his detailed proposals on height limitation to this committee in March 1908, and afterward published them in several articles. He attempted a balanced program that took into account the apparent obstacles to adopting direct limits. Pronouncing the existing unrestricted height contrary to "public interest and private justice," he advocated a height limit of no more than five to six stories in solidly built-up districts. Because a direct height limit elsewhere seemed impossible, the only alternative, he believed, was to limit the floor area above certain heights according to the street width. Specifically, 75 percent of the lot would be limited to a height equal to one and a half times the width of the street, with the maximum at 100 feet. On the remaining one-quarter of the lot, there would be, in effect, no height restriction. All four elevations of the higher building should be given a full architectural treatment, which Flagg thought reconciled the owner's rights with the public good. The limits were designed to provide air and light, minimize congestion and the danger of fire, and improve the aesthetic quality: "Aesthetic considerations, which will undoubtedly have more weight here in the future than they have had in the past, are set at defiance by present methods. Our street facades have a ragged, wild Western appearance, more suitable to a half-civilized community than to a city which claims rank with the other great capitals of the world. Great buildings, having one or two sides ornamented, rear their gigantic walls of naked brickwork far above adjoining buildings, and force their ugliness upon public view."[90]

The debate continued. In November 1908 the Philadelphia architect David K. Boyd proposed limiting height as a function of street width, and advocated "stepped back" facades. Boyd's scheme would have limited height to one and a quarter times the street width. Five years later the heights of buildings commission adopted a proposal that combined aspects of both schemes.[91]

The demolition of the Gillender Building in 1910—only thirteen years after its construction—for a newer, higher, and more prestigious structure exposed another constraint on good design and the creation of an architecture that would serve the public good. The lesson was that a building had become an economic commodity, to be discarded when more profitable possibilities emerged. And it was not an architect who pointed out that fact, but a journal devoted to the celebration of scientific and technical advances:

> So soon as the march of improvement or development renders it certain that there is more profit in "scrapping" an existing machine, plant, or building, and replacing it by another more efficient or of greater capacity, it is a matter of sound business policy to send that machine to the "junk heap" or turn the "wrecking gang" loose upon that building.
>
> The policy is purely utilitarian—brutally so, if you like—a mere question of dollars and cents; but it is a good business policy nevertheless, and, in reality, has been one of the most powerful factors in bringing about the present phenomenal industrial development of the United States.[92]

In essence, then, urban and natural environments may be sacrificed for economic development. The irony was that this policy produced some good architecture: the Singer Tower, for example, which celebrated the city, and the pyramid-roofed Bankers Trust Building, which replaced the Gillender. However, after World War II, the same doctrine of utility brought about the destruction of the Singer for the U.S. Steel Building.

Dissatisfaction with the design of the skyscraper, as much as with its height and density of spacing, continued through the decade. In early 1908, according to the editors of the *American Architect*, the problem was still unsolved: "The great difficulty occasioned by the almost invariable disproportion of breadth to height can hardly be said to have been overcome by the 'columnar' treatment, which has probably been more frequently employed as a general scheme of design than any other."[93] There were two alternatives: dividing the building into two blocks with a common base (like the Hudson Terminal), or expanding the area to a full block twelve to fifteen stories high and adding a tower, campanile, or dome.

The *Architectural Record* leaned the other way, emphasizing, even exaggerating, the effectiveness of a columnar or towerlike quality: "A truer architectural crown to the skyscraper would be gained if the projecting cornice could be *entirely omitted*, and the powerful vertical lines allowed to dominate, unaffected by the abrupt and limiting cornice edge. The designer might then find scope for pleasant fancies in pierced parapets and other open-work, expressing protection and enclosure of the roof, and above all, gain a restful merging of the mass of the structure into infinite space."[94] Contemporary opinions notwithstanding, it is clear that the best architects had created a genuine commercial style of great power and expressiveness, one that allowed for considerable variation, in the early years of the century. These architects understood the problem and the conditions, the functional demands and the exigencies of the site, and their buildings were forceful statements of purpose and form. Under their influence, business could be brought to recognize prior claims of commonwealth, or *bene pubblico*.

The underlying cause of so many dissatisfactions was that the American municipality was ultimately powerless to control the making of its own fabric, its own physical destiny. With few exceptions—like building codes, which reflected the interests of manufacturers and unions as much as the welfare of the people; zoning, which barely touched the surface of the real problems (and was nonexistent in New York); and aesthetic oversight through such organizations as the municipal art commission, which had high standards and the authority to compel adherence but could not generate design—the city lacked the authority to control building, real estate, and financial interests. It was a lack that the Progressive Movement came to be deeply aware of, and the essence of the problem was admirably expressed by Frederic C. Howe in a comparison of German and American cities:

> The American city . . . is in chains. It has great power for evil and but limited power for good. . . . It has to secure the assent of suspicious farmers and hostile financial interests, before it can change the wages or salaries of its officials or alter the method of police administration. . . . The city may be ruined by inadequate terminal facilities, its citizens may be killed by surface crossings, and its trade destroyed by railway discriminations for the advantage of the private speculator. Its waterfront may be monopolized by hostile interests which refuse to develop it. . . . Its unvoiced needs are given less consideration at the State capitol than the demands of a hundred special interests. It is this that strangles the American city; this more than corruption, bad charters or dishonest men.[95]

If the problem was a matter of money—and in part it was—the municipality of New York had potentially unlimited resources. The constant increase in the value of the land, for example, was a great untapped source of revenue for city operations and payment of interest on bonded debt. According to Howe, in the four years of 1905 through 1908, the assessed value of land alone, exclusive of buildings, rose from $3,057,161,290 to $3,843,165,597, an increase of 25.7 percent, for an average annual increment of almost $200 million. If that increase were taxed at a rate of 10 percent, the yield would have been about 13 percent of the average annual municipal budget of $150,000,000 over the same period. This practice was standard in Germany at the time, and was one of the reasons why Howe admired the German cities.[96]

All the unsolved problems, as well as the controversies over possible solutions, were thrown into relief in 1909 by the abortive attempt to revise the New York building code. The building code revision commission, appointed by the board of aldermen, had begun holding hearings by mid-1907. In January of 1908 it presented a new code to the Board of Aldermen, but no action was taken. In mid-May of 1909 the commission issued majority and minority reports, but these provoked so many protests that further public hearings were scheduled. In general, the commission members agreed on which provisions should be carried over from the existing code; the division was over the extent of proposed additions and changes. The new code would have established a board of registration, for example, which would examine and license architects, engineers, builders, and steel erectors; a minority of commissioners wanted to give the board authority over plumbers, steamfitters, and electricians as well. The code would also have granted broad powers to the superintendent of buildings, but the dissenters demanded curbs on those powers.[97]

The new code called for many restrictions on the use of reinforced concrete, including a requirement that the floor slab be able to support five times the design load, a building height limit of 75 feet, and absolute prohibition of the material for any building required to be fireproof. Fireproof construction was limited to segmental floor arches of brick, tile, or plain concrete, and concrete could utilize sand and stone aggregate only, no cinders. The minority argued that some exceptions were necessary. Concrete was placed at a disadvantage throughout; indeed, the proposed code requirements would have barred all of the advanced reinforced concrete work of the early years of the century—the sixteen-story Ingalls Building in Cincinnati (1902–3), for example, and Terminal Station in Atlanta (1903–4). Even as the debate was going on, the National Association of Cement Users at its convention in Cleveland drafted a standard building code for reinforced concrete construction that was far more liberal, limiting neither height nor building type, and that took into account the most recent technical advances to improve the material's performance under stress. The New York code commission appeared to turn its back on these same advances, but while the city was dragging its feet on concrete construction, the steel fabricators were enjoying a bonanza in the skyscraper boom.[98]

Ultimately, the commission adopted the code, which was submitted to the board of aldermen in early July 1909. In spite of considerable opposition, the board adopted it on 13 July, when many of its adversaries were out of the city. The opposition centered on its excessive detail, complexity, restrictions, narrow material specifications, and the fact that, unlike European codes, it did not provide general regulations and set performance standards. But in the end, Mayor McClellan vetoed it.[99] This was an old and familiar story that did not end in 1909; other attempts would be made, but there would be no new code until 1916. The code revision commission, which at one point had as many as thirty members, had represented all the trades and professions. Everyone on it had protected his special interest, then billed the city for services rendered.

11

CULMINATING WORKS AND ENVOYS OF THE FUTURE

The efforts of nearly forty years reached a climax in a series of six skyscrapers, five of them completed, under construction, or projected by 1910, and the sixth, after long consideration, begun in 1913. All revealed the results of technical progress in their spectacular height and culmination of formal mastery along the main avenues of development. In chronological order, they were the Singer Tower, notable for its needlelike form and sheer Beaux-Arts audacity; the soaring and majestic neo-Renaissance campanile known as the Metropolitan Life Tower; the Municipal Building, a monumental demonstration of "Modern Renaissance" classicism; the Bankers Trust Building, a splendid "Grecian" campanile; the watershed Woolworth Building, aptly designated the "Cathedral of Commerce"; and, finally, the new Equitable Building, more notorious than appreciated, but certainly the embodiment of a last blast of the out-of-control density that plagued the city.

The Singer Tower: An Aesthetic and Practical Triumph

When it was completed in 1908, Ernest Flagg's forty-seven-story Singer Tower (1906–8) was the tallest skyscraper yet built—and intentionally so (Figs. 11.1 and 11.2; see also Figs. 8.5 and 8.15). The Singer company set out to overtop all other skyscrapers, proudly announcing in February 1906 that its projected 594-foot-tall tower would be "higher than all existing skyscrapers by from 200 to 300 feet."[1] In the end it would rise 612 feet, and visitors would pay fifty cents each for the thrill of going up to the observation area on the fortieth floor, where they could take in views as far as thirty miles away. Although the Singer would hold the skyscraper height record for less than a year, its dramatic presence in the financial district would set an example for future tower-skyscrapers. It would also demonstrate its architect's "tower solution" to the problem of light and air loss in the densely built-up, narrow streets off Broadway: if it occupied only 25 percent of its site, a tower could rise without restriction.

In actuality, the Singer was a complex comprising two low blocks and a high tower, all designed by Ernest Flagg for the Singer Manufacturing Company but built at different times. By 1908, Flagg had produced a number of major structures, among them the Corcoran Gallery of Art (1892–97) in Washington, D.C.; St. Luke's Hospital (1892–97) and the City and Suburban Homes Company Model Tenements on West 68th and West 69th streets (1896–98; demolished) in New York City; and the United States Naval Academy buildings at Annapolis (1896–1908). Flagg's work for the Singer company began with the initial Singer Building (1897–98), a ten-story, bearing-wall structure in Beaux-Arts style at 149 Broadway on the northwest corner of Liberty Street. In 1898–99 his fourteen-story, skeleton-framed Bourne Building, designed for the Singer company president, Frederick G. Bourne, was built next door at 85–89 Liberty Street. In 1903–4 Flagg's L-shaped Singer Loft Building, a twelve-story structure embellished by intriguingly beautiful green-painted ironwork and orange terra-cotta on its two very open street facades, was constructed at 561–63 Broadway and through to 88 Prince Street. The Singer Loft Building was immediately perceived as "rational" for its French system of ornament expressive of its internal steel frame.[2]

In 1902 Flagg was asked to design an addition to the Singer headquarters building on Broadway, and by early 1903 he was planning a tower of "over thirty-five stories" that would be "the tallest in the world."[3] The Singer company was actively expanding; in 1904 it organized the Singer Sewing Machine Company as the sales agent for its products, which over the years included home knitting machines and various other appliances in addition to sewing machines. By 1906 it had acquired additional property on Liberty Street adjoining the Bourne on the west, and on Broadway adjoining the Singer on the north. Ultimately, Flagg's task involved the creation of a uniform roof line and, consequently, uniform base line of the tower. The old Singer Building was increased in height to match the fourteen-story Bourne. It was also extended northward until it adjoined the site of the City Investing Building, for a frontage of 132.5 feet on Broadway, and the Bourne Building was enlarged by a fourteen-story extension to the west for a total length of 237.5 feet on Liberty Street (Fig. 11.3). The northward extension of the old Singer Building and its reconstruction with steel framing facilitated the construction of a 65-foot-square, forty-seven-story skyscraper tower set back about 30 feet behind the facade of the old, extended building and rising free above its enlarged two-building "base" for thirty-two stories. It should be noted, however, that the uppermost six stories were in the lantern atop the tower roof. The Singer company intended to occupy all the space in the tower above the thirty-first floor and lease out the space below.

It took a large architectural office with its own engineering department, headed by Otto F. Semsch, and two consulting engineering firms, Boller & Hodge (steel structure) and Charles G. Armstrong (mechanical equipment), to design the Singer Tower. And more than forty satellite industries and contractors were required to give it physical embodiment. In lieu of the usual outside general contractor, Flagg's office added a construction department in 1907 to oversee the work on the project. Despite the com-

11.1
Singer Tower (1906–8; demolished), Ernest Flagg, architect.
Museum of the City of New York.

11.2
*View of Broadway
from Thames Street
looking north toward
Singer Tower.
After New York
Illustrated (1914).*

plexity of the undertaking, construction was completed in less than twenty months with no serious accidents. Excavation and foundation work began in mid-September of 1906, and the building officially opened, with only a few interior details left to be completed, on 1 May 1908.[4]

Because the tower was to be so tall and so slender, its wind bracing and the anchoring of its steel framework had to be specially designed. At the time the building was being planned, the problem of determining stresses from wind action in braced framing was receiving new and exhaustive attention; Semsch was undoubtedly aware of all the developments. Bedrock at the site lies as deep as minus 92 feet under an overburden comprising, from the top down, layers of sand, quicksand, clay, boulders, and a stratum of hardpan 20 to 25 feet thick covering the bedrock, and the water level is at minus 20 feet.

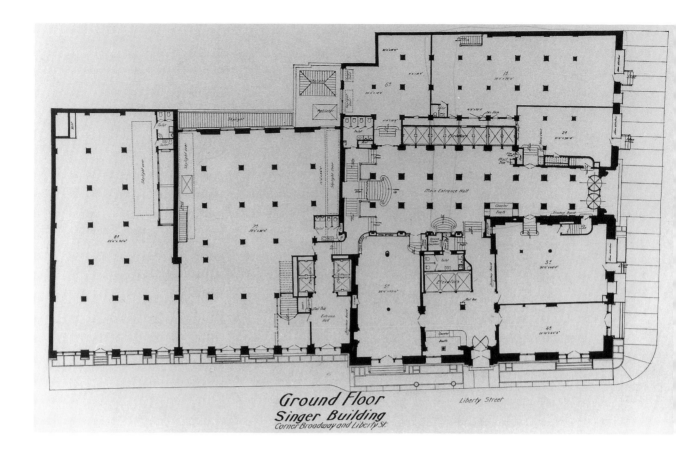

Ground Floor
Singer Building
Corner Broadway and Liberty St.

Liberty Street

11.3

Plan of ground floor, Singer Building. After Semsch, A History of the Singer Building Construction.

The foundation consisted of the usual column footings on concrete piers sunk by pneumatic caissons to bedrock at about minus 85 feet, the caisson piers having been dimensioned to carry a load of 30,000 pounds per square foot. In theory, the Singer Tower's weight alone, calculated at 18,365 tons, could resist the enormous wind pressure of 30 pounds per square foot, as specified in the building code, for a force of 330 tons on each face, but the form and the structure of the tower dictated an innovative anchorage system in the caisson foundation: "The limitations imposed by the architectural treatment of the building have resulted in a wind bracing system of such design that ten of the thirty-six columns supporting the tower showed an 'uplift,' that is, the 'dead weight' carried by items is less than the upward pull exerted on them by the wind bracing systems; thus, in one case, the 'dead load' on the columns is 279 tons and the 'uplift' 480 tons; therefore, this column and the other nine like it had to be anchored down to the caisson to resist an up-lift of 200 tons."[5] To accomplish this feat, eyebars of varying lengths were embedded in the concrete of the caissons. These eyebars, as well as the special bolts and pins that held them together and the cast-steel saddles attached to their top ends and fitted under the columns, were designed in Flagg's office and installed by the Foundation Company. This system was both innovative and costly; the foundation of the Singer Tower cost twice that of the usual skyscraper half its height.

Divided into five 12-foot bays across all dimensions, the tower's steel framework was treated as a trusslike structure with a system of corner bracing that utilized four corner towers in the form of square prisms 12 feet on a side (Fig. 11.4). Full diagonal bracing was confined to the towers; portal bracing was used elsewhere, which left the three central bays in each five-bay elevation free for closely grouped windows and the interior center bays for the elevator shaft tower. The central elevator tower and the four corner towers were tied together by diagonal elements in horizontal frames at the various floors. The steel for the framing was imported from Germany, not, according to an Austrian source, because American steel was inferior but because American workmanship was less reliable than German.[6] The Singer, and the Woolworth Building as well, survived perhaps the most grueling tests in their history in 1912 and 1913, when extreme wind velocities struck the city, reaching 96 miles an hour in 1912 and 90 miles an hour in 1913.[7]

The formal style of the Singer Tower—then termed modern French and now Beaux-Arts—complemented that of the original red-brick, limestone-trimmed, mansard-roofed Singer Building. The effect could be described as one of exuberant elegance. In the words of Flagg scholar Mardges Bacon, the building was "sumptuous, showy, and richly appointed, . . . the kind of office building that corporate clients demanded. Above all else it was good business in an age of big business."[8] Because the tower stood free above the fifteenth floor, all four of its elevations could be treated to the same high quality of design. Its face covering was dark red pressed brick with base courses, sills, copings, and other trim in North River bluestone. Its shaft was emphatically vertical in design, although stone bands divided it horizontally into segments, and iron balconies in the center bay of each face at every seventh floor accented those divisions. The center bay of each face was

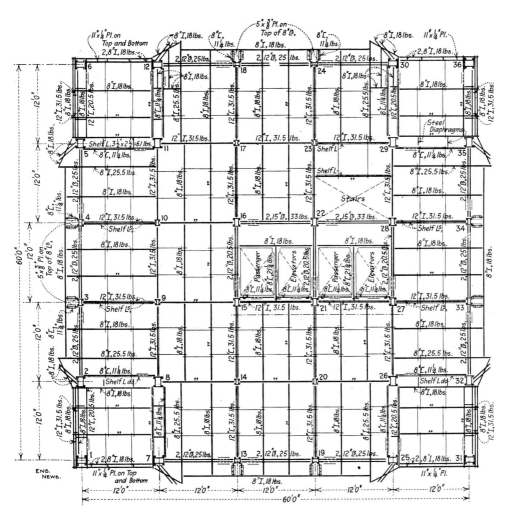

11.4

Typical floor framing plan, Singer Tower. After *Engineering News (1907).*

11.5

*Lobby, Singer Tower.
After Semsch,* A
History of the Singer
Building Con-
struction.

framed by a tall arch that served to outline the dominant framing element, the corner towers of the steel frame, and echo the curved shape of the domed roof. In that rational manner the arches and the dome skillfully maintained a continuity of line in transition from the vertical bands and lines to the horizontal terminators. The ornament of the domed mansard roof, dormers, and lantern was copper sheet, the roof cover slate. In color as in every other way, the Singer stood out from its newer neighbors, all of them uniformly light in color.

The tower's two-story, galleried lobby was an architectural tour de force, with sixteen Italian marble–sheathed columns supporting glazed saucer domes on heavily orna-mented pendentives (Fig. 11.5). It ran from the new main entrance on Broadway to a grand staircase at the rear that led to the former Bourne Building. Along the north side of the lobby was a row of Otis passenger elevators that were driven by horizontal-axis electric motors; the building had sixteen electric elevators, probably the first such installation on this scale.[9]

The Singer Tower was an aesthetic triumph that enriched the city by demonstrating the sculptural possibilities of the steel-framed skyscraper, but it was not generally appreciated in the late 1960s, when tastes ran toward Modernism. No longer the Singer company's headquarters, it was demolished in 1968 to make way for the construction of the United States Steel Building. The Singer might have been spared and another site found for its oppressive fifty-four-story steel and glass replacement, but popular interest in saving it was not strong enough to prevail.[10] The whole affair was an illuminating example of corporate philistine rapacity. Ironically, though, in its demise, the Singer achieved another, more enduring record in becoming the tallest building ever demolished, and the 1916 zoning law incorporated its lesson in the part of the resolution that permits unrestricted height for a skyscraper occupying only 25 percent of its site.

The Metropolitan Life Tower: 700-Foot Wonder

The Metropolitan Life Insurance Company Tower (1907–9) was completed a year later than the Singer Tower. The result was yet another broken record, for its fifty-story, 700-foot height exceeded that of the Singer by three stories and 88 feet. Designed by Pierre L. Lebrun of Napoleon Lebrun & Sons, the new tower rose on the east side of Madison Square, three blocks south of Madison Square Garden and to the east and north of the Flatiron Building (Figs. 11.6 and 11.7). It culminated a complex that embraced the Lebrun firm's original eleven-story building completed in 1893 and harmoniously styled eleven- and twelve-story additions of 1895, 1901, 1902, and 1905 by the same architects (Fig. 11.8). The end result was full-block coverage from 23rd to 24th streets and Madison to Fourth avenues, an impressive series of marble-sheathed arcades and rotundas running through the expanded building from avenue to avenue, and, rising from one corner of its extended base, a stunning skyscraper version of the Campanile of San Marco.

Organized in 1866 and chartered under its current name in 1868, the Metropolitan Life Insurance Company was a latecomer in the life-insurance business relative to its chief rivals, Mutual, New York, and Equitable. Nevertheless, it prospered over the years, especially after 1891, eventually overtaking all of them. In 1906 its assets were still reported as lower than the three older companies, but that same year it obtained a long-coveted site on the corner of Madison Avenue and 24th Street, that of the old Madison Square Presbyterian Church, needed to complete the block. During 1907 Metropolitan Life claimed to have written more policies and "gained more insurance in force than all the other New York companies combined."[11] By then the home-office work force numbered more than 2,800; it was again time to expand and to proclaim the company's importance in an appropriate manner. Whatever space the company did not immediately need would yield rental income in the meantime. The LeBrun firm was commissioned to design the tower, and the experienced Purdy & Henderson firm would serve as structural engineers, with Post & McCord as the steelwork contractors.

The tower form of the corner portion of the addition is said to have been the inspiration of John R. Hegeman, Metropolitan Life's president at the time. Hegeman greatly admired the Campanile of San Marco, whose collapse in 1902—it was reconstructed in

11.6
*Preliminary
rendering,
Metropolitan Life
Tower
(1907–9),
Napoleon LeBrun &
Sons (Pierre LeBrun),
architects.
East side of Madison
Avenue at 24th Street.
In the left distance,
tower of Madison
Square Garden.
After* Metropolitan
Life Insurance
Company *(1908).*

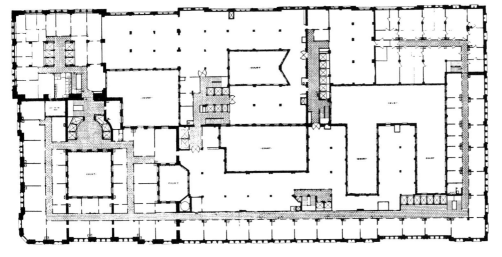

1908—may have induced him and his architect to build the new skyscraper-tower in the form of the cherished Venetian monument.[12] Although the campanile image had for some time past attracted skyscraper architects, most recently in Hornbostel and Post's civic center proposal of 1903, where the projected new municipal building was fashioned after the same model, this would be its first realization. Early in 1907 and in advance of construction, the *Record and Guide* accurately anticipated the effect, observing "how ideally fitting is its location, opposite the open square overlooking the junction and beginning of the two busiest and most important streets of Greater New York."[13] Indeed, the Madison Square area was being actively redeveloped; on the other side of the Square the old Fifth Avenue Hotel would soon be replaced by the massive Fifth Avenue Building. The tower's width was to be about 75 feet on Madison Avenue and 85 feet on 24th Street, its height above the sidewalk 658 feet, and the number of stories forty-eight. The same source, however, in its issue of 18 April 1908, announced that the working drawings had been changed. The tower would instead rise to 700 feet above the sidewalk, and the number of stories would exceed fifty. As completed, although the height did indeed reach 700 feet, the story count remained at fifty above the sidewalk.

No new construction techniques as such were employed, but because the building was to rise so high and require an enormous amount of construction material, its steel framework had to be unusually heavy and its wind bracing extremely rigid. The maximum compressive load on the largest of the twenty columns comprising the framework—four at the corners, two in each wall, eight in the interior—was calculated at 7.5 million pounds. An additional load due to high wind pressure at the specified maximum of 30 pounds per square foot was reckoned at 2.9 million pounds. The total compression of 10.4 million pounds would result in "stresses so large as to be almost or quite unprecedented in this class of construction."[14] Sunk by pneumatic caissons to bedrock at depths varying from minus 28 to minus 46 feet, the concrete piers under the footings transmitted an extremely high unit pressure to the bedrock, reckoned at 50,000 pounds per square foot, which, if correctly reported, transgressed the building code specification of 30,000 pounds maximum.[15] The column support of the steel frame consisted of a cast-steel base plate 7 feet square on the side and 3 feet deep on a grillage of four levels of 24-inch I-beams embedded in concrete. In contrast to the Singer Tower, there was no need to anchor the columns in the footings; the sheer mass of the walls was sufficient anchorage to oppose any uplifting force.[16]

All the columns were box in form, with those at the corners stiffened against bending by two flanges extending from each face. The wind bracing involved built-up spandrel plate girders at each face of the column on the lower twelve floors, where the wind pressure is greatest; double knee braces above and below the corner girders, with triangular gusset plates above and below the girders at other column-and-girder connections, were limited to floors above the twelfth (Fig. 11.9). At the twenty-ninth floor the wall columns were respaced; and at the thirty-first floor, where the walls set back behind an arcaded loggia, these columns were terminated. The corner columns continued up to the thirty-fifth floor, where they ended. At that point, the eight interior columns, which had maintained their vertical alignment from the foundations up, were offset because of reductions in the floor area.

Concrete served as the major fireproofing material, covering all the structural mem-

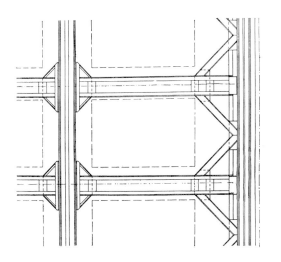
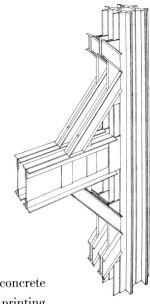

11.9

*Framing details,
Metropolitan Life
Tower. Left: wind
bracing at an end bay.
Right: knee bracing
between a girder and
a corner column.
After American
Architect and
Building News
(1909).*

bers except for the box columns, which were encased in terra-cotta. Reinforced concrete floors of segmental-arch construction were built strong enough to support heavy printing presses and machinery. Marble from Tuckahoe in Westchester County, brick-backed on the lower floors and tightly tied to the structural steelwork throughout, sheathed the full exterior. The interior walls of all public spaces within the building were clad in marble as well. The utilities were largely standardized, but, like the building itself, their installation eclipsed everything that had gone before. After much study by a panel of experts, overhead electric-traction-type elevators manufactured by Otis were installed in the tower rather than the high-speed hydraulic elevators used in the eleven-story base. Taking advantage of the opportunity, in a double-page advertisement the Otis Elevator Company declared that an express trip in the Metropolitan Life Tower's elevators covered "600 feet in 60 seconds."[17]

Though inspired by the San Marco Campanile, the office tower was of necessity far more open and vigorously articulated than its model. The huge structure was divided into three major parts, with proportions roughly corresponding to those of a Doric column and even incorporating a columnlike entasis.[18] The three parts comprised a low, relatively open base, where pairs of columns enframed three large arched openings at the second level; a shaft with triple windows within decorative reveals filling each of three bays and articulated with restrained verticality through continuous piers and rusticated quoins at the corners; and an elaborated capital divided into four strongly demarcated parts. At its lowest level, this spirelike top section comprised a balcony on an ornate double-bracket course surmounted by a loggia with five openings; above that, acting as a transition, a simple recessed block with small discrete windows, barely visible from the street; then a high pyramidal roof punctuated by ocular windows; and, finally, a cupola lantern fitted with electric flashlights for night lighting. Four huge concrete clockfaces, enriched by inlaid blue and white mosaic tile and enframing garlands of fruit and flowers, were mounted high above the street, one on each side of the shaft. A source of great pride, this chiming clock was touted as "the largest four-dial tower clock in the world."[19]

The Metropolitan Life received the American Institute of Architects chapter award of 1909, with a citation for "the general excellence of the result attained, and the extremely successful treatment of one of the most difficult problems now presented to American architects."[20] Although the comment is innocuous, it at least expresses professional admiration and implies an important urbanistic and economic fact, namely, that in structures like this, the business corporation was consciously aiming to express a beneficent civic image, suggesting an altruistic concern with public welfare and the kind of enhancement of the urban milieu that fosters pride in the city.

This comment about the style of the tower, likely supplied by the architect, is similarly indicative of the period: "Whether architects are working toward the right evolution of a tall building, irreverently termed 'skyscraper' style, the verdict of time only can determine. The testimony of the past shows that they have, at every epoch-making period, been sufficiently ingenious to create a special style, giving artistic expression to its dominant characteristics and aspirations. But they have always done so by utilizing and shaping anew the elements of past styles. No worthy *art nouveau* has ever arisen out of a merely eccentric straining after novelty."[21]

Unfortunately, much of the Metropolitan Life Tower's Early Renaissance-style detailing was lost in the early 1960s, when its surfaces were stripped to blend with those of its newly rebuilt base.[22] Yet the tower remains a riveting and distinctive presence and still speaks of the dramatic culmination of the first great skyscraper era—a time when an office building masquerading as a world-famous campanile could invest a great New World city with a semblance of Venetian grandeur. The complex is still owned by the Metropolitan Life Insurance Company and still serves as its home office.

The completion of the 612-foot Singer Tower and the advanced state of construction of the 700-foot Metropolitan Life Tower brought the question of height limitation to the fore once again in 1908. The only limitation at the time was that fixed by the loading criterion for bedrock established by the New York building code. As indicated earlier, for caisson foundations on bedrock the maximum combined dead, live, and wind load was limited to 30,000 pounds per square foot—although the Metropolitan Life tower may have exceeded that limit. With that restriction in mind, and taking into account the existing code regulations for wall thickness—12 inches for the top 75 feet, with an increase of 4 inches for each 60-foot increment of height below—and also the code requirements that the maximum wind load not exceed 30 pounds per square foot and that the overturning moment of wind be less than 75 percent of the stability moment of the structure, O. F. Semsch calculated the maximum allowable height on a 200-foot-square lot. Given the usual 13-foot, 4-inch story-to-story height, the building could rise 150 stories, or 2,000 feet—though the wall thickness at the base would have to be a whopping 140 inches. In other words, if the lone criterion were the bearing capacity of Manhattan bedrock, buildings could rise as high as money would allow. Semsch's estimate of the cost of his hypothetical 150-story building was $60 million.[23]

The Municipal Building: "A Modern 'Colossus of Rhodes'"

For years the city had contemplated the construction of a major office building. By 1880 City Hall was no longer adequate to accommodate the city's office needs, and over the following twenty-five years a number of proposals were advanced: to enlarge the old building, or to acquire existing office space, or to construct an office building. In 1884 Mayor Franklin Edson suggested purchasing the A. T. Stewart Building at the corner of

Broadway and Chambers Street for use as office space. Three years later, city authorities seriously contemplated construction of a building in City Hall Park adjacent to the old City Hall. In 1888 a competition for such a building was held, and Charles Atwood's winning entry called for two large wings flanking City Hall and a tall tower behind it.[24] Had this design been realized, the old City Hall would have been overwhelmed. Strong opposition to building anything in the park put a stop to this plan.

Meanwhile, in the summer of 1887, Arthur M. Wellington, editor-in-chief of *Engineering News*, had advanced an unusual—and prophetic—proposal that called for the construction of a new municipal building over the subway loop for the Manhattan terminal of the Brooklyn Bridge. (The first such combination of loop terminal and overhead office building would in fact be the Hudson Terminal, completed in 1909.) Early in 1890 Mayor Hugh J. Grant recommended the construction of a new municipal building, and later that year the commission appointed to oversee construction of the new building issued a report that listed three acceptable sites on Chambers Street. The commissioners recommended a 55,000-square-foot site on Chambers Street between Centre Street and Park Row and extending to Duane Street. It cost the least, was the largest, and offered the greatest opportunity to build an imposing building. The commissioners also believed that a new building in that location would improve the neighboring property, thereby stimulating other improvements and increasing the tax return—a kind of urban renewal process.[25]

In spite of the commission's strong preference, and after long controversy, a major competition was held in 1893 for a building that would have replaced City Hall. State authorities, responding to a great outcry, intervened to prevent any new construction in City Hall Park and the demolition of City Hall.[26] Early in 1899 George B. Post presented to the Architectural League his project for a new City Hall. A grandiose mansarded and towered office building with ten times the floor area of the old City Hall, it was proposed to be constructed on an elevated terrace just to the north of the site recommended in 1890. The old City Hall would stay where it was.[27] As we have seen, Hornbostel and Post's civic center plan of 1903 called for the construction of a forty-five-story office tower at Chambers and Centre streets, and at long last, in 1907 a competition was announced that ultimately resulted in the current Municipal Building. The new building would rise on a site previously acquired by the city for the enlargement of the Manhattan terminal of the Brooklyn Bridge and for subway lines, the same site that had been recommended in 1890. Centered on Chambers Street, it was bounded by Centre Street, Duane Street, and Park Row. The municipality authorized the commissioner of bridges, with the approval of the Board of Estimate and Apportionment, to take the necessary preliminary steps toward construction.[28]

The competition program was quite specific. Thirteen firms, whose names were listed, had been invited to compete. The competitors were to elect a three-person jury, a procedure that was calculated to ensure a fair judgment but which had been criticized because it prevented publishing the jurors' names in advance. The jury's decision was subject to the approval of the commissioner of bridges, and the art commission would have final approval. The supports of the building were to be positioned so as not to obstruct train tracks and stairways or impede circulation on the platforms, and Chambers Street had to be kept open for vehicular and pedestrian traffic. The first story, to be given over mainly to subway and building entrances and elevator and stair access to the upper floors, had to be at least 20 feet high and completely covered either by floor or by roof; this coverage was to extend over Chambers Street where it passed through the site. There had to be ample access to the subway station and to the building from the streets on all sides, and it was recommended that the floor of the first story be at, or close to, grade level. Inclusion of a mezzanine story for ductwork and mechanical equipment above the first story was advised, and the square footage for each of the departments to be housed in the building was specified, as was a minimum building height of twenty stories.

The program permitted considerable freedom for the architectural styling of the building: "The character of the building and its appointments are to be those of a first-class office building in this city. While a dignified and handsome exterior is desired, a strictly monumental character is not required."[29] Judging from the entries that were published, this instruction was construed as an invitation to go the limit in regard to monumentality. McKim, Mead & White won the competition, and the Howells & Stokes firm seems to have been the runner-up. According to the *Sun*, although many of the designs called for more elaborate exteriors than did the winning entry, it was chosen because it provided the most floor space.[30] As completed, the building contained 1,250,000 square feet of usable space.

The West Street Building was a model for Howells & Stokes' Gothic design (Fig. 11.10). That firm's project, at a height of thirty-three stories to the top of the central tower, is marked by strong verticality. I. N. Phelps Stokes, the partner of John Mead Howells, would later claim that the design influenced the post–World War I tower-skyscraper: "If not actually the prototype of the present upward tapering type of skyscraper with highly accentuated vertical lines, [Howells & Stokes' design] at least marked an important step in this direction, and has had a far-reaching effect upon the design of the modern skyscraper. . . . The only earlier modern building known to the author which shows any indication of this tendency is the West Street building." He then cited Helmle & Corbett's Bush Tower (1916–17), Raymond M. Hood's American Radiator Building (1923–24), and Howells & Hood's Chicago Tribune Building (1923–25) as "recent prominent examples of this general type."[31] But it is doubtful that the Howells & Stokes project had much influence, and in making his assessment Stokes overlooked a great many buildings erected in New York City from 1870 on.

Both McKim, Mead & White's winning design and the building as completed (1909–14) bear a marked resemblance to the same firm's unsuccessful competition entry of 1903 for Grand Central Terminal (cf. Figs. 11.11 and 11.12). Stanford White was responsible for the terminal project. It, too, projected a mammoth structure and called for a tower reminiscent of his Madison Square Garden tower, vaulted passageways that spanned over major streets, and colonnaded treatments of the ground-story arcade, corner towers, and upper level. Had it been realized, it would have been the most sensational of New York skyscrapers, higher by 100 feet than the Woolworth Building and the highest building in the world.[32] Normally the firm was reluctant to enter competitions, but the one for the Municipal Building provided the opportunity to produce a magnificent major skyscraper that would realize the grandeur of White's terminal design. William Mitchell Kendall, one of the firm's partners, is credited with designing the Municipal Building, but Stanford White deserves recognition for his posthumous contribution to its overall imagery. Burt

L. Fenner and Teunis J. Van der Bent were the partners in charge of construction. Purdy & Henderson served as consulting engineers, Alexander Johnson as chief engineer, and the Thompson-Starrett Company as general contractor; construction was supervised by the city's Department of Bridges.

The architects created a visually interesting plan, relating it to the street pattern of the immediate area and providing plenty of outside exposure (Fig. 11.13). Placing the central axis exactly on the center line of Chambers Street, they expertly fitted their huge C-shaped, ten-sided building into its irregular site. The building's frontage on Centre Street was to be 381 feet and its depth 173 feet on the line of Chambers Street. Mayor George B. McClellan applauded the design of "one of the most important projects the City has ever undertaken" and anticipated that many of the city's problems had been satisfactorily solved.[33] The cost of the construction, he stated, would be about $8 million—it would actually cost about $2 million more—and the city would save the approximately $454,000 annual rental it was then paying for the accommodation of the various city departments in other structures. Most of the city departments would be housed in the new building, and the mayor expected some of the courts to move there as well, possibly removing the need for building a new courthouse. That proved overly optimistic; by 1910 proposals were being put forward for a new county courthouse, one no less than a thousand feet high, and a competition would be held in 1912. At 559 feet, the new building, he asserted, would be the city's third-highest office building. That, too, was not to be the case, as the Woolworth Building, completed in 1913, would far overtop it. As it happened, the Brooklyn Bridge terminal was never placed underground; the Interborough Rapid Transit (IRT) and new Brooklyn-Manhattan Transit (BMT) subways, comprising six tracks as well as station platforms, took its place.

Construction of the building, to have twenty-five stories with fifteen more in the tower, posed the most difficult foundation problems ever encountered in any New York City

11.11
Main elevation on 42nd Street, competition entry for Grand Central Terminal (1903), McKim, Mead & White, architects. Drawing signed J. A. Johnson. Collection of The New-York Historical Society.

11.12
Municipal Building
(1909–14),
McKim, Mead & White, architects.
Intersection of Centre and Chambers streets.
After Mujica, History of the Skyscraper.

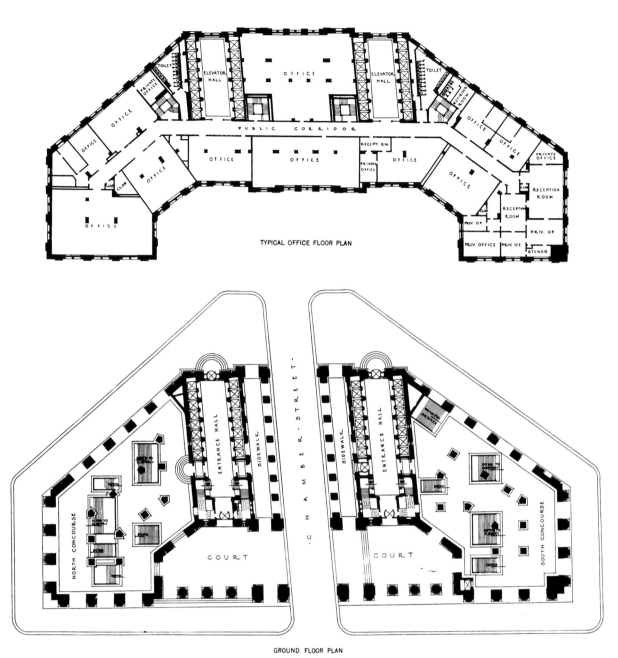

TYPICAL OFFICE FLOOR PLAN

GROUND FLOOR PLAN

SCALE ⊦⊦⊦⊦ FEET·

11.13

*Ground floor and
typical floor plans,
Municipal Building.
After McKim, Mead &
White, A Monograph
of the Work of
McKim, Mead &
White 1879–1915.
Avery Architectural
and Fine Arts Library,
Columbia University
in the City of
New York.*

structure because of the extreme depth of the bedrock, the great variation in its depth,
and the presence of the subway station and lines. At the site bedrock slopes downward
toward the north from minus 136 to minus 178 feet, with much of its area at around
minus 144 feet.[34] All of the foundation work was preceded by extensive borings and load
tests of the soil and rock. The soil, mainly sand and mostly coarse, sharp, and wet, extends
lower than minus 130 feet. Its various layers, with piling, were regarded as adequate
bearing material for the nearby World and St. Paul buildings, and load tests at the
Municipal Building site indicated that the bearing capacity of the sand from minus 85
feet downward was 40,000 pounds per square foot. But the original contract for the
foundation work, let to the J. H. Gray Company, was canceled because the superintendent of buildings doubted that the sand would support this load or any extremely high

loads under the tower portion of the building. The new contract made with the Foundation Company required bedrock caissons except where the depth was prohibitive. It allowed for modifications in work and payments because of the unknown conditions in this unprecedented foundation work.[35] Other variables arose because the World Building, the Hall of Records, the Brooklyn Bridge approach and rail terminal, the Third Avenue elevated line, and the IRT subway line—all in the immediate vicinity—rested on relatively shallow foundations in compact sand.

When confronted with such rock depths, the Foundation Company engineers quickly understood the difficulty. The depth to which pneumatic caissons could be sunk was restricted; the building code specified a pressure limit of 50 pounds per square inch under which men could work safely inside caisson chambers. At the site, that limit was reached at 115.5 feet below mean high water, or 147.5 feet below grade, and would require the deepest caissons ever used. On the southern half of the site, bedrock caissons were sunk to depths varying from minus 136 to minus 144 feet; the extreme depth was at 112 feet below mean high water, which was a record low; the maximum pressure in the caisson work chamber was 47 pounds per square inch, close to the limit. No excavation by the pneumatic method was used below that level. On the northern part of the site, where the bedrock dips down prohibitively low, the pneumatic caissons were enlarged and rested on sand at about minus 74 feet (Fig. 11.14).

The work was done by twenty five-man shifts, each active for forty minutes. Each worker required four hours of decompression between shifts. A physician was in constant attendance, with sanitary and emergency first-aid equipment at the site. The workers were selected on the basis of physical condition and required to follow an exacting diet

11.14
Construction photograph showing tops of caisson piers and column base plates, Municipal Building, 2 November 1910. Hall of Records (1899–1907) in background. Avery Architectural and Fine Arts Library, Columbia University in the City of New York.

and to refrain from all alcoholic consumption. These precautions worked. Although three deaths occurred from construction accidents, one of those from the cave-in of a foundation retaining wall, there were only two cases of caisson disease—the bends—and no deaths from it. The foundations were constructed in less than a year, between December 1909 and early October 1910, by which time the steel framework was being erected.[36]

As massively solid as its granite-covered exterior appears, the Municipal Building is skeleton framed (Fig. 11.15). The most unusual aspect of the frame seems to have been its heaviness and complexity at the first floor. As explained by engineer Norman G. Nims, "Because of the tracks and station platforms below the street level, not only the masonry walls but one-half the steel columns supporting the superstructure had to be stopped at the first floor and carried on steel-plate girders. These girders, in turn, are supported by other steel columns which transmit the entire weight of the building, estimated at 377,319,500 lb., to concrete caissons. The girders at the 1st floor, supporting the columns above, are about 10 ft. in depth and were set in pairs, sometimes three abreast, and were of necessity at all sorts of angles with each other."[37] The largest girders used were the plate girders that carry the framing over the Chambers Street vault. These were 36 feet long with a maximum depth of 11 feet.

Terra-cotta was used for the Chambers Street vault and decorative details above the twenty-fifth floor, and the wall panels below the vault were concrete, but the rest of the building's exterior was clad in light-colored granite. As shown on the plan, there were subway entrances at either end of the building; today only the southern entrance functions. Both were vaulted, using the Guastavino tile-arch system. By 1909 the system, known as Cohesive Construction, was in wide use for vaulting large spaces.[38]

Variously described as Roman Imperial, Italian Renaissance, French Renaissance, or Beaux-Arts, the Municipal Building's style was selected for its "civic character" and because of the proximity of other government structures, "all of them classic, or in styles derived therefrom."[39] A splendid program of bas-reliefs enriches the facades at strategic points. The reliefs are concentrated at the base of the building on the west side, where a giant Corinthian colonnade closes the court at either side of the Chambers Street archway. In the arch spandrels and in roundels, classicizing figures signify the various aspects of civic government—Guidance, Executive Power, and Prudence, for example. Six pairs of standing figures that flank the second-story windows personify the various governmental departments. Cherubs carry garlands in the architrave, and scenes representing Civic Pride and Civic Duty appear above the small arches at either side of the large central archway (Fig. 11.16). The sculptor was the German-born Adolph Alexander Weinman, who had studied with Augustus Saint-Gaudens.[40] Above the plain, vertically articulated shaft, screens of columns reappear in the capital zone, and at that point the building receives its flamboyant, tourelled and multitiered tower topped by Weinman's gilded figure of Civic Fame.

The civic function of this "modern 'Colossus of Rhodes,'" as well as its dominance over the government buildings flanking Chambers Street, is well conveyed by its huge Manhattan-embracing form, its multilevel colonnaded tower, its classical vocabulary, and its sculptural decoration.[41] The building's situation relative to the Brooklyn Bridge, the edge of Manhattan Island, and the mass transportation facilities below and around it all speak to its importance in the scheme of government.[42] The century-old, modestly scaled

City Hall, with its tiny cupola, had been "answered"—if not subjugated—from on high. Moreover, as an early government-office skyscraper, the Municipal Building set a precedent; the Nebraska State Capitol (1920–32), for example, is a successor.

Huge, tightly unified, and strongly rhythmic, the Municipal Building attests to the increasing consolidation of expressive form and imagery in civic and commercial buildings, a quality that also characterized the Singer and Metropolitan towers. The structures that helped bring the first phase of skyscraper evolution to culmination reveal formal mastery and the capacity to exploit the high building to its fullest powers of eloquence. In essence, functional requirements and new structural technology had been realized in aesthetic terms. Claude Bragdon saw this achievement as the expression of both the power and the paradoxes of American civilization:

The tall office building, our most characteristic architectural product, is a symbol of our commercial civilization. Its steel framework, strong, yet economical of metal, held together at all points by thousands of rivets, finds a parallel in our highly developed industrial and economic system, maintained by the labor of thousands of obscure and commonplace individuals, each one a rivet in the social structure. And just as this steel framework is encased in a shell of masonry, bedecked, for the most part, with the architectural imaginings of alien peoples, meaninglessly employed, so are we still encumbered by a mass of religious, political, and social ideas and ideals, which, if we but knew it, impede our free development and interfere with the frank expression of our essential nature.[43]

His statement is informed by allegiance to the organic tradition of Sullivan and Wright, Darwinian agnosticism, and a touch of condescension toward the common man.

The Bankers Trust Building: Halicarnassus Aloft

At 539 feet, the skyscraper that rose on the northwest corner of Wall and Nassau streets became the third-tallest tower in the city, a distinction it held only until the Municipal and Woolworth buildings were completed a year later (Fig. 11.17). The Bankers Trust Company Building (1910–1912) was designed by the partnership of Samuel Breck Parkman Trowbridge and Goodhue Livingston, known as Trowbridge & Livingston and founded in 1894 as Trowbridge, (Stockton B.) Colt, and Livingston. The founding partners were all Columbia School of Mines graduates, and all had worked initially in George B. Post's office. Besides the Bankers Trust Building, a commission it won in competition, Trowbridge & Livingston was to be responsible for the buildings on two of the three adjacent corners of Wall Street: the J. P. Morgan and Company Bank (1913–14) and the New York Stock Exchange addition (1920–22), on the southeast and southwest corners, respectively, of Wall and Broad streets. The venerable Federal Hall, inspired by the Parthenon and built as the New York Custom House in the 1830s, occupies the remaining corner of this architecturally distinguished intersection.

The Bankers Trust Company was organized by a group of bankers in 1903 to compete with existing trust companies, which were taking business away from the commercial banks. The banking laws of the time limited the functions of state and national banks primarily to serving as depositories for business enterprises and did not permit them to execute fiduciary services. Trust companies handled that sort of work, and often these companies also executed transactions that were normally the province of the commercial banks. The new Bankers Trust Company, on the other hand, would perform only fiduciary work referred to it by commercial banks, thus cooperating rather than competing with them. The new company quickly prospered and in 1909 decided to build its own quarters—an undertaking that necessitated the demolition of the nineteen-story Gillender Building, which stood on part of the site. The company's light-gray granite-sheathed office tower was begun in June of 1910 and was ready for occupancy by May of 1912. It rose to roughly twice the height of the Gillender, with thirty-one floors above ground plus six storage floors inside its high roof.[44]

The tower form of the new building, dictated by its almost square lot—about 95 by 107

feet with a small extension at one corner—belongs to the related and well-established column and campanile modes. But the new building departed from earlier such towers by virtue of its granite-clad roof and its specifically Greek architectural motifs. Treated as a giant colonnade resting on a high stylobate, the four-story base was designed to indicate the presence of two different banking offices, Bankers Trust on the two lower levels and the Manhattan Trust Company on the two floors above. (The companies merged in 1912.) The colonnade signified the presence of the main banking room inside, and its order was apparently derived from the famous Erechtheum Ionic. Above the base and two transitional floors, the plainly treated, curtain-walled shaft rises for another twenty stories of rental space. At the twenty-sixth floor, two-story-high engaged columns form the lower portion of a pyramid-topped "temple" that calls to mind the Mausoleum at Halicarnassus (Fig. 11.18). One source described the stepped-pyramid roof, which housed necessary record rooms, storage spaces, and equipment such as the tank for the automatic sprinkler system, as "an expedient . . . here tried for the first time in an office building[,] and its success in this structure prompts the assertion that it will be used a great many times more."[45] Indeed, the distinctive pyramid top became the bank's symbol in 1913 and, subsequently, its registered trademark. The Ionic order used at this level was inspired by that of the wall columns of the propylaea at Palititza in Macedonia.

Simplicity marked the company's public rooms, suggesting that the Greek style was chosen over the more usual and heavier Roman not so much for its historic association with bank architecture but for its ability to provide "simple, clean design, quiet color and an air of businesslike beauty . . . to express as far as possible what should be (and probably is) the spirit of the institution."[46] However, purity was apparently not an issue when it came to designing the coffered, Roman-derived barrel vault of the main floor corridor that led past the elevators to connect with the Hanover Bank Building. Moreover, at either side of the main banking room on the second floor, the Ionic order reappeared, this time in Roman form. The plaster ceilings in both banking rooms displayed Greek motifs.

There were many problems to overcome in constructing the Bankers Trust Building, not least of which were the removal of the Gillender's unneeded caissons, piers, and foundation girders; the need to protect the foundations of adjacent tall buildings; and the presence of treacherous quicksand in the area. Bedrock lies as deep as minus 65 feet under the site, and the usual method of foundation construction would involve sinking caissons to bedrock or to hardpan. The Gillender was founded on large caissons sunk to hardpan, and one of the factors that had made it financially unprofitable early in its short life was that the underground floors were so crowded with columns and braces as to be unusable and certainly unrentable—this for a structure only about 26 feet wide by 74 feet deep. Faced with these difficulties, the architects, the consulting engineer on foundations (T. Kennard Thomson), the general contractors (Marc Eidlitz & Son), and the Foundation Company decided to use a cofferdam foundation similar to that of the German-American Insurance Building but constructed to eliminate the need for interior caissons. A 7-foot-thick concrete cofferdam was created from a wall of narrow, interlocking caissons joined by a watertight web, and the substructure of the Gillender was removed inside this unusually formed enclosure. The footings for the new building's interior columns were placed directly on the rock surface, and its peripheral columns rested on the cofferdam

11.17
Bankers Trust Company Building (1910–12), Trowbridge & Livingston, architects. Northwest corner of Wall and Nassau streets. At right: Hanover National Bank and Equitable Life buildings, with Singer Tower in the distance. In center distance: One Wall Street Building. After Architecture *(1912).*

11.18

Top of Bankers Trust Company Building. After Architecture *(1912).*

wall. The most serious problem occurred when pressure on the cofferdam increased tremendously during the progress of the excavation; temporary timber trusses had to be inserted from wall to wall to prevent a cave-in. Remarkably, this was done in such a way as to permit the new steel framework to be put in place. Not only were the foundations of the Bankers Trust less expensive to construct than the more usual caisson foundations, but they produced additional income by providing four usable underground floors.[47] The steel frame was mostly of the straightforward column-and-girder type, but the setbacks at the second and fourth floors required unusually heavy bracing.[48]

Originated as an adjunct to pure greed like so many of these buildings, this one has remained relatively intact on the exterior even though it has spread by incorporating adjoining properties.[49] It did indeed herald the future: one has only to glance at the lower Manhattan skyline, for example, south toward Bowling Green, where the summit of the rebuilt Standard Oil Building echoes the Bankers Trust pyramid, or to look around midtown, where numerous boldly topped buildings, some recently built, define the skyline.

By 1912 most of the critics, notably Schuyler, favored a vertical design mode as the best means of expressing the steel frame of an office building, and the Gothic style was perceived as offering the ideal solution. The Classical was derived from the post-and-lintel system of construction and was therefore considered inappropriate for a steel-framed office building. An anonymous writer, discussing the relative merits of the expression of the steel frame in the classically styled Bankers Trust Building and in the Gothic Woolworth, denied that Gothic was the better choice:

Every steel building is primarily of post and lintel construction, and just why the Gothic style which is fundamentally arch construction, absolutely at variance with the principles of the actual work it encloses, should be more appropriate than a frank use of mason work as fireproofing, and post [and] lintel classic architecture as decoration is not . . . readily comprehensible. . . . Nor do I think it any more logical that the masonry covering of a steel skeleton should follow exactly its constructive portions than to demand that the human body should actually resemble the bones beneath; at least I have never heard the nose criticised as being illogical because there is no bone at the end of it.[50]

The Woolworth Building: Climax and Conclusion

However much the skyscraper might express the American spirit, however much its triumphs might be applauded, reservations toward it continued to be expressed. In 1910 word of another tower forthcoming led to renewed protests. That F. W. Woolworth intended to build a new office building had been known as early as March 1910, but at first the building was to occupy only the southwest corner of Broadway and Park Place and be modestly tall. The first public announcements of preliminary plans for the Woolworth Building (1910–13), destined to be one of the world's most famous structures, appeared in November 1910. The new tower would rise at 230 Broadway, on the site where Mayor Philip Hone's residence had once stood, conveniently near the center of city government, the financial district, the Brooklyn Bridge, and the old Post Office. Other announced details included the dimensions of the lot, 105 by 197 feet, and the information that the main block would rise twenty-six stories, that it would be surmounted by a nineteen-story, 86-foot-square tower, and that the total height was to be forty-five stories, or 625 feet. Moreover, the apex of the tower was to be so brilliantly lit as to be visible from fifty miles away. Cass Gilbert would be the architect, and the cost was expected to be about $5 million.[51] The announced height and story count would prove to be considerably less than the building that was ultimately constructed, and accordingly the cost would rise to $13.5 million.

On this occasion the demand for a halt came from *Engineering Record* in the form of a heavily editorialized news item: "Just why such a tall structure is considered desirable is something of a mystery, and it has manifest disadvantages to the city. The Singer and Metropolitan towers are advertisements by two of the leading advertisers of the country. There is no such excuse, however, for the rearing of this great pile, shutting off the light of its neighbors, darkening the streets, and containing a population of several thousand people whose concentration on a little piece of ground will add another heavy burden to the transportation facilities in the vicinity."[52] In fact, the Singer and Metropolitan towers, and the Municipal Building as well, had plenty of space around them, secured in the case of the Singer by carrying the tower high above and back from the lower blocks around it. And the Woolworth's mounted, setback tower and fortunate situation overlooking City Hall Park would greatly diminish any negative impact it might have had (Fig. 11.19). Additionally, in order to protect the Woolworth Building itself, two more lots immediately to the west would be acquired, one on Park Place, the other on Barclay Street. Occupied by low buildings, these still function as a light and air zone between the Woolworth and the tall buildings that later rose to the west of it.

As for why so tall a building was "considered desirable," the answer is that its builder, Frank Winfield Woolworth, wanted it to produce the largest income of any property in the world, and his choice of a site that would render his building visible in its entirety facilitated that ambition. Since the opening of his first Woolworth's 5 and 10 Cent Store in 1879, he had built up a spectacularly successful business; by 1910, after a merger with several of his strongest competitors, the F. W. Woolworth Company controlled a mercantile empire of more than six hundred stores. Louis J. Horowitz, head of the Thompson-Starrett Building Company, which constructed the building, explained Woolworth's actions this way: "Beyond a doubt his ego was a thing of extraordinary size; whoever tried to find a reason for his tall building and did not take that fact into account would reach a false conclusion."[53]

The new building was to be the Woolworth company's headquarters and also that of the Irving National Bank; F. W. Woolworth was a director of the bank, and the two businesses collaborated in the development of the site under the name Broadway–Park Place Company.[54] Woolworth wanted his building to rival the Singer Tower, and to rise higher, for it was to function as a huge sign advertising the business of the Woolworth company to the whole world. By late December of 1910, he had decided that it would be the world's tallest skyscraper, and he went so far as to have the Metropolitan Life Tower measured in order to make sure his building would be higher:

> "How high do you want the tower now?" asked Mr. Gilbert.
> "How high can you make it?" Mr. Woolworth asked in reply.
> "It is for you to make the limit," said Mr. Gilbert.
> "Then make it fifty feet higher than the Metropolitan tower."[55]

By January of 1911 Mr. Woolworth had acquired the Barclay Street corner, thanks to the unrelenting efforts of real estate agent Edward J. Hogan, and had instructed his architect to alter the plans so that the building would cover the whole block front. The dimensions of the enlarged building were to be 152 feet on Broadway, 197 feet, 10 inches on Park Place, and 192.5 feet on Barclay, and it would rise to a height of 750 feet—which would give it the fifty feet needed to overtop the Metropolitan Life Tower. But that was still not high enough to suit Mr. Woolworth: when completed, the Woolworth Building soared 792 feet, 1 inch above the sidewalk.[56] The main block rises thirty stories, as do the two west wings, and this part of the building adheres to a U-shaped plan, with a light court above the rear portion of the lobby. The tower adds another twenty-five stories, for a total of fifty-five, and there are two levels below ground. Because the height of the pavilion roof equals five more stories, some accounts give the total number as sixty stories above sidewalk level. According to the information leaflet supplied to visitors in 1995, by later standards there could have been seventy-nine or eighty stories within the building because many of the floors are as much as twenty feet high, and none is less than eleven feet. That this "Cathedral of Commerce," as it was dubbed by the Rev. S. Parkes Cadman at the building's grand opening, which was created to satisfy one man's vainglory, should also be beautiful and influential is owing to three factors: its architect's

11.19
*Woolworth Building
(1910–13),
Cass Gilbert,
architect,
with City Hall Park
in foreground and
Post Office at lower
right.
West side of
Broadway between
Barclay Street and
Park Place.
Photograph by
Wurts Brothers.
Collection of
S. B. Landau.*

genius; the competence of its structural engineers, the Gunvald Aus Company; and Frank W. Woolworth's vision, good taste, and financial resources.

The projected transparency, attenuated verticality, and elegance of the Woolworth's glass-and-terra-cotta envelope intensified the challenging technical problems presented by structural necessities and the process of construction itself. Characteristically for this area, bedrock lies far below the ground surface; the average depth at the site is minus 115 feet, with a range of minus 100 to minus 120 feet; the mean water level is at minus 35 feet. Compounded by the water-saturated burden, the extreme irregularity of the rock surface dictated the use of pneumatic caissons during the laborious and hazardous process of excavating, leveling the rock, and emplacing the concrete footings and steel base plates of the columns (Fig. 11.20). A total of sixty-nine caissons were used, including those that had already been sunk before Woolworth decided to enlarge the building. A major difficulty, in fact, was determining how to make use of the original foundations yet locate the sustaining columns in accord with the new design. Additional caissons were sunk, and, where needed, columns were supported on plate girders between two adjacent caissons. Elsewhere, the columns rested directly on the caissons sunk for the enlarged building. Both round and rectangular caissons were used, the latter primarily along the Barclay Street and rear lot lines, to keep the foundations within the building line.[57]

The architectural design of the Woolworth was certainly affected by aesthetic considerations, but it was heavily influenced by practical requirements and by economic inducements as well. In order to produce the maximum income, as Gilbert later explained, the building had to fill up as much of the lot as possible, and it had to have "many windows so divided that all of the offices should be well lighted and so that partitions might be placed at almost any location."[58] Another major consideration was the ratio of office space to elevator shaft space. At the time of the building's construction, Gilbert stated that the Woolworth's ratio was "the lowest ever provided in any building,"[59] meaning that the building contained the maximum usable floor space. By the time of the Woolworth's construction, the business of skyscraper rentals and building management had become a specialized branch of the real estate industry, so fierce was the competition for tenants. And, as explained by Gunvald Aus, certain practical considerations governed the spacing of the steel framing columns, chief among them the rental agent's insistence on "a certain maximum and minimum size of office" that would be rentable in this location. The spacing of most of the columns in the wings of the building was dictated by those conditions, and that of the tower columns "largely by the architectural requirements, that is to say, the front elevation and the space required by the elevators."[60]

Once the column spacing had been determined, the wind bracing needed to maintain the skyscraper's rigidity had to be addressed, and that too would affect the architectural design. In accordance with a method in use at the time for calculating wind stress, the entire structure was treated as if it were a vertical cantilever bending before the horizontal force of the wind. The sizes of the columns and girders, which had to be massive in order to support heavy loads and comply with building code loading specifications, were a primary consideration.[61] The building's end walls were considered sufficient to resist half the wind load sustained by the lines of columns supporting the walls, and the tower was designed to stand alone under the full wind load from any direction and to provide additional rigidity needed to brace the two west wings. Thus the side and court walls,

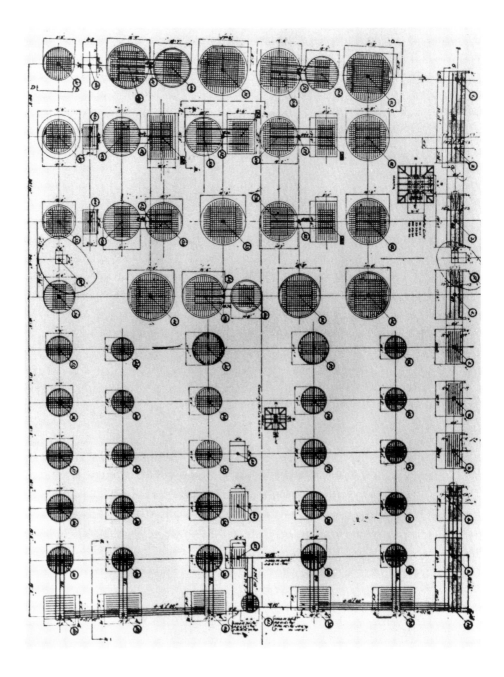

11.20

Plan of caissons and grillages, Woolworth Building.

After American Architect and Building News *(1913).*

together with the interconnecting trusses at every fifth floor between the wings and the rigidity of the tower, were judged adequate to brace the wings. For the tower it was decided that the best method was to use continuous portal-arch bracing from grade level to the twenty-eighth floor—the most extensive application of this relatively expensive system to date—because, as Aus explained, the portal braces "could be concealed in the piers of the exterior walls and in the partitions enclosing the elevators" (Fig. 11.21).[62] The vertical depth of the arch bracing and the width of the massive steel columns fixed the width of the pilasters in the Broadway elevation of the building.

Conventional knee braces and rigid connections of girders to columns were utilized above the twenty-eighth floor. A modification of the portal arches in the facade was used in the column-and-girder frames that extended through the depth of the main block and the two west wings, where technical solutions also controlled the dimensions of the terra-

11.21

Portal-arch bracing,
west elevation,
Woolworth Building.
After American
Architect and
Building News *(1913).*

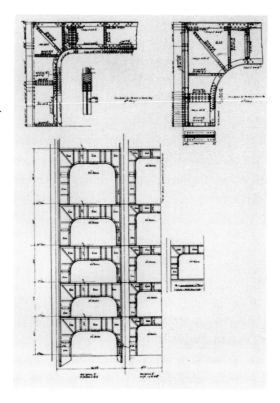

cotta pilasters and the associated window and spandrel proportions. To ensure that the wind shear load below sidewalk level would be transmitted to the retaining walls, reinforced concrete construction was used for the two lowest floors of the building. The more expensive hollow tile was used for all the floors above because of the length of time required to set concrete and the freezing weather conditions under which the setting would have had to be done.

The Woolworth's utilities and safety features were the best that could be had. Except for the shuttle elevator in the tower, which was the electric drum type, the building's twenty-six Otis electric elevators were the same gearless traction type as had been used in the Metropolitan Life and Singer towers. Those that rose the highest traveled 700 feet per minute, the rest 600 feet per minute. As a safeguard against injury, and in their most extensive use to date, Ellithorpe air cushions were installed in the bottom of the elevator shafts.[63] The building's sophisticated and costly water supply involved seven systems—for the mechanical plant, fire protection, the toilet and washrooms, offices with lavatories, the hot-water supply, the swimming pool in the basement, and the restaurant, also in the basement—all interconnected for maximum supply in an emergency.[64] Hoping to attract "lawyers, financial institutions and high-class businesses," Hogan advertised the Woolworth as the "Highest, Safest, Most Perfectly Appointed Office Structure in the World, Fireproof Beyond Question, Elevators Accident-Proof," a business environment that provided "every necessary comfort and convenience, with permanent light and air."[65]

Gilbert was at the same time committed to the aesthetic expression of the building's function and its steel frame; the Woolworth Building would not appear to be a masonry-walled structure. Aus, who considered Gilbert the "leading exponent" of rational design and his Woolworth and West Street buildings excellent examples, was quite clear on the issue: "From an engineering point of view, no structure is beautiful where the lines of strength are not apparent, or in other words, where one cannot follow the distribution of the loads from the top of the structure to its foundations." So successful was Gilbert in achieving this goal that Montgomery Schuyler effusively praised the Woolworth as the "noblest offspring" of skeleton construction; he also admired its retention of the Aristotelian tripartite division as specified in Sullivan's theory, as well as its "success of 'scale.'" Scale and proportion were particular concerns of Gilbert's, so much so that "the study he gave to the Woolworth building destroyed his sense of scale for several years, because of the unprecedented attuning of detail to, for those days, such an excessive height."[66]

The Woolworth Building's tower and Gothic style were requested by Woolworth—who suggested to Gilbert that the Victoria Tower of the Houses of Parliament might be a model—but the decision to use color on the exterior as a means of suggesting shadows and accenting structure was Gilbert's. For Gilbert, the Gothic was the optimal means of expressing the vertical lines of the tower form; however, he was annoyed by the Cathedral of Commerce label and pointed out that his models were secular Gothic, North European town halls with towers. The specific variety of Gothic he chose was the late fifteenth- and sixteenth-century Flamboyant because, in his words, it is "light, graceful, delicate and flamelike, as its name implies, and capable of infinite subdivision."[67] Moreover, it lent itself to verticality and linearity. Terra-cotta, selected as the cladding material for use above the granite-and-limestone-covered base, could be applied thinly and molded and colored effectively. Although from a distance the exterior appears to be uniformly a light cream color, delicate tones of blue, yellow, or green underlie the relief ornament used throughout the exterior. The tower roof was gilded, and Gilbert later recalled that in selecting colors for the roofs and particularly for the gilded tower-top, he intended to make the tower appear taller and also relate it to the changing blue or gray tone of the sky.

The facades are divided into continuous bays by what Schuyler called *reeding:* continuous piers and mullions, exaggerated so that when seen from a sharp angle the openings disappear. The primary, Broadway, facade is given dynamic presence by four thick terra-cotta-clad columns that frame the central section; these are continuous from the base to the first tower setback. On this front, windows are grouped within bays in a rhythmic series of four, two, three, two, and four; and on all facades decorative belt courses tie the reeding together at every fifth story. As Schuyler pointed out, these belt courses counteract any illusion of flimsiness or distortions of perspective that might otherwise have occurred. The building's facades are everywhere fully finished and ornamented, even the court walls. The motivation was visibility: only low structures stood between the Woolworth and the Hudson River, and for years the building was exposed from the back and sides as well as the front.

Proportion as well as program governed the size and placement of the ornament. On the Broadway front, a grand Tudor-arched portal is distinguished by abstract Gothic ornament, heraldic imagery, and allegorical figures in spandrels and niches (Fig. 11.22). Elsewhere, ornament in the form of tracery decorates panels beneath windows and ogee arches over them. It enhances the belt courses and the arched canopies over windows at the twenty-seventh floor and edging the two setbacks of the tower. In a final, glorious outburst at the top, ornament enriches the four tourelles that frame the high roof, and also the dormers, and it transforms the entire surface from the observation deck to the top of the spire into a "fairy filigree" (Fig. 11.23).[68]

Although more sumptuously decorated than its predecessors, the lobby-arcade of the Woolworth Building belongs to a series of grand public spaces in New York skyscrapers that began with the vaulted arcade of the Equitable Building as enlarged in the late 1880s. Other forerunners included the Singer Tower's elegant two-story galleried lobby, City Investing's richly appointed two-story high arcade, the huge, glass-enclosed arcade that swept through the Hudson Terminal Buildings, and the arcades and rotundas that flowed through the Metropolitan Life complex from one avenue to the other. It was the sheer size and ground coverage of these buildings, as well as the perceived advertising value of such impressive public spaces, that motivated their inclusion. The tendency has been to credit the Woolworth Building with inaugurating this feature because the earlier examples, having been destroyed or altered, have been forgotten.

The Woolworth Building's lobby was designed to serve both the Woolworth company and the Irving National Bank. Cathedral-like in its cruciform layout, it incorporates vaulted entrance and elevator halls that function as the Woolworth company's lobby and also as a shopping arcade (Figs. 11.24 and 11.25). Beyond the domed "crossing," and moving westward, the Woolworth lobby opens into a large galleried and skylighted hall with shops opening off of it at either side and, at the center, a grand marble staircase that

11.22
*Entrance portal,
Woolworth Building.
After* Cathedral of
Commerce *(1916).*

11.23
Top of the Woolworth Building tower.
After Cathedral of Commerce *(1916).*

led directly to the Irving Bank offices on the mezzanine level. The walls throughout are sheathed in fine veined marble from the Greek island of Skyros, and the Woolworth lobby ceiling is inlaid with glittering colored-glass tesserae, patterned in the manner of Early Christian and Byzantine mosaics. Traceried marble and bronze trimming, including bronze mailboxes and elevator surrounds and doors, echo the Gothic style of the exterior.

No expense was spared in carrying out a program of abstract and figural ornament that would exalt commerce and finance. At either end of the elevator hall, mezzanine galleries feature allegorical murals that depict Commerce (to the south) and Labor (to the north). The decorative skylight over the great hall displays the dates 1879, when Woolworth founded his company, and 1913, when the building was completed, as well as the names of the world's great commercial nations. The initial *W* occurs at strategic points, and twelve individuals involved in one way or another with the construction of the building appear as grotesques supporting the arcade galleries: these include Woolworth holding a nickel; Lewis Pierson, president of Irving Bank, with a safe deposit box; Gilbert looking

11.24

*First-floor plan,
Woolworth Building.
After American
Architect and
Building News (1913).*

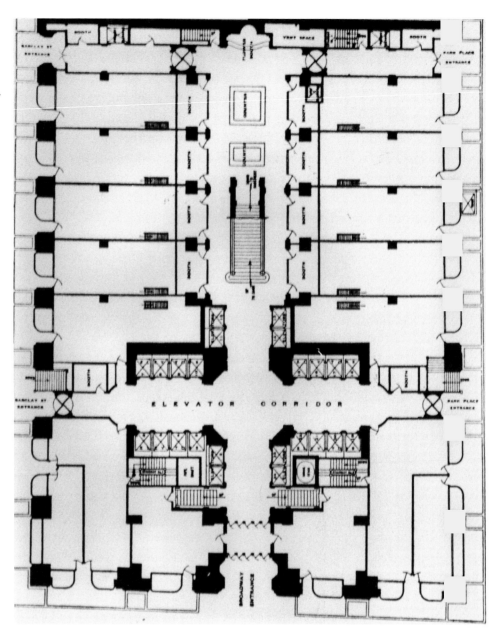

at a model of the building; Aus inspecting a structural beam; Louis J. Horowitz on the
telephone; and Edward J. Hogan, who became the building's rental agent, making a
deal.[69]

F. W. Woolworth not only wanted the highest skyscraper, he wanted it to have the most
original and most phenomenal exterior illumination possible. To get the best and most
expensive, he and Gilbert consulted no fewer than forty illuminating engineers. The
result was made public at precisely 7:30 on the evening of 24 April 1913, when President
Woodrow Wilson pressed a button in the White House, causing the new building to be
flooded with light inside and out and activating alternating flashing red and white lights
at the top.[70] This sensational opening ceremony celebrated a masterpiece whose aus-
picious siting, graceful form, linear design treatment, light coloration, and, above all, lofty
height ensured its domination of the surrounding area—just as Mr. Woolworth had intended. Now, as then, the building towers over the park, dwarfing the first skyscraper

district on the other side and overtopping the Park Row Building and the Municipal Building as well.

The mounted tower and masterful structural technology of Cass Gilbert's romantic, Gothic-styled Woolworth Building brought the first skyscraper era to what was at once a soaring climax, a grand conclusion, and the onset of a new era. The Woolworth would hold the record as the world's tallest office building until 1930. It is tempting to surmise, as many have, that it was conceived as a setback skyscraper in anticipation of the 1916 zoning law. But Gilbert specifically denied that connection, stating that "the tower was simply a response to Mr. Woolworth's desire for a high structure of commanding proportions."[71] Its great height, the form of its tower, and its corporate status value and stirring presence would make the Woolworth Building a prototype for future skyscrapers. It has remained the headquarters and the property of its original corporate owner; in that respect it and the Metropolitan Life Tower are anomalies.

Finale: The New Equitable Building and the
Report of the Heights of Building Commission

Signal events in the year 1913 marked the end of the city's first great skyscraper era. In addition to the completion and occupancy of the Woolworth Building, these included the sinking of the concrete cofferdam-walled, pneumatic-caisson foundations for the new Equitable Life Assurance Society Building (1913–15) and, at the close of the year, publication of the *Report of the Heights of Buildings Commission*, which contained recommendations that would form the basis of the zoning law passed two and a half years later.

Other than extraordinary bulk, the new Equitable Building offered little that was original in the way of architectural design (Fig. 11.26). The designer, Peirce Anderson of the firm of Graham, Burnham & Company, adopted the H-plan that had been used by his firm's predecessor, the D. H. Burnham & Company, for the twenty-eight-story Eighty Maiden Lane Building (1911–12).[72] In Anderson's version of the H-plan, the crossbar of the H rises the full height of the building, leaving open courts at either end above the seventh floor. The Hudson Terminal and Emigrant Industrial Savings Bank buildings had initiated a more open version of the plan in which only the base of the building formed the crossbar. The tripartite design of the new Equitable's granite-, brick-, and terra-cotta-clad exterior, as well as its Beaux-Arts style, repeated a formula that had long been standard and could be readily appreciated in the new building's seventeen-year-old neighbor across Pine Street, the American Surety Building. Not even the grand arcade inside that stretched from street to street was new to the city; it reinstated, albeit at a grander scale, that of Post's enlarged Equitable Building.

Plans to replace the old building had been under consideration since at least 1907, when it was announced at the end of the year that D. H. Burnham & Company had submitted preliminary sketches for a thirty-three-story office building. When the same firm filed plans in June of 1908 for what was described as the highest building yet—to be taller than the Singer and Metropolitan Life towers and exceeded only by the Eiffel Tower—it was suggested that the builder might be afraid of "restrictive legislation" and had therefore moved more quickly than expected. The height of the main block was to be thirty-four stories, with a twenty-eight-story tower rising above that to a record height of 909 feet above the sidewalk. The building was expected to contain "more floor space than any other building in the world."[73] Opposition may well have caused this plan to be dropped, but there were also practical impediments. Two years later, in 1910, it was reported that the plans had been altered and that the Equitable Company now expected to construct a building with only thirty-two stories on the site of its old building as soon as it was able to dispose of its stock in the Mercantile Trust and Mercantile Safe Deposit companies. The fire that destroyed the old Equitable building on 9 January 1912 cleared the way for a new one, for which Equitable would remain the major tenant but not the owner; the new site owner and builder was Thomas Coleman du Pont of the famous American industrial family, a member of the syndicate that developed the Hotel McAlpin.[74]

Momentum had long been gathering, but the threat of a 909-foot-high Equitable Building undoubtedly contributed to the mounting pressure for height restriction. So did foreknowledge of the densely built Equitable Building that was ultimately constructed; covering the entire site from street to street, it would rise thirty-eight-stories and also

11.26
*Equitable Building
(1913–15),
Graham, Burnham &
Company, architects.
Rendering, c. 1912.
Collection of The
New-York Historical
Society.*

include a two-story penthouse for the housing of systems equipment. The real estate industry anticipated a negative impact on surrounding properties many months before construction actually began. George T. Mortimer, who was vice president of the U.S. Realty Company, which owned the Trinity and U.S. Realty buildings across the street—and who served on the Heights of Buildings Commission and would later sit on the zoning law commission—led a group of owners and occupants of surrounding buildings in an attempt to persuade the owner to make a park on the site. Clearly, the building was perceived as a menace: "Here is an instance in which the owners of a particular piece of property are allowed by law to erect a building which bulks so large and so tall compared with adjacent buildings that it will cause several irremediable losses to many neighboring property owners.... It covers a whole block, shuts off the light on four streets and brings into existence an amount of rentable space that is disproportionate to the area of vacancies which would accumulate in any one or in any five years."[75] The *Report of the Heights of Buildings Commission* includes a diagram of the new building as compared to a design calling for three setbacks in accord with the proposed code and which would have greatly reduced the bulk. Under the terms of the 1916 zoning law, the height of the new Equitable, if built straight up from the lot lines, could be two and a half times the width of Broadway; for each foot that it set back from the street line, however, 5 feet could be added to the overall height, or to the setback portion. As expected, the completed building—with no setbacks—excited plenty of criticism, including the oft-quoted observation that it cast a noonday shadow four blocks long and six times its own size.

At least the new Equitable Building conformed to the highest standards of fireproofing. The fire that had devastated the old building and put the whole financial district at risk in 1912 was the subject of a thorough investigation and a report by the New York Board of Fire Underwriters. Six people had lost their lives, and more might have been killed had the fire not started early in the morning before workers were due to arrive. The report called attention to the deficiencies of the old building's fire protection system that had hindered the fire department's efforts to fight the fire in the upper stories—specifically the lack of "adequate standpipe equipment in conjunction with smoke-proof stair towers"—and recommended that the height of buildings "be limited in proportion to the effectiveness of their fire protection if life and property are to be conserved."[76] Automatic sprinklers, fire doors at every floor, interior fire walls, adequate stairways and exits, and protection against the spread of fire from adjacent buildings were recommended for buildings over 50 feet or four stories high. This was more conservative than the building code, which required only buildings taller than 75 feet to be fireproof. The new building was provided with all of the report's recommended features, as well as an effective alarm system. In conformance with code requirements, its steel framing members and its floors were protected by fire-resistant materials such as terra-cotta and concrete; elevator shafts were brick, and elevator cars were metal with steel and asbestos fire doors.

The Equitable was the last of the city's unregulated gargantuan office buildings.[77] As revealed by the heights of buildings commission in its report, the besetting problem was not the number of skyscrapers per se, but their concentration within a small area of lower Manhattan below Chambers Street and between Pearl and Whitehall streets on the east and State, Greenwich, and West Broadway on the west (Fig. 11.27). At the end of 1912, 1,048 of Manhattan's 92,749 buildings were over ten stories high. Fifty-one were over twenty stories, nine were over thirty, and one, the Woolworth, exceeded fifty. Other tall buildings were under way or in the planning stage, including Francis H. Kimball's thirty-two-story Adams Express Company Building at 61 Broadway (1912–14) and his projected but never constructed 901-foot-high Pan American States Association Building.[78]

Numerous loft buildings twelve to twenty stories high were populating the rapidly developing wholesale and dry goods center in the vicinity of Fourth Avenue from 20th to 34th streets and also the retail and manufacturing center between 23rd and 36th streets and Fifth and Seventh avenues. Office and apartment buildings and hotels were gravitating toward Madison, Fourth, and Lexington avenues, especially around the new Grand Central Station precinct. Pennsylvania Station, too, was attracting development: McKim, Mead & White's new central Post Office Building was completed in 1913 just to the west, on Eighth Avenue at 33rd Street. Attracted by the northward movement of the population—which in Manhattan numbered nearly 2.5 million people by 1913—and facilitated by the IRT subway, high-rise automobile business buildings were concentrated around 59th Street and Broadway. Carrère & Hastings' handsome twenty-story United States Rubber Company Building had been completed at the southeast corner of Broadway and 58th Street (1911–12). The theatre district, which had gradually moved north during the nineteenth century, was busily entrenching itself in the Times Square area, with Broadway as its spine.

Lower Manhattan was fully developed—overdeveloped, many believed—although as of late 1912 nearly half the buildings lining Wall Street were five stories or lower. Transportation and mail facilities had centered in midtown. Clearly, midtown offered the opportunity for the tallest skyscrapers yet, and for the application of Skyscraper Gothic, as witnessed by the narrow, thirty-story World's Tower Building at 110 West 40th Street between Sixth Avenue and Broadway (1912–13). This terra-cotta-clad Woolworth clone, designed by Buchman & Fox for developer Edward West Browning, still presents four fully developed sides to view, due in part to the limiting provisions of the zoning law and in part to the fact that the properties at either side—a six-story loft building to the east and an open lot to the west—are under the same ownership as the World's Tower. It was publicized as being the "tallest office building ever built in the world" on a lot of its size—50 by 100 feet.[79] Clearly, midtown was the new frontier, but its tallest and finest skyscrapers were still years away.

World War I began in 1914, engaging the nation's resources if not its immediate participation. And at long last in 1916, after many public hearings and much haggling over district boundaries, the city passed a zoning law mandating height limitations by district and requiring setbacks that would transform the New York skyscraper. In the end it was not architects or planners or even those concerned with health and safety who got the law passed. It was the real estate men, the corporate owners, the syndicators, and the investors—the very financial interests that had created the skyscraper in the first place, those whose primary concern was to protect property values.

The saga of the New York skyscraper and the controversy surrounding it would continue, but its first great age was over. Although ambitious proposals for high buildings were advanced after the war, not until the mid-1920s would economic circumstances permit the construction of skyscrapers comparable in size and quality to the Woolworth

11.27

Bird's-eye view of lower Manhattan, c. 1911. Collection of The New-York Historical Society.

Building. The era that had witnessed the dramatic rise from the five-story commercial building to the fifty-five-story skyscraper had produced both admirable and questionable results. It had created monuments, memories—of those early tall buildings that had already yielded to taller ones, and of many more that would later disappear—and problems, some of which may never be fully resolved. These were the years when the skyscraper was born and grew to maturity, when architecture was put securely in the service of engineering and the profit motive, and when the identity of New York City became inextricably associated with its skyline.

COPR. DETROIT PUBLISH

Culminating Works, Envoys of the Future 397

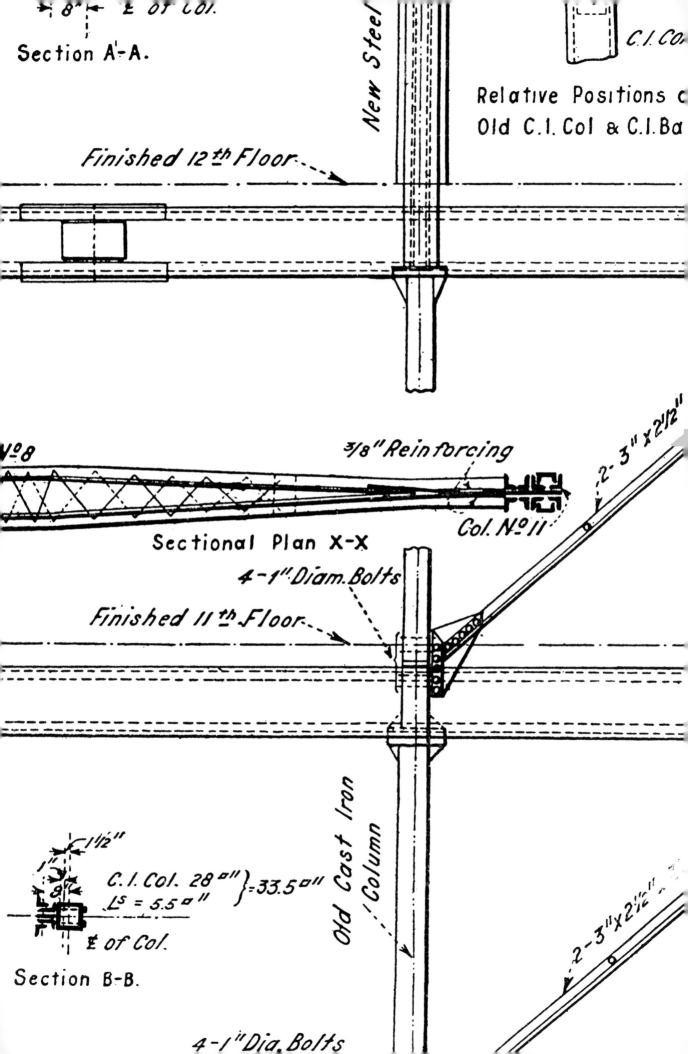

Section A-A.

Finished 12ᵗʰ Floor.

New Steel

C.I. Col

Relative Positions of
Old C.I. Col & C.I. Ba

Nº 8

³/8" Reinforcing

2-3" x 2½"

Sectional Plan X-X

Col. Nº 11

4-1" Diam. Bolts

Finished 11ᵗʰ Floor.

Old Cast Iron Column

1½"
1"
8"

C.I. Col. 28 ◻" }= 33.5 ◻"
Lˢ = 5.5 ◻"

℄ of Col.

Section B-B.

2-3" x 2½"

4-1" Dia. Bolts

NOTES

The following abbreviations are used in the notes:

American Architect   American Architect and Building News
Record and Guide   Real Estate Record and Builders Guide
JSAH   Journal of the Society of Architectural Historians
NBD   New-building dockets (building permit abstracts) in the New York City
      Building Records Collection, Municipal Archives, New York City

Preface

1. "Our 'Sky-Scrapers,'" *Record and Guide* 53 (23 June 1894), 1008.

2. "Building Skyward" (To the Editor), *Record and Guide* 31 (20 January 1883), 28; and "Sky Building in New York," *Building News* 45 (7 September 1883), 363–64. On usage of the word *skyline* in the 1870s and 1880s, see Thomas A. P. van Leeuwen, *The Skyward Trend of Thought: The Metaphysics of the American Skyscraper* (Cambridge: MIT Press, 1988), 85.

3. The second edition of the *OED* also records citations in 1888 (the "sky-scrapers of Chicago") and 1891 ("How the sky-scrapers are built"); and *Morris' Dictionary of Chicago* (1891), as cited in Daniel Bluestone, *Constructing Chicago* (New Haven: Yale Univ. Press, 1992), 112, refers to Chicago as "a city of 'sky-scrapers.'" See also a letter to the editor published in the 12 December 1891 issue of the *American Architect and Building News*, in which the civil engineer F. H. Kindl refers to buildings "now termed 'sky-scrapers.'"

4. As reported by the (anonymous) builder in "Tall Buildings in Former Years," *New York Tribune*, 18 July 1886.

5. At heights of 100 and 130 feet and constructed with iron floor beams and iron columns, just as New York City's large buildings were, these were completed in 1875 and 1877. They were served by a hydraulic elevator. Following efforts said to have been sparked by Queen Victoria's annoyance over the height of this complex, a law was enacted in 1894 restricting London building height to 80 feet; it would remain in force for the next sixty years. The flats were demolished in 1972: Nicolas Taylor, "Unheavenly Mansions," *Architectural Review* 139 (April 1966), 310–12.

6. "The Most Notable Work of the Era: Chicago's Largest Office Building," *Record and Guide* 84 (24 July 1909), 164.

7. Montgomery Schuyler, "The Sky-line of New York, 1881–1897," *Harper's Weekly* 41 (30 March 1897), 295.

8. On the historiography of the skyscraper, see Rosemarie Haag Bletter, "The Invention of the Skyscraper: Notes on Its Diverse Histories," *Assemblage* 2 (February 1987), 110–17.

9. Thomas Bender and William R. Taylor, "Culture and Architecture: Some Aesthetic Tensions in the Shaping of Modern New York City," in *Visions of the Modern City*, ed. William Sharpe and Leonard Wallock (1983; rpt., Baltimore: Johns Hopkins Univ. Press, 1987), 189–219.

10. "Rents in Downtown Office Buildings," *Record and Guide* 88 (29 July 1911), 117.

1. The Urban Context and the Office Building, 1850–70

1. The city was limited to Manhattan Island until 1874, when the western section of the Bronx was annexed. In 1895 the rest of the Bronx was added, and in 1898, with the enlargement of the municipality and the adoption of a new charter, Manhattan became one of the five boroughs of New York City.

2. Much of the statistical data provided in this chapter is from United States Department of Commerce, Bureau of the Census, *Historical Statistics of the United States* (Washington, D.C.: Government Printing Office, 1975), and from *A History of Real Estate, Building and Architecture in New York City during the Last Quarter of a Century* (1898; rpt. ed., New York: Arno, 1967), chapter 1.

3. *Miller's New York As It Is* (1866; rpt. ed., New York: Schocken, 1975, as *The 1866 Guide to New York City*), 24.

4. The elevated rail chronology is as follows:

(1) Greenwich Street, Battery to Cortlandt Street (Charles T. Harvey's experimental system), opened 10 May 1868 and completed to 83rd Street and Ninth Avenue 9 June 1879; (2) Sixth Avenue, opened 5 June 1878; (3) Third Avenue, 26 August 1878; (4) Second Avenue, 1 March 1880; (5) Second Avenue extension to the Bronx, 17 May 1886 to 18 July 1891.

5. *New York Illustrated* (New York: D. Appleton, 1869), 20, 34.

6. According to Carin Drechsler-Marx and Richard F. Shepard, *Broadway from the Battery to the Bronx* (New York: Harry N. Abrams, 1988), 8, the current length of Broadway in Manhattan is closer to seventeen miles.

7. "Editor's Easy Chair," *Harper's New Monthly Magazine* 2 (February 1862), 409.

8. "Office Building," in Russell Sturgis, *A Dictionary of Architecture and Building*, 3 (1902; rpt. ed., Detroit: Gale Research, 1966), 11.

9. The *Oxford English Dictionary*'s earliest citation for *counting-house* is dated c. 1440.

10. John D. Stewart, ed., *The Schermerhorn Row Block: A Study in Nineteenth-century Building Technology in New York City* (Waterford, N.Y.: New York State Office of Parks, Recreation and Historic Preservation, 1981), esp. 1–43.

11. Lois Severini, *The Architecture of Finance: Early Wall Street* (Ann Arbor: UMI Research Press, 1983), 20 and passim. Information also provided by Mosette Broderick.

12. Jane B. Davies, Introduction: "Alexander J. Davis, Creative Architect," in *Alexander Jackson Davis, American Architect, 1803–1892*, ed. Amelia Peck (New York: Metropolitan Museum of Art/Rizzoli, 1992), 10.

13. Wight, "A Millionnaire's [*sic*] Architectural Investment," *American Architect* 1 (6 May 1876), 148.

14. H. R. Hitchcock, "Victorian Monuments of Commerce," *Architectural Review* 105 (February 1949), 62.

15. Peter B. Wight, trans., " 'The History of Art and Aesthetics, From the Earliest Times to the Fall of the Roman Empire,' lectures given by E.-E. Viollet-le-Duc at the Ecole des Beaux-Arts in 1864," *Manufacturer and Builder* 2 (November and December 1870), 323–26, 355–57; and (January 1871), 11–13. E.-E. Viollet-le-Duc, *Discourses on Architecture*, trans. H. Van Brunt (Boston, 1875–81).

16. Hitchcock, "Victorian Monuments of Commerce," 62.

17. Summerson, *The Victorian Rebuilding of the City of London* (pamphlet: Russell Van Nest Black Memorial Lecture, Cornell University, 3 May 1974), 7.

18. Nikolaus Pevsner, *A History of Building Types* (Princeton: Princeton Univ. Press, 1976), 173.

19. "Holt's Castle," *Commercial Advertiser*, 4 January 1833. Hotel also described in Theodore S. Fay, *Views in New-York and its Environs . . .* (New York: Peabody, 1831 ff.), 41; and see Vaughn L. Glasgow, "The Hotels of New York City Prior to the American Civil War" (M.A. thesis, Pennsylvania State Univ., 1970), 65–68. The original ground dimensions of Holt's were 100 (Fulton Street) by 76.5 (Pearl Street) by 85.6 feet (Water Street).

20. *Miller's New York As It Is*, 13 (Mercantile and Business Directory), lists thirty-one first-class hotels in 1866.

21. "Hotel Life," *New York Daily Graphic*, 16 January 1874.

22. S. B. Landau, "Richard Morris Hunt: Architectural Innovator and Father of a 'Distinctive' American School," in *The Architecture of Richard Morris Hunt*, ed. S. R. Stein (Chicago: Univ. of Chicago Press, 1986), 61–66.

23. The maximum land value per square foot in the Broadway, Pine Street, Wall Street, Nassau Street, and Park Row area rose from $61.38 in 1873 to $223.39 in 1895, a 264 percent increase. See *A History of Real Estate*, 123–25.

Between 1850 and 1860 the total assessed property valuation in New York more than doubled, from $286 million to $577 million. In 1875 the figure was $1.1 billion, a further increase of 91 percent. Nationwide between 1870 and 1890, population increased by 62 percent, taxable wealth by 116 percent, and railroad mileage by 209 percent. During these years America became a wealthy nation and New York its wealthiest city.

24. Cf. the periods of development distinguished by Michael A. Mikkelson in his discussion of the city's real estate history from the first large speculative building craze in 1868 to 1898: *A History of Real Estate*, 54–58 ff.

2. Technological Preparations

1. Modern cast iron has a tensile strength of 18,000 to 25,000 pounds per square inch (psi) and a compressive strength of 60,000 to 200,000 psi. The chemical and physical proper-

ties of gray cast iron, which is the softest and toughest of cast irons, are 90.8 to 96.7 percent iron, 1.7 to 4.0 carbon, 0.5 to 3.0 silicon, 0.5 to 1.0 manganese, 0.5 to 1.0 phosphorus, and 0.1 to 0.2 sulphur.

2. Typical chemical and physical properties of wrought iron: iron, 97.19 percent; slag (iron silicate), 2.50; phosphorus, 0.12; silicon, 0.12; manganese, 0.03; carbon, 0.02; and sulphur, 0.02.

3. Purdy, "The Use of Steel in Large Buildings," *Journal of the Association of Engineering Societies* 14 (March 1895), 182–83. No longer extant, Sedgwick Hall was probably the building described as the "former county courthouse" by George B. Post, as quoted in "Steel-Frame Building Construction," *Engineering Record* 32 (15 June 1895), 44. Post had done some reconstructive work on the building in 1888: Office Records, George B. Post Collection, The New-York Historical Society.

4. William H. Pierson, conversation with Landau, April 1989. Pierson also stated that Renwick had wanted to use this construction in all the floors, but that the commissioners refused to do so. See Pierson's forthcoming volume in the series *American Buildings and Their Architects*.

5. For details, and also for the New York chronology of iron construction, see Chapter 3. Frequently the Trenton Iron Company is referred to as the Cooper & Hewitt Iron Works, but technically Cooper & Hewitt, though a major stockholder in the Trenton Iron Company, was a separate company created to manage it.

6. See *Plans of Public Buildings in Course of Construction under the direction of the Secretary of the Treasury including the specifications thereof* (1855). The plans reveal brick jack-arched floors with the connections clearly shown. Tipped in the front of the copy owned by Avery Library, Columbia University, is a letter of 25 October 1856 from the secretary of the Treasury to Charles King, S.S.D., president of Columbia College, stating that the "introduction of wrought iron beams and girders in these Edifices instead of the groined arches as formerly used, is, I believe, wholly new." This is the same letter as that sent out by the engineer in charge of construction, Captain A. H. Bowman, under the secretary's name, with other copies on 13 December 1856: see Lawrence Wodehouse, "Ammi Burnham Young, 1798–1874," *JSAH* 25 (December 1966), 277.

7. The repetition of these experiments through the nineteenth century led to the establishment of the formula $P\alpha SV^2$, where P equals pressure in pounds, S equals area of plate in square feet, and V equals velocity in miles per hour.

8. See Francis H. Steiner, *French Iron Architecture* (Ann Arbor: UMI Research Press, 1984), 113–14.

9. The first deepwater cofferdam in the United States was that of the Permanent Bridge (1798–1806), Philadelphia, designed by Timothy Palmer.

10. Reproduced in John C. Doty, "Foundations for Skyscrapers in New York City," Municipal Engineers of the City of New York, *Proceedings for 1906* (New York: Municipal Engineers of the City of New York, 1907), 140; but see also Charles P. Berkey and John R. Healy, "The Geology of New York City and Its Relation to Engineering Problems," no. 62 (21 February 1911), in Municipal Engineers of the City of New York, *Proceedings for 1911* (New York: Municipal Engineers of the City of New York, 1912), 5–34; and Works Progress Administration, *Rock Data Map of Manhattan*, I (Battery Park to 23rd Street; 1937).

11. John Kieran, *A Natural History of New York City* (Boston: Houghton Mifflin, 1959), 23.

12. Christopher J. Schuberth, *The Geology of New York City and Environs* (Garden City: Natural History, 1968), 82.

13. The Collect was a pond of fresh water bounded, at its extremes, by Lafayette and Baxter streets on the east and west and by Duane (Foley Square) and White streets on the north and south.

14. All of these, as well as many of the English and American patents discussed here, are illustrated in Peter B. Wight's "Origin and History of Hollow Tile Fire-proof Floor Construction," *Brickbuilder* (1897; see chapter bibliography). Most of the information on the use of this construction in American buildings comes from this important source.

15. S. B. Landau, *P. B. Wight: Architect, Contractor, and Critic, 1838–1925* (Chicago: Art Institute of Chicago, 1981), 46.

16. N. H. Hutton, "Fire-Proof Construction," *American Architect* 1 (5 February 1876), 43–44 (publication of his 1873 paper); Robert G. Hatfield, "Anti-Fire Construction," *Scientific American* 38 (19 January 1878), 41–42 (publication of his 1877 paper).

17. The ultimate tensile strength was reckoned as follows:

	Cold	572°F	932°F
Charcoal iron	55,366 psi	63,080 psi	65,343 psi
Medium steel	64,000 psi	69,266 psi	68,600 psi

In other experiments silica firebrick withstood a temperature of four thousand degrees Fahrenheit before damage occurred, but later tests contradicted that result: see C. R. Roelker, "Experiments on the Strength of Wrought Iron and Steel at High Temperatures," *Journal of the Franklin Institute* 92 (October 1881), 241–54.

18. Others involved in key inventions include J. J. Walworth of Boston, J. O. Morse of New York, and Thomas T. Tasker of Philadelphia, who introduced variations on the system of closed and sealed circulation to use steam below atmospheric pressure. Niles Greenwood of Cincinnati invented coils or nests of tubes as radiators, which were connected to the boiler by return and supply lines. James Jay of Mapes, New York, introduced a reliable steam trap. Unfortunately, there is no comprehensive history of heating, and dates and other exact data are elusive. An instructive and relatively recent article on the subject is Robert Bruegmann, "Central Heating and Forced Ventilation: Origins and Effects on Architectural Design," *JSAH* 37 (October 1978), 143–60; see also chapter bibliography.

19. "Steam-heating Apparatus in the Manhattan Co.'s and Merchants' Bank Building," *Sanitary Engineer* 11 (12 February 1885), 230–31; (19 February 1885), 250–51.

20. See, for example, R. F. Hartford, "The Quantity of Air Required in the Ventilation of Buildings," *Engineering News and American Contract Journal* 14 (26 December 1885), 411; and "The Efficiency of Ventilating Fans and Blowers," *Engineering News and American Contract Journal* 16 (11 December 1886), 389.

21. See Jeffrey A. Kroessler, "Water for the City," in *The Old Croton Aqueduct: Rural Resources Meet Urban Needs* (Yonkers: Hudson River Museum of Westchester, 1992), 9–16.

22. "The Vertical Railway," *Harper's New Monthly Magazine* 65 (November 1882), 889. The same source credits Tufts with the invention of "the first passenger elevator in the world driven by steam-power": his so-called "Vertical Screw Railway," patented in 1859 and first used in the Fifth Avenue Hotel that same year (p. 890).

23. A 1908 source credits Cooper Union with having the first passenger elevator in the city, but no other evidence has been found to support this claim: John F. O'Rourke, quoted in "The Man of the Hour," *New York Architect* 2 (May 1908), unpaged.

24. "Scientific Notes. Steam Versus Stairs: the Movable Room in the Fifth-Avenue Hotel . . .," *New York Times*, 23 January 1860. See also *Miller's New York As It Is* (1866; rpt. ed., New York: Schocken, 1975, as *The 1866 Guide to New York City*), 70.

25. See Robert M. Vogel, *Elevator Systems of the Eiffel Tower, 1889*, United States National Museum Bulletin 228 (Washington: Smithsonian Institution, 1961); and for a general history of the elevator to 1893, Thomas E. Brown, "The American Passenger Elevator," *Engineering Magazine* 5 (June 1893), 333–48.

26. See, for example, "Gas Fitting in an Office Building," *Sanitary Engineer* 7 (12 April 1883), 435.

27. See Melvin Kranzberg and Carroll W. Pursell, Jr., eds., *Technology in Western Civilization*, 2 (New York: Oxford Univ. Press, 1967), 571; "The Edison System of Wiring Buildings for the Incandescent Electric Light," *Sanitary Engineer* 7 (14 December 1882), 27–28, and (21 December 1882), 50–52; and Henry Schroeder, *History of Electric Light* (Smithsonian Institution, Washington, D.C., 15 August 1923).

28. "A Historical Review of Progress in the Building Craft," chapter 4 of *A History of Real Estate, Building, and Architecture in New York City, 1868–1894*, supplement to the *Record and Guide* 53 (12 May 1894), 98.

3. Toward the Skyscraper

1. Weisman, "A New View of Skyscraper History," in *The Rise of an American Architecture*, ed. Edgar Kaufmann, jr. (New York: Praeger, 1970), 119–120 ff.

2. *The Rejected Addresses . . . on the Opening of the New Park Theatre in the City of New York* (New York: N. Smith, 1821): fold-out woodcut of theatre interior by Lansing, The New-York Historical Society, and reproduced in Nathan Silver, *Lost New York* (Boston: Houghton Mifflin, 1967), 74. On the theatre see also Theodore S. Fay, *Views in New York and Its Environs . . .* (New York: Peabody, 1831 ff.), 33–34; William Dunlap, *History of the American Theatre*, 2 (1832; rpt. ed., New York: Burt Franklin, 1963), 245; and Richard J. Koke, compiler, *American Landscape and Genre Paintings in the New-York His-*

torical Society: A Catalog of the Collection (Boston: G. K. Hall, 1982), 133.

3. According to Margot Gayle, in Daniel D. Badger, *Badger's Illustrated Catalogue of Cast-Iron Architecture* (1865; rpt. ed., New York: Dover, 1981), vii, a building with an iron storefront was advertised for sale in an 1830 New York newspaper.

It should be noted that the lower facade of Town & Davis's Lyceum of Natural History (1835–36) utilized not iron structural members, as has been assumed, but masonry piers. As pointed out by Jane B. Davies (correspondence with Landau, 1990), the building specifications in the A. J. Davis Collection, Metropolitan Museum of Art, indicate that the glass of the two ground-floor shopfronts was to be set into brass or brass frames backed by wood. Davis's inscription on one of the drawings (no. 24.66.392) states that this was "the first metal shopfront ever made in N.Y."

In 1835 Boorman & Johnston, Merchants, who did a large business in iron, received a lot of "immense iron pillars," possibly from Stockholm. Unable to sell the pillars, the proprietors finally incorporated them under the front wall of their store at 119 Greenwich Street: Emily De Forest Johnston, *John Johnston of New York, Merchant* (New York: Gillis, 1909), 115.

4. Miscellaneous Castle Garden Papers, 1844–1850 (including Pollard's interior of 1844–45 with specifications, contracts, other items), Manuscript Division, The New-York Historical Society. From 1815 to 1824 the structure had been known as Castle Clinton. In 1855 it became an immigration depot, and by that time its island site had been absorbed into the mainland by fill. It was remodeled as an aquarium by McKim, Mead & White in 1896–98, and in 1946 it was renamed Castle Clinton and designated a National Monument.

5. "Astor Library, New York," *Gleason's Pictorial Drawing Room Companion* (25 September 1852), 200.

6. Letter to Landau dated 14 April 1986. The building was extended twice by wings completed in 1859 (architect: Griffith Thomas of Thomas & Son) and 1881 (architect: Thomas Stent). Kathleen Curran discussed the Astor Library's mixed iron and timber ceiling construction in a paper presented at a symposium on "American Architecture and the German Connection" at Columbia University on 7–8 April 1989. See also K. Curran, "The German Rundbogenstil and Reflections on the Ameri-can Round-Arched Style," *JSAH* 47 (December 1988), esp. 369–70; and Giorgio Cavaglieri, "The Past is Present: The Adaptive Reuse of Nineteenth-Century Buildings," *Around the Square 1830–1890: Essays on Life, Letters, and Architecture in Greenwich Village*, ed. Mindy Cantor (New York: New York Univ. Press, 1982), 122–33.

7. The interior was destroyed by fire on 21 May 1866: "Academy of Music Destroyed by Fire," *New York Herald*, 23 May 1866. The exterior walls were preserved in the subsequent rebuilding of 1867–68 by the architect Thomas R. Jackson. Saeltzer says that the height of his auditorium was seventy-eight feet "from the middle of the parquet floor to the ceiling" and that he was required to seat 5,500 people; so the exact number is a question: Alexander Saeltzer, *A Treatise on Acoustics in Connection with Ventilation* (New York: D. Van Nostrand, 1872), 70. See also "New York Academy of Music," *New-York Daily Tribune*, 2 October 1854; and "Academy of Music," *Ballou's Pictorial Drawing Room Companion* 10 (29 March 1856), 200.

Saeltzer's nearly contemporary Duncan, Sherman & Company bank building (1855–56) at Nassau and Pine Streets was extensively iron framed: "New Bank Buildings," *Bankers' Magazine* 10 (September 1855), 217–18. This journal provides detailed descriptions of new banks and their construction: see chapter bibliography.

8. See Winston Weisman, "Commercial Palaces of New York, 1845–1875," *Art Bulletin* 36 (December 1954), 285.

9. "Easy Chair Chats," *Harper's New Monthly Magazine* 9 (July 1854), 261. This was written after the building had been enlarged. Originally it was about 90 feet wide (Broadway) by 101 feet deep (Reade Street), and the dome circumference was 70 feet. The building was enlarged in 1850–51 (Trench & Snook), in 1852–53 (Snook and others), in 1872, and after 1884 (Edward D. Harris). It was occupied by the *New York Sun* from 1919 to 1950. See Mary Ann Clegg Smith, "John Snook and the Design for A. T. Stewart's Store," *The New-York Historical Society Quarterly*, 58 (January 1974), 18–33; and James T. Dillon, "A. T. Stewart Dry Goods Store/Sun Building," New York City Landmarks Preservation Commission designation report, 7 October 1986.

10. *New York Evening Post*, 14 October 1848. Using the same source, Weisman somehow de-

duced that iron was not used structurally in the Moffat. The mason was Edward Black; the stonecutter, Abraham McBride; the plumber, Joseph Craig; and the ironwork was supplied by Althouse & Co.

11. Building ground dimensions: 37.5 by 140 feet; floors each 14 feet high. Estimated cost: $40,000. See "New Buildings," *New York Evening Post*, 22 September 1849. New York Life Insurance Co. was the major tenant in 1864. A mansard roof addition was made c. 1869.

12. According to city directories, Dr. Brandreth moved away from 241 Broadway in 1852. Weisman discusses and illustrates the project drawing in "A New View of Skyscraper History," 129.

13. Edward Roche to Messrs. Upjohn & Co., 1 September 1852, Box 6, Upjohn Papers, New York Public Library, emphasis in original. The owners were Bulkley & Claflin and Fearing & Russell. The terra-cotta cornice and sculpted ornament were supplied by the Hudson River Pottery and Terra Cotta Works, 34 Fulton Street. In 1872–73 the building was altered by George B. Post.

14. Ground dimensions: 106 feet (Cortlandt Street) by 56 feet (Broadway). The building and its details are illustrated in *Badger's Illustrated Catalogue*, plate IX.

15. Esmond Shaw, *Peter Cooper and the Wrought Iron Beam* (New York: Cooper Union, 1960), pamphlet; John Cooper, "Structural Iron and Steel in New York, *Record and Guide* 81 (4 April 1908), 596; and see also Jacob Abbott, *The Harper Establishment; or How the Story Books are Made* (New York: Harper, 1855), esp. chapters 1–3.

16. David M. Kahn, "Bogardus, Fire, and the Iron Tower," *JSAH* 35 (October 1976), 186–203.

17. Ellen W. Kramer, "Contemporary Descriptions of New York City and Its Public Architecture, ca. 1850," *JSAH* 27 (December 1968), 273. We look forward to the publication of Margot Gayle's monograph study of Bogardus, now in preparation.

18. According to Cooper, "Structural Iron and Steel in New York," 596, the rolled-iron I-beams intended for the Cooper Union Building "were diverted by request of the United States Government and used in that year [1854] in the U.S. Assay Office Building in Wall Street."

19. Jackson, who had come to the city from England in 1831 and had trained in Richard Upjohn's office, in 1867 designed the new Academy of Music (which replaced Saeltzer's) and also Wallack's Theatre and Tammany Hall. He won the Times Building commission in a competition.

20. "The Times Building," *New York Times*, 26 May 1858. See also "The 'New York Times' Establishment," *Frank Leslie's Illustrated Newspaper* (12 March 1859), 225–26; "The New 'Times' Building," *Scientific American* 59 (25 August 1888), 117; and "The New Times Building," *New York Times*, 29 April 1889.

Building ground dimensions: 65 feet (Spruce Street) by 100 feet (Park Row) by 95 feet (Nassau Street). Height: 86 feet. Construction contractor: J. M. Trimble. Stonework: Masterton, Smith & Sinclair. Masonry superintendent: Dominick Ryder. Iron stairs and vault lights: G. R. Jackson & Co. Iron columns: Jackson & Throckmorton. Plate glass: Noel & Souter. The building was steam-heated.

21. The great depth of the built-up wrought-iron I-beams suggests the use of portal bracing as well as floor support, but full portal bracing was supposedly introduced at the Sheerness Boat Store in England, begun a year earlier. On the construction see Alan Burnham, "Last Look at a Structural Landmark," *Architectural Record* 120 (September 1956), 273–79.

22. Peter B. Wight, "A Millionnaire's [sic] Architectural Investment," *American Architect* 1 (6 May 1876), 148.

23. "Bank Architecture in New-York," *Bankers' Magazine* 9 (February 1855), 582–83.

24. His churches include Grace Church and St. Patrick's Cathedral in New York. Trained by his father, an eminent structural and mechanical engineer who taught at Columbia College, Renwick studied engineering at Columbia. After his graduation in 1836 he joined the engineering staff of the New York and Erie Railroad and the following year that of the Croton Aqueduct.

25. "Recent Bank Architecture in New-York," *Bankers' Magazine* 10 (February 1856), 600. Building ground dimensions: 41 by 88 feet. Height: 75 feet from street level to the top of the cornice. Ironwork: J. B. & W. W. Cornell. Demolished 1903.

26. Other extensively iron-framed banks of the time were the five-story Bank of the Commonwealth (1854) at the corner of Pine and Nassau streets, architect unknown; the Nassau Bank (1854–55) at the corner of Nassau and Beekman streets, designed by Samuel A. Warner and also five stories; and, as already mentioned, Richard Upjohn & Company's six-story

Mechanics' Bank at 35 Wall and Saeltzer's Duncan, Sherman & Company bank building.

27. The girders were built up of two one-quarter-inch web plates and two flanges—the top 1 by 6 inches, the bottom three-quarters x 8 inches—connected by bars set transversely between them and riveted to the plates by tenons hammered into holes in the plates. The webs and plates were spliced with lap joints near the center, and the few smaller girders were built up with single web plates. The floor beams were built up two web plates that curved outward at the ends to form an I-section and were covered with 4-inch-wide flange plates that were one-eighth inch thick at the top and the bottom: "Early Iron Building Construction," *Engineering News* 50 (10 September 1903), 214–15.

28. Description from *History of Architecture and the Building Trades of Greater New York* (New York: Union History, 1899), 1, 39. See also A. J. Bloor to the Editor on "Fireproof Buildings," *New York Tribune*, 7 February 1882; and Montgomery Schuyler, "A Great American Architect: Leopold Eidlitz," in *American Architecture and Other Writings by Montgomery Schuyler*, ed. William H. Jordy and Ralph Coe (Cambridge: Belknap Press of Harvard Univ. Press, 1961), 1, 161–66.

29. According to Christopher Gray, the builder was John A. May, who "net leased the building to Ball, Black & Company until 1874": Gray, "Streetscapes: 565 Broadway," *New York Times*, 18 October 1992. In 1875 Ball, Black & Company became Black, Starr & Frost.

30. Matthew Hale Smith, *Twenty Years Among the Bulls and Bears of Wall Street* (Hartford: J. Burr, 1871), 293, as quoted in S. B. Landau, *Edward T. and William A. Potter, American Victorian Architects* (New York: Garland, 1979), 240, and, on the building, 239–42, 453.

Frederick Diaper competed with Edward T. Potter for the commission. In 1885 the building was enlarged by the addition of three stories (C. W. Clinton); in 1920 it was enlarged again by a five-story addition (Delano & Aldrich). The building was demolished in 1928.

31. John Crosby Brown, *A Hundred Years of Merchant Banking* (New York: n.p., 1909), 228.

32. Alan Burnham, "Forgotten Engineering: The Rise and Fall of the Phoenix Column," *Architectural Record* 125 (April 1959), 222–25; see also bibliography for Chapter 6 under Quimby.

33. Thomas's design was selected over a High Victorian Gothic project submitted by Pe-

ter B. Wight (Wight & Sturgis) in a competition limited to four or five architects. Although Thomas was far more experienced as a commercial designer, Wight had lately achieved considerable recognition for his polychromatic National Academy of Design and other High Victorian Gothic-style buildings. But the ecclesiastical, moral, and aesthetic associations of that style, as well as its medieval derivation, had caused it to become identified with churches and with buildings housing institutional and cultural facilities, although some commercial buildings were designed in the style. Wight's design may have been rejected as much for its style as for any other reason.

34. *D. Appletons' New York Illustrated* (New York: D. Appleton, 1871), 11, as quoted in Weisman, "Commercial Palaces," 297. On the building: "Minutes. The Park Nation'l Bank of New York" (March 1865 to April 1875), Chase Manhattan Bank Archives, R.G. 3, CNB, v. 3, ms.; and John W. Kennion, *The Architects' and Builders' Guide . . .* (New York: Fitzpatrick and Hunter, 1868), 62–67.

The contracting builder was J. T. Smith; the carpentry was executed by Smith & True; the ironwork was supplied by J. B. & W. W. Cornell. The sculpture, by Robert E. Lauritz, included colossal statues representing Commerce and Navigation, Industry and Mechanical Art, and, in the center arc, Justice. Building demolished c. 1902.

35. As noted in the elevator proposal of 23 February 1871 submitted by Otis Brothers for the new Seamen's Bank for Savings Building (1870–71): Seamen's Bank for Savings Records, 1829–1989, South Street Seaport Museum.

From 1867 to 1898 the elevator company founded by Elisha Graves Otis was known as Otis Brothers & Company. In 1898 it was incorporated as the Otis Elevator Company.

36. Information under "Grand Hotel," Quinn hotel files, The New-York Historical Society. See also James T. Dillon, "Grand Hotel," New York City Landmarks Preservation Commission designation report, 11 September 1979.

37. "A Monster Hotel," *New York Times*, 26 August 1870. See also Moses King, ed., *King's Handbook of New York City*, 2d ed. (Boston: Moses King, 1893), 235–36.

38. NBD 619–1868 (Grand Hotel) and NBD 490–1869 (Broadway Central Hotel).

39. Murray Schumach, "Broadway Central Hotel Collapses," *New York Times*, 4 August 1973.

40. James T. Dillon, "Gilsey House," New York City Landmarks Preservation Commission designation report, 11 September 1979.

41. It is described in detail in "Hotel Demolition Reveals Cast & Wrought-Iron Details," *Engineering News-Record* 98 (3 February 1927), 182–84. See also "Hotel," *New York Evening Post*, 10 March 1871; and Deborah S. Gardner, "The Architecture of Commercial Capitalism: John Kellum and the Development of New York 1840–1875" (Ph.D. diss., Columbia Univ., 1979), 1, 216–50. Building ground dimensions: 196.5 feet (Park Avenue) by 205 feet. Height: 102 feet. Court: 94 by 116 feet. General contractor: Stewart & Smith.

4. The "First Skyscrapers"

1. Weisman, "A New View of Skyscraper History," *The Rise of an American Architecture*, ed. Edgar Kaufmann, jr. (New York: Praeger, 1970), 125.

2. A lively discussion of the "first skyscraper" issue as Weisman and others have dealt with it is provided in R. H. Bletter, "The Invention of the Skyscraper: Notes on Its Diverse Histories," *Assemblage* 2 (February 1987), 110–17. See also Weisman, "New York and the Problem of the First Skyscraper," *JSAH* 12 (March 1953), 13–21; Schuyler, "The 'Sky-scraper' Up to Date," *Architectural Record* 8 (January–March 1899), 231–32; and Hitchcock, *Architecture: Nineteenth and Twentieth Centuries* (Baltimore: Penguin, 1958), 239 (repeated in all subsequent eds.).

3. "A Grand Commercial Edifice," *New York Sun*, 4 November 1869; and R. Carlyle Buley, *The Equitable Life Assurance Society of the United States, 1859–1964* (New York: Appleton-Century-Crofts, 1967), 1: 101–8. These sources, as well as newspaper clippings, insurance pamphlets, and brochures in the Equitable Life Assurance Society Archives, have provided much of the descriptive information given here. The site was previously occupied by the Jan Jansen Damen farmhouse, built in 1646.

4. "The Equitable Life Insurance Building," *Record and Guide* 4 (16 October 1869), 19.

5. See John Coolidge, "Designing the Capitol: The Roles of Fuller, Gilman, Richardson and Eidlitz," in New York State Capitol Symposium, *Proceedings of the New York State Capitol Symposium* (Albany: Temporary State Commission on the Restoration of the Capitol, 1983), 22–23.

Gilman had practiced in Boston before moving to New York in 1866. With Alfred Stone he had designed the Hotel Pelham in Boston (1857), possibly the first apartment hotel built in this country, and in partnership with Gridley J. F. Bryant he designed the Boston City Hospital and Boston City Hall. Noted for his interpretation of the Second Empire mode, Gilman was working with Thomas C. Fuller on Fuller & Laver's design for the New York State Capitol at Albany at about the same time that his firm won the Equitable commission. After his return from Paris, Kendall had worked in the office of Gilman's firm, Bryant & Gilman, in Boston. His brief partnership with Gilman lasted only from 1868 until 1871. Following the success of the Equitable Building, he designed other New York commercial buildings, including the important Washington Building on lower Broadway. In collaboration with the engineer William R. Hutton, he served as a consulting architect for the Washington Bridge over the Harlem River (1886–89), the first long-span, two-hinged arch bridge in the United States.

6. Mendel Mesick Cohen Waite Architects, Development Plan: "Troy Savings Bank Music Hall," 1983.

Except for the eight months or so when he served in the Union Army during the Civil War, Post practiced from 1861 until his death in 1913. From 1861 to 1867 he was in partnership with a former fellow pupil in Hunt's studio, Charles Dexter Gambrill. His own firm, founded in 1867, eventually grew to be one of the largest of the century, and overall he was responsible for more than four hundred projects.

Post's office records in The New-York Historical Society list the names of companies and individuals who supplied materials for the building and the amounts paid to them. On the selection of architect see M. A. Brooks, "Reminiscences of the Early Days of Fireproof Building Construction in New York City," *Engineering News* 68 (28 November 1912), 987. Elsewhere, the choice of winner is said to be unanimous, but Post's name is not mentioned: "Opinion of the Press Regarding the Equitable Life Assurance Society of the United States" (pamphlet, c. 1868), 11, Equitable Archives.

7. Burnham quoted in Francisco Mujica, *History of the Skyscraper* (Paris: Archaeology and Architecture Press, 1929), 22.

8. Based on a written statement in the possession of E. Everett Post, Post's grandson, and as recorded by D. L. Havighorst, 10 January 1958, Equitable Archives. See also *Henry Baldwin Hyde: A Biographical Sketch* (New York:

Equitable Life Assurance Society of America, 1901), 119.

9. *Insurance Times Extra*, c. 1870, 2, Equitable Archives.

10. Post is said to have redesigned the ironwork after receiving a bid that he thought could be lowered, and to have succeeded in cutting the cost by half: Brooks, "Reminiscences," 986; see also New York Board of Fire Underwriters, *Report on Fire in the Equitable Building, Broadway . . . , January 9, 1912* (New York, 1912), Equitable Archives, where the framing is described and illustrated with plans, detail drawings, and photographs.

11. "Disputes of Architects: Question About the Invention of the Skeleton Construction," *New York Times*, 19 August 1899. Brooks, "Reminiscences," 987, alludes to a type of "original construction" that could be construed as some type of primitive skeleton construction.

12. Post to Henry B. Hyde, 22 March 1887, Henry B. Hyde Papers, Baker Library, Harvard Business School. See Leeds, *A Treatise on Ventilation: Comprising Seven Lectures Given Before the Franklin Institute, Philadelphia, 1866–68* (New York: John Wiley & Sons, 1876), esp. 205–6.

13. Term used in *Philadelphia Age*, 10 December 1869, Equitable Archives; *Insurance Times Extra*, and echoed in "A Grand Commercial Edifice" ("free of rent").

14. "The New Way of Getting Up Stairs," *New York Evening Post*, 10 February 1870.

15. Brooks, "Reminiscences," 987. Post may not have accepted the offer as his office remained in the building until 1879. The increasing prestige value of top-floor office space in desirable commercial areas of the city is demonstrated by the rapid rent rise for such space between 1868 and 1874: $850 per year in 1868, $1250 in 1869, and $4500 in 1874. The 1874 figure seems especially remarkable considering the depression that followed the financial panic of 1873.

16. "A Grand Commercial Edifice."

17. *Eleventh Annual Report of the Equitable Life Assurance Society*, 22, Equitable Archives. Other cities quickly followed suit; in Rochester, New York, for example, the seven-story, mansarded Powers Building (1865; 1868–1872), designed by Andrew J. Warner and built additively over several years, incorporated an Otis Brothers elevator and was 175 feet tall at its highest point by the time it was completed. That building is still standing at the corner of State and Buffalo Streets: *Powers's Commercial Fire-Proof Buildings in Rochester* (Rochester: James Matthews, 1872).

18. Building ground dimensions as of 1870: 87 by 137 feet. Height: about 142 feet. Contractors and suppliers: Masonry except granite, James B. Smith; granite work, Sheldon. Structural iron: J. B. & J. M. Cornell. Other ironwork: West Point Foundry. Ventilators and heating supervised by Lewis W. Leeds. Marble work: Larmande. Embossed glass: Joseph Cartissier. Patterns and furniture: Léon Marcotte. Utilities included pressure plumbing, steam heat, gas light (with supplemental electric arc lighting installed in corridors, 1878). Cost: $1,152,936.32. The first tenants included the German American Bank, the American Fire Insurance Company, and the Hanover Fire Insurance Company.

19. General contractor for expansion: David H. King, Jr. Architectural sculpture: Ellin & Kitson. Stained glass in great hall barrel vault: Francis Lathrop.

Post seems not to have been the first choice for this job. Hunt was offered it, but declined: Alan Burnham, ed., "The Richard Morris Hunt Papers, 1828–1895," comp. Catharine H. Hunt, 172, typescript, Avery Library, Columbia University. Edward E. Raht, Hunt's associate, was also seriously considered but instead became the architect of Equitable's foreign buildings: Buley, *The Equitable Life Assurance Society*, 1: 312, and passim. Other enlargements (Post) were made in 1890–98 and 1900–1902; and sometime between 1890 and 1897, Post proposed a campanile-like tower addition that would have been more than four hundred feet high with about twenty-five stories: see Winston Weisman, "The Commercial Architecture of George B. Post," *JSAH*, 31 (October 1972), 197–98; and Kenneth Turney Gibbs, *Business Architectural Imagery: The Impact of Economic and Social Changes on Tall Office Buildings, 1870–1930* (Ann Arbor: UMI Research Press, 1985), 112.

20. Brooks, "Reminiscences," 986.

21. "The Largest Mosaic in America," *New York Times*, 3 April 1887.

22. Quotations, in order, from *New York Daily Graphic*, 10 January 1887; *New York Record*, 13 August 1887; and *New York World*, 10 January 1887, all in Post Collection, The New-York Historical Society. Items in the Post Collection have provided a detailed account of this and other Post-designed buildings discussed in this book.

23. Shepard B. Clough, *A Century of American Life Insurance: A History of the Mutual Life Insurance Company of New York, 1843–1943* (New York: Columbia Univ. Press, 1946), 103, 141.

Kellum won the commission in a competition held in 1863; the other competitors were Leopold Eidlitz, Samuel A. Warner, Robert G. Hatfield, and Griffith Thomas. Building ground dimensions: 78 feet (82 feet rear) by 110 feet. Masons: Wm. R. Stewart & Smith. Marble contractors: East-Chester Marble Co. Iron construction components: Trenton Iron Co. and Phoenix Iron Co. Ironwork: J. B. & W. W. Cornell & Co.

24. "The Equitable's Latest Purchase," *Record and Guide*, 40 (15 October 1887), 1288.

25. Such girders were also used in the National Bank of Commerce (1855–57; architect, John W. Ritch), which stood on the northwest corner of Cedar and Nassau streets until demolished in 1896. New York Life's girder form comprised top and bottom flange plates and double vertical strips with ends reduced to tenons and inserted into mortises in plates, the ends riveted down to make the joints fast. At maximum 25 feet long, the girders were spaced 12 to 15 inches apart with web plates in 12- to 15-inch lengths: "Peculiar Old Iron Girders," *Engineering Record* 34 (27 June 1896), 69–70; and NBD 239–1868.

26. Much of the description given here comes from period sources in the New York Life Archives and also from John W. Kennion, *The Architects' and Builders' Guide . . .* (New York: Fitzpatrick and Hunter, 1868), 59; and see also chapter bibliography.

Designs for the building were submitted by Griffith Thomas, Bryant & Gilman, James Renwick, Jr., and Leopold Eidlitz. Avery Library holds a photograph of a perspective by Schulze & Schoen, and drawings by R. G. Hatfield are in The New-York Historical Society's architectural drawings collection. Dimensions: 60 feet (Broadway) by 71 feet (rear) by 96 feet (depth). Height: 90 feet. Contractor: Thomas Gardiner, Jr. Pediment sculpture: John W. Moffitt. Cost: about $1 million. Two stories added 1879–80: Henry Fernbach, architect.

27. "The 50 Largest Life Insurance Companies," *Fortune* 129 (30 May 1994), 212–13.

28. Hunt's project: Hunt Collection, Prints and Drawings Collection, American Architecture Foundation. Two drawings by LeBrun and photograph of Post's early design: collection of Herbert Mitchell. Hathorne's perspective (carte de visite photograph): Avery Library. The invited competitors were Hunt, Leopold Eidlitz, Hatfield, Griffith Thomas, Russell Sturgis, Gilman, Hathorne, LeBrun, and Post. Apparently Eidlitz, Hatfield, and Thomas declined to enter.

29. Hyde was apparently quite interested. A letter from Post to Hyde, 23 March 1874, answers Hyde's questions regarding the relative sizes of the two: Post Letterbook 2, 496, Post Collection.

30. George P. Oslin, publicity director of the Western Union Telegraph Company, to Frank L. Davis, 26 May 1942, Ryerson and Burnham Libraries, Art Institute of Chicago. As of c. 1878 the clock faces on the tower had not been installed: James D. Reid, *The Telegraph in America* (New York: Derby Brothers, 1879), 739.

31. "The Western Union Telegraph Building," *Journal of the Telegraph* 8 (15 February 1875), 51. According to "A New Elevator," *Record and Guide* 14 (12 December 1874), 394, a "telescopic, hydraulic elevator" had just been installed in the Hamilton Building at 229 Broadway. According to Thomas E. Brown, "The American Passenger Elevator," *Engineering Magazine* 5 (June 1893), 343, Otis Brothers had the exclusive right to the Baldwin-Hale hydraulic elevator. Otis supplied the Western Union's other passenger elevators, so it seems likely that Otis provided the hydraulic elevator installed there as well.

32. Whereabouts today unknown. These may have been the work of Launt Thompson, whom Post recommended to Western Union: Post to William Orton, 14 June 1873, Letterbook 2, 227, Post Collection.

33. Weisman, "The Commercial Architecture of George B. Post," 183.

34. Bloor, "Annual Address," *Proceedings of the Annual Conventions of the American Institute of Architects* 10 (12 October 1876), 29–30.

35. Building ground dimensions: 75.5 feet (77.5 feet rear) by 150.5 feet. Foundation and masonry contractors: James B. Smith & Prodgers Co. Ironwork: J. B. & J. M. Cornell. Carpenter: Philip Herman. Quincy granite of basement and polished granite: J. G. Batterson. Westham granite above basement: Andrews, Ordway, & Green, Richmond, Va. Concrete artificial floors: N.Y. & L.I. Coignet Co. Plumbing and gas fitting: Locke & Monroe. Steam-powered elevators: Otis Brothers. Encaustic tiling: Anderson, Merchant & Co. Embossed glass: Joseph Cartessier. Exterior brick from Baltimore, Md. Cost: more than $2 million. Company moved in 1 February 1875. And see also

"The Western Union Telegraph Building," 49–51.

36. "Western Union Stopped: Its Office Burned Out," *New York Tribune*, 19 July 1890; "The Western Union Fire," *Record and Guide* 46 (26 July 1890), 110–11; and "Fire in a Fire-Proof Building," *Engineering Record* 22 (26 July 1890), 114.

37. "The Reconstructed Western Union Building," *Real Estate Record and Builders' Guide* 47 (25 April 1891), 647–48. Hereafter this periodical will be cited as *Record and Guide*.

38. The Braem house, which stood at 15 East 37th Street, is credited as the first "strictly architectural terra cotta building" in New York in *A History of Real Estate, Building, and Architecture in New York City During the Last Quarter of a Century* (1898; rpt. ed., New York: Arno, 1967), 514, where the wrong street address is given. See p. 510 for a photograph.

39. Hunt's penultimate design is illustrated in *American Builder* (October 1873), 235, where the construction is well described, and in *New-York Sketch-Book of Architecture* 1 (January 1874), plate I. His working drawings are in the American Architectural Foundation's Prints and Drawings Collection, hereafter cited as Hunt Collection.

40. "Sky Building in New York," *Building News* 45 (7 September 1883), 364.

41. Bloor, "Annual Address," 24.

42. NBD 465–1873 gives the projected number of stories as eight. Ironically, a signed and dated (1873) watercolor perspective, presumably offered as an alternative to the client at the beginning of the project, proposes a better-unified ten-story building (Hunt Collection).

The new building is described in detail in "The New Tribune," *New York Daily Tribune*, 10 April 1875.

Building ground dimensions as executed: 92 feet (Printing House Square) by 52 feet (Spruce Street) by 27 feet (Frankfort Street). Supervising architect: Edward E. Raht. Granite foundation: Thomas Crane & Co. Masonry and plaster work: Peter T. O'Brien. Floors and partitions: New-York Fire Proof Co. Iron floor beams: Union Iron Co., Buffalo. Iron for stairs and elevator enclosures: J. B. & J. M. Cornell. Steam heating: James O. Morse. Elevators: Melancton Hanford, Boston. Carpentry: W. Germond & Co. Counting room and banking room woodwork: Herter Brothers. Plaster finish halls and counting room: Garibaldi & Co. Marble work: Casone and Isola. Tiling: L. F. & A. Beckwith.

Clock: E. Howard & Co. Supervising architect of addition (1881–83): Edward E. Raht. Nine-story addition to the top and a nineteen-story annex (1903–5): D'Oench & Yost and L. Thouvard, architects. Building demolished 1966.

43. Wight, typescript of "Origin and History of Hollow Tile Fire-proof Floor Construction" (1897), Wight Collection, Burnham Library, Art Institute of Chicago. On this point see also S. B. Landau, "Richard Morris Hunt: Architectural Innovator and Father of a 'Distinctive' American School," in *The Architecture of Richard Morris Hunt*, ed. S. R. Stein (Chicago: Univ. of Chicago Press, 1986), 58, 74 n. 30. Hollow-tile floor arches were also used in Hunt's contemporary Lenox Library, Coal and Iron Exchange, and Roosevelt Building.

44. "Sky Building in New York," 364.

45. Ibid.

46. Weisman, "Commercial Palaces of New York, 1845–1875," *Art Bulletin* 36 (December 1954), 299.

47. "The Coal and Iron Exchange," *New York Daily Tribune*, 28 January 1876. This source and *Description of the Coal and Iron Exchange Building* (New York: Baker and Godwin, 1876) describe the building in detail; these accounts, along with firsthand examination of Hunt's drawings for the building in the Hunt Collection, are the basis for our analysis.

48. "The Coal and Iron Exchange." Building ground dimensions: 144 feet front (135 feet rear) by 105.5 feet deep. Height: 179 feet (including 45-foot flagpole). Cost: $800,000. Supervising architect: Edward E. Raht. Granite: J. G. Batterson. Mason: A. J. Felter & Son. Carpenter: G. Van Nostrand. Iron floor beams: Union Iron Co., Buffalo. Other ironwork: Architectural Iron Works. Stone trimmings: Daniel McMaster. Interior woodwork: Herter Bros.

49. "New York City News: Hathorne vs. The 'Evening Post'—The Case Summed Up," *The New York World*, 9 October 1875. Hathorne had worked in Gambrill & Post's office in the mid-1860s and is remembered chiefly for his High Victorian Gothic work in Springfield, Massachusetts.

50. Bloor, "Annual Address," 24. There is an unsigned elevation drawing for this commission in The New-York Historical Society's collection that might be speculatively attributed to Hathorne: it is remarkably similar to the building as executed but shows a three-story mansard roof.

51. The newspaper account also erroneously notes Stent's association with Thomas Fuller in

the design of the Ottawa Houses of Parliament. The Stent of Stent & Laver, associated with Fuller & Jones on the Ottawa Parliament houses (1859–67), was Thomas's father, F. W. Stent. Thomas Stent practiced in New York in 1867 and from c. 1875 to 1895. See "The Evening Post: Concise Description of the Building," *New York Evening Post*, 1 July 1875: supplement.

52. "The Evening Post: Concise Description."

53. "New Evening Post Building," *Frank Leslie's Illustrated Newspaper* (21 August 1875), 417. Building ground dimensions: 63 feet (front) by 62 feet (rear) by 103.5 feet (depth). Masonry: R. L. Darragh. Iron beams and girders: A. R. Whitney & Bro. All other iron: Architectural Iron Works. Carpenter: Thomas Wilson. Plumbing and gas fittings: John B. Smith. Glass: Morris, Delano & Co. Steam heat: Bramhall, Deane & Co. Original elevators replaced 1878 by hydraulic elevators supplied by Messrs. Galland & Co. Hydraulic elevators replaced by electric c. 1918, when building was reconstructed. Demolished 1937.

54. Investment return reported in "Sky Building in New York," 364.

55. *Marc Eidlitz & Son, 1854–1904* (n.p., 1904); and New York City directories. The firm was absorbed by Vermilye-Brown Co., Inc., after the death of R. J. Eidlitz in 1935.

56. The first provides the recommended weight, distribution, and capacity of rolled iron beams, all supported by much quantitative tabular data, and it likely influenced the requirement in the city's building law of 1871 that all iron beams be tested by actual weight or pressure placed on them before being put into place. The later book discusses nonaxial loads with resultant bending moments, high deflection, and stresses. It also covers in detail theory, design, and construction with rolled iron beams, tubular iron girders, cast-iron girders, framed girders (trussed forms), and roof trusses; and it describes beams, girders, and bridging in iron and wood.

57. "Seamen's Bank for Savings," *Record and Guide* 8 (12 August 1871), 61. The sculpture group survives, as do Seamen's Bank for Savings Records, 1829 to 1989, in the collection of the South Street Seaport Museum. Hatfield, George B. Post, and Renwick & Sands submitted proposals for the new building. The ironwork, which included rolled-iron floor and roof beams, was supplied by Badger's firm, Architectural Iron Works. Building ground dimen-

sions: 61 feet (Wall Street) by 85 feet (Pearl Street) by 82 feet (rear). Height: 91 feet. Cost: approximately $350,000. (NBD 672–1870.)

58. Described in "Specifications of Iron Work," submitted by Architectural Iron Works (1 June 1870) and, in less detail, in Hatfield's proposal to the Seamen's Bank building committee (12 April 1870): Seamen's Bank for Savings Records. Also documented by photographs made in 1925, when the building was being demolished to make way for a new twenty-story bank and office building: "Unusual Combination Trusses in Old Bank Building," *Engineering News-Record* 95 (24 December 1925), 1029. Otherwise the construction was not unusual: the stone foundation walls were 20 to 24 inches thick and extended 10 feet below street level; the interior side wall and the rear wall were the usual masonry, and the iron-beamed floor construction included brick arches and concrete filling.

59. According to the new-building permit (614–1872), New York City Department of Buildings records, the Bennett's floors were supported on timber girders. However, timber-supported floors would have been unusual construction for a building of this size and importance, and on-site inspection reveals instead floors on brick arches that spanned between wrought-iron beams set at 5 feet center-to-center, with wrought-iron tie rods. The maximum span between the interior brick partitions is 20 feet; the beams are set on cast-iron brackets mounted in the brick partitions, and the clear interior height to the soffits of the beams is 12 feet. Original ground dimensions of building: 117.5 feet (Nassau Street) by 75 feet (Ann Street) by 78 feet (Fulton Street). Height: 98 feet.

60. New York City Department of Buildings records; and "A Review of the Year," *Record and Guide* 49 (22 January 1892), 124.

61. "A Review of the Year," 124.

62. *A History of Real Estate*, 159.

63. Also discussed in S. B. Landau, "The Tall Office Building Artistically Reconsidered: Arcaded Buildings of the New York School, c. 1870–1890," in *In Search of Modern Architecture: A Tribute to Henry Russell Hitchcock*, ed. Helen Searing (Cambridge: MIT Press, 1982), 142, 161 n. 21. Post proposed to adapt the unused design to the needs of the Seamen's Savings Bank, which was built on the site instead: proposal submitted to the chairman of the building committee (12 April 1870) by George B. Post, Seamen's Bank for Savings Records.

64. S. B. Landau, "The Old Racquet Club," *Village Views* 3 (Summer 1986), 24–32. Building ground dimensions: 100 by 75 feet. Height: 82 feet. NBD 593-1875. As this book went to press, the fate of the Racquet Club Building was uncertain, with demolition a possibility.

65. "The Orient Building in Wall Street," *Record and Guide* 21 (9 March 1878), 200.

66. "The Orient Building in Wall Street," 201. Contractor: Samuel Lowden. Building ground dimensions: 30.5 by 119 feet. Marble carved work: James Whitehouse. Iron construction members: J. B. & J. M. Cornell. Fireproof construction: Fire Proof Building Co. Iron stairs: Poulson & Eger. Elevators (two): Whittier Machine Co., Boston. Steam heating: E. Rutzler. Interior tilework: Fisher & Bird. Carpentry: Charles F. True. Interior painting: Edward J. Schwals. Cathedral glass in upper windows: R. Hamilton Sons. Ornamental brass: P. & J. Corbin. Plumbing: Timothy Sullivan. Cost: $125,000. Three stories added later. Demolished c. 1906 for Trust Company of America Building.

67. After his own graduation from Yale in 1870, Benjamin Silliman, Jr., had studied architecture for three years in Berlin, and both he and his partner, James M. Farnsworth, had worked for a time in the office of Calvert Vaux, the noted Victorian Gothicist who with Olmsted designed Central Park. The partnership lasted from c. 1877 to 1882. See Benjamin Silliman obituary, *American Architect* 71 (16 February 1901), 49.

68. Hines, *Burnham of Chicago: Architect and Planner* (Chicago: Univ. of Chicago Press, 1979), 50 and 52.

69. "Iron Fronts—New Office Buildings," *American Architect* 6 (5 July 1879), 6.

70. "Recent Buildings in New York. II. Commercial Buildings," *American Architect* 9 (16 April 1881), 183. On the Morse's brickwork see also "Artistic Brickwork," *Carpentry and Building* 1 (June 1879), 101–3; and 1 (July 1879), 121–22.

71. "The Morse Building," *Record and Guide* 23 (18 January 1879), 44–45. Iron stairs: Poulson & Eger. Elevators: Otis Brothers. Gas fitting and plumbing: Robert Enever & Son. Spanish tiles (interior): Chadwick & Beasley. Slate work, marbles, and grates: Penrhyn Slate Co. Roof: Van Orden & Co. Brick: Peerless Brick Co., Phila. Decorative terra-cotta: Boston Terra Cotta Co. Carpenters: Morton & Chesley, Boston. Decorators and painters: Stewart & Vanhorn. Steam heating: Angell & Blake Manuf.

Co. Structural terra-cotta: S. E. Loring, Chicago. Cost $175,000. Raised in 1901 to twelve full stories, the addition, a six-story steel cage clad in matching materials. Architect: Bannister & Schell. Owner and engineer: Charles Ward Hall. General contractor: Hall & Grant Construction Co. On the addition: "Reconstructing the Morse Building, New York," *Engineering Record* 44 (2 November 1901), 422–24.

72. "Sky Building in New York," 364.

73. The subject of a highly critical review, the book was said to be badly organized and to take material uncritically from manufacturers: "New Books," *American Architect* 1 (16 September 1876), 303–4.

5. The Future Revealed

1. The basis for the following description is William I. Taylor's perspective map of Manhattan, which describes the fabric and demography of the island in extraordinary detail, depicting every street, building, bridge, pier, and ship as it existed in 1879: *The City of New York* (map; New York: Galt and Hoy, 1879).

2. He was lifted 806 feet, which means that the average floor-to-floor height of the time was 13 feet: "High Buildings and Elevators in New York," *Scientific American* 45 (17 September 1881), 181.

3. As quoted in "High Buildings in New York," *American Architect* 5 (4 January 1879), 8.

4. "Sky Building in New York," *Building News* 45 (7 Sept 1883), 363.

5. Long quotation from "A Coming Building Question," *Record and Guide* 30 (23–30 December 1882), 135; and see "Building Skyward" (To the Editor), *Record and Guide* 31 (20 January 1883), 28.

6. R. Kerr, "On the Lofty Buildings of New York City," *Sanitary Engineer* 9 (3 January 1884), 113–14; 9 (10 January 1884), 137–38.

7. In 1889 Ware altered the top story and brought the rear section up to fifteen stories. See "Report on Elevated Dwellings in New York City," printed for private distribution on 1 July 1883 (New York: Evening Post Job Printing Office, 1883), 4, The New-York Historical Society. For events leading up to the law passed in 1885 limiting the height of apartment houses and the contents of that law: Building height restrictions (Editorial), *American Architect* 17 (18 April 1885), 181; 17 (20 June 1885), 289; "Height Limitations of Buildings" (news items), *Sanitary Engineer*, 11 (9 April 1885),

398; 11 (21 May 1885), 515; "The Law and the Builders," unidentified newspaper clipping (18 March 1883), small scrapbooks folder, Post Collection; "Proposed Regulation of the Height of Dwelling Houses in New York City," *Sanitary Engineer* 9 (10 April 1884), 447; "The New Building Law for the City of New York" (titles vary), *American Architect* 18 (18 July 1885), 25 and 33; and other sources on the law listed in bibliographies for Chapters 5 and 6.

8. "What the Elevator Has Done," *Record and Guide* 33 (19 April 1884), 402. See also "High Buildings in Cities," *Scientific American* 50 (19 April 1884), 240.

9. The Daly law, also enacted in 1885, nullified the law of 1881, which allowed wood construction above 140th Street. Instead, it prohibited such construction below 149th and also specified new dimensions for brick walls. The 1881 law had required a 24-inch thickness up to 70 feet of height and 20 inches above; the new law established a minimum thickness of 8 inches (small dwelling houses) and required thicknesses for a 110-foot-high apartment building to be 28 inches up to 15 feet, 24 inches for the next 45 feet, 20 inches for the next 30 feet, and 16 inches from there to the top. There were no differences between the 1881 and 1885 laws on specifications for stone and iron lintels and iron beams, and although the depth of iron beams was specified for a given span, the other variables involved were not regulated.

10. "Our Tall Buildings," *Sanitary Engineer and Construction Record* 15 (8 January 1887), 131.

11. Collapse of buildings adjoining excavations (Editorial), *American Architect* 16 (5 July 1884), 1.

12. "Architects and Engineers," *American Architect* 4 (17 August 1878), 54–55; and 4 (24 August 1878), 62–63.

13. Tuthill, "The Office Building," *Building* 9 (10 November 1888), 167.

14. Weisman, "The Commercial Architecture of George B. Post," *JSAH* 31 (October 1972), 186. Consonant with our established method of story counting, we are not including the half-submerged basement.

15. Others are Burnham & Root's office building (1890–91) in San Francisco and two workingmen's hotels in New York designed by Ernest Flagg: Mills House Nos. 1 (1896–97; now known as the Atrium) and 2 (1896–98; demolished).

16. Unidentified newspaper clipping (3 February 1882), large Post scrapbook, Post Collection; and see also "Foundations of High Buildings," *American Architect* 42 (18 November 1893), 88 ff.; and "Underpinning the Old Mills Building, Broad and Nassau Streets, New York City," *Engineering News* 70 (7 August 1913), 257.

17. "The Mills Building," *Record and Guide* 30 (28 October–4 November 1882), 46–47.

Building ground dimensions: 29 feet (Wall Street) by 163.5 feet (Broad Street) by 101 feet (Exchange Place). Stories: nine and one-half on Broad Street, eight on Wall. Contractor: David H. King, Jr. Three hundred offices capable of accommodating more than fifteen hundred people. 1883–85: addition at 53 Exchange Place. Architect: G. B. Post.

18. Ripley also credited Post with the installation of the first passenger elevator in an office building [the Equitable]; the compilation of the first tables of moments of inertia of steel beams; the design of the first building more than twelve stories tall; the idea of hanging scaffolds from openings in the walls rather than building them up from the ground; and the innovation of having floor arches installed as the steel work rose. Ripley also cited Post as the architect of the first twenty-five-story building, the St. Paul Building of 1895–98 (actually twenty-six stories). As listed by Ripley, other early buildings with generating plants were the Dakota and Osborne apartment houses and the Welles Building, all installed in 1885: Ripley, "Life of Building Power Plants" [1914], *American Society of Heating and Ventilating Engineers*, 1–6, Post Collection.

19. Post considered joining his addition "to a building on piles *without a crack* . . . a very considerable engineering feat": To D. O. Mills, Post Letter Book no. 5 (1870–1885), 353. Post Collection.

20. "Sky Building," 364; and "Our Sky Scrapers," *New York, 1895*, 2d ed. (New York: A. F. Parsons, 1895), 55. See also "Out Among the Builders," *Record and Guide* 27 (16 April 1881), 362.

The building had an iron and stone cornice, iron floor beams, and three hydraulic elevators. Building contractor: Richard Deeves. Iron contractors: Post & McCord. Estimated cost: $400,000 (NBD 390–1881). Nassau Bank obtained a twenty-year lease of the large room on the first floor in 1881; stores and offices occupied the rest of building. In 1889–90 Farnsworth enlarged the building for the same owner, Eugene Kelly, using the original south wall as a party wall for an adjoining new structure: NBD 83–1889.

21. The builder of record was H. H. Hunnewell. With entrances on Broadway and at 5–7 Beaver Street, it covered a ground area of 13,690 square feet, was 145 feet high, and contained two hundred offices. Masonry: Smith, Prodgers & Co. Ironwork: Post & McCord. Its base was red granite, and its upper walls red brick: "Sky Building," 364.

22. "The New York Produce Exchange Competition,"*American Architect* 9 (12 March 1881), 123; see also New York Produce Exchange Building Committee to Richard M. Upjohn, 7 October 1880, Upjohn Papers, Manuscript and Archives Division, New York Public Library; and *American Architect* 9 (9 April 1881), 174 (Withers' design, New-York Produce Exchange); 9 (11 June 1881; Atwood design for same); 14 (8 September 1883; Upjohn design for same).

23. Richard Wheatley, "The New York Produce Exchange," *Harper's Magazine* 73 (July 1886), 189–218, esp. 196.

24. Copy of letter from Everett Post to Jules Salmanowitz, president of the New York Produce Exchange, 19 May 1953, Post Collection.

25. New York Produce Exchange, *Origin, Growth, and Usefulness of the New York Produce Exchange* (New York: Historical Publishing, 1884), 56–58 (Post's commentary) and 60. This publication provides a detailed description of the building.

26. "Steel-Frame Building Construction," *Engineering Record* 32 (15 June 1895), 44 (report of Post's address on 5 June to the New York Architectural League), and *New York Evening Post*, 16 December 1897 (dinner given by the Architectural League in Post's honor).

27. Jenney described the construction of his Home Insurance Building as follows: "Iron was used as the skeleton of the entire building except the party walls": "The Construction of a Heavy Fire-Proof Building on a Compressible Soil," *Sanitary Engineer* 13 (10 December 1885), 33. On the Home Insurance Building, see Gerald R. Larson and Roula Mouroudellis Geraniotis, "Toward a Better Understanding of the Evolution of the Iron Skeleton Frame in Chicago," *JSAH* 46 (March 1987), 39–48.

28. Fryer, "A Review of the Development of Structural Iron," *A History of Real Estate, Building and Architecture in New York City During the Last Quarter of a Century* (1898; rpt.

ed., New York: Arno, 1967), 464–65 ff. Without using the term *cage construction*, William H. Birkmire described it as one of several variations of skeleton construction: Birkmire, *Skeleton Construction in Buildings*, 4th ed. (New York: John Wiley & Sons, 1912), 3.

29. E. E. Viollet-le-Duc, *Discourses on Architecture*, trans. Henry Van Brunt (Boston: J. R. Osgood, 1875), 2: 1–2.

30. *New York Produce Exchange: Origin, Growth, and Usefulness*, 57.

31. Quotations, respectively, from Van Rensselaer, "Recent Architecture in America. III. Commercial Buildings," *Century Magazine* 28 (August 1884), 520; "Grouping in Architecture," *Record and Guide* 32 (17 November 1883), 899–900; and "A Foreigner's View of American Architecture," *American Architect* 25 (25 May 1889), 244. The German commentator was C. Hinckeldeyn, technical attaché to the German Legation, Washington.

32. Information supplied by Ivan Karp in a telephone conversation with Landau (9 September 1988).

Further construction data: Brick walls 16 inches (curtain) to 72 inches (bearing) thick. Post's managing agent: Robert Maynicke. Supervisor of foundations: William H. Hazzard. Masons: Moran & Armstrong. Ironworkers: J. B. & J. M. Cornell. Fireproof building materials: Henry Maurer & Son. Steam heating: Baker, Smith & Co. Terra-cotta work: Perth Amboy Terra Cotta Co. Interior wood finish and cabinetwork: Meeker & Hedden.

33. "Liberal Offers to Distinguished Architects," unidentified newspaper clipping (9 September 1881), Scrapbook of New York Chapter, American Institute of Architects, pt. 2, Box 8, RG 801, SR 1.2, American Institute of Architects Archives, Washington, D.C.

34. Van Rensselaer, "Recent Architecture in America," 518; and Moses King, ed., *King's Handbook of New York City*, 2d ed. (Boston: Moses King, 1893), 820.

35. See Walter B. Chambers, "No. One Broadway: The New York Offices of the International Mercantile Marine Company," *American Architect* 120 (12 October 1921), 287–93; and T. Kennard Thomson, "Washington Building Reconstruction: Columns of Lower Story Replaced by Girders," *Engineering News-Record* 87 (10 November 1921), 774–77.

For further data on original building and enlargement of 1886–87: "The Washington Building," *Record and Guide* 43 (27 April

1889), 583; and "Walls Rising in Broadway: A Glance at the New Buildings," *New York Tribune*, 19 September 1886. The original building contractor was W. H. Hazzard & Son.

36. Weisman, "The Commercial Architecture of George B. Post," 191.

37. Water closets: Meyer-Sniffin Co. Urinals: Benton Bros. Cast-iron pipe: Cassidy & Adler. Wrought-iron pipe and fittings: John Simmons. Lead pipe: Leroy Shot and Lead Mfg. Co. Gate valves: United Brass Co. Plumbing (cost, $25,000): Thos. J. Byrne. See *Metal Worker* (31 October 1885), 37–39, small scrapbooks folder, Post Collection; and "The Plumbing and Water Supply of the New York Cotton Exchange," *Carpentry and Building* 7 (December 1885), 228–30. The Post Collection contains items describing the building, and see also NBD 1162–1883. Building demolished 1923.

38. "The Best Ten Buildings in the United States," *American Architect* 17 (11 April 1885), 178.

39. The finest office building (news item), *Engineering News and American Contract Journal* 11 (26 April 1884), 195.

40. New-building permit 672–1884 and other Department of Buildings records; and Curtis Channing Blake, "The Architecture of Carrère and Hastings" (Ph.D. diss., Columbia Univ., 1976), 2: 351.

41. "Vast Apartment Houses," *Record and Guide* 29 (3 June 1882), 550; "The Dakota," *Record and Guide* 34 (13 September 1884), 948; "The Dakota," *New York Times*, 22 October 1884; "The Dakota Apartment House," *Record and Guide* 35 (7 March 1885), 232; and "The Venerable Dakota," *Architectural Forum* 110 (19 March 1959), 122–29.

42. "The Central Park Apartments, Facing the Park . . ." (Prospectus; New York, 1882); "The Central Park Apartment Houses," *Record and Guide* 33 (28 June 1886), 350; "Mammoth Apartment House," *Record and Guide* 28 (6 August 1881), 783; and Spanish Flats (editorial), *American Architect* 24 (8 December 1888), 261.

43. "A New Apartment House," *Record and Guide* 31 (17 February 1883), 63.

44. On the Osborne see Davida Tenenbaum Deutsch, "The Osborne, New York City," *Antiques Magazine* 129 (July 1986), 152–58; and Virginia Kurshan, "Osborne Apartments," New York City Landmarks Preservation Commission designation report, 13 August 1991.

45. John C. Gobright, *The Monumental City,* or *Baltimore Guide Book* (Baltimore: Gobright & Torsch, 1858), 85, as quoted in Kenneth T. Gibbs, "The Architecture of Norris G. Starkweather" (M.A. thesis, Univ. of Virginia, 1972), 7. Starkweather, whose first name is wrongly given as Nathan in recent publications, was not trained as an architect but began his career as a building contractor. Before coming to New York in 1880, the Vermont-born Starkweather had practiced as an architect-builder in Philadelphia (c. 1854–55), then in Baltimore (1855–c. 1861), and later in Washington, D.C. (c. 1868–80), in partnership with Thomas M. Plowman (Starkweather & Plowman). Starkweather's New York partner from 1881 to 1885 was Charles E. Gibbs, formerly of Washington. Starkweather (Starkweather & Gibbs) was responsible for at least one New York City church, the Second Avenue Methodist Episcopal Church at 319–323 East 118 Street (1882–83; demolished). His best-known Italianate house is Camden in Caroline County, Virginia (1857–59), a towered villa built for William Carter Pratt, and he also designed the Fairfax Seminary near Alexandria (1857–60). See N. G. Starkweather to A. J. Bloor, 12 March 1877, American Institute of Architects Archives.

46. *History of Architecture and the Building Trades of Greater New York* (New York: Union Historical Co., 1899), 2: 317.

47. Sunk to minus 22.5 feet, the brick foundation walls were 4 feet thick. These were undoubtedly on separate pier footings; the extreme depth of the bedrock is about minus 100 feet in this area. In the spring of 1915 the piers under the Beekman Street elevation, on the line of the Interborough Rapid Transit (IRT) subway, were underpinned with tubular steel and concrete piles sunk to minus 56–59 feet, or 12 to 15 feet below water level. The material of the overburden is medium-fine sand: "Jacking Tests on Piles," *Engineering News* 74 (16 September 1915), 559.

According to Blanche Potter, *More Memories: Orlando Bronson Potter and Frederick Potter* (New York: J. J. Little & Ives, 1923), 131–32, O. B. Potter had owned the old World Building.

48. The length of the girders ranges from 13 feet, 9 inches to 16 feet, 3 inches, and the floor beams are predominantly 18 feet, 4 inches long, though longer in places to deal with special exigencies. The beams are mostly set 4 feet, 6 inches from center to center, and they rest on the top flanges of the girders: ascertained from examination of Starkweather's floor plans,

framing plans, and details of the Potter Building, office of Hurley & Farinella, Architects, New York.

49. "The Potter Building," *Record and Guide* 35 (20 June 1885), 701–2.

Mason: Thomas Armstrong. Fireproof building materials: Henry Maurer & Son. Ironwork: New York City Iron Works, J. M. Duclos & Co., H. W. Adams & Co, and completed by Lehigh Iron Co. Jackson Architectural Iron Works also participated. Terra-cotta: Boston Terra Cotta Company. Information from NBD 820–1883; "Out Among the Builders," *Record and Guide* 29 (18 February 1882), 142; "A New Building in Park Row", *New York Times*, 20 July 1883; "Prominent Buildings Under Way," *Record and Guide* 33 (22 March 1884), 289; and "The Potter Building," *Carpentry and Building* 7 (September 1885), 161–62. Also, letter to Condit from Walter E. Sam, Hurley and Farinella, Architects, New York, 15 July 1981.

50. From 1884 to 1902. The builder was Smith & Prodgers, and in 1905 John B. Snook & Sons replaced the original brick piers at the first story with cast-iron columns: new-building permit 782–1883; alteration permit 975–1905, Department of Buildings records. The ground floor has recently undergone other, less sympathetic alterations. Hardenbergh also designed another Western Union Building on Broad Street that was completed shortly before this one: "In West Twenty-third Street," *Record and Guide* 33 (28 June 1884), 693; and New York City Landmarks Preservation Commission, "Ladies' Mile Historic District Designation Report," ed. Marjorie Pearson, 2 May 1989, 1: 309–10.

51. About 1878 Cook joined in partnership with George Fletcher Babb, and the six-story warehouse still standing at 173 Duane Street (1879–80) was the new firm's first essay in the arcaded style. Daniel Wheelock Willard entered the firm in 1884. Babb, Cook & Willard's best-known work besides the De Vinne Press Building is the Andrew Carnegie mansion on upper Fifth Avenue (1899–1901), now the Cooper-Hewitt Museum.

52. The women were in fact paid at the same rate as the men—highly unusual for the time: Theodore L. De Vinne, "The Printing of 'The Century,'" *The Century* n.s. 19 (November 1890), 88. See also "The De Vinne Press Building, New York," *Sanitary Engineer* 13 (13 May 1886), 561 and plate.

Original ground dimensions: 100 feet (Lafayette Street) by 73 feet (Fourth Street). Height: 98 feet. Vault for heaviest presses under Lafayette Street sidewalk. Eight-story addition of 1890–91: 44.5 feet (front) by 25 feet (rear) by 100 feet (deep). Height: 96.5 feet. Removal of bulkhead on Lafayette Street, 1911–12: Walter S. Timmis, architect. Other alterations. Information from NBD 203–1885, NBD 439–1890, Alteration permits 2312–1911 and 1270–1915, and other Department of Buildings records.

53. Because Stanford White designed other structures for the owners, Robert and Ogden Goelet, it is tempting to assign the Goelet Building's design to him. The architect of the addition was Maynicke & Franke. See "Ladies' Mile Historic District," 1: 93–97.

54. Its physical and chemical properties are as follows: tensile strength (ultimate) $= 70,000$–$80,000$ psi; tensile strength (yield) $= 40,000$–$48,000$ psi; $C = 0.2$–0.5%; $Mn = 0.5\%$; $Si = 0.25$–0.75%; P (max. allowable) $= 0.5\%$; S (max. allowable) $= 0.06\%$; $Fe = 97.19$–98.49%.

55. Information from NBD 739–1884 (Tenth Avenue stables), NBD 584–1885 (691 Broadway), and NBD 66–1887 (687–89 Broadway).

56. *History of Architecture and the Building Trades*, 2: 198, 201.

57. The bank had previously occupied two successive buildings at the same address, 36 Wall Street. The new building is described in "Recent Building in Wall Street," *Record and Guide* 40 (16 July 1887), 950. The builder was Marc Eidlitz & Son.

58. New-building permit 560–1886, Municipal Archives. Building ground dimensions: 80 to 82 feet wide by 190 feet deep. All of the floors were to be constructed of 15-inch rolled-iron floor beams weighing 125 pounds per yard and spaced 48 inches apart, center-to-center. These beams were to be supported by 15-inch wrought-iron girders and by cast-iron columns. Ironwork: J. B. & J. M. Cornell. Mason: Masterton & Harrison. Cost: $1,500,000. Purchased by Hamburg-American Line in 1907. Top story, left portion, altered 1906 by De Lemos & Cordes when height increased to fourteen stories. Demolished 1971. See also "Walls Rising in Broadway"; and "Aldrich Court," *Record and Guide* 39 (5 March 1887), 288.

59. "The Army Building," *Record and Guide* 40 (29 October 1887), 1348; "The Question of Overbuilding," *Record and Guide* 40 (29 October 1887), 1348–49; and Christopher Gray, "The Old U.S. Army Building on Whitehall Street," *New York Times*, 5 March 1995. In

1986, as part of a reconstruction, the facades were clad in mirror glass.

60. "The Reconstruction of the 'Times' Building," *Harper's Weekly* 32 (27 October 1888), 818.

61. "The New 'Times' Building," *Scientific American* 59 (25 August 1888), 117. The *Scientific American* had had its offices for many years in the old World Building that burned in 1882.

62. "Replacing Girders in a Lower Story of a High Office Building," *Engineering Record* 50 (24 September 1904), 375–77; and "The New 'Times' Building," *Scientific American*, 117.

63. "The New Times Building," *New York Times*, 29 April 1889. Building ground dimensions: 60 feet (Spruce Street) by 102 feet (Park Row) by 96 ft. (Nassau Street) by 104 feet (line of Potter Building). Indiana limestone suppliers: James Gillies & Sons. Granite suppliers: Hallowell (Maine) Granite Works. Ironwork: J. B. & J. M. Cornell. Elevators (hydraulic): Otis Brothers. Plumbing and gaslighting: Byrne & Tucker. Steam heating and ventilating: Baker, Smith, & Co. Carpenter work: V. J. Hedden & Sons. Cabinet work: Pottier & Stymus. Underpinning and enclosure of vaults, foundation piers (due to construction of subway), 1900–1904: Robert Maynicke. Roof removed and raised to fifteen stories, 1905: Robert Maynicke.

64. NBD 442-1888 names S. D. Hatch as architect, but Kimball is named in the professional journals, e.g., on the plate reproduced in *Building* 13 (28 September 1889), and in Montgomery Schuyler, "The Works of Francis H. Kimball and Kimball & Thompson," *Architectural Record* 7 (April–June 1898), 501–2. No family or other relationship has been traced between the two architects.

65. Schuyler, "The Works of Francis H. Kimball," 501–2.

66. See *Western Electric Company, 1869–1944*, souvenir pamphlet, and promotional materials, office of Haines Lundberg Waehler, Architects.

C. L. W. Eidlitz, educated in Geneva, Switzerland, and trained at the Royal Polytechnic School in Stuttgart, Germany, began his career as a draftsman in his father's office and opened his own office in 1885. By then he had produced major public buildings, notably the Michigan Central Railroad Station in Detroit (1882–83), the Dearborn Street Station in Chicago (1885), and the Buffalo, New York, Public Library (1884–85). His New York City telephone company buildings followed, and his successor firms in the twentieth century would continue to serve as principal architects of what became in 1896 the New York Telephone Company. From 1900 to 1910, when he retired, Eidlitz was associated with Andrew Campbell McKenzie as Eidlitz & McKenzie. The successor firm was McKenzie, Voorhees & Gmelin (1910–26), followed by Voorhees, Gmelin, & (Ralph) Walker (1926–38), who produced distinguished telephone buildings in the Art Deco style. Since 1968, the firm name has been Haines Lundberg Waehler.

67. *New York Times*, 29 April 1888; as quoted in I. N. Phelps Stokes, *The Iconography of Manhattan Island* (New York: Robert H. Dodd, 1915–26), 5: 1995–96. See above for a German commentator's positive reaction to the Produce Exchange in 1889.

68. The constant was determined as 0.0027 or 0.003, a pressure of 27–30 pounds per square foot (psf) per 100 mph of wind velocity; the currently accepted value is 0.00256. The techniques and results of other experiments subsequently conducted are summarized by C. F. Marvin in "Wind Pressures and the Measurement of Wind Velocities," *Engineering News* 24 (13 December 1890), 520–21; the authoritative historical review of all experiments and theories back to Newton is W. H. Bixby, "Wind Pressures in Engineering Construction," *Engineering News* 33 (14 March 1895), 175–84. For other sources on this subject, see chapter bibliography.

69. See F. Collingwood, "Fire-Proof Construction," *Sanitary Engineer* 13 (11 February 1886), 248–50; 13 (4 March 1886), 321–22; 13 (8 April 1886), 441–42; 13 (13 May 1886), 561–62; and chapter bibliography.

70. Following an apprenticeship with J. C. Cady in New York, Gilbert served as the chief architect of the New York, Lake Erie and Western Railroad (Erie) under Octave Chanute, one of the distinguished bridge engineers of the time and later a pioneer of airplane flight. In that capacity Gilbert designed many stations and other buildings along the company's lines and, working independently, stations and terminals for other roads as well, notably the Illinois Central Station (1892–93) in Chicago. He was responsible for enlarging and remodeling the old Grand Central Station in New York (1898–99).

71. As quoted in John C. Van Dyke, *The New New York* (New York: Macmillan, 1909), 99–100. Gilbert's reference to a thirteenth story must include the basement and the space within the pavilion roof in his count.

72. "Condition of Frame of Tower Building, New York, after 25-yr. Service," *Engineering News* 71 (2 April 1914), 748–49.

73. "Condition of Frame of Tower Building," 748. The fireproof building materials were supplied by Henry Maurer & Son.

74. The figures shown on the drawing indicate the horizontal shear in bracing elements in thousands of pounds. By extrapolation, the shear in the diagonals from the ninth through the eleventh stories can be estimated at 10,800 lbs. (ninth floor), 8,000 lbs. (tenth floor), and 5,200 lbs. (eleventh floor). The individual diagonal was composed of two angles, each 2 inches by 3 inches by 11/32 of an inch. The technique for calculating the shear was developed by Corydon T. Purdy but not published until 1891.

75. *History of Architecture and the Building Trades*, 1: 101.

76. Fryer, "A Review of the Development of Structural Iron," 471.

77. Quoted in "Early Skeleton Construction," *Engineering Record*, 40 (12 August 1899), 238; and in "The First 'Skeleton' Building," *Record and Guide* 64 (12 August 1899), 239. Here again, the term "steel" may well describe wrought iron.

78. Birkmire, born in Philadelphia and a graduate of the Philadelphia Academy of Music, was trained as an architect in the office of Samuel Sloan, and he first worked with the Penncoyd Steel Works and Rolling Mills in Philadelphia. In New York he worked for the Jackson Architectural Iron Works from 1888 to 1892, and after 1892 for the J. B. & J. M. Cornell Iron Works, where he was also head of construction. Starting in 1895 he practiced independently but was associated on several projects with John T. Williams from 1895 to 1898.

79. Birkmire and Gilbert are quoted in "Disputes of Architects: Question About the Invention of the Skeleton Construction," *The New York Times*, 19 August 1899. See also note 11, Chapter 4. On Buffington's allegations see "Steel Skeleton Construction," *Record and Guide* 74 (29 October 1904), 896–97; and "Inventors of the Skyscraper," *Record and Guide* 79 (23 February 1907), 398.

80. From 1914 until 1926 the Tower's site was occupied by the four-story Standard Arcade Building designed by Severance and Van Alen, covering a larger site at 44–50 Broadway. That building was replaced by a twenty-two-story skyscraper that still stands.

81. Boston's total was $32,400,000. Philadelphia was third with $26,000,000, Brooklyn fourth with $25,679,405, and Chicago fifth with $25,065,000: "Building in 1889," *Scientific American* 63 (20 September 1890), 184.

82. Richard Wheatley, "The New York Banks," *Harper's Magazine* 80 (February 1890), 464; Wheatley, "The New York Maritime Exchange," *Harper's Magazine* 80 (April 1890), 756–66; and Wheatley, "The New York Real Estate Exchange," *Harper's Magazine* 77 (November 1888), 928–44. The Real Estate Exchange had its headquarters in a building at 59–65 Liberty Street that it purchased and expanded in 1884–85.

6. State of the Skyscraper Art, 1889 to the Mid-1890s

1. William H. Birkmire, *The Planning and Construction of High Office-Buildings* (New York: John Wiley and Sons, 1898), 13. This important book was serialized in *Architecture and Building* starting with the 5 December 1896 issue.

2. "Plumbing in the Bank of America Building, New York," *Engineering and Building Record* 20 (3 August 1889), 134; 20 (10 August 1889), 148; 20 (17 August 1889), 162.

3. This was the five-story Demarest Carriage Emporium at the northeast corner of Fifth Avenue and 33rd Street (1889–90; demolished 1920), designed for Margaret L. de Stivers by Renwick, Aspinwall & Russell: L. A. Petersen, *Elisha Graves Otis, 1811–1861, and His Influence Upon Vertical Transportation* (New York: Newcomen Society of England, 1945), 15; and NBD 995–1889. Two years earlier, in 1887, an electric elevator had been installed in a Baltimore building by William Baxter, Jr.: Thomas E. Brown, "Passenger Elevators," *American Architect* 86 (10 December 1904), 83–84.

4. Apparently Otis Brothers had purchased the license to manufacture a special kind of uniform-speed motor invented by Rudolf Eickemeyer of Yonkers. The production of the new elevator coincided with the publication of a comprehensive set of rules for installing lights, motors, and their associated circuits by the Boston Manufacturers Mutual Fire Insurance Company in "Rules for the Installation of Electric Lighting and Motive Apparatus," *Engineering Record* 22 (16 August 1890), 172–73. The first article on the Otis electric drive had appeared in the same journal a month earlier: "The Otis Electric Elevator," *Engineering and Building Record* 22 (5 July 1890), 76.

5. According to Thomas E. Brown, "The

American Passenger Elevator," *Engineering Magazine* 5 (June 1893), 344. Although Brown does not say these were manufactured by Otis, that was likely the case. See also Brown, "Passenger Elevators," 84–85; and John H. Jallings, *Elevators: A Practical Treatise on the Development and Design of Hand, Belt, Steam, Hydraulic, and Electric Elevators* (Chicago: American Technology Society, 1915), 163. The machinery of Lord's Court's five Sprague-Pratt elevators, located in the basement, included two double-deck sets and one single. Each was 28 feet long; the single-deck was 3.5 feet high and the double-deck 7 feet. The hoisting speed of an average load was 500 feet per minute; the cable diameter was three-quarters of an inch; the working tensile strength was 3,200 pounds per cable; and the power supplied by the four engine-generator sets was 100 kilowatts for three, 50 for one: Birkmire, *Planning and Construction*, 250–54.

6. Other defects include eccentric cores, concealed cavities and blow holes, cinders and other impurities, locked-in secondary stresses resulting from unequal cooling of the body of metal, unequal fusion and hence lack of homogeneity of different currents of metal in the mold, and inferior pig iron with excessive impurities. See chapter bibliography, esp. listings for Purdy and Birkmire.

7. Among the steel sections used throughout the 1890s was a curious form known as the Larimer Column after the inventor who patented it in 1891, actually a revival of the old, discredited cruciform section. It was not often used in high buildings: "The Larimer Steel Column," *Engineering News* 28 (28 July 1892), 89.

8. The results accepted in 1890 are reported in William H. Birkmire, *Skeleton Construction in Buildings*, 4th ed. (New York: John Wiley & Sons, 1912), chapter 2.

9. The area and weight of the section was determined by calculating the bending moment from the total load and by a table giving section corresponding to moment: Birkmire, *Skeleton Construction in Buildings*, chapter 4. Birkmire states on pp. 96–97 that the steel bars manufactured for the Home Life Building (1892–94) in New York were required to have an ultimate strength of 58,000 to 60,000 pounds, with an elastic limit of half that.

10. *Proceedings of the Twenty-eighth Annual Convention of the American Institute of Architects* (16 October 1894), 159–178.

11. Howard Constable, "The Fire-Proofing of Buildings and Improvement in Architectural Methods," *Brickbuilder* 4 (December 1895), 257.

12. George Hill, "Some Practical Limiting Conditions in the Design of the Modern Office Building," *Architectural Record* 2 (April–June 1893), 445–47. Hill's firm, Hill & (Thornton F.) Turner, in existence from about 1895 to at least 1903, seems not to have been very productive in New York City architecture, but it did design Euclid Hall (1902–3), a large apartment house still standing on the west side of Broadway between 85th and 86th streets. Some years later Birkmire, whose role in the construction of the Tower Building was identified in the previous chapter, addressed the same subject; his assessment generally supports Hill's: Birkmire, *Planning and Construction*, esp. 66.

13. Hill, "Some Practical Limiting Conditions," 447–50.

14. Hill, "Some Practical Limiting Conditions," 446–51 and 454. As of c. 1897, according to Birkmire, offices measuring between 10 by 12 feet and 15 by 20 feet were priced at $200 to $450 per year and rented more easily than larger offices: Birkmire, *Planning and Construction*, 68.

15. Hill, "Some Practical Limiting Conditions," 455–61 (including Tables I–IX).

16. Hill, "Some Practical Limiting Conditions," 461–68.

17. "The Building of a Sky-Scraper," *Record and Guide* 54 (15 September 1894), 353–54.

18. On the Fuller company: "Fuller Building," New York City Landmarks Preservation Commission designation report, 18 March 1986, 1–2.

19. It required jacking the column, introducing a temporary beam under the column supported at the ends by jacks on wood blocks, excavating around and under the old footing, and deepening the footing by placing brick or concrete under the old footing plane.

20. "New Method of Underpinning High Buildings," *Engineering News* 37 (7 January 1897), 6.

21. "A Serious Blaze in a Fire-proof Office Building," *Engineering News* 29 (6 April 1893), 323; 29 (13 April 1893), 356–57.

In the thirty-seven years prior to May 1891, 41,722 fires occurred in New York, for an annual average of 1,127. The total damage was estimated at $102 million, or $2,445 per fire: "Thirty-seven Years' Fire Statistics for New York," *American Architect* 36 (4 June 1892), 152.

22. "Defects of 'Fireproof' Buildings," *Scientific American* 73 (23 November 1895), 322. The architect was Stephen D. Hatch.

23. This eight-story, neo-Renaissance building stands on the northwest corner of Broadway and Houston Street. Separate foundations were constructed for the railroad engines and machinery at a level 46 feet below Broadway, and the structure was built with an iron "penthouse" on the roof for use as the janitor's apartment. See "The Cable Building," *Record and Guide* 52 (16 December 1893), 761–62; A fire in the Cable Building (news item), *Engineering News* 35 (30 April 1896), 281; and S. B. Landau, "The Tall Office Building Artistically Reconsidered: Arcaded Buildings of the New York School, c. 1870–1890," in *In Search of Modern Architecture: A Tribute to Henry Russell Hitchcock*, ed. Helen Searing (Cambridge: MIT Press, 1982), 158–59 and 164 (n. 54).

24. Himmelwright, "Fire-Proof Construction and Recent Tests," *Engineering Magazine* 12 (December 1896), 460–69; and see Henry A. Goetz, "Dangers from Tall Office Buildings," *Engineering Magazine* 2 (March 1892), 792–801; Edward Atkinson, "Fire Risks on Tall Office Buildings," *Engineering Magazine*, 3 (May 1892), 149–55; and John M. Carrère, "Interior Fireproof Construction," *Engineering Magazine* 4 (October 1892), 95–108.

25. William J. Fryer, "The New York Building Law," *Architectural Record* 1 (July–September 1891), 69–82. See also *A History of Real Estate, Building and Architecture in New York City During the Last Quarter of a Century* (1898; rpt. ed., New York: Arno, 1967), 287–98; and chapter bibliography under *Laws of the State of New York*.

26. In addition to the superintendent of buildings, the board included one member each from the American Institute of Architects and the Board of Fire Underwriters, two from the Mechanics' and Traders' Exchange; and, later, one from the Society of Architectural Iron Manufacturers, one from the Real Estate Owners' and Builders' Association, one from the Real Estate Exchange, and the fire department chief were added: *A History of Real Estate*, 290.

27. For the 1885 code see *The New York City Record for the Year 1886* (New York: Record, 1886); and for this and later codes, William J. Fryer, ed., *Laws Relating to Buildings in the City of New York . . .* (New York: Record & Guide, 1885, 1887, 1892, 1895, 1897); and *Laws of the State of New York*.

28. The Combined Committee (news item),

American Architect 32 (11 April 1891), 17–18.

29. For an accepted table of the bearing capacity of rock and soils from Ira O. Baker, *Treatise on Masonry Construction*, see Birkmire, *Planning and Construction*, 212.

30. Fryer, ed., *Laws Relating to Buildings in the City of New York . . .* (1892), sec. 477, 20.

31. Allowable stresses were as follows: tension or compression in the flanges = 12,000 psi for wrought iron and 15,000 psi for steel; shear in the web = 6,000 psi for iron, 7,000 psi for steel; shear in rivets = 9,000 psi.

32. "Tests and Requirements of Structural Wrought Iron and Steel," *Engineering Record* 24 (7 November 1891), 364; 24 (14 November 1891), 382.

33. "The Influence of Heat on the Strength of Iron," *Engineering Record* 24 (22 August 1891), 185.

34. These included (1) Columbian Fireproofing Co.: steel beams encased in concrete; concrete slab floors with steel bar reinforcing; (2) John A. Roebling's Sons Co.: concrete with flat and arched wire-mesh reinforcing between and around the beams; (3) various arrangements of flat or arched hollow-tile terra-cotta blocks between beams and over flanges; (4) metal arches between the beams leveled up with concrete; (5) steel plate in concrete; (6) Lee tension-rod tile block reinforced with double-twisted bars in the tension zone; (7) flat tiles over a grid of light steel bars; and (8) hollow tubular tile floors: Birkmire, *Planning and Construction*, 130–31.

35. As quoted in "The Engineer in Building," *Record and Guide* 56 (19 October 1895), 515.

36. Purdy, "The Relation of the Engineer to the Architect," *American Architect* 87 (11 February 1905), 43. Purdy, with his partner at the time, Charles G. Wade, had engineered the frame of the second Rand McNally Building in Chicago (1889–90). This was the first all-steel frame and, with the exception of one masonry party wall, full-skeleton construction. Since 1893 Purdy had been in partnership with Lightner Henderson, and their New York office was established in 1894. As our notes and bibliography indicate, Purdy's papers and articles are a useful source of information on building technology and the state of the engineering profession.

37. Without acknowledging his source: Birkmire, *Planning and Construction*, 14–15.

38. Schuyler, "The 'Sky-scraper' Up to Date," *Architectural Record* 8 (January–March 1899), 233 (Union Trust Building); and Schuyler, *The Woolworth Building* (n.p., 1913), as reprinted in

American Architecture and Other Writings by Montgomery Schuyler, ed. William H. Jordy and Ralph Coe, 2: 613 (Cambridge: Belknap Press of Harvard Univ. Press, 1961). On the Union Trust and American Surety buildings, see Chapter 7.

39. Sullivan, "The Tall Office Building Artistically Considered," *Lippincott's Magazine* 57 (March 1896), 403.

40. With justification, Schuyler questioned Sullivan's rationale for combining the first and second stories as the lowest section of the building, observing that in reality the second floor was just like the ones above and that Sullivan's motivation was actually aesthetic, that he wanted a base more in proportion to the total height: Schuyler, "The 'Sky-scraper' Up to Date," 255.

41. "More Views on High Buildings," *Record and Guide* 53 (30 June 1894), 1009.

42. *New York Tribune* [1894]; quoted in Francisco Mujica, *History of the Skyscraper* (Paris: Archaeology and Architecture, 1929), 33.

43. Thomas Hastings, "High Buildings and Good Architecture: What Principles Should Govern Their Design," *Proceedings of the Twenty-eighth Annual Convention of the American Institute of Architects* (16 October 1894), 147.

44. Vincent J. Scully, Jr., *American Architecture and Urbanism* (New York: Frederick A. Praeger, 1969), 144.

45. Kerr, "The Tall Building Question," *Engineering Record* 24 (31 October 1891), 343.

46. "The Manhattan Life Building," *Record and Guide* 53 (16 June 1894), 967.

47. Mujica, *History of the Skyscraper*, 45.

48. News summary, *American Architect* 51 (11 January 1896), 13.

49. *The Building Code as Finally Adopted by the Building Code Commission of the City of New York* (1899), pt. III, sec. 11, 8; and see also "Legislation to Restrict Height of Buildings Advised by Chamber of Commerce," *New York Times*, 3 January 1896.

50. That, however, lasted only until 1902, when the limit was extended to 260 feet. In 1911 it was reduced to 200 feet: Charles M. Nichols, comp., *Studies on Building Height Limitations in Large Cities with Special Reference to Conditions in Chicago* (Chicago: Chicago Real Estate Board Library, 1928), 14.

51. These events are summarized in Harvey A. Kantor, "Modern Urban Planning in New York City: Origins and Evolution, 1890–1933" (Ph.D. diss., New York Univ., 1971), esp. 168–

73. See also chapter bibliography.

52. Architects, including Post, quoted in minutes of A. J. Bloor, secretary, in "New York Chapter, A.I.A.–High Building Limit," *American Architect* 52 (30 May 1896), 86–87.

53. From the New York Board of Trade and Transportation Papers, as quoted in Kantor, "Modern Urban Planning in New York City," 173. The board had also recommended that all buildings over 137 feet have two separate stairways from ground floor to roof and complete fire-fighting equipment, such equipment to be added to existing buildings as well as incorporated in new ones.

54. Flagg, "The High Building Question in New York," *American Architect* 52 (16 May 1896), 61; and Flagg, "The Dangers of High Buildings," *The Cosmopolitan* 21 (May 1896), 70–79, esp. 72.

55. Blackall, "High Buildings," *Brickbuilder* 5 (February 1896), 29.

7. Monuments to Commercial Power and Corporate Prestige, 1889–95

1. "A Great Amphitheatre," *New York Sun*, 8 June 1890. See also Leland M. Roth, *McKim, Mead & White, Architects* (New York: Harper & Row, 1983), 158–65, where the clear spans of the steel truss roof are said to have measured 167 by 277 feet. The proprietors included Andrew Carnegie, Hiram Hitchcock of the Fifth Avenue Hotel, Edward S. Stokes, and Stanford White, among others.

2. Quotation from *New York Recorder*, 14 October 1891, in McKim, Mead & White scrapbook, McKim, Mead & White Collection, The New-York Historical Society.

3. *New York World*, 15 February 1891, in McKim, Mead & White scrapbook.

4. Schuyler, "The Works of R. H. Robertson," *Architectural Record* 6 (October–December 1896), 216–17.

The iron contractor for the building was Jackson Architectural Iron Works. Fireproofing: Raritan Hollow and Porous Brick Co. See also Lisa Konigsberg, "The Lincoln Building," New York City Landmarks Preservation Commission designation report, 12 July 1988; and Andrew S. Dolkart, National Register Nomination for the Lincoln Building, 1983.

5. "The Union Trust Company's New Building," *Record and Guide* 44 (16 November 1889), 1534. See also "The Union Trust Company," *Record and Guide* 45 (1 February 1890), 149.

6. "The Manhattan Life Building," *Record and Guide* 53 (16 June 1894), 968; Russell Sturgis, "The Works of George B. Post," *Architectural Record* Great American Architects Series, no. 4 (June 1898), 20; and also Schuyler, "The 'Sky-scraper' Up to Date," *Architectural Record* 8 (January–March 1899), 233. It should be noted that the building's two street fronts were alike in design, though different in materials.

Building dimensions: 72 feet wide (Broadway) by 77 feet wide (New Street) by 106.5 feet deep. Height: 196 feet (Broadway); 206 feet (New Street). Contractor: David H. King, Jr. Fireproofing: Raritan Hollow and Porous Brick Co. Demolished c. 1930.

7. "The Pulitzer Building," *New York World*, souvenir issue, 10 December 1890.

8. *Mail and Express*, 20 March 1889, in Post small scrapbooks folder, Post Collection, The New-York Historical Society.

9. "The Pulitzer Building."

10. "The New York World Building," *Engineering and Building Record* 22 (1 November 1890), 342–43; 22 (8 November 1890), 358–60. The intermediate foundation piers were 7 feet, 10 inches in height on a 100-foot-9-inch footing. The intermediate subgrade piers were connected by inverted granite arches now specified by code.

11. "The Pulitzer Building."

12. "The Pulitzer Building."

13. Quotations, in order, from "Metropolitan Architecture," *Rochester (N.Y.) Post Express*, 16 August 1890, in McKim, Mead & White scrapbook; and "The New World Building," *Record and Guide* 45 (14 June 1890), 879.

14. United States Federal Works Agency, Work Projects Administration, *New York City Guide* (New York: Random House, 1939), 99. Masonry: R. L. Darragh. Ironwork: J. B. & J. M. Cornell. Fireproofing: Raritan Hollow and Porous Brick Co. Terra-cotta: Perth Amboy Terra Cotta Co. Plumbing and gas fittings: J. A. Rossman. Heating and ventilating: Baker, Smith & Co. Lighting: United States Electric Light Co. Elevators: Otis Brothers. Engineers: Post's engineering staff. Designer in charge: Robert Maynicke. According to *New York World*, 18 December 1894, Richard Morris Hunt served as one of several professional advisers.

15. He designed the plan and houses of Tuxedo Park, New York, an exclusive sporting community undertaken for millionaire Pierre Lorillard IV (1885–86). Emily Post, the famous arbiter of social behavior, was Bruce Price's

daughter. Her husband, Edwin Main Post, was George B. Post's first cousin.

16. Barr Ferree, "A Talk with Bruce Price," *Architectural Record* Great American Architects Series, no. 5, (June 1899), 76. Price also spoke of a revised, thirty-four-story design—likewise unexecuted—that he had subsequently made for another site. Although Price's drawing indicates a midblock site, some sources state that the building was to rise on the site of its old building at the corner of Park Row and Frankfort streets: "That Thirty-two-story Building," *Record and Guide* 47 (18 April 1891), 608.

17. NBD 1552–1889 and *A History of Real Estate, Building and Architecture in New York City During the Last Quarter of a Century* (1898; rpt., New York: Record and Guide, 1967), 471, and see photograph, p. 581.

18. According to Fryer, the frame was steel and the curtain walls only 12 in. thick: William J. Fryer, "A Review of the Development of Structural Iron," in *A History of Real Estate*, 471. However, the building permit (NBD 1 and 2–1890) gives the thickness of Columbia's curtain walls as 20 in., 16 in., and 12 in. and describes the framing members as iron. P. E. Raque, the engineer who consulted on the addition of three stories in 1910, confirmed that the frame was indeed skeleton, and all-iron: "The Extension of the Columbia Building, New York," *Engineering Record* 62 (23 July 1910), 100–102.

19. "The Columbia Building," *Record and Guide* 46 (27 December 1890), 869. Other dimensions: 84 feet wide (Trinity Place). Height: 156 feet. Construction: Union Iron Works. Four hydraulic Otis elevators. Ventilated by electric fans. Demolished 1930.

The Jackson Building (1891–92; demolished), designed by William H. Birkmire for the Jackson Iron Works, was yet another early skeleton-framed building. Erected on the north side of Union Square, it was a narrow, eleven-story infill building that extended from 31 East 17th to 36 East 18th Street. The framing elements were all-iron: see Birkmire, *Skeleton Construction in Buildings*, 4th ed. (New York: John Wiley & Sons, 1912), chapter 7.

20. "Havemeyer Building," *Record and Guide* 51 (28 January 1893), 133.

21. Hand-tamped around the columns and below the footings, the concrete rested on compact wet sand with the footing load spread widely enough for a unit loading of 6,000 psf. The settlement was expected to vary from five-

eighths to 1.5 inches, and a provision was made to counter this unequal settlement by jacking up the low columns and inserting steel shims.

Detailed sources of information on the building's construction include Post's record book entries, esp. 30 April 1891 to 8 August 1893, and Post's specifications for the foundation renewal (c. 1903), both Post Collection. Also NBD 783–1891; and Birkmire, *Skeleton Construction in Buildings*, chapter 6. Building ground dimensions: 51 feet (Cortlandt Street) by 214 feet (Church Street) by 63 feet (Dey Street). Height: 193 feet. Masonry: J. & L. Weber. Ironwork: J. B. & J. M. Cornell. Carpentry: V. J. Hedden & Sons. Terra-cotta work: Perth Amboy Terra Cotta Co. Plumbing and gasfitting: Byrne & Tucker. Heating and ventilating: Baker, Smith & Co. Cost: $1,300,000. The earliest tenants included Consolidated Wire Works Co., National Tube Works Co., Delamater Iron Works, Westinghouse Air Brake Co., Henry Abbott (jeweler), L. & E. Weber (mason builders), and the Café Cottentin. Storefronts altered 1912–13 by Post. Demolished 1933.

22. The box columns, which had outside dimensions of 10¼ by 13 inches, were composed of four plates joined by angles. The girders were mostly I-section, 12-inch at 20, 32, and 40 pounds per foot. Beams were mostly 9-inch at 27 pounds per foot, with varying spans of around 20 feet. The diameters of the wrought-iron bracing rods diminished from 1¼ inches, from grade level to the eleventh floor, to 1 inch on the twelfth floor, to three-quarters of an inch on the thirteenth. The specified physical properties of the wrought iron used in the frame were an elastic limit of 24,000–26,000 psi and an ultimate tensile strength of 48,000–50,000 psi; of the steel, an elastic limit of 28,000–30,000 psi and an ultimate tensile strength of 60,000 psi.: Birkmire, *Skeleton Construction in Buildings*, 112–115, 118, 123–24.

23. Havemeyer Building accident (news item), *American Architect* 36 (14 May 1892), 93.

24. "Havemeyer Building," 133–34.

25. "The Havemeyer Building—A Type," *Record and Guide* 51 (29 April 1893), 655, 657.

26. J. C., "An Irrepressible Conflict," *Record and Guide* 54 (6 October 1894), 461. On both buildings see Charles Savage, "Home Life Insurance Company Building (incorporating the former Postal Telegraph Building) . . . ," New York City Landmarks Preservation Commission designation report, 12 November 1991.

27. Reginald Pelham Bolton, *The High Office-Buildings of New York* (London: Institu-

tion of Civil Engineers, 1901), 28. See also "The Postal Cable and Telegraph Company and the Home Life Insurance Company Buildings in Broadway," *Record and Guide* 49 (26 March 1892), 469.

28. "The Postal Cable and Telegraph Company and the Home Life Insurance Company Buildings in Broadway," 469; and "The Home Life Building Competition," *Record and Guide* 49 (14 May 1892), 764–65. The other invited competitors were McKim, Mead & White; Babb, Cook & Willard; Carrère & Hastings; and Brunner & Tryon.

29. Pierre LeBrun's Free Church of St. Mary the Virgin (1894–95), New York City, was heralded as the first steel-framed church: *New York Evening Post*, 7 December 1895. On Napoleon LeBrun & Sons: Charles C. Savage, "Metropolitan Life Insurance Company Tower," New York City Landmarks Preservation Commission designation report, 13 June 1989.

30. Birkmire, *Skeleton Construction in Buildings*, 84, 85. According to Moses King, ed., *King's Handbook of New York City*, 2d ed. (Boston: Moses King, 1893), 674, the building was begun in June 1892. Apparently the building permit was filed only later: NBD 349–1892. Ground dimensions: 55 feet front by 30 feet rear by 107.5 feet deep. Originally the building was to have had only a 30.5-foot frontage on Broadway, but early in 1893 the company acquired 25 additional feet from the Merchants' Exchange National Bank, and the original elevation was then altered: *King's Handbook*, 674. Contractor: John Downey.

31. "The Exposure Fire in the Home Life Insurance Building, New York City," *Engineering News* 40 (8 December 1898), 366–67; "The Home Life Building Fire: An Object Lesson," *Record and Guide* 62 (10 December 1898), 864–65; "Cement Floors: A Lesson from the Broadway Fire," *Record and Guide* 62 (10 December 1898), 866–67; and I. N. Phelps Stokes, *The Iconography of Manhattan Island* (New York: Robert H. Dodd, 1915–26), 5: 2071.

32. "The Mail and Express Building," *Record and Guide* 49 (2 April 1892), 506; and "The Place of Marble in Modern Architecture," *Record and Guide* 52 (23 December 1893), 196. See also Robert A. M. Stern, Gregory Gilmartin, and John Montague Massengale, *New York 1900: Metropolitan Architecture and Urbanism 1890–1915* (New York: Rizzoli, 1983), 150.

33. "Architectural Development," *Record and Guide* 49 (11 June 1892), 916.

34. Lisa Konigsberg, "The Union Building

(Former Decker Building)," New York City Landmarks Preservation Commission designation report, 12 July 1988. Of cage construction with a cast-iron and steel frame, the Decker is about 30 feet wide by 138 feet deep.

35. As quoted in S. B. Landau, "The Tall Office Building Artistically Reconsidered: Arcaded Buildings of the New York School, c. 1870–1890," in *In Search of Modern Architecture: A Tribute to Henry Russell Hitchcock*, ed. Helen Searing (Cambridge: MIT Press, 1982), 160.

36. In the mid-1980s the firm of Warner, Burns, Toan & Lunde converted the building, renamed the Archives, to residential use with retail space on the ground floor. Analysis of the building's structure was facilitated by examination of architectural drawings in the firm's collection and by Teitelbaum Group et al., "The Archives: A Redevelopment Plan," (n.p., [1985?]). Edbrooke's original design is illustrated in "New Appraiser's Stores," *Record and Guide* 53, supplement (12 May 1894), 103; see also Marjorie Pearson, memo dated 9 June 1977 appended to New York City Landmarks Preservation Commission, "United States Federal Building," designation report, 15 March 1966.

37. Montgomery Schuyler, "The Works of R. H. Robertson," *Architectural Record* 6 (September–June 1897), 216–17. See also "Extension of the Corn Exchange Bank Building, New York," *Engineering Record* 45 (14 June 1902), 557–59; and Christopher S. Gray, "A 'Noble Monument to Thrift' with an Unusually Modern Air," *New York Times*, 1 November 1987. Also NBD 213–1893; Alteration docket 377–1902; and *King's Handbook of New York*, 729–30. Mason: Robert L. Darragh. Carpenter: John Downey.

38. "A Picturesque Sky-Scraper," *Architectural Record* 5 (January–March 1896), 299, 302.

39. "Architectural Competition for the Manhattan Life Building," *Record and Guide* 49 (14 May 1892), 765–66. The invited competitors were C. W. Clinton; G. B. Post; J. R. Thomas; Wood & Palmer; Babb, Cook & Willard; Edward Kendall; S. D. Hatch; Carrère & Hastings; and Kimball & Thompson. J. C. Cady & Company and Lamb & Rich also submitted designs, presumably in the second stage of the competition.

40. Fryer, "A Review of the Development of Structural Iron," 479; and Wendell Buck, *From Quill Pens to Computers in an Account of the First One Hundred and Twenty-Five Years of the Manhattan Life Insurance Company of New York* (New York: Manhattan Life Insurance, [1974?]), 32–33.

41. Francis H. Kimball, "The Construction of a Great Building," *Engineering Magazine* 8 (February 1895), 879. NBD 110–1893, however, records a much longer time, perhaps including the finishing of the interiors and certainly the time it took for the building inspector to get to the site. It states that the building was begun 3 September 1893 and completed 15 August 1895.

42. See "Pneumatic Foundations for the Manhattan Life Building, New York," *Engineering News* 30 (7 December 1893), 458–59; and chapter bibliography.

Charles Sooysmith was the president of his own New York City company, Sooysmith & Co., civil engineers and contractors, from 1884 to 1900; he served as a consultant on the construction of the New York City subway system. His father, the bridge engineer William Sooy Smith, had recommended the use of (well-type) caissons for the foundation of Adler & Sullivan's Stock Exchange (1893–94), which was the first Chicago building to have such a foundation. Smith was also instrumental in developing a successful piling system for the foundations of Chicago skyscrapers, and he improved the construction of the pneumatic caisson.

43. Around 1928 the Central Union Trust Company bought the building. The new owner, which required large vaults for its bank securities, in 1929 undertook the enlargement of the basement, a project that involved underpinning and inserting new columns. When the foundation structure was removed in the course of this work, it was discovered that "most" of the brick piers and concrete caissons did not extend to bedrock, as had been indicated in the engineering press at the time of construction, but to hardpan at an average elevation of minus 37 feet, above the minus 40- to minus 54-foot bedrock level. Apparently the belief at the time of construction was that hardpan was equivalent to bedrock in bearing capacity: George W. Glick, "Underpinning 17-Story Building . . . ," *Engineering News-Record* 103 (8 August 1929), 214–18.

44. "Manhattan Life Insurance Company [building] . . . Foundations," *American Architect* 39 (4 February 1893), 66; and Charles Sooysmith, "The Caisson Foundations of the Manhattan Life Insurance Building" (letter to editor), *American Architect* 39 (18 February 1893), 111.

45. Transmitted to the United States and

manufactured by Rafael Guastavino, the remarkably durable Guastavino system of construction is described in George R. Collins, "The Transfer of Thin Masonry Vaulting from Spain to America," *JSAH* 27 (October 1968), 176–201. On the details of the framing and conditions of loading: "Manhattan Life Insurance Building, New York City," *Engineering Record* 30 (17 November 1894), 408–10; and see chapter bibliography under title of this article.

The loading factors were as follows: floor (contents plus structure), 175 psf; wind load of main block, 30 psf; wind load of dome, 50 psf. The maximum wind velocity at the site to date of construction was 84 mph, equivalent to a pressure of 35 psf according to the formula used by the structural engineer Charles O. Brown ($P = 0.005V^2$). The load would at present be calculated as 18.1 psf ($P = 0.00256V^2$).

46. "The Manhattan Life Building," *Record and Guide*, supplement (12 May 1894), 140.

47. Schuyler, "The Works of Francis H. Kimball and Kimball & Thompson," *Architectural Record* 7 (April–June 1898), 510. See also "The Manhattan Life Building," 968, for earlier comments of the same nature and also criticism of "the brute masses of common brick" that formed the side walls.

48. "Enlarging and Remodeling the Manhattan Life Building," *Engineering Record* 47 (4 April 1903), 338–42.

Contractor (original building): Richard Deeves. Fireproofing: Raritan Hollow and Porous Brick Co. Terra-cotta: New York Architectural Terra Cotta Co. Ornamental copper work: James White, Brooklyn. Electric Power Plant: New York Electric Equipment Co. Ventilation: Gillis & Geoghegan. Glass: VanHorne, Griffen & Co. Plumbing: J. N. Knight & Co. Addition of 1903–4 with Boller & Hodge as structural engineers. T. Kennard Thomson, C.E., was also involved. General contractor: Arthur McMullin & Co.

49. He also charged a lower fee than the standard 5 percent of construction costs agreed to by the other competitors: Nancy Goeschel, "Former New York Life Insurance Building," New York City Landmarks Preservation Commission designation report (10 February 1987), 8, 15 n. 15.

50. The sculpture group has been removed. Height of building: 188 feet (to top of tower, 270 feet). While Hatch was still listed as architect of the addition, the following firms were engaged in the construction. Masonry and foundations: Lancelot W. Armstrong. Marble front: Norcross Brothers. Carpentry and cabinetwork: Rudolph Hildebrand. Fireproofing: Perth Amboy Terra Cotta Co. Cost of foundations: $1 million. Builder: Charles T. Wills. Since 1967 owned by the City of New York.

51. See Moses King, ed., *King's Photographic Views of New York* (Boston: Moses King, 1895), 326.

52. "The American Tract Society Building," *Record and Guide* 57 (29 February 1896), 343.

53. "Erection of the American Tract Society's Building, New York," *Engineering Record* 31 (15 December 1894), 44–46; and, on the foundations, "Reconstructing the Morse Building, New York," *Engineering Record* 44 (2 November 1901), 422–24. See also NBD 538–1894.

Building ground dimensions: 100.5 feet (Nassau Street) by 94.5 feet (Spruce Street) by 94 feet (rear). Contractor: John Downey. Estimated cost: $900,000. Structural engineer for design of frame: W. W. Crehore. Iron contractor: Keystone Bridge Works of Carnegie Steel Co. Steel erection: Atlas Iron Construction Co.

54. Barr Ferree, "The Modern Office Building," *Inland Architect and News Record* 27 (June 1896), 45.

55. "American Tract Society's 20-Story Office Building," *Engineering News* 32 (27 December 1894), 526. See also Schuyler, "The Works of R. H. Robertson," 217.

56. "Fall of Passenger Elevator in New York City" (titles vary), *Engineering News* 38 (16 September 1897), 183; 38 (23 September 1897), 202–4; 38 (30 September 1897), 218–19; also "The Elevator Accident in the American Tract Society Building," *Engineering Record* 43 (21 November 1896), 456.

57. Quotations from Barr Ferree, "Latest Ideas in High Buildings," *New York World*, 18 February 1894.

58. Ferree, "Latest Ideas in High Buildings."

59. Russell Sturgis, "A Critique of the Works of Bruce Price," *Architectural Record* Great American Architects Series, no. 5, (June 1899), 4; and Barr Ferree, "A Talk With Bruce Price," 75–76.

60. William H. Birkmire, *The Planning and Construction of High Office-Buildings* (New York: John Wiley and Sons, 1898), 98–101. See also on construction features, American Surety Co. building (news item), *Engineering News* 32 (26 July 1894), 71; "The American Surety Building," *Scientific American* 73 (23 November 1895), 329; and "The American Surety Building," *Engineering Record* 34 (13 June 1896), 28–29.

61. The first course of the grillage that covered the brick piers comprised ten 24-inch I-beams, each weighing 80 pounds per foot and extending entirely across the pier; the second course, which ran transverse to the first, consisted of five 20-inch I-beams, each weighing 64 pounds per foot and covering the central areas of pier tops. The column loads were: minimum, 1,326,000 pounds; maximum, 2,560,000 pounds. For the columns on cantilevers: minimum, 1,326,000 pounds; maximum, 1,492,000 pounds. All dead and live loads were distributed over a total of thirty-two columns: "Caisson Foundation Piers of the American Surety Company's Building in New York City," *Scientific American* 71 (25 August 1894), 113, 120.

62. Under the modern formula, the allowable wind drift at maximum is 0.003H (height); a 312-foot building would be allowed 11.23 inches of drift, or 5.62 inches on either side of the central axis. At the time, the bending moment on the building under an 82 mph wind would have been calculated as 71,790,134 foot-pounds, ascertained by first multiplying the area of the front elevation, in this case 26,417 square feet, by a pressure of 27 psf ($P = 0.004V^2$). The total pressure would, therefore, equal 713,259 pounds. If the resultant of the wind load acts at the midpoint of the area (actually somewhat below), the bending or over-turning moment would equal 111,268,404 foot-pounds, too high by contemporary standards. Using the modern formula of $P = .00256V^2$, the unit pressure equals 17.2 psf, yielding a total pressure of 454,372.4 lbs. and a bending moment of 70,882,094.4 foot-pounds. The code would now specify 20 psf.

63. Ferree, "A Talk with Bruce Price," 75 (quotation), 78–79. Although Price did not say so, the *Record and Guide* reported that at the level of the "capital," the glass was returned to the plane of the wall: "The American Surety Building," 57 (14 March 1896), 428. The same source noted the "Chicagoan spirit" of the tripartite design.

64. See "Proposed Treatment of Figures to Be Placed on the American Surety Company's Building . . . ," *American Architect* 48 (25 May 1895), 83.

Site cost: $1,435,000. Estimated building cost: $1,250,000 (new-building permit 529-1894). Foundations: Foundation & Contracting Co. Builder: Charles T. Wills. Iron contractor: Jackson Iron Works. Fireproof materials: Henry Maurer & Son. Five elevators. "Revised Floor Plans" dated 1 July 1895 are in the collection of Avery Library.

65. Editorial, *Record and Guide* 57 (16 May 1896), 833; and *New York Standard Guide: New York, the Metropolis of the Western World* (New York: Foster & Reynolds, [1909?]), 110–11. Alterations of 1896 by Price and Wills connected the two buildings. According to Gail Fenske and Deryck Holdsworth, "Corporate Identity and the New York Office Building: 1895–1915," in *The Landscape of Modernity: Essays on New York City, 1900–1940*, ed. David Ward and Olivier Zunz (New York: Russell Sage Foundation, 1992), 134, the American Surety Company bought the Schermerhorn Building in 1919.

66. Alteration permit 205–1920: Raised to 26 stories (338 feet) and in 1920–22 widened by four bays on Broadway and Pine Street. New dimensions: 123 feet wide (front) by 118 feet wide (rear) by 126 feet deep (Pine Street) by 100 feet deep (south side). Builder: Cauldwell Wingate Co. Ground-story entrance and other alterations made in 1975 by Kajima International, designers, and Welton Becket Associates, architects, for the Bank of Tokyo: "The Bank of Tokyo: New Image with Old Roots," *Architectural Record* 159 (June 1976), 89–94.

8. The Syndicate-Built Skyscraper, Technical Advances, Continuing Debate, 1895–1900

1. The address is 27 William Street and 40 Exchange Place. In 1903 four stories were added: "The Question of the Skyscraper," *Record and Guide* 72 (29 August 1903), 374. One more was added at some later time, and the lower stories have been altered. Building ground dimensions: 107 feet (Exchange Place) by 70.5 feet (William Street) by 182 feet (south side).

2. Sand at that level was test-loaded to 13,000 psf, which was followed by a maximum settlement of 9 to 13 inches. From then on, the sand was stable. From the bottom up, the foundations consisted of a 12-inch-thick bed of concrete over the entire area to keep the unit load at 2,400 feet per column and a double grillage of steel beams with footings above. On the foundations: "Hydraulic Jacks as Part of a Permanent Foundation," *American Architect* 52 (4 April 1896), 1–2; 52 (18 April 1896), 21; and also "Preliminary Foundation Tests for the St.

Paul Building," *Engineering Record* 33 (2 May 1896), 388.

3. Portal-arch bracing had been used in the frame of the Venetian Building in Chicago (1891–92; Holabird & Roche), which was probably engineered by Corydon T. Purdy. See Purdy, "The Steel Skeleton Type of High Building," *Engineering News* 26 (26 December 1891), 606. Purdy had also been responsible for the use of portal-arch bracing in the Old Colony Building (1893–94), also in Chicago. On the St. Paul Building's frame: "Improved Steel Column and Girder Construction," *Engineering Record* 32 (15 June 1895), 43–44. For a full account of the construction details, "The St. Paul Building, New York City," *Engineering News* 35 (7 May 1896), 310–12.

4. "Plumbing in the St. Paul Building, New York City," *Engineering Record* 35 (13 February 1897), 232–33. The plumbing contractor was Rossman & Bracken Co.

5. Post working drawings for St. Paul Building, Post Collection. The New-York Historical Society.

Building ground dimensions, from NBD 1337-1895: 39 feet (Park Row) by 28 feet (Broadway) by 54 feet (rear) by 83 feet (Ann Street) by 104 feet (inside) deep. Total cost: $1,089,826.10. Demolished 1958.

6. "The Tall Buildings of New York," *Munsey's Magazine* 18 (March 1898), 841.

7. "The Most Modern Instance," *Record and Guide* 59 (5 June 1897), 962.

8. On the gallery and the architects see David Van Zanten, "The Architecture of the Layton Art Gallery," in *1888: Frederick Layton and His World* (Milwaukee: Milwaukee Art Museum, 1988), 242–55. Credited with having designed many buildings for American cities, G. A. Audsley was responsible for the Church of St. Edward the Confessor and the Joan of Arc School in Philadelphia: *New York Times*, 24 June 1925. Known as the "organ-architect," he made the St. Louis Exposition organ (1904), which was later purchased by John Wanamaker for his famous Philadelphia store.

9. It may be significant that George Foster Peabody (1852–1938) was related to the American philanthropist George Peabody (1795–1869). George Peabody had lived in London, where he had financed housing for the urban poor; nothing indicates foreign financing for the Bowling Green Offices, however. Spencer Trask & Company had numerous American branches but none in England or Europe, and there seems to be no connection to Frederick Layton, who encountered the architect brothers on board ship while crossing the Atlantic to Liverpool in 1883. Fragmentary evidence from the McKim, Mead & White records suggests the possibility of an invited competition. In 1894 the lawyer Joseph F. Stier paid that firm a flat fee of $5,000 for a commercial building project for 5–11 Broadway: Leland M. Roth, *The Architecture of McKim, Mead & White, 1870–1920: A Building List* (New York: Garland, 1978), 145. Trask himself was so interested in the Bowling Green area that he published a short history of it: Spencer Trask, *Bowling Green*, in *Half Moon Series* (New York: G. P. Putnam's Sons, 1898), vol. 2 (May 1898). On Trask's company: [Eugene Koop,] *History of Spencer Trask & Co* (n.p., 1941).

10. "Giants of Broadway," *Mail and Express*, 2 May 1896.

11. George Ashdown Audsley, "The Designing of Tall Office Buildings" (c. 1896), in "Note Books of George Ashdown Audsley (188-?–1924)," vol. 3, collection Music Division, Performing Arts Research Center, New York Public Library.

12. Spencer Trask & Company, *Bowling Green Offices* (New York: Spencer Trask, 1896), unpaged, New York Public Library. Period sources give the height as sixteen stories, but the building rose a full seventeen stories above the sidewalk on the Greenwich Street side, and sixteen and three-quarters on Broadway.

13. "The Bowling Green Building," *Record and Guide* 59 (15 May 1897), 826; see also *Bowling Green Offices* and Van Zanten, "The Architecture of the Layton Art Gallery," 247–48.

14. Judging from NBD 1439-1895, where it is recorded "Tower abandoned," the original intention was to include a tower as part of the design. Estimated cost $1,800,000. 1912–13: stoops and encroachments removed from front by Ludlow & Peabody. 1917–20: enlarged by Ludlow & Peabody to include a full eighteenth story and above that a four-story tower set back from the front of the building. Builder: M. P. Smith. Information from Department of Buildings records.

15. According to Birkmire, the foundation was begun on 10 July 1896; the steel work was started on 7 August and completed on 23 October; as of 9 December the building was enclosed, and by the end of that month it was ready for occupancy: William H. Birkmire, *The Planning and Construction of High Office-Buildings* (New York: John Wiley and Sons,

1898), 81. Yet NBD 1439–1895 (26 July) records dates of completion in April and August of 1897. Even allowing for a delay in the arrival of the buildings department inspector, this seems too much of a discrepancy.

16. The passenger elevators incorporated large hydraulic cylinders and operated with a maximum working water pressure of 150 psi, so that the ascending and descending speeds, with the maximum car load of 1,000 pounds going up and 2,000 going down, were 600 and 450 feet per minute, respectively: Birkmire, *Planning and Construction*, 246–47.

17. Birkmire, *Planning and Construction*, 81–82. By 1911 the building was known as Citizens' Central National Bank.

18. Berg, who had studied at the Ecole des Beaux-Arts, was also responsible for other buildings in the city, for town houses, for the renovation of St. John's Evangelical Lutheran Church in 1886, and for the ostentatiously "Parisian" Windsor Arcade built on the east side of Fifth Avenue between 46th and 47th streets (1901; demolished).

19. NBD 240–1896; "Record Price for Manhattan Land," *Record and Guide* 84 (18 December 1909), 1128; "The Gillender Building," *Engineering Record* 35 (16 January 1897), 140–44, 146; and "Pneumatic Caisson Foundations for the Gillender Building, New York City," *Engineering News* 37 (7 January 1897), 13–14. Consulting engineer: Henry W. Post. Steel fabricators: Maryland Steel Co. and Pencoyd Bridge Co. Steel erectors: Post & McCord.

20. The $600 to $700 range is given in "Record Price for Manhattan Land," 1128. Three years later the same journal gives the sale price as $813 per square foot: "Wall Street Ready for Building Movement," *Record and Guide* 90 (9 November 1912), 850. A less reliable source reports the sale price as $825 per square foot and calls it "the highest price ever paid anywhere in the world": Moses King, comp., *King's Views of New York, 1896–1915, & Brooklyn, 1905* (rpt., New York: Arno, 1977), 1915, p. 26.

21. "A 16-Story Steel Frame Building to Be Demolished," *Engineering News* 63 (14 April 1910), 432; "The Third Tallest Tower," *Record and Guide* 85 (23 April 1910), 864; "Wrecking the Gillender Building, New York," *Engineering Record* 61 (11 June 1910), 755–56.

22. The specifications always called for coating the steel before shipping with linseed oil and primer paint, but it is questionable whether this had much value. See "The Gillender Building Sound," *Record and Guide* 85 (28 May

1910), 1141; Maximilian Toch, "The Condition of the Steel of the Gillender Building," *Engineering News* 64 (14 July 1910), 54–55; Charles H. Nichols, "The Condition of the Steelwork in the Gillender Building" (letter), *Engineering Record* 62 (5 November 1910), 531–32; and Maximilian Toch, "The Condition of the Steel of the Gillender Building; Final Report," *Engineering News* 66 (17 April 1911), 204.

23. Described in "The Tallest Building in New York," *Record and Guide* 57 (6 June 1896), 972; "The Park Row Building, 30 Stories High; New York City," *Engineering News* 36 (8 October 1896), 226–29; and "Towns under a Single Roof: A Common Building Operation," *Record and Guide* 66 (27 October 1900), 531. Information also from NBD 291–1896 and Department of Buildings records.

24. Excavations were made to minus 34 feet; four thousand piles were then driven through compact sand to depths varying from minus 55 to minus 59 feet, and the total live and dead weight of the completed building was 50,000 tons, yielding a load per pile of 25,000 pounds. The piling was capped with a 10-inch layer of concrete with granite aggregate, and the footings are brick pyramids 4 feet, 9 inches high with granite caps. Atop the pyramids rests a grillage comprising steel I-beams and a complex arrangement of massive distributing box girders added to distribute the load uniformly. The girders varied in length from 8 to 47 feet and from 4 to 8.5 feet in depth: "New York's Tallest Office Building," *Carpentry and Building* 20 (September 1898), 216; and "The Park Row Building, 30 Stories High," 226–27.

25. The specifications called for medium carbon steel with an ultimate tensile strength of 60,000 to 68,000 psi and an elastic limit greater than half the ultimate strength. The minimum elongation of an 8-inch bar was set at 20 percent of its length, and it had to be possible to bend the bar, when cold, to 180 degrees without rupturing the outside fibers of the metal. Tests of 890 sample sections were conducted by Hallsted and McNaugher in Pittsburgh and New York. Of those, 870 were accepted, for a rejection rate of 2.25 percent: "Inspection of Steel for a 30-Story Building" (letter to editor), *Engineering News* 39 (27 January 1898), 61.

26. "Hollow Tile Fireproofing in the Park Row Syndicate Building" (titles vary), *Engineering News* 39 (14 April 1898), 234–35, 240; 39 (2 June 1898), 358.

27. "The Park Row," *Record and Guide* 62 (27 August 1898), 287–88. In spite of all the

criticism, several well-known artists and photographers have chosen to represent the building in paintings and photographs, among them Joseph Pennell, John Marin, and Charles Sheeler: Erica E. Hirshler, "The 'New New York' and the Park Row Building: American Artists View an Icon of the Modern Age," *American Art Journal* 21 (1989), 26–45.

28. "New Building for Park Row," *Record and Guide* 75 (3 June 1905), 1220. Belmont's application for a permit to build the smaller structure was initially filed in mid-1899.

The lot immediately south of the Park Row Building, now vacant, contains the Park Row Building's air conditioning equipment.

29. The current for their operation was supplied by a Westinghouse 200-kilowatt generator driven by three compound horizontal steam engines, and the maximum power consumed by a fully loaded moving car was 3.5 kilowatt hours per car-mile: "The Elevator Equipment of the Ivins Syndicate Building, Park Row, New York," *Engineering News* 41 (27 April 1899), 273–75.

30. The first such gearless traction machine was installed in 1903 in the fifteen-story Beaver Building (1903–4; Clinton & Russell, architects at the intersection of Pearl and Beaver streets; just below Wall Street. The new elevator was described in a paper, "Passenger Elevators," read by Thomas E. Brown before the International Engineering Congress sponsored by the American Society of Civil Engineers in 1904. See chapter bibliography under Thomas E. Brown.

31. On the building: NBD 1232–1895; "The Syndicate Building," *Record and Guide* 57 (25 April 1896), 698 (illustrated); "Syndicate Building," *Mail and Express*, 2 May 1896; and *History of Architecture and the Building Trades of Greater New York* (New York: Union History, 1899), 2: 553.

32. "Building in Lower New York City," *Record and Guide* 58 (17 October 1896), 541.

33. "The Work of George Edward Harding & Gooch," *Architectural Record* 7 (July–September 1897), 114. See also "Cement Floors in High Buildings," *Record and Guide* 57 (6 June 1896), 869–70; and "Substructure of the Commercial Cable Building," *Engineering Record* 35 (17 April 1897), 427–29; 35 (8 May 1897), 493–95.

Cost of lot (7,536 square feet at $149.32 per square foot): $1,125,275.50. Elevators: Sprague Electric Co. In 1905 a sixteen-story addition designed by Stokes & Howells extended the building to the corner of New Street and Exchange Place: "Building Operations South of Chambers St.," *Record and Guide* 75 (4 February 1905), 243. Foundation consultant: T. Kennard Thomson, C.E. Caisson laying: Foundation Co. Steel framework: James Stewart & Co. By 1932 owned by the New York Stock Exchange and known as the Postal Building. Demolished c. 1954.

34. "Underpinning the Stokes Building, New York City," *Engineering Record* 34 (8 August 1896), 183–84; and "Handling a Heavy Foundation Girder in a Tall Building," *Engineering Record* 34 (17 October 1896), 369. Structural engineer: John Bogart. Contractor: Arthur McMullen & Co. Building ground dimensions: 41 by 69 feet. Building illustrated in "New Skyscrapers," *Record and Guide* 58 (24 October 1896), 586. Today the sites of the Queen Insurance and Stokes buildings are occupied by the glass-walled Chase Manhattan Bank Tower, completed in 1960.

35. "Column and Girder Construction in Dun Building, New York City," *Engineering Record* 39 (3 December 1898), 9–10.

The owner had filed a new-building permit for a twenty-three-story building in May of 1896, but the application was withdrawn and refiled in 1897 (NBD 176), with the number of stories reduced to fifteen. The building contractor of record is W. A. & F. E. Conover. Ground dimensions: about 61 by 130 feet. From about 1975 to 1992 the site was part of a city-owned parking lot, and since then a large federal office building has been completed on the site. The ground area of the new building has been curtailed somewhat by the recent discovery and official landmarking of extensive remains of an eighteenth-century African burial ground on the site and covering a large section of the civic center area.

36. "A Really Fire-Proof Building," *Record and Guide* 65 (17 March 1900), 451 (illustrated). This article has all the earmarks of a paid advertisement. See also "Fireproofing Company Urges Repeal," *Record and Guide* 76 (4 November 1905), 688–89.

37. Montgomery Schuyler, "The Works of Francis H. Kimball and Kimball & Thompson," *Architectural Record* 7 (April–June 1898), 511. See also Blanche Potter, *More Memories: Orlando Bronson Potter and Frederick Potter* (New York: J. J. Little & Ives, 1923), 355.

38. F. H. Kimball, "The Architectural Relations of the Steel-Skeleton Building," *Engineering Magazine* 13 (July 1897), 562; and

NBD 2179–1895. See also Charles O. Brown, "Engineering Problems of the Tall Building," *Engineering Magazine* 13 (June 1897), 413.

Ground dimensions: 78 feet (front) by 50 feet (rear) by 224 feet deep. Ground area: 14,000 square feet. Foundations: Foundation & Contracting Co. Contractor: Marc Eidlitz & Son. By 1932, the building was owned by 71 Broadway Corp. and reported to have a rental area of 190,000 square feet and to accommodate 2,200 people: W. Parker Chase, *New York, The Wonder City, 1932* (c. 1931; rpt., New York: New York Bound, 1983), 176.

39. A test of the Ellithorpe air cushion (news item), *Engineering News* 40 (28 July 1898), 56–57; "Elevator Air Cushions in Office Buildings," *Carpentry and Building* 20 (September 1898), 217–19; and "The Elevator Air-Cushion in the Empire Building, New York," *Iron Age;* reprinted in *American Architect* 63 (11 February 1899), 48.

40. Sturgis, "A Critique of the Works of Bruce Price," *Architectural Record* Great American Architects Series, no. 5 (June 1899), 12. See also "The St. James," *Record and Guide* 62 (10 September 1898), 349–50.

41. C. L. W. Eidlitz's handsome Townsend Building (1896), which is twelve stories tall and also tripartite, stands to the south of the St. James Building. The two are separated by a one-story store that in c. 1908 replaced a "hold-out" town house: Andrew Alpern and Seymour Durst, *Holdouts!* (New York: McGraw-Hill, 1984), 27–30.

42. "Views of the Washington Life Building . . . in Process of Construction from May 1st 1897 to May 1st 1898," photographs by F. E. Parshley of Brooklyn, N.Y., collection Avery Library; and "Sinking Foundations," *Record and Guide* 66 (11 August 1900), 178.

43. "The Washington Life Building," *Record and Guide* 61 (30 April 1898), 778.

Ground area: 9,500 square feet. Depth of foundation below curb: minus 75 feet. Height above curb: 279 feet. Estimated cost: $1,000,000: NBD 49-1897. Site now part of Liberty Plaza park (1974).

44. Narciso G. Menocal, "The Bayard Building: French Paradox and American Synthesis," *Sites* 13 (1985), 4–24, esp. 7–8.

45. The mortgage was recalled in June 1899. Perhaps not coincidentally, the rental prospectus for the Bayard includes a history of the Bank for Savings, illustrations of its old and new buildings, and a listing of its officers: *The Bayard Building* (New York: Rost, n.d.), un-paged. Robert Avery was the president of the United Loan & Investment Company.

46. Lyndon P. Smith, "The Schlesinger & Mayer Building: An Attempt to Give Functional Expression to the Architecture of a Department Store," *Architectural Record* 16 (July 1904), 53–60; and Smith, "The Home of an Artist-Architect, Louis H. Sullivan's Place at Ocean Springs, Mississippi," *Architectural Record* 17 (June 1905), 471–90. Smith's office was in the Bayard from 1900 to 1902.

Consulting engineer: George S. Hayes. Steel-work supplier: Passaic Rolling Mill Company. Sprague-Pratt elevators: Sprague Electric Company. Terra-cotta cladding of brick curtain walls: Perth Amboy Terra Cotta Company. Boilers: Heine Safety Boiler Co. Information from *The Bayard Building,* rental prospectus.

47. New-building permit 744-1897 (17 September).

48. Charles T. Wills purchased the Condicts' interest in 1900 and remained the owner until 1920. Interestingly, the 1901 Trow's City Directory (compiled in 1900) lists the Bayard as 65–67 Bleecker Street and the Condict as 69 Bleecker. The Bayard, however, covers both of those addresses. It has therefore been suggested that for a time the Bayard may have been internally divided between two owners: New York City Landmarks Preservation Commission, "Bayard-Condict Building," designation report, 25 November 1975, 4.

49. Plans are reproduced in William H. Jordy, "The Tall Buildings," *Louis Sullivan: The Function of Ornament,* ed. Wim de Wit (New York: W. W. Norton, 1986), 81, 118. The site adjoins that of the Manhattan Savings Bank Building, rebuilt in 1899 (Kimball & Thompson, architects), and at the rear opens onto Shinbone Alley, which was originally a mews lane when the street was built up with row houses.

50. Schuyler, "The 'Sky-scraper' Up to Date," *Architectural Record* 8 (January–March 1899), 257. On the building see also Russell Sturgis, "Good Things in Modern Architecture," *Architectural Record* 8 (July–September 1898), 101–2; "The Bayard Building," *Record and Guide* 62 (15 October 1898), 531–32; and Joseph Pell Lombardi, with Mary B. Dierickx, "The Bayard (Condict) Building: Louis H. Sullivan, Architect," New York, 1975?, collection Avery Library.

51. Schuyler, *The Woolworth Building* (n.p., 1913), as reprinted in William H. Jordy and Ralph Coe, *American Architecture and Other*

Writings by Montgomery Schuyler (Cambridge: Belknap Press of Harvard University Press, 1961), 2: 614. According to James T. Dillon, the building "may be the earliest extant example of the use of this material [polychromatic glazed terra-cotta] for a commercial building in the city": Dillon, "Broadway Chambers Building," New York City Landmarks Preservation Commission designation report, 14 January 1992, 10 n. 18.

52. Guy Kirkham, "Cass Gilbert, Master of Style," *Pencil Points* 15 (November 1934), 545. See also "Plumbing in the Broadway Chambers Building, New York," *Engineering Record* 41 (7 April 1900), 325–26; "The Broadway Chambers," *Architects' and Builders' Magazine* 33 (October 1900), 45–52; and George A. Fuller Company, *Broadway Chambers, A Modern Office Building* (New York: Andrew H. Kellogg, 1900), pamphlet distributed at Paris Exposition. The Fuller Company had established a branch office in New York City in 1896, and by 1900, taking advantage of the skyscraper building boom and the opportunity to build structures of unlimited height, had moved its main office there.

53. "Building Skyscrapers, Described by Cass Gilbert, Architect," *Record and Guide* 65 (23 June 1900), 1087, 1091.

Dimensions: 51 feet wide by 93 to 95 feet deep. Granite: John Peirce, Stony Creek, Connecticut. Bricks: T. B. Townsend Brick Co., Zanesville, Ohio. Iron and steel: Carnegie Steel. Terra-cotta: Perth Amboy Terra Cotta Co. Fireproofing: National Fireproofing Co. Ornamental ironwork and elevator cages: Hecla Iron Works. Lighting fixtures: J. B. McCoy & Son. Woodwork: Henry Taylor Lumber Co. Electric wiring: Brooklyn Electrical Equipment Co. Plumbing contractor: T. J. Byrne. Consulting engineer for electrical work: Reginald P. Bolton. Otis hydraulic elevators. Estimated cost (NBD 264–1899): $700,000. Renovated 1981.

54. "Building Skyscrapers," 1087.

55. Kimball, "The Architectural Relations of the Steel-Skeleton Building, 562, and see also 555.

56. Kimball, "The Architectural Relations of the Steel-Skeleton Building," 564–65.

57. George W. Steevens, as quoted in Montgomery Schuyler, "The Skyscraper Problem," *Scribner's Magazine* 34 (August 1903), 255.

58. S. Henbest Capper, "The American Tall Building from a European Point of View," *Engineering Magazine* 14 (November 1897), 239–52.

59. A. D. F. Hamlin, "The Tall Building from an American Point of View," *Engineering Magazine* 14 (December 1897), 437.

60. Hamlin, "The Tall Building from an American Point of View," 442–43.

61. Peter B. Wight, "Architectural Practice: Mutuality, Not Individuality," *Scribner's Magazine* 29 (February 1901), 253–56; and see "Tradition in Architecture," *Scribner's Magazine* 21 (June 1897), 787–88.

62. J. Lincoln Steffens, "The Modern Business Building," *Scribner's Magazine* 11 (July 1897), 55.

63. "Does the Sky Scraper Pay?" *Record and Guide* 59 (12 June 1897), 1006.

64. "Thirty Years of Office Building," *Record and Guide* 61 (9 April 1898), 642.

65. Jesse Lynch Williams, "The Water-Front of New York," *Scribner's Magazine* 26 (October 1899), 391–92.

66. Schuyler, "The 'Sky-scraper' Up to Date," 231.

67. Inspired by the Campanile of San Marco in Venice and by Price's Sun Building project, Post proposed campanile-skyscrapers for the Equitable Life Assurance Company (c. 1897) in New York and for Prudential Life (1899) in Newark, New Jersey. The first would have embraced about thirty-two stories (400 to 450 feet), the second about forty-two (approximately 600 feet). Both appear to have been influenced by Sullivan's aesthetic. The technology was available to build and operate them safely and efficiently. Discussed and illustrated in Winston Weisman, "The Commercial Architecture of George B. Post," *JSAH* 31 (October 1972), 197–98.

9. Skyscrapers and the Urban Scene at the Turn of the Century

1. "New York Building Statistics," *American Architect* 89 (13 January 1906), 16.

2. Bolton, "The Equipment of Tall Office Buildings in New York City," *Engineering Record* 39 (13 May 1899), 550–51.

3. "New York's Most Valuable Buildings," *American Architect* 75 (1 March 1902), 72; and "The Highest-Priced Site in New York City," *American Architect* 87 (17 June 1905), 196.

4. We have adjusted the story numbers to accord with our reckoning and method of counting and have included the World Building, which is omitted from some lists, possibly because its height was disputed. Certain disparities should be noted: the rental prospectus

for the Bowling Green Offices reports the height of the Broadway facade as 235 feet. The ground slopes at the foot of Broadway, and the Greenwich Street side may have been higher, either of which could account for the number recorded here. The actual space given over to usable floors in the Manhattan Life Building was less, possibly as little as 270 feet. The number reported for the New York Life Building takes in the clock tower. See "The Heights of Tall Buildings," *Engineering Record* 42 (8 September 1900), 217; and "The Height of Buildings," *Engineering Magazine* 20 (October 1900), 117–18; and also "Building Heights" (titles vary), *New York Times*, 11 December 1896, 18 December 1896, 22 December 1896, 31 December 1896.

5. "Skyscrapers in 1902," *Record and Guide*, 71 (3 January 1903) 2–3; Skyscraping buildings (news item), *Engineering News* 49 (2 April 1903), 288; and "Tendencies in Office Building: Increased Breadth with Height Combined: A Late Development," *Record and Guide* 70 (2 November 1902), 720.

6. Herbert Croly, "New York as the American Metropolis," *Architectural Record* 13 (March 1903), 198.

7. Honoré de Balzac, *La Rabouilleuse* (1842), trans. Donald Adamson (New York: Penguin Books, 1970), 62. The greatest American literary treatment of urban gluttony at the highest levels of finance is in Theodore Dreiser's Cowperwood novels, *The Financier* (1912) and *The Titan* (1914), although Philadelphia and Chicago are the settings.

8. Henry Adams, *The Education of Henry Adams* (1918; rpt., New York: Modern Library, 1931), 499.

9. Caffin, "Municipal Art," *Harper's Magazine* 100 (April 1900), 656.

10. *A History of Real Estate, Building, and Architecture in New York City During the Last Quarter of a Century* (1898; rpt., New York: Record and Guide, 1967), 577.

11. *A History of Real Estate*, 587–88.

12. "The Design of Our Tall Office Buildings—the Latest Phase," *Architectural Record* 11 (October 1901), 705.

13. "The Lowest Common Denominator in Office Building Design," *Record and Guide* 68 (5 October 1901), 405–6.

14. "The New Building Commissioner Asks Aid of Architects," *American Architect* 75 (4 January 1902), 1.

15. Jean Schopfer, "American Architecture from a Foreign Point of View: New York City," *Architectural Review* 7 (March 1900), 30.

16. Sydney Brooks, "London and New York," *Harper's Magazine* 104 (January 1902), 297.

17. E. Kilburn Scott, "A Britisher's Impression of the Skyscraper," *Engineering Record* 50 (1 October 1904), 412.

18. Henry James, *The American Scene* (1907; Bloomington: Indiana Univ. Press, 1968), 95–96.

19. Henry James, "New York Revisited," *Harper's Magazine* 112 (February 1906), 401–2.

20. Julius F. Harder, "The City's Plan," *Municipal Affairs* 2 (March 1898), 24–45, esp. 38–39.

21. Quoted in Robinson, "Improvement in City Life. III. Aesthetic Progress," *Atlantic Monthly* 86 (June 1899), 772.

22. See Henry F. Hornbostel, "Proposed Brooklyn Bridge Terminal and City Offices," *Architects' and Builders' Magazine* 4 (August 1903), 483–89. On the Municipal Art Society: Gregory F. Gilmartin, *Shaping the City: New York and the Municipal Art Society* (New York: Clarkson N. Potter, 1995), published when our book was already in the production process. On the art commission: *The Art Commission of the City of New York, 1898–1989* (1989), pamphlet.

23. New York City Improvement Commission, *Report to the Honorable George B. McClellan of the City of New York & to the Honorable Board of Aldermen of the City of N.Y.*, January 1907 (New York: Kalkhoff, 1907).

24. Ernest Flagg, "The Plan of New York, and How To Improve It," *Scribner's Magazine* 36 (August 1904), 253–56.

25. George Hill, "The Economy of the Office Building," *Architectural Record* 15 (April 1904), 313–14.

26. Hill, "The Economy of the Office Building," 317.

27. Hill, "The Economy of the Office Building," 318–22.

28. Ideally, according to Hill, the space should accommodate three similar boilers, one for summer and two for winter, with one in reserve; and the engine driving a generator should be high-speed, automatically controlled, and of the simple expansion type. A feedwater heater was essential. Pump ratings should be determined exactly by the operating requirements of the hydraulic elevators, the boiler feedwater circulation, and with a carefully calculated emergency reserve capacity: Hill, "The Economy of the Office Building," 323–25.

29. Hill, "The Economy of the Office Building," 325–27. In 1928–29 the subject of sky-

scraper economy in relation to height was extended in detail, yielding conclusions that for the most part apply to the whole twentieth-century development. See W. C. Clark and J. L. Kingston, *The Skyscraper: A Study in the Economic Height of Modern Office Buildings* (New York: American Institute of Steel Construction, 1930).

30. Neilson, "The Effects of Wind Pressure on Structures," *Engineering Magazine* 24 (January 1903), 548–62.

31. The matter was discussed by Edward W. De Knight in a paper read before the Western Society of Engineers in Chicago in November 1906 and again in an article in the *New York Herald*, 4 August 1907, neither of which identified the building. See "To Save the Skyscrapers," *Architecture* 16 (15 October 1907), 163–65. Alexander Brociner, C.E., "A Few Words About Structural Steel and Architecture," *Record and Guide* 79 (2 March 1907), 441, addresses the topic in relation to steel construction.

32. "The Permanence of Iron and Steel Structures." *Engineering Record* 43 (5 January 1901), 1.

A potentially valuable innovation in the steel frame was proposed early in the century, but its adoption was delayed for more than fifty years. In August 1903 the engineer Louis L. Calvert proposed the adaptation of the balloon frame to steel construction. In place of the usual widely spaced wall columns with massive spandrel girders, he suggested the use of a dense array of small columns spaced 6 feet center-to-center to conform to the customary floor-beam spacing. Heavy girders running 20 inches and more in depth were to be replaced by beams no more than 6 inches deep. For floor loads of 80 pounds dead plus 120 pounds live and roof loads of 70 pounds dead plus 50 pounds live, he estimated the saving in the weight of the frames in the wall plane at 25 percent. The technique would also have simplified construction and so reduced cost in that respect as well. See Calvert, "'Balloon Construction' for Steel Skeleton Structures," *Engineering News* 50 (27 August 1903), 183–84. Apparently the proposal was not implemented until the invention of the load-bearing screen wall in concrete and the design of the Vierendeel-truss walls of the World Trade Center towers.

33. "Collapses of New Brick Buildings . . . ," *Engineering Record* 51 (25 March 1905), 339.

34. Concrete building construction in New York City (news item), *Engineering News* 48 (18 December 1902), 521. By late 1904 others had been completed or were under construction, including a three-story stable in the Bronx, a mercantile building in Brooklyn, and a group that the *Record and Guide* called the first concrete buildings in Manhattan, constructed by the Guy B. Waite Co. as shops and offices at 31st Street and the East River. The Waite Company specialized in fireproof and concrete construction. See "The First Reinforced Concrete Mercantile Building in the City," *Record and Guide*, 74 (15 October 1904), 777; "First Concrete Buildings in Manhattan," *Record and Guide* 75 (4 February 1905), 245; and William H. Burr, "The Reinforced Concrete Work of the McGraw Building," *Engineering Record* 56 (26 October 1907), 455–60.

35. "Structural Details in the Farmers' Loan and Trust Building, New York," *Engineering Record* 59 (20 February 1909), 206–8; "Derricks and Sheet Pile Drivers for Foundation Work," *Engineering Record* 50 (27 August 1904), 254–56; "Steel Derricks for Erecting Tall Buildings," *Engineering Record* 59 (27 March 1909), 347–48; and "The Use of Compressed Air in Building Construction," *Record and Guide* 69 (7 June 1902), 1038–39. Because steel frames offered many anchor points for cranes, the derricks that were most frequently used were those with a fixed steel-guyed post and boom, both usually of open latticework form at the sides and with the maximum cross-sectional area at the midpoint. The midpoint was the place of maximum bending because the boom was hinged at one end but free to rotate at the other, like a two-hinged arch (not a cantilever, as it seems to be, because of the hinged end).

36. Barr Ferree, "The Art of the High Building," *Architectural Record* 15 (May 1904), 445 (quotation), 453 ff.

37. Ferree, "The Art of the High Building," 455, 462, 465–66.

38. Thomas Hastings, "Architecture and Modern Life," *Harper's Magazine* 94 (February 1897), 404.

39. New York City Heights of Buildings Commission, *Report of the Heights of Buildings Commission to the Committee on the Height, Size and Arrangement of Buildings of the Board of Estimate and Apportionment of the City of New York, December 23, 1913* (City of New York, 1913), 32–34, 134 ff.

40. Harvey A. Kantor, "Modern Urban Plan-

ning in New York City: Origins and Evolution, 1890–1933" (Ph.D. diss., New York Univ., 1971), 173–74.

41. "The Convention of the American Society of Civil Engineers," *Engineering Record* 42 (21 July 1900), 65.

42. "The Success of the Skyscraper and What It Means," *Record and Guide* 66 (10 November 1900), 618.

43. "The Tallest Sky-scraper Yet," *American Architect* 71 (9 February 1901), 48.

44. "The Reaction Against High Buildings in New York," *American Architect* 80 (4 April 1903), 1.

45. "The New Fifth Avenue Considered Architecturally," *Record and Guide* 73 (4 June 1904), 1309–11.

46. Allowable stresses for metals were specified in detail as follows. Rolled and cast steel: compression = 16,000 psi; tension = 16,000 psi. Wrought iron: compression = 12,000 psi; tension = 12,000 psi. Cast iron: compression = 16,000 psi; tension = 3,000 psi. Steel rivets: compression = 20,000 psi; shear = 10,000 psi. Wrought-iron rivets: compression = 15,000 psi; shear = 7,500 psi. Steel-web plates: shear = 9,000 psi. On the code and its provisions: "A New Building Code for New York City" (titles vary), *Engineering News* 39 (13 January 1898), 32; 39 (20 January 1898), 39–40; 39 (28 April 1898), 280; 39 (19 May 1898), 313; The new building law (news item), *Engineering News* 42 (7 September 1899), 145; "The New Building Code of New York," *Engineering Record* 40 (9 September 1899), 333; "The Proposed New Building Code of New York City," *Engineering News* 42 (14 September 1899), 174–76; 42 (12 October 1899), 247; "Structural Regulations of the New York Building Law," *Engineering Record* 40 (16 September 1899), 367–69.

47. The minimum bearing capacity of the earth was specified as follows: soft clay = 2,000 psf; wet clay and sand mixed = 4,000 psf; dry clay or fine sand = 6,000 psf; coarse sand, stiff gravel, or hardpan clay = 8,000 psf. The load limit for a single pile was specified as 40,000 pounds. The loading factor for the roof was set at 50 psf minimum; and, as in the 1892 code, the maximum wind load factor was specified as 30 psf. The maximum overturning moment exerted by the wind had to be less than 75 percent of the moment of stability. See *The Building Code as Finally Adopted by the Building Code Commission of the City of New York* (1899), sections 23, 25, 130, 140.

48. *The Building Code*, sections 36, 37.

49. The regulations specified the proportions of the concrete (one part cement, two parts sand, four parts aggregate), its minimum resistance to crushing (2,000 psi after hardening for twenty-eight days), and the strength of the cement (300 psi tensile strength after one day in the air, 500 psi after one day in the air and six days in the water, 600 psi after one day in the air and twenty-seven in the water). The figures seem high. Specifications for the quality of the sand and the stone were the usual. The allowable stresses were as follows: extreme fiber stress on concrete in compression = 500 psi; shearing stress in concrete = 50 psi; concrete in direct compression = 350 psi; tension in steel = 16,000 psi; shear in steel = 10,000 psi. The adhesion between the concrete and the steel was assumed equal to the shear strength of the concrete. The prescribed ratio of the moduli of elasticity of the concrete and the steel was 1:12. All the beams were to be simple, with no allowance for continuous construction. (This was a curious restriction inasmuch as the first English patent for concrete [Wilkinson, 1854] showed continuous beams with reinforcing correctly placed for transitions from positive to negative bending.) The maximum ratio of the length to the radius for columns was to be 12, with hoop reinforcing at appropriate intervals to be no more than the diameter of the column. Finally, load tests could be required at any time. See *Report of the Department of Buildings of the City of New York for the Borough of Manhattan for the Quarter and Year Ending December 31, 1904* (New York: McConnell, 1905); and The reinforced concrete regulations (news item), *Engineering Record* 59 (5 June 1909), 703; and "Reinforced Concrete Regulations in Building Codes," *Engineering Record* 61 (12 February 1910), 173.

50. "Skyscrapers in 1902"; and "Lower West Street's Prospects," *Record and Guide* 71 (18 April 1903), 754.

10. The Skyscraper Comes of Age, 1900–1910

1. Information from material in Mutual Life Insurance Co. Archives, and see Chapter 2 bibliography. Addition of 1900–1904 (NBD 1687–1899): Consulting engineer: Alfred Noble. Foundation consultant: T. Kennard Thomson. Foundation contractor: Arthur McMullen & Co. Caisson foundations. Steel-skeleton framed.

Later further enlarged. Demolished c. 1950.

2. "Sinking Foundations: Great Engineering Feats Involved," *Record and Guide* 66 (11 August 1900), 178. The other unusual, if not unique, feature of the building was that instead of the common cantilever girder normally used in cage framing, it had a steel-cage frame; hinged trusses were used to carry the columns adjacent to the party wall of the neighboring building. The aim was to allow the outermost columns to rotate without bending under wind deflection. All structural steel columns were Z-bar form: "The Atlantic Mutual Insurance Company's Building," *Engineering Record* 42 (18 August 1900), 157–59, and also NBD 604–1900. Foundation engineer and contractor: John F. O'Rourke. Structural engineer: S. C. Weiskopf. General contractor: Thompson-Starrett Co.

3. Forty-two Broadway (1902–3), the Broad-Exchange's closest rival in this respect, was a twenty-one-story skyscraper that incorporated 257,796 square feet of rentable space. Known as the Empire Trust Building and still extant, though altered, it was designed by Henry Ives Cobb and constructed by the George A. Fuller Company. The building is distinguished architecturally by its five-story-high "Jacobethan" ornament above the entrance. For plans, see McVickar, Gaillard Realty Company, *Forty-Two Broadway* (New York: McVickar, Gaillard Realty, n.d.), real estate prospectus, Avery Library, Columbia University, and also "Tendencies in Office Building: Increased Breadth with Height Combined a Late Development," *Record and Guide* 70 (15 November 1902), 720.

4. "Towns under a Single Roof . . . ," *Record and Guide* 66 (27 October 1900), 532. Located at 25–33 Broad Street and 44 Exchange Place. Developer: Alliance Realty Co. Estimated cost: $3,500,000. Height: 276 feet (NBD 2143-1899.

5. According to "A Wonderful Building," *New York Tribune Illustrated Supplement*, 29 June 1902.

6. New-building permit: 1356–1901; New York City Landmarks Preservation Commission, "Ladies' Mile Historic District," designation report, ed. Marjorie Pearson, 2 May 1989, 1: 296–300; Christopher Gray, "Flatiron Building," in *C. P. Company* (Ravarino, Italy: C. P. Company, 1991), 57; Paul Starrett, *Changing the Skyline* (New York: McGraw-Hill, 1938), esp. chapters 6, 7, and 9; and New York City Landmarks Preservation Commission, "Fuller Building" (593–599 Madison Ave.), 18 March 1986.

On the demise of the Fuller Company: *Crain's New York Business* 10 (29 August 1994), 1, 21.

7. John Zukowsky and Pauline Saliga, "Late Works by Burnham and Sullivan," *Museum Studies* (Art Institute of Chicago) 11 (Fall 1984), 73.

8. The primary framing members were 36 built-up box columns with a cross-sectional area yielding a maximum working stress of 12,500 psi. Built-up columns were becoming increasingly common. The pneumatic riveter was used in constructing the steel frame. Steel fabricator: American Bridge Co. See "The Flatiron Building, New York," *Engineering Record* 45 (29 March 1902), 296–300. The exterior terra-cotta cladding was supplied by the Atlantic Terra Cotta Company of Tottenville, Staten Island.

9. Christopher Gray, "Suddenly a Landmark Startles Again," *New York Times*, 20 July 1991; and "Winds Play Havoc with Women at the Flatiron," *New York Herald*, 31 January 1903.

10. As quoted in Dorothy Norman, *Alfred Stieglitz, An American Seer* (New York: Random House, 1973), 45.

11. The Bank of the Metropolis was absorbed by the Bank of Manhattan in 1918, and in 1955 the Bank of Manhattan merged with Chase National Bank to become Chase Manhattan Bank. By 1994 the upper floors of the building housed offices and apartments, and the Metropolis Cafe on the ground floor had incorporated many of the banking hall's features in its decoration. See New York City Landmarks Preservation Commission, "The Bank of the Metropolis," designation report, 12 July 1988.

12. The Blair Building's structural columns, which bore on concrete foundation walls shared with other buildings, rested on bases supported by 36-inch-deep distributing girders, which spread the column loads uniformly over the length of the walls rather than concentrating them under the column bases. The bracing was portal with girders doubled on either side of the columns, and with the beams in the peripheral bays doubled, one for the wall load, one for the floor load. The structural engineer was Henry W. Post, who had engineered the Gillender Building. Building ground dimensions: 76.5 feet front by 85 feet deep. Estimated cost: $650,000. General contractor: Andrew J. Robinson Co. Carpenter contractor: Sloane & Moeller. Electric work: Joseph P. Hall. Elevators: Otis Elevator Co. Heating: Johnson & Morris. Plumbing: James Armstrong. Iron con-

tractors: American Bridge Co. Information from NBD 371–1902 and "The Blair Building, New York," *Engineering Record* 46 (6 September 1902), 227–29.

13. Dimensions: 61 feet wide (Wall Street) by 191 feet wide (Pine Street). Height: 352 feet. Estimated cost: $1,250,000. Builder: Charles T. Wills. (NBD 650–1903.) Demolished 1970s.

14. "Twenty-eight Story Building, the First Skyscraper Ever Designed: A Prophecy That May Come True Next Year," *Record and Guide* 74 (12 November 1904), 1027; see also "Steel Skeleton Construction," *Record and Guide* 74 (29 October 1904), 896–97; 74 (31 December 1904), 1490. In 1932 Clinton & Russell's successor firm, known by the same name, completed a sixty-seven-story addition—actually a separate building—on the north side of Pine Street. It was connected to the old building by a bridge and an underground passageway. For years the new Sixty Wall Tower, known as the Cities Service Building, was the tallest building in lower Manhattan, and its Gothic-style tower is still a striking feature on the skyline.

15. *New York Times Building Supplement*, 1 January 1905, 3.

16. The fourth and most northerly of these sites is just below Columbus Circle, where Broadway and Eighth Avenue intersect between 58th and 59th streets. Also motivated by the opening of the new subway, the *New York American* newspaper apparently considered building a forty-story, 555-foot-high tower on that site in 1904. Designed by Barney & Chapman, the unexecuted design incorporated an elevator core from which the offices radiated outward, all within a wildly elaborated Gothic exterior. See "The Work of Barney & Chapman," *Architectural Record* 16 (September 1904), 204–8.

17. Montgomery Schuyler reproduces an early design, made before a hotel at the southern end of the site was acquired and subsequently demolished, which places the tower in the center of building and crowns it with a cupola. See Schuyler, "The Evolution of a Skyscraper," *Architectural Record* 14 (November 1903), 333.

18. *New York Times Building Supplement*, 8.

19. *New York Times Building Supplement*, 10.

20. *New York Times Building Supplement*, 11–12.

The loading factors were as follows: subbasement floor, 250 psf; basement, 150 psf; floors above the basement, 85 psf dead plus 90 psf live; wind, 50 psf. The wind-loading factor was

extremely high according to the current formula, equivalent to a wind of 140 mph. See "The New York Times Building," *Engineering Record* 49 (21 May 1904), 648–49; 49 (11 June 1904), 742–44; and also chapter bibliography under same title.

21. The *Times* reported that eight months were lost during the construction period due to strikes by laborers. There was only one fatality and a surprisingly low number of injuries during construction: *New York Times Building Supplement*, 19.

Area of building lot: 5,405 square feet. Total area including vaults: 17,633 square feet. Estimated cost: $1,500,000. Excavation: Degnon-McLean Contracting Co. Ironwork contractor: Rickey, Brown & Donald of Maspeth, L.I. Carpentry: John C. Orr & Co. Interior ironwork: Theodore Westing. Terra-cotta: Perth Amboy Terra Cotta Co. Plastering: John J. Roberts. Marble Work: John H. Shipway & Brother. Plumbing: Wells-Newton Co. Steel: American Bridge Co.

22. The twins are well documented in Elisa Urbanelli, "Trinity Building," New York City Landmarks Preservation Commission designation report, 7 June 1988; and Urbanelli, "U.S. Realty Building," New York City Landmarks Preservation Commission designation report, 7 June 1988.

23. "Foundations for Trinity Building," *Record and Guide* 73 (20 February 1904), 383. See also "Constructing the Foundations of the Trinity Building, New York," *Engineering Record* 50 (3 September 1904), 283–85; "An Interesting Foundation," *Record and Guide* 78 (14 July 1906), 53; and chapter bibliography.

24. The elevators were supplied by the Standard Plunger Elevator Company. See U.S. Realty and Improvement Co., *Trinity Building, 111 Broadway, and United States Realty Building, 115 Broadway* (New York: U.S. Realty and Improvement, [1907?]), real estate prospectus, 29; and Cecil D. Elliott, *Technics and Architecture: The Development of Materials and Systems for Buildings* (Cambridge: MIT Press, 1992), 338.

Building dimensions (from NBD 131–1904, alteration docket 1555–1906, and NBD 638–1906): 68 feet to 75 feet wide (with addition) by 260.5 feet to 267 feet deep by 280.5 feet high (Trinity); 61 feet wide by 269.5 feet to 275 feet deep by 282 feet high (U.S. Realty). General contractor: George A. Fuller Co. Structural engineers: S. C. Weiskopf and Purdy & Henderson. Marble Work: John H. Shipway & Brother. Total cost (including land): $15,000,000. These buildings were renovated and carefully restored in 1987–88, and they continue to be used as office space.

25. "A Tribute: Mr. [Robert E.] Dowling's Speech," *New York Architect* 2 (May 1908), unpaged.

26. Other initial tenants of the Trinity Building were Deyo, Duer & Beuerdorf; Rogers, Brown & Company; the Stirling Company; the General Fire Extinguisher Company; the Hudson Company; Henry Morgenthau; Whitehouse & Co.; Charles G. Gates & Co.; the National Electric Co.; S. P. McConnell; C. E. Schwab; the Magnus Metal Co.; Charles Harris; Marsh & Wever; W. L. Stow & Company; the City Investing Company; Harriman & Company; and the Republic Iron and Steel Company: "The Trinity Building Renting Well," *Record and Guide* 25 (22 April 1905), 868. See also "U.S. Realty Building," *Record and Guide* 79 (4 May 1907), 860.

27. "Number One Wall Street," *Record and Guide* 77 (16 June 1906), 1140; and also "The Highest-Priced Site in New York City," *American Architect* 87 (17 June 1905), 196.

28. One Wall's builders were investors represented by the Mercantile Trust Company of St. Louis, and the general contractor was the Westlake Construction Company of St. Louis. Cost of construction: $237,080. See "Wall Street and Broadway to Be Improved with an Eighteen-Story Structure," *Record and Guide* 77 (10 February 1906), 233; and "A Remarkable Building...," *Engineering Record* 53 (23 June 1906), 755.

29. "Number One Wall Street."

30. "Real Estate and Building in 1905," *Record and Guide* 77 (6 January 1906), 1.

31. "Foundations of the U.S. Express Co. Building," *Record and Guide* 76 (23 December 1905), 997; see also "The United States Express Company's Building, New York City," *Engineering Record* 54 (28 July 1906), 108–11.

Building width (front): 118 feet, 7 inches. Estimated cost: $1,600,000. Structural engineer: J. H. Wells. General contractor: Thompson-Starrett Co. (NBD 860–1905). Later (by 1932) known as Electric Bond and Share Co. Building.

32. "Skyscraper Builders in Gigantic Race," *Record and Guide* 77 (30 June 1906), 1237. The Evening Post Building (1906–7), however, is only thirteen stories high. Designed by Robert D. Kohn and located at 20 Vesey Street, it is a rare New York City work in the Vienna Secession style. Its vertically designed, unusually

open shaft is crowned by a high mansard, below which are a series of four figures associated with printing history, two sculpted by Gutzon Borglum and two by Kohn's wife, Estelle Rumbold Kohn.

33. "Skyscrapers in Manhattan," *Record and Guide* 78 (18 August 1906), 294.

34. "Five gigantic office buildings . . . ," *Record and Guide* 78 (1 December 1906), 899.

35. According to Sharon Irish, who provides a detailed account of the events leading up to the building's construction, other syndicators were Walter Roberts of the John Peirce Company and Judge S. P. McConnell, who had been Harry Black's legal counsel in Chicago. Formerly a stone contractor, Peirce had supplied the granite for the Broadway Chambers Building: Sharon Lee Irish, "Cass Gilbert's Career in New York, 1899–1905" (Ph.D. diss., Northwestern Univ., 1985), 212, 221; on the building see also Sharon Lee Irish, "A 'Machine That Makes the Land Pay': The West Street Building in New York," *Technology and Culture*, 30 (April 1989), 376–97.

36. As recounted by Irish, the Metropolitan Life Insurance Company, which underwrote the project, challenged the use of piles. As a result the Peirce Company also consulted engineers Boller & Hodges and Purdy & Henderson. A. P. Boller recommended the additional precautions of sheet piling and collaring: Irish, "Cass Gilbert's Career in New York," 227–30. See also "Waterproofing the Substructure of the West Street Building," *Engineering Record* 53 (12 May 1906), 601; and "The Substructure of the West Street Building, New York," *Engineering Record* 54 (29 December 1906), 710–13.

37. Quotations from Schuyler, "The Woolworth Building," in *American Architecture and Other Writings*, ed. William H. Jordy and Ralph Coe (Cambridge: Belknap Press of Harvard Univ. Press, 1961), 2: 616, 615, respectively.

38. Guy Kirkham, "Cass Gilbert, Master of Style," *Pencil Points* 15 (November 1934), 548.

39. Building dimensions (NBD 1376–1905): 158 feet wide (front) by 102 to 119 feet deep by 300 feet high. Excavation work, pile driving, foundation work (in part): John Monk & Sons. Mechanical engineer: Burt Harrison. Terracotta: Atlantic Terra Cotta Co. Marblework: Empire Marble Co. Steel fabricator: Milliken Brothers. Elevators: Standard Plunger Elevator Co.

In 1923 the building was sold to James Cox Brady, founder of the Brady Security and Realty Company, to which title was transferred, and renamed the Brady Building. It remained profitable until the depression began to take its toll in the early 1930s. Extensive renovation was undertaken in 1933–34, including the lobby, corridors, lighting (which had improved radically over the previous twenty-five years), elevators, plumbing, and power plant: "Costs Were Held Down in Modernizing the Brady Building . . . ," *Architectural Forum* 60 (March 1934), 21. In 1985 the exterior of 90 West Street, as the building is known today, was cleaned, the gold-leafing on the mansard roof renewed, and the top lighted at night.

40. Information from New York City directories and "Robert E. Dowling Dies: Realty Firm Head," *New York Times*, 17 March 1943.

41. Francis H. Kimball, "City Investing Building," *New York Architect* 2 (May 1908), unpaged. The passenger elevators were manufactured by the Standard Plunger Company, and the two additional freight elevators were Otis electric. See also Broadway-Cortlandt Company, *The City Investing Building, Broadway-Cortlandt and Church Streets . . .* (New York: Chasmar-Winchell, 1907), real estate prospectus.

42. Donn Barber, editorial, *New York Architect* 2 (May 1908), unpaged.

43. "The Largest Buildings of the Year," *Record and Guide* (4 January 1908), 38. The steel frame alone weighed 12,000 tons, or 14 percent of the total; thus the unit weight of the steelwork equaled 48 psf of floor area. (This figure was to rise to over 50 psf and then be drastically reduced with the introduction of the braced cantilever in 1965 (Hancock Building, Chicago). See "The Pneumatic Foundations of the City Investing Building, New York," *Engineering Record* 55 (2 March 1907), 267–70, and chapter bibliography for accounts of the building's construction.

Building height: 486 feet (NBD 932–1906). Total cost: $10,000,000. Structural engineers: Weiskopf & Stern. Electrical and mechanical engineers: Griggs and Holbrook. Sanitary engineer: Wm. C. Tucker. General contractor: Hedden Construction Co. Foundation contractor: O'Rourke Engineering and Construction Co. Steel fabricator: American Bridge Co. Steel erection: Post & McCord. Stonework: William Bradley & Sons. Ornamental iron: Hecla Iron Works. Terra-cotta and other tilework: National Fireproofing Co. Plumbing: Wells & Newton. Marble work: J. H. Shipway & Bros. From 1919 to 1937 known as the Benenson Building.

44. Kimball, "City Investing Building."

45. "The Most Notable Work of the Era," *Record and Guide* 84 (24 July 1909), 163–64.

46. At full capacity the Hudson Terminal could accommodate 687,000 people per day; in comparison, Pennsylvania Station (1902–11) was designed with a capacity of 500,000. In its first seven years of operation, from 1908 to 1915, the Hudson & Manhattan company carried 329,357,277 passengers, for a weekday average of about 147,000: C. W. Condit, *The Port of New York* (Chicago: Univ. of Chicago Press, 1980), 255.

47. The seventeen-story Emigrant Industrial Savings Bank Building (1909–12), designed by Raymond Almirall, and still extant at 51 Chambers Street, was mistakenly identified as the first H-plan skyscraper: "The 'H' Plan for Office Buildings," *Record and Guide* 84 (7 August 1909), 254.

An interesting attempt at improved interior courtyard lighting is the Fifth Avenue Building, Maynicke & Franke's fourteen-story store and loft building at 200 Fifth Avenue (1908–9), which replaced the Fifth Avenue Hotel at the intersection of 23rd Street, Broadway, and Fifth Avenue. It can be seen on the right in Fig. 11.7. There the courtyard walls are set back, making the court three times as wide at the top as at the bottom: "New Kind of Light Court," *Record and Guide* 82 (1 August 1908), 227.

48. William V. Ramsey, *A Story of the Church Street Terminal Buildings of the Hudson & Manhattan Railroad Company* (New York: Wynkoop Hallenbeck Crawford, 1909), unpaged real estate prospectus.

49. Ramsey, *A Story of the Church Street Terminal Buildings*.

The loading factors were as follows: dead, 98 psf; live, 105 psf; wind, 30 psf. The maximum allowable stress in the columns was equal to 13,000 psi. See "The Construction of the Hudson Companies' Buildings, New York," *Engineering Record* 57 (4 April 1908), 476–78; and "The Hudson Companies' Building, New York," *Engineering Record* 56 (3 August 1907), 121–23.

Foundations: O'Rourke Engineering and Contracting Co. Structural engineers: Purdy & Henderson. Tunnel engineers for New York and Jersey Railroad Co. and Hudson and Manhattan Railroad Co.: Charles M. Jacobs and J. Vipond Davies. Steel fabricator: American Bridge Company.

50. Chesebrough, with his father Robert A. Chesebrough, was responsible for developing a

number of properties in the immediate vicinity, including the Chesebrough, Battery Park, and Maritime buildings on State and Pearl streets.

51. "Newest of the City's Structural Giants," *Record and Guide* 82 (5 September 1908), 461; and 84 (4 December 1909), 994.

52. "Rents in Downtown Office Buildings," *Record and Guide* 88 (29 July 1911), 117. In 1931 the tenants of the buildings, many said to have been there for a long time, included the Gulf Refining Co., Tide Water Oil Co., United States Weather Bureau, U.S. Internal Revenue Dept., and the Penn Coal & Coke Company: W. Parker Chase, *New York, The Wonder City, 1932* (c. 1931; rpt., New York: New York Bound, 1983), 169.

53. "Pneumatic Caisson Foundations, Whitehall Building, New York," *Engineering Record* 61 (18 June 1910), 792–94; "Progress at the 'Whitehall,'" *Record and Guide* 85 (25 June 1910), 1354; and "Construction of the Whitehall Building Extension," *Engineering Record* 62 (3 September 1910), 277–78.

Dimensions of 1903 building (NBD 258–1902): 181 feet wide by 63 to 69 feet deep. Height: 259 feet. Front: granite, brick, and limestone clad. Estimated cost: $1,000,000. Dimensions of 1911 building (NBD 109–1908): 306 feet deep by 104 to 115 feet wide. Height: 415 feet. Front: granite, brick, and terra-cotta clad. Thirty elevators. Estimated cost: $4,600,000. Consulting structural engineers: Purdy & Henderson. Steel fabricator: Brown-Ketcham Iron Works. Steel erection: A. E. Norton Co. Total ground area both buildings: 51,515 square feet. General contractor for both: George A. Fuller Co.

54. At the turn of the century, McGraw published and printed the *American Telephone Journal*; *Electrical World*; *Electrochemical and Metallurgical Industry*; *Engineering Record*, which was the leading journal of the construction industry; and *Street Railway Journal*, which covered the whole domain of electric railroad motive power, construction, and operations.

55. "A Concrete Office Building," *Record and Guide* 78 (28 July 1906), 170. See also new-building permits 796–1906 and 1201–1911; and William H. Burr, "The Reinforced Concrete Work of the McGraw Building," *Engineering Record* 56 (26 October 1907), 455–60. The standard interior column section was between 2 feet, 2 inches and 2 feet, 5 inches on the side, in place of the standard Considère column with hoop reinforcing, and the bay span measured 14 feet, 8 inches by 21 feet, 9 inches. The mechanical engineer was Walter S. Timmis, and the Underwriters Engineering and Construction Company handled the reinforced concrete work for the general contractor, Frank B. Gilbreth.

56. E. P. Goodrich, "The Construction of the Thirty-Ninth Street Building, New York," *Engineering Record* 57 (4 April 1908), 390–93.

57. The maximum depth of the distributing members was reported as 5 feet, 9 inches; the bearing capacity of the soil was 8,000 psf. The general contractor was C. P. Willis, and the steel was fabricated by J. B. and J. M. Cornell: "Cantilever and Raft Foundations for a Twelve-Story Building," *Engineering Record* 59 (27 March 1909), 362–63.

58. Frederick P. Hill, "A Criticism," *Architecture* 19 (10 February 1909), 19.

59. "The German-American Insurance Building," *Record and Guide* 81 (4 January 1908), 25. See also "The Downtown Flatiron Building," *Record and Guide* 79 (25 May 1907), 1017; and NBD 320–1907.

60. Knowles later designed Mecca Temple (1924; now City Center of Music and Drama) at 135 West 55th Street. Masonic Hall is fully documented in "Ladies' Mile Historic District," 2: 936–39.

61. The construction of this auditorium, which is on the third floor, necessitated that columns for six stories be carried on two longitudinal trusses with an out-to-out depth of 31 feet, one-half inch, with columns bearing on paired transverse plate girders 4 feet deep; the galleries and mezzanine balconies required much cantilever construction. The excavation was reduced to a minimum because here the bedrock is near the surface, which accounts for the power plant's being in the attic. The engineer was Purdy & Henderson and the general contractor the Wells Brothers Company: "The Extension to Masonic Hall, New York City," *Engineering Record* 59 (13 March 1909), 284–86.

62. "The Bryant Building Substructure," *Engineering Record* 61 (21 May 1910), 665–67; also "Bryant Foundations Finished," *Record and Guide* 84 (16 October 1909), 678; and "Steelwork of the Bryant Building, New York," *Engineering Record* 61 (26 March 1910), 357–59.

63. "Manhattan''s Latest Tower Building," *Record and Guide* 83 (3 April 1909), 654. A similar description is given in *The Liberty Tower, New York* (New York: Liberty-Nassau

Building, 1910), unpaged real estate prospectus.

64. "Architectural Criticism," *Architecture* 22 (15 August 1910), 117.

65. *The Liberty Tower, New York*. The murals no longer exist. See also Lydia Latchinova, "Liberty Tower," New York City Landmarks Preservation Commission designation report, 24 August 1982.

The building's thirty-three stories include the three stories above the thirtieth story in the roof: the attic story, superintendent's floor, and tank story. Building ground dimensions (new-building permit 367–1909): 58 feet (Liberty Street) by 86 feet (Liberty Place) by 65.5 feet (rear) by 82 feet (Nassau Street). Height: 385 feet. Foundation contractor: Foundation Company. Terra-cotta: Atlantic Terra Cotta Co. Elevators (five high-speed): Otis. Plumbing: W. J. Cornell Co. Estimated cost: $800,000. From 1919 until 1945, owned by the Sinclair Oil Co. and known as the Sinclair Oil Building. In 1979 converted to cooperative apartments by Joseph Pell Lombardi & Associates.

66. Quinn hotel files, The New-York Historical Society; "Still Not Enough Hotels," *New York Times*, 19 October 1890; May N. Stone, "Hotel Pennsylvania: Strictly First-Class Accommodations at Affordable Rates" (M.S. thesis, Columbia Univ., 1988), 5; "The New York Hotel and Its Mission," *Record and Guide* 87 (13 May 1911), 899. An informative and well-illustrated presentation of hotels of the period, including those discussed in this chapter, is provided in Robert A. M. Stern, Gregory Gilmartin, and John Montague Massengale, *New York 1900: Metropolitan Architecture and Urbanism, 1890–1915* (New York: Rizzoli International, 1983), 252–79.

67. New York City Heights of Buildings Commission, *Report of the Heights of Buildings Commission to the Committee on the Height, Size and Arrangement of Buildings of the Board of Estimate and Apportionment of the City of New York, December 23, 1913* (City of New York, 1913), 17.

68. On the extensive steel trusswork of the Astoria's ballroom and lobby: N. A. Richards, "Steel Framing for Long-Span Construction," *Architectural Forum* 30 (January 1919), 23–27; and "A Large Truss in the Waldorf Hotel Extension, New York City," *Engineering News* 35 (5 March 1896), 152, 157–58. See also W. G. Mitchell, "The Hotel Waldorf-Astoria, New York," *American Architect* 60 (2 April 1898), 3–4. Purdy & Henderson served as the structural

engineers, and J. B. & J. M. Cornell fabricated the steel.

69. Moses King, ed., *King's Handbook of New York City*, 2d ed. (Boston: Moses King, 1893), 218. On the New Netherland see also items in Corsa hotel files, The New-York Historical Society. On the Hotel Savoy: O. D. Kisner, *Hotel Savoy Illustrated* (New York: Hotel Savoy, [c. 1893]).

70. Said to have been steel framed, the Hotel Manhattan was enlarged by Hardenbergh in 1901 and altered about 1920 by McKim, Mead & White for office use: items in Corsa hotel files. See also Montgomery Schuyler, "Henry Janeway Hardenbergh," *Architectural Record* 6 (January–March 1897), 364.

71. The building contractors were Thompson-Starrett and Marc Eidlitz & Son. See "Heating and Ventilating Plant . . . Power Plant of the Hotel St. Regis, N.Y.," *Engineering Record* 54 (25 August 1906), 220–24; 54 (8 September 1906), 265–68; *The St. Regis Hotel, Fifth Avenue and Fifty-Fifth Street, New York City* (New York: St. Regis Hotel, 1905); "A Trade Review of the Work Achieved in the Hotel St. Regis," *Architectural Record* 15 (June 1904), 601–24; Arthur C. David, "The St. Regis–the Best Type of Metropolitan Hotel," *Architectural Record* 15 (June 1904), 552–600; and James T. Dillon, "St. Regis Hotel," New York City Landmarks Preservation Commission designation report, 1 November 1988.

72. The architect was Hiss & Weekes, and the Gotham is now the Peninsula Hotel. See William Hutchins, "New York Hotels. II. The Modern Hotel," *Architectural Record* 12 (November 1902), 622; "The Hotel Gotham," *Architects' and Builders' Magazine* 38 (November 1905), 45–56; "The Mechanical Equipment of the Hotel Gotham," *Architects' and Builders' Magazine* 38 (November 1905), 81–84; and James T. Dillon, "Gotham Hotel," New York City Landmarks Preservation Commission designation report, 6 June 1989.

73. "Hotel Belmont," *Engineering Record* 47 (7 February 1903), 146–51; 47 (4 April 1903), 351; items in Corsa hotel files; H. W. Frohne, "The Hotel Belmont," *Architectural Record* 20 (July 1906), 63–69; see also "The Mechanical Plant of the Hotel Belmont, New York City," *Engineering Record* 52 (30 December 1905), 739–42; 53 (6 January 1906), 9–13; 53 (13 January 1906), 56–58; 53 (20 January 1906), 81–83; 53 (19 May 1906), 631–33.

74. The Plaza replaced an eight-story hotel of the same name on the site. Hardenbergh's

building was extended on the 58th Street side in 1921. See especially "Construction of the New Plaza Hotel, New York," *Engineering Record* 54 (17 November 1906), 553–55; "Structural Details in the Plaza Hotel, New York," *Engineering Record* 55 (30 March 1907), 418–20; H. W. Frohne, "Newest Great Hotel," *Record and Guide* 80 (14 September 1907), 398; "Designing a Metropolitan Hotel: The Plaza," *Architectural Record* 22 (November 1907), 349–64; and "Heating and Ventilation of the Hotel Plaza, New York," *Engineering Record* 59 (13 March 1909), 304–8; 59 (20 March 1909), 329–31.

75. Stern et al., *New York 1900*, 267. See also Ritz-Carlton, under "Architectural Criticism," *Architecture* 23 (15 June 1911), 1–2, plates 7–8; "The Ritz-Carlton Hotel," *Engineering Record* 61 (12 February 1910), 186–87; and Corsa hotel files.

76. The Knickerbocker Hotel was financed by John Jacob Astor and designed by Marvin & Davis, with Bruce Price as consulting architect; Trowbridge & Livingston took over as architects for the (delayed) completion of the building in 1905–6. In 1920–21 it was converted to office use. For further information: Kevin McHugh, "Knickerbocker Hotel," New York City Landmarks Preservation Commission designation report, 18 October 1988; and "Heating and Ventilating the Hotel Knickerbocker, New York City," *Engineering Record* 56 (13 July 1907), 41–44.

The Hotel Rector was designed by D. H. Burnham & Company. See "The Hotel Rector, New York," *American Architect* 99 (18 January 1911), 25–29.

77. David E. Tarn, "New York's Newest Hotel," *Architectural Record* 33 (March 1913), 236. Also "World's Largest Hotel," *Record and Guide* 91 (4 January 1913), 57; "Hotel McAlpin, New York City, F. M. Andrews & Co., Inc., Architects," *Architectural Review* 11 (April 1913), 82–85, 93, 109–11, 132–33; Corsa hotel files; and Stone, "Hotel Pennsylvania," 11–13. The hotel replaced a building known as the McAlpin that was erected c. 1886 as bachelors' apartments and studios by D. H. McAlpin. McAlpin House, as the 1912 building is called today, is now a rental apartment house.

78. Skeleton framing was the preferred form of construction because it readily permitted the deep floor heights then considered appropriate for residential use: "The Metropolitan Apartment House and Hotel," *Record and Guide* 73

(supplement, 11 June 1904), 1464–66.

79. The Ansonia was designed by Graves & Duboy for W. E. D. Stokes. See Lori Zabar, "The Influence of W. E. D. Stokes's Real Estate Career on West Side Development" (M.S. thesis, Columbia Univ., 1977), 53–73; and Stern et al., *New York 1900*, 384–85.

80. "The Use and Abuse of 'Sky-Scrapers,'" *Record and Guide* 70 (18 October 1902), 561; and see also "The Spread of the 'Sky-Scraper,'" *Record and Guide* 70 (6 September 1902), 317.

Under the building code, mercantile buildings could in theory exceed 150 feet, but the mandatory fireproofing and other requirements were such that it had not proved profitable to build them above that height. The highest of these, therefore, such as the new Wanamaker Store (1904; D. H. Burnham & Co.), were eleven or twelve stories only: "The Making and the Makers of America's Metropolis," *Record and Guide* 73 (supplement, 11 June 1904), 1429.

81. It increased from 4.22 to 9.87 percent: W. C. Clark and J. L. Kingston, *The Skyscraper: A Study in the Economic Height of Modern Office Buildings* (New York: American Institute of Steel Construction, 1930), 30.

82. Seymour I. Toll, *Zoned American* (New York: Grossman, 1969), 74, 145–46; and New York City Improvement Commission, *Report to the Honorable George B. McClellan of the City of New York & to the Honorable Board of Aldermen of the City of N.Y.*, January 1907 (New York: Kalkhoff, 1907).

83. These efforts are reviewed in Anthony Sutcliffe, *Towards the Planned City, Germany, Britain, the United States and France, 1780–1914* (New York: St. Martin's, 1981), 113–14 and passim.

84. George B. McClellan, Annual Message to Board of Aldermen, 7 January 1907, quoted in I. N. Phelps Stokes, *The Iconography of Manhattan Island* (New York: Robert H. Dodd, 1915–26), 5: 2065, 2068.

85. "To Have Six Complete Underground Floors," *Record and Guide* 82 (28 November 1908), 1018; "'Earthscraper' New Word Coined," *Record and Guide* 82 (26 December 1908), 1299; and "Building Planned 1,000 Feet High," *Record and Guide* 82 (18 July 1908), 127–28.

86. Quote from "Skyscrapers in Manhattan," 294; see also "Limit Building Height," *Record and Guide* 79 (16 March 1907), 532–33.

87. William O. Ludlow, "Reasons for Limit-

ing the Height of Buildings," *Record and Guide* 79 (25 May 1907), 1015.

88. John M. Carrère, "Must Skyscraping Cease?" *Record and Guide* 80 (28 September 1907), 472. See also "The President of the New York Board of Fire Underwriters . . . ," *American Architect* 92 (14 September 1907), 81–82.

Louis Sullivan is credited with having originated the setback solution, but he recognized William LeBaron Jenney as having pioneered it in the Manhattan Building (1889–91). Dankmar Adler, Sullivan's partner, argued in favor of setbacks in "Light in Tall Buildings," *Engineering Magazine* 4 (November 1892), 171–86. See Donald Hoffmann, "The Setback Skyscraper City of 1891: An Unknown Essay by Louis H. Sullivan," *JSAH* 29 (May 1970), 181–87, and Paul E. Sprague, "Adler & Sullivan's Schiller Building," *The Prairie School Review,* 2:2 (1965), 5–20.

89. "Sky-scrapers," *Architectural Review* 14 (October 1907), 217.

90. Ernest Flagg, "The Limitation of Height and Area of Buildings," *American Architect* 93 (8 April 1908), 125. See also Flagg, "A Scheme for Limiting Building Height, *Record and Guide* 81 (14 March 1908), 441.

91. On this issue, see Mardges Bacon, *Ernest Flagg: Beaux-Arts Architect and Urban Reformer* (New York: Architectural History Foundation, 1986), 221–23.

92. "New Skyscrapers for Old," *Scientific American* 102 (21 May 1910), 414.

93. "Problems of the Skyscraper," *American Architect* 93 (18 January 1908), 24.

94. Charles Cressey, "The Crown of the Skyscraper," *Architectural Record* 27 (May 1910), 434.

95. Frederic C. Howe, "The German and the American City," *Scribner's Magazine* 49 (April 1911), 486.

96. Howe, "The German and the American City," 489; see also Howe, "In Defense of the American City." *Scribner's Magazine* 51 (April 1912), 484–90.

97. See "Building Code Revision," *Record and Guide* 79 (4 May 1907), 860–61; A proposed new building code (news item), *Engineering News* 58 (26 December 1907), 705; "The Proposed New York Building Code," *Engineering Record* 59 (29 May 1909), 673; The building code revision in New York City (news item), *Engineering Record* 59 (22 May 1909), 647; The new building code (news items), *Engineering News* 62 (15 July 1909), 85; 62 (22 July

1909), 107; and "The New York Building Code" (titles vary), *Engineering Record* 60 (10 July 1909), 30–31, 56; 60 (17 July 1909), 58; 60 (24 July 1909), 87; 60 (31 July 1909), 45; 60 (7 August 1909), 167.

98. By 1909 advanced performance codes had been adopted in Boston, Portland, Washington, Minneapolis, Cincinnati, Louisville, and Los Angeles, as well as in Switzerland. These offered considerable latitude in the permissible stresses. Most called for load tests, but with a wide range of allowable results; the specifications for columns were equally broad and erratic. The inconsistencies revealed the need for further experiment and reliable national standards: The reinforced concrete regulations (news item), *Engineering Record* 59 (5 June 1909), 703; and "Reinforced Concrete Regulations in Building Codes," *Engineering Record,* 61 (12 February 1910), 173; "Standard Building Regulations for the Use of Reinforced Concrete," *Engineering Record* 61 (5 March 1910), 268–70; "Tests of Reinforced Concrete Columns," *Engineering Record* 61 (5 March 1910), 270–72.

99. The new building code (news item), *Engineering News* 62 (29 July 1909), 125–126, 131; and 62 (30 December 1909), 729.

11. Culminating Works and Envoys of the Future

1. As quoted from the *New York Times* in Anthony W. Robins, "Top This One: The Continuing Saga of the Tallest Building in the World," *Architectural Record* (January 1987), 56.

2. H. W. Desmond, "A Rational Skyscraper," *Architectural Record,* 15 (March 1904), 274–84; and Mardges Bacon, *Ernest Flagg: Beaux-Arts Architect and Urban Reformer* (New York: Architectural History Foundation, 1986), 185–96. Bacon's book is the definitive study of Flagg's career.

3. From the Arthur T. Sutcliffe Diary, 26 February 1903, collection Avery Library, Columbia University, as quoted in Bacon, *Ernest Flagg,* 215.

4. Otto F. Semsch, ed., *A History of the Singer Building Construction: Its Progress from Foundation to Flag Pole* (New York: Trow, 1908), 37.

5. "Anchorage of Singer Building Tower," *Record and Guide* 79 (27 April 1907), 824. And see also "The Foundations . . . Structural Details of the Singer Building, New York" (titles

vary), *Engineering Record* 55 (2 February 1907), 116–18; 55 (2 March 1907), 275–76; 55 (4 May 1907), 542–43; 55 (18 May 1907), 599–602; 55 (25 May 1907), 630–32; and chapter bibliography.

6. H. Pudor, "Durability Test," *Zeitschriften des Östereichischen Ingenieur und Architekten Vereines*, 2 June 1911; quoted in "Why Steel Is Imported," *Engineering News* 65 (22 June 1911), 765. The steelwork was constructed by Milliken Brothers, Inc. Two timber derricks were used for setting the steel, one of special wood construction with a capacity of 40 tons and a 75-foot mast and 65-foot boom, and the other of 25 tons' capacity: Semsch, *A History of the Singer Building Construction*, 28.

7. "A High Wind . . . New York City," *Engineering News* 69 (9 January 1913), 90.

8. Bacon, *Ernest Flagg*, 212.

9. "Elevators in the Singer Building," *Record and Guide* (28 September 1907), 475.

10. "End of Skyscraper: Daring in '08, Obscure in '68," *New York Times*, 27 March 1968.

11. *The Metropolitan Life Insurance Company: Its History, Its Present Position in the Insurance World, Its Office Building and Its Work Carried on Therein* (New York: Metropolitan Life Insurance, 1908), 12. In 1991, the company became "the first North American insurer to achieve one trillion dollars . . . of life insurance-in-force": flyer entitled "1991 Annual Report Highlights."

12. Suggested by Charles C. Savage in his "Metropolitan Life Insurance Company Tower," New York City Landmarks Preservation Commission designation report, 13 June 1989, 7.

13. "Manhattan's Highest Skyscraper," *Record and Guide* 79 (26 January 1907), 169.

14. "Heavy Columns in the Metropolitan Tower, New York," *Engineering Record* 56 (13 July 1907), 40.

15. The figure of 50,000 psf appears in an article written by the engineer in charge of the project: John L. Hall, "Description of the Structural Steel Framework for the Tower of the Metropolitan Life Insurance Building, New York City," *American Architect* 96 (6 October 1909), 130.

16. Amazingly, as of mid-1908 none of the construction crew had been hurt: "Seven Hundred Feet Aloft," *Record and Guide* 81 (30 May 1908), 1006.

17. Advertisement, *Record and Guide* 82 (12 September 1908), 524–25; and also *The Metropolitan Life Insurance Company: Its History . . .*, 24. The power plant incorporated nine Bab-

cock and Wilcox boilers for steam engines that drove electric generators and provided heating and hot water.

The construction machinery that was used was also sophisticated. It included two state-of-the-art steel derricks, the larger having a 90-foot mast and a 75-foot, 30-ton boom that reached from the center of the excavation site to the street, where it unloaded material from trucks. The smaller, at the thirty-third story, had a 65-foot, 12-ton boom that handled the steel setting above that level. All of the hoisting was done by means of an enclosed, 50-horse-power engine permanently installed on the ground floor of the tower; it was regulated by signal bells that facilitated control of the main drums and the swinging gear. Early in the construction the machinery for two elevators was installed and their use by the workers increased efficiency of construction: "The Erection of the Metropolitan Life Building Tower, New York," *Engineering Record* 57 (4 April 1908), 439–41.

18. According to Hall, "Description of the Structural Steel Framework," 131, the entasis on the short axis of the shaft was 1.5 feet, that on the long axis 2 feet, with "the outside faces of the walls gradually approach[ing] the column centers as they rise."

19. *The Metropolitan Life Insurance Company: Its History, Its Present Position in the Insurance World, Its Office Building and Its Work Carried on Therein* (New York: Metropolitan Life Insurance, 1914), 47.

20. Quoted in Montgomery Schuyler, "The Work of Napoleon Le Brun & Sons," *Architectural Record* 27 (May 1910), 380–81.

21. *The Metropolitan Life Insurance Company: Its History . . .* (1908), 26–27.

22. The reconstruction of the lower part of the building began in 1952, and the renovation of the tower was accomplished in 1960–64, with Lloyd Morgan & Eugene V. Meroni as architects.

General contractor: V. J. Hedden & Sons Co. Construction engineer: J. B. Clermont. Steel work: Ambridge plant of American Bridge Co. and J. B. & J. M. Cornell Co. Steel and iron work: Jackson Architectural Iron Works; Levering & Garrigues. Floor-construction fireproofing and tunnel lining: Reinforced Concrete Construction Co.

23. "Limit of Height for Tall Buildings." *Scientific American* 99 (25 July 1908), 59.

24. Charles B. Atwood, "Accepted Design for New Municipal Buildings in the City of New-York," *Building* 9 (29 December 1888), plates;

and "Accepted Design for the New Municipal Building in the City of New York, to Be Erected in City Hall Park," *American Architect* 9 (29 December 1888), 233 and plates.

25. "The Original Proposal for a High Building for New York Municipal Headquarters," *Engineering News* 66 (27 July 1911), 117 (Wellington proposal); "The New Municipal Building," *Record and Guide* 46 (25 October 1890), 543–44; 46 (22 November 1890), 685–86; and The new municipal building commissioners (news item), *Engineering News* 24 (22 November 1890), 470.

26. Richard Morris Hunt, Napoleon LeBrun, and William Robert Ware served as expert advisers, and there were 134 entries. One of the finalists, John R. Thomas, was in 1897 commissioned to adapt his proposal to serve as the new Hall of Records. See Editorials, *American Architect* 39 (4 February 1893), 66; 39 (18 March 1893) and 44 (26 May 1894), 81; Robert A. M. Stern, Gregory Gilmartin, and John Montague Massengale, *New York 1900: Metropolitan Architecture and Urbanism, 1890–1915* (New York: Rizzoli International, 1983), 61–63; and *Illustrated History of the Manhattan Municipal Building* (City of New York, 1989), 5–6.

27. The center axis would have been between Duane and Pearl streets. Post also proposed a grand plaza for the Manhattan end of the proposed new East River (Manhattan) Bridge: see "Architect George B. Post's Project for a Glorified Manhattan Island," *New York World*, 8 January 1899, Post Collection, The New-York Historical Society.

28. Competition plans for a municipal office building (news item), *Engineering News* 58 (26 December 1907), 704–5.

29. "Program of a Competition for the Selection of the Architect for the Office Building of the City of New York," *American Competitions* 2 (Philadelphia: T-Square Club, 1908), 3. The invitees were J. Stewart Barney; Carrère & Hastings; Clinton & Russell; J. H. Freedlander; Cass Gilbert; Heins & La Farge; Helmle & Huberty; Hoppin & Koen; Howells & Stokes; H. R. Marshall; McKim, Mead & White; Trowbridge & Livingston; and Warren & Wetmore. Of those, twelve submitted designs, and Cass Gilbert was said to have withdrawn from the competition.

30. "23 Story Municipal Building," *New York Sun* (29 April 1908). The jurists were William A. Boring, who had worked in McKim, Mead & White's office in the late 1880s; Francis H. Kimball; and an architect whose name was given only as Day (Frank Miles Day?): *Illustrated History of the Manhattan Municipal Building*, 9. The winning entry, along with those of Carrère & Hastings, Howells & Stokes, and Clinton & Russell, was published in *American Architect* 93 (27 May 1908).

31. I. N. Phelps Stokes, *The Iconography of Manhattan Island* (New York: Robert H. Dodd, 1915–26), 5: 2067.

32. Before the Municipal Building, and aside from the Madison Square Garden tower, McKim, Mead & White had produced but one major skyscraper, and it was completed only in 1911. This was the Downtown Building for the Knickerbocker Trust Company (1907–9; 1909–11; demolished), later the Columbia Trust Company Building, which fronted on Broadway at Exchange Place and extended back to New Street. It belonged to the long-established column-skyscraper genre: see Leland M. Roth, *McKim, Mead & White Architects* (New York: Harper & Row, 1983), 305, 307.

33. From his speech made on 4 January 1909 to the board of aldermen, and as quoted in Stokes, *Iconography*, 5: 2073.

34. A recent publication reports the extreme depth as minus 209 ft. at the north end of the site, and as minus 289.9 ft. just outside the lot: *Illustrated History of the Manhattan Municipal Building*, 16. The contemporary engineering journals, however, all of which reported the construction of the foundations in great detail, as well as the Works Progress Administration, *Rock Data Map of Manhattan*, I (Battery Park to 23rd Street; 1937), give the extreme depth as minus 177.8 ft. on the north side of the Municipal Building site.

35. The total compensation to the Foundation Company was $1,443,147, or about $820,000 more than that for the Gray Company to make a sand foundation: "A Composite Sand and Rock Foundation for a Tall Building," *Engineering News* 63 (6 January 1910), 24–26.

36. "An Unusual Example of Pneumatic Caisson Work," *Engineering Record* 62 (5 November 1910), 506; "Completion of the Foundations for the Municipal Building, New York," *Engineering Record* 62 (5 November 1910), 522–25; "Foundations of the Municipal Building, New York City," *Engineering News* 64 (17 November 1910), 523–29. On the building's caisson foundations and substructure (titles vary), see also *Engineering Record*, 61 (2 April 1910), 375, 448–49; 61 (11 June 1910), 745; 62 (9 July 1910), 46–48; 62 (16 July 1910), 57–58.

37. Nims, "The Municipal Building of the City of New York," *The Municipal Engineers in*

the City of New York, Proceedings for 1913 (New York: Municipal Engineers of the City of New York, 1914), 288–89. Overall the framework incorporated 129 primary columns of box section resting on cast-steel and cast-iron pedestals on the caisson tops, with distributing girders and grillages for those most heavily loaded, and another 124 secondary columns in the basement and the mezzanine story between the station area of the basement and the first floor. Because of the plan's unusual shape and its oblique angles, the columns had to be distributed irregularly, with most spaced 12 to 18 feet center-to-center. See also "Steelwork in the New York Municipal Building," *Engineering Record* 61 (19 March 1910), 320–24; "Progress on the New York Municipal Building," *Engineering Record* 63 (25 March 1911), 326–28; "The Municipal Building, New York City; An Office Building for the City Government," *Engineering News* 66 (27 July 1911), 99–100; "Remarkable Building Construction," *Engineering Record* 66 (7 September 1912), 254–55; and "Construction of the New York Municipal Building," *Engineering Record* 66 (7 September 1912), 256–59.

38. The marble and other interior-finish materials are described in detail, as are all aspects of the building, in Nims, "The Municipal Building," 290–91, and in other sources. There were thirty-three elevators, counting the shuttle elevator in the tower, of the overhead traction type; these were manufactured by Robert Wetherill & Company, not by Otis.

39. "Problems in Designing the Municipal Building," *Record and Guide* 81 (9 May 1908), 858.

40. On the Municipal Building sculpture: Charles H. Dorr, "A Sculptor of Monumental Architecture: Notes on the Work of Adolph Alexander Weinman," *Architectural Record* 33 (June 1913), 518–29.

41. Described as a "modern 'Colossus of Rhodes'" because it spans across Chambers Street as the huge Greek sculpture supposedly stood astride the harbor entrance: Dorr, "A Sculptor of Monumental Architecture," 519.

42. The Municipal Building has recently (completed 1992) undergone a thorough facade restoration. Corners had developed vertical cracks, joints had opened, and the granite and terra-cotta cornice was dangerously deteriorated, but no foundation problems were discovered. As part of the work, Civic Fame was rehabilitated and regilded. Wank Adams Slavin Associates did this work.

43. Bragdon, "Architecture in the United States, III: The Skyscraper," *Architectural Record* 26 (August 1909), 96.

44. On the company and its well-documented building, see *Twenty Years of Bankers Trust Company: March 30 1903–1923* (New York: Bankers Trust, 1923), pamphlet, collection The New-York Historical Society; Bankers Trust Company, New York, *Twenty-five Years of Bankers Trust Company . . . 1903–1928* (New York: Bankers Trust, 1928), especially 7–11; and "The Bankers' Trust Building, Some of the Unique Features of Its Construction," *Real Estate Magazine* 1 (August 1912), 17–27.

45. "The Bankers Trust Building," *Architecture* 25 (15 May 1912), 70. See also "Campaniles, Medieval and Modern: The Bankers' Trust Building—Successful Solution of a Difficult Architectural Problem," *Scientific American* 105 (1 July 1911), 6–7.

46. "The Bankers Trust Building," 70.

47. Allen S. Beals, "A New Source of Rent in Tall Buildings: The Type of Foundation Invented for the Bankers' Trust Building Means a Saving of $60,000 and a Handsome Yearly Income," *Record and Guide* 87 (27 May 1911), 997–98; and also "A Novel Method for Jacking Caisson Piles for Underpinning," *Engineering News* 64 (15 September 1910), 286; and "The Substructure of the Bankers' Trust Company Building," *Engineering Record*, 62 (10 December 1910), 677–79.

48. The bracing was achieved mainly by using solid triangular gusset plates above and below the girders and twin girders at the second floor, one above the other and spaced about 6 feet apart between the adjacent flanges. Heavy rectangular gusset plates were used between the girders at the columns: Bankers' Trust Company building, steel and structural details (titles vary), *Engineering Record* 63 (11 February 1911), 152–54; 63 (11 March 1911), 284–86; 63 (29 April 1911), 476–78; 64 (19 August 1911), 221–23.

49. In 1917 Bankers Trust became a commercial bank, and two years later it acquired the adjoining Hanover Bank Building and also 10–12 Wall Street and 7–9 Pine Street for its use. In 1931, the company demolished the Hanover Building and in its place constructed an L-shaped addition (1931–32) designed by Shreve, Lamb & Harmon that takes in all those properties. The Bankers Trust Company sold the building in 1986 but remains the major tenant. By 1993 the building was owned by General Electric Investment Properties.

Original building consulting engineers: Bassett Jones, W. E. S. Strong. Consulting engineer for structural steel: S. C. Weiskopf. Vault engineer: Fred S. Holmes. Equipment engineer: Thomas Bruce Boyd. Steelwork: Post & McCord. Interior marble work: Batterson & Eisele. Granite: New England Granite Works. Eleven gearless traction elevators and five drum-type elevators: Otis. Vault lift: Standard Plunger Elevator Company. Plumbing: W. G. Cornell Co. Offices of J. P. Morgan & Co. on 31st floor.

50. "The Bankers Trust Building," 69.

51. "F. W. Woolworth to Build," *Record and Guide* 85 (12 March 1910), 546; "New Woolworth Building," *Brickbuilder*, 19 (November 1910), 261–62; and Advance Reports: Contract Practically Let for Third Highest Building in the World (news item), *Record and Guide* 86 (19 November 1910), 833.

Extensively documented in the Gilbert papers in The New-York Historical Society, the Woolworth Building has been the subject of two doctoral dissertations as well as two thoroughly researched designation reports written by Anthony W. Robins for the New York City Landmarks Preservation Commission in 1983 (see chapter bibliography). See also Gail Fenske and Deryck Holdsworth, "Corporate Identity and the New York Office Building: 1895–1915," in *The Landscape of Modernity: Essays on New York City, 1900–1940*, ed. David Ward and Olivier Zunz (New York: Russell Sage Foundation, 1992), 143–46.

52. Another skyscraper, under "Notes and Comments," *Engineering Record* 62 (19 November 1910), 563.

53. Louis J. Horowitz and Boyden Sparkes, *The Towers of New York: The Memoir of a Master Builder* (New York: Simon and Schuster, 1937), 120.

54. After a merger in the 1920s, the bank became the Irving Trust Company, and in 1988 it merged with the Bank of New York, which continues to occupy space in the building.

55. From Leo L. Redding, "Mr. F. W. Woolworth's Story" (interview with Woolworth), *World's Work* 25 (April 1913), 665. Redding explains that he learned of this conversation from "another source," not from his own interview (p. 664). See also "New Woolworth Will Over-Top Metropolitan Tower," *Record and Guide* 87 (21 January 1911), 108.

56. That footage and the total number of stories, however, vary from account to account. NBD 231–1911 (24 April) gives the height as 750 feet and the story count as fifty-one, and

the Woolworth company's own visitors' brochures differ. One published in 1913 gives the height above ground as 784 feet; another published in 1916 gives it as 792 feet, 1 inch, probably including the flagpole. The 1995 information leaflet states that it is 792 feet high above the pavement and has sixty stories "from subbasement to tower."

57. As explained by S. F. Holtzman of the Gunvald Aus Company, those on Barclay Street had to comply with a city ordinance enacted between the time the initial building permit was obtained (7 November 1910) and the first caissons sunk, and the filing of the application for a permit to cover the enlarged, redesigned building (24 April 1911): Holtzman, "Design of the Woolworth Building," *Engineering Record* 68 (5 July 1913), 22. See also "The Woolworth Building Foundations," *Engineering Record* 64 (26 August 1911), 256–57; and "The Steel Substructure of the Woolworth Building in New York City," *Engineering Record* 65 (17 February 1912), 177–78.

58. Cass Gilbert, "The Tenth Birthday of a Notable Structure," *Real Estate Magazine* 11 (May 1923), 344.

59. George T. Mortimer, "The Woolworth Building, Most Modern Example of the Fireproof Skyscraper—How It Was Built," *Real Estate Magazine* 1 (July 1912), 56.

60. Aus, "Engineering Design of the Woolworth Building," *American Architect* 103 (26 March 1913), 159–60.

61. The city building code allowed S. F. Holtzman to calculate the wind forces in the columns as equal to 50 percent of the forces derived from dead and live gravity loads and treated as an addition to such loads. On this basis he determined the column section as approximately 3 by 4 feet if the stress was to remain within the allowable unit stress of 19,000 psi: Holtzman, "Design of the Woolworth Building," 23. See also "Frame and Wind Bracing of the Woolworth Building," *Engineering News* 72 (30 July 1914), 231–33.

62. Aus, "Engineering Design of the Woolworth Building," 160.

63. "Six Hundred-Foot Drop Tests Woolworth Building Elevators," *Engineering Record* 70 (5 September 1914), 266–67.

64. "Water Supply System in the Fifty-Five Story Woolworth Building, New York," *Engineering Record* 68 (12 July 1913), 44. The water was taken directly from the city main, metered, filtered, and pumped to storage tanks for gravity flow, except for the water used below the

second floor, which was pumped to the fixtures. The storage tanks were located at the fifty-third floor (No. 1), the fiftieth (No. 2), the thirty-eighth (No. 3), the twenty-seventh (No. 4), and the fourteenth (No. 5). The water was extensively recycled; that used for lavatories, cooling, and condensation was filtered and stored for use in the toilets, supplemented by outside supply.

65. Advertisement, *Record and Guide* 89 (23 March 1912), 587.

66. Quotations, in order, from Aus, "Engineering Design of the Woolworth Building," 158; Schuyler, "The Woolworth Building," in *American Architecture and Other Writings*, ed. William H. Jordy and Ralph Coe (Cambridge: Belknap Press of Harvard Univ. Press, 1961), 2: 608, 620; and Julia Finch Gilbert, *Cass Gilbert: Reminiscences and Addresses* (New York: Scribner, 1935), 14.

67. Gilbert, "The Tenth Birthday," 344.

68. Schuyler, "The Woolworth Building," 620.

From 1977 to 1981 a major facade and structural restoration was carried out by the Ehrenkrantz Group. The terra-cotta blocks were cleaned and repointed, and deteriorated blocks were replaced with precast cement blocks colored to match the original: "The Woolworth Tower: A Technology Revisited, a Material Understood, a Landmark Restored," *Architectural Record* 169 (Mid-August 1981), 90–95.

69. The sculptor was the caricaturist Tom Johnson, the muralist Paul Jenewein. For further details: Anthony W. Robins, "Woolworth Building, first floor interior . . . ," New York City Landmarks Preservation Commission designation report, 12 April 1983.

70. Said to involve eighty-thousand lights, the illumination was produced by "specially designed nitrogen lamps of great candle-power set in mirrored reflectors"; the effect at the top was described as that of "an immense ball of fire, giving the effect of a gorgeous jewel resplendent in its setting of rich gold . . . [visible to] mariners forty miles at sea": *The Cathedral of Commerce* (New York: Broadway Park Place, 1916), unpaged. This lighting has been replaced.

71. Gilbert, "The Tenth Birthday," 345.

Dimensions of tower at its base: 84 by 86 feet. Foundations: Foundation Company. Steel fabricator: American Bridge Co. Stone and interior marble contractors: Bradley & Son. Stone masonry: J. & D. Angus. Water supply and sanitary systems: designed by consulting engineer Albert L. Webster. Plumbing installation: W. G. Cornell Co. Terra-cotta: Atlantic Terra Cotta Co.

72. "Plans for Fire Insurance Building," *Record and Guide* 87 (22 April 1911), 735–36.

73. "Particulars of Equitable Building Plans," *Record and Guide* 82 (4 July 1908), 27. The announcement first appeared on the front page of the *New York Times*, 30 June 1908, under the headline, "909-Foot Skyscraper to Tower Above All." The base would have had a cruciform plan with the following overall dimensions: Broadway frontage, 167.1 feet; rear, 152.3 feet; sides, 304.2 feet and 312.3 feet; height, 489 feet. See also Editorial, *Record and Guide*, 82 (4 July 1908), 1–2; and "Plans for the New Equitable Building," *Record and Guide* 80 (28 December 1907), 1046.

74. "Equitable Plans," *Record and Guide* 86 (2 July 1910), 8. The Mercantile Safe Deposit Company's long-term lease on the basement was said to be one of the impediments to redevelopment of the site. See also Horowitz and Sparkes, *The Towers of New York*, 133–35.

75. "Building to the Limit," *Record and Guide* 90 (7 December 1912), 1064. On Mortimer's involvement: Earl Shultz and Walter Simmons, *Offices in the Sky* (Indianapolis: Bobbs-Merrill, 1959), 78–79; and Seymour I. Toll, *Zoned American* (New York: Grossman, 1969), 149.

76. The New York Board of Fire Underwriters, *Report on Fire in the Equitable Building, Broadway, Pine, Nassau and Cedar Streets, New York City, January 9, 1912* (New York: 1912), 10, Equitable Archives. See also Sally A. Kitt Chappell, *Architecture and Planning of Graham, Anderson, Probst and White, 1912–1936: Transforming Tradition* (Chicago: Univ. of Chicago Press, 1992), part 2, "Equitable Building," 106. The old building was not insured for fire, because, according to Roscoe Carlyle Buley, *The Equitable Life Assurance Society of the United States: One Hundredth Anniversary History, 1859/1959* (New York: Appleton-Century-Crofts, 1959), 164, it was valued at less than the cost of insuring it over the years.

77. Thompson-Starrett served as general contractors. Today the building is no longer regarded as an evil, but rather as an important contribution to the development of the financial district. From 1983 to 1990 it underwent a massive facade restoration carried out by Ehrenkrantz, Eckstut, & Whitelaw.

78. New York City Heights of Buildings Commission, *Report of the Heights of Buildings*

Commission to the Committee on the Height, Size and Arrangement of Buildings of the Board of Estimate and Apportionment of the City of New York, December 23, 1913 (City of New York, 1913), 15; and "Will Be the World's Highest Skyscraper," *Record and Guide* 92 (4 October 1913), 613 (projected Pan American States As-sociation Building).

79. Moses King, comp., *King's Views of New York, 1896–1915, & Brooklyn, 1905* (rpt., New York: Arno, 1977), 65 (1915). See also "A Tall, Thin One," *Record and Guide* 89 (1 June 1912), 1185.

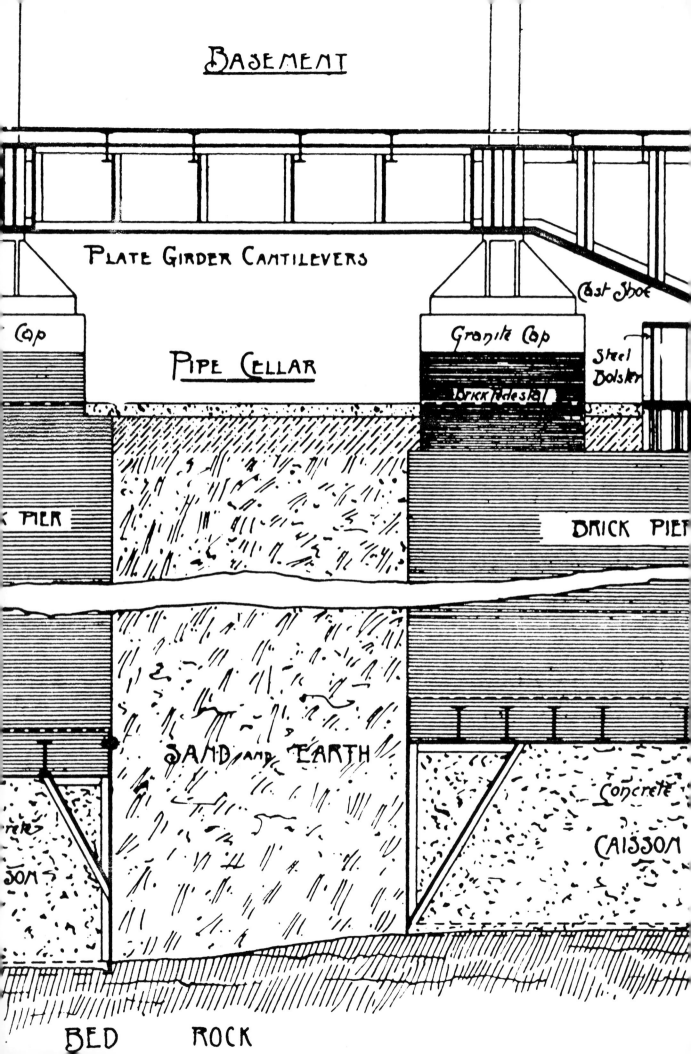

BIBLIOGRAPHY

Note: This list contains frequently cited and generally useful sources; chapter bibliographies follow general references. For sources used only for specific items of information, see endnotes. For key to abbreviations see page 399.

General References

Baedeker, Karl. "New York." In *The United States, with Excursions to Mexico, Cuba, Porto Rico, and Alaska,* 10–74. Leipzig: Karl Baedeker, 1909.

Banham, Reyner. *The Architecture of the Well-Tempered Environment.* Chicago: Univ. of Chicago Press, and London: Architectural Press, 1969.

Berkey, Charles P. "Engineering Geology in New York City." In *Guidebook of Excursions,* ed. Agnes Creagh. New York: Geological Society of America, 61st Annual Meeting, 10–14 November 1948.

Birkmire, William H. *The Planning and Construction of High Office-Buildings.* New York: John Wiley and Sons, 1898.

—. *Skeleton Construction in Buildings.* 1893. 4th ed. New York: John Wiley and Sons, 1912.

Bonner, William Thompson. *New York. The World's Metropolis, 1623–24–1923–24.* New York: R. L. Polk, 1924.

Boyer, M. Christine. *Manhattan Manners: Architecture and Style, 1850–1900.* New York: Rizzoli, 1985.

Burt, Henry J. "Growth of Steel-Frame Buildings: Origin & Some Problems of the Skyscraper," *Engineering News-Record* 92 (17 April 1924), 680–84.

Chase, W. Parker. *New York, The Wonder City, 1932.* C. 1931. Rpt., New York: New York Bound, 1983.

Clark, W. C., and J. L. Kingston. *The Skyscraper: A Study in the Economic Height of Modern Office Buildings.* New York: American Institute of Steel Construction, 1930.

Condit, Carl W. *American Building: Materials and Techniques from the First Colonial Settlements to the Present.* Chicago: Univ. of Chicago Press, 1968. 2d ed., 1982.

—. *The Port of New York: A History of the Rail and Terminal System from the Beginnings to Pennsylvania Station.* Chicago: Univ. of Chicago Press, 1980.

—. "The Wind Bracing of Buildings." *Scientific American* 230 (February 1974), 92–105.

Darton, N. H., et al. *New York City, New York–New Jersey, Geologic Folio.* United States Geological Survey Publication No. 83. Washington: Government Printing Office, 1902.

Dictionary of American Biography. New York: Charles Scribner's Sons, 1928–80.

Dolkart, Andrew S. *Forging a Metropolis: Walking Tours of Lower Manhattan Architecture.* New York: Whitney Museum of American Art, 1990.

Dunlap, David W. *On Broadway: A Journey Uptown Over Time.* New York: Rizzoli, 1990.

Elliott, Cecil D. *Technics and Architecture: The Development of Materials and Systems for Buildings.* Cambridge: MIT Press, 1992.

Ellis, Edward Robb. *The Epic of New York.* New York: Coward-McCann, 1966.

Fisher, Donald W., et al. *Geologic Map of New York: Lower Hudson Sheet.* Albany: Univ. of the State of New York, State Education Department, 1961.

FitzSimons, Neal, ed. "History of Tall Buildings." *Planning and Design of Tall Buildings,* Chapter PC-2. Bethlehem, Pa.: Council on Tall Buildings and the Urban Habitat, Committee on the History of Tall Buildings [c. 1987].

Flinn, Alfred Douglas. *Engineering Achievements and Activities of New York City.* New York: American Society of Civil Engineers, 1913.

Francis, Dennis Steadman. *Architects in Practice, New York City, 1840–1900.* New York: Committee for the Preservation of Architectural Records, 1979.

Goldberger, Paul. *The Skyscraper.* New York: Alfred A. Knopf, 1981.

History of Architecture and the Building Trades of Greater New York. 2 vols. New York: Union Historical, 1899.

A History of Real Estate, Building and Architecture in New York City During the Last

Quarter of a Century. New York: Real Estate Record Association, 1898. Rpt. ed., New York: Arno, 1967.

Hitchcock, Henry-Russell. *Architecture: Nineteenth and Twentieth Centuries*. 4th ed. Harmondsworth: Penguin, 1977.

Hornbostel, Caleb. *Materials for Architecture: An Encyclopedic Guide*. New York: Reinhold, 1961.

Huxtable, Ada Louise. *The Tall Building Artistically Reconsidered: The Search for a Skyscraper Style*. New York: Pantheon, 1984.

Jordy, William H. *American Buildings and Their Architects: Progressive and Academic Ideals at the Turn of the Century*. Garden City, N. Y.: Doubleday, 1972.

Jordy, William H., and Ralph Coe, eds. *American Architecture and Other Writings by Montgomery Schuyler*, 2 vols. Cambridge: Belknap Press of Harvard Univ. Press, 1961.

King, Moses, ed. *King's Handbook of New York City*. 2d ed. Boston: Moses King, 1893.

—, ed. *King's Photographic Views of New York*. Boston: Moses King, [c. 1895].

—, comp. *King's Views of New York*. Boston: Moses King, [c. 1908].

—, comp. *King's Views of New York*. New York: Moses King, 1915.

—, comp. *King's Views of New York, 1896–1915 & Brooklyn, 1905*. Rpt., New York: Arno, 1977.

Kranzberg, Melvin, and Carroll W. Pursell, Jr., eds. *Technology in Western Civilization*. 2 vols. New York: Oxford Univ. Press, 1967.

Landau, Sarah Bradford. "The Tall Office Building Artistically Reconsidered: Arcaded Buildings of the New York School, c. 1870–1890." In *In Search of Modern Architecture: A Tribute to Henry Russell Hitchcock*, ed. H. Searing, 136–64. New York: Architectural History Foundation, and Cambridge: MIT Press, 1982.

Leeuwen, Thomas A. P. van. *The Skyward Trend of Thought: The Metaphysics of the American Skyscraper*. Cambridge: MIT Press, 1988.

Lobeck, A. K., and Erwin Raisz. *The Physiography of the New York Region*. New York: Geographical Press of Columbia Univ., 1930.

Moran, David E. "Foundation Development During Fifty Years." *Engineering News-Record* 92 (17 April 1924), 670–73.

Mujica, Francisco. *History of the Skyscraper*. Paris: Archaeology and Architecture Press, 1929. Rpt., New York: DaCapo, 1977.

Murphy, J. J., and T. W. Fluhr. "The Subsoil and Bedrock of the Borough of Manhattan as Related to Foundations." *Municipal Engineers Journal* 30 (1944), 119–23. Map.

National Cyclopaedia of American Biography. New York: James T. White, 1891–1987.

Nevins, Allan, and John A. Krout, eds. *The Greater City: New York, 1898–1948*. New York: Columbia Univ. Press, 1948.

New York City building plans and permits. New York City Department of Buildings, Manhattan.

New York City buildings and street views: drawings, photographs, prints, newspaper and periodical clippings, miscellaneous documents. Department of Prints and Photographs, Museum of the City of New York.

New York City Department of Buildings docket books and records. New York City Municipal Archives.

New York City Heights of Buildings Commission. *Report of the Heights of Buildings Commission to the Committee on the Height, Size and Arrangement of Buildings of the Board of Estimate and Apportionment of the City of New York, December 23, 1913*. City of New York, 1913.

New York City Landmarks Preservation Commission. Designation reports for individual landmarks and for historic districts. [Listed under specific titles in endnotes.]

New York City maps and landbooks, 1852–1994. Especially *Miniature Atlas of the Borough of Manhattan in One Volume*. New York: E. Belcher Hyde, 1912.

New York City photograph collection of buildings and street views. Department of Prints, Photographs, and Architecture, The New-York Historical Society.

Nimmons, George C. *Studies of Building Height Limitations in Large Cities*. Chicago: Chicago Real Estate Board, 1923.

Pevsner, Nikolaus. *A History of Building Types*. Princeton: Princeton Univ. Press, 1976.

Placzek, Adolf K., ed. *Macmillan Encyclopedia of Architects*. 4 vols. New York: Free Press, 1982.

Post, George B. Collection. Record books, letterbooks, scrapbooks, clippings folder, drawings, photographs, and specifications. Department of Prints, Photographs, and Architecture, The New-York Historical Society.

Scott, Mel. *American City Planning Since 1890*. Berkeley: Univ. of California Press, 1969.

Shultz, Earl, and Walter Simmons. *Offices in the Sky*. Indianapolis: Bobbs-Merrill, 1959.

Silver, Nathan. *Lost New York*. Boston: Houghton Mifflin, 1967.

Singer, Charles, et al., eds. *A History of Technology*. Vols. 4 and 5. Oxford: Clarendon, 1958.

Starrett, W. A. *Skyscrapers and the Men Who Build Them*. New York: Charles Scribner's Sons, 1928.

Stern, Robert A. M., Gregory Gilmartin, and John Montague Massengale. *New York 1900: Metropolitan Architecture and Urbanism, 1890–1915*. New York: Rizzoli, 1983.

Stokes, I. N. Phelps. *The Iconography of Manhattan Island, 1498–1909*. 6 vols. New York: Robert H. Dodd, 1915–26. Rpt., New York: Arno, 1967.

Sturgis, Russell. *A Dictionary of Architecture and Building*. 3 vols. 1902. Rpt., Detroit: Gale Research, 1966.

United States Department of Commerce, Bureau of the Census. *Historical Statistics of the United States*. Washington: Government Printing Office, 1975.

——. *Statistical Abstract of the United States*. Washington: Government Printing Office, 1879–1911.

United States Federal Works Agency, Work Projects Administration. *New York City Guide*. New York: Random House, 1939.

Ward, James. *Architects in Practice, New York City, 1900–1940*. New York: Committee for the Preservation of Architectural Records, 1989.

Weisman, Winston. "The Commercial Architecture of George B. Post." *JSAH* 31 (October 1972), 176–203.

——. "A New View of Skyscraper History." In *The Rise of an American Architecture*, ed. Edgar Kaufmann, jr., 115–60. New York: Praeger, 1970.

Willensky, Elliot, and Norval White. *AIA Guide to New York City*. 3d ed. San Diego: Harcourt Brace Jovanovich, 1988.

Wright, Carol von Pressentin. *Blue Guide: New York*. London: Ernest Benn, and New York: W. W. Norton, 1983.

Zeisloft, E. Idell, ed. *The New Metropolis*. New York: D. Appleton, 1899.

1. The Urban Context and the Office Building, 1850–70

Albin, Robert G. *The Rise of New York Port (1815–1860)*. New York: Charles Scribner's Sons, 1939.

Brown, Henry Collins. *Fifth Avenue Old and New, 1824–1924*. New York: Fifth Avenue Association, 1924.

Browne, Junius Henri. *The Great Metropolis: A Mirror of New York*. Hartford, Conn.: American, 1869.

Disturnell, John. *New York as It Was and as It Is*. New York: D. Van Nostrand, 1876.

Gardner, Deborah S. *Marketplace: A Brief History of the New York Stock Exchange*. New York: New York Stock Exchange, 1982.

Hamlin, Talbot. *Greek Revival Architecture in America*. 1944. Rpt., New York: Dover, 1964.

Hardy, John. *Manual of the Corporation of the City of New York, 1870*. New York: John Hardy, 1871.

Hutchins, William. "New York Hotels: The Hotels of the Past." *Architectural Record* 12 (October 1902), 459–71.

Janvier, Thomas A. "The Evolution of New York." *Harper's Magazine* 86 (May 1893), 813–29; 87 (June 1893), 15–29.

Kennion, John W. *The Architects' and Builders' Guide: An Elaborate Description of All the Public, Commercial, Philanthropic, Literary & Ecclesiastical Buildings Already Constructed and about to be Erected Next Spring in New York and Its Environs, with Their Cost Respectively, and the Names of the Architects and Builders*. New York: Fitzpatrick and Hunter, 1868.

Kouwenhoven, John A. *The Columbia Historical Portrait of New York*. New York: Doubleday, 1953.

Kramer, Ellen W. "Contemporary Descriptions of New York City and Its Public Architecture, ca. 1850." *JSAH* 27 (December 1968), 264–80.

Lockwood, Charles. *Manhattan Moves Uptown: An Illustrated History*. Boston: Houghton Mifflin, 1976.

Miller's New York as It Is; or Stranger's Guide-Book to the Cities of New York, Brooklyn and Adjacent Places. 1866. Rpt., New York: Schocken, 1975, as *The 1866 Guide to New York City*.

New York City Landmarks Preservation Commission. "Fraunces Tavern Block Historic District Designation Report," 14 November 1978.

——. "South Street Seaport Historic District Designation Report," 10 May 1977.

——. "Tribeca West Historic District Designation Report," 7 May 1991. [The warehouse as a building type.]

New York Illustrated. New York: D. Appleton, 1878.

Peterson, Charles E. "Ante-Bellum Sky-scraper." *JSAH* 9 (October 1950), 27–28. [Jayne Building.]

——. "The Jayne Building Again." *JSAH* 10 (March 1951), 25.

Quinn Hotel Files. The New-York Historical Society Library.

Rideing, William H. "The Metropolitan News-paper." *Harper's Magazine* 56 (December 1877), 43–59.

Spann, Edward K. *The New Metropolis: New York City, 1840–1857.* New York: Columbia Univ. Press, 1981.

Taylor, William I. *The City of New York.* New York: Galt and Hoy, 1879. Map.

"Three Hundred Years of New York." *Scientific American* 101 (25 September 1909), 224–26.

Van Pelt, Daniel. *Leslie's History of the Greater New York.* New York: Arkell, 1898.

Weisman, Winston. "Commercial Palaces of New York, 1845–1875." *Art Bulletin* 36 (December 1954), 285–302.

——. "Philadelphia Functionalism and Sullivan." *JSAH* 20 (March 1961), 3–19.

Zeisloft, E. Idell, ed. *The New Metropolis.* New York: D. Appleton, 1899.

Zelizer, Viviana A. Rotman. *Morals and Markets: The Development of Life Insurance in the United States.* New York: Columbia Univ. Press, 1979.

2. Technological Preparations

Badger, Daniel D. *Illustrations of Iron Architecture, Made by the Architectural Iron Works of the City of New York.* New York: Architectural Iron Works, 1865.

Bannister, Turpin C. "Bogardus Revisited." *JSAH* 15 (December 1956), 12–22; 16 (March 1957), 11–19.

Bixby, W. H. "Wind Pressures in Engineering Construction." *Engineering News* 33 (14 March 1895), 175–84.

Bogardus, James. *Cast Iron Buildings: Their Construction and Advantages.* New York: J. W. Harrison, 1856.

Box, Thomas A. *A Practical Treatise on Heat, as Applied to the Useful Arts.* 2d ed. London: E. and F. N. Spon, 1876.

——. *A Practical Treatise on the Strength of Materials.* London: E. and F. N. Spon, 1883.

Briggs, Robert. "American Practice in Warming Buildings by Steam." *Sanitary Engineer* 7 (5 April 1883), 416; 7 (12 April 1883), 436; 7 (26 April 1883), 485; 7 (3 May 1883), 508; 7 (24 May 1883), 582; 7 (31 May 1883), 607; 8 (14 June 1883), 37.

Brown, Thomas E. "The American Passenger Elevator." *Engineering Magazine* 5 (June 1893), 333–48.

Bruegmann, Robert. "Central Heating and Forced Ventilation: Origins and Effects on Architectural Design." *JSAH* 37 (October 1978), 143–60.

Condit, C. W. "The Two Centuries of Technical Evolution Underlying the Skyscraper." In *Second Century of the Skyscraper,* ed. Lynn S. Beedle for Council on Tall Buildings and Urban Habitat, 11–24. New York: Van Nostrand Reinhold, 1988.

Fairbairn, William. *On the Application of Cast and Wrought Iron to Building Purposes.* New York: John Wiley, 1854.

Ferguson, Eugene S. "A Historical Sketch of Central Heating, 1800–1860." In *Building Early America,* ed. Charles E. Peterson, 165–85. Radnor, Pa.: Chilton, 1976.

"Fire-Proof Columns." *American Architect* 1 (22 January 1876), 29–31. [Tests on Drake & Wight patent column.]

Francis, James B. *On the Strength of Cast Iron Pillars, with Tables for the Use of Engineers, Architects, and Builders.* New York: D. Van Nostrand, 1865.

Gayle, Margot, and Edmund V. Gillon, Jr. *Cast-Iron Architecture in New York.* New York: Dover, 1974.

Gratacap, L. P. *Geology of the City of New York.* 1901. 3d ed. New York: Henry Holt, 1909.

Hatfield, Robert G. *Fire-Proof Floors for Banks, Insurance Companies, Office Buildings and Dwellings. Tables, Shewing the Distances from Centres at Which Rolled Iron Beams Should Be Placed, and the Weight of Metal per Superficial Foot of Floor.* New York: American Institute of Architects, Committee on Library and Publications, 1868. Pamphlet.

Henrici, Olaus M. F. E. *Skeleton Structures, Especially in Their Application to the Building of Steel and Iron Bridges.* New York: D. Van Nostrand, 1867.

"A Historical Review of Progress in the Building Craft." Chapter 4 of *A History of Real Estate, Building, and Architecture in New York City, 1868–1894. Record and Guide* 53. Supplement (12 May 1894), 98–117.

Humber, William. *Strains in Girders: A Handy Book for the Calculation of Strains in Girders and Similar Structures, and Their Strength.* New York: D. Van Nostrand, 1869.

Jewett, Robert A. "Solving the Puzzle of the First American Structural Rail Beam." *Technology and Culture* 10 (July 1969), 371–91.

——. "Structural Antecedents of the I-Beam, 1800–1850." *Technology and Culture* 8 (July 1967), 346–62.

Joynson, Francis Herbert. *The Metals Used in Construction.* New York: D. Van Nostrand, 1868.

Landau, Sarah Bradford. *P. B. Wight: Architect, Contractor, and Critic, 1838–1925.* Chicago: Art Institute of Chicago, 1981.

Larson, Gerald R. "Fire, Earth and Wind: Technical Sources of the Chicago Skyscraper." *Inland Architect* 25 (September 1981), 20–29.

Morris, Tasker and Company. *Illustrated Catalogue.* 4th ed. Philadelphia: Morris, Tasker, 1861.

——. *Price List.* Philadelphia: Morris, Tasker, 1858.

Otis Elevator Company. *The First Hundred Years.* New York: Otis Elevator, 1953.

Petersen, L. A. *Elisha Graves Otis, 1811–1861, and His Influence Upon Vertical Transportation.* New York: Newcomen Society of England, 1945. Pamphlet.

Peterson, Charles E. "Ante-Bellum Skyscraper." *JSAH* 9 (October 1950), 27–28.

——. "The Jayne Building Again." *JSAH* 10 (March 1951), 25.

Pierson, W. H., Jr. *American Buildings and Their Architects: The Corporate and Early Gothic Styles.* Garden City, N.Y.: Doubleday, 1970.

Stone, May N. "The Plumbing Paradox: American Attitudes toward Late Nineteenth-century Domestic Sanitary Arrangements." *Winterthur Portfolio* 14 (Autumn 1979), 283–309.

Sturges, Walter K. "Cast Iron in New York." *Architectural Review* 114 (October 1953), 232–37.

Sutherland, R. J. M. "The Introduction of Structural Wrought Iron." *Transactions of the Newcomen Society* 36 (1963–64), 67–84.

Viollet-le-Duc, Eugene E. *Discourses on Architecture.* 2 vols. Trans. Henry Van Brunt. Boston: J. R. Osgood, 1875.

Vogel, Robert M. "Building in the Age of Steam." In *Building Early America,* ed. Charles E. Peterson, 119–34. Radnor, Pa.: Chilton, 1976.

——. *Elevator Systems of the Eiffel Tower, 1889.* United States National Museum Bulletin 228. Washington: Smithsonian Institution, 1961.

Webster, J. Carson. "The Skyscraper: Logical and Historical Considerations." *JSAH* 18 (December 1959), 126–39.

Wight, Peter B. "The Fire Question." *American Architect* 1 (17 June 1876), 195–97; (24 June 1876), 203–5; (1 July 1876), 211–12; 3 (2 March 1878), 76.

——. "The Johnson System of Floor Construction." *Brickbuilder* 11 (October 1902), 214–17.

——. "Origin and History of Hollow Tile Fireproof Floor Construction." *Brickbuilder* 6 (March 1897), 53–55; 6 (April 1897), 73–75; 6 (May 1897), 98–99; 6 (June 1897), 117–23; 6 (July 1897), 149–50.

Wolf, A. *A History of Science, Technology, and Philosophy in the Eighteenth Century.* 2d ed. London: George Allen and Unwin, 1952.

3. Toward the Skyscraper

Abbott, Jacob. *The Harper Establishment; or How the Story Books Are Made.* New York: Harper, 1855.

Badger, Daniel D. *Illustrations of Iron Architecture Made by the Architectural Iron Works of the City of New York.* New York: Architectural Iron Works, 1865. Rpt. with new introduction by Margot Gayle, New York: Dover, 1981.

Bannister, Turpin C. "Bogardus Revisited." *JSAH,* 15 (December 1956), 12–22; 16 (December 1957), 11–19.

Bogardus, James. *Cast Iron Buildings: Their Construction and Advantages.* New York: J. W. Harrison, 1856.

Brandon, Ruth. *A Capitalist Romance: Singer and the Sewing Machine.* Philadelphia: J. B. Lippincott, 1977.

Brown, John Crosby. *A Hundred Years of Merchant Banking.* New York: 1909.

Burnham, Alan. "Forgotten Engineering: The Rise and Fall of the Phoenix Column." *Architectural Record* 125 (April 1959), 222–25.

Clymer, Ernest Fletcher, ed. *1856–1917: Some Mile-Stones in the History of the National Park Bank of New York.* New York: William Edwin Rudge, 1917.

Gayle, Margot, and Robin Lynn. *A Walking Tour of Cast-Iron Architecture in SoHo.* New York: Friends of Cast Iron Architecture, 1983. Pamphlet.

Kramer, Ellen W. "Contemporary Descriptions of New York City and Its Public Architecture ca. 1850." *JSAH* 27 (December 1968), 264–80.

New bank buildings in New York (various titles). *Bankers' Magazine* 9–12 (July 1854–August 1857).

Phoenix Iron & Steel Company records and trade catalogs. Hagley Museum Library.

Richmond, John Fletcher. *New York and Its Institutions, 1609–1872* . . . New York: E. B. Treat, 1872.

Shannon, Joseph. *Manual of the Corporation of the City of New York, 1869.* New York: E. Jones, 1870.

Shaw, Esmond. *Peter Cooper & the Wrought Iron Beam.* New York: Cooper Union, 1960. Pamphlet.

Smith, Mary Ann Clegg. "The Commercial Architecture of John Butler Snook." Ph.D. diss., Pennsylvania State Univ., 1974.

Upjohn Papers. Including letters, specifications, and other materials dated 1852–56. Manuscripts and Archives Division, New York Public Library. [Trinity Building; Mechanics' Bank.]

4. The "First Skyscrapers"

Adams, George H. *New Columbian Railroad Atlas and Pictorial Album of American Industry.* New York: Asher and Adams, 1876.

Alexander, William. *Description of the New Equitable Building, 120 Broadway, New York, with Illustrations and Plans.* New York: J. K. Lees, 1887.

——. *The Equitable Life Assurance Society of the United States: 65 Years of Progress and Public Service, 1859–1924.* New York: [Equitable Life Assurance Society], 1924.

Baker, Paul R. *Richard Morris Hunt.* Cambridge: MIT Press, 1980.

Brooks, M. A. "Reminiscences of the Early Days of Fireproof Building Construction in New York City." *Engineering News,* 68 (28 November 1912), 1986–87. [Post and first Equitable Building.]

Buley, Roscoe Carlyle. *The Equitable Life Assurance Society of the United States, 1859–1964.* Vol. 1. New York: Appleton-Century-Crofts, 1967.

Burnham, Alan. "The New York Architecture of Richard Morris Hunt." *JSAH* 11 (May 1952), 9–14.

Clarke, T. C. "On Certain Principles of Iron Construction." *American Architect* 1 (8 July 1876), 219–20.

Clough, Shepard B. *A Century of American Life Insurance: A History of the Mutual Life Insurance Company of New York, 1843–1943.* New York: Columbia Univ. Press, 1946.

Curran, Kathleen A. *A Forgotten Architect of the Gilded Age: Josiah Cleaveland Cady's Legacy.* Hartford, Conn.: Watkinson Library and Department of Fine Arts, Trinity College, 1993.

"The Destruction of the Equitable Building by Fire, January 9, 1912." *Engineering News* 67 (18 January 1912), 123–24.

The Equitable Life Assurance Society of the United States Archives.

"The Extension of the Tribune Building, New York." *Engineering Record,* 55 (1 June 1907), 642–46.

Fryer, William J. *Architectural Iron-Work: A Practical Work for Iron-Workers, Architects, and Engineers.* New York: John Wiley and Sons, 1876.

Gibbs, Kenneth Turney. *Business Architectural Imagery: The Impact of Economic and Social Changes on Tall Office Buildings, 1870–1930.* Ann Arbor: UMI Research Press, 1984.

Hardy, John. *Manual of the Corporation of the City of New York, 1870.* New York: John Hardy, 1871.

Hatfield, Robert G. *The Theory of Transverse Strains, and Its Application to the Construction of Buildings.* New York: John Wiley and Sons, 1877.

Historic American Buildings Survey. No. 7 (July 1969). New York City Architecture. HABS No. NY-5468. [Tribune Building.]

Hudnut, James M. *History of the New-York Life Insurance Company, 1895–1905.* New York: New York Life Insurance, 1906.

——. *Semi-Centennial History of the New-York Life Insurance Company, 1845–1895.* New York: New York Life Insurance, 1895.

Hunt, Richard Morris. Collection. Prints and Drawings Collection, The Octagon Museum, American Architectural Foundation.

Landau, Sarah Bradford. "Richard Morris Hunt: Architectural Innovator and Father of a 'Distinctive' American School." In *The Architecture of Richard Morris Hunt,* ed. S. R. Stein, 46–77. Chicago: Univ. of Chicago Press, 1986.

Leeds, Lewis W. *A Treatise on Ventilation: Comprising Seven Lectures Given Before the Franklin Institute, Philadelphia, 1866–68.* 2d ed. New York: John Wiley and Sons, 1876.

Mausolf, Lisa. "A Catalog of the Work of George B. Post Architect." M.S. thesis, Columbia Univ., 1983.

Mutual Life Insurance Company Archives. [Especially *Annual Reports, 1864–86*.]

"The Nassau-Beekman." *Architectural Record* 12 (May 1902), 93–98. [Morse Building.]

The New York Board of Fire Underwriters. *Report on Fire in the Equitable Building, Broadway, Pine, Nassau, and Cedar Streets, New York City, January 9, 1912.* New York, 29 February 1912. Equitable Life Assurance Society Archives.

New York Illustrated. New York: D. Appleton, 1878.

New York Life Insurance Company Archives.

The New-York Tribune: A Sketch of Its History. New York: 1883. Pamphlet.

Schumann, F. "Fire-proof Construction." *American Architect* 3 (29 June 1878), 224–25; 4 (6 July 1878), 4–5.

Schuyler, Montgomery. "A Review of the Work of Richard Morris Hunt." *Architectural Record* 5 (October–December 1895), 97–180.

Seamen's Bank for Savings records, 1829–1989. Collection, South Street Seaport Museum.

Shaughnessy, Jim. *Delaware & Hudson.* Berkeley, Calif.: Howell-North, 1967.

"Sky Building in New York." *Building News* 45 (7 September 1883), 363–64. [Tribune, Western Union, Evening Post, and Morse buildings.]

Sturgis, Russell. "The Works of George B. Post." *Architectural Record* Great American Architects Series. No. 4., June 1898.

Weisman, Winston. "Commercial Palaces of New York, 1845–1875." *Art Bulletin*, 36 (December 1954), 285–302.

———. "New York and the Problem of the First Skyscraper." *JSAH* 12 (March 1953), 13–21.

5. The Future Revealed

Alpern, Andrew. *Apartments for the Affluent: A Historical Survey of Buildings in New York.* New York: McGraw-Hill, 1975.

———. *Luxury Apartment Houses of Manhattan: An Illustrated History.* New York: Dover, 1992.

"Another Victorian Vanishes: The New York Produce Exchange, 1884–1957." *Architectural Forum* 106 (June 1957), 142–49.

"Building Laws Condemned." *New York Times*, 6 June 1881.

Collingwood, F. "An Examination into the Method of Determining Wind Pressures." *Engineering News* 8 (15 October 1881), 416–18.

"Competitive Design for an Office Building . . . for Cyrus Field, Esq." *American Architect* 13 (21 April 1883), 186–87. [Charles Atwood's design.]

"Condition of Frame of Tower Building, New York, after 25-yr. Service." *Engineering News* 71 (2 April 1914), 748–49.

"Corner Stone of New [Produce Exchange] Building Laid." *New York Times*, 7 June 1882.

Cromley, Elizabeth Collins. *Alone Together: A History of New York's Early Apartments.* Ithaca: Cornell Univ. Press, 1990.

"Early Iron Building Construction." *Engineering News* 50 (10 September 1903), 214–15.

"The Edison System of Wiring Buildings for the Incandescent Electric Light." *Sanitary Engineer* 7 (14 December 1882), 27–28; 7 (21 December 1882), 50–52.

"Foundations of High Buildings." *American Architect* 42 (18 November 1893), 88–90. [Mills, Washington, and Manhattan Life buildings.]

Gibbs, Kenneth T. "The Architecture of Norris G. Starkweather." M.A. thesis, Univ. of Virginia, 1972.

Graether, Leonard F., comp. *Atlas of the Illustrated Building Laws of the Principal Cities of the United States.* Vol. 1: *Building Laws of the City of New York, in Force in 1896, Including Amendments up to 1898 Inclusively.* New York: Leonard F. Graether, 1898.

"The Growth of New York." *New York Times*, 19 January 1879, 26 January 1879. [Building statistics for ten years.]

Hawksley, T. "On the Pressure of Wind upon a Fixed Plane Surface." *Engineering News* 8 (8 October 1881), 408.

The invention of skeleton construction (news item). *Engineering News* 42 (24 August 1899), 113.

"Maximum Wind Pressure." *Engineering News and American Contract Journal* 14 (10 October 1885), 235.

"Mode of Fire-Proofing Iron Columns and Girders." *Engineering and Building Record and Sanitary Engineer* 18 (15 September 1888), 189–90.

"Most Costly Buildings Enumerated." *New York Times*, 5 October 1890.

"New [Produce Exchange] Building: Opening" (titles vary). *New York Times*, 4 May 1884, 6 May 1884, 7 May 1884.

"The New Building of the Mutual Life Insurance Company of New York." *New York Times*, 26 June 1884.

"New Buildings of Prominence in New York City." *Scientific American* 50 (10 May 1884), 292.

"New Down-Town Buildings." *Record and Guide* 32 (29 September 1883), 729. [Mutual Life Building, 1883–84.]

New York City Landmarks Preservation Commission. "Ladies' Mile Historic District Designation Report," ed. Marjorie Pearson, 2 May 1989, 2 vols. [Especially Architects' Appendix; also Western Union and Goelet buildings.]

New York Produce Exchange. *Origin, Growth, and Usefulness of the New York Produce Exchange.* New York: Historical Publishing, 1884.

New York's "original skyscraper," impending demolition (news item). *Engineering News* 54 (13 July 1905), 41. [Tower Building.]

"Office of United States Trust Company, New York, N.Y." *American Architect* 23 (16 June 1888). Plate.

"The Origin of the Skeleton Type of High Building." *Engineering News* 29 (5 January 1893), 15.

Plunz, Richard. *A History of Housing in New York City: Dwelling Type and Social Change in the American Metropolis.* New York: Columbia Univ. Press, 1990.

"The Post Building." *Record and Guide* 30 (11–18 November 1882), 72–73.

Post scrapbooks and clippings folder. George B. Post Collection. The New-York Historical Society. [Mills Building, Produce Exchange, Cotton Exchange, Times Building.]

"Report on Elevated Dwellings in New York City." Printed for private distribution on 1 July 1883. New York: Evening Post Job Printing Office, 1883.

Rosenberg, Theodore. "Fire-Proof Buildings." *Journal of the Association of Engineering Societies* 5 (February 1886), 121–26.

Schuyler, Montgomery. "The Evolution of the Skyscraper." *Scribner's Magazine* 46 (September 1909), 257–71. [Includes Tower Building.]

———. "Henry Janeway Hardenbergh." *Architectural Record* 6 (January–March 1897), 335–75.

———. "Recent Buildings in New York." *Harper's Magazine* 67 (September 1883), 557–78.

———. "A Review of the Works of Cyrus L. W. Eidlitz." *Architectural Record* 5 (April–June 1896), 411–35.

———. "The Works of Cady, Berg and See." *Architectural Record* 6 (April–June 1897), 517–53.

"Sky Building in New York." *Building News* 45 (7 September 1883), 363–64. [United Bank, Mills, Temple Court, Welles, and Washington buildings.]

Starkweather, Norris G. Floor plans, framing plans, and details, Potter Building, c. 1885.

Stokes, Henry. "Incombustible Materials for Buildings." *American Architect* 11 (4 March 1882), 105–6.

"The Strength of Wrought Iron and Steel at High Temperatures." *American Architect* 11 (20 May 1882), 238.

Sturgis, Russell. "The Warehouse and the Factory in Architecture." *Architectural Record* 15 (January 1904), 1–17; 15 (February 1904), 123–33.

———. "The Works of George B. Post." *Architectural Record* Great American Architects Series. No. 4, June 1898.

Taylor, William I. *The City of New York.* New York: Galt and Hoy, 1879. Map.

"Thirty-seven Years' Fire Statistics for New York." *American Architect* 36 (4 June 1892), 152.

"The Tower Building and the 'Skeleton-construction' Controversy." *American Architect* 65 (26 August 1899), 65.

Tunick, Susan. "Architectural Terra Cotta: Its Impact on New York." *Sites* 18 (1986), 4–38. [Especially Potter Building.]

Van Rensselaer, Mariana Griswold. "Recent Architecture in America. III. Commercial Buildings." *Century Magazine* 28 (August 1884), 511–23.

"Vast Apartment Houses." *Record and Guide* 29 (3 June 1882), 550.

Waid, D. Everett. "A History of Steel Skeleton Construction." *Brickbuilder* 3 (August 1894), 157–59.

Wheatley, Richard. "The New York Chamber of Commerce." *Harper's Magazine* 83 (September 1891), 502–17.

———. "The New York Produce Exchange." *Harper's Magazine* 73 (July 1886), 189–218.

"Wind Pressure." *Engineering News and American Contract Journal* 14 (1 August 1885), 65.

"Wind Pressure and Velocity." *Engineering News* 18 (29 October 1887), 308.

"Wind Pressure Constant." *Engineering News*

21 (23 March 1889), 255.

"Wind Pressure Formulas." *Engineering News* 25 (31 January 1891), 111.

6. State of the Skyscraper Art, 1889 to the Mid-1890s

Adler, Dankmar. "Tall Office Buildings—Past and Future." *Engineering Magazine* 3 (September 1892), 765–73.

Allen, Leicester. "Heating and Ventilating Tall Buildings." *Engineering Magazine* 9 (June 1895), 476–82.

Berg, Louis De Coppet. "Iron Construction in New York City." *Architectural Record* 1 (April–June 1892), 448–68.

Birkmire, William H. *Architectural Iron and Steel and Its Application in the Construction of Buildings*. New York: John Wiley and Sons, 1891.

——. *Compound Riveted Girders, as Applied in the Construction of Buildings*. New York: John Wiley and Sons, 1893.

Blackall, C. H. "The Endurance of Structural Metal Work." *Brickbuilder* 3 (November 1894), 217–19.

——. "High Buildings." *Brickbuilder* 5 (February 1896), 28–29.

Breithaupt, W. H. "On Iron Skeletons for Buildings." *Engineering Record* 25 (5 March 1892), 226.

"Cast and Wrought Iron for Frame Work of Buildings." *Scientific American* 71 (15 December 1894), 370–71.

"A City of High Buildings." *Record and Guide* 53 (17 March 1894), 405–7. [Architects' views on high buildings.]

"Do 'Sky-scrapers' Pay?" *American Architect* 44 (12 May 1894), 58.

"Fireproof Construction." *Engineering and Building Record* 22 (9 August 1890), 148.

Flagg, Ernest. "The Dangers of High Buildings." *The Cosmopolitan* 21 (May 1896), 70–79.

Freitag, Joseph Kendall. *Architectural Engineering with Especial Reference to High Building Construction, Including Many Examples of Prominent Office Buildings*. 2d rev. ed., New York: John Wiley and Sons, 1901.

Fryer, William J. "The New York Building Law. *Architectural Record* 1 (July–September 1891), 70–82.

——, ed. *Laws Relating to Buildings in the City of New York* . . . New York: Record and Guide, 1885, 1887, 1892, 1895, 1897.

Graether, Leonard F., comp. *Atlas of the Illustrated Building Laws of the Principal Cities of the United States*. Vol. 1: *Building Laws of the City of New York, in Force in 1896, Including Amendments up to 1898 Inclusively*. New York: Leonard F. Graether, 1898.

"Height and Areas of Buildings." *Record and Guide* 49 (16 January 1892), 66–67.

Height limitation of buildings, law regulating (news item). *Engineering News* 35 (23 January 1896), 49; 35 (20 February 1896), 128; 35 (19 March 1896), 192; 37 (21 January 1897), 32; 37 (8 April 1897), 208.

"High Buildings of Steel Skeleton Construction." *Engineering News* 32 (27 December 1894), 535–37. [Includes extensive bibliography of subsidiary articles on structural design, *Engineering News* 29–32 (1893–94).]

Hill, George. "The Heating of Buildings." *Architectural Record* 5 (October–December 1895), 204–11.

——. "Some Practical Limiting Conditions in the Design of the Modern Office Building." *Architectural Record* 2 (April–June 1893), 445–68.

"Is Skeleton Construction an Experiment Only?" *Record and Guide* 53 (9 June 1894), 923–24.

Jallings, John H. *Elevators: A Practical Treatise on the Development and Design of Hand, Belt, Steam, Hydraulic, and Electric Elevators*. Chicago: American Technology Society, 1915. [Especially on Sprague-Pratt elevator.]

Kantor, Harvey A. "Modern Urban Planning in New York City: Origins and Evolution, 1890–1933." Ph.D. diss., New York Univ., 1971. [Pavey bill and other height restriction efforts.]

Laws of the State of New York Passed at the Eighty-third Session of the Legislature, Chapter 470 (Albany, 1860). *Laws . . . Eighty-fifth Session . . .*, Chapter 356 (1862). *Laws . . . Eighty-ninth Session . . .*, Chapter 873 (1866). *Laws . . . Ninety-fourth Session . . .*, Chapter 625 (1871). *Laws . . . Ninety-seventh Session . . .*, Chapter 547 (1874). *Laws . . . One hundred and Eighth Session . . .*, Chapter 456 (1885). *Laws . . . One Hundred and Fifteenth Session . . .*, Chapter 275 (1892). [New York City Building Codes.]

"Live-Loads and Supports in Office-Buildings." *American Architect* 43 (10 March 1894), 118–19. [Letters by Fritz von Emperger and William Le Baron Jenney.]

Longfellow, William P. P. "The Architect's Point of View." *Scribner's Magazine* 9 (January 1891), 119–28.

"The New York Building Law." *Engineering Record* 25 (30 April 1892), 360, 368.

"Operation of the New Building Law: Opinions of Prominent Builders as to Its Probable Effect on Business." *Record and Guide* 50 (2 July 1892), 3.

Petersen, L. A. *Elisha Graves Otis, 1811–1861, and His Influence Upon Vertical Transportation.* New York: Newcomen Society of England, 1945. Pamphlet.

Purdy, Corydon T. "The Steel Skeleton Type of High Building." *Engineering News* 26 (5 December 1891), 534–36; 26 (12 December 1891), 560–61; 26 (26 December 1891), 605–8; 27 (2 January 1892), 2–5.

Quimby, Henry H., et al. "Wind Bracing in High Buildings." *Engineering Record* 26 (19 November 1892), 394; 27 (31 December 1892), 99; 27 (14 January 1893), 138; 27 (21 January 1893), 161–62; 27 (28 January 1893), 180; 27 (25 February 1893), 260; 27 (11 March 1893), 298–99; 27 (18 March 1893), 320.

Sooysmith, Charles. "Foundation Construction for Tall Buildings." *Engineering Magazine* 13 (April 1897), 20–33.

"The Stability of High Buildings." *Engineering Record* 26 (1 October 1892), 273; 26 (15 October 1892), 312; 26 (22 October 1892), 329; 26 (5 November 1892), 362; 26 (26 November 1892), 407; 27 (28 January 1893), 180.

"Stability of Lofty Buildings." *Scientific American* 74 (21 March 1896), 178.

"Steel Columns vs. Cast-Iron Columns." *Record and Guide* 49 (6 February 1892), 200–201.

"Steel Foundations of Tall Office Buildings." *Scientific American* 71 (8 December 1894), 353, 359.

"Steel-Frame Building Construction." *Engineering Record* 32 (15 June 1895), 44.

"The Tall Building Question." *Engineering Record* 24 (31 October 1891), 343; 35 (12 December 1896), 23.

"To Limit the Height of Tall Buildings." *Scientific American* 76 (23 January 1897), 50.

"To Restrict the Height of Buildings." *Engineering Record* 33 (22 February 1896), 203.

Twenty-story office buildings (editorial). *Engineering News* 31 (22 March 1894), 240.

Waite, Guy B. "Wind Bracing in High Buildings." *Engineering News* 32 (20 December 1894), 506–7.

"Wind Bracing in High Buildings." *Engineering Record* 32 (8 June 1895), 30; 32 (15 June 1895), 42; 32 (13 July 1895), 119; 32 (20 July 1895), 136–38; 32 (27 July 1895), 155–56; 32 (3 August 1895), 173–74.

"A Year's Building in Three Great Cities." *American Architect* 31 (14 February 1891), 112.

7. Monuments to Commercial Power and Corporate Prestige, 1889–95

"Architectural Development." *Record and Guide* 49 (11 June 1892), 916.

"The Architectural League Exhibition." *Record and Guide* 41 (14 January 1893), 36–37. [Competition drawings for Manhattan Life Building.]

Bolton, Reginald Pelham. *The High Office-Buildings of New York.* London: Institution of Civil Engineers, 1901. Illustrated pamphlet.

Buck, Wendell. *From Quill Pens to Computers in an Account of the First One Hundred and Twenty-Five Years of the Manhattan Life Insurance Company of New York.* New York: Manhattan Life Insurance, [1974?].

Cortissoz, Royal. "Landmarks of Manhattan." *Scribner's Magazine* 18 (November 1895), 531–44.

Ferree, Barr. "An 'American Style' of Architecture." *Architectural Record* 1 (July–September 1891), 39–45.

———. "The High Building and Its Art." *Scribner's Magazine* 15 (March 1894), 297–318.

———. "The Modern Office Building." *Inland Architect and News Record* 27 (February 1896), 4–5; 27 (March 1896), 12–14; 27 (April 1896), 23–25; 27 (May 1896), 34–36; 27 (June 1896), 45–47.

———. "A Talk with Bruce Price." *Architectural Record* Great American Architects Series. No. 5, June 1899.

———. "Tendencies in Recent Architecture." *Engineering Magazine* 1 (September 1891), 784–802.

"Foundations of High Buildings." *American Architect* 42 (16 November 1893), 88–89. [Manhattan Life Building.]

Hudnut, James M. *Semi-Centennial History of the New-York Life Insurance Company, 1845–1895.* New York: New York Life Insurance, 1895.

Kimball, Francis H. "The Construction of a

Great Building." *Engineering Magazine* 8 (February 1895), 877–92. [Manhattan Life.]

"The Lofty Buildings of New York City." *Scientific American* 75 (10 October 1896), 277, 285–86.

"Manhattan Life Insurance Building, New York City." *Engineering Record* 29 (20 January 1894), 122–25; 30 (18 August 1894), 189–90; 30 (17 November 1894), 408–10; 30 (24 November 1894), 428; 31 (1 December 1894), 5–6; 31 (26 January 1895), 152–154; 31 (27 April 1895), 388–390.

Manhattan Life Insurance Company's building (news items). *Engineering News* 29 (2 February 1893), 97; 29 (18 May 1893), 455.

McKim, Mead & White. *A Monograph of the Work of McKim, Mead & White, 1879–1915.* Vol. 1. New York: Architectural Book, [c. 1914–17].

McKim, Mead & White Collection. The New-York Historical Society. [Scrapbook clippings on Madison Square Garden, New York Life, World, and other buildings; files, photographs, and drawings relating to New York Life Insurance Company Building.]

New York Life Insurance Company Archives. [Photographs, plans, "Specifications and Contracts for Rebuilding Home Office, 346–348 Broadway."]

"The New York World Building." *Engineering and Building Record* 22 (1 November 1890), 342–43; 22 (8 November 1890), 358–60; 22 (15 November 1890), 374.

"Old and New Buildings of New York." *Scientific American* 71 (13 October 1894), 228–29.

Parsons, H. de B. "The Tall Building under Test of Fire." *Engineering Magazine* 16 (February 1899), 767–83.

"The Pulitzer Building." *The New York World*, souvenir issue, 10 December 1890.

"Recent Brickwork in New York." *Brickbuilder* 1 (October 1892), 78. [Havemeyer Building.]

Record and Guide 53. Supplement (12 May 1894), 98–138.

"A Review of the Year." *Record and Guide* 49 (23 January 1892), 111–24.

Schuyler, Montgomery. "Henry Janeway Hardenbergh." *Architectural Record* 6 (January–March 1897), 335–75.

——. "The Work of N. Le Brun and Sons." *Architectural Record* 27 (May 1910), 365–81.

——. "The Works of Francis H. Kimball and Kimball & Thompson." *Architectural Record* 7 (April–June 1898), 401–518.

——. "The Works of R. H. Robertson." *Architectural Record* 6 (October–December 1896), 184–219.

Seitz, D. C. *Joseph Pulitzer: His Life and Letters.* New York: Simon & Schuster, 1924.

Sturgis, Russell. "A Critique of the Works of Bruce Price." *Architectural Record* Great American Architects Series. No. 5, June 1899.

——. "The Works of McKim, Mead and White." *Architectural Record* Great American Architects Series. No. 1, May 1895.

Swanberg, W. A. *Pulitzer.* New York: Charles Scribner's Sons, 1967.

"The Tall Buildings of New York." *Munsey's Magazine* 18 (March 1898), 833–48. [Height of Manhattan Life Building.]

"That Thirty-two-story Building." *Record and Guide* 47 (18 April 1891), 608. [Project for Sun Building.]

Troubles . . . high office-buildings in New York [news item]. *American Architect* 50 (19 October 1895), 25. [American Surety Building cornice.]

"The Work of George Edward Harding & Gooch." *Architectural Record* 7 (July–September 1897), 104–17.

8. The Syndicate-Built Skyscraper, Technical Advances, Continuing Debate, 1895–1900

"The Art Critic and the Tall Building." *Scientific American* 80 (28 June 1899), 50.

Audsley, George Ashdown. "Note Books of George Ashdown Audsley (188-?–1924)." Music Division, Performing Arts Research Center, New York Public Library.

The Bayard Building. New York: Rost, n.d. Rental prospectus.

Blackmore, J. J. "Systems and Apparatus for Heating Buildings by Steam." *Engineering Magazine* 15 (April 1898), 28–38.

Bolton, Reginald P. "Electrical Equipment of Office Buildings." *Engineering Magazine* 19 (June 1900), 381–90.

——. "The Equipment of Tall Office Buildings in New York City." *Engineering Record* 39 (13 May 1899), 550–51.

Brown, Charles O. "Engineering Problems of the Tall Building." *Engineering Magazine* 13 (June 1897), 406–18.

Brown, Thomas E. "Passenger Elevators." *American Architect* 86 (12 November 1904), 51–54; 86 (26 November 1904), 67–71; 86 (3 December 1904), 78–79; 86 (10 December 1904), 83–86; 86 (17 December 1904), 91–94.

Bryan, William H. "The Mechanical Plant of a Modern Commercial Building." *Engineering News* 41 (5 January 1899), 2–8.

"Building on Scientific Principles." *Record and Guide* 53. Supplement (12 May 1894), 140–41. [On John T. Williams.]

"Building Skyscrapers, Described by Cass Gilbert, Architect." *Record and Guide* 65 (23 June 1900), 1087–91.

Capper, S. Henbest. "The American Tall Building from a European Point of View." *Engineering Magazine* 14 (November 1897), 239–52.

Coyle, David C. "Alterations Involving a 26-Story Self-sustaining Wall." *Engineering News-Record* 96 (13 May 1926), 774–76. [Commercial Cable Building.]

Freitag, Joseph Kendall. *Architectural Engineering with Especial Reference to High Building Construction, Including Many Examples of Prominent Office Buildings.* 2d rev. ed., New York: John Wiley & Sons, 1901.

——. *The Fire-proofing of Steel Buildings.* New York: John Wiley and Sons, 1899.

George A. Fuller Company. *Broadway Chambers, a Modern Office Building.* New York: Andrew H. Kellogg, 1900. [Pamphlet distributed at Paris Exposition.]

Hamlin, A. D. F. "The Tall Building from an American Point of View." *Engineering Magazine* 14 (December 1897), 436–43.

Irish, Sharon Lee. "Cass Gilbert's Career in New York, 1899–1905." Ph.D. diss., Northwestern Univ., 1985.

Kimball, F. H. "The Architectural Relations of the Steel-Skeleton Building." *Engineering Magazine* 13 (July 1897), 551–66. [Manhattan Life, Empire, and others.]

New York Illustrated, rotogravure edition. New York: C. Souhami, 1914.

One Hundred and Sixty Glimpses of Greater New York. Boston: John F. Murphy, 1904.

"Pneumatic Caissons for the Mercantile Building, New York City." *Engineering News* 38 (15 July 1897), 38–39. [Dun Building.]

Schuyler, Montgomery. "The 'Sky-scraper' Up to Date." *Architectural Record* 8 (January–March. 1899), 231–57.

——. "The Works of Francis H. Kimball and Kimball & Thompson." *Architectural Record* 7 (April–June 1898), 401–518.

"Some Entrances to the Skyscraper." *Architectural Record* 9 (April 1900), 363–74. Plates.

Spencer Trask & Company. *Bowling Green Offices.* New York: Spencer Trask, 1896. Rental prospectus.

Steffens, J. Lincoln. "The Modern Business Building." *Scribner's Magazine* 22 (July 1897), 37–61.

"The Tall Buildings of New York." *Munsey's Magazine* 18 (March 1898), 833–48.

"The Tallest of the Modern Office Buildings." *Scientific American* 79 (24 December 1898), 401, 409–10. [Park Row Building.]

"The Work of George Edward Harding & Gooch." *Architectural Record* 7 (July–September 1897), 104–17.

9. Skyscrapers and the Urban Scene at the Turn of the Century

Barney, J. Stewart. "The Ecole des Beaux-Arts, Its Influence on Our Architecture." *Architectural Record* 22 (November 1907), 333–42.

Bolton, Reginald Pelham. *The High Office-Buildings of New York.* London: Institution of Civil Engineers, 1901. Pamphlet.

The Building Code as Finally Adopted by the Building Code Commission of the City of New York. 1899.

Caffin, Charles H. "Municipal Art." *Harper's Magazine* 100 (April 1900), 655–66.

"Coal Consumption in Large Buildings." *Engineering News* 41 (16 February 1899), 103.

Corbin, John. "The Twentieth Century City." *Scribner's Magazine* 33 (March 1903), 259–72.

"The Cost of the High Office Building." *American Architect* 64 (10 June 1899), 82.

Croly, Herbert. "New York as the American Metropolis." *Architectural Record* 13 (March 1903), 193–206.

Ferree, Barr. "The Art of the High Building." *Architectural Record* 15 (May 1904), 445–66.

Frohne, H. W. "Engineering in Architecture." *Architectural Record* 22 (July 1907), 57–60.

Greater New York Illustrated: Over One Hundred and Fifty Photographic Views of the Foremost City of the Western Hemisphere. Chicago: Rand, McNally, 1898.

"A Halt Called on 'Sky-scrapers.'" *Scribner's Magazine* 19 (March 1896), 395–96.

Henry Maurer and Son. Catalogue of fireproof building materials. New York: Henry Maurer and Son, 1898.

Hill, George. "The Economy of the Office Building." *Architectural Record* 15 (April 1904), 313–27.

James, Henry. "New York Revisited." *Harper's Magazine* 112 (February 1906), 400–406; 112 (March 1906), 603–8; 112

(May 1906), 900–907.

King, Moses. *New York: The American Cosmopolis, the Foremost City in the World.* Boston: Moses King, 1894.

"Legislation to Restrict Height of Buildings Advised by Chamber of Commerce." *New York Times*, 3 January 1896, 6.

Lewis, Nelson P. "Municipal Engineering Work in New York City in 1904." *Engineering News* 53 (9 February 1905), 144–45. [City improvement commission.]

Manhattan Electrical Supply Company Catalogue. New York: Manhattan Electrical Supply, 1897.

Meyer, Henry C., Jr. "The Ventilation and Heating of Tall Buildings." *Engineering News* 41 (26 January 1899), 63.

Monroe, William S. "Electric Lighting of Modern Office Buildings." *Architectural Record* 6 (October–December 1896), 105–13.

"The Need of Improved Methods for Extinguishing Fire in High Buildings." *Engineering News* 40 (22 December 1898), 396–97.

"Reasons for the Development of High Buildings in Lower New York." *American Architect* 74 (12 October 1901), 9.

"The Regulation of Tall Building Construction." *Engineering Record* 35 (2 January 1897), 96–97.

Rhodes, Harrison. "New York: City of Romance." *Harper's Magazine* 119 (November 1909), 914–25.

Robinson, Charles Mulford. *Modern Civic Art; or The City Made Beautiful.* New York: G. P. Putnam's Sons, 1903.

Russell, A. D. "The Architect and the Engineer." *Architecture* 5 (15 June 1902), 190–94.

Schneider, Charles C. "The Structural Design of Buildings." *Proceedings of the American Society of Civil Engineers.* Rpt. in *American Architect* 86 (15 October 1904), 21–22; 86 (22 October 1904), 27–29; 86 (29 October 1904), 35–37; 86 (31 December 1904), 110–12; 87 (25 February 1905), 64–67.

Schopfer, Jean. "American Architecture from a Foreign Point of View: New York City." *Architectural Review* 7 (March 1900), 25–30.

Schuyler, Montgomery. "The Skyscraper Problem." *Scribner's Magazine* 34 (August 1903), 253–56.

Shanor, Rebecca Read. *The City That Never Was.* New York: Viking, 1988.

"The Use of Concrete-Steel Construction in New York." *American Architect* 82 (17 October 1903), 21. [Building code regulations.]

10. The Skyscraper Comes of Age, 1900–1910

Bolton, Reginald Pelham. "The Engineer, the Architect, & the General Construction Company." *Engineering Magazine* 27 (August 1904), 768–74.

Boyd, David K. "The Skyscraper and the Street." *American Architect* 94 (4 November 1908), 161–67.

Bragdon, Claude. "Architecture in the United States. III. The Skyscraper." *Architectural Record* 26 (August 1909), 84–96.

Broadway-Cortlandt Company. *The City Investing Building, Broadway-Cortlandt and Church Streets . . .* New York: Chasmar-Winchell, 1907. Real estate prospectus.

"Building and Machinery Foundations in Quicksand." *Engineering Record* 53 (3 March 1906), 247–48.

"Building Operations South of Chambers St." *Record and Guide* 75 (4 February 1905), 243. [Sixty Wall, Trinity, and U.S. Express buildings.]

Concrete building construction in New York City (news item). *Engineering News* 48 (18 December 1902), 521.

"The Construction of the City Investing Building, New York." *Engineering Record* 57 (4 April 1908), 444–47.

"The Construction of the Trinity and United States Realty Buildings, New York." *Engineering Record* 55 (2 March 1907), 302–4; 55 (4 May 1907), 539.

Corsa hotel files. The New-York Historical Society Library.

David, Arthur C. "The New Fifth Avenue." *Architectural Record* 22 (July 1907), 1–14.

De Leeuw, Rudolph M. *Both Sides of Broadway.* New York: De Leeuw Riehl, [c. 1910].

"Derricks and Sheet Pile Drivers for Foundation Work." *Engineering Record* 50 (27 August 1904), 254–56. [Trinity Building.]

Desmond, H. W. "A Beaux-Arts Skyscraper: The Blair Building, New York City." *Architectural Record* 14 (December 1903), 37–43.

Droege, John A. *Passenger Terminals and Trains.* New York: McGraw-Hill, 1916.

Dubin, Lydia S. "The Hotels of New York City, 1885–1900." M.A. thesis, Pennsylvania State Univ., 1969.

"An Eighteen-Story Steel Cage Building" (titles vary). *Engineering Record* 54 (22 September 1906), 333–34; 54 (1 December 1906), 598–99. [One Wall Street Building.]

"Erecting Tall Buildings in Congested Streets."

Engineering Record 63 (25 March 1911), 317–18.

"Erection of the City Investing Company's Building." Engineering Record 55 (15 June 1907), 696–97.

"The Erection of the Trinity Building, New York." Engineering Record 50 (3 December 1904), 662–63.

Flagg, Ernest. "The Limitation of Height and Area of Buildings in New York." American Architect 93 (8 April 1908), 125–26.

"The Foundations of Buildings." Engineering Record 51 (15 April 1905), 421.

"The Foundations of the Trinity Annex and Boreel Buildings, New York." Engineering Record 54 (3 November 1906), 482–85.

Granger, Alfred H. "A Plea for Beauty." Architectural Record 18 (August 1905), 161–66. [Blair Building et al.]

"The Height of American Office Buildings." Engineering Record 50 (1 October 1904), 382.

"Hotel St. Regis, New York." Architecture 9 (15 June 1904), 81–91, plates 42–50.

Howe, Frederic C. "The German and the American City." Scribner's Magazine 49 (April 1911), 485–92.

——. "In Defense of the American City." Scribner's Magazine 51 (April 1912), 484–90.

Hubbard, Charles L. "Power and Heat for Office Buildings." Engineering Record 54 (1 December 1906), 614–16.

Hutchins, William. "New York Hotels. II. The Modern Hotel." Architectural Record 12 (October 1902), 459–71; 12 (November 1902), 621–35.

"The Invasion of New York City by Darkness." Record and Guide 81 (6 June 1908), 1056–57.

Irish, Sharon Lee. "A 'Machine That Makes the Land Pay': The West Street Building in New York." Technology and Culture 30 (April 1989), 376–97.

Jallings, John H. Elevators: A Practical Treatise on the Development and Design of Hand, Belt, Steam, Hydraulic, and Electric Elevators. Chicago: American Technology Society, 1915. [Especially on the Standard Plunger elevator.]

Kantor, Harvey A. "The City Beautiful in New York." The New-York Historical Society Quarterly 57 (April 1973), 149–71.

Kimball, Francis H. "City Investing Building." New York Architect 2 (May 1908), unpaged.

Knowlton, Howard S. "Modern Elevator Types and Elevator Practice." Engineering Magazine 28 (November 1904), 241–48.

Kreitler, Peter Gwillim. Flatiron: A Photographic History of the World's First Steel Frame Skyscraper, 1901–1990. Washington, D.C.: American Institute of Architects Press, 1990.

"The Largest Single Office Building in the World." Scientific American 97 (23 November 1907), 373, 378. [City Investing Co. Building.]

The Liberty Tower, New York. New York: Liberty-Nassau Building, 1910. Real estate prospectus.

"A Mammoth Office Building Dissected." Scientific American 103 (6 August 1910), 102. [City Investing Co. Building.]

"A Metropolitan Standard of Buildings." Record and Guide 73. Supplement (11 June 1904), 1395–1473.

"Modern Foundations." Architectural Record 21 (June 1907), 459–67.

"New York Building Statistics." American Architect 89 (13 January 1906), 16. [Covering the years 1870–1905.]

New York City Improvement Commission. Report to the Honorable George B. McClellan of the City of New York & to the Honorable Board of Aldermen of the City of N.Y., January 1907. New York: Kalkhoff, 1907.

New York City's high buildings [news item]. Engineering News 58 (14 November 1907), 528.

New York Illustrated, rotogravure edition. New York: C. Souhami, 1914.

"The New York Times Building" (titles vary) Engineering Record 49 (30 April 1904), 550–52; 49 (7 May 1904), 594–96; 49 (14 May 1904), 612–14; 49 (21 May 1904), 648–49; 49 (28 May 1904), 683–85; 49 (4 June 1904), 719–22; 49 (11 June 1904), 742–44.

New York Times Building Supplement, 1 January 1905. [Times Building.]

"Number of New York Skyscrapers." American Architect 92 (14 December 1907), 200.

Purdy, Corydon Tyler. "The 'New York Times' Building." Excerpt, Minutes of Proceedings of the Institution of Civil Engineers, 178, Session 1908–9, part 4. London: Institution of Civil Engineers, 1909.

Ramsey, William V. A Story of the Church Street Terminal Buildings of the Hudson & Manhattan Railroad Company, New York. New York: Wynkoop Hallenbeck Crawford, 1909. Real estate prospectus.

"Real Estate and Building in 1905." Record

and Guide 77 (6 January 1906), 1–3.

Schuyler, Montgomery. "The Evolution of a Skyscraper." *Architectural Record* 14 (November 1903), 329–43. [Times Building.]

——. "Some Recent Skyscrapers." *Architectural Record* 22 (September 1907), 161–76.

"The Skyscraper." *Engineering Record* 61 (26 March 1910), 345.

"Some Structural Features of the City Investing Company's Building, New York" (titles vary). *Engineering Record* 54 (24 November 1906), 566–68; 54 (1 December 1906), 603–5.

Starrett, Paul. *Changing the Skyline*. New York: McGraw-Hill, 1938.

"The Steel Framework of the Trinity Building, New York." *Engineering Record* 51 (14 January 1905), 44–46.

"The Structural Framework of the Astor Hotel, New York City." *Engineering News* 36 (24 December 1896), 412–15. [Waldorf-Astoria Hotel.]

Sturgis, Russell. "A Review of the Works of Clinton and Russell." *Architectural Record* 6 (April–June 1897), 4–61.

Thomson, T. Kennard. "The Foundations of the New Mutual Life Insurance Building, New York." *Engineering News* 45 (28 March 1901), 221–27.

"Three Great Contracts." *Record and Guide* 77 (2 June 1906), 1043. [Hudson Terminal, Trinity, U.S. Realty buildings.]

"Times Tower's Era Ends with Removal of '04 Cornerstone." *New York Times*, 6 March 1964.

The towering skyscraper (news item). *Engineering Record* 61 (12 February 1910), 175.

"Two New Record-Breaking Office Buildings in New York City . . . Singer Building . . . City Investing Building." *Engineering News* 58 (5 December 1907), 595–603.

U.S. Realty and Improvement Company. *Trinity Building, 111 Broadway, and United States Realty Building, 115 Broadway*. New York: U.S. Realty and Improvement, [1907?]. Real estate prospectus.

Van Dyke, John C. *The New New York*. New York: Macmillan, 1909.

The West Street Building. New York: Cruikschank, [1907?]. Pamphlet.

"The West Street Building, New York City." *Architectural Record* 22 (August 1907), 102–9.

Wilson, A. C. "Wind Bracing with Knee Braces or Gusset Plates." *Engineering Record* 58 (5 September 1908), 272–74.

"The Works of Messrs. Carrère and Hastings." *Architectural Record* 27 (January 1910), 1–120.

11. Culminating Works and Envoys of the Future

Adams, Thomas. *Buildings: Their Uses and the Spaces about Them*. New York: New York Regional Plan Association, 1931.

Aus, Gunvald. "Engineering Design of the Woolworth Building." *American Architect* 103 (26 March 1913), 157–70.

Aus, Gunvald, and Cass Gilbert. Woolworth Building framing plans. New York: Office of Gunvald Aus, 1911, 1912. Collection, Dept. of Civil Engineering, National Museum of American History, Smithsonian Institution.

Bacon, Mardges. *Ernest Flagg: Beaux-Arts Architect and Urban Reformer*. New York: Architectural History Foundation, and Cambridge: MIT Press, 1986.

"The Bankers Trust Building." *Architecture* 25 (15 May 1912), 69–78 and plates.

Beals, Allen E. "Edward J. Hogan, Agent: The Inside Story of How World's Tallest Structure Came to Be Built, and How the Site Was Procured." *Record and Guide* 90 (9 November 1912), 869–70. [Woolworth Building.]

——. "Has the New York Skyscraper Reached Its Limit? Prospective Effects of the Removal of the Post Office: Manhattan's 'Billion-Dollar Mile' and Its Relation to Commercial Migration Uptown." *Record and Guide* 87 (24 June 1911), 1185–86.

Bein, Arthur G. "Famous Prototypes of New York Towers." *American Architect* 97 (16 February 1910), 81–84. [Includes Metropolitan Life Tower.]

Bruce, H. Addington. *Above the Clouds and Old New York*. Privately printed, 1913. Woolworth Building visitors' brochure.

Buley, Roscoe Carlyle. *The Equitable Life Assurance Society of the United States: One Hundredth Anniversary History, 1859/1959*. New York: Appleton-Century-Crofts, 1959.

Burnham, Alan. "Forgotten Pioneering." *Architectural Forum* 106 (April 1957), 117–21. [Singer Building.]

"A Campanile 700 Feet High." *Scientific American* 98 (2 May 1908), 305, 310. [Metropolitan Life Tower.]

The Cathedral of Commerce. New York: Broadway Park Place, 1916. Woolworth Building visitors' brochure.

Chappell, Sally A. Kitt. "A Reconsideration of the Equitable Building in New York." *JSAH* 49 (March 1990), 90–95.

Commission on Building Districts and Restrictions: Final Report, June 2, 1916. City of New York, Board of Estimate and Apportionment, Committee on the City Plan, 1916. Zoning law.

"Construction of the Woolworth Building." *Engineering Record* 66 (27 July 1912), 97–100.

Desmond, H. W. "The Works of Ernest Flagg." *Architectural Record* 11 (April 1902), 1–103.

"The Equitable Building." *Architecture and Building* 47 (May 1915), 165–80.

Equitable Office Building Corporation. *Equitable Building: New York.* New York: 1914. Real estate prospectus.

"Erecting Columns in Occupied Offices." *Engineering Record* 57 (4 April 1908), 427. [Singer Building.]

"The Erection of the 612-Foot Singer Building." *Scientific American* 97 (7 September 1907), 168–69.

"Extension of the Metropolitan Life Insurance Building." *Engineering Record* 53 (3 March 1906), 310–12.

"A 40-Story Building in New York City." *Engineering Record* 54 (8 September 1906), 261–63. [Singer Building.]

A forty-story tower . . . for the Singer Building (news item). *Engineering News* 55 (1 March 1906), 249; 56 (30 August 1906), 239.

Gilbert, Cass. "The Tenth Birthday of a Notable Structure." *Real Estate Magazine of New York* 11 (May 1923), 344–45.

Horowitz, Louis J., and Boyden Sparkes. *The Towers of New York: The Memoir of a Master Builder.* New York: Simon and Schuster, 1937.

Jones, Robert Allen. "Cass Gilbert, Midwestern Architect in New York." Ph.D. diss., Case Western Reserve Univ., 1976.

——. "Mr. Woolworth's Tower: The Skyscraper as Popular Icon." *Journal of Popular Culture* 7 (Fall 1973), 408–24.

King, Moses, ed. *King's How to See New York.* New York: Moses King, 1914.

Koeper, Frederick H. "The Gothic Skyscraper: A History of the Woolworth Building and Its Antecedents." Ph.D. diss., Harvard Univ., 1969.

McKim, Mead & White. *A Monograph of the Work of McKim, Mead & White, 1879–1915.* Vol. 4. New York: Architectural Book, [c. 1914–17].

McKim, Mead & White records. Avery Library, Columbia University. [Municipal Building.]

The Metropolitan Life Building, New York. New York: Metropolitan Life Insurance, [1909?].

The Metropolitan Life Insurance Company: Its History, Its Present Position in the Insurance World, Its Office Building and Its Work Carried on Therein. New York: Metropolitan Life Insurance, 1908 and 1914 editions.

"Metropolitan Life Insurance Co. Building, New York." *Architecture* 10 (15 October 1904), 152, 154, 156, 157, plates 75–79.

"The Metropolitan Tower." *American Architect* 96 (6 October 1909), 125–29.

"Metropolitan Tower Going Higher." *Record and Guide* 81 (18 April 1908), 700.

Mortimer, George T. "The Woolworth Building, Most Modern Example of the Fire-proof Skyscraper: How It Was Built." *Real Estate Magazine* 1 (July 1912), 54–69.

"A Municipal Building of the City of New York." *Scientific American* 103 (16 July 1910), 41, 46.

The New York Board of Fire Underwriters. *Report on Fire in the Equitable Building, Broadway, Pine, Nassau, and Cedar Streets, New York City, January 9, 1912.* New York, 29 February 1912. Equitable Life Assurance Society Archives.

Nims, Norman G., "The Municipal Building of the City of New York." In *The Municipal Engineers in the City of New York, Proceedings for 1913*, 285–302. New York: Municipal Engineers of the City of New York, 1914.

"An Office Building 612 Feet High: The Loftiest Masonry Structure in the World." *Scientific American* 95 (8 September 1906), 169, 174. [Singer Building.]

"Program of a Competition for the Selection of the Architect for the Office Building of the City of New York." *American Competitions* 2. Philadelphia: T-Square Club, 1908.

"Real Estate as an Investment." *Record and Guide* 84 (18 December 1909), 1084–98. [Assessment of future of midtown.]

Redding, Leo L. "Mr. F. W. Woolworth's Story." *World's Work* 25 (April 1913) 659–65.

Robins, Anthony W. "Woolworth Building." New York City Landmarks Preservation Commission designation report, 12 April 1983.

——. "Woolworth Building, first floor interior . . . ," New York City Landmarks Preservation Commission designation report, 12 April 1983.

Roth, Leland M. *McKim, Mead & White Archi-*

tects. New York: Harper & Row, 1983.

Schuyler, Montgomery. "The Towers of Manhattan and Notes on the Woolworth Building." *Architectural Record* 33 (February 1913), 98–122.

———. "The Work of N. Le Brun and Sons." *Architectural Record* 27 (May 1910), 365–81.

Semsch, Otto F., ed. *A History of the Singer Building Construction: Its Progress from Foundation to Flag Pole.* New York: Trow, 1908.

"The Structural Features of the Singer Building, New York." *Engineering Record* 56 (16 November 1907), 530–32.

"The Tallest Office Building in the World: Erection of the Woolworth Building, New York." *Scientific American* 108 (8 March 1913), 224–25, 233.

"Testing Foundations at the Municipal Building, New York." *Engineering Record* 63 (18 February 1911), 196–97.

[Thompson, Mary Lee.] *Illustrated History of the Manhattan Municipal Building Published on the Occasion of Its 75th Anniversary.* City of New York, 1989.

Toll, Seymour I. *Zoned American.* New York: Grossman, 1969.

"The Tower of the Metropolitan Life Building, New York" (titles vary). *Engineering Record* 55 (12 January 1907), 51; 55 (26 January 1907), 97–99; 55 (9 February 1907), 146–50.

"A Twentieth Century Campanile." *Scientific American* 96 (30 March 1907), 270. [Metropolitan Life Tower.]

"Two New Record-Breaking Office Buildings in New York City . . . Singer Building . . . City Investing Building." *Engineering News* 58 (5 December 1907), 595–603.

Van Dyke, John C. *The New New York.* New York: Macmillan, 1909.

Ward, David, and Olivier Zunz, eds. *The Landscape of Modernity: Essays on New York City, 1900–1940.* New York: Russell Sage Foundation, 1992.

Weiss, Marc A. "Skyscraper Zoning: New York's Pioneering Role." *Journal of the American Planning Association* 58 (Spring 1992), 201–12.

INDEX